Scottish Life and Society

An Introduction to Scottish Ethnology

Publications of the European Ethnological
Research Centre

Scottish Life and Society: A Compendium of Scottish Ethnology
(14 Volumes)

Already published:
Volume 2 *Farming and the Land*
Volume 3 *Scotland's Buildings*
Volume 4 *Boats, Fishing and the Sea*
Volume 5 *The Food of the Scots*
Volume 6 *Scotland's Domestic Life*
Volume 7 *The Working Life of the Scots*
Volume 8 *Transport and Communications*
Volume 9 *The Individual and Community Life*
Volume 10 *Oral Literature and Performance Culture*
Volume 11 *Education*
Volume 12 *Religion*
Volume 13 *The Law*
Volume 14 *Bibliography for Scottish Ethnology*

GENERAL EDITOR:
Alexander Fenton

Scottish Life *and* Society

A COMPENDIUM OF SCOTTISH ETHNOLOGY

AN INTRODUCTION TO SCOTTISH ETHNOLOGY

Edited by
Alexander Fenton
and Margaret A Mackay

JOHN DONALD
in association with
THE EUROPEAN ETHNOLOGICAL RESEARCH CENTRE

First published in Great Britain in 2013 by
John Donald, an imprint of Birlinn Ltd
West Newington House
10 Newington Road
Edinburgh
EH9 1QS

www.birlinn.co.uk

Hardback ISBN: 978 1 906566 06 7
Paperback ISBN: 978 1 906566 70 8

British Library Cataloguing-in-Publication Data
A catalogue record for this book is available on request from the British Library

Typeset by Mark Blackadder

Printed and bound in Britain by CPI Antony Rowe, Chippenham

Contents

List of Figures

List of Contributors

PROFESSOR ANDREW BLAIKIE
Chair in Historical Sociology,
History, University of Aberdeen

DR VALENTINA BOLD
Reader in Literature and Ethnology and Director,
the Solway Centre for Environment and Culture,
University of Glasgow, Crichton Campus, Dumfries

DR DAVID BROWN
National Records of Scotland

MR JOHN BURNETT
Independent scholar

DR KATHERINE CAMPBELL
Director of Research, Celtic and Scottish Studies,
University of Edinburgh

PROFESSOR HUGH CHEAPE
Cùrsa MSc, Sabhal Mòr Ostaig,
University of the Highlands and Islands

PROFESSOR EDWARD J COWAN
Emeritus Professor of Scottish History,
University of Glasgow

PROFESSOR ALEXANDER FENTON†
Emeritus Professor, Celtic and Scottish Studies,
University of Edinburgh

MR IAN FRASER
Honorary Fellow, Scottish Place-Name Survey,
Celtic and Scottish Studies, University of Edinburgh

† deceased contributor

DR HEATHER HOLMES
Independent Researcher and Scottish Government

DR NEILL MARTIN
Lecturer, Celtic and Scottish Studies, University of Edinburgh

DR CATRIONA MACKIE
Lecturer in Manx Studies, University of Liverpool

MISS MORAG MACLEOD
Senior Lecturer, retired, Scottish Ethnology, University of Edinburgh

DR MARGARET A MACKAY
Honorary Fellow, Celtic and Scottish Studies, University of Edinburgh

DR LICIA MASONI
Department of Education Sciences, University of Bologna

DR ALEXANDER MURDOCH
Senior Lecturer, Scottish History, University of Edinburgh

MS LORNA PIKE
Co-òrdanaiche a' Phròiseict / Project Co-ordinator, Faclair na Gàidhlig

MR BOB POWELL
Principal Museums Officer, Highland Folk Museum, Newtonmore

DR WENDY UGOLINI
Lecturer, History, University of Edinburgh

DR DOREEN WAUGH
Honorary Fellow, Scottish Place-Name Survey,
Celtic and Scottish Studies, University of Edinburgh

DR GARY J WEST
Senior Lecturer in Scottish Ethnology,
Celtic and Scottish Studies, University of Edinburgh

DR KEITH WILLIAMSON
Research Fellow, University of Edinburgh

DR ANDREW WISEMAN
Senior Research Associate on the Calum Maclean Project,
University of Edinburgh

Preface

An Introduction to Scottish Ethnology is the final volume to appear in the fourteen-volume series *Scottish Life and Society: A Compendium of Scottish Ethnology*, prepared and published by the European Ethnological Research Centre (EERC) from its foundation in 1989. The overall aim of the series is to examine the interconnecting elements in Scottish history, language and culture which have shaped the identity of Scotland and Scots at local, regional and national level and to place these in an international context. This volume provides an overview of ethnology, its genesis as a subject, the sources and resources for its study, and insights into the way in which its constituent parts may be researched, used and understood in the wider context of European Ethnology.

The series was the child of the visionary founder of the EERC, the pioneering ethnologist Professor Alexander Fenton (1929–2012). A scholar committed to fieldwork and associated archival research, whose capacity for participant observation arose from personal experience of home and work and community life, Sandy Fenton engaged with Scotland's material and linguistic culture from his early years and went on to explore its parallels in other cultures. Following his university studies in Aberdeen and Cambridge, and National Service between 1953 and 1955, he worked for four years as a senior assistant editor on the *Scottish National Dictionary*, assisting the new School of Scottish Studies, founded in 1951, with the preparation of questionnaires and other work on the relationship between words and things. From 1959 he pursued a career in the National Museum of Antiquities of Scotland, becoming its Director in 1978 and its Research Director from 1985. He lectured in Material Culture at the University of Edinburgh from 1974, and between 1990 and 1994 he held the first Chair of Scottish Ethnology in the School of Scottish Studies, where he had been an Honorary Fellow from 1969.

Much of the inspiration for his work in and on Scotland derived from his contacts in other European countries where the formal study of ethnology was well developed through national and university institutions, through local, regional and national museums and through the contribution of individuals and groups grounded in their culture and eager to value and to share it. Publications were key to his work on behalf of Scottish Ethnology. He was himself a prolific and indefatigable author at home and abroad, as the *Bibliography* published by the EERC to mark his eightieth birthday[1] demonstrates, and from its foundation the EERC has been dedicated to making the fruits of research available through its journal, the *Review of Scottish Culture* (*ROSC*), and a publications programme

Professor Alexander Fenton (1929–2012)

embracing editions of local records, autobiographical accounts and other outputs.

He was attracted by the *Magyar Néprajzi Lexikon*, the *Historical Lexicon of Hungarian Ethnography*, edited by Gyula Ortutay et al. from 1977 onwards, and determined that Scotland should have something similar. It is right that Sandy Fenton's debt to Hungarian scholars and the models provided by their work should be gratefully acknowledged here, for he often did this himself. He knew the language, enjoyed fieldwork with colleagues there and did much to make their research better known beyond Hungary's borders. A poet himself, he also took great delight in translating the poetry of Sándor Weöres for the pleasure of new audiences.

But the *Compendium* is not a lexicon or an encyclopedia. It aims to present the research of established and rising scholars into the institutions, both formal and informal, which constitute Scottish society, and their work on the lived experience of its people, in a series of thematic volumes. Each save one volume, *The Food of the Scots*, for which Fenton was the sole author, is multi-authored. Each offers solid evidence from a variety of sources for its assertions and suggestions for further research.

An Introduction to Scottish Ethnology falls into four main sections. Part One looks at ethnology as a subject of systematic study, its history in Scotland, and at a central feature of its method, ethnological fieldwork. Part Two has its focus on the preservation, presentation and rediscovery of its materials in museums, archives and other centres and in the work of organisations such as local history societies. Part Three examines individually a range of ethnological genres, their associated methodologies and theoretical and analytical approaches, drawing on case studies and providing guidance on appropriate sources. Part Four concentrates more closely on the range of sources and resources used by the ethnologist, oral, written, visual, and Scotland's languages past and present.

This volume aims to be a practical guide to ethnology, its theory and practice and the sources for its study, for the student, the scholar and the interested lay person alike. Ethnology has at its heart life as it is lived by individuals in society, in and through time and place, and it is a subject for all, for it begins with ourselves. As Sandy Fenton himself wrote:

> It is a subject that relates to each and every one of us and there is no one who cannot be a practitioner. It is one in which personal roots, the home and environment within which the researcher is brought up, become part of the research apparatus of national identity.

Margaret A Mackay

NOTES

1 A Fenton. *Bibliography 1955–2009*, Edinburgh, 2009.

Acknowledgements

Trustees of the European Ethnological Research Centre and others in the wider ethnological world offered advice in the preparation of this volume and their help is gratefully acknowledged. Warm thanks go to the chapter authors and to those who were invited to contribute but found themselves unable to do so.

Mark Mulhern and Kenneth Veitch of the EERC have given unfailing and generous assistance to the editors and the contributors. So too have staff in several libraries and repositories including Arnot McDonald in the Scottish Studies Library and Cathlin Macaulay, Caroline Milligan and the late Ian MacKenzie in the School of Scottish Studies Archives, from which a number of the illustrations in this volume come. The following institutions have also given reproduction permissions: the Kunsthistorisches Museum, Vienna (Figure 14.3: *The Battle between Carnival and Lent* by Peter Brueghel, 1559); the National Folklore Collection, University College Dublin (Figure 24.1); the National Trust for Scotland (Figure 25.1); National Museums Scotland (Figure 25.2).

Birlinn staff and those working with them have been supportive throughout and sincere thanks are due in particular to Mairi Sutherland, Jacqueline Young, Sarah Campbell and Linda Sutherland. The Scotland Inheritance Fund has provided financial support for the preparation and production costs.

This volume, whilst being an *Introduction* both to the subject of ethnology and to the series as a whole, is the last to be published. It is therefore appropriate to add here thanks to all who have contributed to the *Compendium of Scottish Ethnology* over the years: members of the EERC staff and Guest Editors, the many authors of chapters, those who have provided funding for individual volumes and those who have dealt with the practical side of producing these at all stages. Each volume includes a more detailed acknowledgement of these.

The EERC has had two homes over the years during which the volumes of the *Compendium* have appeared, the National Museums of Scotland at first and more recently Celtic and Scottish Studies in the School of Literatures, Languages and Cultures at the University of Edinburgh. Both of these have offered appropriate environments for the production of the series.

Throughout its history the *Compendium* has received sustained and substantial support for the costs associated with its preparation and production from the Scotland Inheritance Fund. The confidence and interest of the SIF trustees has ensured the appearance of the series as a whole and the achievement in its fourteen volumes of the aims of its creator and General Editor, Professor Alexander Fenton (1929–2012). It is acknowledged here with deepest gratitude.

Abbreviations

APS	*The Acts of the Parliaments of Scotland*, eds T Thomson and C Innes, 12 vols, Edinburgh, 1814–75
BALH	British Association of Local History
BL	British Library
DASG	Digital Archive of Scottish Gaelic
DOST	*A Dictionary of the Older Scottish Tongue, from the Twelfth Century to the Seventeenth*, ed. W A Craigie, 12 vols, Chicago and Oxford, 1937–2002
DSL	*Dictionary of the Scots Language*
EERC	European Ethnological Research Centre
IASA	International Society of Sound Archives
IFC	Irish Folklore Commission
ISAD(G)	General International Standard Archival Description
ISFNR	International Society for Folk Narrative Research
ISO	International Standards Organisation
JSNS	*Journal of Scottish Name Studies*
NAS	National Archives of Scotland
NLS	National Library of Scotland
NMS	National Museums Scotland
NRS	National Records of Scotland
NS	*Northern Scotland*
NSA	*New (Second) Statistical Account of Scotland*
NYCRO	North Yorkshire County Record Office
OED	*Oxford English Dictionary*
OSA	*Old (First) Statistical Account of Scotland*
PP	*Parliamentary Papers*
PRO	Public Record Office
PSAS	*Proceedings of the Society of Antiquaries of Scotland*
RCAHMS	Royal Commission on the Ancient and Historical Monuments of Scotland
RCS	Royal Conservatoire of Scotland
RINA	Rail Industry National Archive
ROSC	*Review of Scottish Culture*
RSGS	Royal Scottish Geographical Society
SA	*Scottish Archives: The Journal of the Scottish Records Association*
SCAN	Scottish Archives Network

SCRAN	Scottish Cultural Resources Access Network
SESH	*Scottish Economic and Social History Journal*
SGJ	*Scottish Geographical Journal*
SGM	*Scottish Geographical Magazine*
SIEF	International Society for Ethnology and Folklore
SLA	Scottish Life Archive, National Museums Scotland
SLHF	Scottish Local History Forum
SND	*Scottish National Dictionary*, eds W Grant and D A Murison, 10 vols, Edinburgh, 1931–76
SPNS	Scottish Place-Name Society
SS	*Scottish Studies*
SSPCK	Society in Scotland for Propagating Christian Knowledge
TDGNHAS	*Transactions of the Dumfriesshire and Galloway Natural History and Antiquarian Society*
TELAFNS	*Transactions of the East Lothian Antiquarian and Field Naturalists' Society*
TGSI	*Transactions of the Gaelic Society of Inverness*
UHI	University of the Highlands and Islands

Introduction

Introduction

MARGARET A MACKAY

Scotland is a country rich in variety of all kinds. Its geology, geography, history, demography and languages all contribute to the story of its people, both individually and in groups, and the shaping of their identity or, more properly, their identities.

For its size, Scotland's geology is older and more varied than that of any other part of the world. And it is the geology, 'the structure below', which dictates the topography, the nature of the soil and its qualities, shaping the areas which are most attractive for human settlement and for cultivation. On the coastline it determines the location of harbours and the communities which depend on them. It separates one dale or strath and its inhabitants from another, channelling the lochs, streams and rivers which both connect and divide and which are sources of power. It provides the deposits which produce minerals and fuels such as coal and oil, spurring on extractive industries. It is the source of the very stones which have served to house and shelter and defend its people, their stock and their crops, in countryside and burgh and city. All this was laid down before the beginning of human time.[1]

At the opposite end of the time-frame, Scotland is a nation which has long been at the forefront of providing resources for the study of its people. These range from the *Statistical Accounts* initiated by Sir John Sinclair in the 1790s, gathering data of use to the state, attempting to gauge the extent to which the lives of the population had been improved in a period which had seen developments in trade, technology, industry and agriculture, and providing a comprehensive parish-by-parish picture of Scottish life, to the array of online data sets now provided by several national institutions in digital form which reflect the lives of its people in written documents, visual images and sound recordings.

The geography of Scotland shows a country of variety and contrasts, island–mainland, highland–lowland, urban–rural, inland–coastal, which can furnish a framework for comparative approaches to its study. The primary concern of ethnology is with the experience of the individual in all the stages of life, within family, neighbourhood, community, region and nation, interacting with its environment, with institutions, work opportunities, and expressing itself in various forms of communication. Local resources dictate the nature of the local economy; their abundance or scarcity may prompt population movement – a feature of life in times present as well as past. Equally, decisions made and issues arising in the international or global sphere can have a profound impact on lives at the local level. It is not surprising that in many countries, including

Scotland, ethnologists have been nurtured in the discipline of geography, or that comparative and regional approaches to ethnology have proved fruitful ones.

The ethnologist, for whom themes of continuity and change in human experience are fundamental, may choose to look at phenomena in a synchronic way, that is, with a focus on a particular point in time, or in a diachronic way, that is, through a period of time. In both cases, there is a concern with time and thus with history. These two disciplines are close allies and make use of similar methods of source criticism. The history of settlement in Scotland from the earliest periods onwards provides the basis for studies of land division and resource allocation, of responses to climatic conditions and their changing patterns, and of the imprint of daily life and ritual in the landscape. Here the work of the archaeologist illuminates 'prehistoric' time, a word introduced to English by the Scot Daniel Wilson,[2] before the written word becomes a form of evidence. Historical information from Roman times onward, the annals produced in monastic communities, early legal documents, maps and a growing body of written records from the medieval period to the present provide the ethnologist with a knowledge of the political, economic and institutional context for life at the local level, on land and sea, in village, burgh and city. Evidence from non-written sources, from the material culture and from oral testimony, local and family history, contributes in unique ways to an understanding of the past and the present. The interplay of evidence from written sources, private and public, and from oral material and visual sources, makes a powerful contribution to our knowledge of Scottish life.

A similar combination of sources, including place-names, helps to plot demographic change and enables us to see the present-day population of Scotland, with its mixture of cultures, ethnicities and faiths as part of a continuum of inward migration evident from the earliest times. Scotland has been peopled by Celts, Angles, Scandinavian and Franco-Norman settlers, has seen influences from the Low Countries, and in more recent periods became home to incomers of Irish, Jewish, Italian, Lithuanian, Polish and other European backgrounds and to settlers from India and Pakistan, China and Malaysia. Now there are few parts of the world which are not represented in the Scottish population, for there are more people on the move in the world today than at any previous point in its history.

Within the country, population shifts have been evident. In the eighteenth and nineteenth centuries the rise and growth of industrial and manufacturing centres drew individuals and families from country districts where agricultural improvement had an impact on the workforce required on the land. Growing cities became melting-pots where new identities and distinctive urban speech and culture were created. Improved communications and work opportunities brought Highlanders to the Clyde, Shetlanders and Orcadians to Leith. Women and men following the herring found marriage partners from other fishing communities. And inward migration had its mirror in outward migration, both temporary and permanent, to every continent.

Another strand in Scottish life, and one which runs through all of the volumes in this series, is language. Again, Scotland offers great variety. It may be in the languages which are evident in the Scottish place-name record, reflecting the peoples who have settled in Scotland over many centuries. It may be in the languages used today, Gaelic, Scots, Scottish English and British Sign Language (BSL), and dialects of these, and the many home languages of incomers which make Scotland and Scottish communication distinctive within a global culture of dominant languages. The work of Scotland's lexicographers and linguistic atlas-makers has produced, and continues to produce, outstanding dictionary and related resources which document its languages and their vocabularies through time, with new items continuing to be created. It may be in the local and regional variations in language which have been charted through the work of the Linguistic Surveys of Scotland, illustrating, for example, how many different words there are for the same phenomenon, tool, bird or insect throughout the country. It may be in the specialist terminology of a profession or a craft or trade, essential in the workplace and a badge of identity for those within the group concerned. It may be in the language used in storytelling or song or ritual drama or sermons, with their own richness of register. The ethnologist must be alert to all of these and to the resources which enable a connection to be made between 'words' and 'things' and thus their context and meaning.

All of these elements contribute to an understanding of Scotland and its people in and through time. Very quickly a blank map of Scotland begins to be populated with the details of geology, topography and human history. In his song 'These old stone walls', song-maker and drystane dyker Dave Goulder reflects on the way the geology of Scotland and the varied types of stones used for wall-building in the different terrains illustrate this variety, urging the hearer to 'look and discover'.[3] It could be a suitable motto for this series, itself such a splendid quarry.

SCOTTISH LIFE AND SOCIETY: A COMPENDIUM OF SCOTTISH ETHNOLOGY

Throughout his long career, it was always the aim of Professor Alexander Fenton (1929–2012) to place Scottish data within a wider European and more broadly international context and to provide Scottish material for comparative use.[4] He readily acknowledged the profound influence which scholars in other countries had on his own work and approaches, and the impact of field and archival work elsewhere – his own and that of others – on his analysis of Scottish phenomena. His vision for *Scottish Life and Society: A Compendium of Scottish Ethnology* was that it should be a comprehensive resource, providing insights on life and society based upon the research of seasoned scholars and acknowledged experts as well as rising ones and covering those topics which reveal individual experience through the lens of place, time and social milieu. It would, he hoped, set a baseline for the story of Scottish culture and society at the end of one millennium and the beginning of another.

Its fourteen volumes, including this *Introduction* and the *Bibliography,* incorporate several studies with a very specific focus. Material culture is dominant in *Scotland's Buildings* (Volume 3), *The Food of the Scots* (Volume 5) and *Scotland's Domestic Life* (Volume 6). But it will be readily seen that each of these volumes also contains information on social interaction, oral tradition, festivities and rites of passage. The same is the case with those volumes which have work and resources at their heart, *Farming and the Land* (Volume 2), *Boats, Fishing and the Sea* (Volume 4), *The Working Life of the Scots* (Volume 7), and *Transport and Communications* (Volume 8). This interplay, which reflects the realities and the actualities of human life, where the tangible and the intangible constantly meet, is skilfully transmitted as well in Volumes 9 and 10, *The Individual and Community Life* and *Oral Literature and Performance Culture*. Three volumes deal with the institutions which have a distinctive Scottish character, *Education* (Volume 11), *Religion* (Volume 12) and *The Law* (Volume 13).

AN INTRODUCTION TO SCOTTISH ETHNOLOGY:
WHAT IS IN IT AND HOW TO USE IT

This volume is both an introduction to the subject of ethnology and to the *Compendium* as a whole. Like all the volumes in the series it stands alone but the student of ethnology or anyone with particular interests in certain subjects within the ethnology of Scotland will want to consult individual volumes of the series where these are dealt with as a main focus. Some chapters here have a very direct relationship with other volumes.

What can be called the earliest textbook for ethnology in Scotland, or indeed the UK, is *The Past in the Present: What is Civilisation?* by Dr, later Sir, Arthur Mitchell (1826–1909), of 1880, in which he published the first series of Rhind Lectures which he delivered to the Society of Antiquaries of Scotland in 1876 and 1878. In it he examined objects such as hand querns, spindle whorls and types of pottery which were still in use much as they had been since earlier times and used these as a means of understanding the past by working back from the present, engaging in the debate about the nature of 'civilisation' which was much in the air in the later part of the nineteenth century.

An Introduction to Scottish Ethnology has been designed to be both a reference book and a textbook for the twenty-first century. It thus differs somewhat from the other volumes in the series, including guidance on how to conduct fieldwork, how to identify and analyse sources and study many of the topics which ethnology embraces. Part One deals with the history of ethnology, its theoretical and analytical approaches, and its methodologies. Chapter 1 sets out the wider context for Scottish ethnology within the development of ethnological thinking elsewhere, examining the influences which have come from approaches in other countries and from other disciplines. Ethnology has also been borrowed by other disciplines, as can be seen in the use of oral evidence by historians.

Chapter 2 provides an overview of ethnology as it has developed in Scotland. Significant individuals and institutions which have played a role in nurturing ethnological investigation in Scotland are introduced, and the work of those who have built up collections. A distinguishing feature of ethnology is the capacity of its practitioners to create bodies of material for others to use. Throughout this volume there are references to these collections and their locations, details of publication if in printed form, and means of access if in digital format.

Trends in ethnology in Scotland have reflected those elsewhere in Europe and in the USA, while Scotland has been well placed to develop regional ethnology and to harness its linguistic diversity for ethnological purposes. Located as it is at the crossroads of the North Atlantic, it is not surprising to see the impact of Celtic and Scandinavian contact both in early Scotland and in recent times. In the development of ethnology as a discipline in Scotland in the twentieth century, scholarship and models from Ireland and Sweden were of particular importance, and the role of key figures is described.

Fieldwork is a vital element of ethnological methodology, and the issues it raises are explored in Chapter 3. Here the author of the chapter makes helpful use of a case study drawn from her own research. This approach is found in a number of the chapters in the volume, illustrating the combination of theory and method in actual examples. Each author in the *Introduction* speaks with his or her own voice and on the basis of first-hand experience of the topic, the genre or the resource concerned.

Part Two has its focus on themes of preservation, presentation and rediscovery. Its chapters examine material culture (Chapter 4) and the role of museums (Chapter 5), including the open-air museum movement (Chapter 6). These are followed by studies of archival sources and ethnology (Chapter 7), the local history movement (Chapter 8) and the heritage industry (Chapter 9).

Part Three looks at a further range of ethnological genres and, importantly, how they may be studied. Folk narrative (Chapter 10), traditional music, referring to music which is instrumental in nature (Chapter 11), Scots song (Chapter 12), and Gaelic song (Chapter 13) are all genres which are also included in Volume 10 of the Compendium, on *Oral Literature and Performance Culture*, but looked at there from other perspectives. Part Three continues with custom, belief and traditional drama (Chapter 14), social organisation (Chapter 15) – another chapter where the reader will benefit from delving into other volumes in the series, Volume 9, *The Individual and Community Life*, in particular – and onomastics, name studies, mainly concentrating on place-names, in Chapter 16.

Part Four offers insights on a range of types of sources and resources which can be consulted in ethnological enquiry. These include oral sources (Chapter 17), written evidence in the form of personal and public accounts (Chapters 18 and 19), and prose and poetry (Chapter 20). Chapbooks, broadsides and the periodical press are dealt with in Chapter 21, which includes a case study. Linguistic and lexicographical resources and how they may be used are outlined with regard to Gaelic in Chapter 22 and to Scots in Chapter 23. A case study describing the creation of an electronic resource is presented in Chapter 24. Visual evidence, concentrating on photographs, is the theme of Chapter 25.

Each chapter includes a bibliography as well as relevant further reading on the topic where appropriate. There are many interconnecting strands linking the chapters and guidance which is applicable across genres. It will readily be seen that there are common methodological approaches here. For example, both Chapters 11 and 14 illustrate the importance of film in ethnological research. Seeking answers to basic questions such as those posed as essential for enquiry from classical times onwards but enumerated most famously by Rudyard Kipling in his *Just So Stories* as 'six honest serving-men' – what, why, when, how, where and who – will serve the ethnologist well in analysing and contextualising a source whether it is the contents of a painting, a piece of written or oral evidence, a song, an item of clothing, a film or a customary practice.

FUTURE DIRECTIONS FOR ETHNOLOGY IN SCOTLAND

The European Ethnological Research Centre embarked in 2011 on its next major enterprise, the Regional Ethnology of Scotland Project. This will consist of regional studies which have as their hallmark close interaction with local residents and organisations carrying out ethnological research as well as academics with similar interests.

The first study is based on Dumfries and Galloway and the lives of its people through time. Outputs will include online resources, a multi-authored book and contributions to the EERC's *Flashbacks* series. Topics of study within the Project include family, occupations, place-names, dialect, farming, land management, fishing, industries, population movement, emigration and immigration, communications, education, local administration, sports, religious expression, literature, visual art, instrumental music, song, oral narrative and calendar customs. It is hoped that through its methodology each regional study will leave a legacy locally that will ensure that further exploration of the ethnology of Scotland will take place.

The work of staff and students in ethnology in Scotland's institutions of higher education will continue to reflect life and society in contemporary Scotland as well as features seen through time in a diachronic fashion. Graduates with degrees in Scottish Ethnology since the 1980s have taken up employment in a range of institutions in Scotland and beyond, and are bringing an ethnological perspective to activities in many fields. Applied ethnology will be more and more seen as an important component in making government policy, whether in relation to Scotland's increasingly diverse population, arts and cultural provision and support, or in relation to equality issues to do with language and communication. These are all areas in which an understanding of what goes into the creation of individual and group identity is crucial to good decision-making.

Student and staff mobility within Europe and beyond holds great potential for comparative and collaborative work. ERASMUS and TEMPUS schemes offer the opportunity for students of ethnology to follow courses or further their research in ethnology departments elsewhere. Staff similarly have the chance to be based elsewhere for short periods, contributing a comparative dimension to the host department's teaching programmes and engaging in research with colleagues and resources there. Degrees to which several departments contribute are under discussion.

Collections such as those of the School of Scottish Studies Archives continue to be a dynamic source of inspiration for singers, instrumentalists and storytellers, and increasingly for visual artists and those working in other multi-media contexts. A project to film the stories from the sound archive translated into British Sign Language has been initiated and will be developed further.[5] The potential here is great, and is assisted by the conversion of analogue recordings to digital versions through the Tobar an Dualchais / Kist o Riches Project. These resources now also form the basis for the development of a wide range of teaching resources responding to and supporting new curricular initiatives in Scottish education at all levels. Museum resources are also ready to be exploited for similar purposes in a range of innovative ways.

Discussions are underway towards creating enhanced access to sound collections held in a range of Scottish repositories through a dispersed Scottish Sound Archive. The resources of the Scottish Screen Archive, administered by the National Library of Scotland and encompassing material on many themes and places from the earliest days of the moving image in Scotland to the present, offer much scope for research.

The creation of large corpora of linguistic and ethnological material to which programmes can be readily applied opens up new uses for collections and possibilities for comparative analysis and research which have been impossible hitherto.

New modes of communication mean that scholars can be in touch with each other and have access to research findings and collections in ways which enhance collaborative work with a potential never experienced before. This does not mean that gatherings will not continue. International ethnological organisations meet at regular intervals to ensure that there continue to be opportunities for comparative endeavour and Scottish input. The congress workshops and working groups of the International Society for Ethnology and Folklore (SIEF) are effective in taking research forward in specific topics, such as those for Ballad Studies, Cultural Heritage and Property, the Ethnology of Religion, Food Research, The Ritual Year, Place Wisdom, Ethnocartography, and Historical Approaches to Cultural Analysis. New groups are established as needs are perceived. The International Society for Folk Narrative Research (ISFNR) and the International Society of Sound Archives (IASA) also meet regularly.

Applied ethnology can have very practical outcomes in terms of the healing which takes place through the sharing of experiences in contexts of trauma. The folklorist Carl Lindahl and colleagues in Houston, Texas, have worked with the survivors of the hurricanes Katrina and Rita, which devastated New Orleans in 2005, in the 'Surviving Katrina and Rita in Houston' Project, offering training and payment to enable the survivors themselves to engage with others in telling their stories. This is the first large-scale project in which the survivors of a major disaster have taken the lead in documenting it.[6] In situations of displacement, which are all too frequent in our present world, whether through natural disaster or human conflict, there is a role for the response and support which the ethnologist can give, among hurricane survivors in Houston or asylum-seekers in Edinburgh. Time, place, social milieu and memory are foregrounded. Ethnology, with human experience at its heart, allows us to understand each other in ways which are positive and creative, across national cultures and other divides, and is needed now more than ever before.

NOTES

    1 For an excellent introduction to this see Ralston and Edwards, 1997.
    2 Ash, 1999, 60.
    3 Goulder, 1986, track 15.
    4 Fenton, 2009.
    5 Robertson and McLean, 2012. This BSL dvd was an output of the British Sign
       Language UPTAKE (University Partnership Towards Accessible Knowledge
       Exchange) Project. Two stories told in Scots by Stanley Robertson from the School of
       Scottish Studies Sound Archive were translated into British Sign Language by
       Frankie McLean.
    6 Ancelet et al., 2013.

BIBLIOGRAPHY AND FURTHER READING

Ancelet, B J, Gaudet, M and Lindahl, C, eds. *Second Line Rescue: Improvised Responses to Katrina and Rita*, Jackson, MS, 2013.
Ash, M. Old books, old castles, and old friends: The Making of Daniel Wilson's *Archaeology and Prehistoric Annals of Scotland*. In Hulse, E, ed., *Thinking with Both Hands: Sir Daniel Wilson in the Old World and the New*, Toronto, 1999, 60–80.
Fenton, A. *Bibliography*, Edinburgh, 2009.
Goulder, D. 'These Dry Stone Walls', *The January Man*, Drystone Records CD01, UK, 1986.
McKirdy, A, Gordon, J and Crofts, R. *Land of Mountain and Flood: The Geology and Landforms of Scotland*, Edinburgh, 2009.
Ralston, I and Edwards, K J, eds. *Scotland: Environment and Archaeology 8000 BC – AD 1000*, New York, 1997.
Robertson, S and McLean, F. *Storytelling as a Family Activity* and *The Old Woman Who Sold Her Soul to the Devil*, BSL dvd, Edinburgh, 2012. See also <www.bsluptake.org.uk/info/ ?cat=756> [accessed 10 April 2013].
Scottish Natural Heritage. *Scotland: The Creation of its Natural Landscape*, Edinburgh, 2011.
West, G. *Voicing Scotland: Folk, Culture, Nation*, Edinburgh, 2012.

PART ONE

●

Ethnology

1 Ethnology as a Subject

ALEXANDER FENTON

Ethnology as a subject, as taught in European universities, can be more precisely described as European or regional ethnology, and is regarded as lying within the orbit of general ethnology. Its three basic defining characteristics have been expressed as those of time, place and social milieu; that is, there is a historical dimension and it has relationships with localities and their demographic structure. This was sufficient in the period when ethnological research concentrated on peasant farming and fishing communities, on the grounds that survivals of traditional aspects of culture were most likely to be found in such rural or maritime areas, but gradually the impact of industrialisation was taken into account, along with the accompanying urbanisation. The older view, for example, was expressed by Dr Iorwerth C Peate, former director of the Welsh Folk Museum, who did not consider that folklife research applied to industrialised areas.[1] Nowadays other factors are also considered, notably the movement of ethnic groups and the consequences for the localities to which they came (and from which they originated), and the phenomenon of globalisation. Inevitably, ethnology has had to change its ground, in line with an ever-widening remit. The process of 'folk culture' is in a constant state of transition, and it has kept up-to-date by taking on board methodologies of approach borrowed from the social sciences. However, European ethnology is a historical discipline, and the basic concepts of time, place and social milieu remain as essential distinguishing elements.

Importantly, study of past oral traditions and of aspects of material culture that have become obsolete or obsolescent should not lead to fossilisation of the subject studied, since a gradual, almost imperceptible, process of endogenous change over time is a constant factor, even in the seemingly most primitive communities. However, it can happen in museum displays, for example of house interiors, purporting to represent specific periods. All items belonging to times outside the period are weeded out, and a fossilised and sanitised picture is presented. Similarly, collectors of folksongs, folktales and other oral material can tinker with the texts as they got them and publish their 'amended' versions, which are then accepted as the standard. The realities of everyday life and human culture are that traces of the past are always present in some way, along with pointers to the future, whether in the furnishings of rooms in the dwelling house, or in the miscellaneous clutter of knowledge held in every human brain. Any definition of ethnology, therefore, must take into account this constant process of change.

This is especially necessary with globalisation and the levelling effects of the creation of bodies such as the European Union, with accompanying change in attitudes to national and regional boundaries. At the same time there has been a counter-movement that lays stress on regional identity, and this may lead to the promotion of views of the past that are selective of certain features and that do not allow for change. It is a task of ethnology to try to establish the realities of the human situation, past and present, through intensive, unbiased research. In this way, it can act as a means of validating data presented in the more political forms of history. The three-dimensional evidence of material culture can also be used for this purpose. It has been noted that students and established historians, brought up to cope with flat documents, find it hard to accept that objects in the round can also be interpreted like documents.

As the subject of ethnology has grown wider, there has been an increasing degree of specialisation in specific aspects. A major divide has been that between folklore and folklife, which can be broadly construed as oral tradition on the one hand and the study of material and social culture on the other. In Norway, for example, there are separate university institutes of folklore (*folkeminnevitskap*) and of ethnology (*folkelivsgransking*), with separate professorships.[2] In Finland, this division in the discipline was marked by the setting up of a chair in folklore in 1908, and another in ethnology in 1921.[3] Similar divisions exist elsewhere, and can also be found in the titles of societies such as Société Internationale d'Ethnologie et de Folklore (SIEF; formerly CIAP, Commission Internationale des Arts et Traditions Populaires).

Professor Sigurd Erixon in Sweden, a leading figure in the development of European ethnology, wrote in 1967 in the first issue of the journal *Ethnologia Europaea* that:

> Every country and independent territory has its own history and therefore also to a certain degree its own ethnology. The same applies, or should apply, to research workers and their schools.[4]

Teaching of European ethnology at university level should take this into account. Researchers and teachers should aim at establishing the multifarious factors that go into the concept of national and regional identity, whilst also examining wider ethnological perspectives, within which the national or regional experience can be evaluated through comparison with other geographical areas or culture zones. These can also be related to the general principles of approach that have been worked out for neighbouring disciplines, such as cultural anthropology, cultural sociology, philology, cultural history, musicology, art and architecture, agriculture, history, etc. It can appear, however, that the subject tries to be all things to all men; Professor Günter Wiegelmann in Germany, for example, has noted that the thematic breadth of the subject and the number of neighbouring sciences make the study of the subject relatively difficult, which in turn makes it hard for university students to acquire an overview and basic knowledge of it.[5] The home territory of a would-be ethnologist is the best possible base for gaining experience and choosing a future research direction.

The breadth of ethnology as a subject is in part due to its historical development out of a variety of culture-related disciplines in different countries, amongst them anthropology, philology, historical geography and antiquarianism. It is a matter of importance for any subject to have a distinguishing name, and there were different names for 'ethnology' in different countries. These are discussed below.

The question of a standard international name, however, led to much discussion in learned circles. In 1969, an important meeting took place between Scandinavian and Finnish scholars at Jyväskylää in Finland, at which the proposal was made that '*etnologi*' should be adopted as the official academic name for the subject, in place of 'folklife studies'.[6] This was agreed, and in 1970–1 a questionnaire circulated in the Germanic language-speaking areas brought responses in which the majority were in favour of the change, though keeping the well-established '*Volkskunde*' and adding the words 'European Ethnology' in brackets.[7] In this way an international term was established, which could be used alone or in parallel with pre-existing terms. It also implicitly recognised the existence of a general ethnology, within the bounds of which a 'European' or 'Scottish' or 'Finnish' or any other regional ethnology could and should operate.

The adoption of the term 'European ethnology' as a standard mark of identity of the subject as practised in Europe raises the question of what Europe is. It is not enough to define it as the group of countries belonging to the EU, since this grouping does not constitute a fixed entity. Besides, there are different national schools of ethnology, including schools within individual nations that have different approaches to the teaching of ethnology, and often focus still on 'cultural themes within politically drawn boundaries'.[8]

This concept of Europe as an ethnological region was already to be found in a presidential address to the Folk-Lore Society, delivered in 1914 by Robert Ranulph Marett (1866–1943), and published in 1920 in his book on *Psychology and Folk-Lore*. He spoke of the difficulty of establishing an 'ethnological province', within which the culture could be divided into chronological strata, the order of which would tell how development had proceeded. But he was wary of this approach:

> ... what has this so-called 'ethnological method' done, or is it likely to do, for folklore? In the first place, how are you going to define your ethnological province? I suppose all Europe at the very least must be regarded by the folklorist as his special area of characterization.[9]

THE VARIOUS NAMES OF ETHNOLOGY

In trying to define the subject of ethnology, it is helpful to examine the names by which it has been known. Each name illuminates a different aspect or fashion of approach according to time and place, and the range of names demonstrates the extent to which it is a process in a constant state of transition, though at different rates in different countries and regions.

Ethnology, Ethnography, Völkerkunde

In the nineteenth century, 'ethnology' was understood as the study of the human races, their physical, intellectual and moral characters, their languages and historical traditions. This, for example, was the target of interest of the Société d'Ethnologie de Paris, founded in 1839 by William Frédéric Edwards and a group of geographers with the aim of establishing what were the different human races.[10]

The word *'ethnologie'* appears to have been coined by the Frenchman André-Marie Ampère, who saw it as a division in his classification of the sciences. He used it in a letter to his son dated 9 June 1830, and in a book published in 1856 he related the application of the subject to the territories occupied by the nations, the races from which they took their origins, the monuments left by their predecessors, the history of their rise and decline, and the religions they professed.[11] Archaeology and history were seen as the background to ethnological studies. He therefore placed ethnology, in his taxonomic classification, amongst the group of sciences that studied human societies and all the circumstances of their existence, past and present.

Ampère also drew a distinction between 'ethnology' and 'ethnography', locating the former with comparative ethnology and the latter with elementary ethnology, with its documentary and descriptive functions, i.e. the gathering stage, which could lead to the establishment of archives and museum collections, and eventually university departments. The *Oxford English Dictionary* defines ethnology as 'the science which treats of races and peoples, and of their relations to one another, their distinctive physical and other characteristics, etc'; and ethnography as 'the scientific description of nations or races of men, with their customs, habits, and points of difference', which is more or less in line with Ampère. Between the time of Ampère's letter of 1830 and 1871, 'ethnology' was beginning to appear regularly in publications and in the titles of societies in several countries of Europe and in the United States: Société ethnologique de Paris (1839); Ethnological Society of New York (later the American Ethnological Society) (1842); Ethnological Society of London (1843); Societá italiana di antropologia e di etnologia (Florence, 1871).[12]

Ethnology was understood at this time as a subject that dealt with non-European races and archaic phenomena that characterised the early developmental stages of human society. British anthropologists regarded it as the study of races and languages and prehistoric archaeology,[13] in line with this view. But the difference between ethnology and ethnography, as indicated by Ampère, is not observed in some countries. For example, Russia uses 'ethnography' in the sense of the study of archaic phenomena, and does not separate the subject into two disciplines, one comparative and theoretical, and the other purely descriptive.[14]

In Germany, the *Deutsches Universalwörterbuch* defines *'ethnologie'* as 'general (comparative) *Völkerkunde* in which the findings of ethnography are compared with each other' and 'Science that deals with the social structure and culture of (primitive) societies', and *Ethnographie* as 'part of *Völkerkunde*, which systematically describes the features of the different peoples and cultures; descriptive *Völkerkunde*'.

Völkerkunde is defined as the 'science of the culture and forms of life of (primitive) races'.

Further detail comes from the *Wörterbuch der deutschen Volkskunde*. The term *'Völkerkunde'* first appeared in 1778. In the eighteenth and nineteenth centuries it was equated with 'anthropology', as is still sometimes the case in the West European and Anglo-Saxon countries and in the USA. In Germany a separation from anthropology and prehistory took place around 1928 with the founding of the *Gesellschaft für Völkerkunde*.[15] The emphasis in sense lies on the study of non-European peoples that are more or less lacking in documented background history, whence the need for ethnographic research through fieldwork to establish the data on which further analysis can be based.

Volkskunde

This term, recorded from 1787 in Germany, but from 1783 in the Netherlands,[16] is used in the Germanic language-speaking countries. The *Wörterbuch der deutschen Volkskunde* has a long entry under this heading, outlining the various fortunes of the subject as well as the range and period covered by researchers, from the years before AD 1000, when the German people and territory were taking shape. It was not until the threshold of the modern period that scientific attention began to be paid to the characteristics and shaping of the *'Volksgeist'* (spiritual self-awareness of the people). Leading up to the present, topics investigated have included settlement patterns, buildings and equipment, dress, ornament and sculpture, as well as song, games and dance, beliefs and customs, riddles, proverbs, droll stories, etc. Material and oral culture were complemented by more sociologically oriented studies of social organisation, viewed as a layered pyramid with a broad base consisting of the rural and eventually urban populations.

The Romantic Period brought a great deal of activity, particularly in the field of folksongs and ballads. Bishop Thomas Percy (1729–1811) published *Reliques of Ancient English Poetry* in 1765, and this collection influenced Johann Herder (1744–1803) in Germany, who emulated Percy and published *Stimmen der Völker in Liedern* (voices of the people in songs) in 1778–9. Here he demonstrated his love for the songs of the people, for unsophisticated human nature. He was responsible for coining the word *'Volkslied'* (folksong), as well as *'Volksseele'* (soul or spirit of the people) and *'Volksglaube'* (folk belief). In Scotland, James Macpherson (1736–96) published *Fragments of Ancient Poetry Collected in the Highlands of Scotland* in 1760, followed by *Fingal, an Ancient Epic Poem*, in 1761 and *Temora, an Ancient Epic Poem*, in 1765. When *The Poems of Ossian* appeared in 1773, the book became a literary sensation, being seen as 'folk poetry', the authentic voice of the nation. It was translated into Danish, French, German, Italian, Polish, Russian and Swedish,[17] and exercised a considerable influence on European poetry and attitudes to the past.

With the activities of the Brothers Grimm (Jacob Ludwig Carl, 1785–1863 and Wilhelm Carl, 1786–1859), *Volkskunde* became a much more professional subject. Their collection of folktales, *Kinder- und Hausmärchen* (1812, 1816, 1818), helped to lay a more academic basis for the science, though with emphasis on the collecting of customs and usages, traditions, legends and tales. These were to be interpreted for the archaic content which, it was assumed, they contained. Research into local history and geography, *Heimatkunde* (first used 1816), provided another source for the growth of *Volkskunde* through local studies which, first pursued at home, could lead to a better understanding of the wider world, the nation.[18] To some extent, these parallel the community studies discussed later in this chapter.

The rise of *Volkskunde* as a science or discipline stems largely from the second half of the nineteenth century, and is marked by the establishment of societies, institutions and journals concerned with the subject in various European countries, and with an expansion of such activities in the first half of the twentieth. The roots of this development lie in the eighteenth century, however, and are in great part based on the belief that rural (and coastal) communities, comprising ordinary people, had retained their age-old cultures and had been less influenced by outside forces, though others considered that the concept of 'folk' should include all social strata.[19]

With the Grimms, fairy tales, stories and songs that had been seen as lying within grandmother's domestic domain began to be studied for their literary, aesthetic and ideological significance, and a substantial literature on fairies was produced and continues to appear. A further orientation, especially in Germany and Russia in the 1770s–80s, was the ethnographic description and exploration of ways of living, customs and usages, material culture and languages of dwellers in various new lands, with scientific expeditions providing basic data.[20] From this, it was a fairly easy step for similar activities to be undertaken or intensified in European countries, with their long historical backgrounds.

Folklore

'Folk-lore' (later, 'Folklore') was coined by William John Thoms in the issue of the *Athenaeum* for 22 August 1846, as an equivalent for 'popular antiquities, antiquitates vulgares'. The term spread in the course of the nineteenth century and later, especially in the Romance language-speaking countries and was applied, as in Britain and America, primarily to oral traditions – stories, myths, proverbs, song, music, popular lore, custom and belief, wellerisms, etc. For example, *'folclore'* was used first in Portugal in 1875, and has subsequently been treated as an equivalent for 'oral literature'.[21] In 1891, the second International Folk-Lore Congress was held in London, at which the Scot Andrew Lang (1844–1912) gave the Presidential Address. Speaking of folklore, he said:

> When the word was first introduced, by Mr Thoms, it meant little, perhaps, but the observing and recording of various superstitions, stories, customs, proverbs, songs, fables, and so forth. But the science has gradually increased its scope, till it has taken almost all of human life for its province.[22]

Thus, Lang was on the one hand aware of the changing sense of 'folklore', and on the other he was finding it difficult to distinguish it from anthropology.

There was, however, some difficulty in adopting folklore as a university subject. In Britain in 1969, following the Anglo-American Folklore Conference held at Ditchley Park, Oxford, a resolution was published which sought to 'draw public attention to the unfortunate neglect in the British educational system of Folklore as a serious academic subject'. Folklore, it stated, 'though often regarded as a matter of fun and frivolity', was properly 'one of the humanities and social sciences, related to anthropology, literature, history, psychology, and human geography, but with its own methods, goals and scholarship'.[23]

Folklife, Folkliv

This term first appeared in the early 1900s. It was adopted at three Swedish universities, Lund, Stockholm and Uppsala, under the title *Nordisk och jämförande folklivsforskning* (Nordic and Comparative Folklife Research). It was accepted in academic circles in Scandinavian countries as the normal name for the subject, and the title of the influential journal, *Folkliv*, gave it a further boost. This was the first journal to be dedicated entirely to European ethnology. It first appeared under the editorship of Professor Sigurd Erixon in 1937.

'Folklife' was adopted in Britain also. It appeared in the titles of journals, e.g. *Ulster Folklife*, first issued by the Committee on Ulster Folklife and Traditions in 1955. There was at first some unease about the use of the term. At a symposium on 'The Scope and Methods of Folk Life Research', held at the School of Scottish Studies in Edinburgh in September 1959, some delegates took the view that the term 'folk life' should be abandoned, on the grounds that it did not reflect the whole community and that association with 'folklore' and 'folksong' gave it a 'false and indeterminate value'. It was suggested that it should be replaced by 'ethnography', since that occurred in the title of the British Ethnography Committee, but this was not adopted.

There was a tendency to restrict 'folklore' to oral traditions, and 'folklife' to studies of material and social culture, so inhibiting the holistic study of folk traditions. In Norway, for example, ethnology was regarded as two disciplines, folklife for the study of material and social culture, and folklore for the study of the spiritual heritage.[24] In Finland there was a similar division.[25] In Denmark, a Chair in Material Folk Culture was set up in 1959, but folklore continued to be dealt with separately.

The development of folklife in Britain and the Scandinavian countries owes a good deal to museum-based individuals, whose work with collections tended to place an emphasis on material culture. This in turn was in the first instance concerned with peasant culture, in particular of a pre-industrial nature, in the belief that survivals from the past were most likely to be found in the lower strata of the social hierarchy. One solid outcome of the folklife phase was the build-up of archives and collections in museums, so that 'a great harvest has been brought into the barn for coming generations'.[26]

There was a quick response, suggesting that there had been a good deal of dissatisfaction with the old terms, which by stressing the element 'folk' had tended to perpetuate the old restriction to the lower and middle classes. The

Chair in Material Folk Culture in Denmark became the Chair of European Ethnology in 1971. In Sweden, a similar change was made at Lund, and the journal *Folkliv* was replaced by *Ethnologia Scandinavica*, marking a concentration of the main research area on the Scandinavian countries. In Germany, '*Europäische Ethnologie*' was adopted at Marburg, and '*Kulturanthropologie und Europäische Ethnologie*' at Frankfurt. In Austria, at Innsbruck and Vienna, '*Volkskunde*' continued to be used alongside '*Europäische Ethnologie*'. In middle Europe, the Comenius University in Bratislava (Slovakia) launched a new journal, *Ethnologia Slavica*, in 1969, published in German, French and English, in an effort to internationalise. In Britain, the Society for Folk Life Studies published a journal, started in 1963, entitled *Folk Life. Journal of the Society for Folk Life Studies*. It was proposed at a conference in Glasgow in the early 1970s that the name should be changed. There was some opposition, but it was eventually agreed to keep the name *Folk Life*, and to add the sub-title, *A Journal of Ethnological Studies*. This was implemented in Volume 11 for 1973. The European journal, *Ethnologia Europaea*, was established in 1967 with all of Europe in its remit, *Ethnologia Fennica* in Finland in 1971, and *Ethnologia Polona* for Poland in 1975. Some existing journals had their names changed: for example, the French *Arts et Traditions Populaires* became *Ethnologie française* with the 1971 issue.[27]

There was, therefore, a surge of activity in the 1960s–70s, and this was also marked by efforts to open up international debate and to facilitate comparative studies, for example, by using English, French, German and Russian to summarise journal articles in less familiar languages.

DEFINING ETHNOLOGY

The definition of ethnology has evolved over time, in step with changes in society, and relates to a process that is in a constant state of transition, as implied by the range of names that have been applied to it. The variations are significant in this respect, highlighting differences between countries, stressing different aspects, such as oral and material forms of culture and pointing to the nature of the discipline at particular time periods. As a matter of fact, it is difficult to find any concise definition of ethnology in the literature. An early statement was made in 1898 by the then president of the Folk-Lore Society, Alfred Nutt, in line with the view that the subject had chiefly to do with survivals: 'The sense which I attach to the term folklore . . . is that of elements of culture surviving among the less advanced sections of the community, but discarded by the more advanced.'[28]

Also in 1898, the anthropologist Alfred C Haddon (1855–1940) published *The Study of Man*, and in the Introduction he attempted some definitions:

> Ethnography is the description of a special people, whether it be a small tribe, the natives of a restricted area, or a large nation: it includes a comparative study of human groups, and has for its aim the elucidation of the interrelationship of tribes, races and other bodies of men; thus it deals with the classification of peoples, their origin and their migrations.
>
> Ethnology may also be divided into several branches, the four more

important of which are: Sociology, Technology, Religion, and Linguistics.

Sociology is the study of human communities, both simple and complex, and an attempt is now being made to trace the rise of simple communities and their gradual and diverse evolution to the complex civilizations of ancient and modern times. History . . . deals more especially with the later stages of this metamorphosis . . . The physical conditions of a country, including the climate, the vegetation . . . and the indigenous animals, affect the life of the human inhabitants of that country; in other words, the mode of life of a primitive people is conditioned by its environment. The method of living affects the family life, and so we find that certain types of family organization are related to definite habits of life. As civilization advances, the State acquires powers and regulates families as well as individuals, but the characteristics of different forms of government are themselves due to the type of family organization which obtains among those various peoples . . .

Other fruitful lines of study are to be found in tracing the evolution of tools, weapons – in fact, all manufactured objects.[29]

Haddon also found the study of designs and patterns to be relevant, and he wrote a book on the subject: *Evolution in Art, as Illustrated by the Life-Histories of Designs*, 1895. He was concerned to find ways of establishing how our forefathers thought and what they believed. One possibility was to investigate people at different stages of culture in relation to different degrees of geographical isolation, and carry out a comparative study of customs, ways of thought, and religion. Another was to use folklore to probe into the past, since he went along with the general view of the time that the 'folk' bore 'the same relation to educated people that savages do to civilized communities':

> They are the backward people among ourselves. The same value applies to their actions and modes of thought as to the investigation of savages. But folk-lore is the investigation of psychical survivals within a more or less civilized society, and thus by its means we are largely enabled to study the practices and beliefs of our forefathers, for in an attenuated form many of these actually persist amongst us. By appealing to comparative custom and religion we can often form a pretty good idea as to what those actions really signified, and so we can recover our ancestral religion.[30]

Richard Weiss, in his book *Volkskunde der Schweiz* (1946), defined *Volkskunde* as the science of *Volksleben* (folklife), which consists of the interrelationships between the people and popular culture, insofar as these are conditioned by community and tradition. He described the subject as a young and developing science, and claimed that this volume presented for the first time a unified and scientifically based overview for Switzerland, which not only indicated the richness of the subject, but also the variety of the research topics: settlement forms, buildings, clothing, ceramics, hand tools, folksongs, folktales, devotion, superstition, legal survivals and customary ways of life. He could have added others, such as food, which in recent years has become increasingly a subject for ethnological study.[31]

Descriptions of the subject can be helpful in trying to establish a definition. In 1977, Wiegelmann described the subject as follows:

> *Volkskunde* researches cultures in the area of Europe, chiefly those of the middle and lower classes. Historically, it goes as far back as written sources will allow, i.e. roughly to the Middle Ages. In terms of time, it links up with pre- and early history, especially in relation to material culture research. Since information on the lower and middle echelons of society begins to flow more strongly in modern times, ethnological research is mainly concentrated on the period following 1500.
>
> From the systematic point of view, it has the same focus as *Völkerkunde* and Cultural Anthropology, namely, culture. The difference lies only in the orientation. *Völkerkunde* concentrates on non-European and pre-literate societies, cultural anthropology researches cultures worldwide and in general culture and its laws. Since there has been since the Middle Ages in Europe a hierarchical layering of society with a leading upper class culture, the other group of neighbouring sciences consists of those which study the areas of culture that have most relevance to the upper classes: art, music, literature and architecture.[32]

In 1979 in Finland, Ilmar Talve produced a comprehensive survey of every aspect of Finnish folk culture, the bulk of which could apply to any country, whether in Europe or not, apart from a number of purely regional elements, unique to the area concerned. The Introduction dealt with the setting of geography, history, religion, land ownership, towns. The individual chapters covered settlement and buildings; traditional occupations, including farming, hunting, fishing, forestry work and handicrafts; communications and trade, including seafaring; food; dress; textiles and folk art; social and economic institutions; life-cycle rites; special days in the year; folk belief and folk medicine; folklore, mainly of an oral nature; folk music, dance and games; the towns and industrial communities; and a general picture of folk culture in its main periods and as it varied regionally.[33]

Talve provided an almost encyclopedic coverage of themes that could be considered relevant to ethnological study. A volume published in Sweden in 1966, an 'introduction to folklife research', by Professor Sigfrid Svensson, adopted a more theoretical approach and dealt with the methodology of research. His chapters related to courses taught at the University of Lund in Sweden, and comprise folk culture and early (prehistoric) culture; folk culture and primitive culture; typology, mapping and dating; cultural regions, cultural zones (which can be smaller parts of cultural regions) and distribution maps; relict- and peripheral zones, functional and social retreat; words and things; the dissemination of tradition and culture contact; economic high periods and cultural fixation; folk culture and central direction; pattern, copying and re-modelling; the meaning of the pattern (model?), reality and invention; function and milieu; totality and change; and Nordic and comparative folklife research as a university subject.

He included a chapter on how folklife research was carried out at his university.[34] Some of these elements were further explored by Wiegelmann in 1990, in a book on theoretical concepts in European ethnology.[35]

PREHISTORIC AND DARK AGE ETHNOLOGY

In discussing the history of ethnological research in the eighteenth and nineteenth centuries, Wiegelmann stated that *Volkskunde* dealt with cultures in the area of Europe, primarily in relation to the middle and lower classes of society. He recognised, however, that ethnological research could go back as far as written sources allow, i.e. to the Middle Ages, and for earlier times archaeological evidence could provide much data, especially from material culture, which includes remains of fauna and flora.[36] There is therefore a case for viewing ethnology as a discipline that can cover a very long time span, though it must adapt its approach to periods and situations where there is no written record, for example by using later ethnological evidence as a means of interpreting the past, and indicating how gaps might have been filled in areas – such as easily perishable items, or the techniques of use of specific hand tools – for which no evidence survives. So, for example, examination of the widespread finds of hazelnut remains in prehistoric excavations suggests that hazelnuts were not only a food source, but they could also play a role similar to hard grains (wheat, maize, rice, etc) that could be dried and stored, and used in due course in an economy based on barter and therefore acting as a trade link between early communities,[37] in effect giving a possible glimpse into the way early communities worked and the level of economic sophistication they had attained. Survivals can also have quite a sophisticated story to tell, incorporating techniques of use as well as similarities in form. The method of baking bannocks against a stone set at the side of the fire on festival occasions is an example of retention into the late nineteenth century in north-east Scotland of a much older technique that had otherwise disappeared with the spread of the flat girdle on which oatcakes were baked above the fire.[38] In relation to prehistory, therefore, and to a considerable extent also to the so-called Dark Ages, ethnological research into the tools, techniques and all the paraphernalia of everyday life under whatsoever administrative system, of any later literate societies, can perform a useful function in interpreting the past. The archaeologist Professor Grahame Clark understood this:

> Archaeological evidence can only yield history when it has been interpreted, and . . . it can only be interpreted adequately by taking account among other things of survivals from the past . . . When one passes beyond the range of recorded history the difficulty of understanding past ages is magnified, since one finds oneself deprived of that direct access to the thought of earlier generations which only the written word allows.

And he added the proviso:

> Before assuming that any particular element of Folk-Culture is in fact a

survival from ancient times, therefore, it is essential to be sure that continuity has in fact been established between the features under comparison. By means of a critical historical method, it should be possible to strip away the civilized accretions and reveal the essential barbarian core.[39]

Demonstrable continuity from early times, however, is a scarce luxury, and though it may come closest to being realised in relation to certain aspects of buildings, such as circular as against rectangular forms,[40] there will always remain a gap. This is where study of later ethnological material, including techniques of use of tools, alongside comparative research in other countries or regions, can lead to more secure interpretation, so that the researcher can begin to fill out, however provisionally, the dark period of the gap, using earlier archaeological and later ethnological and comparative evidence.

In the aforementioned symposium held at the School of Scottish Studies in 1959, the archaeologist Charles Thomas gave a lecture on 'Archaeology and Folk-Life Studies'. He saw folklife as dividing into two categories. *Pure* folklife studies embraced the 'material remains of contemporary or "sub-recent" communities, expanded by similar study of their popular beliefs, sayings, traditions, stories, songs and music'. They tended to concentrate on rural communities, especially those in peripheral zones. *Applied* folklife studies were a means whereby the pre- or proto-historian,

> faced with evidence of the use of objects, of domestic custom, or of rural technology, which he cannot explain in terms of the objects or customs themselves, turns to the context of supposedly similar things, practices, or machinery in use to-day, and looks for a solution there.[41]

Arthur Mitchell's book, *The Past in the Present* (1880), is cited as an example of the use of obsolete or obsolescent objects in interpreting the past.[42]

ANTIQUARIANISM

One of the roots of the ethnological method lies in the field of antiquarian learning, which produced a substantial literature that took into account aspects of both material culture and oral traditions. The pattern of antiquarianism was set in the sixteenth and seventeenth centuries. John Leland (1506–52) styled himself 'antiquarius', and was appointed King's Antiquary by Henry VIII in 1533, with powers to seek out records of antiquity in ecclesiastical establishments throughout England. He was followed by William Camden (1551–1623), whose survey of British topography and antiquities, *Britannia*, was first published in Latin in 1586,[43] and then in expanded English versions in 1695 and 1789. In his *Remaines of a Greater Worke, Concerning Britain*, he included descriptions of old costumes and coins, as well as a list of proverbs.[44] Francis Grose (1731?–91) was an active antiquarian, who regarded the study of antiquities as 'a serious branch of national learning'. He made it clear in the journal he founded and ran from 1775 to 1784, *The Antiquarian Repertory*, that the earlier concept of antiquities related to 'physical and visual remains and scenes and to the memorials of the great rather than the lowly'.[45] He worked hard at justifying the study of antiquities, which it had been the fashion to laugh at as 'the idle amusement of a few humdrum fellows', and explained its worth in the Introduction to the first volume of his journal:

> Without a competent fund of Antiquarian Learning, no one will ever make a respectable figure, either as a Divine, a Lawyer, Statesman, Soldier, or even a private Gentleman, and that it is the *sine qua non* of several of the more liberal professions, as well as many trades; and is besides a study to which all persons in particular instances have a kind of propensity, every man being, as Logicians express it, '*Quoad hoc*', an Antiquarian.[46]

Grose wrote a *Treatise on Ancient Armour and Weapons* (1785–89), maintaining the old concern for the material culture of the élite classes, but he also produced much of a philological nature: *A Provincial Glossary, with a collection of Local Proverbs, and Popular Superstitions* (1787) and *A Classical Dictionary of the Vulgar Tongue* (1785). In this way, he linked words and things in his collecting activities, and brought language and dialect into play as a further element in the study of antiquities.

John Aubrey (1626–97) added to the range by seeking out local traditions in Wiltshire and Surrey that included supernatural experiences and conceptions. In his *Miscellanies* (1696) he gathered together much occult information:

> fatalities occurring at predestined times and places, omens, dreams, apparitions, prophecies, marvels, magic, knockings, blows invisible, visions in a glass, glances of love and envy, converse with angels and spirits, transportation in the air, second-sighted persons.[47]

As a country squire collecting, amongst other things, such memorates, which the American folklorist Richard Dorson describes as 'in form . . . casual and conversational, lacking the taut structure of fictional folktales',[48] Aubrey was expanding the concept of 'antiquity', as implicit in the writings of Leland and Camden, to include local traditions and customs.[49]

Aubrey was followed by the clergyman Henry Bourne (1694–1733), who published *Antiquitates Vulgares; or, the Antiquities of the Common People. Giving an Account of several of their Opinions and Ceremonies. With proper Reflections upon each of them; shewing which may be retain'd, and which ought to be laid aside*, in 1725. He was zealous in seeking to clean up the holy days and other occasions of ceremony, which, he claimed, the common people marked by revelry and loose conduct. In his efforts against papistry and heathen ideas, he sought the origins of calendar customs and the like in early Latin writings, the books of scripture, classical authors (e.g. Socrates, Plutarch, Virgil and Cicero), and English chroniclers, in effect creating a handbook of sources. He also drew on his own observations of Midsummer's Eve bonfires, of the visiting of wells and springs for superstitious purposes, etc. *Antiquitates Vulgares* was published again in 1777, with extensive commentaries added to each chapter by John Brand (1744–1806), under the title

Observations on Popular Antiquities. A two-volume edition, edited by Sir Henry Ellis (1777–1869), secretary of the Society of Antiquaries, appeared in 1813, entitled *Observations on Popular Antiquities: Chiefly Illustrating the Origin of our Vulgar Customs, Ceremonies and Superstitions.* According to Dorson, 'this mighty work laid the foundations for a science of folklore, and became a landmark in the history of English thought', and 'by his range of illustrative examples, Brand had defined an unknown and unsuspected area of civilization, the traditional culture of the common people, rooted in a pagan antiquity, and so of interest to the educated gentry'.[50]

Brand found his material in sources of all kinds, including dictionaries, glossaries and collections of proverbs, like Grose at an earlier date. For Scotland, the *Statistical Accounts* of the 1790s in twenty-one volumes were a further rich source of regional information, with sections on antiquities and the manners and customs of the people, which came close to being a national survey.[51] Joseph Strutt (1749–1802) was another important figure, whose copious writings were dedicated to the study of antiquities, including arms, dress, games and pastimes, and Brand made much use of them. Another source which was becoming frequent at the period was the growing literature on tours and travels, such as *A Tour in Scotland, MDCCLXIX* (1769) by Thomas Pennant (1726–98), a Welsh naturalist, who travelled widely in Britain and Ireland and the continent of Europe and was a keen observer of agricultural practices, industry, buildings, antiquities and amusements.[52]

Brand was basically an excerptor of data from printed sources; the next 'step forward in transmuting the concept of popular antiquities into the science of folklore, however, would be the direct soliciting of eye-witness accounts and personal reports of rural ceremonies and usages'.[53] This approach was adopted by William Hone (1780–1842), bookseller, who initiated the practice of having a number of contributor–correspondents, or informants. He roused interest by reprinting descriptions of popular customs in his *Every-Day Book* (Jan. 1825–Dec. 1827), *Table-Book* (1827) or *Year-Book* (1831–32). His informants were encouraged to send him descriptions of similar phenomena that they had witnessed personally. In this way he was also able to record local variations, which he published in his weekly, making it a storehouse of past and present manners and customs.[54]

By the second half of the nineteenth century, the academic subject range and research methods of approach had been largely established. 'Popular antiquities' had become 'folklore', and there was a growing literature on the subject, covering an increasingly wide range of subjects. There was even an ethnological novel, Thomas Carlyle's *Sartor Resartus* (the tailor retailored), first published in 1833, which used clothes as the symbolic theme and was divided into two parts, 'Historical-Descriptive', and 'Philosophical-Speculative', which correspond pretty well to 'ethnographical' and 'ethnological'. Carlyle, who had a deep knowledge of German literature, wrote about aspects of ethnology with which modern ethnologists are familiar, for example, the symbolic quality of the material aspects of human culture: 'Not a Hut he builds but is the visible embodiment of a Thought; but bears visible record of invisible things; but is, in the transcendental sense, symbolical as well as real.' He was also aware of changing fashion: Homer's Epos does not cease to be true, but it is not our Epos. Its truth is of another era, and it has to be reinterpreted for succeeding generations.[55] Such reinterpretation is one of the major tasks of ethnology, and for this reason it is important to establish the historiography of the subject.

THE GROWTH OF 'FOLKLORE' AS A SCIENCE

In the course of the nineteenth century, antiquarianism as such was gradually replaced by the developing subject of anthropology, and antiquaries evolved into 'Antiquary-Folklorists'. Those specified by Richard Dorson were the Irishmen Thomas Crofton Croker (1798–1854) and Thomas Keightley (1789–1872), Francis Douce (1757–1834), Thomas Wright (1810–1877), James Orchard Halliwell-Phillipps (1820–1889) and William John Thoms (1803–1885). Croker had been collecting songs and legends of the Irish peasantry from his boyhood and eventually published *Fairy Legends and Traditions of the South of Ireland* in 1825. The book drew widespread attention, internationally as well as at home. It was the first intentional field collection to be made in Great Britain, as Dorson points out, and it drew the attention of Sir Walter Scott in Scotland and the Grimms in Germany, one of whom translated the book into German.

Keightley's volume on *The Fairy Mythology, Illustrative of the Romance and Superstition of Various Countries* (1850) was an exercise in comparative folklore, marking on the one hand an increasing level of international folklore research, and on the other a new respect for the sanctity of the oral tradition, and avoidance of added literary touches. In examining 'folklore's perpetual puzzle, how to explain the similarity of widespread tales',[56] he classified legends into three groups: those that were clearly transmitted, those of apparently independent formation, and a group whose origins could not be established.[57]

The erudite Francis Douce did not produce books to any extent, but his polymathic knowledge was frequently and freely made available to others, including Brand and Ellis. Uniquely amongst folklorists of the time, he took a learned interest in folk dance, and produced a treatise 'On the Ancient English Morris Dance'.

Wright was influenced by Jacob Grimm in Germany, and saw in popular mythology and superstitions clues to 'the early formation of nations, their identity or analogy, their changes, as well as the inner texture of the national character'. He followed Grimm in seeking out relics of pagan beliefs in medieval documents, in an effort to reconstruct the pagan mythology.[58]

The main thrust of Halliwell-Phillipps' folklore research was nursery rhymes. He published *The Nursery Rhymes of England, Collected Principally from Oral Tradition* in 1842, for the Percy Society, and *Popular Rhymes and Nursery Tales* in 1849, adding another dimension to folklore studies. He also edited dictionaries of dialect words, and reprints of jestbooks, ballads and fairy beliefs, so making available much valuable source material.[59]

Thoms, the begetter of the term 'folklore', first used the *Athenaeum* to communicate with the public in the collection of folklore material, 'garnering the few ears which are remaining, scattered over that field from which our fore-fathers might have gathered a goodly crop'. But this was a journal more concerned with literature, science and the arts and accordingly, in 1849, he founded *Notes and Queries* to deal more effectively with antiquarian and folklore matters. He considered that anyone studying the manners, customs, observances, etc. of earlier times must reach two conclusions: 'The first, how much that is curious and interesting in these matters is now entirely lost – the second how much may yet be rescued by timely exertion.' This is a plea that has been repeated time and again throughout the history of the subject, though it incorporates the danger that too great a concentration of attention on survivals from the past can tend to fossilise the past. It is better to regard the past and the present, leading on to the future, as a continuing process, ever incorporating new sets of circumstances and subjects of study and adopting new methodologies, often in partnership with neighbouring disciplines. Nevertheless, the collection of evidence from all possible types of source remains a basic necessity. Thoms expressed the hope that the *Athenaeum* would

> gather together the infinite number of minute facts, illustrative of the subject . . . which are scattered over the memories of its thousands of readers, and preserve them in its pages, until some James Grimm shall arise who shall do for the Mythology of the British Islands the good service which that profound antiquary and philologist has accomplished for the Mythology of Germany. The present century has scarcely produced a more remarkable book . . . than the second edition of the '*Deutsche Mythologie*': and, what is it? – a mass of minute facts, many of which, when separately considered, appear trifling and insignificant, – but, when taken in connexion with the system into which his master-mind has woven them, assume a value that he who first recorded them never dreamed of attributing to them.[60]

By the mid nineteenth century, the subject was being shaped in Britain. It was no longer a question of simple antiquarianism, it had a name, 'folklore', and had entered a phase of substantial activity by a number of individuals that continually widened its scope. There was much discussion about origins, and means of transmission, and knock-on effects on literary productions. Sir Walter Scott (1771–1832) was prominent amongst those who created literature out of folklore and antiquities; other Scots figuring in this development were Allan Cunningham (1784–1842), writer and poet, and Robert Chambers (1802–1871), publisher, whose *Traditions of Edinburgh* (1824) was an exercise in urban folklore well before that topic became part of the folklorists' quiver.

In 1892, the British Association set up a committee to conduct 'Ethnographical Investigations in the British Isles'. The committee was backed by the Society of Antiquaries of London, the Folk-Lore Society, the Anthropological Institute and the Dialect Society. In its first circular, it stated its purpose, which was to record from selected 'typical' villages and their surrounding districts the following material:

1. Physical types of the inhabitants
2. Current traditions and beliefs
3. Peculiarities of dialect
4. Monuments and other remains of ancient culture
5. Historical evidence as to the continuity of race

An Ethnographical Survey of Ireland was undertaken at the same period by a Dublin Committee, supported by the Royal Irish Academy, in whose *Proceedings* four reports had already been published between 1893 and 1898, mainly on sea-delimited island areas, along the following lines:

> I. *Physiography of the district investigated.* II. *Anthropography.*– 1. Methods; 2. Physical characters with lists of measurements; 3. Vital Statistics (general and economic), (A) Population, (B) Acreage and Rental, (C) Language and Education, (D) Health; 4. Psychology; 5. Folk names. III. *Sociology.*– 1. Occupations; 2. Family Life and Customs; 3. Food; 4. Clothing; 5. Dwellings; 6. Transport. IV. *Folk-lore.*– 1. Customs and Beliefs; 2. Legends and Traditions; 3. Leechcraft. V. *Archaeology.*– 1. Survivals; 2. Antiquities. VI. *History.* VII. *Ethnology.* VIII. *Bibliography.*

Instructions were given for compiling the data. Hair and eye colour, the shape of the head and the shape of the nose were noted. Folklore aimed at comparing and collecting survivals of archaic beliefs, customs and traditions in modern times. The schedule of the Ethnographical Committee advised that:

> Every item of Folk-lore should be collected, consisting of customs, traditions, superstitions, sayings of the people, games, and any superstitions connected with special days, marriages, births, deaths, cultivation of the land, election of local officers, or other events.[61]

The English Dialect Society was accustomed to identifying dialectal boundaries, and it was suggested in a lecture by Miss Charlotte Burne in 1890 that the same could be done for folklore items. Her advice on the personal collecting of folklore was that:

> If you wish to understand folk-lore you must learn to understand the folk. You must know what the folk think, and how they act on subjects such as folk-lore touches, and observe how their minds form the natural background to the superstitions they act on, the customs they practise, the tales they tell.[62]

There was, therefore, a good deal of ethnological activity based on learned institutions, with an emphasis on collection.

Also in the Victorian period, the subject of anthropology was being formed. At Oxford University, Edward Burnet Tylor (1832–1917), keeper of the University Museum and reader in Anthropology, became the first Professor of Anthropology, from 1895 till 1909, and was knighted in 1912. He has been described as 'the father of anthropology and godfather of the anthropological school of folklorists'. In his view, there was a difference between mythology, which 'preserved the explanations in story form which all peoples, from the primitive to the highly developed, fashioned to account for their supernatural origins', and folklore, which 'represented the contemporary superstitions and nursery tales of civilized peoples . . . [and] belonged only to the last and highest stage of cultural progression and embodied survivals from the earlier stages'. [63]

In his influential two-volume work on *Primitive Culture* (1871)[64] Tylor discussed his theories of survivals and of animism, both relating to the development of religious ideas, including superstitions. He pinpointed survivals in a wide range of folklore categories: 'Children's games, nursery tales, proverbs, riddles, blessings, taboos, witchcraft.'[65] He marked a major divide in scholarship between the antiquarians and the new generation of folklorists, whose scientific approach was partly based on anthropology, and some of whom, like Andrew Lang, were his pupils. There followed a period of intense activity, during which the leading figures, each following his own specialisation within the field of folklore, and capable of commenting on his fellows' views, in contradiction or otherwise, nevertheless saw as their central subject man as a tradition bearer, even if it was man as a 'contemporary savage', from the less sophisticated layers of society, that formed the main thrust of investigation.

FORMALISATION OF FOLKLORE/ETHNOLOGY AS A SCIENCE

An important stage in the formalisation of the subject as a science in Britain was the founding of the Folk-Lore Society in London in 1878. It provided a focal point for discussion and drew together the contemporary 'anthropological folklorists', of whom several served terms as president: Andrew Lang in 1888–89, George Laurence Gomme in 1890–94, Edward Clodd in 1895–96, Alfred Nutt in 1897–99, and Edwin Sidney Hartland in 1900–01. These and others

> produced a whole library of folklore writings, from multi-volumed treatises to pithy articles, prefaces, lectures, addresses, reviews, and notes. Co-operating closely with each other, they formed a 'great team' whose collective efforts wrote a brilliant chapter in the history of modern thought.[66]

They sought to define the subject, and evolved methodologies of approach that not only considered printed or manuscript sources, but also included accurate, systematic field research. Since they all – in spite of their differing research emphases – looked on folklore as offering a key to identifying the stages in the ascent of man from savagery to civilisation, the question of survivals loomed large. These were recorded and studied by all possible means, with specialisations appearing: e.g. archaeologists studied material culture and established distribution patterns and levels of organisational development of early human groupings, and folklorists did the same with immaterial, mainly oral, survivals. There was much discussion of the question of diffusion from a centre, as against spontaneous creation of similar phenomena, such as folktales, ballads, etc., from a variety of centres. Early forms of village and tribal institutions were studied, as well as questions of continuity between medieval Celtic literature and modern Gaelic folklore. It was realised that fragmentary survivals were also to be found in the higher levels of civilisation. Andrew Lang summed up the situation:

> There is a science, Archaeology, which collects and compares the material relics of old races, the axes and arrow-heads. There is a form of study, Folklore, which collects and compares the similar but immaterial relics of old races, the surviving superstitions and stories, the ideas which are in our time but not of it. Properly speaking, folklore is only concerned with the legends, customs, beliefs of the Folk, of the people, of the classes which have least been altered by education, which have shared least in progress. But the student of folklore soon finds that these unprogressive classes retain many of the beliefs and ways of savages, just as the Hebridean people used spindle-whorls of stone, and bake clay pots without the aid of the wheel . . . The student of folklore is thus led to examine the usages, myths, and ideas of savages, which are still retained, in rude enough shape, by the European peasantry. Lastly, he observes that a few similar customs and ideas survive in the most conservative elements of the life of educated peoples, in ritual, ceremonial, and religious traditions and myths.[67]

A major new element in the early 1900s was 'the voice of the social sciences asking for scrutiny of the processes affecting change and stability in folklore'.[68] At the same time, broadening of the subject with new themes and concepts continued, along with efforts to classify and systematise. For example, the Orcadian William Alexander Clouston (1843–1896) sought to demonstrate that migration and trade had played a leading role in the Asiatic origins of certain European popular tales. He emphasised the importance of medieval translations in such diffusion, and signalled the interplay between written texts and oral storytelling. Francis Hindes Groome (1851–1902) studied gipsy folktales and superstitions and the Romanian rabbi Moses Gaster (1856–1934), who came to England in 1885, had a wide knowledge of eastern European languages which led him to believe that there was an easy transmission of folk narratives across language boundaries. Groome and Gaster were diffusionists, as against Lang and Tylor, who pinned their faith on a more evolutionistic approach. Gaster also differed from earlier folklorists in that he regarded fairy tales as the end of a literary process, rather than as pointers to the mentality of primitive people. Jacob Jacobs (1854–1916) was a diffusionist who postulated two lines of trans-mission, lateral and vertical; borrowing proceeded laterally, and survivals descended vertically. This theory allowed the viewpoints of the cultural evolu-tionists and diffusionists to come together, though in practice there was the weakness that it was not easy to tell if borrowings had come from outside.[69]

There was a further broadening of the subject of folklore. The archaeologist

David McRitchie argued that oral legends could retain a core of historical truth, and he linked fairy legends with prehistoric underground dwellings as proof of the former existence of a pigmy race.[70] Robert R Marett (1866–1943) re-invigorated the doctrine of survivals. He considered that study of the process of change in living folklore could lead to better understanding of what had led up to it. He advocated participation: 'Let the field folklorist observe, analyse, and even participate in custom, dance, game, and song, to understand their inner content for modern people and so the better to comprehend their meaning to savages.'[71]

There was also, broadly in the second half of the nineteenth century, a considerable infusion of comparative oral material from other countries, Iceland and Norway, Russia, Italy, India and Burma, and elsewhere. George Webbe Dasent (1817–1896) specialised in Scandinavian studies, and translated into English the *norske-eventyr* (Norse tales) gathered from the Norwegian peasants by Peter Christen Asbjörnsen and Jörgen Moe. He wrote a long Introduction on 'the Origin and Diffusion of Popular Tales' for his *Popular Tales from the Norse*, in which he followed the Grimms in relating the tales to mythological antecedents.[72] William Ralston Shedden-Ralston (1828–1889), a co-founder of the Folk-Lore Society, published books on Russian folktales, epic poems (*byliny*) and songs, with explanatory texts on the 'old Slavic pagan mythology that lay half buried in the peasant oral literature'.[73] Like Dasent and Thom, he was much influenced by Jacob Grimm. The Englishwoman Rachel Harriette Busk (1881–1907), whose second home was in Italy, set about collecting Italian folktales, and published folktales and folksongs from various localities within Italy, including the urban setting of Rome. Richard Carnac Temple was an army colonel and civil administrator in India and Burma, who published a good deal of Indian folklore and lectured to the Folk-Lore Society on the subject. He also analysed his material, and worked out tables that displayed 'practically the whole machinery of popular Indian story-telling'.[74] Mary Henrietta Kingsley (1862–1900) was a promulgator of African folklore. She believed in 'the practical value of folklore studies in contributing to successful imperial government', and thus demonstrated what could be an important function for ethnological studies.

There were also those who were called by Dorson the 'Celtic Folklorists': John Francis Campbell of Islay (1822–1885) and Alexander Carmichael (1832–1912) in Scotland; Sir John Rhys (1840–1915) in Wales; and Douglas Hyde (1860–1949) in Ireland. Their work spawned a number of academic institutes in Britain and Ireland, but also brought to the forefront questions of nationalism, such as have been discussed by the sociologist Michael Hechter, who saw the phenomenon of Celtic nationalism as a political response to the persistence of regional inequality, allied to questions of language and religious affiliation and levels of industrialisation.[75]

The underlying motivation of such Celtic folklorists was an anxiety to protect and conserve what was seen as a disappearing language and culture, under constant pressure from the country's prosperous core. Campbell's *Popular Tales of the West Highlands Orally Collected* appeared in two volumes in 1860, and two more were added in 1862.[76] Under the influence of the Grimm brothers in Germany, and of Scandinavian, but especially Norwegian, scholars, Campbell set about collecting in 1859, and teamed up with competent writers of Gaelic, notably Hector Maclean, the Islay schoolmaster, and John Dewar, a maker of fences, to ensure that he was getting the exact words in Gaelic of the storytellers. He also collaborated with Alexander Carmichael, exciseman for Islay, Skye, Uist and Oban, whose collections were published in six volumes under the title *Carmina Gadelica. Hymns and Incantations With Illustrative Notes on Words, Rites, and Customs, Dying and Obsolete; Orally Collected in the Highlands and Islands of Scotland*.[77] Campbell presented his own folk inheritance with intellectual detachment. He was

> conscious of practical method and underlying theory, scrupulous in furnishing information on his tellers and the storytelling situations, alert to the possibility of the storytelling situations, alert to the possibility of literary influences, aware of comparative narratives outside Scotland and of variations within the Highland hoard, and sensitive to the problems of translation.[78]

Carmichael's strong subject area was that of religious folk poetry, parallel in some respects to the archaic prayers that Zsuzsanna Erdélyi collected in Hungary.[79]

Carmichael's collecting activity lay mainly in the period from 1855 to 1899. His material has been classified under the following headings:

> invocations (e.g. prayers for protection, prayers before going to sleep: addresses to the saints, seasonal hymns, including genuine Christmas carols, blessings for everyday tasks (banking up the fire for the night, reaping, grinding, milking, herding, and hunting); incantations used in healing; prayers to the sun and moon; rhymes about animals and birds; blessings on cattle and other livestock; miscellaneous songs, e.g. praise-songs, love-songs, milking songs, fairy songs, waulking songs; auguries, with notes on the augurers' methods; and much incidental information on custom and belief in general . . . [much of which comprised] the things which were said when the door was closed, and the lights were out.[80]

Rhys was a philologist and archaeologist, who published material on Welsh and Manx folklore, notably in the two volumes of *Celtic Folklore, Welsh and Manx*. Whereas his work was academic (he was the first Professor of Celtic at Oxford), that of Douglas Hyde in Ireland was positively nationalistic. He was founder in 1893 of the Gaelic League, which promoted the active use of the Irish language and of Irish cultural institutions. The use of Irish was made compulsory for matriculation purposes in the National University of Ireland in 1913, and the Irish Parliament, the Dáil Éireann, was committed to the language from its first meeting in 1919. This is an example of the use of a language, with its content of folklore, not to reconstruct the thoughts of prehistoric savages, but to act as a stimulus to the revival of a nation.[81]

Developments during the twentieth century in folklore and folkloristics are included elsewhere in this work.

By the first half of the twentieth century, the antiquarian phase in folklore, which had been common to all of Britain as well as to other countries in Europe, began to change into a more decentralised approach, with emphasis on 'national' cultures. Running through both phases, however, are other strands besides antiquarianism and folklore. Philology and etymology played a considerable role in relating folklore survivals to, for example, Aryan traditions, and providing evidence for links that supported evolutionist thinking amongst nineteenth-century scholars. The study of language and dialect, and the compilation of dictionaries and glossaries based on scrutiny of printed sources and on question-naires and field research, meanwhile built up a database of great ethnological value. Rustic speech was seen as a direct key to folklore studies, 'opening windows into the covert beliefs of English countrymen through the living language of their local dialects'.[82] It became a vehicle for occupational studies, as of drift-net fishermen and coal miners.[83]

Dialectal material in linguistic atlases could throw up distribution patterns that were relevant to the establishment of ethnological culture zones. For example, the investigators who gathered data for Georg Wenker's *Deutscher Sprachatlas* (German linguistic atlas) had expected to find clearly distinguished dialectal boundaries, but in the event, the atlas 'revealed a continuum in which forms of language made up, map by map, a complex of overlapping distribution'.[84] Wenker (1852–1911) issued a questionnaire that went to 40,000 points in Germany, starting in 1876, and later as a supplementary exercise to Austria, Luxemburg, Switzerland and part of the then Czechoslovakia. Publication of the German linguistic atlas began in 1926 at Marburg, under the editorship of Ferdinand Wrede. The fairly dense network of points was necessary, because of the way Germany was made up of a number of territorial units and towns with specific speech districts in and around them. In France, on the other hand, the centralising pressures of Paris allowed the use of a wider-meshed net and so the linguistic atlas of France (*Atlas linguistique de la France*) was completed more quickly, under the editorship of Gilliéron and Edmont. Linguistic atlases, therefore, can provide practical clues to the establishment of culture zones, and to differences between them resulting from the underlying forms of administrative or political organisation. They are useful tools in ethnological research.

Language and lore came to be a focus in centres established in the twentieth century at the Universities of Sheffield and Leeds in England.

HISTORICAL GEOGRAPHY, ANTHROPOLOGY AND SOCIOLOGY

In Britain, historical geography, anthropology and sociology played a part in the development of ethnological studies, wittingly or otherwise. Individuals within these disciplines could be inspirational – for example, the polymathic Professor Herbert John Fleure (1877–1969) who, after studying at Aberystwyth in Wales and Zürich in Switzerland, in 1910 became Professor of Zoology and also lecturer in Geography at Aberystwyth. In 1917 he became the first Chair of Geography and Anthropology, the second element in the title being his own choice. In 1940 he moved to Manchester as Professor of Geography and retired from there in 1944. His wide-ranging view of the interaction of man with his environment is neatly summed up in his book *A Natural History of Man in Britain*.[85] His influence was great, and a number of his pupils became pioneers in shaping the study of folklife and local community studies and the development of folk- and open-air museums.

One of them was Iorwerth Cyfeiliog Peate (1901–1982). The son of a carpenter and teacher of arts and crafts, he studied under Fleure at Aberystwyth, and graduated in 1921. Fleure spoke of his

> ... dedication of himself to the study of the life of the people, their thought and art as well as their material equipment and economic activities. For him there was no separation of folklore and folk-life, and his use of the word 'folk' was far above the sugary sentiment that it connotes in some minds. For Peate it was to be the study of the life of the people, the humble as well as the rich, the language as well as the houses and villages.[86]

Peate joined the National Museum of Wales in 1927, working in the Department of Archaeology, which had a collection of 'bygones'. His work on these led to the publication in 1929 of his *Guide to the Collection of Welsh Bygones*, in two parts. In the first, he described the 'old-fashioned life in Wales', to provide a historical and cultural guide to the collection. This was effectively an agenda for the study of folklife in Wales, covering not only material culture but also oral traditions, customs and folklore. In the second part, the catalogue proper, he demonstrated how objects could be used to illuminate the culture as a whole. The *Guide*, therefore, was a pioneering publication for museums as well as for folklife studies.

In 1932, as a result of his perseverance, the Sub-Department of Folk Culture and Industries was established in new galleries, and the collections were officially recognised as the 'National Folk Collection'. It was laid down that the collections should only include items of post-1536 date, this being the year of the Act of Union of Wales with England.

When the estate of St Fagans was given to the National Museum of Wales, he was able to develop the site as the Welsh Folk Museum, founded in 1947, containing, for example, re-erected traditional building types with period rooms, a woollen mill, a tannery, a non-conformist chapel and various craft workshops, in which craftsmen could demonstrate traditional techniques. This was, in its conception and practice, greatly indebted to the 'open-air museums' of Scandinavia, of which a leading example, popularly known as 'Skansen', was founded by Artur Hazelius in 1891.[87] Others were the Danish Folk Museum, 1881; the Norsk Folkemuseum, Oslo, 1887; the Sandvigske Samlinger, Lillehammer, Norway, 1887; and Den Gamle By, Denmark, 1909. By Scandinavian standards, the British open-air museums came much later in time. The influence of the Scandinavian open-air museum movement can be symbolised by the fact that the term 'Skansen' is used generally elsewhere. The Hungarian Open-Air Museum, for example, is called 'Skanzen'.[88]

A feature of the Welsh Folk Museum was a full-scale department dealing with the Welsh language and its various forms. It undertook 'the collection of data relating to all aspects of the Welsh oral tradition, e.g. vocabularies – domestic, craft agricultural, etc. – (with tape recordings), folktales, lore and customs, and all information possible concerning the spiritual background of Welsh life and culture'.

Peate was also the founder in 1956 and editor of the ethnological journal *Gwerin* (Welsh for 'folk'). This half-yearly journal was a personal initiative and one of the earliest in Britain, along with *Ulster Folklife* (1955) and *Scottish Studies* (1957), to have specifically ethnological content. It was replaced by the journal *Folk Life*, the organ of the recently formed Society for Folk Life Studies, in 1973, which, like *Gwerin*, covered the whole of the British Isles and Ireland.

Iorwerth Peate is an important figure both in the spread of the open-air and folk museum movement in Britain in the second half of the nineteenth century, and in the promotion of ethnological research, especially along historical–cultural lines, following the Scandinavian model of the period.[89] However, he regarded folklife as 'the study of the way of life of communities and of nations which are comparatively unaffected by a high degree of industrialization', and he thought that highly industrialised areas and the heavy industries associated with them should be excluded.[90] The more recent view is that such areas are probably most in need of study.

Another influential pupil of Fleure was Emyr Estyn Evans (1905–1989). A Welshman who spent the bulk of his working life in Ulster, he was one of the main founders of folklife studies in Ireland. He was Professor of Geography and director of the Institute of Irish Studies at Queen's University, Belfast, president of the Ulster Folklife Society and chairman of the Board of Trustees of the Ulster Folk and Transport Museum (founded in 1958), in the formation of which he had played a substantial role.[91]

Fleure's teaching was the major influence on his academic work, with its emphasis on the interaction between culture and environment, and 'achieving an understanding of the evolution of human life in the past as a key to interpreting life in the present'. Evans came to folklife through fieldwork in archaeology and geography, during which he kept a sharp eye on the material culture of the countryside. His first articles on ethnological subjects appeared in archaeological journals, the *Ulster Journal of Archaeology* and *Antiquity*, in 1939, on material culture survivals, and in the geographical journal *Geography*, on 'Some survivals of the Openfield system'. He did not forget oral evidence, and a selection of folktales was published in 1941. His books on folklife started with *Irish Heritage* (1942), dedicated to H J Fleure, and lavishly illustrated with his own sketches. This ran into numerous subsequent editions, and it could well be regarded as the earliest attempt in English to systematise the subject, though it avoids the 'controversial realms' of religion and politics. In his *Irish Folk Ways*, first published in 1957, he expanded and further systematised the material and added a bibliography and references, making it a more academic work. Other books mark clearly his integrated view of geology and geography, settlement patterns and land use, buildings, tools and equipment, crafts, the produce of land and sea, etc., whether relating to a specific area such as *Mourne County* (1951) or to the larger entity of Ireland, as in *The Personality of Ireland. Habitat, Heritage and History* (1973).[92]

Though he was very influential through his books and the various culture-related positions he held, via which he was able to facilitate the establishment of the Ulster Folk and Transport Museum, he was aware that much of his recording and collecting work was still very much at the beginning of things, and might more accurately be described as 'ethnographical', in Ampère's sense of the word (see above). In this respect, he can be seen as a role model for trainee ethnologists, who should begin by getting to know their own environment and community. This is a factor that Jacob Grimm recognised also. When A H Hoffmann von Fallersleben visited him in 1819, and told him that he planned to travel to Italy and Greece to study the remains of ancient forms of art, Grimm replied: *'Liegt Ihnen Ihr Vaterland nicht näher?'* (Isn't your fatherland closer?).[93]

Peate and Evans both played a direct and important role in the development of folklife studies and folk museums in Britain. Another student of Fleure who made an impact of a different but related kind was R U Sayce, who became an orthodox anthropologist, working in South Africa before taking up employment in the Manchester Museum. In 1933, he published his book on *Primitive Arts and Crafts, An Introduction to the Study of Material Culture*, noting that: 'For some years past British anthropologists have devoted most of their attention to the sociological side of their subject, and comparatively little has been published in this country on the material culture of primitive peoples.' Though the bulk of the book is concerned with the tools and equipment of non-European peoples, nevertheless the chapters discuss a variety of approaches, covering, for example, the relationship of material culture with the environment, inventions and civilisation, diffusion by trade and emigration, the effects of prestige, and of the differences between the sexes.[94] He was also interested in food, and wrote a lengthy article on food through the ages,[95] so providing an early example of the use of food in anthropological studies. Sayce's work could well provide a basis for the construction of a theory of material culture applicable to European conditions.

A scholar who held the Chair of Geography and Anthropology at Aberystwyth for a time, but who was not one of Fleure's pupils, was C Daryll Forde, whose book *Habitat, Economy and Society. A Geographical Introduction to Ethnology* (1934) is well known. It was 'intended as an introduction to the ethnography and human geography of non-European peoples', and dealt with the 'economic and social life of a number of groups at diverse levels of cultural achievement and in different regions of the world, and with the rise of new crafts and organizations in the growth of civilization'. Forde deliberately concentrated on economic life, and largely left out religious and ceremonial life. This work, although it would be classed as ethnography according to Ampère's definition, nevertheless demonstrates the important influence that human geography can have on ethnological research, especially in relation to the study of material culture,[96] which is intimately related to the social organisation of the community.[97]

The various types of background to the growth of the subject of ethnology so far discussed have been largely cultural–historical, on the analogy of the Swedish practice, in which Sigurd Erixon and his journal *Folk-Liv* had set the pattern (though Erixon came to carry out massive research projects in industrial situations also). Swedish ethnologists had in turn been influenced by German ethnology of the pre-1914 period, for example through Fritz Graebner and his book *Methode der Ethnologie*.[98] Aberystwyth was a focal point for the development of university ethnology and ethnology-related activities in Britain. One of these activities was the planning in the 1930s by the Department of Geography and Anthropology of a series of community studies dealing with social relations and institutions, using a geographical dimension as well as adapting the intensive methods and holistic approach developed by anthropologists for the study of small-scale entities to units of society set with clear geographical bounds within larger societies. Field research was carried out in the 1940s–50s, and the programme produced a number of studies that have considerable ethnological value.

Alwyn D Rees, a student of C Daryll Forde, produced *Life in a Welsh Countryside* (1950). Applying a historical perspective (using census data, agricultural returns, legal codes and texts, etc.), and with the use of questionnaires completed by every household in the parish, he was able to compile statistical data. Rees examined the local social life and structure of a rural community which was not a sharply defined area with clear physical boundaries, and set it within the context of the general culture of Wales. It included a serious study of the material culture of a community, one of the earliest examples in the British Isles. It demonstrated the application of anthropological techniques to contemporary life in Wales, and it surveyed the economy, homes and hearths, farmsteads, family and kindred, religion, status and prestige. An interesting finding was the lack of focus and of a village tradition on the English pattern in his community.[99]

Another book, of much interest for its view of farming communities, was David Jenkins' *The Agricultural Community in South-West Wales at the Turn of the Twentieth Century* (1971). This study, based on the south Cardiganshire area, discusses the relationship between 'farm practice and social structure'. At this period of change, before the coming of harvesting and tractor technology, smallholders and landless cottagers supplied the essential additional harvest labour for the bigger farmers, in return for which, according to the number of days worked, they were allocated so many drills of potatoes, grown on the farmer's land. In this symbiotic relationship, the farmer secured his crop and ensured food supplies for his family and stock, and the cottager got a store of potatoes for his family and pigs. In other areas, seasonal harvest labour would be hired at the cross in the village.[100] Further examples of such symbiosis were the dependence of small units on large farms for the services of a bull, which were paid for by the provision of help during the grain, hay and potato harvests, normally at the rate of one day's free labour for each cow served. Or a horse might be borrowed to make up a plough team, with payment again in the form of harvest labour.

These two community studies are perhaps the best of the five that were inspired from Aberystwyth.[101] A common feature that relates to the ethnological method is the awareness of background history, at a time when anthropologists like A R Radcliffe-Brown were not viewing history as relevant to the study of society. On the other hand, little or no attempt is made to record vanishing customs for their own sake. The impact of borders is prominent, in this case the English/Welsh border, marked by a basic English/Welsh opposition. But 'the community studies carried out in Wales and published between 1950 and 1971 showed few signs of a systematic development of theory'. The community study approach has not been continued, and 'has come to be regarded as a somewhat intractable concept despite the sociologist's obvious concern with social bonds in everyday life'.[102] Nevertheless, the volumes reflect the ethnologists' concern for time, place and social milieu. Man as an individual cannot function outside some kind of social framework, and the community studies volumes have drawn attention to several aspects of human interaction within social frameworks of a variety of kinds, such as the role of incomers in decision making, the function of recreational groups, the part played by gossip, boundaries between secular and religious matters, status distinctions, etc. They also take into consideration the question of material culture in interpreting status, economic level, and dependence relationships. In terms of the use of historical data and analyses of material culture, they come close to the methodology of ethnology, and demonstrate how sociology, anthropology and ethnology can be integrated into a rounded research method.

But the real importance of the Aberystwyth Chair lies with the students of Professor Fleure, who became involved in establishing the major open-air or folk museums, with archives, and systematised the production of ethnological data in journals and books, often on the basis of questionnaires. Their training in historical geography has had a lasting influence on the practice of ethnology in Britain. Iorwerth Peate, who was first director of the Welsh Folk Museum, studied under Fleure. In Ulster, the work of Professor E Estyn Evans was instrumental in establishing the Ulster Folk Museum, with George Thompson, also a pupil of Fleure, its first director. As a result, such individuals and museums have played an important role in shaping the modern concept of ethnology in Britain.

THE IMPACT OF NEIGHBOURING DISCIPLINES

Sociology (a name first coined by the Frenchman Auguste Comte in 1864) and social anthropology tend to deal with current themes or situations on the basis of field research and participant observation and are less concerned with historical depth. There are exceptions, though – for example, the study by Norbert Elias, *The Civilising Process*, is described by the historian turned sociologist Peter Burke as 'a book which may perhaps best be described as a sociological interpretation of European history from the Middle Ages onwards, though the authors of such historically oriented studies were "swimming against the stream"'.[103] History, on the other hand, is, according to Burke, 'the study of human societies, with the emphasis on the differences between them and on the changes which have taken place in each one over time', while sociology was 'the study of human society, with the emphasis on generalising about its structure'.[104]

Clearly, history, sociology, social anthropology and other neighbouring disciplines, including peasant studies, have much to offer ethnology, and ethnology has much to offer in return. For example, in community studies, the basic unit was the individual and the family. In pre-industrial times and in peripheral areas, collaboration between family members and between separate families in work activities (such as tilling the soil, harvesting) was a necessity for subsistence purposes. The intricacies of inheritance systems, which could impinge on forms of land use, were also fundamental to the structure of the family, particularly in relation to land ownership and ownership of the means of making a living.[105] The study of the family and of earlier social structures was the purpose of the Cambridge Group for the History of Population and Social Structure, founded officially in 1964 through the enterprise of two people in particular, E A Wrigley and Peter Laslett. Laslett's book, *The World We Have Lost*, first published in 1965, and written before the group came into being, began as an attempt to write out in a straightforward way the introductory facts about the structure of English society as it was before the Industrial Revolution, and to make some comparison with its structure in the twentieth century.

The raw material for this type of sociological analysis came from account books, parish registers of births, baptisms and weddings, census returns, etc., which provided the statistical data that enabled scholars to reconstruct the 'family' at earlier periods. Amongst the better off, including craftsmen and tradesmen, the concept of family could include servants and apprentices as well as the biological group. The data assembled in Cambridge for studying the size and structure of the domestic group is extensive – parallel work has been proceeding in, for example, France, Japan, Serbia, and colonial North America – so that it requires the computer and the conjoint input of a group of scholars, such as the Cambridge Group, to analyse it. This has introduced scientific, quantitative controls into the art of social history, though allowance has to be made for the differing nature of the sources, which may be incomplete or subject to administrative or political bias. It would make sense, therefore, for social scientists of all kinds, such as sociologists, social and cultural anthropologists, historians and historical geographers to collaborate with ethnologists in trying to achieve a truer or fuller picture of family and community at particular points in time and space, each contributing their particular specialisms and methods of approach. Examples of such an interdisciplinary mélange of approaches are Kussmaul's study of the functioning of the English countryside through investigation of servants in husbandry in early modern England, Spufford's study of English villagers in the sixteenth and seventeenth centuries, and Wrightson's volume on English society over the same period.[106] Scotland does not as yet have the same coverage, though it is evident that sources such as the testamentary records held in the National Records of Scotland could, if treated with the same partnership process, provide an enormous amount of information on the social history of the family with the associated material culture, economics, composition and disposal of stock and crops, the lending of money, family interactions, inheritance patterns and regional variations in pre-industrial times. The conjoint approach in Cambridge has had an effect on historical studies, and can provide a statistical basis for the work of researchers in neighbouring disciplines, including ethnology.[107]

Laslett distinguished three types of household: the 'simple family household', consisting of a married pair or a widow with her children; the 'extended family household', which included one or more relatives other than offspring; and the 'multiple family household', containing two or more conjugal units connected by kinship or marriage.[108] This, however, oversimplifies the situation, for the household can expand as children are born, and contract as they marry and move out, so changing the classification; or a group of relatives might live together and exploit a piece of property in common. A newly married couple might live in a rented room, but this did not necessarily mean a move to a new lifestyle, for the wife might spend much of her time back in the parental home when her husband was working, and the two households were treated, in effect, as one extended household.[109] An ethnological study of the furnishings and equipment of households of different types would add significantly to the value of such investigations, and give them greater depth.

Another concept that ethnology is concerned with is that of 'ecology'. The term was first used in 1870 by the German zoologist Ernst Haeckel, and was adopted by human geographers, notably Paul Vidal de la Blache in France and Friedrich Ratzel in Germany, in their considerations of the relationship between man and his environment. It was developed by anthropologists as a means of also viewing cultural processes, and ethnologists found it useful in assessing the 'balance between human achievement (within the capabilities offered by technology, economy and social organization) and the restrictions and opportunities offered by the natural environment (by terrain, geology, climate, soil and vegetation)'.[110] In pre-industrial times, ecological adaptations were complex and wide-ranging: for example, Orvar Löfgren in Sweden, in a study of 'Peasant Ecotypes', speaks of peasants of the plain, cultivating grain, woodland peasants who exploited forest resources, peasant fishermen who combined fishing and farming, cattle-raising peasants for whom dairying and seasonal migration to different pastures were important, mining peasants who combined small-scale pre-industrial mining with farming, and the mountaineer peasant whose economic focus was hunting and cattle raising. In Denmark, Bjarne Stoklund has shown how landscape change over long periods, for example through deforestation, could lead to change from woodland peasant to peasant of the plains. Numerous subsistence strategies were undertaken for economic survival, filling cultural or economic niches, such as charcoal-burning, tar extraction (especially in Finland), making hazel hoops for barrels, etc. As farming became more prosperous farmers might abandon certain niches, which were then filled by landless cottagers. The landless were also dependent on the farmers, who gave them harvest employment, saw to their transport needs, and provided a market for hand-made craft goods, which could also be peddled seasonally over long distances.[111]

In the late eighteenth century and the nineteenth century, according to Peter Burke, 'the "people" or "folk" became a subject of interest to European intellectuals', just at the time when traditional forms of popular culture were beginning to disappear. J G Herder and the brothers Grimm were 'extremely influential' in furthering the concept of national folksongs, of which many collections appeared from a variety of countries, for example Russia, Germany, Sweden, Serbia, and Finland, where Elias Lönnrot arranged songs collected from oral tradition into an epic, the *Kalevala*, published in 1835. Herder actually used the term 'popular culture' (*Kultur des Volkes*) as against 'learned culture' (*Kultur der Gelehrten*).[112]

It is in relation to popular culture that a difference can be found between the development of ethnology in Britain and in much of the rest of Europe. Folksongs and other aspects of popular culture were associated with the national liberation movements and quest for self-definition in several countries of Europe from the late eighteenth century, sometimes in the spirit of Romanticism. Hobsbawm has distinguished three phases for nineteenth-century Europe. The first is related to cultural, literary and folkloric developments that did not have political or nationalist overtones. The second is when strong supporters of the concept of 'nation' begin to campaign actively for their ideals. The third is when the mass of people give their support for nationalist programmes.[113] These movements came to change the map of Europe to a considerable degree, and the discipline of ethnology changed with them. In Britain, however, its development led back mainly to antiquarianism, and less to nationalist strivings. And whereas in the early days European ethnology evolved through the interest taken by intellectuals in survivals amongst the less advanced layers of society of fragments of evidence that could help to interpret earlier stages in the development of civilisation, now in more recent times it is analysis of human society at any level that is of primary importance. It is, therefore, very appropriate that 'for several years ethnology has located its field of research just at the crossing point where history and anthropology today meet one another'.[114] The subject is almost limitless in its scope and has absorbed so many different strands, from antiquarianism to popular culture, that it perforce contains within itself many specialisations, and makes at least partial use of the methodologies of numerous related disciplines. It may be best to view it as a discipline of partnership, adding its own dimension to research into the past and present condition and environment and forms of culture of mankind through the ages. Professor Sigurd Erixon defined it as 'a comparative cultural research on a regional basis with a sociological and historical orientation and with certain psychological implications'.[115] It would appear as if this definition remains valid.

NOTES

1 Peate, 1959, 99.
2 Kolsrud, 1967.
3 Räsänen, 1992, 7.
4 Erixon, 1967, 3.
5 Wiegelmann, 1990.
6 Bringéus, 1968; Bringéus, 1969.
7 *Dgv-Informationen*, 80:1 (1971).

8 Bendix and Löfgren, 2008, 5–6.
9 Marett, 1920, Chapter 1, quoted in Dorson, 1968a, II, 564.
10 Heine-Geldern, 1964, 407.
11 Ampère, 1834, 254, quoted in Rohan-Csermak, 1967, 179.
12 Rohan-Csermak, 1967, 183–4.
13 Radcliffe-Brown, 1972, 276.
14 Bromley, Y V. 'Ethnography and contiguous disciplines', typescript, n.d., privately held (collection of Alexander Fenton).
15 Erich and Beitl, 1914, 96, 862–3.
16 Dekker, 2002, 6.
17 Keay and Keay, 1994, 670–1.
18 Hugger, 1992, I, 18.
19 Dekker, 2002, 3, 5.
20 Dekker, 2002, 4.
21 Dias, 1967, 300.
22 Jacobs and Nutt, 1892, 3.
23 The Ditchley Park Conference Resolution, *Journal of the Folklore Institute*, 7 (1970), 2–3.
24 Kolsrud, 1967, 297.
25 Räsänen, 1992, 7.
26 Stoklund, 1972, 7.
27 See Fenton, 1973, 9–10; Wiegelmann, Zender and Heilfurth, 1977, 9–10.
28 Nutt, 1898, 31.
29 Haddon, 1898, xvii–xix.
30 Haddon, 1898, xxi–xxii.
31 Weiss, 1946, 8, 11.
32 Wiegelmann, 1977, 9.
33 Talve, 1997. Three previous editions had appeared in Finnish in 1979, 1980 and 1990.
34 Svensson, 1966; this was translated into German (Svensson, 1973).
35 Wiegelmann, 1990.
36 Wiegelmann, 1977, 9.
37 Fenton, 2007, 25–7.
38 Fenton, 2007, 192–3.
39 Clark, 1951, 49–50, 56–7.
40 Fenton, 2003, 9–23.
41 Thomas, 1960, 7.
42 Thomas, 1960, 8.
43 Camden, 1586.
44 Camden, 1605.
45 Dorson, 1968a, I, 1–2.
46 Quoted in Dorson, 1968a, I, 2.
47 Dorson, 1968b, 7.
48 Dorson, 1968b, 9.
49 Dorson, 1968b, 11.
50 Dorson, 1968b, 17, 18–19.
51 See Chapter 19, 'Public Accounts', for an outline of these.
52 For lists of such tours in Scotland, see Mitchell and Cash, 1917; Hancock, 1959, I, 13–21; Holmes and MacDonald, 2003, 1–41.
53 Dorson, 1968b, 34.
54 Hone, 1825–27; Hone, 1827; Hone, 1832.
55 Carlyle, 1987, 170, 231.

56 Dorson, 1968b, 55.

57 Keightley, 1828, I, ix–xi.

58 Wright, I, 1846, 237.

59 Dorson, 1968b, 66–74.

60 *Athenaeum*, no. 982 (August 1846), quoted in Dorson, 1968a, I, 53.

61 Haddon, 1898, 434–75 (Chapter 16).

62 Burne, 1890, 313.

63 Dorson, 1968b, 187.

64 Tylor, 1958.

65 Dorson, 1968b, 197.

66 Dorson, 1968b, 202–3.

67 Lang, 1901, 11.

68 Dorson, 1968a, II, 469.

69 Dorson, 1968b, 309.

70 Dorson, 1968a, II, 549.

71 Dorson, 1968a, II, 561.

72 Dasent, 1859, lxxxvi, cviii, cxvii–clx.

73 Dorson, 1968a, II, 599.

74 Temple, quoted in Dorson, 1968a, II, 642.

75 Hechter, 1975, 161.

76 Campbell, 1860–62; reissued London, 1890–3.

77 Carmichael, 1941–76.

78 Dorson, 1986a, II, 655.

79 Erdélyi, 1978; see, for an example, Fenton, 1985.

80 MacInnes, 1992, 8–10.

81 Dorson, 1968a, II, 698–9; Fanning, 1983, 80–2.

82 Wright, 1913; Dorson, 1968a, II, 561.

83 Wakelin, 1972.

84 McIntosh, Samuels and Benskin, 1986, I, 4.

85 Fleure and Davies, 1971.

86 Fleure, 1969, xv.

87 See Chapter 6, 'Scotland's Open Air Museums'.

88 See Cseri, Horváth and Szabó, 2007. See Chapter 6, 'Scotland's Open Air Museums'.

89 See Stevens, 1986; Kavanagh, 1990, 22–4; Editorial Notes, *Gwerin*, 1:1 (1956); The Welsh Folk-Life Survey, *Gwerin*, 1:1 (1956), 47–8; Peate, 1941, 45–50; Peate, 1972, 17.

90 Peate, 1959, 100. This was the presidential address delivered to Section H at the Glasgow meeting of the British Association, 1 September 1958.

91 Some of the detail is given in Evans, 1965.

92 See Buchanan, 1990, 1–3; Evans, 1951; Evans, 1957; Evans, 1958; Evans, 1973; Evans, 1988.

93 Hoffmann von Fallersleben, 1968, I, 125, quoted in Roodenburg, 1994, 268.

94 Sayce, 1933; for an example of a study of the material culture of Bantu-speaking peoples who had been affected by the building of the Kariba Dam, see Reynolds, 1968.

95 Sayce, 1946, 1–25.

96 Forde, 1964, v–vi.

97 See Nicolaisen, 1963, 281.

98 Graebner, 1911.

99 Rees, 1950.

100 Jenkins, 1971.

101 The others were Davies and Rees, 1960; Emmett, 1974; Frankenberg, 1957.

102 For a detailed analysis of the Welsh community studies, see Owen, 1985.
103 Elias, 1994; Burke, 1980, 23.
104 Burke, 1980, 13.
105 See, for example, Goody, Thirsk and Thompson, 1979.
106 Kussmaul, 1981; Spufford, 1979; Wrightson, 1982.
107 For an example of analysis of a number of seventeenth-century testaments, see Michie, 2000, Chapter 4.
108 Laslett and Wall, 1972.
109 See, for example, Hagan, 2008, 559–63.
110 Owen, 1981, 9.
111 Löfgren, 1976; Stoklund, 1976, 84–9; Fontaine, 1996; Talve, 1997, 88–90.
112 Burke, 1980, 8.
113 Hobsbawm, 1995, 3, 12.
114 Stoklund, 1983, 26.
115 Quoted in Owen, 1981, 5.

BIBLIOGRAPHY AND FURTHER READING

Ampère, A-M. *Essai sur la philosophie des sciences ou exposition analitique d'une classification naturelle de toutes les connaissances humaines*, Paris, 1834.
Bendix, R and Löfgren, O. Rethinking Europe as a field for European ethnology, *Ethnologia Europaea*, 38:1 (2008), 5–6.
Bringéus, N-A. Studieplan I Folklivsforskning, Institutionen for folklivsforskning vid Lund, *Meddelanden*, 49 (December 1968).
Bringéus, N-A. Traditionsvetenskapen I Undervisning och Forskning vid de svenska Universiteten, Institution for folklivsforskning vid Lunds Universitet, *Meddelanden*, 52 (October 1969).
Buchanan, R H. Obituary. Emyr Estyn Evans, 1905–1989, *Ulster Folklife*, 36 (1990), 1–3.
Burke, P. *Sociology and History*, London, 1980.
Burne, C S. The collection of English folk-lore, *Folk-Lore*, 1 (1890), 313–30.
Camden, W. *Britannia*, London, 1586.
Camden, W. *Remaines of a Greater Worke, concerning Britaine*, London, 1605.
Campbell, J F. *Popular Tales of the West Highlands*, 4 vols, Edinburgh, 1860–62; reissued London, 1890–3.
Carmichael, A. *Carmina Gadelica, Hymns and Incantations. With Illustrative Notes on Words, Rites, and Customs, Dying and Obsolete: Orally Collected in the Highlands and Islands of Scotland*, 6 vols, London and Edinburgh, 1941–76.
Carlyle, T. *Sartor Resartus*, ed. K McSweeney and P Sabor, Oxford, 1987.
Clark, G. Folk-culture and the study of European prehistory. In Grimes, W F, ed. *Aspects of Archaeology in Britain and Beyond. Essays presented to O. G. S. Crawford*, London, 1951, 49–65.
Cseri, M, Horváth, A and Szabó, Z. Kiállításvezetō. *Szabadtéri Néprajzi Múzeum*, Szentendre, 2007.
Dasent, G W. *Popular Tales from the Norse*, 2nd edn, Edinburgh, 1859.
Davies, E and Rees, A D, eds. *Welsh Rural Communities*, Cardiff, 1960.
Dekker, T. *De Nederlandse Volkskunde. De verwetenschappelijking van en emotionele belangstelling*, Amsterdam, 2002.
Dias, J. The academic position of European ethnology in Portugal, *Ethnologia Europaea*, 1:4 (1967), 300–1.
Dorson, R M. *Peasant Customs and Savage Myths. Selections from the British Folklorists*, 2 vols, London, 1968a.

Dorson, R M. *The British Folklorists. A History*, London, 1968b.

Elias, N. *The Civilising Process. The History of Manners and State Formation and Civilization* [1939], Oxford, 1994.

Emmett, I. *A North Wales Village*, London, 1974.

Erdélyi, Z. *Hegyet hágék, lötöt lépek*, Budapest, 1978.

Erich, O A and Beitl, R, with Beitl, K. *Wörterbuch der deutschen Volkskunde*, 3rd edn, Stuttgart, 1914.

Erixon, S. European ethnology in our time, *Ethnologia Europaea*, 1:1 (1967), 3–11.

Evans, E E. *Mourne Country*, Dundalk, 1951.

Evans, E E. *Irish Folk Ways*, London, 1957.

Evans, E E. *Irish Heritage* [1942], Dundalk, 1958.

Evans, E E. Folklife studies in Northern Ireland, *Journal of the Folklore Institute*, 11:3 (December 1965), 355–63.

Evans, E E. *The Personality of Ireland. Habitat, Heritage and History*, Cambridge, 1973.

Evans, E E. The early development of folklife studies in Northern Ireland. In Gailey, A, ed., *The Use of Tradition. Essays Presented to G B Thompson*, Holywood, 1988.

Fanning, R. *Independent Ireland*, Dublin, 1983.

Fenton, A. The scope of regional ethnology, *Folk Life*, 11 (1973), 5–14.

Fenton, A. 20,000 prayers for Roxália Babos, *Aberdeen University Review*, 174 (Autumn 1985), 215–8.

Fenton, A. Continuity and change. In Stell, G, Shaw, J and Storrier, S, eds, *Scottish Life and Society. A Compendium of Scottish Ethnology, Volume 3: Scotland's Buildings*, East Linton, 2003, 9–23.

Fenton, A. *Scottish Life and Society. A Compendium of Scottish Ethnology, Volume 5: The Food of the Scots*, Edinburgh, 2007.

Fleure, H J. Introduction. In Jenkins, G, ed., *Studies in Folk Life. Essays in Honour of Iorwerth C Peate*, London, 1969.

Fleure, H J and Davies, M. *A Natural History of Man in Britain*, London, 1971.

Fontaine, L. *History of Pedlars in Europe*, Durham, 1996.

Forde, C D. *Habitat, Economy and Society. A Geographical Introduction to Ethnology* [1934], London, 1964.

Frankenberg, R. *Village on the Border*, London, 1957.

Goody, J, Thirsk, J and Thompson, E P. *Family and Inheritance. Rural Society in Western Europe 1200–1800* [1976], Cambridge, 1979.

Graebner, F. *Methode der Ethnologie*, Heidelberg, 1911.

Haddon, A C. *The Study of Man*, London, 1898.

Hagan, H. 'It's Ma Job tae Work and it's Yours tae Make it go Roun': Aspects of the female experience in Port Glasgow between the wars. In Coull, J R, Fenton, A and Veitch, K, eds, *Scottish Life and Society. A Compendium of Scottish Ethnology, Volume 4: Boats, Fishing and the Sea*, Edinburgh, 2008, 545–70.

Hancock, P D. *A Bibliography of Artworks relating to Scotland, 116–1950*, 2 vols, Edinburgh, 1959.

Hechter, M. *Internal Colonialism. The Celtic Fringe in British National Development, 1536–1966*, London, 1975.

Heine-Geldern, R. One hundred years of ethnological theory in the German-speaking countries: some milestones, *Current Anthropology*, 5:5 (December 1964), 407–18.

Hobsbawm, E J. *Nations and Nationalism since 1780* [1990], Cambridge, 1995.

Hoffmann von Fallersleben, A H. *Mein Leben. Aufzeichnungen und Erinnerungen* [My Life. Sketches and Memories], Hannover, 1968.

Holmes, H and MacDonald, F, eds. *Scottish Life and Society. A Compendium of Scottish Ethnology, Volume 14: Bibliography for Scottish Ethnology*, East Linton, 2003.

Hone, W. *Every-Day Book; or Everlasting Calendar of Popular Amusements, Sports, Pastimes, Ceremonies, Manners, Customs, and Events*, 3 vols, London, 1825–27.

Hone, W. *Table-Book*, London, 1827.

Hone, W. *Year-Book*, London, 1832.

Hugger, P. *Handbuch der schweizerischen Volkskultur*, 3 vols, Basel, 1992.

Jacobs, J and Nutt, A. *The International Folk-Lore Congress 1891*, London 1892.

Jenkins, D. *The Agricultural Community in South-West Wales at the Turn of the Twentieth Century*, Cardiff, 1971.

Kavanagh, G. *History Curatorship*, London, 1990.

Keay, J and Keay, J. *Collins Encyclopaedia of Scotland*, London, 1994.

Keightley, T. *The Fairy Mythology, Illustrative of the Romance and Superstition of Various Countries*, London, 1828.

Kolsrud, K. The academic position of European Ethnology in Norway, *Ethnologia Europaea*, 1:4 (1967), 295–7.

Kussmaul, A. *Servants in Husbandry in Early Modern England*, Cambridge, 1981.

Land, A. *Custom and Myth*, London, 1901.

Laslett, P and Wall, R. *Household and Family in Past Time: Comparative Studies in the Size and Structure of the Domestic Group over the Last Three Centuries in England, France, Serbia, Japan and Colonial North America, with Further Materials from Western Europe*, Cambridge, 1972.

Löfgren, O. Peasant ecotypes. Problems in the comparative study of ecological adaptation, *Ethnologia Scandinavica*, 4 (1976), 100–16.

MacInnes, J. Preface. In *Carmina Gadelica. Hymns and Incantations*, Edinburgh, 1992, 8–10.

Marett, R R. *Psychology and Folklore*, London, 1920.

McIntosh, A, Samuels, M L and Benskin, M, eds. *A Linguistic Atlas of Late Middle English*, 4 vols, Aberdeen, 1986.

Michie, M F. *Glenesk. The History and Culture of an Angus Community*, ed. A Fenton and J Beech, East Linton, 2000.

Mitchell, A and Cash, C G. *A Contribution to the Bibliography of Scottish Topography*, 2 vols, Edinburgh, 1917.

Nicolaisen, J. *Primitive kulturer. Nogle hovedtræk af etnologiens historie* [Primitive cultures. Some main lines in the history of ethnology], Copenhagen, 1963.

Nutt, A. The discrimination of racial elements in the folklore of the British Isles, *Folklore*, 9 (1898), 30–52.

Owen, T M. Folklife studies. Some problems and perspectives, *FolkLife*, 19 (1981), 5–16.

Owen, T M. Community studies in Wales. An overview, *Ethnologia Europaea*, 15:1 (1985), 27–52.

Peate, I C. The place of folk culture in the museum, *Museums Journal*, 41 (1941), 45–50.

Peate, I C. The study of folklife: and its part in the defence of civilization, *Gwerin*, 2:3 (1959), 97–109.

Peate, I C. *Tradition and Folk Life. A Welsh View*, London, 1972.

Radcliffe-Brown, A R. Historical note on British social anthropology, *American Anthropologist*, 54 (1972), 275–7.

Räsänen, M. *Pioneers. The History of Finnish Ethnology*, Studia Fennica Ethnologica 1, Helsinki, 1992.

Rees, D A. *Life in a Welsh Countryside*, Cardiff, 1950.

Reynolds, B. *The Material Culture of the Peoples of the Gwembe Valley*, Kariba Studies volume 3, Manchester, 1968.

Rohan-Csermak, G de. La première apparition du terme 'ethnologie', *Ethnologia Europaea*, 1:3 (1967), 170–84.

Roodenburg, H. Tussen 'volksgeest' en 'volksverheffing'. Over volkskunde en nationale identiteit aan het begin van de negentiende eeuw [Between national spirit and national improvement. On Volkskunde and national identity at the beginning of the nineteenth century]. In Dekker, T, Post, P and Roodenburg, H, eds, *Antiquaren, liefhebbers en professoren, Momenten uit de geschiedenis van de Nederlandse Volkskunde* [Antiquaries, amateurs and professors. Moments from the history of the Volkskunde of the Netherlands], *Volkskundig Bulletin*, 20:3 (December, 1994), 268–89.

Sayce, R U. *Primitive Arts and Craft. An Introduction to the Study of Material Culture*, Cambridge, 1933.

Sayce, R U. Food through the ages, *The Montgomeryshire Collections* (Transactions of the Powys-land Club), 16:2 (1946), 1–25.

Spufford, M. *Contrasting Communities. English Villagers in the Sixteenth and Seventeenth Centuries* [1974], Cambridge, 1979.

Stevens, C. *Writers of Wales: Iorwerth C Peate*, Cardiff, 1986.

Stoklund, B. Europäische Ethnologie zwischen Skylla und Charybdis, *Ethnologia Scandinavica*, (1972), 5–14.

Stoklund, B. Ecological succession: reflections on the relations between man and environment in pre-industrial Denmark, *Ethnologia Scandinavica*, (1976), 84–9.

Stoklund, B. *Folklife Research: Between History and Anthropology*, Cardiff, 1983.

Svensson, S. *Introduktion till Folklivsforskningen*, Malmö, 1966.

Svensson, S. *Einführung in die Europäische Ethnologie*, Textbücher zur Europäischen Ethnologie, ed. Günter Wiegelmann, Meisenheim am Glan, 1973.

Talve, I. *Finnish Folk Culture*, Studia Fennica Ethnologica 4, Helsinki, 1997.

Temple, R C. The folk-lore in the legends of the Panjab, *Folklore*, 10 (1899), 384–443.

Thomas, C. Archaeology and folk-life studies, *Gwerin*, 3:1 (1960), 7–17.

Tylor, E B. *Primitive Culture*, 2 vols, New York, 1958.

Wakelin, M F, ed. *Patterns in the Folk Speech of the British Isles*, London, 1972.

Weiss, R. *Volkskunde der Schweiz*, Erlenbach-Zürich, 1946.

Wiegelmann, G, Zender, M and Heilfurth, G. *Volkskunde. Eine Einführung*, Berlin, 1977.

Wiegelmann, G. Geschichte des Forschung im 18. und 19. Jahrhundert. In Wiegelmann, Zender and Heilfurth, 1977, 9–26.

Wiegelmann, G. *Theoretische Konzepte der Europäischen Ethnologie*, Grundlagen der Europäischen Ethnologie, vol. 1, Münster Hamburg, 1990.

Wright, E. *Rustic Speech and Folklore*, Oxford, 1913.

Wright, T. *Essays on Subjects Connected with the Literature, Popular Superstitions, and History of England in the Middle Ages*, 2 vols, London, 1846.

Wrightson, K. *English Society 1680*, London, 1982.

2   A History of Ethnology in Scotland

ALEXANDER FENTON AND
MARGARET A MACKAY

While ethnology shares theories, methods and analytical approaches with other related disciplines, one characteristic which separates it from these is that typically ethnologists have created, in a disinterested fashion, collections for others as well as themselves to use and analyse. These may take the form of descriptions, texts, maps, plans, drawings, collections of objects, transcriptions, sound recordings, photographs, questionnaires, films or other materials.

The beginnings of ethnological practice may be said to date from the renaissance period, when the rediscovery of the classical world made scholars look more closely at the relics of the past closer at hand. Exploration beyond these islands brought contact with new peoples, and the opportunity to compare and contrast their mores with those of the inhabitants at home. Even earlier, the Crusades had brought Scots into contact with other peoples, while guides for pilgrims en route to places such as Santiago de Compostela were noting the particular features of the communities through which one might pass, making comparisons and noting contrasts.

Medieval Scottish literature and other sources of the period also include references which show how differences were viewed – between Highland and Lowland Scots, for example – while medieval laws and annals contain data of ethnological interest. Early descriptions of Scotland are found in reports by foreign visitors, from papal envoys to continental courtiers, and other correspondence contains observations on customary practices and diverse ways of life in the nation of Scotland. We learn of the distribution of coals to the poor at church doors in this way. A satirical description of a Gaelic-speaking Highland bard in the mid-fifteenth century *Buke of the Howlat*, a poem by an Orkney-born cleric, Richard Ratter (styled Ricardus de Holandia or Richard from the farm of Holland/Ha-land), tells of awareness of difference within the nation.

An invaluable source for this period is *A Dictionary of the Older Scottish Tongue* (DOST). Charting the evidence of Scots from the earliest period to 1700, DOST is a veritable encyclopedia of medieval and early modern Scottish life. Examples of how this source can be used to illuminate topics such as social relations, food and drink, shipping law, weights and measures, and building construction may be found in a volume which celebrated the completion of DOST at the beginning of the twenty-first century, *Perspectives on the Older Scottish Tongue*.

Early descriptions of Scotland by Scots show the development of a comparative approach such as can be found in the writings of the philosopher John Major or Mair (c.1467–1550) who published his *De Gestis Scotorum* in Paris in

1521, and the cleric Donald Monro (*fl.* 1526–74) who wrote his *Description of the Western Isles of Scotland* in 1563. William Camden (1551–1623), the English historian, antiquarian and topographer, first published his *Britannia*, a county-by-county description of Great Britain and Ireland, in 1586, compiled with the help of corre-spondents and tracing evidence of the past in the landscape. A century later, Sir Robert Sibbald (1641–1722), antiquary, physician, botanist and Geographer Royal from 1682, embarked on a description of Scotland, publishing a circular which asked for information. While this was never completed, he did publish his *Scotia Illustrata*, a natural history of Scotland, in 1683. The Skyeman Martin Martin (?1665–1719) answered his call, however, with his two publications *A Late Voyage to St Kilda* (1698) and *A Description of the Western Isles of Scotland* (1703). In 1707 Edward Lhuyd (1660–1709) published his *Archaeologia Britannica*, including data on language, history and customs he had collected in Scotland.

THE EIGHTEENTH CENTURY
AND THE EARLY NINETEENTH CENTURY

The eighteenth century witnessed great interest in those remnants of the past which had survived into the present, including objects, material remains and structures. 'Popular antiquities', aspects of language, song or lore, were a topic of study. The public museums of later times owe their origins to the 'cabinets of curiosities' assembled for the private study and enjoyment of those with the means to do so, and word lists and song collections were assembled and published in similar fashion.[1]

Thomas Ruddiman (1674–1757) can be said to have been responsible for the introduction of Scots lexicography, linking the glossaries and word lists of earlier times, which were mainly concerned with understanding Latin sources, with the rediscovery of texts in Older Scots. His edition of Gavin Douglas's 1513 translation into Scots of Virgil's *Aeneid*, published in Edinburgh in 1710, included 'A Large Glossary, Explaining the Difficult Words, Which may serve for a Dictionary to the old SCOTTISH language'.[2]

Along with Ruddiman, a key figure at the time in Scots lexicography, as well as in the publication of both the poetry of earlier periods and songs collected in his own time, was Allan Ramsay (1686–1758). His anthology *The Ever Green: A Collection of Scots Poems Wrote by the Ingenious Before 1600,* and his five-volume collection entitled *The Tea-Table Miscellany* were both published in 1724 and both included glossaries. The trend set by Ruddiman and Ramsay was to be followed subsequently by other anthologists.[3]

The collecting of oral tradition was given impetus by James Macpherson's publications of the products of the Gaelic bard Ossian in the 1760s.[4] Rapidly translated into many European languages, these promoted the link between poetry and identity and encouraged collections to be made elsewhere. Closer to home, debates on their authenticity did not stifle but rather promoted attention to oral sources. Robert Burns (1759–1796) was not only a gifted poet but should rightly be remembered as a collector as well as an adapter of the texts and melodies of others which he heard on convivial occasions or on his travels.[5] He too provided glossaries of Scots. Sir Walter Scott (1771–1832) and his friends, family and associates were collectors as well as sources of song and lore and Scott's role in the establishment of Scottish identity is well attested.[6]

The Scottish Enlightenment, that period of intellectual ferment, fostered systematic data collection, and the vision of Sir John Sinclair (1754–1835) for gathering, parish by parish, 'statistical' accounts (that is, information of use to the state) on the effects of scientific development, industrial advances and agricultural improvement on the lives of Scotland's people, was put into practice by employing the methodology of the questionnaire and encouraging respondents to apply a comparative approach. The *Statistical Accounts* gathered and published in the 1790s are, in European terms, an unrivalled source for the ethnologist, as are the later series.

The establishment of the Society of Antiquaries of Scotland (SAS) in 1780 marked another milestone in the gathering and dissemination of knowledge of the past, fostering that spirit of enquiry which characterised the time. Its collections of artefacts, which the archaeologist, anthropologist, ethnologist, historian and artist Daniel Wilson (1816–1892), one of the Society's secretaries, was to reorganise in the 1840s according to the tripartite Stone, Bronze and Iron Age system of archaeological classification used by the Danish scholars Thomsen and Worsaae,[7] formed the core of the Museum of Antiquities of the next century. Both the Royal Society of Edinburgh, Scotland's national academy of science and letters, which Sibbald had advocated decades earlier, and the Society of Antiquaries of Scotland were incorporated by Royal Charter confirmed by charter in 1783, and have worked closely ever since.

An interest in country life material goes back to the founding of the Society of Antiquaries of Scotland. The first lecture delivered to the Society after its formation on 18 December 1780 was on 'The Antient [sic] State of Agriculture in Scotland', though this leant heavily on classical authors. A single-stilted plough from Orkney was the first implement to be acquired, in 1782, and many articles of everyday life were added to the Society's collections, which were passed to the government in 1858 to form the National Museum of Antiquities. There was, however, no systematic collecting and research programme, except insofar as the concept of survivals from earlier times motivated collection and the choice of items to mark the progress of civilisation. One hundred years after the creation of the SAS, Dr, later Sir, Arthur Mitchell's book *The Past in the Present* (1880), based on his Rhind Lectures, was to exemplify this concept well for in it he discusses many of the items which he and others had donated to the Society's museum as symbols of such progress, a theme which was current in scholarship at the time.

However, the Highland and Agricultural Society of Scotland, founded in 1784, had amongst its primary aims the advancement of agriculture and it offered 'premiums' for inventions likely to further this. The first to receive an award of ten guineas, on 6 December 1793, was the Rev. Alexander Campbell, for his newly-invented plough suitable for Highland farms. A replica was placed in the lobby of the Society's hall in Albyn Place in Edinburgh and this is regarded as the start of the Society's Museum.

It consisted of the implements that had been submitted for premiums. In

1831 it was decided to gather in a series of models of the 'most approved' implements of the time. Problems of space led to the erection of a new museum on George IV Bridge in the city, which opened in 1841. A 'Catalogue of Models and Machines in the Museum of the Highland Society' was published in 1832 and this was included in the 1841 Catalogue of the Museum, in which it covered fifty-four pages.[8]

A fire destroyed part of the contents in 1851. Meantime, the Industrial Museum, later called the Museum of Science and Art, with subsequent re-namings down the years, was being erected in Chambers Street. It was completed in 1859 and was headed by George Wilson, brother of Daniel. The Highland Society transferred to it its collection of models and geological specimens. The agricultural side was not continued, however, and in 1928 the models were transferred to the Science Museum in London on loan. The one-third life sized paintings of animals commissioned by the Directors of the Highland Society were also dispersed.

So ended the first Agricultural Museum, which had been in existence from 1793 until 1855 in Edinburgh. Outside the capital city there was also some museum activity. Messrs Drummond and Sons set up a highly-praised Agricultural Exhibition at Stirling in 1831. By 1833 it had become Drummond's Agricultural Museum, showing seeds and plants as well as implements and demonstrating the role that horticulture played. It produced reports in 1831, 1833 and 1835 in which much valuable information was presented, including James Smith of Deanston's important study of underground tile drainage and subsoil ploughing, and data on Patrick Bell's reaping machine. At this period, Agricultural Improvement was well advanced and a knowledgeable German traveller wrote in the early 1840s that 'Scotland was one of the best cultivated countries in the world'.[9]

Drummond's Agricultural Museum in Stirling ran to at least 1844. The firm opened an establishment in Dublin in 1843 and formed a second Agricultural Museum there at 10 Dawson Street. Like the one in Stirling, this was a commercial venture, 'for the exhibition and sale of the newest and most improved implements of husbandry, and agricultural machinery; to which will be added a repository and assortment of seeds, roots and grasses, carefully classified and arranged'.[10]

These early agricultural museums had a great effect on the agricultural practices in their vicinity for they kept them before the eyes of the farmers and were regularly updated. Inventions or adaptations of implements could be put on display and discussed by observers and sometimes, as at Stirling, the latest literature on farming was on view too. These museums had a practical purpose and they played a considerable part in the period of Agricultural Improvement.

FURTHER ACTIVITIES IN THE NINETEENTH CENTURY
AND THE EARLY TWENTIETH CENTURY

The clergyman and antiquarian John Jamieson (1759–1838) was an active member and, for a time, joint secretary of the Society of Antiquaries of Scotland. He was one of the ministers who contributed to the *Statistical Account*. He met Scott, who was to become a great supporter, as a young man and wrote a poem for Scott's *Minstrelsy of the Scottish Border*. His theological writings were highly valued in his own time. But he is chiefly known for his pioneering *Etymological Dictionary of the Scottish Language* published in two volumes in 1808 with a later *Supplement* in 1825.

He meticulously consulted manuscripts and printed volumes and sought assistance from specialists in certain subjects such as botany and the law, but also – importantly – gathered Scots words from oral sources, seeking voluntary contributors from across the country in order that his evidence could be based 'on the authority of the nation at large'.[11] He provided references and, where possible, context in the form of illustrative quotations so that his *Dictionary* contains invaluable details not only on the usage of terms but also on the practice of customs, beliefs and many other aspects of Scottish life. The longest entry, for example, is that for 'Yule', with copious descriptions and references.

In 1824 Robert Chambers (1802–1871) began to publish his *Traditions of Edinburgh*, a pioneering work of urban ethnology, following it with *The Popular Rhymes of Scotland* in 1826 and *Scottish Jests and Anecdotes* in 1832. His working life was taken up with book editing, publishing and selling, and much later, in 1863–4, he brought out his monumental *Book of Days* in two volumes, which he described as a miscellany of popular antiquities in connection with the calendar. He could be said to stand on the cusp between the 'miscellany' collectors of the past, such as John Aubrey, John Brand and William Hone, to whom he pays tribute, and a new approach to collecting and publishing.

In 1846 the antiquary William John Thoms (1803–1885) had coined the term 'Folk-Lore' as an alternative to the phrase 'popular antiquities' in a letter to the *Athenaeum* of 22 August.[12] He saw this as an aspect of living, contemporary culture and he encouraged those with an interest to gather examples wherever they could. Just three years before Chambers published his *Book of Days*, John Francis Campbell of Islay (1822–1885) had begun to publish his *Popular Tales of the West Highlands*, a work which marked a more scientific and systematic approach to folklore collecting. He had been challenged by George Webbe Dasent to do for Scotland what the brothers Grimm had done for German-speakers and Asbjornsen and Moe for Norwegians. With the help of assistants, he began to take down the oral narratives of Gaelic-speakers word for word. Contextual information was gathered as well and in some cases, Campbell, a skilled artist, also sketched the tellers and their settings, as he did on his visits to Scandinavia and other parts of the world.[13]

Others followed him in Gaelic Scotland, such as Alexander Carmichael (1832–1912)[14], the Reverend John Gregorson Campbell (1836–1891), Robert Craig Maclagan (1839–1919), Frances Tolmie (1840–1926)[15], Marjory Kennedy-Fraser (1857–1930)[16], Lucy Broadwood (1858–1929)[17], Father Allan MacDonald (1859–1905)[18], Amy Murray (1865–1947) and Lady Evelyn Stewart Murray (1868–1940)[19].

The foundation of The Folk-Lore Society in 1878 was a further spur to collecting in Scotland and it was the Reverend Walter Gregor's *Notes on the Folk-Lore of the North-East of Scotland* of 1881 that was the Society's first published field collection, gathered with the help of its guidelines. Robert Craig Maclagan's work,[20] co-ordinated while a busy doctor, was inspired by a call from the Society in 1889 and carried out with the help of correspondents in the West Highlands between 1893 and 1902, resulting in over 9,000 manuscript pages. Another doctor,

David Rorie (1867–1946), who was a poet and song composer as well, practised in the coalfields of Fife and in rural Aberdeenshire, and gathered customs and beliefs concerning mining, health and illness as well as much more.[21]

A figure who should not be forgotten in the history of ethnology in Scotland is the visionary Patrick Geddes (1854–1932), biologist, sociologist, geographer and town planner, who fostered integrated ways of looking at the relationships between human beings and their environment, the links between 'place', 'work' and 'folk', and the use of the 'Valley Section' to study the connection between resources and types of community.

KEY TWENTIETH-CENTURY DEVELOPMENTS

The impetus which ethnology and folklore studies had gathered in the last decades of the nineteenth century and the early years of the twentieth, much of it carried out through the encouragement of The Folk-Lore Society and the work of several collectors active in Scotland, was curtailed with the outbreak of World War I and in the years which followed. Those who might have developed the profession found themselves at the front or in support roles, and not all survived. Others poured their energy into war work at home. It was not until its end that moves were seen to take these and associated subjects forward once more.

In 1919 Sir William Craigie (1867–1957), one of the editors of the *Oxford English Dictionary*, proposed the creation of 'a dictionary of the Older Scots language from its earliest appearance to 1700', on historical principles, and began to edit this himself from his then base at the University of Chicago. *A Dictionary of the Older Scottish Tongue* (DOST) was published between 1931 and 2002.[22]

Craigie also encouraged a sister project for it in the form of a dictionary of Scots from 1700 onwards and in 1907 called for the collection of Scots words, ballads, legends and traditions from oral sources as being integral to such work.[23] The English Association set up a Scottish Dialects Committee at once, with William Grant (1863–1946) playing a leading role with the help of volunteers until the Scottish National Dictionary Association was established in 1929 to take the work forward with Grant as editor. The first part appeared in 1931.

Grant was succeeded as editor by David Murison (1913–1997) and brought the *Scottish National Dictionary* (SND) to completion in 1976. The *Concise Scots Dictionary* (CSD) brought resources from the two historical dictionaries into a single useful volume. The creation of Scottish Language Dictionaries Limited in 2002 united the aims of DOST and SND to provide a new edition of the CSD, specialist dictionaries, school resources, and on-line access to Scotland's Scots lexical wealth through electronic editions of DOST and SND in *The Dictionary of the Scots Language* (DSL).[24] A project for similar lexical provision for the Gaelic of Scotland has been underway for several years.[25]

Ethnology and Folklore in the First Half of the Twentieth Century

Efforts towards a systematic framework for the collection, study and dissemination of Scottish folklore and folklife materials were instigated by the Anthropological and Folklore Society of Scotland, which had its origins in the Edinburgh and Lothians Branch (founded in 1922) of the Royal Anthropological Institute. This body brought together individuals with interests in comparative cultural study, drawn from the university sector, the museum world, the membership of the Society of Antiquaries of Scotland, and the ranks of retired colonial officials. Within ten years, a Scottish Anthropological Society had been created, with 'Folklore' added to its title in 1936. The Society's *Proceedings*, published between 1934 and 1956, provide a useful record of its aims and programmes.

The 1930s were a time of much activity elsewhere. Margaret Fay Shaw (1903–2004) had come to live in South Uist and to photograph and film the life of the townships there. Skilled in musical notation, she was able to take down the songs of the district, while John Lorne Campbell (1906–1996) undertook sound recordings of Gaelic material with the most advanced equipment available to him. They were to marry in 1935 and from 1938 make the island of Canna their home and a very special cultural domain.[26] Werner Kissling (1895–1988), the German diplomat and anthropologist who had settled in Britain, filmed and took photographs in Eriskay and other Hebridean islands.[27] Aage Roussell came from Denmark to study the vernacular buildings of the Western and Northern Isles in 1931, publishing his *Norse Building Customs in the Scottish Isles* in 1934. The Swedes Sven T Kjellberg and Olof Hasslöf travelled in the Hebrides in that year to study buildings, crofting and fishing.[28]

Influences and encouragement from Scandinavia and from Ireland were to prove immensely valuable for Scottish developments and cooperation continues to this day. By 1935 the Irish Folklore Commission, successor to the Irish Folklore Institute (1930–5), had come into being and its Director, James Hamilton Delargy (1899–1980), was anxious that Scotland should have an institution similar to his own and took a keen interest in the Society. So, too, did the Swedish ethnologist Åke Campbell (1891–1957) of the University of Uppsala, who was invited to lecture and initiate research work in the Institute which the Society created in the Free Church College in Edinburgh, where instruction for certificate and diploma studies was offered by members and associates.

The Society established a Folk-Museum Committee early in the 1930s and later in the decade there are references in its *Proceedings* to the desirability of a Survey of Scottish Dialects and the creation of a 'research laboratory' to be called the Scottish Archive for Ethnological, Folkloristic and Linguistic Studies. In 1937 it hosted a conference of the International Association for European Ethnology and Folklore created at Lund in Sweden in 1935. Participants included Campbell and other leading Swedish scholars, Professor Sigurd Erixon (1888–1968) of Stockholm and Dr Carl Wilhelm von Sydow (1878–1952) of Lund.

Once more war intervened to bring these cooperative ventures to a halt but links were re-established following World War II and the activities of the 1930s very much prefigured what would come into being with the founding of the School of Scottish Studies and the Linguistic Surveys of Scotland.[29]

The School of Scottish Studies at the University of Edinburgh

The story begins in 1948 when Angus McIntosh (1914–2005) was appointed the first holder of the Forbes Chair of English Language and General Linguistics at the University of Edinburgh. A scholar of medieval dialectology, he brought with him war-time experience which was directly relevant to the projects he was to foster there. As part of the Bletchley Park code-breaking team, he had seen the potential in new technology such as magnetic tape, the portable tape recorder and the computer for linguistic study and research. Added to this, he had experienced the benefits to be achieved by teamwork in the completion of a major project of data collection and analysis.

The friendship of McIntosh and the Campbells, engendered in the 1930s and lasting for life, provided a vital catalyst. In 1947 John Lorne Campbell had founded the Folklore Institute of Scotland (FIOS), its initials supplying the Gaelic word for 'knowledge' and the use of 'Institute' reflecting the name of the forerunner of the Irish Folklore Commission, to promote the collecting and study of Scotland's oral traditions. James Hamilton Delargy had taken an interest in Campbell's work and gave support to the aims of FIOS. But more importantly, he had encouraged Calum Maclean (1915–1960) of Raasay to become a folklore collector and to undertake work of this sort in Scotland under the aegis of the Commission. In 1948 Maclean was in the Hebrides on fieldwork and with him was Åke Campbell, who had been there first in 1939 but who was in Scotland in 1948 for a festival of folk music and dance organised by the Scottish Anthropological and Folklore Society.

McIntosh had been on Barra and in Nova Scotia and Cape Breton with the Campbells. He saw clearly how the collection of lore and language could go together and, soon after his arrival, set in motion the establishment of the Linguistic Surveys of Gaelic and Scots. In this he had the support of the Principal and Vice-Chancellor of the time, Sir Edward Victor Appleton (1892–1965), who sought to bring fresh ideas to old disciplines and fostered the development of new ones. At McIntosh's instigation, a memorandum was drawn up by representatives of a range of subjects and on 15 May 1950, the University Court approved the creation of a School of Scottish Studies as a focus for interdisciplinary research on aspects of Scottish life and culture. Place-names, oral traditions, music, material culture, anthropology and Scots Law were to figure in its activities, with archival provision and a supporting research library assured.[30] It began to function in 1951. Other departments gradually took over the work of the last two subjects, and FIOS and the Scottish Anthropological and Folklore Society soon came to an end.

McIntosh received both encouragement and practical help from Delargy, who invited him to see the work of the IFC at first hand and advised on library acquisitions. Assistance came from colleagues in Sweden such as Campbell and Professor Dag Strömbäck (1900–1978), who was Head of the Dialect and Folklore Archive at Uppsala and from 1948, Professor of Nordic and Comparative Folklore there. Calum Maclean was sent from Dublin to be the first full-time collector in the School of Scottish Studies, and with him a handsel – a gift at the start of an enterprise – in the form of copies of all the material he had collected for the IFC in Scotland. Though he embarked on recording immediately in 1951, later in the year he was to leave for a nine-month period of intensive study of fieldwork methods and archival practice in Sweden under the guidance of Campbell and Strömbäck.

Calum Maclean was to work in the School of Scottish Studies for only ten years, for he died in 1960 aged 45. But his years were characterised by great productivity and the emphasis in the School on the primacy of field recording, the establishment of strong community connections, and maintaining high technical standards, was to create a distinctive ethos which has lasted through the decades. Maclean's collecting was not limited to the Gaelic-speaking areas of the country. He undertook fieldwork in the Borders and as far north as Shetland.

He was soon joined in the School by Stewart Sanderson as Secretary-Archivist, by the musicologist Francis Collinson (1898–1984), who collaborated closely with John Lorne Campbell and published on Scotland's instrumental traditions, and by the poet and song specialist Hamish Henderson (1919–2002), who brought an international outlook based on his pre-war and wartime experience to his work throughout a long career, during which, amongst many activities, he brought to the fore the traditions of the Scottish Travelling People and agricultural workers, and was an instrumental force in the Scottish Folk Revival.[31] Audrey Henshall was followed by Ian Whitaker in the area of material culture. Onomastics, name studies, were represented by W F H (Bill) Nicolaisen, who joined the staff in 1956. James Ross (1923–1971) researched Gaelic song and was succeeded by John MacInnes. Located in the premises of the School of Scottish Studies from 1954, and sharing library and other resources with the School's staff until their completion, were the two dictionary projects, *DOST* and *SND*.

In 1957, Ulster-born Basil Megaw (1913–2002), Director of the Manx Museum, was appointed the School's first Director. He was an advocate of fieldwork, undertaking it himself with others in places such as the Highland township of Smearisary, and of disseminating research results through conferences, symposia and publication. In that year the journal *Scottish Studies* began to appear, with early issues containing the fruits of several such conferences. The holdings of the sound and photographic archives grew as songs, tales, instrumental music, customs, beliefs, place-names, and information on ways of life, crafts, trades and buildings were gathered in. The Northern Scholars Scheme, proposed by the School of Scottish Studies as a means of bringing scholars from Scandinavia (and more recently from the Baltic countries) to the University of Edinburgh, was launched in the mid-1950s and has fostered links in the ethnological and related fields for over sixty years.

The 1960s saw some departures and the arrival of new staff members. Appointments included Anne Ross (1925–2012) specialising in custom and belief, Iain Crawford succeeding Ian Whitaker in material culture, ethnomusicologist Thorkild Knudsen from Denmark and Donald Archie Macdonald (1929–1999) to succeed Calum Maclean, with a main but not exclusive focus on oral narrative. He was to contribute almost 900 recordings to the sound archive in the course of his career and to create, with the assistance of Cathie Scott, a comprehensive

Tale Archive containing tales recorded or published in Scotland classified according to international systems.

Morag MacLeod worked in the area of Gaelic song while Alan Bruford (1937–1995) was appointed Research Archivist and was an active fieldworker, editor and author. Ian Fraser came to the Scottish Place-Name Survey and Daphne Hamilton to assist with *Scottish Studies*. Eric Cregeen (1921–1983), of Manx background, opened up the field of social organisation. Peter Cooke succeeded Knudsen and within his remit took forward the publication of the *Scottish Tradition* LP series of archive material. Ailie Munro (1918–2002) was to write on the folk song revival, in which the School of Scottish Studies played a vital role.

In the course of this decade the School came to be more closely associated with the Faculty of Arts, having previously reported directly to Senatus and Court, and reached out to other departments through offering limited contributions to their courses. The desirability of an undergraduate degree programme in Scottish Ethnology, using that title, was mooted but this was to be a project for the future. Term-long teaching commitments would put constraints on fieldwork programmes and related work, still the main function of the School at the time. A Postgraduate Diploma in Scottish Studies was instituted, however, combining teaching by staff and a research-based dissertation.

Basil Megaw retired in 1969, though he remained an Honorary Fellow to the end of his life, and Professor John MacQueen was appointed Director, holding that position for close to two decades. He had held the Masson Chair of Medieval English and Scottish Literature at the University of Edinburgh and brought with him an interest in place-names and in narrative sources including saints' lives and a family background in the south-west of Scotland. He was named to a personal chair of Scottish Literature and Oral Tradition in 1972. Undergraduate teaching and postgraduate supervision moved on in this decade.

In the 1970s filming was added to the means by which oral and material culture might be recorded, with the assistance of The Gannochy Trust in acquiring a 16 mm camera. Subjects included the re-creation of a *luadh* (waulking) session in South Uist, the participants all having done such work as younger women, an outdoor baptism on the Island of Tiree, the making of a Shetland *kishie* (basket), dancing, fiddling and storytelling in Gaelic and Scots.

The *Scottish Tradition* LP series began to be published, first by Tangent Records and later by Greentrax Recordings Limited, each accompanied by a full brochure with extensive notes based on research into the subject featured, an individual singer, the instrumental or vocal music of a particular region or a genre of oral tradition. LPs had first been published in the 1960s to illustrate aspects of the School's collections to date but the series, numbering well over twenty publications by 2012, has brought these to a world-wide audience.

1971 saw the launch of the archive publication *Tocher* (a word meaning a dowry in Scots and Gaelic). This innovative means of disseminating original material in transcription and, where required, translation, supported by notes and photographs, complemented the *Scottish Tradition* LPs in sharing the voices of those recorded for the archive with the wider public, including – importantly – those communities in which the recordings had been made. The pioneering nature of this outlet for the School's work cannot be underestimated.[32] Much credit is due to Mary MacDonald (1911–1999) for the inspiration behind the inception of *Tocher*, and she assisted Alan Bruford in editing it for many years. Its ethos would lie behind the PEARL Project ('Providing Ethnological Resources for Research and Learning') of the 1990s and Tobar an Dualchais/Kist o Riches in the decade following.

Another significant innovation in this decade came in the form of the School's one-year course 'Oral Literature and Popular Tradition', open to students in the Faculty of Arts as part of their degree curriculum and harbinger of the full degree in Scottish Ethnology which was developed in the 1980s. The course gave students an overview of the subject, drawing on the expertise of members of the School staff and using for illustration recordings and photographs made in the field as well as the work of ethnologists and folklorists elsewhere. A second year was added in due course. Once more, this was a pioneering endeavour in the Scottish context and more widely. Supervision of students for postgraduate degrees, already initiated, was further promoted. Alexander Fenton taught material culture in the Department of Scottish History in this period.

This decade also saw the first instance of UK research board support in the School when Eric Cregeen secured funding for the Tiree Project from the Social Science Research Council (SSRC), later the Economic and Social Research Council (ESRC), for work incorporating oral and documentary evidence for the study of a Hebridean island community and its emigrant offshoots in the eighteenth and nineteenth centuries. The oral history movement was gathering impetus at the time and he was instrumental in furthering research of this kind in Scotland through the founding of the Scottish Oral History Group in 1978 and notable contributions to the work and publications of the Oral History Society. The School's work and collections showed how oral tradition as well as individual experience could illuminate the past and many oral history projects initiated in Scotland in this period received methodological, analytical and technical guidance from School staff and this type of engagement was to continue. A number of these projects have been deposited in the School of Scottish Studies Archives as well as others such as the South East of Scotland Working People's History recordings.

The momentum of the 1970s was further realised in the 1980s with the inauguration of the first full four-year degree in Scottish Ethnology, at both single honours and joint honours levels. Students could study for a joint degree in Scottish Ethnology with Celtic, Scottish History, Archaeology, English Literature, English Language, Linguistics and Scandinavian Studies. Two staff members were appointed, Margaret Bennett and Margaret Mackay, to take this initiative forward, through course planning and co-ordination, the preparation of materials and liaison with participants beyond the department, as well as to undertake work in their own specialties, custom and belief and social organisation respectively.

The degree programmes attracted both school-leavers and mature students, as the university was increasingly engaged in access and other entry arrangements for candidates in the latter category. Many brought work or other experience highly relevant to the study of ethnology. All found that the emphasis from year one on original research provided a welcome feature of this discipline, the opportunity to use one's own family, or home place, or other interests as topics for study. Using the Swedish motto 'Dig where you stand!', students were trained in ethnological research methods and analysis and began to bring new kinds of data into the archives as their projects and dissertations were deposited and accessioned on a regular basis. The principle of SAMDOK, an acronym for Swedish *samtids dokumentation* and known in the museum context in connection with the collection and display of items representing current times, was also one which they often called into play, documenting contemporary phenomena in their work.

This period also saw the start of the publication of the eight-volume *Greig-Duncan Folk Song Collection* with Emily B Lyle as General Editor following the death of Patrick Noel Shuldham-Shaw (1917–1977), who had begun the task. In a sequence lasting two decades, over three thousand song texts and tunes collected in the north-east of Scotland by Gavin Greig (1856–1914) and the Reverend James B Duncan (1848–1917) were edited by Lyle and other specialist scholars.

A Board of Scottish Studies was created to embrace representation from the subject areas with which Scottish Ethnology had joint degrees, and other departments in the University. It was instrumental in undergraduate and postgraduate recruitment initiatives such as *Studying Scotland at Edinburgh*. It should also be noted that although the programmes of the School of Scottish Studies were pioneering in their provision, subjects such as Scottish folklore and song were included in curricula at several other universities including Aberdeen, Stirling and Glasgow.

Alexander Fenton was appointed to the first Chair of Scottish Ethnology in 1989 on the retirement of John MacQueen and held the position until 1994. The placing of Scottish Ethnology within its wider European context was a priority during this period and when Margaret Mackay became Director of the School of Scottish Studies on Fenton's retiral, she co-ordinated a programme of Visiting Professors of Ethnology over the next five years which brought distinguished ethnologists and folklorists to the department from Scandinavia and beyond. Each contributed to undergraduate teaching at all levels, including an honours course incorporating theory, methods and material in his or her area of special expertise, and interacted creatively with staff and postgraduate students, as well as using the School's resources and networks for comparative purposes in their own fields. They were W F H Nicolaisen, who had returned to Scotland after a sojourn in the USA from 1969 (onomastics and folkloristics), Linda Dégh from the University of Indiana (oral narrative), Bjarne Stoklund from the University of Copenhagen (material culture), Nils-Arvid Bringéus of the University of Lund (religious ethnology and *bildlore*, the use of visual sources in ethnology), and Åse Enerstvedt from Norway (childlore and children's culture).

Another major focus in this period was archive development, including the initiation of online access to archive holdings through the PEARL Project, in close collaboration with the university's computing services. Original sound items selected from those already published in *Tocher* enabled the testing of technological approaches which were to be used further in the decade following. New appointees to the teaching and research staff were Gary West (material culture), who had graduated from the School's undergraduate and postgraduate programmes and thus signalled the new continuity of scholarship engendered by the department, Mark Trewin (ethnomusicology) and John Shaw (oral narrative).

The 1990s additionally saw the foundation of The Elphinstone Institute at the University of Aberdeen. The importance of the north-east of Scotland and of north-eastern scholars and enthusiasts in the development of ethnology can not be stressed too highly and the Elphinstone Institute brought a focus to these. James Porter, who had worked in the School of Scottish Studies early in his career, was appointed Professor of Scottish Ethnology there. The Royal Scottish Academy of Music and Drama in Glasgow, now the Royal Conservatoire of Scotland, launched its undergraduate Scottish Music degree with the provision of archive resources from the School of Scottish Studies. In the Universities of Stirling and Glagow and the University of the Highlands and Islands, folklore and ethnology were integrated into curricula as well.

Two main features dominate the story of the School of Scottish Studies in the first decade of the twenty-first century. One of these is university re-structuring, which brought a merger of Celtic and Scottish Studies into a single subject area. The School of Scottish Studies Archives and the European Ethnological Research Centre (EERC), described below, are located within it in a new School of Literatures, Languages and Cultures, and a new College of Humanities and Social Science. The other is the further development of online provision of archive resources. Building on the PEARL project of the 1990s and utilising digital technology in new ways, Tobar an Dualchais/Kist o Riches is a partnership of three archive-holders, The School of Scottish Studies, BBC Radio Scotland, and The National Trust for Scotland (Campbell of Canna Collection), co-ordinated by Sabhal Mòr Ostaig, University of the Highlands and Islands, for ensuring preservation and access to three major collections of Gaelic and Scots oral tradition. Neill Martin (custom and belief), Katherine Campbell (Scots song and ethnomusicology) and Will Lamb (oral narrative and Gaelic song) were appointed and Donald Meek was named to a Personal Chair in Scottish and Gaelic Studies.

The diamond jubilee of the founding of the School of Scottish Studies took place in 2011 and the staff of Celtic and Scottish Studies and the School of Scottish Studies Archives have entered the seventh decade of activities with further funding for work on the Calum Maclean website, already well developed in a previous project; the Alexander Carmichael Project continuing; a joint project with the University of Mainz on Scott's *Minstrelsy*; the Maclagan Manuscript Index nearing completion; and new courses in the offing at undergraduate and postgraduate levels.

Scottish Museums in the Second Half of the Twentieth Century

The history of ethnology within the university context and the work of the School of Scottish Studies and others should be seen alongside the important parallel developments in the museum world.

The establishment of the Country Life Section of the National Museum of Antiquities of Scotland (NMAS) in 1959 aimed to build up and document collections of rural material, carry out essential field research, work towards the creation of an open-air museum of country life and generally to 'expand the Museum's activities, particularly in recording and illustrating passing ways of country life and agriculture'.[33] The NMAS thus completed the range of cultural periods over which it had responsibility, from prehistoric archaeology through the Middle Ages to the Agricultural Improvement period and so on to the present day, fulfilling its role as the 'national' museum.

The concept of a museum of Scottish country life had been in the air since at least 1929, when reference was made to it in a Report of the Royal Commission on Museums and Galleries. This was probably inspired by the Scandinavian folk museums, of which the earliest was Nordiska Museet, founded in 1872 by Artur Hazelius in Stockholm, Sweden, and widely imitated.[34] Am Fasgadh, the Highland Folk Museum created by Dr Isabel Frances Grant (1887–1983) first on Iona, then at Laggan and finally in Kingussie (1944), had its first flowering in a 'Highland Exhibition' which she organised in Inverness in 1930.[35] It has already been noted that the Scottish Anthropological (and Folklore) Society established a Folk-Museum Committee in the early 1930s.

In 1951 the development of a national 'folk museum' was recommended by the Secretary of State for Scotland's Advisory Committee on Education, in a Report on Libraries, Museums and Art Galleries. In the same year an exhibition was held at the Royal Scottish Museum as a contribution to the Festival of Britain. Entitled 'Living Traditions', it presented Scottish crafts and vernacular architecture, and included Gaelic singing by Flora MacNeil of Barra, recently recorded for the School of Scottish Studies, to illustrate the songs which accompanied the waulking of handwoven woollen cloth.

The urgent necessity for such a museum was discussed the following year at a conference of the School of Scottish Studies about which a report appeared in The Scotsman on 31 May 1952. It welcomed the appointment of Ian Whitaker as Research Fellow in Contemporary Material Culture in the School from 1 July of that year as 'an entirely new departure in the British Isles'. The importance of combining information on process through sound, photograph and object was stressed and the advice to 'Collect, collect all the time' had come from Dr Iorwerth C Peate (1901–1982) of the Welsh Folk Museum at St Fagan's, Cardiff, which had been set up in 1947, and from Professor J H Delargy of the Irish Folklore Commission, both conference participants. Later that decade Margaret (Greta) Fairweather Michie (1905–1985) opened the Glenesk Museum in 1955, a project influenced by the work of I F Grant and Artur Hazelius before her.[36]

A few more years passed until in 1959, the Trustees of the NMAS appointed an Assistant Keeper to organise the new Country Life Section of the NMAS. The person appointed to this position was Alexander Fenton (1929–2012). Born in Lanarkshire and raised in Aberdeenshire, the rural life he experienced in the Auchterless and Turriff areas was to influence his future career profoundly. He gained his MA (Hons) in English and French at the University of Aberdeen in 1951 and his BA in the University of Cambridge Archaeological and Anthropological Tripos in 1953. Following National Service in Germany from 1953 to 1955, his first post was as Senior Assistant Editor of the *Scottish National Dictionary*, working with David Murison (1913–1997) and honing his *Wörter und Sächen* ('words and things') approach to the study of material culture.[37] The SND project was housed within the School of Scottish Studies complex and he worked closely with its staff, helping to devise early questionnaires.

Alexander (Sandy) Fenton's museum career lasted thirty years. He went on to become Deputy Keeper in the NMAS, then its Director and finally Research Director of the National Museums of Scotland, before being appointed the first Chair of Scottish Ethnology at the University of Edinburgh and Director of the School of Scottish Studies in 1989. In 1959, the immediate need was seen to be the setting up of an Archive. It was conceived on what might be called 'lexico-graphical' principles, which fitted in well with his experience on the *SND*. Any theme entered in the Archive had full extracts from the sources to support it. Slips of paper measuring 250 × 130 mm were fed into specially-made binders, in chronological order, and located according to the old counties and parishes as used in the *Old* (1790s) and *New* (1845) *Statistical Accounts of Scotland*. In effect, this was following the ethnological principles of time and place.

The slips were big enough to take half-plate photographs as well as a reasonable amount of information, which could come from any source: extracts from printed books and papers, newspaper cuttings, letters, oral information, drawings, dialect terms etc. Ease of access to the stored information was an important criterion and the binders facilitated this, for they could be lifted off a shelf and used at desk or table. As all possible pieces of information were brought together under each heading, their value as tools for research increased as more and more data was added to them.

Although the indexing system of the Archive at the Landsmal och Folkmin-nesarkiv in Uppsala was widely emulated and, having been studied by Calum Maclean during his Swedish study period, adapted for use in the sound archive of the School of Scottish Studies, it was decided that a pre-existing system from another land should not be adopted for the Museum's Country Life Archive but rather that one should be created that was suited to the needs of ethnological research in Scotland. On the basis of the consultation of books containing data for each parish or county, including the two *Statistical Accounts* and the series of *General Views* of agriculture in different districts, also instigated by Sir John Sinclair, a natural set of thematic headings was evolved in keeping with the character of Scotland.

Not surprisingly, the bulk of the headings coincided with those in ethno-logical archives elsewhere, built up by those who had long been actively engaged at an academic level with ethnological research and folk museums. The emphasis, however, was on material culture, complementing the School of Scottish Studies Archives, where there was a strong emphasis on oral tradition, Scots and Gaelic song, tales, instrumental music and custom and belief. In sound, photograph and film, however, the School's collections also include a great deal of information on material culture, work, crafts, trades, buildings and ways of life.

By 1988, when a Guide to the Archive was published after twenty-nine years of ingathering of data, there were c.500 binders, c.100,000 photographs, c.6,000 transparencies, and an A4 archive for items too big for the binders, a manuscript archive for diaries and notebooks with questionnaire answers, a catalogue archive containing trade literature, and special collections. These include the collection of the travel writer Alasdair Alpin MacGregor, containing c.4,000 negatives and prints, and Ian Fleming's collection of c.700 transparencies from the Scottish Agricultural Industries Work Study in Agriculture.[38]

A second Index and Guide was published ten years later, in 1998, with a greatly enlarged series of entries, especially in the subject areas of agricultural engineering, boats, buildings, cattle, communications and transport, dairy, dress, farm workers, food, fuel, grain, health and welfare, housing, hunting, trapping, and breeding. A postcard collection of c.5,000 items had been added and a small audio-visual collection of c.100 audio tapes and films, in particular films made by the East of Scotland College of Agriculture in the 1940s and 1950s.[39] An attempt was made to fit in with the work of the Social History Curators' Group, which had developed a Social History and Industrial Classification (SHIC). The Archive was renamed twice, as the Scottish Ethnological Archive and now as the Scottish Life Archive, for it aims to cover every aspect of life including urban and industrial material.

Along with the establishment of the Archive came the work of assessing existing material in the NMAS collections, the gathering of further objects and the creation of exhibition displays. There was a close connection between the build-up of the collections, the growth of the Archive and the temporary thematic exhibitions which began to be mounted almost immediately in the Museum Gallery at 18 Shandwick Place in Edinburgh. Once a theme had been chosen, all relevant background research notes were fed into the Archive.

A series of eleven exhibitions were held there from 1960 to 1970 on the most important themes in the daily round. There were:

1960 *Agricultural implements and techniques.* Ropes and rope-making, including a linguistic map of the terminology of rope-twisters; a reconstructed smiddy; harness and harness cleaning; the history of the plough; grain processing; turf and peat spades.

1961 *Old Scottish Crafts.* Smithing; woodworking; leather working; straw work and basket work.

1962 *Scottish Country Life and Work.* Dairying, byres and cattle-fastenings.

1963 *Peat Cutting and Land Improvement.* The processing of peat for fuel; drainage of fields; enclosing; manuring; farm societies and clubs; a Caithness kitchen reconstruction with a peat fire.

1964 *Fishing, Fowling and Hunting.* Inshore fishing; angling and poaching; fowling; trapping and hunting.

1965 *The History of Harvesting.* Sowing; shearing; stacking; threshing; winnowing; drying; grinding.

1966 *Hearth and Home.* Traditional house types; hearths; thatching; cooking and baking; washing and mangling; lighting; settlement patterns; ironmongers' catalogues.

1967 *Hearth and Home.* This was an expansion of the 1966 exhibition.
1968 *St Kilda.*
1969 *Islands of the North and West.*
1970 *Caithness and the Northern Isles.*

In 1965 an opportunity arose for preparing much larger exhibitions than could be mounted in the Museum Gallery and with much greater exposure to the public. An invitation came from the Secretary of the Royal Highland and Agricultural Society, Mr Dick Lemmon, to mount agricultural displays in the Showground at Ingliston on the west side of Edinburgh. These were very successful and led to the establishment of a building and workshop in the Showground. However, with a small staff it became difficult to mount exhibitions in both the Museum Gallery and at Ingliston, so there was some repetition of displays in the Gallery. They ceased in 1970 and concentration was turned fully on Ingliston.

The Ingliston phase of the Scottish Agricultural Museum was a productive one for displays of rural life and a highlight each year for visitors to the Royal Highland Show, but there was still the need for a permanent and more extensive site where interpretation could take place and the extensive collections find an appropriate home. The Scottish Country Life Museums Trust was set up to gather funds and the Carnegie UK Trust paid for a roving curator to give support to several independent museums.[40] These included the West Highland township museum at Auchindrain in Argyll, established in 1964, the site having been recognised by Marion Campbell of Kilberry, Alexander Fenton and Eric R Cregeen as a unique surviving pre-crofting settlement.

Material culture studies were given further impetus at the time by the Society for Folk Life Studies, which attracted an active Scottish membership. Founded in 1961, from 1963 it published its journal *Folk Life*, successor to *Gwerin*, which Iorwerth C Peate had edited between 1956 and 1962. The Scottish Vernacular Buildings Working Group was established in 1972 and aimed then and since to develop expertise in this area through conferences, study visits, its journal *Vernacular Building* and monographs.

The search for a suitable permanent home for a Scottish Agricultural Museum was resolved with the development of the farm of West Kittochside, between East Kilbride and Carmunnock in Lanarkshire, by the National Trust for Scotland and the National Museums of Scotland. Home for ten generations of the Reid family, whose history on the land from 1567 onwards is very thoroughly documented, the farm was gifted to the Trust in 1992 by Mrs Margaret Reid, who had worked it with her late husband James, the last of the Reid line there.

It opened in 2001 as the Museum of Scottish Country Life and was renamed the National Museum of Rural Life in 2006. It features the Georgian buildings of the farm itself, fields and hedgerows around them and an events area as well as a 50,000 square foot purpose-built museum and visitor centre designed by Page & Park Architects and displaying artefacts illustrating the main themes of land, tools and people. The models from the Highland Society have been relocated there and other unique exhibits include the oldest known surviving threshing mill in the world. The farm carries a herd of cattle and a flock of sheep, and ploughing, sowing, haymaking and harvesting are demonstrated. Activity days are held throughout the year.

The European Ethnological Research Centre

In 1989 the European Ethnological Research Centre was founded by Alexander Fenton as a focus for the publication of research on Scottish topics, setting these in a wider European and comparative context. Initially located within the National Museums of Scotland, the EERC moved later to the University of Edinburgh and the Department of Celtic and Scottish Studies, which also houses the School of Scottish Studies Archives and Library. Its major projects to date have been the *Compendium of Scottish Ethnology*, the journal *Review of Scottish Culture (ROSC)*, which began publication in 1984, *Sources in Local History* and the *Flashbacks* series. A comprehensive ethnological study of Dumfries and Galloway has now been launched by the EERC, the first in a proposed series of cultural landscape investigations.

FUTURE PROSPECTS

Ethnology is carried forward in Scotland at several levels – in national and local museums and in institutions of higher education as well as in schools where the new curricula embrace local resources and encourage research with online access to national collections such as those of the Royal Commission on the Ancient and Historical Monuments of Scotland, the National Archives of Scotland, and SCRAN (Scottish Cultural Resources Access Network). The Scottish Screen Archive, with its rich fare for the ethnologist, is now administered through the National Library of Scotland. Local organisations which collect and display or otherwise use objects, photographs and information from oral sources and other sources, often create digital resources of interest both at home and abroad. Such media mean that opportunities for comparative study have never been greater, all the more so as Scotland's population becomes increasingly diverse and cultures meet and interact here. The key remains community engagement, a hallmark of ethnology in this country. The international nature of our subject gives it a dimension in which all can find a place. That gives it a real relevance and applicability in our contemporary world.

Please note that dates have been provided, where known, only for those individuals not living at the time of publication.

NOTES

1 See Dorson, 1968, 1–43 for an account of this period of antiquarian activity and the book as a whole for a survey of the subject.

2 McClure, 2012, 35.

3 McClure, 2012, 40.

4 Gaskell, 1996 and 2004.

5 Brown, 1976, 45–67.

6 Dorson, 1968, 107–18.

7 Ash, 1999, 72.

8 *Transactions*, 1832, 385–400.

9 Kohl, 1844, x.

10 Fenton, 1962, 7.

11 Rennie, 2012b, 70. For a full account of Jamieson see Rennie, 2012b, 60–84 and Rennie, 2012a.

12 Dorson, 1968, 1.

13 Dorson, 1968, 393–402.

14 Dorson, 1968, 402–5.

15 Bassin, 1977.

16 Kennedy-Fraser, 1929 and 2011.

17 Bassin, 1965, 145–52.

18 Campbell, 1958.

19 Robertson and Young, 1996.

20 The Maclagan MSS have been lodged by The Folklore Society in the School of Scottish Studies Archives, where an electronic index is under preparation.

21 Buchan, 1994.

22 Dareau, 2012, 116–43. This work carried on under the editorships of A J (Jack) Aitken (1921–1998), James A C Stevenson (1917–1992), Harry Watson, Marace Dareau and Lorna Pike.

23 Macleod, 2012a, 144–71.

24 Macleod, 2012b, 172–96.

25 Gillies and Pike, 2012, 252–9.

26 Shaw, 1999; Perman, 2010.

27 Russell, 2003.

28 Fenton with Mulhern, 2012.

29 Mackay, 2013, 1–33.

30 The Memorandum can be found in Senatus Papers for May of 1950.

31 Neat, 2007, 2009.

32 Lindahl, 2013, 227–9.

33 National Museum, 1960.

34 Bringéus, 1974, 5–16.

35 Grant, c.1950, 2007.

36 Cant, 1987, 1–3; Michie, Fenton and Beech, 2000.

37 Steensberg, 1993.

38 Fenton et al., 1988.

39 Langler and Kidd, 1998.

40 Fenton, 1990b.

Ash, M. Old books, old castles, and old friends: The making of Daniel Wilson's *Archaeology and Prehistoric Annals of Scotland*. In Hulse, E, ed., *Thinking with Both Hands: Sir Daniel Wilson in the Old World and the New*, Toronto, 1999.

Bassin, E. Lucy Broadwood, 1858–1929: Her contribution to the collection and study of Gaelic traditional song, *Scottish Studies*, 9:2 (1965), 145–52.

Bassin, E. *The Old Songs of Skye: Frances Tolmie and her Circle*, ed. D Bowman, London, 1977.

Bringéus, N-A. Artur Hazelius och Nordiska Museet, *Fataburen* (1972), 7–32.

Bringéus, N-A. Artur Hazelius and the Nordic Museum, *Ethnologia Scandinavica* (1974), 5–16.

Bringéus, N-A. *Åke Campbell som etnolog*, Uppsala, 2008.

Bringéus, N-A. *Carl Wilhelm von Sydow: A Swedish Pioneer in Folklore*, Helsinki, 2009.

Brown, M E. 'The Joy of My Heart': Robert Burns as folklorist, *Scottish Studies*, 20 (1976), 45–67.

Buchan, D, ed. *Folk Tradition and Folk Medicine in Scotland: The Writings of David Rorie*, Edinburgh, 1994.

Campbell, J L, ed. *Gaelic Words from South Uist Collected by Fr Allan MacDonald*, Dublin, 1958.

Cant, R G. Margaret Fairweather Michie 1905–1985: A memoir, *Review of Scottish Culture*, 3 (1987), 1–3.

Chambers, B, ed. *The Carrying Stream Flows On: Celebrating the Diamond Jubilee of the School of Scottish Studies*, Kershader, 2013.

Cheape, H, ed. *Tools and Traditions: Studies in European Ethnology Presented to Alexander Fenton*, Edinburgh, 1993.

Dareau, M G. Dictionary of the Older Scottish Tongue. In Macleod, I and McClure, J D, eds, *Scotland in Definition: A History of Scottish Dictionaries*, Edinburgh, 2012, 116–43.

Dorson, R. *The British Folklorists: A History*, London, 1968.

Fenton, A. Scottish Agricultural History Museums, *Transactions of the Royal Highland and Agricultural Society of Scotland*, 7 (1962), 1–9.

Fenton, A. Historical ethnology in Scotland, *Ethnologica Europea*, 1:1 (1967), 1–5.

Fenton, A. The scope of regional ethnology, *Folk Life*, 11 (1973), 5–14.

Fenton, A, Kidd, D, Langler, E and Hendry, C. *The Scottish Ethnological Archive*, National Museums of Scotland Information Series, No 2, 1988.

Fenton, A. Phases of ethnology in Britain with special reference to Scotland, *Ethnologia Europaea*, 20:2 (1990a), 177–88.

Fenton, A. *On Your Bike: Thirteen Years of Travelling Curators*, Edinburgh, 1990b.

Fenton, A. Crossing the Rubicon (Inaugural lecture for the Chair of Scottish Ethnology), *Scottish Studies*, 31 (1993), 1–8.

Fenton, A. *Bibliography*, Edinburgh, 2009.

Fenton, A with Mulhern, M A, eds. *A Swedish Field Trip to the Outer Hebrides, 1934*, Edinburgh, 2012.

Gaskell, H. *The Poems of Ossian and Related Works*, Edinburgh, 1996.

Gaskell, H, ed. *The Reception of Ossian in Europe*, London, 2004.

Gillies, W and Pike, L. Gaelic lexicography: The last hundred years. In Macleod, I and McClure, J D, eds, *Scotland in Definition: A History of Scottish Dictionaries*, Edinburgh, 2012, 236–59.

Grant, I F. *Am Fasgadh, the Highland Folk Museum*, c.1950.

Grant, I F. *Highland Folk Ways*, London, 1961.

Grant, I F. *The Making of 'Am Fasgadh'*, Edinburgh, 2007.

Hulse, E, ed. *Thinking with Both Hands: Sir Daniel Wilson in the Old World and the New*, Toronto, 1999.

Kennedy-Fraser, M. *A Life of Song*, London, 1929. Reprint with introduction by P Ahlander, Kershader, 2011.

Kohl, J G T. *Travels in Scotland*, London, 1844.

Langler, E and Kidd, D. *The Scottish Life Archive*, Department of Social and Technological History, National Museums of Scotland, 1998.

Lindahl, C. The School of Scottish Studies, an Island Community. In Chambers, B, ed., *The Carrying Stream Flows On: Celebrating the Diamond Jubilee of the School of Scottish Studies*, Kershader, 2013, 226–46.

Kay, C J and Mackay, M A, eds. *Perspectives on the Older Scottish Tongue*, Edinburgh, 2005.

Mackay, M A. The First Sixty Years of the School of Scottish Studies: An Overview. In Chambers, B, ed. *The Carrying Stream Flows On: Celebrating the Sixtieth Anniversary of the School of Scottish Studies*, Kershader, 2013, 1–33.

Maclean, C I. *The Highlands*, London, 1959.

Macleod, I and McClure, J D, ed. *Scotland in Definition: A History of Scottish Dictionaries*, Edinburgh, 2012.

Macleod, I. Scottish National Dictionary. In Macleod, I and McClure, J D, eds, *Scotland in Definition: A History of Scottish Dictionaries*, Edinburgh, 2012a, 144–71.

Macleod, I. Other twentieth and twenty-first century Scots dictionaries. In Macleod, I and McClure, J D, eds, *Scotland in Definition: A History of Scottish Dictionaries*, Edinburgh, 2012b, 172–96.

McClure, J D. Glossaries and Scotticisms: Lexicography in the eighteenth century. In Macleod, I and McClure, J D, eds, *Scotland in Definition: A History of Scottish Dictionaries*, Edinburgh, 2012, 35–59.

Michie, M F with Fenton, A and Beech, J. *Glenesk: the History and Culture of an Angus Community*, Edinburgh, 2000.

National Museum of Antiquities of Scotland, *Sixth Annual Report*, HMSO, 1960.

Neat, T. *Hamish Henderson: A Biography. Volume One, The Making of the Poet (1919–1953)*, Edinburgh, 2007; *Volume Two, Poetry Becomes People (1952–2002)*, Edinburgh, 2009.

Perman, R. *The Man Who Gave Away His Island*, Edinburgh, 2010.

Rennie, S. *Jamieson's Dictionary of Scots: The Story of the First Historical Dictionary of the Scots Language*, Oxford, 2012a.

Rennie, S. Jamieson and the nineteenth century. In Macleod, I and McClure, J D, eds, *Scotland in Definition: A History of Scottish Dictionaries*, Edinburgh, 2012b, 60–84.

Robertson, S and Young, P. *Daughter of Atholl; Lady Evelyn Stewart Murray (1868–1940)*, Dundee, 1996.

Robertson, S and Dilworth, T, eds and trans. *Tales from Highland Perthshire collected by Lady Evelyn Stewart Murray*, Aberdeen, 2009.

Roussell, A. *Norse Building Customs in the Scottish Isles*, London, 1934.

Royal Commission on the Ancient and Historical Monuments of Scotland. *Wester Kittochside, the Museum of Scottish Country Life* (broadsheet 7), Edinburgh, 2001.

Russell, M. *A Different Country: The Photographs of Werner Kissling*, Edinburgh, 2003.

Shaw, M F. *Folksongs and Folklore of South Uist*, London, 1955.

Shaw, M F. *From the Alleghenies to the Hebrides: An Autobiography*, Edinburgh, 1999.

Steensberg, A. Wörter und Sächen / Terms and Realities. In Cheape, H, ed. *Tools and Traditions: Studies in European Ethnology Presented to Alexander* Fenton, Edinburgh, 1993, 16–21.

Stewart, D W, ed. *The Life and Legacy of Alexander Carmichael*, Kershader, 2009.

Transactions of the Highland Society of Scotland, 9 (1832), 385–400.

West, G. *Voicing Scotland: Folk, Culture, Nation*, Edinburgh, 2012.

JOURNALS

Folk Life, 1963–present
Gwerin, 1956–62
Review of Scottish Culture (*ROSC*), 1984–present
Scottish Studies, 1957–present
Tocher, 1971–present
Tools and Tillage, 1968–present
Vernacular Buildings, 1975–present

ONLINE RESOURCES

Celtic and Scottish Studies, <http://www.ed.ac.uk/schools-departments/literatures-languages-cultures/celtic-scottish-studies>
Dictionary of the Scots Language, <www.dsl.ac.uk>
Elphinstone Institute, <www.abdn.ac.uk/elphinstone>
School of Scottish Studies Archives, University of Edinburgh, <www.ed.ac.uk/schools-departments/literatures-languages-cultures/celtic-scottish-studies/archives>
Scottish Screen Archive, <www.ssa.nls.uk>
Tobar an Dualchais / Kist o Riches, <www.tobarandualchais.co.uk>

3　Ethnological Fieldwork

WENDY UGOLINI

This chapter aims to provide an overview of ethnological fieldwork, addressing the main issues and debates surrounding the use of in-depth interviewing as a research technique and exploring some of the key issues which arise. These issues include the interpersonal dynamics between interviewee and researcher, the centrality of reflexivity and the importance of conducting fieldwork within an ethical and legal framework. It will draw, in particular, on my experiences of undertaking fieldwork amongst the Italian community in south-east Scotland at the close of the twentieth century.[1]

Oral history is the name given to the act of recording people's memories – either their accounts of particular historic events or their life stories. As Michael Richards summarises, historical information gleaned from the study of memory is essentially of two types. First, memory reveals positive facts about past events and about the experience of those events, be they wars, revolutions or everyday realities in 'times of normality'. Second, it tells us how recollections of events are acquired and subsequently altered in the constant forming and reforming of identities. Memory is shaped by our changing surroundings and the way we interpret them.[2] Until the late 1970s, the use of personal testimonies was largely promoted by pioneering oral historians as a way of accessing and retrieving factual information and gathering fresh data about the lives of previously marginalised groups; this was a period defined by Michael Roper as 'the reconstructive mode' of oral history.[3] The guiding principle behind much of the earliest and well-known oral history publications such as Paul Thompson's *The Edwardians* and Mary Chamberlain's *Fenwomen*[4] rested on a political commitment to recover the lives of those who were traditionally 'hidden from history', such as women and the working classes.[5] However, academic studies which made use of oral testimonies faced ongoing criticisms from documentary historians who believed memory to be unreliable as a historical source because it was distorted 'by the deterioration of age, by personal bias and nostalgia, and by the influence of other, subsequent versions of the past',[6] leading to what Penny Summerfield terms a 'methodological defensiveness' whereby oral historians felt the need to adopt the quantitative research methods of sampling and tabulation.[7]

In the early 1980s, however, there was a significant methodological shift when publications by Italian historians such as Luisa Passerini and Alessandro Portelli and American historian Ron Grele collectively identified the *process* of remembering as the key to exploring the subjective meanings of lived experience and the nature of individual and collective memory.[8] The work of Passerini, in particular, stressed the need to pay particular attention to the 'cultural and symbolic import' of people's stories as well as their factual content.[9] As Chamberlain notes, oral historians such as Alessandro Portelli and anthropologists such as Elizabeth Tonkin, most famously in *Narrating our Pasts: The Social Construction of Oral History*, argue that oral testimonies, like other narrative forms, are governed by genres which the scholar can 'identify and codify, and clue back into an understanding of historical reckoning or imagining'.[10] This approach, which Roper defines as 'oral history in the interpretive mode',[11] led to a new understanding of oral history as a powerful tool for exploring 'how people make sense of their past, how they connect individual experience and its social context, how the past becomes part of the present, and how people use it to interpret their lives and the world around them.'[12] Grele was instrumental in arguing that researchers who use personal testimonies need to grasp 'the underlying structure of consciousness which both governs and informs oral history interviews' and to look at the dominant themes which emerge from an interview, how people organise their lives into historical narratives and to have an awareness of the 'deeper meaning' of personal narratives.[13] Portelli emphasised the ways in which 'oral history is intrinsically different, and therefore specifically useful':

> The unique and precious element which oral sources force upon the historian and which no other sources possess in equal measure . . . is the speaker's subjectivity: and therefore, if the research is broad and articulated enough, a cross section of the subjectivity of a social group or class. They tell us not just what people did, but what they wanted to do, what they believed they were doing, what they now think they did.[14]

Ethnography has come to be associated with some distinctive methodological ideas, such as the importance of understanding the perspectives of the people under study, and of observing their activities in everyday life.[15] The methodology of ethnology is used by anthropologists, oral historians, sociologists and folklorists as well as students of cultural studies, educational studies and religious studies.[16] Within these disciplines, researchers will employ a range of methods when conducting fieldwork, including interviewing, photography, field notes and recording. Lareau and Shultz allude to the varying definitions of ethnographic studies which exist, ranging from the use of participant observation to studying a community for an extended period of time, the portrayal of the community from the perspective of the participants and a focus on the lived culture of the setting.[17] As Hammersley and Atkinson note, the traditional perception is that the ethnographer participates, overtly or covertly, in people's daily lives for an extended period of time, watching what happens, listening to what is said, asking questions; in fact, collecting whatever data are available to throw light on the issues with which he or she is concerned.[18] As in-depth interviewing and participant observation are the most widely used fieldwork techniques within ethnological research, they will form the focus of this chapter.

In their ethnography textbook, Lareau and Shultz outline the generally held consensus on good ethnographic practice: that researchers using participant observation 'should build rapport, gain the trust of the people in the study, provide detailed and accurate field notes, interpret the results in a theoretically informed manner and write it up in a vivid and engaging style'.[19] The term 'participant observation' is most commonly identified as the central research method of social and cultural anthropologists, but practitioners also use the term to encompass the general approach of fieldwork in ethnographic research or as 'a cover term for all of the observation and formal and informal interviewing in which anthropologists engage'.[20] For DeWalt and DeWalt, participant observation is one of several methods that fit into the general category of qualitative research, along with other qualitative methods including structured and semi-structured interviewing, observation and the collection and analysis of texts. They write:

> While much of what we call fieldwork includes participating and observing the people and communities with whom we are working, the method of participant observation includes the use of information gained from participating and observing through explicit recording and analysis of this information. That is, all humans are participants and observers in all of their everyday interactions, but few individuals actually engage in the systematic use of this information for social scientific purposes.[21]

Fundamentally, as Hammersley and Atkinson argue, all social research takes the form of participant observation: 'It involves participating in the social world, in whatever role, and reflecting on the products of that participation.'[22]

THE PRINCIPLE OF REFLEXIVITY

Hammersley and Atkinson define the spirit of ethnography as 'what we have come to call the principle of reflexivity.'[23] Reflexivity encompasses both the researcher's reflection on how their presence in the field impacts on the material being collected and the essentially dialogical nature of fieldwork rooted in participant observation and in-depth interviewing. By stressing 'the reflexive character' of ethnological research, Hammersley and Atkinson assert one of its most fundamental aspects: 'There is no way in which we can escape the social world in order to study it . . . We cannot avoid relying on "common-sense" knowledge nor, often, can we avoid having an effect on the social phenomena we study.'[24] The anthropologist Kevin Dwyer has identified the central paradox of much ethnological work: that the observation of an event is influenced by the observer's presence. He refers to 'the inevitable tie between what is studied – the "Object" – and who studies it – the "Subject": neither can remain unaffected by changes in the other'.[25] Hammersley and Atkinson stress that embracing the notion of reflexivity is an essential part of ethnological research, requiring an 'explicit recognition of the fact that the social researcher, and the research act itself, are part and parcel of the social world under investigation'.[26]

They also point out that, rather than engaging in futile attempts to eliminate the effects of the researcher, we should set about understanding them. As they note:

Once we abandon the idea that the social character of research can be standardized out or avoided by becoming a 'fly on the wall or a full participant', the role of the researcher as active participant in the research process becomes clear. He or she is the research instrument *par excellence*.[27]

The fact that behaviour and attitudes are often not stable across contexts, and that the researcher may play an important part in shaping the context, becomes central to the analysis.[28] As Hammersley and Atkinson conclude, it is a distinctive feature of social research that the 'objects' it studies are in fact 'subjects' and themselves produce accounts of their world.[29] The fact that as oral historians or ethnologists our key sources are living, breathing humans has major implications not just in the evidence we collect but also the ways in which we use the material. The ethical dilemmas that often arise from this dynamic will be discussed later in this chapter.

NARRATIVES AS CULTURAL CONSTRUCTIONS

Life histories contain not simply the particular events of the life of a single individual but also the picture of a community, society and historical situation filtered through the texture of an individual life.[30] The sociologists Daniel Bertaux and Isabelle Bertaux-Wiame, when conducting fieldwork amongst bakers in France, realised as they carried out their interviews that a process was taking shape, with every new life story confirming what the preceding ones had shown. They define this as 'a process of saturation' and conclude that several life stories taken from the same set of sociostructural relations can support each other and make up, all together, a strong body of historical evidence.[31] Indeed, Samuel Schrager notes how, when 'congruences' in the accounts of different tellers convey commonalities in the events being described, this underlines how the single account 'belongs to an entire narrative environment'.[32] Furthermore, as well as providing rich empirical data, personal narratives are now recognised as 'important cultural constructions in themselves'.[33] Hammersley and Atkinson make the insightful point that 'the more effectively we can understand the account and its context – who produced it, for whom and why – the better able we are to anticipate the ways in which it may suffer from biases of one kind or another as a source of information. Indeed, separating the question of truth or falsity of people's beliefs, as currently assessed, from the analysis of those beliefs as social phenomena allows us to treat participant knowledge as both resource and topic.'[34] A question is often raised about the truthfulness of accounts narrated in interview settings, but as Hamersley and Atkinson make clear, the aim of in-depth interviewing is not to gather 'pure' data that are free from potential bias: 'Rather, the goal must be to discover the correct manner of interpreting whatever data we have.'[35] As the Personal Narratives Group asserts: 'Rather than labelling any story as true or untrue, interpreters need to look for the reasons *why* narrators tell their stories.'[36] Passerini agrees that 'the guiding principle could be that all autobiographical memory is true; it is up to the interpreter to discover in which sense, where, and for which purpose'.[37]

It is useful to be aware that, as Schrager points out, 'the oral historian is an intervener in a process that is already highly developed . . . most of what is told has been said before in a related form'.[38] He insists that this should not be discouraging:

> An account's previous tellings give it validity apart from the moment of the interview. If it belongs to the teller's repertoire of narrative, it is grounded in his or her life and in the social world in which that life is lived. What the oral historian does is to provide a new context for the telling of mainly pre-existent narrative.[39]

When linked together, personal narratives have a cumulative value because they provide a powerful, collective account of lived experience.

INTERVIEWING TECHNIQUES

The two main types of interviewing are the standardised and structured form of interview, most typically survey-based, and the semi-structured interview, which allows for more flexibility and fluidity. Hammersley and Atkinson state that ethnographers do not decide beforehand the questions they want to ask, nor do they restrict themselves to a single mode of questioning. They point out that on different occasions, or at different points in the same interview, the approach may be non-directive or directive, depending on the function that the questioning is intended to serve.[40] However, using a questionnaire has many advantages: it gives direction, focus, and a chronological shape. But it is important to remember Passerini's maxim that 'to respect memory also means letting it organise the story according to the subject's order of priorities'.[41] Essentially, within an interview setting, respondents should be encouraged to relate their story and place emphasis on those areas which are important to them. The sequence in which the informant brings subjects up may be particularly revealing. As Hammersley and Atkinson note, the researcher must be an 'active listener' who listens to what is being said in order to assess how it relates to the research focus and how it may reflect the circumstances of the interview.[42] Furthermore, during the course of the fieldwork a number of issues can be identified with more precision, and new categories of questions developed. Initial fieldwork suggests a number of potentially important aspects to be identified more thoroughly and some potentially useful analytical ideas.[43]

NEGOTIATING ACCESS

Most general ethnography textbooks agree on the fundamental decisions which the ethnographer has to make at the outset of their research: when and where to observe, who should be interviewed, how much time should be spent in the field and how the data should be collected.[44] Having chosen a question, write Lareau and Shultz, the researcher must set about, 'the delicate process of negotiating entry into the setting in which the research will be carried out. This complicated task often sets the tone for the remainder of the research project.'[45] Hammersley and Atkinson point out that the process of achieving access is not merely a practical matter and make the important point that, 'the discovery of obstacles to access, and perhaps of effective means of overcoming them, themselves provide insights into the social organisation of the setting'.[46]

CASE STUDY – PERSONAL FIELDWORK EXPERIENCE

In my own work with the Italian community[47] in south-east Scotland, which focused on Edinburgh, I found it difficult to find people willing to be interviewed as part of my research project. As I received a poor response to public appeals made in the media and other community settings, I had to increasingly rely on the 'snowballing' method of locating interviewees via word-of-mouth recommendation. This limited response was in itself indicative of important communal dynamics in relation to cultural memory of World War II. My research explored the experiences of second-generation Italians who were living in Scotland when Italy declared war on the United Kingdom in 1940. The British government implemented a policy of internment and deportation of Italian men within certain categories, as well as the enforced relocation of Italian women from coastal 'protected areas'. These policies, coinciding with the enlistment of Italian Scottish men into the British armed forces, often meant that only second-generation women, as British subjects, were permitted to stay in their homes. They therefore took on the responsibility for their family's livelihood and welfare – running shops and cafes, and attempting to keep businesses operating at a time of intense anti-Italian hostility.[48] The community historian Terri Colpi comments that the war had such a devastating and traumatic impact on the Italian community that older members are reluctant to dwell on or remember this period.[49] She writes that Italians who lived through the anguish of the war, 'do not like to talk about their experiences . . . The old Italians have over the years tried to put the war behind them and to forget about it.'[50] Another historian of the period, Brian Simpson, agrees that Anglo-Italians 'seem to have wished to forget the whole awful affair'.[51] During fieldwork, I also discovered a deep reluctance, a level of subtle resistance or noncompliance, to the idea of discussing the war and its impact on Italian families, particularly amongst the older members of the community.

Leydesdorff et al. point out that a life-story approach to interviewing provides an opportunity to explore the relationship between personal and collective experience, by focusing on remembering and forgetting as cultural processes.[52] They acknowledge that 'trauma is not an isolated event in a life story but may in itself often play a decisive role in a person's perception of life afterwards, interpretations of subsequent events, and consequently, memories of preceding experiences'.[53] A major factor in my research has been the veil of silence which appears to have been drawn over wartime events. Organisers of 'Una Storia Segreta' (A Secret History), a recent exhibition highlighting the experiences of Italian Americans during World War II, acknowledge that the story remained hidden for decades because silence had been 'adopted as *protective cover* by those affected'.[54] It would appear that, like the rural dwellers encountered by Smith,

Perks and Smith during their fieldwork in Ukraine, individuals were afraid of speaking openly about their experiences and were reluctant 'to disrupt a close-knit community which had come uneasily to terms with its past'.[55] I have found many survivors of the period, particularly women, either unwilling to be interviewed or apprehensive about making a public account of something which has remained largely private. Not only was there a negligible response to requests for information that I placed in the media, but many other people simply refused to talk. However, I could draw some significance from this, most notably the fact that that the war was a hugely traumatic period in the lives of my sample interview group, and that it had a hitherto under-acknowledged long-term psychological impact.

There are very few formal community associations for older Italians in Scotland, and whilst this made it more difficult to locate interviewees at the outset, it possibly had long-term research advantages. As Isabelle Bertaux-Wiame notes, migrant societies often give access to the most visible of migrants only, i.e. 'those who have succeeded in life'.[56] As the existing literature already reflected the experiences of the community elite, I was keen to approach less well-known people and to avoid the 'big names' in the community. Whilst still contacting high-profile organisations such as the Italian Consulate and the Italian Cultural Institute, I also decided that placing adverts in newspapers was a particularly useful way of reaching those members of the community who might not readily engage in organised 'community' activities. I initially advertised the project in two local free newspapers and a parish newsletter, specifically targeting the age group of Italian Scots who would have been adolescents or adults at the outbreak of World War II. The response to these adverts attracted only three interviewees. Letters sent to the wardens of sheltered accommodation and old people's homes resulted in only three interviews with women in this setting. A poster circulation which sought interviewees throughout a regional library service elicited just one response. In an attempt to reach those members of the Italian community who had served in the British armed forces during the war, I also contacted veteran organisations such as the Royal Pioneer Corps Association, the British Legion, the Women's Land Army and the Scots at War Trust but, unfortunately, there were no respondents through these channels. Overall, as a result of the difficulties encountered locating willing interviewees, I inevitably did not reach those who no longer perceived themselves as Italian.

When undertaking fieldwork with a long-established migrant group, it is often difficult to avoid an over-reliance on interviewing 'professional informants' within the community. Respected and high-profile individuals are frequently called upon to speak on behalf of the wider community, particularly by the popular media. They tend to be nominated by others within the community as the most effective spokespeople. However, this tendency for communal history to be defined and represented by a rather narrow pool of interviewees – often male – who are successful and articulate raises questions of authenticity, requiring the researcher to consider who speaks on behalf of a community and why. Spokespeople such as these can fail to reflect gender, generational or even political difference within a migrant community, and may have their own vested interests in promoting a particular strand of communal narrative. These respondents were more likely to provide polished or 'fixed' public performances[57] reminiscent of Alistair Thomson's Anzac interviewee who told the stories he wanted to tell, regardless of Thomson's questions.[58] Two former internees I interviewed recounted with pride the number of television and radio programmes in which they had participated, as well as the visits they had received from postgraduate students. It can often be frustrating, within a fieldwork setting, to revisit previously published stories and anecdotes and, in my case, I redoubled my efforts to try and contact women and other neglected groups I had identified in order to ensure I collected a broader range of historical perspectives and narratives.

Unfortunately, locating female respondents proved to be problematic. Adverts placed in popular national publications such as *The People's Friend* and the *Scots Magazine* resulted in only two responses. By far the most effective method of finding women was via personal recommendation, whereby one interviewee would put me in touch with another. Interestingly, this accords with the experience of research undertaken in America on mental health amongst different ethnic groups, in which researchers found a greater reluctance amongst Italian, as opposed to Jewish and Slavic women, to be interviewed, with 'the traditional Italian reserve and sense of family loyalty' quite frequently winning out.[59] These researchers acknowledged the importance of using personal intermediaries to gain access, noting that:

> Italian women did not respond to the concept of 'research or history', but did respond to a personal contact. As a result, most of the Jewish and Slavic women were located through organisations or institutions, while most of the Italian women were friends of a friend, or relatives of someone the co-ordinator knew.[60]

Amongst those of Italian descent in Scotland there is a widespread reluctance to discuss the role and function of Italian Fascist clubs, established outside Italy in the interwar period as a direct result of the Italian Fascist regime's decision to view Italian emigrants as 'Italians abroad' who were to remain loyal to Italy. As a result of this general reticence, I was unable to interview any surviving members of the women's committee of the Edinburgh *fascio* club, and within this context I also encountered the phenomenon of relatives or friends acting as 'gatekeepers' who turned down or refused interviews on behalf of someone else. The fieldworker needs to respond sensitively to these dynamics and respect the decision of individuals not to participate, including their desire not to be approached with an interview request. In my fieldwork, a couple of female contacts who had served in the British forces also turned down interviews, including one who cancelled an arranged interview at the last minute, expressing her apprehension about 'saying the wrong thing'.

In order to find more respondents, I decided to extend my fieldwork beyond Edinburgh to other parts of south-east Scotland, such as Fife and Stirling, and also travelled to other Scottish towns and cities if contacted by a respondent who fell into one of my target categories. An early intention to set up a reminiscence group as part of my fieldwork had to be abandoned because of a general reluctance to discuss the past in a public forum. As I developed contacts amongst the Italian presence in Edinburgh, I discovered that two Italian Scottish women had already attempted to set up reminiscence groups amongst older women, but both these initiatives had been discontinued. However, during the course of my fieldwork I was told about a language class provided by the Italian Consulate which created a forum where women attendees apparently felt able to discuss the war together. I occasionally sensed that my desire, as an academic researcher, to make an external public account of wartime Italian Scottish experience was at variance with an embedded belief that it was safer for certain things to remain unsaid.[61] Over a five-year period I was able to interview forty-four people of Italian origin: twenty-five women and nineteen men. The respondents were born between 1906 and 1940. Whilst this age range effectively encompasses two generations of Italian Scots, the bulk (twenty-three) of respondents were born in the decade 1920–29. The average age of the male interviewees in 1940 was eighteen, the women slightly younger at thirteen.

INTERSUBJECTIVITIES

As Hammersley and Atkinson note, 'the interview is not impermeable to outside influences'. They point out that the ways in which these roles are played will depend considerably upon the latent identities that the participants invoke and attribute to one another.[62] As Josselson and Lieblich state, narrative approaches to understanding bring the researcher more closely into the investigative process than do quantitative and statistical methods:

> Through narrative, we come in contact with our participants as people engaged in the process of interpreting themselves. We work then with what is said and what is not said, within the context in which the life is lived and the context of the interview in which words are spoken to represent that life. We must decode, recognise, recontextualise or abstract that life in the interest of reaching a new interpretation of the raw data of experience before us.[63]

It is now widely acknowledged by those working in the field that the interview is not simply an attempt to gather historical evidence or data but an interaction between two people. Many practitioners include an overview of their actual fieldwork in their final publications. In the field of oral history, for example, material collected via in-depth interviewing is predicated on an active human relationship between researchers and their sources which can transform the practice of history in several ways.[64] As the Personal Narratives Group write: 'Both interpreters and narrators approach the process of creating a personal narrative with their own agendas. These, too, affect the shape and focus of the text.'[65]

The anthropologist Juha Pentikäinen defends the intimate nature of some fieldwork encounters, acknowledging 'the right of the scholar to be human . . .

to study human phenomena in a human way'.[66] Summerfield has highlighted the importance of the 'interpersonal dynamics' at work in an oral history interview:

> the interviewer's style of dress, accent, tone of voice, demeanour, body language, spoken and unspoken attitudes give clues to the interviewee not just about the interviewer's research frame, but also what else might be preoccupying them, and whether narrator and interviewer hold shared values.[67]

She has written frankly of interviewing an elderly aunt about her wartime experiences and sensing an undercurrent or awkwardness when they came to address the aunt's decision to stop working to look after her children. This female relative was personally aware that Summerfield had children but had chosen to return to her academic career rather than look after them and, Summerfield argues, possibly she felt challenged within the interview setting about her own life choices.[68] In her intensive fieldwork involving hospital-based participant observation and numerous interviews with first-time mothers, Ann Oakley found herself unable to avoid questions relating to birth and motherhood directed towards her as a woman.[69] The anthropologist Peter Collins agrees that an interview is 'a highly complex social interaction' wherein multiple dialogues are conducted between jointly negotiated selves. He believes it is pointless to try and deny the roles one is expected to play: 'The interviewee will evaluate, judge and generally size us up, no matter what we do.'[70]

Although DeWalt and DeWalt can now boldly state that 'no one argues that the researcher enters the research setting as a neutral research tool',[71] previously there was a widely held belief that it was best for those undertaking social science research to remain neutral and objective in the interview encounter in an attempt to replicate the social survey method of gathering standardised 'scientific' data. Any material produced in this period, therefore, was often presented without any discussion of the interviewer's role or presence in the field. However, in a groundbreaking article published in 1981, Ann Oakley challenged the traditional paradigms of interviewing practices, suggesting that it was necessary to share aspects of yourself as an individual with your interviewees, and that this in turn has implications for the use and reproduction of the material. As a feminist writer, she identified, in particular, a gap between what she viewed as the masculine model of the neutral social scientist and the practical messy reality of interviewing people intimately in their homes, particularly for women interviewing women.[72] Oakley felt that topics traditionally left out of sociological research included the social or personal characteristics of those doing the interviews; interviewees' feelings about being interviewed; interviewers' feelings about the interviewees; the quality of interviewer–interviewee interaction; hospitality offered to interviewers by interviewees and the extension of interviewer–interviewee encounters into more broadly based social relationships.[73] Oakley asserts that, as a feminist interviewing women, she feels the interviewer has to be prepared 'to invest his or her own personal identity in the relationship'.[74]

Following on from Oakley, Janet Finch in 1984 examined her own role as a researcher and raised concerns over the 'extreme ease' with which a woman researcher can elicit material from other women, believing that the ability to get women to talk in an interview situation depends not so much on one's interviewing skills but on one's identity as a woman.[75] She argued that a female researcher interviewing other women was conducive to an easy flow of information, making women 'especially vulnerable as subjects of research'.[76] Both Finch and Oakley were highly influential, not just within feminist literature but in challenging researchers more generally to examine their relationship to the people they interview. In a more recent addition to the debate, however, psychologist Miriam Zukas cautions against the development of wider social relations beyond the interview context. In particular, she perceives interviews as encouraging the construction of 'quasi friendships', in which we encourage the telling of stories and analysis of the past with the intention of extracting as much from the interviewee as possible.[77] In an article adopting a critical and reflective overview of her research on women's friendships, Zukas concludes:

> I felt very ambiguous about the openness and trust of the women I interviewed, although this was the very atmosphere I was trying to create. Four of the women I spoke to were in tears at some point in the interview and were clearly confiding very intimate experiences.[78]

Zukas believes that empathy in interviewing leads to the expression of warmth and concern which are not only largely a 'front' on behalf of the researcher but, furthermore, are more 'appropriate to a friendship rather than a research relationship.'[79] In a more extreme interpretation, Stephen A Tyler identifies duplicity at the core of the interviewer–interviewee relationship, rooted in ethnographic notions of the observed 'other':

> Some ethnographers have tamed the savage, not with the pen, but with the tape recorder, reducing him to a 'straight man', as in the script of some obscure comic routine, for even as they think to have returned to 'oral performance' or 'dialogue', in order that the native have a place in the text, they exercise total control over her discourse and steal the only thing she has left – her voice.[80]

As Fortier notes, ethnographers are 'inevitably caught up in a web of demands that come from different directions at once: academia, personal interests (career oriented, the immediate requirements of the inquiry, family related, economic concerns), and the interests of the subjects (who may be sponsoring the study or hoping for public visibility, or looking for an advocate of their 'cause', and so on)'. In her opinion, 'deception and role playing are part and parcel of participant observation'.[81]

In my own research with members of the Italian community in Scotland who lived through World War II, I have, at times, been caught off-guard by the willingness of some women to relate distressful and intimate details of their past. This heightened my sense of responsibility and also my apprehension about the ways in which the material could be used. I found that, because they were placing their trust in me as an individual, many respondents were quite relaxed about signing the copyright clearance form at the end of the interview. I felt I had a responsibility to ensure that they were fully aware of the different ways in which the material could be used in the future. I always recommended to respondents that they should take the option of being informed if any material was to be published and offered the choice of anonymity to those who raised concerns and anxieties about potential 'repercussions' if their words were published. I also made a determined effort to keep post-interview lines of communication open, so that respondents felt they could contact me at any time. I always transcribed the interviews myself and made sure I returned transcripts to my interviewees. This served a practical purpose in that I was able to ask people to check spellings and factual accuracy, but it also served the more important function of providing a physical record of the interview, which could reassure those who may have been worrying about what they had divulged in the intimacy of the interview encounter. Sometimes problems would arise at this stage as other members of the family read the transcripts and raised their own concerns about publication.

The American oral historian Grele points out that oral history 'allows us to enter people's lives in the most extraordinarily intimate ways'.[82] My interviews often took place at night in people's homes and I suspect that the dynamic of an oral history interview, with a younger woman appearing and taking an interest in your life, can create an environment which encourages confidences. Summerfield argues that when entering 'an oral history contract', most people nowadays are familiar with the genre of the narrative interview via various modes of popular culture such as television documentaries and films.[83] However, I am not so convinced that all interviewees fully anticipate or appreciate the ways in which their contributions will ultimately appear, particularly with the omnipresence of the internet and the use of digital recording devices in collecting. Portelli argues that the passage from field testimony to published text, in 'transforming the informants' speech from one directed to a *determined* addressee, the field-worker, to one addressed to an *undetermined* and multiple one, the historian's audience' further undermines the 'myth of non-interference' by a neutral and detached interviewer.[84] Similarly, Summerfield acknowledges the potential tensions surrounding the 'mediation' between the interviewee's text arising from the interview and the author's published interpretation.[85]

INSIDER–OUTSIDER

An ethnographer's degree of access to another culture is often associated with his degree of incorporation into the group or sub-group under study.[86] Hammersley and Atkinson note that while ethnographers may adopt a variety of roles, the aim throughout is to maintain a position of marginality. Citing Lofland, they state that the researcher generates 'creative insight' out of this marginal position of simultaneous insider–outsider. Summarising the key texts on ethnography, Hammersley and Atkinson observe that the ethnographer must be intellectually poised between familiarity and strangeness, while socially he or she is poised between 'stranger' and 'friend'.[87] On one level of ethnographic research, the fieldworker exists 'in a liminal state, separated from his own culture yet not incorporated into the host culture'.[88] As Norris Brock Johnson emphasises, ethnographic fieldwork can require a transitional rite of passage that leads to a more incorporative stage of research.[89] Fortier, who carried out a social anthropological study of London Italian community groups, refers to her position as being on the 'threshold', denoting a position that is not quite outside or inside, and suggesting that 'there is always movement and change in the nature of the relationships between researcher and the research setting'.[90]

I am not of Italian origin myself, but there is no doubt that the fact that I am married to a third-generation Italian Scot, whose grandparents and father were all born in Italy, influenced the way that I was viewed by interviewees and had methodological implications for my fieldwork. The question of 'passing' as an Italian, first raised by Fortier in her study of institutional representations of London Italian identity, was also relevant.[91] Numerous interviewees commented on how, with my physical appearance of dark hair and dark eyes, I appeared to 'be Italian', and the use of my married surname served to reinforce this impression. A few respondents recognised my surname because my father-in-law had been a professional footballer in the immediate post-war years. One respondent had been interned with my husband's grandfather; another had served with my husband's uncle in the Pioneer Corps. Being viewed as a representative of my husband's family undoubtedly conferred upon me some degree of 'Italian affiliation'.[92] Furthermore, although I would be explicit at the outset of interviews that it was my husband who had the Italian connection, in interviews this distinction would often become blurred. This sense of shared experience helped me build up a relationship of trust with those I interviewed, which proved invaluable, as many were recalling traumatic and painful memories. Essentially, I benefited from being perceived as an 'insider' whilst remaining fundamentally an outsider.

ETHICAL QUESTIONS

Lareau and Schultz acknowledge the 'unevenness' of the fieldwork process, remarking that regardless of all the guidance and advice available on the ideal way to undertake ethnological research there is, inevitably, a 'gap between instruction and implementation'.[93] Student handbooks on ethnography now commonly underline the need for researchers to 'attend closely to the relationships they establish with those being studied and, in particular, with ethical concerns that might arise as a result of this interaction'.[94] Yet, as the historian Joan Sangster makes clear, the use of living people as a source for our research can involve complex and often 'uncomfortable' ethical issues.[95] Indeed, working with living people can both inspire and inhibit when you reach the point of academic interpretation. In the 1970s, feminist historians seized upon oral history as a particularly effective way of rescuing women from their marginalised position in the historical record by enabling researchers to speak directly to women, value their memories and recover their 'voices'. However, doubts and concerns have developed over time about the inherent power imbalance between researcher and researched – the fact that ultimately, whatever your gender or beliefs, the relationship between interviewer and informant is fundamentally imbalanced, with the power resting in the student or academic who collects oral narratives, testimonies and life histories and then goes away to use the texts, often to establish their own credentials in the academic world, and adopting language and terminology which is frequently alien to those whose words have been recorded.

This dilemma has been most effectively addressed in the collection *Women's Words* edited by Sherna Berger Gluck and Daphne Patai. The two editors raise their concerns that any control exercised by the narrators during the interview, when they are able to negotiate the terrain, usually ends once the session is completed. They identified a 'real separation' between the original narrator and the feminist scholar, with distinct imbalances in power and privilege highlighting how, contrary to the feminist ideal of empowerment, the individual narrators were rarely true partners in the process. In particular, there could be a tension arising from the scholar's desire to use the material in an academic way to further his or her career, which may alienate the original narrator. They were particularly concerned by the fact that 'a story or statement, in its oral form, is "by" the speaker but very often reaches the public in the form of a "text" written by the scholar, whether as a life history or as excerpts used by the scholar to illustrate a line of argument'.[96] As the anthropologist Peter Collins admits, 'even the most well-intentioned academic gains or at least hopes to gain prestige and perhaps even promotion through publishing their research findings'.[97]

One of the most crucial issues in oral history and ethnological scholarship – the question of who controls the text[98] – has been addressed by the folklorist Katherine Borland in an absorbing case study of her own fieldwork. Discussing the angry response of her grandmother to a text analysing her experiences and (mis)representing her as a feminist, Borland identifies the key tension:

> Presumably, the patterns upon which we base our interpretations can be shown to inhere in the 'original' narrative, but our aims in pointing out certain features, or in making connections between the narrative and larger cultural formations, may at times differ from the original narrator's intentions. This is where issues of our responsibility to our living sources become most acute.[99]

Amanda Coffey notes that whilst it is increasingly fashionable for individual researchers to 'personalise' accounts of their fieldwork, 'research texts remain relatively silent on the ways in which fieldwork affects us, and we affect the field'.[100] In particular, Coffey believes that the emotional aspects of fieldwork are often underplayed. She urges recognition of 'the emotional and identity work that frame the fieldwork experience' – the fact that personal and emotional factors permeate the whole research process.[101] The pressure on academics to publish can often put them into conflict with their informants, particularly in relation to disclosure and the desire not to cause offence. An excellent collection of essays produced by ethnographers and social anthropologists, *When They Read What*

We Write (1993), directly addresses the anxieties many researchers experience relating to the politics of audience reception, 'whether real or imagined'.[102] In confronting the dilemmas arising from publishing material based on personal testimonies, one academic who studied the Dublin intelligentsia admits that, inevitably, some level of 'self-censorship' begins to occur in the writing process when researchers start to anticipate informants' reactions.[103] Another academic, R P Horwitz, admits that at times he is 'torn between my respect, if not affection, for individual informants and my sense of professional duty as a critic of the cultures to which they/we belong'. On the one hand, he aims to please, 'but on the other to challenge – print what "helps" even if it hurts'.[104] Coffey's belief that 'fieldwork is personal, emotional and identity *work*' is relevant here, as the authors are attempting to negotiate the tensions between their academic selves and their sense of personal obligation to those whom they have researched. As she concludes:

> In writing, remembering and representing our fieldwork experiences we are involved in processes of self presentation and identity construction. In considering and exploring the intimate relations between the field, significant others and the private self we are able to understand the processes of fieldwork as practical, intellectual and emotional accomplishments.[105]

There is also the issue that, on occasion, the researcher may be stirring traumatic and painful memories which lead to the '*dis*composure' of both the narrator and their life-story narrative.[106] This could be as a direct result of the remit of the research project itself or it may occur spontaneously and catch the researcher off-guard. The historian Kathryn Anderson admits that often in her interviews with rural farming women her interview strategies 'were bound to some extent by the conventions of social discourse':

> My fear of forcing or manipulating individuals into discussing topics they did not want to talk about sometimes prevented me from giving women the space and the permission to explore some of the deeper, more conflicted parts of their stories. I feared, for good reasons, that I lacked the training to respond appropriately to some of the issues that might be raised or uncovered.[107]

Ultimately, the oral historian has to tread carefully when probing areas of memory surrounding personal trauma because, as Thomson succinctly puts it: 'Unlike the therapist, oral historians may not be around to put together the pieces of memories that have been deconstructed and are no longer safe.'[108]

The assumption underlying much of the literature on oral history methodology is still the ideal of empowering cultural minorities, yet there is less discussion about what happens when one ultimately offers an interpretation that some will find challenging, uncomfortable and even unwelcome. Thomson has confronted the tensions arising when a more critical analysis of a historical topic 'collides with powerful emotional investments in the past'.[109] As he eloquently summarises:

> On the one hand, oral historians may feel that they have no right to use people's memories to make histories which are challenging or critical towards their narrators, that this involves a breach of trust and confidence. On the other hand, oral historians may feel that they have another duty to society and history, a responsibility to challenge historical myths which empower some people at the expense of others. Perhaps all researchers live with this dilemma, but for oral historians it is particularly acute because we have personal relationships with our sources.[110]

Fundamentally, as Thomson recognises, 'narrators and researchers often have contradictory aims'.[111] Furthermore, Hanna Diamond reminds oral historians wrestling with the ethical dilemmas of power imbalances that they should not 'underestimate the power of the informant who creates the life story as s/he organises and tells it', and points out that the informant always has the option of placing restrictions on their narrative.[112] Joanna Herbert, reflecting on her recent research with South Asian communities living in Leicester, comments: 'My experiences showed that the respondents were not simply powerless but were able to communicate their message and the perception that the researcher has the power and the respondent does not simply ignores how power is relational.'[113]

The final interpretation and analysis of interview texts rests with the researcher and not with those who have shared their life stories. Sangster also argues that we need to be realistic about the fact that there will always be an inherent imbalance of power within the researcher–subject relationship, as we gain access to people's memories not as friends but as professional researchers:

> We can honour feminist ethical obligations to make our material accessible to the women interviewed, never to reveal confidences spoken out of the interview, never to purposely distort or ridicule their lives, but in the last resort, it is our privilege that allows us to interpret.[114]

Indeed, as the anthropologist Anthony Cohen concluded after years of fieldwork with the islanders of Whalsay, researchers can only offer their 'version' of the past, an interpretation, which is neither more nor less 'privileged' than those already current.[115]

PHOTOGRAPHY AND VIDEO RECORDING

Video, film and photographs can also be useful research documents within ethnological fieldwork, either acting as a trigger for eliciting information or providing an original document. P Loizos demonstrates how photographic images can be utilised in a number of potential research applications. Fundamentally, of course, photographs can provide documentation of the specificity of historical change – 'every still photograph, from the moment it has been taken, is a historical document'.[116] However, as Loizos points out, various kinds of oral history interviews might be facilitated if the researcher goes to an interview armed in advance with some relevant photographs. The photograph could act as 'a trigger to elicit memories of people an interviewee might otherwise not spontaneously recall, or access important "passive" memories rather than the more "active" ones'.[117] He writes that 'images are resonant with submerged memories, and can help focus interviewees, free up their memories, and create a piece of shared "business" in which the researcher and the interviewee can talk together, perhaps in a more relaxed manner than without such a stimulus'.[118] A further use of historical photographs might involve reading them for implicit cultural or historical information.[119]

Similarly, with video and film recording in research, it is also important to distinguish between visual data that the researcher analyses unaided and visual data serving to focus, or elicit, interviewees' comments.[120] As Loizos notes, video has an obvious data-recording function whenever some set of human actions is complex and difficult for a single observer to describe comprehensively while it unfolds (religious ritual, life stage ceremonials such as weddings) but he also cautions that, whereas with purely written information the promise to conceal personal names may guarantee ethical protection against identification, the situation is more difficult with images.[121]

CONCLUSION

Ethnographic fieldwork is a fundamentally worthwhile and rewarding endeavour, enabling the researcher to learn more about the world and the individuals within it, and contributing significantly to our historical understanding. Yet, as this chapter has indicated, ethnography is also a serious undertaking that needs to take into account the full ethical and legal implications of using living human beings as key sources. There is a need to proceed sensitively, act respectfully towards those who agree to participate in fieldwork, and to think critically and reflexively about the nature of the oral testimonies being collected and recorded.

NOTES

1 Ugolini, 2006.
2 Richards, 2002, 93–4.
3 Roper, 1996, 346.
4 Thompson, 1975; Chamberlain, 1975.
5 Thompson, 1988, 2.
6 Thomson, 1995, 227.
7 Summerfield, 1998, 17.
8 Thomson, Frisch and Hamilton, 1994, 33. See Grele, 1991; Passerini, 1979; Portelli, 1981.
9 Passerini, 1987, 4.
10 Chamberlain, 2000, 157.
11 Roper, 1996, 347.
12 Frisch, 1990, 188.

13 Grele, 1991, 213.
14 Portelli, 1981, 99.
15 Hammersley and Atkinson, 1983, ix.
16 Lareau and Schultz, 1996, 2.
17 Lareau and Shultz, 1996, 3.
18 Hammersley and Atkinson, 1983, 2.
19 Lareau and Shultz, 1986, 2.
20 DeWalt and DeWalt, 2002, 2.
21 DeWalt and DeWalt, 2002, 2.
22 Hammersley and Atkinson, 1983, 16.
23 Hammersley and Atkinson, 1983, ix.
24 Hammersley and Atkinson, 1983, 15.
25 Dwyer, 1979, 205.
26 Hammersley and Atkinson, 1983, 234.
27 Hammersley and Atkinson, 1983, 18.
28 Hammersley and Atkinson, 1983, 17–18.
29 Hammersley and Atkinson, 1983, 105.
30 Niedermüller, 1988, 470.
31 Bertaux and Bertaux-Wiame, 1981, 187.
32 Schrager, 1998, 288–9.
33 Chamberlain, 1997, 10.
34 Hammersley and Atkinson, 1983, 107.
35 Hammersley and Atkinson, 1983, 112.
36 Personal Narratives Group, 1989, 203. This is a multidisciplinary research
    group, affiliated with the Centre for Advanced Studies at the University of
    Minnesota, which gathered together essays on a wide range of women's personal
    narratives.
37 Passerini, 1989, 197.
38 Schrager, 1998, 284.
39 Schrager, 1998, 285.
40 Hammersley and Atkinson, 1983, 113.
41 Passerini, 1987, 8.
42 Hammersley and Atkinson, 1983, 113.
43 Hammersley and Atkinson, 1983, 39.
44 Hammersley and Atkinson, 1983, 37–45; Lareau and Shultz, 1986, 5.
45 Lareau and Shultz, 1986, 4.
46 Hammersley and Atkinson, 1983, 54.
47 A full account of this research is given in Ugolini, 2011, 5–13.
48 Ugolini, 2006.
49 Colpi, 1991, 100.
50 Colpi, 1991, 99.
51 Simpson, 1992, 194.
52 Leydesdorff et al., 1999, 13.
53 Leydesdorff et al., 1999, 15.
54 Distasi, 2003, n.p.
55 Smith, Perks and Smith, 1998, 5.
56 Bertaux-Wiame, 1982, 188.
57 Thomson, 1995, 210.
58 Thomson, 1995, 14.
59 Colecchia, 1978, 253.

60 Krause, 1978, 263.
61 Ugolini, 2004.
62 Hammersley and Atkinson, 1983, 119.
63 Josselson and Lieblich, 1995, ix.
64 Perks and Thomson, 1998, ix.
65 Personal Narratives Group, 1989, 202.
66 Pentikäinen, Preface.
67 Summerfield, 2000, 102.
68 Summerfield, 2000, 99.
69 Oakley, 1981, 43.
70 Collins, 1998, para. 3.33.
71 DeWalt and DeWalt, 2002, 83.
72 Oakley, 1981, 31.
73 Oakley, 1981, 31.
74 Oakley, 1981, 41.
75 Finch, 1984, 78.
76 Finch, 1984, 81
77 Zukas, 1993, 78–9.
78 Zukas, 1993, 78.
79 Zukas, 1993, 79.
80 Tyler, 1986, 128.
81 Fortier, 2000, 9.
82 Grele, 1991, Preface.
83 Summerfield, 2000, 93.
84 Portelli, 1997, 12.
85 Summerfield, 1998, 26.
86 Johnson, 2007, 76.
87 Hammersley and Atkinson, 1983, 100.
88 Johnson, 2007, 76.
89 Johnson, 2007, 76.
90 Fortier, 2000, 9.
91 Fortier, 2000, 6–7.
92 Fortier, 1996, 310.
93 Lareau and Schultz, 1986, 2.
94 Lareau and Shultz, 1986, 5.
95 Sangster, 1998, 92.
96 Berger Gluck and Patai, 1991, 2.
97 Collins, 1998, 3.3.
98 Borland, 1991, 70.
99 Borland, 1991, 64.
100 Coffey, 1999, 1.
101 Coffey, 1999, 2, 3.
102 Brettell, 1993, 3.
103 Sheehan, 1993, 77.
104 Horwitz, 1993, 137.
105 Coffey, 1999, 1.
106 Summerfield, 2000, 93.
107 Anderson, 1991, 13.
108 Thomson, Frisch and Hamilton, 1994, 34.
109 Thomson, 1995, 5.

110 Thomson, Frisch and Hamilton, 1994, 35.
111 Thomson, Frisch and Hamilton, 1994, 34.
112 Diamond, 1997, 65.
113 Herbert, 2007, 265.
114 Sangster, 1998, 93.
115 Cohen, 1987, 4.
116 Loizos, 2001, 293.
117 Loizos, 2001, 294.
118 Loizos, 2001, 295.
119 Loizos, 2001, 296.
120 Loizos, 2001, 299.
121 Loizos, 2001, 301.

BIBLIOGRAPHY AND FURTHER READING

Anderson, K and Jack, D C. Learning to listen: Interview techniques and analyses. In Berger
    Gluck and Patai, 1991, 11–26.
Berger Gluck, S and Patai, D, eds. *Women's Words: The Feminist Practice of Oral History*,
    London, 1991.
Bertaux, D and Bertaux-Wiame, I. Life stories in the bakers' trade. In Bertaux, D, ed.,
    Biography and Society. The Life History Approach in the Social Sciences, London, 1981, 169–89.
Bertaux-Wiame, I. The life history approach to the study of internal migration: How women
    and men came to Paris between the wars. In Thompson, P, ed., *Our Common History*,
    London, 1982, 186–200.
Borland, K. "That's Not What I Said": Interpretive conflict in oral narrative research. In
    Berger Gluck and Patai, 1991, 63–76.
Brettell, C B, ed. *When They Read What We Write. The Politics of Ethnography*, Westport, 1993.
Chamberlain, M. *Fenwomen. A Portrait of Women in an English Village*, London, 1975.
Chamberlain, M. *Narratives of Exile and Return*, London, 1997.
Chamberlain M. The global self. Narratives of Caribbean migrant women. In Cosslett, T,
    Lury, C and Summerfield, P, eds, *Feminism and Autobiography. Texts, Theories, Methods*,
    London, 2000, 154–66.
Coffey, A. *The Ethnographic Self. Fieldwork and the Representation of Identity*, London, 1999.
Cohen, A. *Whalsay. Symbol, Segment and Boundary in a Shetland Island Community*, Manchester,
    1987.
Colecchia, F. Women, ethnicity, and mental health: The Italian woman, impressions and
    observations. In Boyd, C B, Harney, R F and Tomasi, L F, eds, *The Italian Immigrant Woman
    in North America. Proceedings of the Tenth Annual Conference of the American Italian Historical
    Association*, Toronto, 1978, 252–8.
Collins, P. Negotiating selves: Reflections on "unstructured" interviewing, *Sociological
    Research Online*, 3:3 (1998), <http://www.socresonline.org.uk/3/2/2.html> [accessed
    November 2012].
Colpi, T. *The Italian Factor*, Edinburgh, 1991.
DeWalt, K M and DeWalt, B R. *Participant Observation. A Guide for Fieldworkers*, Lanham,
    2002.
Diamond, H. Oral history: An assessment. In Perry, S and Cross, M, eds, *Voices of France.
    Social, Political and Cultural Identity*, London, 1997, 59–72.
Distasi, L, ed. *Una Storia Segreta: The Secret History of Italian American Evacuation and Intern-
    ment during World War II*, online edition, 2003, Preface <http://www.segreta.org/>
    [accessed November 2012].

Dwyer, K. The Dialogic of Ethnology, *Dialectical Anthropology*, 4:3 (1979), 205–24.

Finch, J. "It's great to have someone to talk to": The ethics and politics of interviewing women. In Bell, C and Roberts, H, eds, *Social Researching. Politics, Problems, Practice*, London, 1984, 70–87.

Fortier, A M. Troubles in the field: The use of personal experiences as sources of knowledge, *Critique of Anthropology*, 16:3 (1996), 303–23.

Fortier, A M. *Migrant Belongings. Memory, Space, Identity*, Oxford, 2000.

Frisch, M. *A Shared Authority. Essays on the Craft and Meaning of Oral and Public History*, Albany, NY, 1990.

Grele, R J. Listen to their voices: Two case studies in the interpretation of oral history interviews. In Grele, R J, *Envelopes of Sound. The Art of Oral History*, 2nd edn, New York, 1991, 212–41.

Hammersley, M and Atkinson, P. *Ethnography. Principles in Practice*, London, 1983.

Herbert, J. Negotiating boundaries and the cross-cultural oral history interview. In Rodger, R and Herbert, J, eds, *Testimonies of the City: Identity, Community and Change in a Contemporary Urban World*, Aldershot, 2007, 251–68.

Horwitz, R P. Just stories of ethnographic authority. In Brettell, 1993, 131–44.

Jaffe, A. Involvement, detachment, and representation on Corsica. In Brettell, 1993, 51–66.

Johnson, N B. Sex, Color, and Rites of Passage in Ethnographic Research. In Robben, A C G M and Sluka, J A, eds, *Ethnographic Fieldwork. An Anthropological Reader*, Oxford, 2007, 76–91.

Josselson, R and Lieblich A, eds. *Interpreting Experience. The Narrative Study of Lives*, Vol. 3, London, 1995.

Krause, C A. Oral history in Pittsburgh – Women, ethnicity, and mental health: Rationale, procedure and methodology. In Boyd, C B, Harney, R F and Tomasi, L F, eds, *The Italian Immigrant Woman in North America*, Toronto, 1978, 260–8.

Lareau, A and Schultz, J, eds. *Journeys Through Ethnography. Realistic Accounts of Fieldwork*, Colorado, 1996.

Leydesdorff, S, Dawson, G, Burchardt, N and Ashplant, T G. Introduction: Trauma and life stories. In Lacy Rogers, K, Leydesdorff, S and Dawson, G, eds, *Trauma and Life Stories*, London, 1999, 1–26.

Loizos, P. Video, film and photographs as research documents. In Bryman, A, ed., *Ethnography*, volume 3, London, 2001, 290–303.

Niedermüller, P. From the stories of life to the life history: Historic context, social processes and the biographical method. In Hofer, T and Niedermuller, P, eds, *Life History as Cultural Construction/Performance*, Budapest, 1988, 451–73.

Oakley, A. Interviewing women: A contradiction in terms. In Roberts H, ed., *Doing Feminist Research*, London, 1981, 30–61.

Passerini, L. Work ideology and consensus under Italian fascism, *History Workshop Journal*, 8 (1979), 82–108.

Passerini, L. *Fascism in Popular Memory*, Cambridge, 1987.

Passerini, L. Women's personal narratives: Myths, experiences and emotions. In The Personal Narratives Group, 1989, 189–97.

Pentikäinen, J. Oral repertoire and world view. An anthropological study of Marina Takalo's life history, *Folklore Fellows Communications*, 93:219 (1978).

Perks, R and Thomson, A, eds. *The Oral History Reader*, London, 1998.

Personal Narratives Group, eds. *Interpreting Women's Lives. Feminist Theory and Personal Narratives*, Indianapolis, IN, 1989.

Portelli, A. The Peculiarities of Oral History, *History Workshop Journal*, 12 (1981), 96–107.

Portelli, A. *The Battle of Valle Giulia: Oral History and the Art of Dialogue*, Madison, WI, 1997.

Richards, M. From war culture to civil society: Francoism, social change and memories of the

Spanish Civil War, *History & Memory*, 14:1/2 (2002), 93–120.

Roper, M. Oral history. In Brivati, B, Buxton, J and Seldon, A, eds, *The Contemporary History Handbook*, Manchester, 1996, 345–52.

Sangster, J. Telling our stories. Feminist debates and the use of oral history. In Perks and Thomson, 1998, 87–100.

Schrager , S. What is social in oral history? In Perks and Thomson, 1998, 284–99.

Sheehan, E A. The student of culture and the ethnography of Irish intellectuals. In Brettell, 1993, 75–90.

Simpson, A W B. *In the Highest Degree Odious. Detention without Trial in Wartime Britain*, Oxford, 1992.

Smith, T, Perks, R and Smith, G. *Ukraine's Forbidden History*, Stockport, 1998.

Summerfield, P. *Reconstructing Women's Wartime Lives*, Manchester, 1998.

Summerfield, P. Dis/composing the subject. Intersubjectivities in oral history. In Cosslett, T, Lury, C and Summerfield, P, eds, *Feminism and Autobiography. Texts, Theories, Methods*, London, 2000, 91–106.

Thompson, P. *The Edwardians. The Remaking of British Society*, London, 1975.

Thompson, P. *The Voice of the Past*, Oxford, 1988.

Thomson, A, Frisch, M and Hamilton, P. The memory and history debates: Some international perspectives, *Oral History*, 22:2 (1994), 33–43.

Thomson, A. *Anzac Memories: Living With the Legend*, Oxford, 1995.

Tyler, S A. Post-modern ethnography: From document of the occult to occult document. In Clifford, J and Marcus, G E, eds, *Writing Culture. The Poetics and Politics of Ethnography*, Berkeley, 1986, 122–40.

Ugolini, W. The internal enemy 'other': Recovering the World War Two narratives of Italian Scottish women, *Journal of Scottish Historical Studies*, 24:2 (2004), 137–58.

Ugolini, W. 'Communal myths and silenced memories: The unremembered experience of Italians in Scotland during World War Two', PhD thesis, University of Edinburgh, 2006.

Ugolini, W. *Experiencing War as the 'Enemy Other': Italian Scottish Experience in World War II*, Manchester, 2011.

Zukas M. Friendship as oral history: A feminist psychologist's view, *Oral History*, 21:2 (1993), 73–9.

•

PART TWO

Preserving, Presenting and Rediscovering – Museums, Archives, Societies and Heritage

4 Material Culture

HUGH CHEAPE

TERMINOLOGY

The study of 'material culture' is central to many areas in both the humanities and the sciences and is recognised as an autonomous field of intellectual endeavour. Material culture studies as a genre have evolved among archaeologists, anthropologists, historians, social scientists, geographers, natural scientists and others, inferring perhaps that they are not susceptible to ready or conclusive definition within the unity of a single discipline or within an institutional identity. The history, institutional configurations and national boundaries of academic disciplines with their attendant specialisms tend to a situation where shared interest may not always lead to cross-fertilisation of theoretical or methodological approaches, despite the obvious commonalities that exist in the study of an area fundamental to the construction of our physical and social worlds. Other hindrances to the flow, sharing and adoption of ideas may be inferred from academic labels and terminology of disciplines within the human sciences such as anthropology, its variety of usages and differences in interpretation between, for example, continental Europe and North America. A prime example of this dissonance arises in the intelligibility and varied usages of 'ethnology' between subject areas such as cultural anthropology and folk life studies.

MUSEUM COLLECTION

An apparent pluralism, even heterodoxy, indicates perhaps that material culture studies occupy an interdisciplinary field, and certainly a multidisciplinary field, in that they generally draw on the perspectives of both cognate and different disciplines and variously adopt a diversity of approaches. A substantial literature emerging since the 1980s bears witness to this heterogeneity.[1] Such a field, consisting of the study of things and their relationships to people and environmental contexts, is bound to be wide or even without readily definable limits. The concept of the 'collection' offers practical limits and an intellectual framework for material culture. Material culture studies organically linked to the museum 'collection' form the perspective of this exploration; their purpose is to describe and evaluate the material past with methodologies for placing the material record in context and for developing its interpretation.[2] In modern museums, that context tends to lay emphasis on people and their relationship to the objects they have created and used. Methodologies for interpreting the concrete elements of everyday life and the uses to which they are put will tend to draw on contemporary and prevailing paradigms in history and the social sciences and lift the study of material culture above simple description and 'antiquarianism', interpret it for modern understanding and give it a scholarly and disciplinary relevance and rigour.

THINGS AND WORDS

Material culture, however, is not restricted to objects found in museums or preserved mutely from the remote past. It embraces potentially all conceivable objects and all historical periods or prehistory, against a backdrop of landscape and environment. The study of material culture therefore requires a methodological balance to take account of the diversity of its evidence between objects, text and other media, and sources such as language itself. It would reject a simplistic distinction claiming that material culture treats only with 'things' whereas conventional history looks at words and texts. It requires an understanding of the objects themselves for interpretations of how and why they have been made and used, to the extent that the evidence from objects should augment our view and understanding of context and of people, and the absence of such evidence can be said to diminish such perspectives. It might be claimed that without things, our understanding of people is impoverished.

It is now widely accepted that every kind of evidence, both durable and ephemeral, is open for assessment, depending on the topics being addressed and the research questions being asked; it might be synchronic historical or archaeological evidence throwing light on human activity and relationships in a specific place or time, interpreting, for example, a detritus of post-medieval pottery and metalwork; or it might take an artefact such as the quern or hand-mill as an abundant (and durable) diachronic element of the everyday record in Scotland from the Neolithic to the end of the second millennium.[3] It might be topographical evidence in the form of extensive ridge and furrow or 'lazybeds' on the margins of the modern landscape, exploring marks of land-use through centuries for human impact or the relationship between people and their environment, the interpretation of which should employ an understanding of plough and spade and techniques of use.[4] It might be food and diet with changing dietary patterns over time owing to economic or geographical factors and coastal or inland settlement patterns.[5] It might be dress and jewellery, growing out of functional items such as dress fasteners to become expressions of wealth and status or of faith and love.[6] It might be architectural evidence in terms of buildings or the 'archaeology of buildings', using the survival and greater visibility of buildings to construct material analogies for collateral evidence in other subjects in human experience and endeavour. Scholars have been unpicking evidence for startling architectural genres in Scotland such as Renaissance 'palaces' of the sixteenth century, with pointers to shifts in architecture, dress, food and language as a result of political and dynastic links with France.[7] These diagnostic trends became absorbed into what are seen as national styles and effectively have become less evident or even invisible. The treatment of physical space can be analysed for issues of 'intangible cultural heritage', for example, to throw more light on language, story, belief and ritual, music or song. Church buildings, for instance, offer insights into divine service and liturgical practices in the ways that the interior spaces were created and arranged. Material culture studies here offer opportunities for seamless academic enterprise, and rewards are in proportion.

Communicating information about things will test language, in interpreting how an object was made and used and what it was called. The naming of things sits among the diversity of evidence for a material world and the recording of names normally belongs in the critical framework surrounding the museum collection. Experience shows that in Scotland the naming of things will often depart from Standard English and will employ Scots or Gaelic or dialects of these.[8] They have benefited in recent years from a growing awareness of the importance of 'minority languages' within the European Union as demonstrated by its Bureau for Lesser Spoken Languages. Different values have come to be put on them and their integrity is now recognised. Both Scots and Gaelic have splendid and resounding oral and literary traditions, but for generations they were variously suppressed languages and used as tools for social exclusion. Now, increasingly, they are being seen as rich languages, markers of national identity and subjects for study at all levels at home and abroad. Scots must be the most distinctive of anglophone varieties of speech. It can still be claimed to be a distinct 'national language', having been a separate language in both a social and political sense and thriving, for example, in the fifteenth and sixteenth centuries. It has an important linguistic history, with a large vocabulary and borrowings from Gaelic, Norse, Dutch, Flemish, Norman-French, French and English. The significance and integrity of Scottish Gaelic as a language has now been reasserted. It has its range of dialects and registers, complex phonetics and a substantial literary as well as oral tradition. The Linguistic Survey of Scotland began collecting Scottish Gaelic dialect material in the late 1940s and, at the time, indigenous Gaelic speakers lived in almost all areas forming what we perceive as the Highlands and Islands, from Sutherland and parts of Caithness in the north to Braemar, Angus and East Perthshire in the east, and to Arran and Kintyre in the south. The geographical limits of Gaelic-speaking Scotland, the *Gàidhealtachd*, had remained stable for centuries.

The study of material culture is germane to geology and natural history and related disciplines, as well as to archaeology and history, in other words, in both the sciences and humanities. In its turn, the concept of 'material culture' has been conventionally and widely used to describe the area of work of the archaeologist, in all physical aspects of human life and society from portable artefacts such as dress to the equipment of production, structures and spatial layouts. In this prehistoric context of the exclusivity of objects, the concept and significance of material culture can be better appreciated. Material culture is central to archaeology, where objects have an 'authority' generally unalloyed by language and text. The success of archaeology in recent decades, its confidence in why archaeology matters and its transformation into a global discipline, may sometimes work against sustaining a domain or discourse and against pragmatic alliances with other disciplines such as history, literature and language. Modern pedagogy deserves such broader alliances. A slight example from the material culture record throws up significant detail from a language context: Duncan Campbell's description of shielings and animal husbandry in Upland Perthshire in the 1860s identified the circular folds for cattle, sheep and goats – what he termed *crodhan* – as circular and without necessarily any associated hut structures. His cautionary tale of recognition of these features seems aimed at archaeologists:

> [The *Crò*] was generally surrounded by a strong wall, but in bushy districts it was often fenced in by rough wicker-work, which when it disappeared, only left the circular floor to mark the place . . . The folds were in pairs, or sometimes in double pairs, because milking and cheese-making purposes required that calves, lambs and kids should be kept separate from their mothers. What are called 'hut circles' seem to me to be in many, but not perhaps in all cases, the floors of wicker-work folds, which were too near permanent abodes to be associated with regular shieling huts.[9]

Cross-disciplinary reach characterises examples such as this and may be more easily appreciated as a natural domain of museum work, that is, in simple terms, the collecting, classifying, study and interpretation of artefacts. Museums on the whole state their purpose in terms of their collections, how these are nurtured and displayed, and of the pursuit and dissemination of knowledge by communication with as wide audiences as possible, as well as with audiences within specialisms. While some collections are more static, preserving typically for public edification the fruits of a philanthropist's hobby or obsession, most grow and are sustained by research and scholarship. This essential dynamic may not be immediately evident on the public side of the display of objects in glass cases and the controlled environment, but it is keenly felt and passionately pursued by museum 'professionals' such as curators and conservators. The care and treatment of museum objects is subsumed within 'conservation', a profession that emerged to prominence in the second half of the twentieth century. Processes of rebuilding objects for museum display or reinstating lost parts, formerly standard museum practice, have been replaced by sophisticated treatments to arrest decay and to stabilise, and the control of the environment to minimise decay. The museum is a public showcase committed to the public service but should for long-term survival also be a scholarly institution employing the world's leading scholars in their fields. For most professionals, the core of their work in the public domain is the painstaking assembling and systematic interpretation of permanent museum collections, that is, of material culture.

NATIONAL COLLECTIONS

Material culture is the driver of processes of research and education in museums, since material culture study has grown up and matured with the establishment of great museum collections, themselves based on the esoteric but generally intellectually driven collecting, classifying and interpretation of artefacts. The

Wallace Collection in London and the Burrell Collection in Glasgow are examples of esoteric and eclectic interests and driven collecting habits of individuals converted ultimately to public benefit. The establishment of the large public museums in the nineteenth century then created a concept and an ideology with a following both popular and academic. Public interest in museums grew and public expenditure was lavished on them in the second half of the nineteenth century. Architecture on a grand scale, such as in London's museum cluster in South Kensington, as well as the collections within these 'national museums' helped to put such institutions firmly in the public eye and have laid down potent markers for the representation of 'national culture' or 'national cultures'.[10] Objects enshrined in grand buildings serve the ambition of museum curators to educate and fire the imagination. Object 'literacy' on the other hand poses questions about what or how much an audience can read critically into an object as presented formally in a museum or elsewhere. The opening of the Museum of Scotland, now the National Museum of Scotland, on Saint Andrew's Day 1998 is a good example of the longer-term meaning and function of 'national collections' and the values perceived to be enshrined in national museums. These are in turn part of a more recent dialectic seeking to explore and explain cultural representation and markers of identity as responses to modern realities of globalisation and multiculturalism.

GREAT EXHIBITIONS

Museums have flourished in the last fifty years in Britain and Ireland, in common with museums in Europe and Scandinavia, and have been at the core of a renaissance in the study of Scotland's past. A generation of historians and archaeologists has given this an academic rigour for modern scholarly discourses, and the combination in museums of the intellectual dimension with the institutional dimension makes for an extraordinarily effective process both of dissemination and of public consumption. The opening of the National Museum of Scotland in 1998 and the Museum of Scottish Country Life, Wester Kittochside, in 2001 symbolises this quickening, but the role of museums in popular education and entertainment as opposed to collecting for its own sake has a longer history and evolves with the temporary exhibition. This genre begins with the Great Exhibition in London in 1851 with its 6 million visitors from 1 May until 15 October of that year. This was a spectacular shop window for a country which had built itself as a trading nation on the back of the 'Industrial Revolution'. It was a demonstration of what was perceived by its perpetrators as the highest pitch of human social and technical evolution, and a licence for imperial dominance. One of the organisers, Sir Henry Cole (1808–1882), summed up the event with a note of confidence born of the time: 'The history of the world, I venture to say, records no event comparable in its promotion of human industry, with that of the Great Exhibition of the Works of Industry of all Nations in 1851. A great people invited all civilised nations to a festival, to bring into comparison the works of human skill.'[11]

A narrower but significant aspiration, attributed to Prince Albert, was the creation of a cultural and education centre from the profits of the Great Exhibition, and the purchase of a site and a nucleus of objects from the exhibition brought the South Kensington Museum, now the Victoria and Albert Museum, into existence. Sir Henry Cole was effectively its first director from 1853 until 1873. In addition to the fixed capital of sites and buildings, temporary exhibitions fuelled mass entertainment. An early example of the popular appeal of museums was the display of the Prince and Princess of Wales' wedding presents in 1863 at the South Kensington Museum. It has continued to more recent crowd-pulling events such as the Tutankhamun exhibition of the early 1970s and current expediencies such as ticketing to control visitor numbers. These seasonal and perennial events attract huge publicity and serve many purposes. Curators may bask in their short-term reflected glow and the plaudits of reviewers and then return to nurse the permanent collections, many regretting a mentality that focuses on popular exhibitions and an opportunistic pursuit of popularity for its own sake.

MUSEUM IDEOLOGIES

If London offered an exhibition dynamic for museum methodology, Scotland drew also on Scandinavia for museum ideology. The vigorous study of early history and prehistory in the Nordic countries, overlaid with nineteenth-century Romanticism, inspired an appetite for traditions and customs and for the explanation of origins and distinctiveness of 'national character'. Scottish scholars had drawn inspiration from the study and evaluation of the Viking diaspora throughout the North Atlantic region in the researches of Scandinavian scholars such as Grímur Thorkelin in the 1780s and 1790s.[12] A number of Nordic societies formed themselves in the 1850s and 1860s to investigate and preserve local antiquities, leading to the founding of provincial 'cultural history' museums, the first of which was established in 1867. The study of German language and literature by the brothers Jacob and Wilhelm Grimm in the early nineteenth century lent an intellectual dimension to national Romanticism as a virtually pan-European movement. The Swedish scholar and philologist Artur Hazelius (1833–1901), with a keen personal interest in Swedish history and the spoken language, wanted to encourage the widest possible contemporary interest in these subjects and opened an exhibition of costume and folk art in Stockholm in 1873 that was to develop into the Nordiska Museet. The progress of industrialisation in contemporary Scandinavia was considered to be leading to the wholesale destruction of a traditional culture and its replacement by mass-produced factory goods. Household furniture and utensils, clothes, goods and tools of all kinds had been made in accordance with traditional methods and patterns, and these forms of self-reliance and subsistence were seen as characterising a 'peasant culture', essentially a rural and non-élite phenomenon, which lay at the heart of the 'true spirit of Swedish tradition'. Cement, colour and coherence were given to this traditional culture by the social and economic organisation of village and parish life and festivals, customs and beliefs, which were all studied in detail. Hazelius himself shared in a mid nineteenth-century academic fashion for a pan-Scandinavian or 'Nordic' view embracing all the Scandinavian countries and, in the early years of its existence, Nordiska Museet's naming and collections reflected this fashion. The building also, completed and opened in 1907, reflected a Danish–Dutch 'Nordic renaissance' architectural style. The representation of a national culture included the consideration of vernacular architecture, and building structures and interiors, both ancient and modern, had been an ingredient of European national trade exhibitions such as the World Exhibition in Paris in 1878. An 'open-air museum' with buildings from different periods and regions was opened on a 75-acre site at Skansen in 1891 and added the collection of buildings to material culture studies. Folk and open-air museums followed the inspiration of Nordiska Museet and Skansen throughout Europe, including initiatives to preserve and collect the old buildings of districts and settlements in Sweden itself, creating over 800 'Skansens' or community museums.[13]

A museum exhibition programme, whether for temporary or permanent exhibitions, has been a dynamic vehicle for research and acquisition. The annual exhibitions mounted by the National Museum of Antiquities of Scotland at the Royal Highland Show from 1965, for example, assembled the fundamental evidence for the history of Scottish country life, with the focus firmly on its material culture. The assembling of the material culture for the agricultural history of Scotland was the product of an earlier initiative to found a 'national folk museum' or open-air museum of Scottish country life, drawing inspiration from Scandinavian and European examples. The National Museum created a curatorial post in 1959 and appointed Alexander Fenton to develop a 'Scottish Country Life Section' and to collect, display and research the material needful for an open-air museum. The material was the obsolete and obsolescent agricultural tools and equipment and mainly horse-drawn machinery, the tools and products of local craftsmen, and domestic – including dairying – equipment, especially where this showed regional forms and variety. The exhibitions ranged over cultivation and ploughing, harvesting, farm stock, land improvement, food and diet, and illustrated variety and change over time between Lowland and Highland Scotland and differences in material, life and work styles and traditions within regions and between parishes or islands. Staged within the principal national agricultural event, the Royal Highland Show, these exhibitions 'spoke' to an informed audience, the farming population of Scotland, a fact that accelerated the process of research and collection. Most farms in Scotland were moving to greater mechanisation, and the men and women who had worked the land by hand and with horse power had stories to tell. The history of Scottish country life was then written by its new 'Keeper', Alexander Fenton, and distributed as exhibition leaflets to a receptive and knowledgeable Highland Show audience. The first exhibition, 'Ploughs and Ploughmen of Scotland', 22–25 June 1965, broke new ground in Scottish museum exhibitions:

> The oldest plough on display is an 'old Scots' plough dating back to about 1790, on loan from the County Museum in Stranraer. This one was probably pulled by 4 animals but in some areas the team might be as big as 12, as for the 'twal-ousen' (12 ox) plough of Aberdeenshire, with one man holding the plough and another leading the team. It was the plough of pre-enclosure

days, when the unfenced land was ploughed into a series of high-backed ridges resembling corrugations. The furrows between the ridges allowed for surface drainage.[14]

These were topics nowhere else in print, and exemplars of material culture studies. The exhibition leaflet, 'price three pence', accompanying 'Peat Cutting and Land Improvement' at Stand 312 at Ingliston 18–21 June 1968, for example, summarised drainage for the first time, in a deft 200 words, for Scottish history and material culture:

> The present day arable fields of Scotland largely owe their dry, level appearance to the regular system of underground tile drainage that developed after c.1820–30. Before that, though some drainage was done by means of box or stone drains and open ditches, the main method was surface drainage, by ploughing the soil into high, raised ridges, between which water could run off. Numerous examples can still be seen on the lower slopes of many hills.
>
> Hand-made horse-shoe shaped tiles, known as 'saddle-back' or 'mug' tiles, generally resting on soles of tile or wood, began to be used c.1820 for field drainage, and are still functioning in many places. This was the type used by James Smith of Deanston, a pioneer in systematic underground drainage, though he also used stone drains about 2½ ft. deep, filled with stones in graded sizes, then turf, and finally, soil. Smith also patented a mole-plough that broke the hard-pan below the surface, so as to let water percolate away. The improvement of his land was so great that his system of 'thorough drainage', and the use of the mole-plough, spread very rapidly. Cylindrical drain-pipes, at first of small bore (2 in.), did not come into use till the late 1840s.[15]

Access to authentic material lies at the heart of museums' claims to social and cultural significance, and this is subject to changes in fashion. One might cite the move from densely packed displays, in which more or less the whole collection might be visible, to the sparse and meticulously designed highlighting of single objects chosen to stand for processes or events that characterises the modern museum. The need for today's museums to draw the public through their doors might even lead to a recognisable paradox in the presentation of the singular spectacular object under the spotlight, of the shapely and beautiful but perhaps historically insignificant against the dull and distasteful but significant. It might lead also to the confusion of élite and popular cultures. The significance of the visually dull, however, is captured in the stored research collections of the larger museums, a detail of museum culture that has drawn public and media criticism over 'treasures in the cellars' and 'hidden national treasure'. The unique attribute of the museum remains the object. The challenge to the museum curator is to acquire the object or group of objects, both dull and appealing, and to present them in their own right to enthral and to affirm knowledge by understanding them *per se* and in context. To conventional exhibition is now added digital media in the form of screens, film projections, interactive displays and websites as mechanisms to maximise accessibility. The object is given 'authority' by an object message which the museum wants to convey, relating it on the one hand to its context and origins and on the other to its audience. Sir Henry Cole's claim for the 'history of the world' being written in an exhibition has been reconfigured in the Director of the British Museum's *History of the World in 100 Objects* in 2010, by which a 100-part series on BBC Radio built fundamental and far-reaching connections for human history exclusively through objects. The effectiveness and significance of material culture can be enhanced by its presentation, its interpretation and its power to engage, surprise and enlighten, as the Director, Neil MacGregor, has claimed.[16]

ANTIQUARIAN STUDIES

Modern methodologies for preservation and presentation, and the development of museums and museum collections, have deep roots in European culture. Material culture studies in both individual and institutional contexts have a long history. The study of things and their cultural and environmental contexts drew inspiration from the humanist notion of collecting and the Renaissance fashion of the 'cabinet of curiosities', the *Kunstkammer*, which would hold a mirror to the taste and sensibility of the cultivated prince.[17] Collecting and study increased with the voyages of geographical discovery and 'new worlds' of the sixteenth century, the 'scientific revolution' of the seventeenth century, and the polymathy of eighteenth-century Enlightenment inquiry and what was seen as the advance towards the 'enlightened' state. Objects of mystery such as fossils or drift seeds came to be explained while retaining an aura in popular belief as charms and amulets.[18] When European explorers and traders brought objects from the Americas, Asia and the South Pacific in the sixteenth century, natural phenomena aroused wonder and widespread curiosity. Objects and material such as shells, eggs, coconuts and corals that are now commonplace were considered rare and wonderful and became coveted and collected objects. Ostrich eggs and coconut cups were crafted with settings, mounted in silver and gold and turned into ornaments and treasures in sixteenth- and seventeenth-century Europe. Silver-mounted coconut cups have survived in Scotland from this time, and a seemingly unique and beautifully crafted nautilus shell, the 'Heriot Loving Cup', was prepared by an Edinburgh goldsmith about 1612.[19]

The curiosities and souvenirs of merchants and traders also offered clues to the past which were recognised by scientists and antiquaries, and analogies and resemblances were perceived between exotic material and objects found in the home soil. A 'cabinet of curiosities' which acquired fame throughout Europe was the collection of physician and natural scientist Sir Hans Sloane (1660–1753), the influence of whose inheritance as a Protestant Ulsterman of Scots parentage remains to be explored. His all-absorbing interest and his life's work was the formation of collections that he wished to be kept together and offered to the nation following his death. Accepted under the terms of an act of parliament in June 1753, his collections were housed in Montagu House in Bloomsbury and opened to the public in 1759 as the British Museum and the 'national museum of archaeology, ethnography and natural history'. The museum had matured from the recherché 'cabinet of curiosities' to the democratic opportunity for reasoned enquiry, study and comparison.

A by-product of 'new learning' in the seventeenth century and the Enlightenment of the eighteenth century was the intensive and extensive collecting, classification and description of prehistoric and historic material in the course of the nineteenth century. The study of such physical evidence followed the early work of the 'antiquaries', a 'profession' that came later to elicit caricature and ridicule but which instigated the study of material culture. The obsessions of scholars such as William Stukeley and John Aubrey with physical antiquities tells us that they then understood they had crossed the boundaries of what literary sources could tell them about objects from the ground and monuments in the landscape. They studied and recorded 'antiquities' in the field and drew on the new approach to history and historical method of William Camden (1551–1623) whose Britannia was first published in 1586.[20] The antiquaries worked to make sense of the past for the writing of history from the detailed examination of evidence and to establish a scientific basis for the study of the past from empirical evidence rather than from myth, as another contemporary, Sir Francis Bacon (1561–1626), demonstrated. They argued from the evidence on the ground rather than deducing from a priori theory. They began to reveal deep-time measured in millions of years, cautiously enlarging perceptions of time based exclusively on the timeframe of the Bible. The corollary of collecting was dividing into parts with the systematic arranging and classifying of this new corpus on Aristotelian principles, thereby constructing an intellectual rationale and taxonomies for a new museum movement and an institutional framework for the study of material culture. The Society of Antiquaries of Scotland had initiated the process in the 1780s, following the earlier examples of the Society of Antiquaries of London (1707) and the emergence of the British Museum (1753), though looking also to Scandinavia for links and analogies. The Scottish Society of Antiquaries appeared to take a distinctly independent course, vigorously defining a role for a national museum and recommending its patriotic purpose, but failing, however, to gain government support before 1851. Leading scholars such as Daniel Wilson (1816–1892) argued for the importance of objects as evidence, not only for the interpretation of prehistory and for the building of theoretical foundations but also for augmenting the records of a nation whose culture had been neglected and even wilfully destroyed. In this context, the National Museum of Antiquities of Scotland developed a distinctively Scottish dialectic in the late nineteenth century, for which 'ethnology' and other terms began also to serve a purpose of scholarly definition.[21]

THE HISTORIANS' TRADE

Modes of working belonging to the museum profession and the sums of working knowledge engendered by them have added a cross-disciplinary and complementary component of 'material culture' to the historian's techniques and toolkit.

For the practitioner, the study of material culture towards an understanding of the past and present adds significantly to other sources and might now be said to be part of the historians' trade. In the longer term, this was more enthusiastically acknowledged and embraced in Scandinavian and continental academies than in the more conventional British schools of history. One of the Swedish Nordiska Museet's duties was to provide academic instruction in the University of Stockholm, and Chairs for comparative folk life research or 'ethnology' were established here and at the Universities of Lund and Uppsala. The ethnologist Sigurd Erixon (1888–1968) was the distinguished second holder of the Chair in Stockholm.[22] Erixon's perspective was that folklife studies and ethnology grew on the back of material collections and fieldwork, writing in 1962 that:

> For a number of decades our Swedish folk-life researchers have devoted, with almost hectic zeal, a great deal of time and energy to the collection of material. We have attached particular importance to the study of, *inter alia*, material culture, at first with special interest for dateable objects, and later perhaps above all for their distribution. For this purpose we have had to study them in their respective localities and, finally, in the now more than a thousand local museums.[23]

Scandinavian historians and social scientists, as pioneer 'ethnologists', also used the concept of material culture for the classification and comparison of historical evidence, borrowing more perhaps from cultural anthropology than from other areas of the social sciences, and their example was adopted by Scottish museum scholars and researchers. Ethnology therefore may now be defined as a form of cultural anthropology, dealing with comparative and analytical studies of culture and tailored to some extent to local circumstances and social milieu. In this latter area of discourse, it has been distinguished in the literature with the label 'regional ethnology', behaving as a historical discipline in relation to concepts of time, place and social circumstances.

In twentieth-century Britain as a whole, a virtual mantra of conventional historical study – no documents, no history – meant that there was still little study of an undocumented past, so that material culture studies remained more or less confined to archaeology. Exceptions to this ingrained professional divide have lain on the borderline of history and archaeology in, for example, Scotland of the Picts, Vikings and Gaels, and England of the Anglo-Saxons and Danes. 'Who are the Picts?', for example, posed an enticing and compelling question, and answers continue to draw on historical and philological evidence for the interpretation of an impressive material culture; arguments then enter arenas of contention around the understanding of prehistoric societies and processes of reasoning and induction from object and production to motivation behind it. Fallacies too arise from applying ethnic labels to prehistoric objects, so that 'Pictish' or 'Celtic' will appeal to the modern mind and fit into accepted taxonomies but can be fundamentally flawed. Material culture studies as in archaeology can be used to further illuminate history, literature, language, religion or other areas of study such as mythology, although hypotheses and conclusions are still limited. The early historical period offers examples: the historically attested 'twelfth-century renaissance' as a European phenomenon indicates the development of towns and trade, institutions of government and centralised political control in Scotland, associated by historians with the driving force of David I (1124–1153) and Norman-French and Flemish settlers as new landholders forming a military caste. Surviving and excavated material culture suggests economic change in this period and the appearance of a new range of material in, for example, ceramics, metalwork, coinage and items such as seal matrices signifying trade and exchange, markers of status and of new protocols and language for recording transactions. Archaeologically, the story is vividly one of change, though 'continuum' is proffered in the literature as a characteristic of the medieval period.[24]

Historians in general have still been reluctant to challenge the exclusive status of text to provide evidence or to imbue objects with the same authority as written texts, and there may have been sufficient reasons to accept such a view. The historian's craft was seen as making sense of the written word and literary sources, and history as an academic field to be practised as a literary genre. This narrower discourse was shaken in the twentieth century by extensive social analysis and a widening of the range of questions asked of history. Present fashions for a more holistic approach and a readiness not to be constrained by disciplinary boundaries have extended historical studies to explore the edges of the discipline beyond word-generated documentation and to critique long-standing conventions. The study of material culture fits comfortably into this expansion of the domain, and the research of Dr Stana Nenadic in publications such as *Lairds and Luxury: The Highland Gentry in Eighteenth-Century Scotland* provides an excellent example.

A dominant anglophone historical narrative characterised nineteenth- and twentieth-century historical studies, emerging from the confidence and certainties of Britain's imperial role and doctrinaire concepts of the 'civilised' society. This era is convincingly in the past, but the 'British Empire', the infrastructure of empire and a world economic dominance all cast a long shadow; it is still contested territory and a matter of academic debate. From the perspective of Scotland's material culture it is tangible, with the long-term import of raw materials such as cotton and jute and the export more or less worldwide of the products of the 'industrial revolution', whether cast-iron pots and utensils from Carron, ploughs and implements from Uddingston, locomotives from Springburn, or ships from the Clyde. The study of material culture has profited from the more recent shift to analyses of human behaviour and away from a conventional and narrow focus on political and constitutional history in which 'history' was the history of parliamentary institutions and political élites. It has profited also from continued but changing emphasis on the role of history in the schools' curriculum, the enthusiastic pursuit of history in the broadcasting media, and the more eclectic reach for ideas and educational material to inspire responses to demotic and 'political' questions of identity and origins, of who we are and where we come from. Beyond the bounds of the academies there is a keen interest in oral history and family history, and everyone is encouraged to be their own historian. The democratisation of history is often inspired by material culture, by the discovery of family heirlooms and ancient souvenirs, or the revelations of local history, offering individuals and communities a sense of identity and belonging and of their own past. Objects and material culture are triggers for research and lines of historical thought, when a family Bible, a wedding dress lovingly folded away in previous generations, a shoe last and old tools, or a collection of medals, as military or civil awards, usually inscribed with name and date, surprise and inspire discussion and reconnection with person and event.

ETHNOLOGICAL STUDIES

Outside the narrower or conventional domain of history, the establishment of great museum collections was also part of the theoretical debates of the day; for example, on concepts of 'progress' and 'civilisation', crystallised as we have seen by contemporary representation of the Great Exhibition. Artefact studies were seen as offering benchmark measurements of technical progress or empirical bases for grand schemes of social evolution, diffusion or acculturation. Prehistory then offered opportunities to regress evolutionary schemes, since archaeologists could only describe and evaluate a culture from its material and artefacts. Cultural significance in prehistory therefore belonged almost exclusively to the object, and degrees of interpretation of what the object might symbolise for its maker and user varied accordingly. How people represented and wrote about objects consequently varied, and this becomes more evident in the Enlightenment when the literature of 'improvement' roundly condemned the ancient and outmoded, and mocked 'folk belief'. Scholars in the field in the late nineteenth century, largely the early anthropologists, began to study and collect the material culture of indigenous peoples whose tools and techniques seemed to them to differ little from those used by Neolithic or even Mesolithic folk, as revealed by their archaeological remains. Colonies of 'primitive peoples' were objects of Victorian curiosity, compassion and condescension, and curiosity might be heightened when the objects of study, charity or Christian mission were located not in the South Seas but within a day's journey of Britain's new centres of civilisation. This was characterised by some as the survival of the 'past in the present' in nineteenth-century Scotland, and it inspired an important book by that name and also laid the foundations for the ethnological or 'folklife' collections of the National Museums.

Sir Arthur Mitchell (1826–1909), having trained in medicine, was an architect of this human science. He published a set of his lectures, given as the Rhind Lectures in the National Museum in 1879, under the title *The Past in the Present: What is Civilisation?*, with more than a hint of irony in the subtitle. He went out into the field and identified, drew, measured and published what he regarded as primitive survivals, to be found significantly in Scotland's Central Belt as well as in perceived remoter parts and islands of the north and west of Scotland. He was a prolific contributor to the Society of Antiquaries' *Proceedings*, as well as donor to the national collections of a wide selection of tools, goods and chattels such as ploughs, spades, querns, spinning and weaving equipment and pottery. He examined contemporary observable phenomena which could be deemed to throw light on prehistoric material and techniques, from a viewpoint more anthropological than archaeological. His descriptions and analysis rested on assumptions such as continuity, inheritance and an unbroken succession from a remote past of particular phenomena such as stone hand tools or pottery making. 'Ethnology' in the sense in which it was then used as a 'human science' was not used by Mitchell in this context; he coined his own terminology by which he described

> an archaic character chiefly in respect of a certain rudeness in their form and purpose, but they are in reality not archaic, having all been made and used in this country by persons of this time. They have therefore been called neo-archaic, and the study of them throws light on the study of many objects which are really archaic.[25]

This version of material culture studies founded on archaeology, but moving out into new disciplines in the human sciences, re-emerged as 'ethnology' in museums in the second half of the twentieth century. This period saw enlargement of the role of museums, both in social and in intellectual contexts, the carefully studied pursuit of 'collection development', an exponential growth in specialist knowledge and its publication, the espousal of interdisciplinary methodologies and a more rigorous critique. The significance given to material culture required a creed to propagate a rationale and wider usage, and levels of professionalism were defined for museum work and interdisciplinary and multidisciplinary principles applied. By the late twentieth century, the largely Scandinavian version of 'ethnology' had come to supply a paradigm and conceptual framework for the formation of collections in the National Museum and in other museums in Scotland. The paradigm, recognised in contemporary scholarly literature under the broad label of 'European Ethnology', derived from the museum nexus and teaching in Scandinavian and European universities. The term was adopted to a limited but important extent in Scotland to provide a rationale and interpretive tools for the collection and description of material culture, initially under the influence of museum-based archaeology and particularly in the then National Museum of Antiquities of Scotland.[26]

The student of this subject is faced with a wealth of material, between museum and research collections and the subsisting social and economic environment and its study. It is difficult to define the scope of this field, as evidenced by the variety of terminology such as 'ethnology' or 'folklife studies' adopted or employed in different discourses, for example in Europe and North America. As the folk museum movement spread in Scandinavia and Germany, ethnology grew out of it in the 1930s to become a university discipline, as we have seen, and, under the guiding intellect of Professor Sigurd Erixon and others, the subject developed substance and methodology. This has been crystallised, for example, not only in national museum collections but also in international journals such as *Ethnologia Europaea* founded in 1967. A systematic approach to the study of the traditional ways of life of the people of Scotland, as they were in the past and as they are now, drew inspiration and intellectual vigour from the Scandinavian 'school'. Ireland experienced the same process, where 'ethnology' was grafted onto the work of the Irish Folklore Institute (later Commission) and mediated particularly through a school of historical geographers. Estyn Evans, Professor of Geography in Belfast, published the first 'modern' book on Irish folklore in 1942 and followed it with *Irish Folk Ways* in 1957; most aspects of rural life are described, not as isolated objects but as part of a structure and rooted both in the environment and history. Professionalism to match the work in Scandinavia began modestly in Scotland with the founding of a number of folk museums – for example, the Highland Folk Museum in Iona (1935) and later at Kingussie (1944), the Angus Folk Museum at Glamis (1950), the Glenesk Museum (1955) – and took a major step forward with the opening of the School of Scottish Studies at the University of Edinburgh (1951) and then the setting up of the Country Life Section in the former National Museum of Antiquities of Scotland (1959), with its remit to collect and study the material culture of all the regions of Scotland.

To a limited extent, such models entered into the mainstream of the discipline of history, at least in the context of British social history. The growing interest of academics in the second half of the twentieth century in society, social and physical environments and beliefs began to fill out the picture. Hitherto, a dearth of research into many aspects of society and its history was true of England and certainly true of Scotland. The development of a Marxist dialectic in the 1960s widened the range and depth of focus, albeit within a doctrinaire model of a dynamic and ultimately self-destructive capitalism. Studies of the 'labour process' and definition of 'modes of production' required a diversity of approach and might be said to have transformed the teaching and practice of history. E P Thompson's *The Making of the English Working Class*, published in 1963, added a robust Marxist social analysis to the historical narrative with the thesis of an organised and insurgent working class. Behind these intellectual changes were influences often more implicit than explicit, such as the interdisciplinary methodologies of the *Annales* school of Lucien Febvre (1878–1956) and Marc Bloch (1886–1944), their cachet deriving from the journal they founded in 1929. 'Structuralism' supplied a further major influence, the name given to an analytical methodology associated with the anthropologist Claude Lévi-Strauss (1908–2009), which sought explanations of culture through deeper structures of meaning and relationships in all or most human activity. An interest in the artefact belonged to structuralism, but the emphasis tended to shift in academic debate from 'material' to 'culture' with semiotics and meanings dominating over form and function. In this often fiercely competitive intellectual atmosphere, the debate might be strong on theory but weak on substance, and the documentation of objects brief and partial.

A RURAL PAST

Material culture studies have still profited from leads given by social and economic historians in the twentieth century, taking us beyond the more typical economic history focus on trade, industry and the industrial centres, communications and the growth of towns and cities. T C Smout's *A History of the Scottish People 1560–1830*, published in 1969, opened up new perspectives with a social history of Scotland since the Reformation. It was, however, significant that Christopher

Smout proposed that it was 'impossible to understand the social development of Scotland without a background of political history', a proposition aligning himself with contemporary British historiography and implying that Scottish history had been poorly served in this respect. The attenuation of Scottish historical studies in the eighteenth century and following the Union of 1707 was proposed as a substantial reason for the founding of the Society of Antiquaries and a national collection in the 1780s. A surge in research and scholarship in the Scottish History academic field in the second half of the twentieth century began to rectify an imbalance and to expand the role and potential of a national history. This shift can be identified in a plethora of new published work but more simply detected in a comparison between *A Dictionary of Scottish History* of 1977 with its roots firmly in 'Scottish Kings' (1906) and 'The Scots Peerage' (1904–1914) and the *Oxford Companion to Scottish History* of 2001 with 188 contributors and an exponential reach into agriculture and industry, rural and urban society, the family, birth, marriage and death, housing, health, food and diet, dress, sport, music, song, oral tradition, custom and belief.[27] The most important premise of the *History of the Scottish People* for our purposes was Smout's emphasis on the circumstances of 80 or 90 percent of Scots living on the land and depending for their livelihood on its productivity. The more strictly material conditions and accessories of this rural life were not explored.[28]

An earlier product of research in Scotland was narrower in focus but more inclusive in its grasp of evidence. Isabel Grant's *Every-day Life on an Old Highland Farm* (1924) interpreted the bare details of a farm account book for the Davoch of Dunachton in Strathspey to provide evidence of material culture and people's everyday lives, and a more detailed understanding of the changing landscape. Her thesis of interpretation enlarged on the attenuated manuscript evidence of the account book over little more than a decade in the 1770s through her own kinship with and proximity to the folk of the locality and a deeply imbued familiarity with the landscape setting. Her recognition of the role of material culture and the ways that objects shed light on people's experience and shifting worlds convinced her of the importance of forming a collection in the public domain; her legacy is the Highland Folk Museum in Kingussie and Newtonmore.[29] When Isabel Grant was researching the account book, she drew on the memories and experience of families in the district to explain farming processes and terms referred to in the manuscript. The annual seasonal migration from the townland to the upland grazings had long ceased but was still remembered: 'The older people can remember their parents' stories of the great migration up to the shielings.' The term 'tathing', for example, defined the folding or enclosing of cattle and sheep at night on selected areas of pasture or 'outfield' to fertilise it with their dung, and the turf wall enclosure would be moved on after eight or ten nights. This practice had been carried on around Kingussie within the memory of those living there in the early twentieth century.[30] Old tools and implements were then passing into obscurity but could still be explained. *Caibe làir* was still known locally as the term for the 'flauchter spade' or turfing spade that was used for skinning the turf for cultivation and opening peat banks, building turf walls or for roofing buildings. When she began to collect material for the museum in the 1930s, she acquired a number of this type of spade blade, suggesting that it had been commonly used until relatively recently.[31] For her, these objects played an important part in an understanding of the past and making of the present. Her later book, *Highland Folk Ways* (1961), brought material culture to the fore in her account of the different spheres of life and work within the household, on the land and at sea in the Highlands and Islands.

Material culture was firmly positioned in historical studies in the wider Scotland with the publication of Alexander Fenton's *Scottish Country Life* in 1976. This pioneering work opened up the field of material culture studies by drawing for its premises on fieldwork of collecting and research, the detailed documentation of museum collections, and the Highland Show exhibition series of the 1960s and 1970s. Scottish farming and, more broadly, 'Scottish country life' over the preceding 250 years were scrutinised to define a transition from a traditional and mainly subsistence economy to a highly mechanised one. It offered a detailed examination of tools and implements for cultivating and harvesting and the description and analysis of the techniques of their use, the processing of cereals, milk and milk products, the food people ate, forms of transport, types of buildings, processes of change and impacts of technology. Paradoxically, perhaps, the 'agricultural revolution' of the late eighteenth and early nineteenth centuries had less to do with machinery than with cheap and plentiful labour, so that the planting, care and harvesting of crops, for example, were sustained by teams of men, women and children with hand tools. Significant markers of technological change were identified, with associated social and economic influences and consequences both national and international, in, for example, James Small's 'swing plough' of 1767, Andrew Meikle's threshing mill of 1786, the Rev. Patrick Bell's reaping machine of 1827, and the spread of systematic underground field drainage as created by James Smith of Deanston. Only with the levelling of the ground surface with field drains was it possible for machinery such as Bell's reaper to come into use and promote the mechanisation of agriculture. Alexander Fenton sets out the parameters of his study with a confidence and emphasis born of thorough research added to personal experience:

> A knowledge of Scottish country life amounting to accurate historical insight derives in the end not only from studying the broad patterns and trends that come through official statistics, not only from recording the lives and actions of men like Lord Kames or Sir John Sinclair, not only from plotting on a map the diffusion of James Small's plough or Andrew Meikle's threshing mill, but also from learning about the everyday activities in byre and barn, home and workshop, about small-scale equipment and its techniques of use, and about the unspectacular, indigenous changes that took place in these over a period of time in response to local conditions.[32]

MATERIAL DETAIL

This has acted as a prompt for using material culture and the 'unspectacular, indigenous changes' to revisit textual sources in order to link their content to physical things and the landscape. Early printed and manuscript sources, as in the collections of the National Records of Scotland and the National Library, are often 'top-down' views of people's lives and administrative in bias and purpose. An understanding of their contents can be improved by an understanding of their material culture meaning. An Inventory of a farm in Lochwinnoch parish in 1826 lists tools from a labour-intensive and arable regime before 'improvement'. These – flaughter spade, spades and shovels, sowing sheet, clippers, scythes and sneds, flails, peat spades, peat barrows, sled or 'car', cows' boyns, milk cogs, stacks of oats and barley, and so on – can be readily identified and visualised from surviving regional examples and the nature of their use explored.[33] Copious legal evidence, for example in statute and the acts of parliament, can be linked to economic and material evidence and the appearance of the landscape. The parliamentary statutes which provided a basis in law for agricultural change can be better understood by being located in material contexts. Acts of 1661, 1685 and 1695 ruled for the enclosing of lands lying run-rig, for the division of 'commonties' and for the planting of trees.[34] The effect of such radical legislation was different in Scotland than in England, and subdivision of open-field or 'enclosure' tended not to raise legal proceedings as in England, since rights in 'commonties' were matters of joint ownership or occupancy. Legal evidence that more vividly relates to material culture and daily life can be sourced in the records of the baron courts, for example, in their granting of authority for fairs and markets, or regulating the seasonal tasks of their communities, and behavioural and environmental changes can be tracked. The 'acts of the Laird of Glenorchy' in his baron court in 1621 included oversight of muirburn, the repair of head-dykes and fauld dykes, the hunting of wolves, peat cutting, manuring and composting, the grinding of barley or 'bere' meal, and prescribing dates for going to and returning from the shielings.[35]

The close attention to detail in the study of material culture will tease out information otherwise glossed over or ignored, and offer correctives to a tendency to oversimplify or over-romanticise; it may even challenge the imposition of grand narratives with which we feel comfortable. The terminology of legal records such as inventories or court proceedings can be interpreted through their material culture, the interpretation developed through deeper engagement, evidence led from the objects or context, and assumptions or conclusions challenged. The history of crops, as the fundamental element of food and survival, reveals extensive variation over time and adjustment to local conditions. The balance between barley and oats changed, for example, and this might have been influenced by climate as well as geography. Barley or 'bere', for instance, was the enduring component of the dietary staple and the food crop for growing on poorer and more acidic soils. It was better adapted to the climate of Scotland, being sown in May and harvested in late August and therefore needed only a relatively short growing season. It was not only a subsistence crop but also could be the source of malt for distilling and, until the eighteenth century, and later in some parts, small-scale distilling based on barley was universal. The winning of the crop in harvest was a critical process, with a complex of economic and social indicators. It was the focal point of the effort of most of Scotland before the eighteenth century and usually invisible in the textual record outside the blight of famine. Harvesting implements were the sickle (for centuries) and scythe, and they were used with grain stack and rope-making tools. A sickle with a toothed blade was used for cutting the grain. It was the woman's harvesting tool until the nineteenth century, used by taking hold of a bundle of stalks and cutting them with a sawing action. Customarily three to five women worked together along the rig, and a man followed to tie the sheaves. This method produced the harvesting team known as the 'bandwin' that would be hired for shearing the harvest. The sheaves were tied with 'bands' formed from the stalks of grain. The toothed sickle came to be replaced by a larger, smooth-bladed sickle adapted from cutting grass or hay, and the scythe was adopted as the harvesting implement in the nineteenth century.[36]

Recent years have seen an upsurge of interest in material culture, obliquely, perhaps, through popularisation of museums for education and entertainment, and with archaeology programmes as broadcast themes, and also as concomitant to landscape and environment study. The *Compendium of Scottish Ethnology* is the affirmation of such interest, a marker of its significance and a guide to the material culture of Scotland in its European setting. While debates over definitions, methods and concepts continue in the academic field and material culture is picked over by different disciplines in the pursuit of changing research cultures and concerns, the pursuit of material detail in a land of different parts and pasts, peoples and languages offers a unique challenge to material culture at the heart of the ethnological project. This integration of sources is no doubt what prompted the comment of a Celtic Studies scholar in 1930, when contemplating the significance in a folktale of a 'spancel' or cow-fetter used to hobble a cow when being milked:

> . . . on the *buarach*, a long article might be written.[37]

NOTES

1 See Hicks and Beaudry, 2010, *passim*; Buchli, 2002, 13, 15, 18–19.
2 In the light of ongoing debates, the choice of the 'collection' as benchmark may seem overly conservative, static or even reductionist but it chimes with the origins and aims of the series *Scottish Life and Society. A Compendium of Scottish Ethnology*.
3 McLaren and Hunter, 2008, 105–28; Curwen, 1937.
4 Halliday, 69–81; Fenton, 1963, 264–317.
5 Fenton, 2007.
6 Stevenson, 1979.
7 McKean, 2000, 3–21.
8 Fenton, 1974, 243–58; Fenton, 1987.
9 Campbell, 1899, 69.
10 See, for example, Stearn, 1981.
11 Gibbs-Smith, 1981, 7.
12 Cant, 1981, 23–4.
13 Rehnberg, 1957, 7.
14 See also Fenton, 1964, 80–4.
15 Typically in the course of the exhibitions, information would be added to the sum of knowledge by word of mouth; for example, that there were further types of narrow pipe and collar tile known colloquially as 'Gladstone drains'.

16 See Cheape, 2011, v–x.
17 Findlen, 1989, 60.
18 Cheape, 2008, 104–18.
19 Dalgleish and Fothringham, 2008, 39–41.
20 Piggott and Robertson, 1977.
21 Cheape, 2010, 357–73; Cheape, 2009, 3–14; Anderson, 1881; Hulse, 1999.
22 Rehnberg, 1957, 67; see Storå, 1992, 85–102, for the academic framework of
     ethnology in Finland. I am most grateful to Raila Kataja, National Museum of
     Finland, for this reference.
23 Erixon, 1962, 279–80.
24 Caldwell, 2006, 14–27; Caldwell, 1982.
25 Mitchell, 1898, 181.
26 Fenton, 1985–86.
27 Donaldson and Morpeth, 1977; Lynch, 2001.
28 Smout, 1969; see also Smout and Fenton, 1965, 73–93.
29 Grant, 2007.
30 Grant, 1924, 40–1, 60.
31 Cheape, 1986, 120.
32 Fenton, 1976, v; see also Fenton, 2002, 13–24.
33 Pryde, 1951, 153–6.
34 *APS* vol. 7, 263–4; *APS* vol. 8, 488; *APS* vol. 9, 421, 462.
35 Innes, 1855, 359–66.
36 Fenton, 1976, 50–64.
37 Murchison, 1960, 172.

BIBLIOGRAPHY AND FURTHER READING

Anderson, J. *Scotland in Early Christian Times*, Edinburgh, 1881.
APS [*Acts of the Parliaments of Scotland*], vol. 7 (*s.a.* 1661); vol. 8 (*s.a.* 1685); vol. 9 (*s.a.* 1695).
Bell, A S, ed. *The Scottish Antiquarian Tradition. Essays to Mark the Bicentenary of the Society of Antiquaries of Scotland, 1780–1980*, Edinburgh, 1981.
Buchli, V. *A Material Culture Reader*, Oxford, 2002.
Caldwell, D, ed. *Angels, Nobles and Unicorns. Art and Patronage in Medieval Scotland*, Edinburgh, 1982.
Caldwell, D. Continuity and change in twelfth- and thirteenth-century Scotland: An archaeological view, *ROSC*, 18 (2006), 14–27.
Campbell, D. Highland shielings in the olden times, *Transactions of the Inverness Scientific Society and Field Club*, 5 (1895–99), 62–90.
Cant, R G. David Steuart Erskine, 11th Earl of Buchan: Founder of the Society of Antiquaries of Scotland. In Bell, 1981, 1–30.
Cheape, H. 'Convivial and anomalous conversations': The Society of Antiquaries and their Museum, *ROSC*, 21 (2009) 3–14.
Cheape, H. Touchstones of belief: The Charms and Amulets collection of the National Museums Scotland, *ROSC*, 20 (2008), 104–18.
Cheape, H. Introduction: Ethnology and object-based research, *ROSC*, 23 (2011), v–x.
Cheape, H. The Society of Antiquaries of Scotland and their museum: Scotland's national collection and a national discourse, *International Journal of Historical Archaeology*, 14 (2010), 357–73.
Cheape, H. Dr I F Grant (1887–1983): The Highland Folk Museum and a bibliography of her written works, *ROSC*, 2 (1986), 113–25.

Curwen, E C. Querns, *Antiquity*, 11:2 (1937), 133–51.

Dalgleish, G and Fothringham, H S. *Silver. Made in Scotland*, Edinburgh, 2008.

Donaldson, G and Morpeth, R S. *A Dictionary of Scottish History*, Edinburgh, 1977.

Erixon, S. Folk-life research in our time, *Gwerin*, 3 (1962), 275–91.

Fenton, A. Early and traditional cultivating implements in Scotland, *PSAS*, 96 (1962–63), 264–317.

Fenton, A. *The Shape of the Past. Essays in Scottish Ethnology*, 2 vols, Edinburgh, 1985–86.

Fenton, A. The scope of regional ethnology, *Folk Life*, 11 (1973), 5–14.

Fenton, A. Lexicography and historical interpretation. In Barrow, G W S, ed., *The Scottish Tradition*, Edinburgh, 1974, 243–58.

Fenton, A. *Wirds an' Wark 'e Seasons roon on an Aberdeenshire Farm*, Aberdeen, 1987.

Fenton, A. How did the pre-improvement landscape and society work?, *ROSC*, 15 (2002), 13–24.

Fenton, A. *Scottish Life and Society. A Compendium of Scottish Ethnology, volume 5: The Food of the Scots*, Edinburgh, 2007.

Fenton, A. The Chilcarroch plough, *Scottish Studies*, 8 (1964), 80–4.

Findlen, P. The museum: Its classical etymology and Renaissance genealogy, *Journal of the History of Collections*, 1 (1989), 59–78.

Gibbs-Smith, C H. *The Great Exhibition of 1851*, London, 1981.

Govan, S, ed. *Medieval or Later Rural Settlement in Scotland: 10 Years on*, Edinburgh, 2003.

Grant, I F. *Every-day Life on an Old Highland Farm, 1769–1782*, London, 1924.

Grant, I F. *The Making of Am Fasgadh*, Edinburgh, 2007.

Halliday, S. Rig-and-furrow in Scotland. In Govan, ed., *Medieval or Later Rural Settlement*, 69–81.

Hicks, D and Beaudry, M C. *The Oxford Handbook of Material Culture Studies*, Oxford, 2010.

Hulse, E, ed. *Thinking with Both Hands : Sir Daniel Wilson in the Old World and the New*, Toronto, 1999.

Innes, C, ed. *The Black Book of Taymouth. Papers from the Breadalbane Charter Room*, Edinburgh, 1855.

Lynch, M, ed. *The Oxford Companion to Scottish History*, Oxford, 2001.

McKean, C. The Scottish château, *ROSC*, 12 (1999–2000), 3–21.

McLaren, D and Hunter, F. New aspects of rotary querns in Scotland, *PSAS*, 138 (2008), 105–28.

Mitchell, A. A description of some neo-archaic objects, *PSAS*, 32 (1897–98), 181–94.

Murchison, T M, ed. *Prose Writings of Donald Lamont, 1874–1958*, Edinburgh, 1960.

Nenadic, S. *Lairds and Luxury: The Highland Gentry in Eighteenth-Century Scotland*, Edinburgh, 2007.

Piggott, S and Robertson, M. *Three Centuries of Scottish Archaeology*, Edinburgh, 1977.

Pryde, G S. Papers relating to a Renfrewshire farm, *Miscellany of the Scottish History Society*, 8, Edinburgh, 1951, 139–62

Rehnberg, M. *The Nordiska Museet and Skansen*, Stockholm, 1957.

Smout, T C. *A History of the Scottish People 1560–1830*, London, 1969.

Smout, T C and Fenton, A. Scottish agriculture before the improvers: An exploration, *Agricultural History Review*, 13 (1965), 73–93.

Stearn, W T. *The Natural History Museum at South Kensington. A History of the British Museum (Natural History) 1753–1980*, London, 1981.

Stevenson, R B K. *Brooches*, 2nd edn, Edinburgh, 1979.

Storå, N. Five ethnologies. The rise of Finnish ethnology from a Finland–Swedish point of view. In Räsänen, M, ed., *Pioneers. The History of Finnish Ethnology*, Helsinki, 1992, 85–102.

5 Museums and Ethnology

JOHN BURNETT

INTRODUCTION: LISTING, COLLECTING AND UNDERSTANDING

The mid fifteenth-century poem 'Cokelbie [or Colkelbie] Sow' listed the people asked to a feast:

> A forfarn falconer
> A malgratious millare,
> A berward, a brawler   [bear ward]
> And ane aip ledar,
> With a cursit custumar.[1]   [customs officer]

This miscellaneous assemblage is deliberately ludicrous in its use of different categories (behaviour, trade, personality) to describe people – similar to the all-encompassing museum which holds different things for different reasons, some of the reasons having been forgotten. Working in and with museums is a continual process of making new patterns in the disorder.

One method for reducing the disorder is to produce a catalogue of the collection and change the problem of dealing with physical objects into a more manageable one of handling words and numbers. Patterns are then more easily detected. Another method is to choose a part of the collection and start to examine it thoughtfully, comparing objects with one another and relating them to their original context – in other words, to carry out purposeful research with the aim of producing a document which advances understanding both of the objects and of some more general question. These generalisations can be applied not only to collections of objects, but to words, images, events, social roles and many other things.

The purpose of this chapter is to explore some of the links between museums and ethnology. In the remainder of this introduction, the connection between collecting, ethnology and the antiquarian tradition is examined. This is followed by a discussion of some aspects of the nature of material culture, the reality which shapes what museums might collect, and an outline of museum history. Next, I examine the question of the extent to which different kinds of museum are to various degrees ethnological, and the chapter ends with brief comments on the importance of museums, and of ethnology.

The collecting and ordering of information was a distinguished learned tradition from classical antiquity. In the Hellenistic period, this antiquarianism included the collecting of traditions about individual cities, sanctuaries, gods and institutions; the systematic description of marvels; the recording of inscriptions; and the establishing of chronologies. The antiquarian tradition, as a way of approaching the past, was distinct from the study of the history of power and politics, which some argue stemmed from Thucydides. When the tradition was revived in the sixteenth and seventeenth centuries, its empirical basis was emphasised, and the collectors of Roman coins and the assemblers of the first local histories saw Galileo as an inspiration, because he confronted dogmatic theology with his own astronomical and physical observations. Being an antiquary meant being objective.[2]

Travel literature was part of the same tradition, exemplified by the collection of accounts of voyages: Englishman Richard Hackluyt, to name the most famous editor, assembled descriptions of obscure places so that they could be compared and understood in the light of others, and so guiding exploration and assessing the opportunities for manufacture and commerce. This activity is similar to the detailed descriptions of familiar places by scholars such as the Dane Ole Worm and the Englishman Robert Plot.[3] In Scotland, Martin Martin's accounts of the Western Isles (1703 and 1716, the second edition omitting some material that is in the first) are the first in this genre, and are notable for their bias towards folklore.[4]

The systematic collection of the people's culture began in the second half of the eighteenth century. Peter Burke's list of important books in this area, which covers the whole of Europe, includes seven relating to Scotland in his first twenty-three (dating from 1760 to 1803), including the ballad collections of Herd, Pinkerton and Walter Scott.[5] Museum collections of folklife start considerably later – Burke notes that 'a serious interest in folk-art did not develop until after 1850, perhaps because popular artefacts were not threatened by mass-production until this time'.[6] One hesitates to accept this explanation: in Britain, at least, cheap pottery, glass and textiles had minimised the place of objects made in the community and the home before 1825. It is certainly true that élite culture in the nineteenth century was based on texts rather than objects and images.

MATERIAL CULTURE: THE STUFF THAT GETS INTO MUSEUMS

'Material culture' is an ambiguous phrase which has been used at various points on a scale between two extremes. At one pole it is a synonym for 'objects', and at the other it includes not only the objects used by a culture but also everything to do with them, including their making, plus other aspects such as their place in ritual and their role as markers of status. In the latter case 'material culture' can come close to 'culture'. Nevertheless, it is still something distinct, because the object and issues to do with it are always in the foreground.

To what extent is material culture a museum subject? The question is worth asking, because although museums are thought of as storehouses of objects, in fact most objects do not end up in museums, and the contents of museums are hardly representative of the selection of objects in the real world and their relative numbers. In addition, many objects, including almost all food, are made to be ephemeral, and many more, such as clothes, are only preserved with strenuous effort or great good luck. Important objects are sometimes so large that they can only be preserved with vast resources – like the warship *Vaasa* (1628) in Stockholm, which is housed in a museum of its own, a building containing one object, and a notably unsuccessful one at that, for the badly designed ship sank at the beginning of her first voyage. Although open-air museums collect and display buildings, they are usually fairly small and traditional, and buildings are typically preserved where they were built and not in museums.

In the sense that there are far more objects, and types of object, in the globalising world of the twenty-first century, material culture has changed since the smaller world of (say) a seventeenth-century Scottish parish, where the range of tools, utensils and clothes was quite small. However, the material culture was just as rich as it is now, although far more of it originated in the skilled use of simple tools, in making objects in the community, and in mending and maintaining them – hence the regional variations in tools and implements. Knowledge and skill are essential parts of material culture.

The material aspect of a culture includes a number of subcultures, often based on work. Each of the traditional trades had a material subculture, mostly consisting of tools – the contents of the smithy or the joiner's workshop – some of which became extensive in the nineteenth century. The blacksmith, who made almost all of his own implements, normally had a wide range of tools from the late eighteenth century onwards, when iron became cheap. Some aspects of leisure had many different objects associated with them. Curling is a clear example: by the middle of the nineteenth century the play involved not only the stones, but also tee markers and a smith-made iron footboard to stand on; some clubs had badges and uniforms, and almost all played for medals; and in the evening the curlers dined with trophies and perhaps the club's snuff mull on the table. It is perhaps unsurprising that the Royal Caledonian Curling Club, for example, plans to open a museum to display its collection: some of the most successful small museums focus on a single sport or occupation, such as the Musée de l'Archerie at Crépy-en-Valois or the Deutches Hirtenmuseum (shepherding) at Hersbrück, near Nuremberg.

Objects are evidence of the past, but they can be difficult to read. Whether a ceramic pot has been made by a master craftsman, or – as in the case of a piece of *crogan* – by someone with no specialist skills, is usually evident. Moving from there to a certain knowledge of the reason why the object was made, why it was made in this way, who made it and where, and what its cultural significance was, is a long journey and perhaps an impossible one. Tiny details can be significant. Wear marks on spade shafts can help to interpret the way they were used, and the direction of movement of plough pebbles through the soil can be established by looking at the striations on them, and the existence of leading and training edges.

Sometimes progress can be made by examining groups of objects. For example, good thermometers (that is, ones that give the same readings as others made by the same craftsman) were being made in the Netherlands by Daniel Fahrenheit by 1720 and in Scotland or England by about 1740. Did the Scots, and in particular Alexander Wilson of St Andrews, learn the technique from the Dutch or the English? The scale on Fahrenheit's instruments was divided every four degrees, and so were Wilson's, but the English thermometers are divided at 5-degree intervals, making it highly probable that the Scots learned from Amsterdam.

There are two kinds of aids to the examination of objects.[7] First, scientific analysis can produce data which relate to the manufacture of objects: for example, X-ray fluorescence on the glaze of ceramics can show which pieces came from the same pottery. Pattern-recognition software has been used to make an objective assessment of which Lewis chessmen are closely similar to one another and therefore probably made by the same craftsman or group of craftsmen, and which are different.[8] Second, archaeological and, in particular, anthropological theory can be used to evaluate the way in which the objects related to their social environment. Exchange theory, which stems from Marcel Mauss' *Essai sur le Don* (1925), can be used to look at the reasons why gifts and prizes are given and accepted.[9] Mary Douglas has shown that the changing views of people living in a culture as to the ideal form of that culture can be used to explain changes in the decorative arts.[10]

Often, objects are better treated as sources of questions than as packages of evidence. Why is it like this? Why is it different from that one? The objects themselves may point to answers, as in the case of the thermometers. Sometimes progress can be made by imagining the object in use in a real situation, and understanding what the ploughman or the angler was trying to do. However, usually the most fruitful approach is to move from the object to text, seeking there an explanation for its use, clues which suggest its cultural importance, and also the vocabulary of its parts and its use. When studying subcultures which still exist, or which are clearly remembered by those still living, there is also the opportunity, if not an imperative, to talk.

MUSEUM HISTORY AND THE AIMS OF MUSEUMS

When the museum emerged in the Renaissance as an art form in which a wealthy gentleman could indulge himself, it immediately appeared in a number of forms. Some collections consisted of the strange productions of nature, from unicorns' horns (in fact narwhal tusks) to meteorites. The Germans had a name for each one: the *Wunderkammer*, *Schatzkammer*, and so on. With these, we are far from ethnology, because the motives for making the collections ranged from showing the owner's wealth and taste to exemplifying the power and creativity of God. When public collections were made by the universities, such as Oxford's Ashmolean Museum (1683), the curators promoted reverence for their subject matter (art, or history, or classical Greece, say), a serious approach to it, and a wide-ranging intellectual curiosity. The museums were something like a temple, and their legacy is the idea that a museum can be contemplated upon, brooded over, and so be the birthplace of thoughts.

In the eighteenth century, French Enlightenment thinkers disliked antiquarianism, seeing it as a fascination with details rather than a focus on the great project of reason confronting superstition. In addition, antiquarianism was concerned only with the past. The great *Encyclopédie* (1751–65) of Diderot and d'Alembert, which, significantly, had no biographical entries, placed itself in the present through tactics such as the detailed description of how each type of tradesman carried out his work. It also tried to tackle the whole world, not just some antiquarian corners. The *Encyclopédie* became the model for nineteenth-century technical museums, including the Industrial Museum of Scotland (1854), which metamorphosed in stages into the Royal Scottish Museum (1903). The first director, George Wilson, sought sequences of objects from the raw material to the finished product: the bar steel, the roughly hammered blade, and the polished and mounted lancet ready to be sold. Wilson's aim was to educate and inspire the people who designed and made things; museums have had links with social and economic goals which go far beyond the museum's display cases.

One way of assessing the collections in museums is to ask how well they cover their field. Specialist museums are always aware of what it would take to form a comprehensive collection. Natural history collections can have the same aim – to have one of everything, a kind of dead ark. In the nineteenth century, archaeological museums, including that of the Society of Antiquaries of Scotland, had a similar goal: to collect as much as possible so that it became clear what was common and what was rare, and so that the variation within a type could be studied. Other institutions sought sufficient material to enable thinking on a problem: the Pitt Rivers Museum at Oxford collected all over the globe to promote the understanding of other civilisations and the relationships between them, and ultimately of the nature of humankind.

Removing an object from context changes it and limits it, and this is a very strong argument for recording in detail and in situ. The issue is less acute in the instance of objects that were made to be looked at, and indeed some objects were created to look meaningful in a situation not unlike a museum – in a church or temple, say, or in the parlour of a Victorian industrialist. Leaving aside these exceptions, there are two linked issues: how to explain the significance of a museum object to the public; and how to create and sustain a rich understanding for the specialist, including museum staff, and ranging from the present into the distant future. Both are difficult once personal contact with the culture in question has been lost – once we are dealing, say, with something that dates from before our parents' lives. The method therefore is to absorb the facts and evaluate their significance – which takes us into the slippery and evasive area of meanings and emotions – and then to write in a concise and sensitive way. This is a counsel of perfection.

Open-air museums are discussed elsewhere in this volume,[11] while agricultural museums are discussed elsewhere in the series.[12] They are central to ethnography as it is practised in Britain at the moment, so here I will make only two points to set them in perspective. First, the way such museums are viewed has changed over time. The museum of the Highland and Agricultural Society was intended to promote modern farming methods that were bringing about increased productivity, but now it is a distant link with a phase of change which took place over 150 years ago. The second point arises from the fact that the models in this particular collection are important, for the full-size objects do not survive. A central problem with agricultural and open-air museums is that machinery and buildings can only be collected in limited numbers because of their size, and this emphasises the need for careful choice, and for as much recording in the field as possible.

'Folk art' is an uncomfortable concept which has only limited application in Scotland. In most parts of Europe, attractive objects were produced by country people for their own consumption in the pre-industrial world. Catholic and Orthodox church buildings and their contents were sources of colour, design and imagery. As soon as a market appeared for them in the cities, production was skewed towards the most saleable things, and urbanites started to wear or collect them. Intermediaries appeared, cutting the maker and the purchaser off from one another, such as the firms that bought Shetland knitting and exploited the knitters by paying them in goods rather than money, until the Truck Act of 1872. 'Folk art' is an unhelpful term because it moves attention onto the object as an object (to be sold and bought) and away from the world in which it was created and the meanings that it contained. There is a rich tradition, for example in Eastern Europe, of the bride and groom wearing elaborate clothes on their wedding day; but it is more productive to think of the meaning of marriage, the rituals and the changes of status involved, rather than looking only at the clothes. The introduction of visual representations, including images of the human figure, into the homes of working people in Scotland did not start until cheap transfer-printed pottery began to be manufactured around the end of the eighteenth century. One way of looking at this is to say that folk art in Lowland Scotland was very limited and was probably made up largely of clothes; alternatively, we might say that before and after the introduction of industrially made ceramics, the interesting art form was the home itself, laid out with plain objects made by the blacksmith, the joiner, and at home (and, later, bought in shops) and assembled thoughtfully into a practical and visual whole.

Museums collect objects both actively and passively. The latter form of acquisition depends on what is offered to the collections and so is not systematic, though randomness and opportunism have the virtue of getting away from the curator's personal bias. Active collecting is based on knowledge of a subject area: it is almost impossible to define boundaries and implement thoughtful collecting without knowledge. It is a truism that ethnological writing is preceded by ethnographic research – description comes before analysis and explanation. Ethnographic research also precedes collecting.

MUSEUMS AND ETHNOLOGY

To what extent are museums ethnological? Three questions can help to make an assessment. Does the museum approach its subject with its focus at the level of the individual and the small group, the latter usually being the family, the work group (say on a farm) or a voluntary association? Does it try to explain the way in which people lived, either looking at their whole lives or at some distinct part of them – or, to put it more intellectually, does it express functionalist anthropology? Does it enable comparison between life in different places or at different times? These questions can be applied to a museum's collections, to its displays as a whole, and to individual galleries.

Some countries have national ethnological museums. In Budapest, the displays in the Néprajzi Múzeum (Museum of Ethnography) are sufficiently large to give an overview of traditional life, including farming methods. Most striking is a huge map of Hungary as it was before World War I, from the Adriatic to Transylvania, indicating the areas where the different racial groups lived. The Heeresgeschichtliches (Army) Museum in Vienna makes a point about the diversity of the Austro-Hungarian Empire by showing pamphlets giving basic instructions to new recruits about 1910, all with the same content but in fifteen languages – illustrating how social perspectives can appear in unexpected places. The National History Museum at St Fagans, west of Cardiff, has been re-displayed in the twenty-first century to address the whole of life in Wales and the nature of Welshness. Whilst the result is admirable, one cannot but regret the loss of an earlier gallery which described the intensively worked countryside of the nineteenth century with, for example, different designs of hedging tools from different counties – a good piece of functionalist anthropology. In all of these museums, the displays pass the tests I have set. In national institutions, however, one must be aware of the possibility of political bias. Muzeul Taranului Roman (the Romanian Peasant Museum) in Bucharest has extensive displays on the traditional lives of the Romanian people, which is not the same as the people of Romania, where there are several important racial minorities involved, particularly Hungarian and German ones in Transylvania, whose cultures are distinct.

The Museum of Scotland (opened 1998) is an example of a general history museum that is ethnological in three senses. Obviously, it contains a wide selection of objects, and they have been chosen and displayed in such a way as to act as a compendium of Scotland's material culture. Second, the objects include material that relates to the history of popular culture, including basketwork, farming implements and sporting equipment. Finally, the objects are related to their context through extensive publication in journals (for more than 200 years), monographs and exhibition catalogues, and to the Scottish Life Archive. This kind of presentation, in which the cultures of the élite and the ordinary people are shown together, is typical of local museums all over Europe, and of regional museums such as the Musée Dauphinois in Grenoble and most of the German Landesmuseums, but is not common at the national level – although the marvellous Germanisches Nationalmuseum in Nuremburg displays farmhouse models, ex votos, a huge collection of the work of country craftsmen in the same building as archaeological material, and paintings by Albrecht Dürer.

The local museum has the role of showing what is distinctive about this one place, and this means showing not only what is different about it – which museums often try to do – but also illustrating the ways in which it is similar to other places. The latter is done less often, and it is a shortcoming of publications on local history. A step halfway towards illustrating similarity is to relate the local to the regional and the national, but explicit comparison, a key tool of ethnology, is usually a more revealing method.

A specialist museum seems to examine one aspect of society, but usually it says a lot about society as a whole by commenting on one specific aspect ('the world in a grain of sand'). For example, food museums (there are ones concentrating on asparagus, potato dumplings, pasta, cider, bread and much more) typically discuss farming, economics, transport, industrial processing and changing taste. Their displays are often strongly ethnological, because their subject is production and consumption, or they are about cultural expression and this, plus the obvious concentration on objects, means that their concern is with the local.

The Musée International du Carnaval et du Masque at Binche (Belgium) gives an account of Binche's own carnival, and of other Belgian ones, and also explores other European traditions of donning masks and dressing up.[13] Its clear focus enables it to show the richness and strangeness of masqueing, the creativity of the members of the community who made the disguises, the civic pride in continuing the processions and rituals year after year, and the range of responses to the dominating fears in life: of the failure of the community, the death of the individual, the blighting of crops, extreme weather, and the instability of this false world. As well as material from Belgium, it displays costume from most of Europe, and there is a little African material too. Photographs and video show the processions, dances and other rituals in which the costume is worn. The displays in this museum are based on the comparative method, and are complemented by well-illustrated publications which take the context-setting further.

Of course, it is possible to have a satisfactory specialist museum which does not use the comparative method: the Museum of Childhood in Edinburgh is purely about the British experience of childhood, and the National Railway Museum at York is almost entirely concerned with railways in Britain, its excellent library holding little on Europe or the rest of the world. Words that give a museum national status ('National', 'Scottish', etc.) usually point to the exclusion of material from elsewhere. 'International', however, suggests cultural comparison, as at Binche, the Musée International de l'Horlogerie at La Chaux-de-Fonds (Switzerland), or the International Slavery Museum in Liverpool.

Art galleries contain special, high-status objects which may interest the ethnologist in two ways. Paintings made for churches have both a ritual purpose and also contain elaborate symbolism that relates to wider issues of religious belief and practice. Alternatively, a painting can be examined for the evidence it contains about contemporary life – dress, agricultural methods, and much more. These details may be incidental – the harness of the donkey in a *Flight Into Egypt*, say – or in a genre painting they may be deliberate, as in the work of Scots such as Alexander Carse or David Allan. Evidence is to be handled warily, for the painters were thoughtful about what they were doing and were always likely to be steering the viewer towards what the painter wanted them to see and feel. Of course, what has been said in this paragraph concerns the ethnologist as visitor to an art gallery: most art historians are ethnologists by another name, concerned with the conception, production and distribution of one kind of object.

We can now return to the question of to what extent museums are ethnological. The first answer is that, as I have outlined, museum displays vary in their ethnological nature. Second, the prepared visitor can make any visit ethnological: an afternoon in an aquarium could be spent studying 'pure' natural history, but the visitor could also use the experience to learn more about fish and shellfish that have been caught and collected, and gain insights into human issues by looking at the behaviour of aquatic animals. So for the ethnologically inclined (and this includes many people who do not recognise the word or the idea of ethnology, but enjoy trying to see the world from someone else's point of view) any museum is more ethnological to the ethnologist than it is to the non-ethnologist. Finally, all collections are ethnological because there is an ethnology of collecting as a purposeful cultural activity.

CONCLUSION: CONTACT WITH ANOTHER REALITY

Museums are enjoyable because they are both focused on their subject and are highly interdisciplinary, and at the same time they relate outwards to museum visitors. In Alan Bennett's play *The History Boys*, whose subjects are education and healthy ambition, the central character is a teacher who several times says of knowledge: 'Pass it on! Pass it on!' Thus in the museum too. Museums are important: they are part of our civilisation, and part of passing it on.

Museums are central to the ethnological endeavour because, through real objects, they give access to the ways in which people lived – the life of a fishwife, a ploughman or a cooper. An understanding of how people functioned leads to the beliefs upon which they based their lives, the love of land, the fear of the sea, the importance of the family, the respect for craftsmanship, the awareness of nature and the need to work with it, and often a scepticism coupled with loyalty towards the laird and the minister. Historical ethnology is about lost forms of reality, and it bears a similar relation to our lives in Scotland in the present day as life in exotic cultures. The task of the ethnologist and the anthropologist is to understand these cultures as living wholes, complete meshes of ideas and objects; as, for the novelist, it involves the attempt to live in others' minds.

ACKNOWLEDGEMENTS

I am grateful to Dorothy Kidd for her comments on a draft of the chapter, and to Sarah A Laurenson.

NOTES

1 Bannatyne, 1873–1901, IV, 1025.
2 Momigliano, 1990.
3 Worm, 1655; Plot 1677 and 1686.
4 Martin, 1703; 1716.
5 Burke, 1979, 287–8.
6 Burke, 1979, 7.
7 Kingery, 1996.

8 Caldwell, Hall and Wilkinson, 2010.

9 Mauss, 1990.

10 Douglas, 1996, 50–76.

11 See Chapter 6, 'Scotland's Open Air Museums'.

12 Dornan and Fenton, 2011.

13 Revelard, 1991, 90–5.

BIBLIOGRAPHY AND FURTHER READING

Alexander, E P. *Museum Masters: Their Museums and their Influence*, Nashville, 1983.

Bannatyne, G. *The Bannatyne Manuscript*, 4 vols, Glasgow, 1873–1901.

Brown, I G. *The Hobby-Horsical Antiquary*, Edinburgh, 1980.

Burke, P. *Popular Culture in Early Modern Europe*, London, 1979.

Caldwell, D H, Hall, M A and Wilkinson, C M. The Lewis hoard of gaming pieces: A re-examination of their context, meanings, discovery and manufacture, *Medieval Archaeology*, 53 (2009), 155–202.

Dornan, D M and Fenton, A. Agricultural museums. In Fenton, A and Veitch, K, eds, *Scottish Life and Society. A Compendium of Scottish Ethnology, Volume 2: Farming and the Land*, Edinburgh, 2011, 924–44.

Douglas, M. *Thought Styles. Critical Essays on Good Taste*, London, 1996.

Fenton, A. Schottische Volkskunst. In Deneke, B, ed., *Europäischer Volkskunst*, Frankfurt, 1981.

Graham, A. Records and opinions: 1780–1930, *PSAS*, 102 (1969–70), 241–84.

Kingery, W D, ed. *Learning from Things: Method and Theory of Material Culture Studies*, Washington, DC, 1996.

Martin, M. *A Description of the Western Islands of Scotland*, London, 1703; 2nd edn, London, 1716.

Mauss, M. *The Gift*, trans. W D Hills, London, 1990.

Momigliano, A. *The Classical Foundations of Modern Historiography*, Berkeley, 1990.

Murray, D. *Museums: Their History and Use*, 3 vols, Glasgow, 1904.

Plot, R. *The Natural History of Oxford-shire*, Oxford, 1677.

Plot, R. *The Natural History of Stafford-shire*, Oxford, 1686.

Revelard, M. *Musée Internationale du Carnaval et du Masque, Binche*, Brussels, 1999.

Worm, O. *Museum Wormianum*, 2 vols, Leyden, 1655.

6 Scotland's Open Air Museums

BOB POWELL

Scotland's open air museums provide unique resources for ethnological research and education and have led the way in introducing innovative means of communicating information about Scotland's material culture in its social context. The word 'museum' can summon up a vision of a single building, sometimes purpose built, with glass cases, perhaps filled with thematic or iconic specimens. Here, the visitor is probably excluded from direct contact with the artefact, receiving information through a label or other non-personal interaction. Further, the interpretive experience, either personal or received, is probably sensory-limited, including few opportunities for engagement with features, staff, or activities. This was the case in the UK into the twentieth century, though in recent decades substantial efforts have been made to enhance the visitor experience in conventional museums. However, a visit to an open air museum offers a marked contrast.

THE START OF THE OPEN AIR MUSEUM MOVEMENT

Towards the end of the nineteenth century, a new approach to museum display was introduced in Scandinavia, with pioneering museums in Norway and Sweden. Artur Hazelius is generally regarded as the father of the movement. Born in Stockholm in 1833, Hazelius – teacher, publisher, patriot and visionary – in common with other observers of the time, noted how improvement, industrialisation and emigration were having a radical effect on the traditional rural life and agricultural practices of the Swedish countryside. This spurred him to start collecting examples of rural material culture in the 1870s and, in 1873, to open his first museum, the Scandinavian Ethnographic Collection in Stockholm.[1] It was his approach to interpretation that differed from the norm for he displayed his collection in recreated interiors and where relevant, incorporated life-size manikins in traditional costumes. Such techniques won him awards such as that at the 1878 Paris World Exhibition. Indeed, the role of the international exhibition in constructing national identity in the period is an important one in the history of the open air museum movement.[2]

The ever growing collections made by Hazelius were ultimately to find their place in the Nordiska Museet. The impetus of this museum was still tending towards the traditional and gave Hazelius little scope for acquiring, displaying and interpreting larger items and particularly buildings. Professor Nils-Arvid Bringéus has written that Hazelius 'was moving even further towards realism by rebuilding or reconstructing whole houses and courtyards. No one had ever thought about building such a collection as a permanent educational exhibition for the public. The response he received at home and abroad shows that this was something new.'[3] Following his acquisition of the Mora Cottage from Dalarna in 1885, he worked towards the purchase of a site on which to construct an open-air museum. Hazelius explained 'it was hither that my thoughts removed of founding a museum which was unlike any existing museum, namely, an open-air museum devoted to folklore and the history of civilization'.[4]

Hazelius inaugurated his open air museum at Skansen on 11 October 1891. The site, the name of which refers to a small stockade, was located in the Swedish capital and grew to thirty hectares in area. Buildings and smaller artefacts supported by interpreted environments, livestock, demonstrations of traditional crafts and festivities including music and dance aimed 'to present folk life in living brushstrokes'.[5] So influential did this concept become that 'Skansen' was adopted as a generic term for an open air museum in many cultures. By the time of his death in 1901, Hazelius had initiated a movement with international ramifications.

THE UNITED KINGDOM MOVEMENT STARTS IN SCOTLAND

Professor Bjarne Stoklund has described the importance of international exhibitions in the development of displays of national identity with particular reference to northern Europe.[6] The Scottish Exhibition of National History, Art and Industry held in Glasgow's Kelvingrove Park in 1911 featured 'An Clachan', a recreated Highland village with a range of vernacular buildings providing a setting for a display of crafts including spinning and blacksmithing.[7] This was an early attempt in Scotland to offer an open-air museum experience and was repeated at the Empire Exhibition (Scotland) held in Bellahouston Park in Glasgow in 1938.[8]

If Hazelius displayed a passion for encouraging Swedes to know themselves, for 'Know Yourself' was his museum's motto, the same was to be reflected by Isabel Frances Grant (1887–1983), the equally passionate and determined founder of the Highland Folk Museum, the first UK mainland open-air museum. Isabel Grant's story is well documented in her own memoir *The Making of 'Am Fasgadh'* (2007) and elsewhere.[9] Briefly, Isabel Grant, who had Highland family roots, was born in Edinburgh on 21 July 1887 but raised in London where her Aunt Fan[10] took her to the London galleries and museums, where she viewed and criticised 'serried ranks of specimens'.[11] As she was to declare in later life, 'Things look so much more at home if not imprisoned in glass cases.'[12]

When she was seventeen, Isabel's parents took her to Antwerp where she viewed the Musée Plantin, a realistically recreated and interpreted print works of seventeenth-century origin. That visit, where 'a feeling of continuity with the past became more and more potent'[13], was a revelation to Isabel. Some time later, Isabel started on the transcription of the account book of her great-great-great-grandfather, William Mackintosh, who had farmed at Dunachton in Badenoch for over fifteen years from 1768. This task gave Isabel an insight into early Highland agriculture and was ultimately to culminate in the publication of her first book, *Every-day Life on an Old Highland Farm, 1769–82*, in 1924. It was about that time Isabel was taken on a cruise that included Stockholm where 'we went to Skansen and I saw my first folk museum'.[14] 'In eager delight I wandered from one to another of the little houses . . . Then I began to notice that among the other visitors there were a great many obviously of the country – some of them real country people and suddenly I thought, "Oh! I do wish that there was a Highland Folk Museum for Highland people to see."'[15] 'I could never hope for anything more rewarding than to create a museum adequately preserving the setting of the past life of the stock of which I am sprung – the people of the Highlands.'[16] This was the start of a journey for Isabel Grant that was to dominate her life and create a milestone in British museum development.

Buoyed by this vision, Isabel Grant's aspiration was to rescue those objects which were being discarded as 'old troke', and no longer considered relevant for a twentieth-century lifestyle.[17] Her first opportunity to put this material on public display came in 1930 with the mounting of a Highland Exhibition in Inverness Town Hall, composed of everyday items from her own growing collection and loaned objects, augmented by associated songs, narratives and demonstrations. She hoped that this would encourage support for the creation of a folk museum but, in spite of the popular interest, the support was not forthcoming.

Undeterred, Grant next purchased a redundant church building on the island of Iona in 1935 with a view to creating a museum herself. She decided to call it *Am Fasgadh*, Gaelic for 'the shelter', for it was to be a place where 'the vanishing relics of our past … could be kept and cared for'.[18] The majority of these items were still relatively small, yet Grant was aware of other larger elements of the material culture including buildings, regretting that she had no opportunity to re-erect them on Iona.

Grant was unable to envisage taking the Museum any further on Iona; it was impractical for her purposes and, knowing that the mainland offered greater opportunities, she resolved to look for a new site. This she found at Laggan in Badenoch – another empty church – and she moved her collection there in the autumn of 1938.

By now Grant realised that the days of her 'most active collecting were over, though (she) was to go on learning more and more about the social conditions that had brought about the material setting that (she) was so anxious to reproduce'.[19] Grant thought more about what she had observed and learned. She felt that 'the Scandinavian open-air folk museums . . . seemed to represent a static state of society that has never existed in the Highlands' and 'in the Highlands . . . any attempt to preserve the setting of life in the past ought to take into account those well-marked periods into which it falls'.[20] She further realised some of the limitations: 'A folk museum can only try to indicate the vast changes in the ways of life of the country people that the Agricultural Revolution brought about.'[21]

The relocation to Laggan was only a temporary sojourn and a time of 'arrested development' owing to the outbreak of World War II.[22] The prospects at Laggan were unlikely to help her achieve her vision. However, the Pitmain Lodge site in nearby Kingussie became available and she was able to purchase it in 1943: 'It is a pleasant, Georgian house close to the station at Kingussie. The layout is particularly suitable for displaying a collection and it has three acres of ground for the erection of cottages.'[23] In establishing *Am Fasgadh* in Kingussie, Grant used the interior of the Lodge to display much of her collection in a traditional format. She also used the stables as the base for her reconstruction of an old dairy. Most significant, influenced by what she had seen at Skansen, was her opportunity to recreate rather than reconstruct four Highland and Island buildings. In an achievement remarkable in wartime, Grant opened her Highland Folk Museum on 1 June 1944. It was the first open-air museum on the British mainland.

Dr Grant's achievement (she was awarded an Honorary LLD by the University of Edinburgh in 1948) was a remarkable one, for she kept steadfastly to her vision and worked very much as an individual, without institutional support, devoting her time and her own resources to securing this museum for Scotland. To see how the founding of *Am Fasgadh* fits into the wider picture of major open air institutions in the United Kingdom, it should be noted that Cregneash, now the National Folk Museum on the Isle of Man, pre-dated it. At its inception in 1938, however, it comprised only the cottage of crofter and Manx speaker Harry Kelly. St Fagans, the Welsh Folk Museum situated near Cardiff and now known as St Fagans National History Museum, opened in 1948. The 170 acre Folk Museum which is part of the Ulster Folk and Transport Museum at Cultra near Belfast was instituted by Act of Parliament in 1958 but did not open until 1964. In England, the Weald and Downland Open Air Museum at Singleton, West Sussex, was founded in 1965 by Roy Armstrong but did not open until 1970. The concept for Beamish, the North of England Open Air Museum, was proposed as early as 1958 but it was not until 1970 that it came into being under the directorship of Frank Atkinson, opening to visitors in 1972.

The buildings recreated by Grant were first a 'cottage' which she considered characteristic of Inverness-shire. This thatched building was destroyed circa 1960 in a fire started by a spark from a passing steam train. Second, and ultimately an icon for the Museum, was a Lewis 'Black House', built under the close personal direction of a native of that island. The third structure was not a house but a Norse-style horizontal mill whose principal mechanism Grant had obtained from Lewis in return for a donation to the Stornoway hospital. Finally, her last cottage she described as being a later type of Highland dwelling.

With her buildings, Grant was able to achieve her vision of saving 'the old setting of our daily life'.[24] In them she used her collection as aids to their interpretation, employing objects in context as realistically as she could to evoke a sense of time and place and to stimulate memory. Real fires added a strong sensory experience. She employed very small-scale farming, feeling that 'the work of hay-making and presence of livestock played an important part in giving a homely feel to the Museum'.[25] Her livestock included a goat and Kirstie the cow, kept in the Lewis cottage byre, along with the milking stool and pail. Grant encouraged friends to contribute to the activities and she herself was often to be found engaging with her visitors whilst demonstrating traditional crafts.

As Isabel Grant grew older, she considered *Am Fasgadh*'s future, including its possible sale. In 1955, through the intervention of the Pilgrim Trust, she agreed to the Museum being managed by a Highland Museum Trust composed of representatives of the universities of Edinburgh, St Andrews, Glasgow and Aberdeen. It was Aberdeen University which was to take the lead in the Museum's administration, appointing George 'Taffy' Davidson as its first Curator.

Grant continued to take an active interest in the history and culture of the Highlands and in writing and publishing. Her first book had appeared in 1924, *Every-day Life on an Old Highland Farm, 1769–82*, based on the papers of an ancestor, and she was keenly interested in economic as well as social history. She had, in fact, honed her research skills as an assistant to John Maynard Keynes in London as a young woman. In 1961 she published *Highland Folk Ways*, which used the collections of *Am Fasgadh* to illustrate aspects of Highland life over the centuries. E Estyn Evans' *Irish Folk Ways* had appeared four years earlier.

The Highland Museum Trust and Davidson continued adding to Grant's significant collections but did not add to the vernacular structures. The Museum was strengthened, however, by the gift of the adjacent Churchill House in 1957 by the MacRobert Foundation, which the Trust redesigned to create a formal gallery space. By the 1970s the Trust was struggling to finance the Museum. In 1975 its administration briefly transferred to Badenoch District Council before later that year transferring in its entirety to Highland Regional Council, later Highland Council.

In 1976, R Ross Noble, who had been a roving curator for the Scottish Country Life Museums Trust, was appointed as curator and a process of rejuvenation began. Noble introduced open, thematic displays within the farming museum and visitor numbers grew as craft-based 'heritage in action' days enlivened Grant's structures. A travellers' 'gelly', a temporary shelter made of canvas over willow wands, would be erected for basket-making and story-telling sessions. Although no further permanent structures were added to the site, Noble did add one in 1980. This was an experimental timber cruck-framed, turf-walled, Central Highland-style house.[26] The house was put to various tests and although it did not survive, it was to become instrumental in later Highland Folk Museum developments.

THE HIGHLAND FOLK MUSEUM (NEWTONMORE)

The 1980s saw a major change for the Highland Folk Museum when Highland Regional Council and Noble began to investigate the opportunities that having a larger open-air museum site would create, including the chance to take Grant's original vision further forward. Several locations were considered but the one chosen and subsequently purchased in 1987 was the current 32 hectare site at Newtonmore, three miles south-west of the Kingussie site. This site was initially called the Highland Folk Park to differentiate it from the parent site.

Between 1987 and 1995, the infrastructure of the mile-long park was put in place. The site was subdivided, roads were created, field boundaries erected, woodland planted and an outline interpretation plan developed that in original outline would represent Highland rural life from the period of prehistory through to the twentieth century. When Bob Powell joined the Museum staff at the start of 1997, the principal vernacular structures in place were the original *in situ* early 1880s Aultlarie farm steading and the relocated Leanach Church from near Inverness. This is a 'tin tabernacle', a sectional building supplied by Spiers of Glasgow circa 1890 and rescued from demolition at the end of the 1980s. Simultaneously, an independent body, the Highland Vernacular Buildings Trust (HVBT), was established at the Park. In partnership with the Highland Folk Museum, its objectives included the teaching of traditional building skills that contributed to the Park's development, especially the timber-framed and heather-thatched 1700s Raitts Township reconstruction.

During development, issues arose from a local perception that 'nothing was happening'. In reality, a great deal was happening but the concept was not fully understood nor the effort involved fully appreciated. The time and work required for dismantling, moving, repairing and re-erecting one period structure is considerable but the result may appear insignificant. For the open-air museum curator, the site is the 'glass case' of the more traditional museum and time is needed to achieve results. The fact that open-air museums elsewhere had depended upon a similar time-frame was not always recognised by critics. The older Kingussie site was still open and attracting reasonable numbers of visitors. Smaller and compact, it still had much appeal, especially for the older visitors familiar with many of the items displayed. Some questioned the need for a new development.

But gradually the Park developed. The unique township grew and attracted interest not only from visitors for its portrayal of 1700s Highland life but also from academics and public bodies for the valuable experimental work carried out there relating to materials, techniques and structures in vernacular architecture. At Aultlarie farm, interpersonal engagement and interpretation centred on 1930s implements, machinery, crops and livestock. Over time more buildings were re-located including a Kingussie joiner's shop, Knockbain School, the Glenlivet post office, a Newtonmore tailor's shop, and others. In 2012 the interpreted structures number around thirty, with one or two being added each year. Daluaine Summer House opened in 2009, the township's Cottar's House in 2010, both the Highland Cottage and the Craig Dhu Tweed Cottage opened in 2011, and the Boleskine Shinty Pavilion was completed in 2012.

Eventually, there were further changes for both the Kingussie site and the Newtonmore park. Both sites were operated by the same permanent staff, numbering about nine, and at the start of 2002 Ross Noble retired and Bob Powell succeeded him as curator. The Highland Vernacular Buildings Trust, having become unviable, ceased operation and two of the craft workers transferred to the museum team. Steadily, the Park's reputation was growing as was an appreciation of its concept and ethos. As buildings were added and its living history interpretation developed, visitor numbers and accolades also grew. More people appreciated the hands-on sensory experience, interactive engagement and activities, especially the opportunities for learning, understanding, inspiration, enjoyment and – critically – relevance for younger people. Early awards included Scottish Museum of the Year in 2000 and the Sandford Award for Heritage Education in 2001, while more recently, the Association of Scottish Visitor Attractions (ASVA) selected it for its 2010 Award for Best Visitor Experience.

Inevitably, the Kingussie numbers started to decline as the Park's numbers increased. The balance point was reached in about 2001 but the Park's attendance figures increased significantly and by 2006 they were three times greater than those for Kingussie. Thereafter, factors including changes in visitors' interpretation preferences, the physical decline in the Kingussie buildings and the conflict in operating two related, similar sites so closely together led to an appraisals study in 2006 to establish the best way forward. The conclusion resulted in the closure of the Kingussie site by 2008, with resources concentrated on Newtonmore, which was re-established as the Highland Folk Museum. This logical move saw visitor numbers exceed 50,000 in 2010, over 25 per cent above those in 2009.

Further changes occurred in October 2011 when the administration of the Highland Folk Museum changed from the Highland Council to High Life Highland. This is a charitable company limited by guarantee which has a twenty-five year service delivery agreement to manage, develop and provide access to the site and the collections. Highland Council has, however, continued to invest in the Museum. In 2012 construction began at the site on the £3.7 million Am Fasgadh collections facility comprising collections storage, conservation laboratory, library, study and meeting areas.

AUCHINDRAIN

In a Scottish context, the next open-air museum to open to the public was the preserved Auchindrain (Gaelic for 'the field of the thorn tree') Township situated near Inveraray, Argyll. Here on the estate of the Duke of Argyll were the remains of a *baile* or township where a succession of joint tenants and cottars had lived for centuries. The complete or partial remnants of over twenty buildings and their associated adjacent fields, with rigs still obvious in the landscape, could be seen. With a documented history stretching back to circa 1470, the township was home to farming tenants until 1963 when the last tenant, Edward (Eddie) McCallum who had cultivated the fields until the mid-1950s, retired.

The significance of Auchindrain as one of the last surviving and accessible examples of the type of multiple tenancy community which characterised the Highlands and Islands of Scotland before the introduction of crofting, was recognised by three key people. These were Marion Campbell of Kilberry (1919–2000), Argyll historian, author and archaeologist, who had known the township for many years; Eric Cregeen (1921–1983), then Resident Tutor in Argyll for the University of Glasgow and a pioneer scholar of Highland social organisation, subsequently on the staff of the School of Scottish Studies at the University of Edinburgh; and Alexander Fenton (1929–2012), then Keeper at the National Museum of Antiquities of Scotland, who was introduced to the site by Miss Campbell.[27]

The timing for securing Auchindrain could probably not have been more auspicious since the sole remaining tenant was about to retire. The Duke of Argyll was approached by Campbell who agreed to the preservation of the township. This was followed by the establishment of the Auchindrain Committee who, having sought further advice from the Royal Commission on the Ancient and Historical Monuments of Scotland and others, subsequently transferred their responsibilities to the trustees of the newly formed Auchindrain Trust in 1964. The Trust included representatives from several local and national bodies including the National Museum of Scotland, the Countryside Commission, the National Trust for Scotland, and the Universities of Glasgow and Edinburgh. Auchindrain benefited early in its museum life from the attention of the Scottish Country Life Museums Trust.[28]

At Auchindrain, the buildings are *in situ* where originally erected over a period of two hundred years, the most recent being a Colt House built for the last tenant in the middle of the twentieth century. A plan of the township from the late eighteenth century shows the layout then, and continuing research in relevant documentary sources and through oral testimony and memory have enabled a picture of the Auchindrain families to be built up and information on the changing ways of life to be assembled. Artefacts directly connected to the site are still donated or acquired from time to time, most recently a marriage kist and the first 'wee grey Fergie' (Ferguson tractor) used there, to be restored for practical use on the site.

The designation of the Auchindrain township as a 'Recognised Collection of National Significance to Scotland' in 2008, under a scheme administered by Museums Galleries Scotland on behalf of the Scottish Government, has generated support for much of the recent research and development on the site. An active friends organisation gives much assistance with events and activities which animate and enliven the township and there is active engagement with the local community in ways which are mutually supportive. It is still managed by the Auchindrain Trust. In 2014 it will see its fiftieth anniversary, the year in which the Highland Folk Museum will see its seventieth, or its eightieth if one goes by the date, 1934, which Dr Grant gives as the year in which the idea of founding the Museum first came to her.[29]

PRIVATE COLLECTIONS AND THE DEVELOPMENT
OF SMALL RURAL LIFE MUSEUMS

It is interesting to reflect that by the 1960s there was a growing private interest in the preservation of agricultural heritage through the collection and working of traction engines, tractors, horse and other equipment. Part of this was undoubtedly fired by nostalgia and a harking back to earlier farming times, particularly associated with earlier industrialisation which even by the 1950s was remarkably different from that of the early part of the century. Farm machinery preservation societies developed and a growing number of farm-related collections, often on farms, and a willingness to display, demonstrate and interpret collections for interested people. It was logical that such collections should spur on the development of farming or rural life museums associated with existing buildings and often owned by private individuals. Several such enterprises developed during the 1970s and 1980s. These might not be defined as open-air museums but the principles and interest in them, in some ways similar or connected, were also ripe for helping further open-air museums to develop.

Adamston Agricultural Museum

A classic example was the opening of the Adamston Agricultural Museum in 1972 at Adamston, by Huntly, Aberdeenshire. The Museum's owner was Hew McCall-Smith, who on his farm exhibited over 500 items 'illustrative of the way of life and work on the land over the last 100 years' of the North-East.[30] McCall-Smith's collection comprised ploughs and other cultivation implements, horse harness, barn and dairying equipment, domestic utensils and so forth. An additional link to open-air museums was that McCall-Smith also 'went that extra mile' by holding events such as the 1979 'Farming Yesterday' weekend where working exhibits included threshing, horse ploughing, cheese- and butter-making, while non-material culture was represented by a Bothy Concert Party compèred by the broadcaster Robbie Shepherd, who introduced Eric Bell, then the Scottish Accordion Champion.[31]

The Adamston collection remained open to visitors until the early 1980s. It was in 1983 that Moray District Council was contemplating establishing an open-air farming museum, and Bob Powell was employed to help the subsequent development for which the proposal included the possible inclusion of the Adamston collection. Relevant contacts were made. However, the development of the Museum was not progressed and Powell subsequently moved on to the Weald & Downland Open Air Museum in West Sussex. This was not the end of the Adamston collection, however, for it was to go on to play a role in the development of another open-air museum.

Aden, the North East of Scotland Agricultural Heritage Centre

The North East of Scotland Agricultural Centre, more recently known as the Aberdeenshire Farming Museum, is situated within Aden Country Park near Mintlaw and nine miles west of Peterhead. Developed by Banff and Buchan District Council, the initial impetus in 1976 was to restore the unique semi-circular home farm situated within the developing Country Park on the Aden Estate. This was part of 'a growing awareness of the importance of preserving the region's farming heritage'.[32] Notably, in 1983 the District Council sought to enhance the already popular Aden Estate display by purchasing the significant agricultural collection amassed by Hew McCall-Smith of Adamston, Huntly.[33] By bringing together the Aden farm steading and the Adamston collection, the council went a long way to establishing the groundwork for another rural life museum within the public domain and with the possibility to develop its open-air potential. The latter was taken further forward by the addition of the Hareshowe Working Farm. Hareshowe of Ironside is a typical small Buchan farm steading, originally located nine miles from Aden Country Park and owned by the Barron family from 1935 until the late 1980s. It was dismantled stone by stone and rebuilt on its present site in 1990–1, where it was returned to its mid-1950s character. The fact that the steading was dismantled and relocated takes it into the open-air museum category of incorporating both *in situ* and relocated structures. Associated with Hareshowe are twenty acres of land for the related interpretation of traditional farming practices. The Hareshowe farm house as well as the bothy kitchen within the curved steading may both be used to interpret domestic life. An account of the development of Aden may be found in Andrew Hill's[34] contribution to *Tools and Traditions*, the Festschrift presented in 1993 to Alexander Fenton, who had been an important source of encouragement and practical assistance in its development.

Ladycroft Farm Museum

Another example with similarities to Adamston is a private collection of primarily horse-drawn agricultural equipment which was amassed by Charlie and Moira Spence near Rothes, Moray, by the early 1980s. The small museum at the owner's home was available for visitors and the collection was locally well received. By the later 1980s, through the auspices of Moray Council, the Spences and their collection were moved to the nearby Ladycroft steading at Archiestown. The steading was owned by Moray Council and Bob Powell was initially involved with the proposal that would have established the collection in the steading, interpreted and supported by working activities. The intended result would have been, like many other similar venues, more of a working croft rather than an open-air museum. But Ladycroft did not fulfil its potential and by the early 1990s it was closed and much of the collection was moved under the care of Moray Council's museums into storage in Elgin. From there, in 1997, when Powell joined the Highland Folk Museum staff, the collection was transferred to Highland Council where it was to contribute to the developing Highland Folk Museum site at Newtonmore.

KITTOCHSIDE, THE NATIONAL MUSEUM OF RURAL LIFE

Kittochside, first known as the Museum of Scottish Country Life when it opened in 2001 and since 2006 as the National Museum of Rural Life, is located near East Kilbride and includes a working farm as well as collections facilities, exhibition display areas and other visitor amenities.

The origins of the Museum lie within the National Museum of Antiquities collections which were used to form the Scottish Agricultural Museum adjacent to the Royal Highland Showground at Ingliston near Edinburgh. Managed by the National Museums' Country Life Section, the Museum formed part of the remit of the Scottish Country Life Museums Trust, whose roving curator assisted at other museums such as Auchindrain. Within the management of the national museum there was an interest in developing an open-air version of the Scottish Agricultural Museum, where the permanent collections could be complemented by working exhibits, live interpretation and events. Different potential sites were investigated and the solution came in a partnership with The National Trust for Scotland, to whom the 170 acre farm of Wester Kittochside was donated in 1992 by Mrs Margaret Reid, whose late husband's family had farmed there since the sixteenth century.

The site offered potential to illustrate farming practice, provide interpretation and add further buildings including accommodation for the rural life collections of the National Museum. The latter was designed by the architectural firm of Page and Park and reflects the rural vernacular of a barn while using modern materials such as concrete in place of timber. While the exhibition building comprehensively reflects the material culture of Scottish agriculture and the people engaged in it from the sickle to the combine harvester, it is the open-air interpretation at Kittochside that adds an extra dimension. When the buildings were gifted, several elements, both domestic and working, related to the late eighteenth century period of agricultural improvement and onwards. However, the Dutch barn constructed in 1949 and parts of the house reflecting the 1950s were instrumental in the decision to select an early 1950s date for the focus of interpretation. This way it was possible to include both horse and tractor operations, maintain a herd of Ayrshire cattle milked by machine, and so forth.

Critically, this decision brought the period of interpretation into living memory for more people, addressed issues such as the need for 'modern' collecting and the declining availability of people with certain 'traditional' skills of working the land and managing livestock. Another key factor was that the development and, particularly, the interpretation complemented other open-air museums within Scotland.

A RURAL LIFE TRAIL

Informally and uniquely, interpretive and cooperative strategy opportunities for Scottish rural open-air museums have been created. This was in earlier days supported by the Scottish Country Life Museums Trust and more recently by Scottish members of the UK-wide body formerly known as the Rural Life Museums Action Group (RuLMAG), now the Rural Museums Network.

In effect, there is potential for the creation of a national rural open-air museums trail, not only a physical one reflecting regional variations but also one that reflects Scottish agriculture through time. In a simple overview, the Highland Folk Museum currently represents the eighteenth century and the first half of the twentieth; Auchindrain, a wide span but in particular the nineteenth and first half of the twentieth centuries; Aden, up to the 1950s; and Kittochside, clearly the 1950s but with collections that represent both earlier times and more recent technology. The interpretation time distinctions are not wholly clear but there is enough to afford variety and avoid a degree of duplication of effort in, for example, vernacular architecture, agricultural practices and non-material culture. A principal benefit is the opportunity afforded to define Scottish 'nationally distributed collections' and to take a holistic approach to collecting, interpretation and promotion. That the approach can work was demonstrated when, in the early 2000s under the aegis of the National Museums, a shared promotion policy was undertaken that included the Highland Folk Museum alongside Kittochside.

DIFFERENT APPROACHES

If there is to be one contrast between open-air or living history museums and the more traditional museums with, to paraphrase Dr Grant, their glass cases full of serried ranks of specimens, it is that the former may provide comprehensive sensory experiences. The 'real thing' may inspire wonder and learning in both types, but the former can trigger emotions mixed with nostalgia, and aligned with the senses of seeing, feeling, touching, hearing, smelling and even tasting. Whether it is an original artefact or a re-creation, the value lies in the experience of context, the opportunity for first hand engagement or interaction, perhaps seeing something in action or, better still, having the chance to participate actively.

A common perception is that open-air museums are either partly or wholly rural in nature, literally in the open air. Many, like the original Skansen, started on green field sites where any original structures were rural, such as the farm buildings and homes at the Highland Folk Museum, Auchindrain, Aden and Kittochside. However, the open-air or living history interpretation of urban landscapes or industrial life bears consideration.

The open-air museum interpretation of a large scale *in situ* urban landscape has not yet occurred in Scotland. Worthy examples would include Gamla Linköping in Sweden or Colonial Williamsburg in Virginia, USA. In the Scottish context, urban interpretation includes the National Trust for Scotland's Tenement House at 145 Buccleuch Street, Garnethill, Glasgow.

For the interpretation of industrial life there are several examples where there are structures, associated artefacts (some in working order) and interpretation by means of displays and live interpreters. The twenty-two acre Museum of Scottish Industrial Life at Coatbridge, known as Summerlee, is built around one of Scotland's principal hot blast process ironworks founded in 1836 by the Neilson family. The ironworks continued until 1926 and subsequently, the site was used for engineering operations, including the Hydrocon Crane Works, until it was acquired for the Museum in 1987. Since then, the Museum has developed its interpretation and expanded in open-air museum style. In addition to displays of its industrial collections, the Museum has added a reconstructed mine, miners' cottages and a sawmill, all of which are connected by an electric tramway. As with the other principal open-air museums, Summerlee incorporates retail and visitor facilities along with educational services, interpretive and interactive programmes.

The National Mining Museum Scotland, located at the Lady Victoria Colliery in Newtongrange, Midlothian, offers an experience of mining work, history and life through site visits, displays and opportunities for interaction with members of the local community, where the industry was dominant for many years and where housing pattern and the local 'Goth', a tavern whose profits were fed into community projects on the Gothenburg principle, bear witness to this connection.

At New Lanark, the cotton mills and purpose-built village and associated institutions founded in 1785 by David Dale and developed by his son-in-law Robert Owen (1771–1858) has been named a UNESCO World Heritage Site. Owen was a reformer and campaigner for working conditions beneficial to the employees including the provision of education and health care. Here his own home, the mill buildings, workers' tenements, school and shop are subject to interpretation. Retail and visitor services as well as businesses are located here and there is a hotel and other visitor accommodation on site.

It might be argued that as society migrates from its rural past (and perhaps a perceived rural idyll), there may be more need for living history or open-air interpretation of the built environment. If this reflects what current and future generations are increasingly comfortable with and consider relevant to their lives, is this an option for the future?

At present we are in a period of national austerity, with museums and other heritage attractions affected by budget cuts, staff reductions and closures. It is difficult to predict the future. As in the case of the Highland Folk Museum, the transfer from local authority to arm's length organisations (ALOs) may become more general, with trust status offering a degree of independence. The future is challenging for all of Scotland's open-air museums in terms of funding and the stewarding of resources, balancing commercial considerations with the need to be educational, inspiring and relevant to established and new audiences. Tourism is vital to Scotland and our cultural industries are important for the local and the national economy as well as for the well-being of all our people. Museums play a significant role in and for their immediate community and for the community of visitors. One thing is certain – the continuing appreciation of the experience of engaging, multi-sensory interpretation based on sound research that the open-air or living history museum can offer.

NOTES

1 Bringéus, 1974, 10.
2 Stoklund, 1990, 1993, 1994.
3 Bringéus, 1974, 10.
4 *Skansen*, 5.
5 *Skansen*, 6.
6 Stoklund, 1993, 1994.
7 Kinchin, Kinchen and Baxter, 1988, 121–3. The 1911 Exhibition also displayed an 'Auld Toon', with replicas of a range of urban buildings (101–4).
8 Kinchin, Kinchen and Baxter, 1988, 156–7. The architect of the 1938 Clachan was Dr Colin Sinclair, author of *The Thatched Houses of the Old Highlands*, Edinburgh, 1953. He also included a house in An Clachan conforming to contemporary building standards, which he proposed as a type for the Highland home of the future.
9 Cheape, 1986.
10 Grant, 2007, 8.
11 Grant, 2007, 12.
12 Grant, 2007, 175.
13 Grant, 2007, 13.
14 Grant, 2007, 15.

15 Grant, 2007, 15.
16 Grant, 2007, 19.
17 Grant, 2007, 16.
18 Grant, 2007, 33.
19 Grant, 2007, 59.
20 Grant, 2007, 58.
21 Grant, 2007, 49.
22 Grant, c.1950, 3.
23 Grant, c.1950, 3.
24 Grant, c.1950, 3.
25 Grant, 2007, 178.
26 Noble, 1983–4.
27 Fenton, 1979, 2.
28 Fenton, 1979, 3.
29 Grant, c.1950, 3.
30 McCall-Smith, c.1980.
31 McCall-Smith, 1979.
32 Fenton, 1987.
33 Fenton, 1987.
34 Hill, 1993, 37–42.

BIBLIOGRAPHY AND FURTHER READING

Bringéus, N-A. Artur Hazelius och Nordiska museet, *Fataburen* (1972), 7–32.

Bringéus, N-A. Artur Hazelius and the Nordic Museum, *Ethnologia Scandinavica*, 4 (1974), 5–16.

Cheape, H. Dr I F Grant (1887–1983): The Highland Folk Museum and a bibliography of her written works, *ROSC*, 2 (1986), 113–25.

Cheape, H, ed. *Tools and Traditions: Studies in European Ethnology Presented to Alexander Fenton*, Edinburgh, 1993.

Fenton, A. *A Farming Township: Auchindrain, Argyll*, Perth, 1979.

Fenton, A. *North East Farming Life, A Companion to the Exhibition 'The Weel Vrocht Grun'*, Macduff, 1987.

Grant, I F. *Every-day Life on an Old Highland Farm, 1769–82*, London , 1924

Grant, I F. *Am Fasgadh, The Highland Folk Museum at Kingussie, Inverness-shire*, n.p., c.1950.

Grant, I F. *Highland Folk Ways*, London, 1961.

Grant, I F. *The Making of 'Am Fasgadh'*, Edinburgh, 2007.

Hill, A. Aden – A Case Study in the Presentation of Regional Ethnology. In Cheape, H, ed., *Tools and Traditions: Studies in European Ethnology Presented to Alexander Fenton*, Edinburgh, 1993, 37–42.

Kinchin, P, Kinchin, J and Baxter, N. *Glasgow's Great Exhibitions*, Bicester, 1988.

McCall-Smith, H. *Farming Yesterday*, n.p., 1979.

McCall-Smith, H. *Adamston Agricultural Museum*, n.p., ca 1980.

Noble, R R. Turf-walled houses of the Central Highlands: An experiment in reconstruction, *Folk Life*, 22 (1983–4), 68–83.

Rentzhog, S. *Open Air Museums: The history and future of a visionary idea*, Östersund, 2007.

Skansen, Stockholm, 2002.

Stoklund, B. International exhibitions and the new museum concept in the latter half of the nineteenth century, *Ethnologia Scandinavica*, 23 (1993), 87–113.

Stoklund, B. The role of the international exhibitions in the construction of national cultures in the 19th century, *Ethnologia Europaea*, 24 (1994), 35–44.

7 Archival Sources and Scottish Ethnology

DAVID J BROWN

INTRODUCTION

Ethnology is in many ways a 'young' discipline in Scotland. Much of the initial post-war research and writing focused on the material culture of the agricultural community. While this 'first wave' of researchers made use of archival resources, the bulk of their evidence derived mainly from a wide variety of printed primary sources. This same period was marked both by a very great expansion in the provision of archive facilities in Scotland and a corresponding increase in the availability of hitherto untapped records created by public and private bodies. In the same way that, over the last forty years, the political, social and economic histories of Scotland have been gradually rewritten using this growing resource, so ethnologists are now increasingly turning to the archives to unearth new material and test older assumptions. But how is the material to be found and accessed? What follows is an attempt to answer this question, partly by looking at individual archives, partly by looking at themes, and principally by giving pointers.

WHAT IS AN ARCHIVE?

The International Standards Organisation's definition of an archive is a good starting point: 'Materials created or received by a person, family or organisation, public or private, in the conduct of their affairs and preserved because of the enduring value contained in them or as evidence of the functions and responsibilities of their creator, especially those materials maintained using the principles of provenance, original order and collective control; permanent records.'[1] To the experienced ethnologist or historian, the description seems only to omit those many records that have happily survived by chance or accident, rather than by design.

   The last fifteen years have seen a quiet revolution in the staffing of Scottish archives. Where once recruits were, like the author, required simply to have a degree in (commonly) an arts subject and were then taught or acquired the principles of cataloguing and records management 'on the job', it is now practically mandatory for new entrants to possess a postgraduate qualification in archives administration. This new 'professional' staffing has been paralleled by the growing recognition and adoption of ISAD(G), the international cataloguing standard.[2] This standard does not, and could not, prescribe how individual types of records should be described, but it has led to a much more uniform framework for setting out catalogue descriptions. Every document in an archive needs to have a unique reference number, a title or basic description, covering dates and other attributes. Not all older catalogues, first created on paper, necessarily met these requirements. As computer cataloguing began rapidly to advance in archiving over the last quarter century, so pre-existing lists had to be shoe-horned into the new format before they could be typed into online catalogues. This transition from the old to the new formats has fortunately not normally led to any loss of information. Even now, however, there are many archives where the catalogues are only partially available in computerised form and, indeed, some where there are still only paper lists.

Even in archives that possess computerised catalogues, younger researchers are surprised that it is still not generally possible electronically to search such catalogues for themes. The phrases 'agricultural revolution' or 'urban renewal' will almost certainly uncover nothing in most archive catalogues, which are generally based on succinct descriptions of the documents' authors and record content. Archivists have not generally tried to use 'concepts' in their descriptions, and the use of subject thesauri, very much the norm in libraries, has had only a limited uptake in archive cataloguing. This is partly because using them tends to be labour-intensive and they are anyway subject to changing 'fashions'. This situation may change with time, or following future developments in internet search algorithms.

Nothing is more calculated to infuriate the staff of an archive than the media pronouncement (it comes in many forms) to the effect that something 'has just been found, lost in an archive' (or worse: 'lost in a dusty archive'; we generally keep our store rooms clean). It is a form of words that usually fails to explain that the 'discoverer' has merely recognised and trumpeted a particular significance in something that was otherwise already freely available for public inspection. They may even have been pointed to it by the archivist in the first place. To be fair, occasionally these are genuine discoveries which take all parties aback, but in many cases they are not.[3]

Self-evidently an archive catalogue is not an index of a record's contents, and in looking for the pithy phrases to summarise a document, or group of documents, cataloguers cannot mention all the topics or information that they have seen. There will always be a requirement for a researcher to trawl through records, sometimes having long fallow periods between making useful, even significant, discoveries.

When archivists and academic users confer, the most frequently voiced wish from the academic side is that the archivist would give much more detail in the cataloguing process. Sadly, this pressure often has to be resisted because the amount of cataloguing work and the time that it takes puts a premium on what an archivist can realistically do. Conversely, it is also the case, although professional archivists try to rein in the effect, that lists, particularly of private papers, inevitably reflect in their content some of the interests of the cataloguer. If the cataloguer has ethnological or material culture interests, this will sometimes be apparent in the finished lists.

The great bulk of what is held in the archives described here is historical material, open to public access. The 'thirty-year rule' that used to close British government records is now gradually falling away as the Freedom of Information (FoI) acts enacted in Edinburgh and London embed a presumption of public access. Only national security, commercial confidentiality or data protection rights are now satisfactory reasons for closing records to public inspection. To be sure, many official files are still notionally 'closed' but this is only because the departments and the archivists involved have yet to surmount the backlog of checking work to ensure that the records can be opened safely without harm to named individuals. Many records held in archives remain private property, however, and some owners place restrictions on users. It is never a good idea to turn up at an archive without first checking for problems beforehand, and this is one of the issues that advance preparation can identify.

There is one last access issue. Documents before the last years of the nineteenth century will almost all be handwritten. There may even be some manuscript catalogues. Handwriting after about 1730 should, with a little practice, be accessible to most researchers. Before this, it can be more problematic. The National Records of Scotland (NRS) and other archives provide tuition in medieval and early modern palaeography, and the NRS provides online tuition.[4] Grant Simpson has published an excellent handbook on the subject, which gives facsimiles of handwriting styles and a very useful glossary.[5]

AN OVERVIEW OF THE ARCHIVE WORLD

For an outline history of the development of archive provision in Scotland, one should turn to an article in the *Scottish Historical Review* for 1974.[6] As of 2013, there are two major Scottish national repositories for archives and manuscripts: the National Records of Scotland (NRS) and the National Library of Scotland (NLS). The Royal Commission on the Ancient and Historical Monuments of Scotland (RCAHMS) has a growing collection, mainly focused on architects' papers. Almost all of the Scottish local authorities make some provision to allow public access to their holdings of public and private records. Most of the universities have professionally staffed archives. Many museums, both local and central, hold significant archival collections. Similarly, some local libraries acquired records of various sorts in the long years before formal archive provision began gradually to take shape in the local authorities following the Local Government (Scotland) Act of 1973.[7]

For a bird's eye view of archives that might contain Scottish material, we inevitably turn first to the internet. This has brought many benefits, but it also serves to expose some shortcomings. At the time of writing some Scottish archives do not have a direct internet presence, and some of those that do, including some major institutions, are unable to provide online access to their full, detailed catalogues. To date, however, over fifty national, local, university and other archives have made summaries of their holdings ('Fonds level entries' in the professional jargon) available through the Scottish Archive Network (SCAN). These give basic details about collections held and may be viewed online.[8]

For many years the Scottish Records Association (SRA) maintained a series of Data Sheets providing much the same information, albeit in a very summary form. Since SCAN was established, the SRA has focused its Data Sheets on libraries, museums and other bodies which, although not formally archives, nevertheless hold manuscripts or other records.[9] Together, these sites cover the great majority of records held in publicly accessible archives in Scotland.

The absence in Scotland of a full, comprehensive online national catalogue comparable with the English and Welsh A2A (see below) is now glaring. In 2011, the Scottish Council on Archives (SCA) was leading a renewed discussion north of the border about plans to bring together an online union catalogue of the contents of Scottish archives. Only time will tell whether funding and resources can be found to advance this.

There is a UK-wide resource, ARCHON, which can be seen through the website of The National Archives in London (TNA, formerly the Public Record Office).[10] This was originally created by the Historic Manuscripts Commission and gives addresses and contact details for all UK archives.[11] TNA has also sponsored A2A, an online catalogue covering about 400 publicly accessible archives in England and Wales. This provides complete catalogue entries (to 'file and item level' in the jargon) but it does not include Scottish repositories.[12] In the London area, AIM25 gives access to the catalogues of 100 higher education institutions and learned societies in the area encircled by the M25 motorway.[13]

It is worth concluding this overview by introducing three important qualifications. Almost none of the Scottish archives, including those in SCAN, give full coverage of their holdings (whether in summary form or as comprehensive catalogues) on the internet. Worse, catalogues (such as exist) of the records and archives held by museums and local libraries are in many cases entirely absent from the internet. Finally, almost all archives, whether in Scotland or elsewhere, have backlogs, sometimes large, of uncatalogued records. This is largely the consequence of the comparatively late development of local authority archives in Scotland. A system of county record offices failed to materialise in Scotland as it did in England in the first half of the twentieth century. In Scotland almost all local archives date from after 1975, and the priority for most of the newly appointed archivists in the decade thereafter was simply to secure and accession large quantities of local government and other records. Most local archives were and are under-resourced and shortage of staff time has prevented cataloguing keeping pace with accessioning. Record cataloguing is exceptionally labour-intensive, even in the computer age, and archivists are now only rarely on top of the mountain of listing work confronting them. While not a shameful secret, the existence of such backlogs will nonetheless commonly not feature even in a summary catalogue. The combined effect of these three qualifications means that it will almost always pay a researcher doing extended research on a subject to cultivate direct links with an archive or library, or museum and its staff. Familiarity between archivist and reader generally breeds advice, assistance and exchange of information. This writer has witnessed and experienced numerous examples of this, both as an archivist in Edinburgh and as a researcher elsewhere.

THE NATIONAL REGISTER OF ARCHIVES FOR SCOTLAND (NRAS)

There remains a vast mass of archival material still held privately in Scotland, whether in family homes or in the stores of commercial and legal companies. In volume and quality, it probably equals the body of private records already held in public archives. The National Register of Archives for Scotland (NRAS), a branch of NRS, has worked since 1946 to identify and list such records, as well as to facilitate access to them.[14] The NRAS also acts as a clearing house for information on collections of private papers deposited in archives, libraries, universities and museums throughout Scotland. It now has over 4,300 surveys, or catalogues, of collections and many can be seen on the NRAS website.[15] They range from the massive archives of the Dukes of Atholl and the Marquesses of Bute all the way down through gentry families and medium-sized companies to the records of small businesses and individuals. Because most are privately held, however, there can be no automatic presumption of a right of access for researchers. In the majority of these cases, it is expected that the enquirer will first approach the staff of the NRAS, who will then approach the owner on their behalf. Similarly, for reasons of privacy or personal security, some owners do not allow lists of their papers to appear online. In these cases the NRAS makes the paper catalogue available to personal callers at their Edinburgh office. All surveys on the Register are also available in the National Register of Archives (NRA), part of The National Archives in London. The NRA's online indexes are extremely useful as a first port of call in tracking collections.

THE NATIONAL RECORDS OF SCOTLAND (NRS)

The oldest established archive in Scotland, the NRS is also the largest, with (currently) 72,000 metres of shelved records.[16] Acting as archivist to the Scottish government and the Scottish law courts, the NRS also holds the sasine (land transfers) and other public registers, together with a large body of private records created by churches, families, companies and individuals. The overwhelming majority of the catalogues for these records may now be seen through an online catalogue,[17] but the indexes to many of the public registers have yet to be converted to electronic form and a few of the lists of family papers still await conversion.

The catalogue is simple to search but it can sometimes be helpful to have an overview of the NRS's holdings. The NRS website has a series of Guides to Records which discuss record types (e.g. burgh records) or subjects (e.g. crime and criminals) and provide reference numbers. Resort should also be made to the published official guide to the records that covers the years to 1707[18] and to a brief, privately published guide by the late Professor Gordon Donaldson, which is particularly strong on the public records before 1600.[19] There are also two self-help books published by NRS for readers tracing Scottish family history and local history.[20] Easily overlooked by researchers, some of whom may foolishly imagine neither to be 'serious' subjects, they give good explanations of the possibilities and pitfalls in the most useful record series and consequently have a real application to wider investigations, including ethnology. For instance, it is here that details can be found of how to use the valuation rolls and the records of the assessed taxes.

It is difficult to exaggerate the importance and variety of the NRS's holdings to researchers, and harder still to summarise them in a short space. Appropriately, the 540 major private collections include the papers of Scotland's first ethnologist, Sir Arthur Mitchell (ref: GD492). They also number many of the archives of the great landed families, such as the Earls of Leven and Melville (GD26), Dalhousie (GD45) and Breadalbane (GD112); and the Dukes of Montrose (GD220) and Buccleuch (GD224). There are papers for many other landed proprietors, as well as for major engineering and other businesses.[21] The Register House series includes two groups of paper records, RH9 and RH15, containing large quantities of private archives which parallel the GDs. They appear to have originated as productions in cases that came before the Court of Session and other courts. Two other series, RH2 and RH4, consist of large numbers of copies (in the form of photocopies and microfilms, respectively) of records of Scottish interest that have been identified either in private hands or in archives outside Scotland. Their ready availability in Edinburgh can save the Scotland-based researcher much travelling time.

It is worth digressing briefly to make some general points about private family archives – points that apply to collections in most archives and not just in the NRS. Until World War I, the landed classes retained a strong grip on society in Scotland, despite the fact that industrialisation after 1820 had begun to create a significant bourgeois class. The landowners had enormous sway over the lives of ordinary people. They might lease them land as tenants or cottars, they might employ them as servants or labourers, or they might do business with them as merchants or tradesmen. In all these relationships there is potential for some sort of written record, whether rentals of tenants, correspondence and accounts by estate managers, or legal papers concerning commercial transactions, services or debts. It is a fact that before civil registration of births, marriages and deaths began in 1855, evidence for the existence of many individual Scots and the lives they led survives only in the records created and maintained by private landowners. Nor was their influence confined to the countryside. Until well into the nineteenth century, many burghs were dominated by the local laird and his influence reached far into the lives and economies of these urban communities. For example, any histories of the life and societies of Elgin, Forres, Grantown or Nairn burghs would be lacking several dimensions if they did not use the family papers of the Earls of Seafield (GD248), now in NRS.

The record series created by the Scottish government departments and now held by NRS are a treasure trove and easily overlooked. The Scottish Office, established in 1885, and its successor from 1999, the Scottish Executive, had (and has) a remit that reaches into all corners of Scottish life, and it inherited the records of predecessor bodies, some going back far into the nineteenth century.[22]

Five broad areas of business are represented in the stream of modern records that started to come to NRS in the 1960s, and these divisions of business have more or less continued down the years: agriculture and fisheries; economic development and regional planning; education; home affairs, including law and order; and health. This wide-ranging administration has created many records on subjects of ethnological interest. Heather Holmes has used records from several departments of the former Scottish Office in her studies of seasonal workers in twentieth-century Scottish agriculture.[23] Among the records of the Planning Division of the former Development Department (ref: DD12) are many files on the design and construction of prefabricated houses, with photographs and technical drawings. The files of the former Department of Agriculture and Fisheries unsurprisingly have extensive materials on the fishing fleet (e.g. series AF62). They also have many records dealing with the farming and crofting communities. The home and health files (ref: HH) have material as varied as the Scottish people's domestic experience of World Wars I and II; crimes, criminals and criminality; the prison community; and the national and local health services.

The archives of the Scottish law courts represent the largest single group of records in NRS. They offer a goldmine of information on the everyday lives of the Scots, but it is only in recent years that their potential has begun to be tapped. Their full extent is discussed elsewhere in this *Scottish Life and Society* series[24] and so this essay will touch briefly on only four record groups: the Court of Session, the High Court of Justiciary, the sheriff courts and the commissary courts.

The Court of Session as the supreme civil judicature in Scotland has left a colossal quantity of records (refs: CS1- CS370) but it is only in the last half century that there has been extended work to make them searchable. Its justice was not the sole preserve of the rich, and it was accessible to people quite far down the social scale. Hamish Fraser has shown how various records generated by the court can give insights into the life and work of various Scottish trades.[25] The High Court of Justiciary, based in Edinburgh but with travelling circuit courts, dealt with the most serious criminal cases. While the court necessarily enmeshed only a tiny part of a (broadly) law-abiding society, the process papers repay trawling for their incidental insights into Scottish life and society. Work on a new, comprehensive computerised index to the court's records began in 2001,[26] and the work to date was released to the public in 2011.

The modern sheriff court system began in 1748, although many of the new courts inherited much older records from predecessor bodies. Starting with twenty-seven courts, there are now forty-nine and they have generated much useful record material. The new sheriffs-depute had a criminal jurisdiction as well as a wide civil one. The process papers in each court are often large in volume and rarely listed in any detail. They are a treasure trove of information, largely unexplored, on the society over which they held (and hold) sway. For the period before the late nineteenth century, they frequently contain material from other local offices. Thus the Inverness Sheriff Court records (ref: SC29) include many criminal precognitions, copies of lost originals that would once have been with the procurator fiscal, the crown agent or the Justiciary Court. It is in the Paisley Sheriff Court records that we find the precognitions relating to the weavers' strike of 1773 (ref: SC58/55/1). There is also much for the researcher in material culture. By way of example, this writer, in sorting the Inverness civil processes for the period 1669–1860 (ref: SC29/10), was struck by the number of disputes concerning grain mills, where full inventories were to be found of a building's contents, fittings and equipment.[27]

The commissary courts, created in 1564 and progressively abolished from 1823, registered wills and testaments. The testaments have long been seen as a major source for Scottish social history.[28] They are indexed and may be searched by the name of the deceased, by their occupation and by their place of death. It is worth noting that for every registered testament before 1824, there was a corresponding warrant (that is, the original papers), many of which have survived. Warrants are arranged separately and rarely consulted but it is sometimes the case that they contain more of the fine detail of the deceased's possessions than is recorded in the registered version. From 1824, testaments were recorded in the sheriff courts, and these do not have associated warrants. The full index to testaments covering both commissary and sheriff courts from 1513 to 1901 may be consulted online.[29]

Since 1960, the Church of Scotland has deposited most of its records with the NRS. The records of the General Assembly, the synods, presbyteries and kirk sessions (refs: CH1, CH2 and CH3) are a central source for many aspects of Scottish national, local and social history. Kirk sessions in particular had a responsibility for the social mores of their parishioners, as well as for the relief of the local poor, and these duties have left an extraordinary series of records giving wonderful insights into the lives of the people under their charge.[30] The NRS, with the Church's permission, has in recent years passed many of these as loans to local archives under the 'charge and superintendence' of the Keeper of the Records of Scotland. In a separate process, NRS is engaged in an immense digitisation programme to image all the presbytery and kirk session records with the eventual intention of making them available over the internet.

Many congregations left ('seceded from') the Church of Scotland over the course of its history, beginning with the Secession Church in the 1730s and culminating in the Disruption of 1843 and the birth of the Free Church. Many of these congregations would rejoin in or after 1929 and their surviving records are listed in the series CH3 at NRS.

NRS also holds less comprehensive series of records for various other religious denominations, including the Methodists and the United Free Church.

The NRS has over 150,000 maps and plans, most of which have been separated out from their parent collections into a single running series, RHP. Together, they constitute the largest collection of original maps and plans of Scotland. Most are topographical, but they include transport, architectural, public utilities and engineering plans, as well as vignettes with agricultural scenes, people at work, buildings and ships. While the full catalogue is available online, there is also a published catalogue covering the first 4,999 plans.[31] Rosemary Gibson used NRS plans and other records to study the development of the Scottish landscape.[32]

The union that created the NRS in 2011 brought with it the Old Parish

Registers (OPRs) of baptisms, marriages and burials kept by the Church of Scotland before 1855, together with the records of the Scottish censuses since 1841. Most Scottish family history guides explain these records and their potential, but researchers should be aware that they will be charged for access to them.

THE NATIONAL LIBRARY OF SCOTLAND (NLS)

The NLS, established in 1925, inherited the marvellous collection of manuscripts acquired over several hundred years by the Advocates' Library. There is a useful published summary catalogue to this,[33] and parts of the collection have subsequently been re-catalogued and expanded although these expansions remain unpublished. As well as the Advocates' Manuscripts, the NLS has since its inception acquired by purchase, donation and loan a large body of business, family, estate and miscellaneous archives. The first eight volumes of their catalogues have been published,[34] and another six are available in typescript only at the NLS. The cataloguing method used is similar to that in the manuscripts department of the British Library. Each collection is arranged into broad subject areas (e.g. 'family correspondence'; 'estate vouchers'; 'committee minute books') and below that into volumes or bundles. These are given a running manuscript number. Each 'manuscript', which may contain dozens of individual documents, is only given a broad contents description, although most of the correspondents (writers and recipients) involved are detailed in indexes appended to each of the successive catalogue volumes. These indexes also include some place-names and a very limited coverage of subjects. In short, they are very useful where a researcher knows that a particular individual is likely to be writing on a subject of interest, but where a theme is more of a social, economic or ethnological bent, the researcher is often left only with the broad-brush contents descriptions and so must undertake much more speculative investigation. The NLS, unlike many institutions, tries to make interim catalogues of new acquisitions available to allow rapid public access in advance of producing more detailed final catalogues. As of 2011, relatively little of their catalogue is visible on the internet, although work is currently in hand to improve this situation.

Although smaller than the NRS collections, the NLS manuscripts are fully as interesting. Their family and estate collections are mainly focused on the east and south of Scotland, although the deposit of the Sutherland papers is an obvious and spectacular exception, and the Mackenzie of Delvine papers have much of Highland interest. The Earl of Minto's papers have much to say about Borders life and society, while the Fletcher of Saltoun papers and the Yester papers are similarly informative about East Lothian. Special interest areas that underpin the NLS collecting policy are the papers of literary figures, of modern political parties and politicians, and of trade unions and other records concerning organised labour.[35] Quite distinct from the archives of landed families, famous writers and worthy institutions, there are innumerable gems scattered through the NLS collections. A personal favourite of this writer are the essays of John Ramsay of Ochtertyre, a Perthshire laird who filled his evenings from the 1780s until about 1810 composing a series of studies of the history of Scotland and of the changing society in which he lived. They are full of acute social observation and much incidental evidence about aspects of material culture and rural working life.[36]

The NLS holds the largest single collection of maps and plans in Scotland, covering all parts of the world. Although they have a small number of manuscript maps, the bulk of their Scottish-related holdings are published. As a copyright library, they have an outstanding collection of Ordnance Survey plans. For many years they have possessed beautiful and useful full-size colour reproductions of General Roy's 1755 military maps of Scotland, the originals of which are in the British Library.

THE ROYAL COMMISSION ON THE ANCIENT AND HISTORICAL MONUMENTS OF SCOTLAND (RCAHMS)

Founded in 1908, and instructed to record the 'life and conditions' of the people of Scotland through their built environment, RCAHMS ('The Commission') works to gather and interpret information on the built, archaeological and maritime heritage of Scotland. It has the particular function of recording those listed buildings and buildings in conservation areas where permission has been given for partial or total demolition. The Commission has accumulated a large body of records and photographs arising from this survey work, and these can be of considerable use in doing research on architecture, rural and urban settlement patterns, as well as providing resources for the material culture of building history. RCAHMS also collects manuscripts, most particularly the personal and business papers of modern architects.[37] One fruit of this has been the Scottish Survey of Architectural Papers, covering practices formed before 1950.[38] Their other holdings include historical, archaeological and architectural research notes compiled by individuals; RCAHMS field investigators' notebooks, containing detailed notes, descriptions and sketches from 1908; archaeological reports and site documentation; inventories of kirk furnishings; graveyard surveys; and research material from both the Scottish Burgh Survey to 1984 and the Scottish Industrial Archaeological Survey. The Commission has very recently taken over the Buildings at Risk register, with its associated documentation. While their catalogues are not fully available online, a sense of the breadth of their coverage may be obtained from searching 'Canmore', the principal search tool on their website.[39] This contains map-based information on buildings and archaeological sites throughout Scotland. The Commission also has a large collection of aerial photographs of Scotland (currently 1.6 million images), acquired from various sources, including the RAF and the Ordnance Survey.

THE NATIONAL TRUST FOR SCOTLAND (NTS) AND HISTORIC SCOTLAND

The National Trust for Scotland has its own administrative archive, including case files relating to its property holdings. At the time of writing this was being recatalogued. The archives of the private families who sometimes live in these properties tend not to belong to the NTS. Catalogues for them can sometimes be found in the NRAS database, however. Historic Scotland has a photographic archive covering the properties in its care as well as holding photographs of some other properties. All are being loaded to its online website. Its drawing office holds working drawings of properties in care. It has only a small archive collection, which includes the records of Biggar Gas Works.

The Local Government (Scotland) Act of 1973, implemented from 1975, swept away numerous burghs, shires and counties, the ancient pillars of Scottish local government, replacing them instead with a system of regional and district councils. These in turn were replaced in 1996 by a system of thirty-two unitary councils following the Local Government etc. (Scotland) Act of 1994.[40] The 1973 Act included (s. 200) the first comprehensive obligation on Scottish councils to make provision for their records, and this was continued in a slightly strengthened form in the 1994 Act (ss. 53–54). By 2011, thirty-one of the thirty-two authorities made some provision for access to their holdings, and it is hoped that the Public Records (Scotland) Act of 2011 will further improve this position.

The local authority archives have consequently inherited an enormous range of records.[41] They can include the records of local burghs, with all the information that these contain about urban society in Scotland.[42] In the nineteenth and early twentieth centuries, the Scottish Burgh Records Society printed selections from among the archives of some of the sixty-six royal burghs, but very much more still remains unpublished in the archives and perhaps elsewhere.[43] As recently as 2008, the eighteenth-century records for Musselburgh, long reckoned lost, were discovered in a forgotten, sealed room in the town's Tolbooth. The records of the Convention of Royal Burghs, the forum where the burgh representatives gathered to apportion tax liabilities and debate common concerns, are now held by Edinburgh City Archives. They are far from being dull administrative records but are only now being seriously mined for the evidence that they contain of Scottish life and society.[44] The records of rural government can include those for the commissioners of supply, predecessors of the later county councils, responsible for levying the land tax and maintaining roads and bridges, as well as the parochial boards established from 1845 to manage poor relief. The Scotch Education Act of 1872 placed renewed responsibilities on the parishes and burghs to maintain schools, and this has left a large body of education records in local archives. From the 1880s onwards, the progressive growth of local government and its responsibilities has left a mass of minutes, accounts, correspondence and other records that allow us to view the lives, environment and material culture of the Scottish people. The local archives have also accumulated large collections of private family and business papers, for instance the Murray Threipland of Fingask papers in the Perth and Kinross Archive and the Forbes of Callendar papers at Falkirk.

Regional police forces were created in 1975 and the fate of the records of their predecessor city, county and burgh constabularies is typical of the effects of local government reform on the survival of historical records. After 1975, some police headquarters' and individual station records were deposited with local archives, while others have been retained by the forces. Sadly, there have also been many losses of records during amalgamations of forces.

It should be remembered that during the twentieth century many local public records found their way to the NRS, where they were taken in for safe keeping. This was particularly true of the records for many of the royal burghs. A large quantity still remains with NRS, but since the late 1970s successive Keepers of the Records have pursued a policy of returning them to the localities, whether as loans on charge and superintendence terms, or increasingly as outright alienations.

It is worth noting that as part of its work in support of the 1973 Act, the NRS undertook a survey of the then-surviving records of the thirty-three Scottish counties and the several dozen royal and other burghs. There is little doubt that many records were destroyed or lost at or after regionalisation, but the survey does provide a clear picture of what there once was and it is still of some use when trying to identify surviving material.[45]

THE SCOTTISH UNIVERSITIES

Almost all the Scottish universities and higher education institutions have archives. Unsurprisingly, the largest and most diverse holdings for the ethnologist are held by the four oldest universities, St Andrews, Aberdeen, Edinburgh and Glasgow, but there are also excellent collections at Dundee, Heriot-Watt and Glasgow Caledonian universities. In 2001 the UK university archives launched the Archives Hub, an online research and access tool covering their holdings.[46] It is the quickest way to identify records held by the higher education sector. Like the SCAN network, the Hub provides full details on how to gain access to collections and the facilities available. Most of the entries are summaries of catalogues, but some lists are detailed down to file and item level. The Hub aspires to bring together full catalogue descriptions from all UK archives in one searchable catalogue, the so-called UK Archive Discovery Network (UKAD). This is likely to be a little way off, but the Hub has already accepted a small amount of content from outside the education sector, such as East Dunbartonshire Archives and the Northamptonshire County Record Office. Again, one has to be aware that not all the collections in a given archive will be summarised. At the very least, however, the site provides contact details and will also point to published guides, websites and other catalogues.

It is not possible to generalise about the universities. All hold administrative records generated by the parent institution, as well as a certain amount of material relating to their localities. Glasgow University is exceptionally strong in company records and in many ways functions as a national business archive for Scotland. Among its many riches, Edinburgh University's archive has at its heart the remarkable collection gathered by the antiquarian David Laing, with documents concerning virtually every period of Scottish history and many aspects of its life and society.[47] The collections of the School of Scottish Studies are described elsewhere in this volume. Glasgow Caledonian University collects records that support its social sciences, social work and childcare teaching programmes, including the Glasgow records for Children 1st (formerly the RSSPCC). The archive also gathers material of national significance on left-wing politics and trade union activity. St Andrews University has some Fife burgh and church records and has a very fine photographic archive.[48] Dundee University Archives collect records on the jute and linen industries among much else. Aberdeen University's archives hold some exceptional private estate archives, most notably those of the Earls of Fife and of Kintore. Together with some estate and literary collections, Stirling University has several archives relating to Scottish film making and broadcasting.

THE HEALTH BOARDS AND MEDICAL RECORDS[49]

Of the fourteen Scottish health boards, only six currently employ the services of archivists, whether directly or indirectly. NHS Lothian, Greater Glasgow and Clyde, and Grampian each employ one or more archivists. NHS Tayside passes its historical records to the Dundee University archives,[50] while NHS Dumfries and Galloway and NHS Highland make theirs accessible through the local authority archives in Dumfries and Inverness respectively. Summaries of their holdings may be seen on the SCAN or Archives Hub websites. The Hospital Records Database maintained by the National Archives at Kew covers hospital records held in archives across the UK but has little coverage of those hospitals that maintain their own archives. It gives summaries of the surviving records for hospitals and the availability of catalogues.[51] 'Finding the Right Clinical Notes', an online project based at Edinburgh University and Lothian Health Services, is designed to identify holdings of personal health records relating to individuals. While many of the records it identifies must remain confidential and so are closed to public examination, there is some content that is open and of interest to the researcher.[52]

The Royal Colleges have records going back several centuries. The Royal College of Surgeons of Edinburgh has origins dating from 1505, while The Royal College of Physicians of Edinburgh dates from 1681 and the Faculty of Physicians and Surgeons in Glasgow was founded in 1599. All of them have important archives, which can be approached either through the SCAN or NRAS catalogues. The Royal College of Nursing, based in Edinburgh, has an extensive archive and this can be searched through the College's website.

RELIGIOUS ARCHIVES

Although grouped under this title, all these collections represent far more than the mere history and theology of their parent churches. The Scottish Catholic Archives, based in Edinburgh, is a perfect case in point, with a grouping of collections that provides a fascinating insight into the world of a community that was actively persecuted until the early eighteenth century, and thereafter only barely tolerated until the early nineteenth. Unsurprisingly, there is little material for the years before 1560.[53]

While many of the congregations that broke away to form the Free Church in 1843 reunited with the Church of Scotland in 1929, a significant number did not and there remains today a continuing Free Church. Some congregations retain their own records; others have passed them to the Church's Edinburgh head office. Such access as is possible is on personal application. The situation of the records for the Scottish Episcopal Church is very similar. Most are held locally, some by the congregations, but some also by local and university archives. The NRAS holds a fairly comprehensive survey covering a majority of the Episcopal congregations made in the 1980s. There are significant bodies of records for the Scottish Quaker community[54] and for the Glasite community, much of the latter of which is now held at Dundee University Archives.[55] In recent years records of the Methodist and Baptist churches have begun to be deposited with local authority and university archives.

The Scottish Jewish Archives Centre at Garnethill Synagogue, Glasgow, documents the full range of the life of the Jewish community in Scotland since the eighteenth century. It holds old synagogue minute books and registers, membership lists, a photographic collection, oral history recordings, annual reports of many communal organisations, and personal papers, as well as numerous artefacts.

Currently, very little is known about any records held by the Scottish Islamic community.

BUSINESS RECORDS

The wider world of work is fully represented in Scottish archives. The Business Archives Council for Scotland (BACS), based at Glasgow University, seeks to identify and catalogue records of Scottish companies and other enterprises.[56] Almost all of their cataloguing output is represented in the NRAS catalogues. Glasgow University's archives have a strong focus on business archives generally and it also supports the Scottish Brewing Archive.[57] The Scotch whisky industry has its own company archives, most notably those of Diageo at Menstrie[58] and John Dewar and Sons, Ltd, in Glasgow. The two major Scottish banks, the Royal Bank and the Bank of Scotland (currently Lloyds Banking Group plc) hold extensive archives, including both business records created in the course of their work, and also records of other banks engrossed by earlier amalgamations. They also hold other more miscellaneous records acquired from various sources.[59]

Of heavy industry, the bulk of the records of the Scottish shipbuilders' archives are split between the NRS and Glasgow University's archives. They are fully catalogued and include several marvellous series of plans and photographs. The records of the nationalised coal industry are almost all with the NRS (ref: CB) and include the surviving records of the pre-1948 companies. It has to be said, however, that the bulk of the records for individual collieries for the period 1948–92 do not survive,[60] and what NRS holds are the copies provided to 'head office' of the minutes and other papers concerning the various local pits. They are still fully adequate to underpin a history of the lives and work of the coal mining communities.

The principal records of the Scottish railway system and its workforce, both the private companies before 1948 and the nationalised industry thereafter, are also at the NRS (ref: BR). The records of the newly privatised industry after 1996 are mostly still with the various franchise operators, although Network Rail, the owner of the working infrastructure, is now gathering its historic and administrative archive at Clifton Moor, near York. The National Railway Museum is currently constructing the Rail Industry National Archive (RINA) at Wroughton, near Swindon, and this collection will include the historic records of the new train operating companies and other bodies. There will be Scottish material in both the Clifton Moor and Wroughton repositories.[61]

The records of British Steel and the constituent pre-nationalisation companies are at the NRS, but they are largely uncatalogued and not easily searchable.

ARCHIVES IN MUSEUMS

We have noted above that many Scottish museums have collections of manuscripts, some created as part of their own institutional work, others given as donations. The NRAS currently holds lists for archives in almost seventy museums. In many cases these give an incomplete picture of the holdings because, as with conventional archives, most museums have backlogs of unlisted material. The SRA Data Sheets give summaries of some museum holdings.

The National Museum of Scotland (NMS) in Edinburgh holds a large body of administrative records, as well as gifted, loaned and purchased material. The recent redevelopment of their main building has included a research library, which will much improve public access to its archival holdings. That said, these remain largely unlisted and consequently unknown to the general public. The exception within NMS is the Scottish Life Archive, which started as the Country Life Archive in 1959. At its core is an artificially created research archive consisting of a large series of ring-binders, arranged by subject and internally by county and parish, containing photographs, drawings and data extracted from published and manuscript sources. Its coverage starts in the late seventeenth century and runs to modern times. It is complemented by a photographic collection of about 100,000 negatives, prints and slides commencing from the 1880s, by a document collection of about 3,000 drawings, prints, manuscripts, diaries and maps and plans, by a postcard collection, and by a small collection of audio tapes and film. This last includes films made by the East of Scotland College of Agriculture in the 1940s and 50s. Although at its outset it was focused on the rural community, the Scottish Life Archive now gathers material on maritime, urban and industrial history. Overall, it is a prime resource for any Scottish ethnological investigation. Almost none of its catalogues are online.

The SRA Data Sheets noted above and the National Register of Archives (see below) cover a few museums not caught in the NRAS catalogues. The variety of finds possible in a local museum is perhaps best suggested by a recent article on the West Highland Museum.[62]

We have already noted several online search systems that are UK-wide. The point to be taken, of course, is that there is much of Scottish interest in national and local archives across the UK. The Union of 1707 removed real power in Scotland to London and this is to some extent reflected in the records, most obviously those held in The National Archives at Kew, but also those held by the British Library (BL) at St Pancras in London.

TNA is much more a 'central government archive' than its Scottish counterpart, and its holdings of private family and business archives are relatively small. All of its catalogues are available through its website, but there is an older and still serviceable published guide to its holdings.[63] In addition, many of its catalogues have been published by the List and Index Society. TNA annually has to deal with enormous numbers of readers and enquiries; consequently they have published or sponsored a considerable body of self-help guides, ranging from small leaflets to substantial books, covering different types of records and areas of research. There is a great deal of material on Scottish life and society scattered through its holdings, especially for the period before the establishment of the Scottish Office in 1885. Inevitably much of it is to do with the mechanics of revenue and tax administration but there is also material on law and order, health, transport and on matters military and naval. The NRS in Edinburgh has photostat copies of some of this material, notably the Home Office records from 1708–1830,[64] as well as duplicates of a large body of Cabinet Office papers for the nineteenth and twentieth centuries.[65] Some TNA series are regularly delved into by Scots researchers; others await their curiosity. The hundreds of boxes of private petitions and official papers submitted to the Treasury since 1707 (ref: T1) are likely to reveal much about the social and economic condition of Scotland, but their very quantity and the inadequacy of the finding aids has hitherto deterred any extended examination of them. As always, there is the prospect of serendipitous finds. It is from a private archive at Kew, the papers of William Pitt the Younger, that we get one of the very few real insights into the framing of the legislation that finally led to the abolition of slavery in the Scottish coal mines in 1799.[66]

The manuscript department of the British Library has a large and ever-growing collection of family, literary, institutional and other archives. There are several series but the largest is the Additional Manuscripts (Add. Mss.), and some of these include Scottish material. There are a few collections that are primarily Scottish, for instance the papers of the MacKenzie family of Suddie and Scatwell in Ross-shire, ranging from the seventeenth to the nineteenth centuries.[67] These are the exceptions, however. Much more common is the situation where an English collection includes documents of Scottish interest. For instance, the Dropmore papers include the archive of William Grenville, Home Secretary 1789–1791. As well as having much on Scottish politics, there is a file of material on the construction of roads in the North Highlands, 1789–1791.[68] As noted earlier, the British Library manuscript catalogues provided the model later adopted by the NLS, and many of them have been published. They may also be viewed and searched through the British Library's website.[69] The Oriental and India Office Collections (OIOC) now at the BL might sound unpromising territory for the Scottish ethnologist, but here are to be found the core records for tracking the lives of those Scots who sought their fortunes with the East India Company. Even less expectedly, the private letter books of the East India Company director David Scott of Dunninald include some of the fine detail of his Scottish estate management in the 1790s. One letter of 1796 gives perhaps one of the earliest references to bathing machines on Scottish beaches, in this case at Boddin near Montrose.[70]

Sometimes Scottish material is found in England because a British family owned properties in one or more countries and chose to centre its archives outside Scotland. Sometimes the family simply decamped entirely from Scotland and took its records to a new home.[71] To take just one example, the Dundases of Zetland through their landholdings in the Northern Isles have good material in their family archive about kelp making in the late eighteenth and early nineteenth centuries. It is all now in the North Yorkshire County Record Office at Northallerton. A letter in the same collection relating to their Stirling estates describes a situation, which may have been more general in Scotland, whereby a newly hired ploughman was to be sent to Dalkeith to oversee the construction of his ploughs there 'and give any directions he may wish'.[72] The archives of the Marquesses of Abercorn, including their Scottish estate records, are all at the Public Record Office of Northern Ireland (PRONI) in Belfast. The archives of the Marquises of Stafford, now in the Stafford Record Office, contain much material on the family's Sutherland possessions and so complement the Sutherland archive deposited in the NLS.

As in Scotland, so in England and Wales there is a vast mass of important archives held privately, whether in manorial cellars or company vaults. The National Register of Archives, part of the Historical Manuscripts Commission now housed in The National Archives at Kew, gathers surveys of such records. Its micro-site[73] forms part of the TNA website and this will often provide links to summary catalogues of the collections it covers.

The Museum of English Rural Life, part of the University of Reading, holds the records of the first Board of Agriculture, 1793–1823. This includes some Scottish material and there is an online catalogue.

SOUND AND VISION

The premier collection of historic films for Scotland is the Scottish Screen Archive (SSA), now part of the NLS. The full catalogue of films held can be seen on the NLS website and it may be searched in a number of ways, perhaps most usefully by subject and place. The NRS generally places its film holdings with the SSA. As noted above, the Scottish Life Archive also has a small collection of films, as does the School of Scottish Studies. BBC Scotland has a film archive in Glasgow which provides a service to members of the public, corporate bodies and other broadcasters. Academic research requests can be submitted to them, but research will be mediated and this is a chargeable service. Following the research and depending on the end use, copies of programmes can be provided, again at a charge.

The School of Scottish Studies has an extensive collection of sound recordings, and many Scottish archives hold small quantities of miscellaneous recordings. At the time of writing, it is understood that the NLS has agreed in principle to take the lead in sponsoring a future national sound archive, to be run in parallel with the SSA.

CONCLUSION

No short essay could do justice to the wealth of archival material that awaits the researcher in Scottish ethnology. This writer is very conscious of the astonishing pace of change that has been unleashed by the digital revolution, which makes writing on these resources akin to aiming at a moving target. This movement has so far been manifested primarily in the development of electronic catalogues and by the appearance of more and more images of original records online. It is worth ending with a needful reminder of what has remained unchanged, however. The benefits of information technology to historical research have hitherto been about improving access to resources. Outside of the narrow field of statistical databases, computerisation has not been able to facilitate or undertake the work of interpretation significantly. This and the work of identifying, considering and selecting evidence will remain a laborious activity. The researcher is assisted but not replaced by the computer, and serendipitous discoveries are the just reward only of the diligent labourer.

It is worth ending with a combined warning and maxim set out over twenty years ago by one of the great historians of early modern Britain:

> What makes a historian master of his craft is the discipline of checking findings, to see whether he has said more than his source warrants. A historian with a turn of phrase, when released from this discipline, risks acquiring a dangerously Icarian freedom to make statements which are unscholarly because unverifiable . . . The absence of archives makes it harder to resist a temptation to sacrifice precision to eloquence.[74]

ACKNOWLEDGEMENTS

For advice and comments on early drafts of this essay, I am grateful to Dr Alan Borthwick, John Burnett; Dr Heather Holmes; John McLintock; Dr Malcolm Bangor-Jones, Dr Alison Rosie and Dr Frances Shaw.

NOTES

1 International Standards Organisation: ISO 16175–1:2010. Information and Documentation: Principles and Functional Requirements for Electronic Records in Office Environments.

2 ISAD(G): General International Standard Archival Description, 2nd edn, Ottawa, 2000.

3 The most significant recent discovery in the NRS was made by a researcher examining a music score in a private collection. A cataloguer had long ago identified it as being by Vivaldi but was unaware that it was an incomplete version of a flute concerto long believed to have been lost. See *Retour*, Issue 15 (Spring 2011), 3–4.

4 Scottish Handwriting.com, maintained by NRS, <www.Scottishhandwriting.com> [accessed April 2012].

5 Simpson, 1998.

6 Imrie, 1974, 194–210.

7 Both Edinburgh and Glasgow had an archive service before 1973 but they were very much the exceptions.

8 See Scottish Archive Network website, <www.scan.org.uk> [accessed April 2012]. I am not profligate in providing internet page addresses, since they change regularly and have all the permanency of the business section of a telephone directory. For similar reasons, I have been selective about what I state as being accessible online.

9 These Data Sheets may be viewed on the Scottish Records Association website, <www.scottishrecordsassociation.org> [accessed April 2012]. Since 1995, the SRA has also published *Scottish Archives*, a journal devoted to studies of records relating to Scotland. It has much exceptionally useful and accessible material, as will be obvious from the footnotes to this essay. The SRA also publishes a regular newsletter, *Retour*.

10 The National Archives website, <www.nationalarchives.gov.uk> [accessed April 2012].

11 See Ritchie, A. ARCHON and Scotland, *Scottish Archives*, vol. 9, (2003), 83–6.

12 'Access to Archives', <www.nationalarchives.gov.uk/a2a/> [accessed April 2012].

13 Aim25 website, <www.aim25.ac.uk> [accessed April 2012].

14 See Rosie, 2004, 109–22.

15 <www.nas.gov.uk/nras> [accessed April 2012].

16 Created in 2011 from a union of the former National Archives for Scotland (NAS) and the General Register Office for Scotland (GROS). National Archives of Scotland ran from 1999–2011, and before that it was called the Scottish Record Office. Even now, some older historians still insist on calling it HM General Register House, the title commonly used before 1948. For simplicity, this long-lived organisation will here be called by its latest name, the National Records of Scotland. Its new website address will be <www.nrscotland.gov.uk>.

17 See the the National Archives of Scotland website, <www.nas.gov.uk> [accessed April 2012].

18 SRO, 1996.

19 Donaldson, 1978.

20 Clarke, 2011 and Sinclair, 1994.

21 Two published volumes, SRO, 1971 and 1976, were the first of a now discontinued series giving very detailed summaries of the first ninety-six of these collections. Although largely superseded by the online catalogue, they still have much value.

22 For a useful structural account of the organisation and its remit, see Milne, 1957. The Highland Destitution Records (HD) are a perfect example of the older legacy of the Scottish Office.

23 Holmes, 2000, 71–82.

24 Borthwick, 2012, 191–230.

25 Fraser, 1988.
26 Longmore, 2004, 39–54.
27 On the usefulness of the sheriff court records, see Blair-Imrie, 2006, 70–80. See also Bigwood, 2004, 26–38.
28 See for instance two recent articles by Sanderson, 2008, 15–26 and Sanderson, 2010, 35–51.
29 See ScotlandsPeople, the online genealogy resource, <www.scotlandspeople.gov.uk> [accessed April 2012].
30 For a flavour of this, see Mitchison and Leneman, 1989; Cage, 1981.
31 Adams, 1966–1988.
32 Gibson, 2007.
33 NLS, 1971.
34 NLS, 1938–1992.
35 It is appropriate to note here MacDougall, 1978. This was very comprehensive at its time of publication and is still extremely useful.
36 NLS, MSS1635-1644. The well known published selection by Allardyce, 1888, scarcely does justice to Ramsay's work and insights.
37 For the issues involved in selecting and interpreting architectural papers, see Watters, 1999, 91–9.
38 See Bailey, 1996.
39 Go to the RCAHMS website at <www.rcahms.gov.uk> [accessed April 2012].
40 There is an account of this and of the first outcome of the 1994 Act in Flett, 1998, 6–10.
41 For a sense of the role of local government and the records it generated, see Whetstone, 1981.
42 A good introduction is Convery, Cripps, and Gray, 1998, 104–10.
43 Ritchie, 2006, 24–7.
44 Most notably by Whatley, 2000.
45 The original survey is kept by NRS in its internal office files in the series G/329. It can be made available on request.
46 <www.archiveshub.ac.uk> [accessed April 2012].
47 It remains largely uncatalogued but there is an excellent report by the Historical Manuscripts Commission, 1925.
48 Reid, 1999, 83–90.
49 Parry, 2005, 13–18 is a most useful summary.
50 Brown, 2005, 116–24.
51 <www.nationalarchives.gov.uk/hospitalrecords> [accessed April 2012].
52 <www.clinicalnotes.ac.uk> [accessed April 2012].
53 A full summary of holdings is in Nicoll, 2006, 105–19.
54 Burton, 2008, 39–46.
55 Murray, 2008, 96–101. See also Retour, no. 15, Spring 2011.
56 <www.gla.ac.uk/archives/bacs> [accessed April 2012].
57 Topen, 1998, 97–103.
58 Birnie and McCarthy, 2006, 95–103.
59 See McDonald, 1997, 30–43.
60 Between 1996 and 1999, this writer was part of the NRS appraisal team selecting the post-1948 Coal Board records for preservation. The ex-Coal Board staff and miners who advised us in our work explained that the local colliery records were usually the last thing to be thrown down each pit shaft before it was capped.
61 The Railway Heritage Committee, established in 1996 but scheduled to be abolished in 2013, was given powers to identify and 'designate' records of historic interest held

or created by the private companies. The anticipation was that these could eventually be steered to public archives for preservation. It has had some notable successes, particularly the rescue of the GNER archive, now destined for RINA. The Committee's powers are to be transferred to the Trustees of the National Museum of Science and Industry.

62 Byrne, 2010, 87–98.

63 PRO, 1963–8.

64 The TNA references for this material are HO102 and HO103; the NRS copies are at RH2/4.

65 Ian Levitt has written two articles exploring Scottish material in the Cabinet Office records for the years 1917–66: Levitt (1999 and 2000a). See also Levitt, 2000b, 37–47.

66 TNA, Chatham papers, PRO/30/8/190, ff. 193–203, letters of William Wilson to William Pitt and to William McDowall, March 1799.

67 BL, Add. Mss. 39,187–Add. Mss. 39,211.

68 BL, Add. Mss. 59,258.

69 <www.bl.uk> [accessed April 2012].

70 BL, OIOC, Home Misc. H/728, pp. 500–1, letter of David Scott to Colonel or Mrs Edwards, 15 Aug. 1796 (copy).

71 For a very good discussion of this, with many useful examples, see Smith, 2007, 32–8.

72 NYCRO, Northallerton, Dundas of Zetland, ZNK/X/2/1/1585, Letter of Charles Innes to Lord Dundas, 9 Jan. 1807.

73 <www.nationalarchives.gov.uk/nra/default.asp> [accessed April 2012].

74 Professor Conrad Russell writing in a review in the *Times Literary Supplement*, 19–25 October 1990.

BIBLIOGRAPHY AND FURTHER READING

Adams, I H. *Descriptive List of Plans in the Scottish Record Office*, 4 vols, Edinburgh, 1966–88.

Allardyce, A. *Scotland and Scotsmen in the Eighteenth Century*, 2 vols, Edinburgh and London, 1888.

Bailey, R, ed. *Scottish Architects' Papers: A Source Book*, Edinburgh, 1996.

Bigwood, F. The courts of Argyll, 1664–1825, *Scottish Archives*, 10 (2004) 26–38.

Birnie, J and McCarthy, C. The Diageo archive – capturing the spirit of the past, *Scottish Archives*, 12 (2006), 95–103.

Blair-Imrie, H. The 'ordinary processes' of the sheriff court: An important source for eighteenth century agricultural and social history, *Scottish Archives*, 12 (2006), 70–80.

Borthwick, A. Records of the Law. In Mulhern, M A, ed., *Scottish Life and Society. A Compendium of Scottish Ethnology, Volume 13: The Law*, Edinburgh, 2012, 191–230.

Brown, C. 'Unlocking the medicine chest' – medical records at the University of Dundee, *Scottish Archives*, 11 (2005), 116–24.

Burton, P F. Using Quaker records for social history, *Scottish Archives*, 14 (2008), 39–46.

Byrne, L. Archives of the West Highland Museum, Fort William, *Scottish Archives*, 16 (2010), 87–98.

Cage, R A. *The Scottish Poor Law, 1745–1845*, Edinburgh, 1981.

Clarke, T. *Tracing Your Scottish Ancestors: A Guide to Ancestry Research in the National Archives of Scotland*, 6th edn, Edinburgh, 2011.

Convery, S, Cripps, J and Gray, I. Aberdeen City Archives: A celebration of 600 years of council registers, *Scottish Archives*, 4 (1998), 104–10.

Donaldson, G. *The Sources of Scottish History*, privately published, 1978.

Flett, I. The genealogy of archives: Root and branch of the tree of administration, *Scottish Archives*, 4 (1998), 6–10.

Fraser, H. *Conflict and Class: Scottish Workers 1700–1838*, Edinburgh, 1988.

Gibson, R M. *The Scottish Countryside: Its Changing Face, 1700–2000*, Edinburgh, 2007.

Historical Manuscripts Commission, the. *Report on the Laing Manuscripts Preserved in the University of Edinburgh*, ed. H Paton, 2 vols, London, 1925.

Holmes, H. Viewing an 'underworld': Sources of evidence for Irish migratory potato workers in early twentieth-century Scotland, *Scottish Archives*, 6 (2000), 71–82.

ISAD(G): General International Standard Archival Description, 2nd edn, Ottawa, 2000.

Imrie, J. The Modern Scottish Record Office, *Scottish Historical Review*, 53 (1974), 194–210.

Levitt, I. Scottish papers submitted to the Cabinet, 1917–45: A guide to records held at the Public Record Office and National Archives of Scotland, *Scottish Economic and Social History*, 19:1 (1999), 18–54.

Levitt, I. Scottish papers submitted to the Cabinet, 1945–66: A guide to records held at the Public Record Office and National Archives of Scotland, *Scottish Economic and Social History*, 20(1) (2000a), 58–125.

Levitt, I. Scottish papers presented to the British Cabinet, 1917–66: Their archival and historical significance, *Scottish Archives*, 6 (2000b), 37–47.

Longmore, B. The High Court of Justiciary databases: A solemn path through crime, *Scottish Archives*, 10 (2004), 39–54.

MacDougall, I. *Catalogue of Some Labour Records in Scotland and Some Scots Records Outside Scotland*, Edinburgh, 1978.

McDonald, S. Bank of Scotland archives: Past, present and future; and Wilkinson, V. Hidden treasures: A brief insight into the Scottish Archives of the Royal Bank of Scotland, *Scottish Archives*, 3 (1997), 30–43.

Milne, D. *The Scottish Office*, London, 1957.

Mitchison, R and Leneman, L. *Sexuality and Social Control*, Oxford, 1989.

Murray, D B. The legacy of a fellowship of independent churches, 1725 to 1989: The voluminous Glasite Archive, *Scottish Archives*, 14 (2008), 96–101.

Nicoll, A. 'One of our main shop windows to the world at large': The Scottish Catholic Archives, *Scottish Archives*, 12 (2006), 105–19.

NLS. *Summary Catalogue of the Advocates' Manuscripts*, Edinburgh, 1971.

NLS. *National Library of Scotland Catalogue of Manuscripts Acquired Since 1925*, 8 vols, Edinburgh, 1938–92.

Parry, C. Web-based access to Scottish Health Records, *Scottish Archives*, 11 (2005), 13–18.

PRO. *Guide to the Contents of the Public Record Office*, 3 vols, London, 1963–8.

Royal Commission on the Ancient and Historical Monuments of Scotland (RCAHMS), <www.rcahms.gov.uk> [accessed April 2012].

Reid, N H. The photographic collections in St Andrews University Library, *Scottish Archives*, 5 (1999), 83–90.

Ritchie, A. Finding Scottish burgh records, *Scottish Archives*, 12 (2006), 24–7.

Rosie, A. 'Something sensible for a change': The National Register of Archives for Scotland, *Scottish Archives*, 10 (2004), 109–22.

Sanderson, M. Lives of the Scottish cottars, 1585–1620: The evidence of their testaments, *ROSC*, 20 (2008), 15–26.

Sanderson, H. Clothing sixteenth-century Scotland: Crafts, clothes and clients, *ROSC*, 22 (2010), 35–51.

Simpson, G G. *Scottish Handwriting 1150–1650. An Introduction to the Reading of Documents*, East Linton, 1998.

Sinclair, C J. *Tracing Scottish Local History in the Scottish Record Office*, Edinburgh, 1994.

Smith, A. 'South of the border'? Some great British family and estate collections, *Scottish Archives*, 13 (2007), 32–8.

SRO. *Lists of Gifts and Deposits in the Scottish Record Office*, Edinburgh, 1971 and 1976.

SRO. *The Guide to the National Archives of Scotland*, Edinburgh, 1996.

Topen, A. The Scottish Brewing Archive, *Scottish Archives*, 4 (1998) 97–103.

Watters, D M. Complexity and diversity: Case studies in Scottish twentieth-century architectural archives, *Scottish Archives*, 5 (1999) 91–9.

Whatley, C. *Scottish Society 1707–1830: Beyond Jacobitism, towards Industrialisation*, Manchester, 2000.

Whetstone, A. *Scottish County Government in the Eighteenth and Early Nineteenth Centuries*, Edinburgh, 1981.

ONLINE RESOURCES

All websites last accessed April 2012.

Aim25, <www.aim25.ac.uk>

Archives Hub, <www.archiveshub.ac.uk>

British Library website, <www.bl.uk>

Business Archives Council of Scotland, <www.gla.ac.uk/archives/bacs>

Clinical Notes website, <www.clinicalnotes.ac.uk>

National Archives, the, <www.nationalarchives.gov.uk>

National Register of Archives for Scotland, <www.nas.gov.uk/nras>

ScotlandsPeople, <www.scotlandspeople.gov.uk>

Scottish Archive Network, <www.scan.org.uk>

Scottish Handriting.com, <www.Scottishhandwriting.com>

Scottish Records Association, <www.scottishrecordsassociation.org>

8   Local History Societies

ALEXANDER MURDOCH

Local historians are often interested in ethnology, even if they are not aware of it, and ethnologists in Scotland have had an interest in recent years in the possibilities of fruitful collaboration with local history and heritage societies. When the University of Edinburgh Department of Adult Education and Extra-Mural Studies organised a residential conference on Local History in Scotland in 1965, Alexander Fenton contributed a paper on the subject of 'Local Investigation and the Museum', which explicitly identified ethnological research as central to the subject. He contrasted an older 'holistic method', as the conference reporter recorded it, which produced a complex account of a locality such as that in John Firth's *Reminiscences of an Orkney Parish*[1] or William Alexander's *Notes and Sketches Illustrative of Northern Rural Life in the Eighteenth Century*,[2] with the more modern idea of carrying out detailed local research that would form the basis of a comparative national work (the word compendium did not appear in the 1966 report on this paper) of ethnology in a Scottish context. 'By patient collection of local detail through on-the-spot fieldwork, from oral sources, from printed and manuscript sources and careful comparative analysis of the results it would be possible to learn a great deal more about local history.'[3]

T C Smout spoke at the same conference, on 'Economic History and Local Study', arguing that 'local and economic historians needed each other badly', echoing an proposition made earlier by George Pratt Insh in a series of essays published under the title *The Study of Local History* in 1932, having previously appeared in the *Quarterly Bulletin* of the Educational Institute of Scotland. Using a case study of two Lanarkshire parishes, Dalziel and Old Monkland, Pratt Insh argued that only local studies could illuminate the history of social and economic change in Scotland, declaring that 'it is on the student of local history that the historian must depend' for the data necessary to understand the modernisation of Scotland; 'then it will be possible to work out a real history of Scotland: a history that will differ from all previous histories of Scotland in being not a record of tribal war and of antiquarian memories but a history of the Scottish people'.[4] It was Professor Smout who carried out the agenda Pratt Insh set out but could not progress. In his famous *A History of the Scottish People 1560–1830*, continuously in print for more than four decades, the notes and list of further reading record just how much Smout had engaged with local history throughout the country in attempting to write a national social and economic history of early modern Scotland. Although few publications of local history articles are cited, a myriad of primary sources published by the Scottish historical clubs, as well as the great

Statistical Accounts for Scotland of the eighteenth and nineteenth centuries, enabled Smout to capture something of the compelling human drama of social and economic change in early modern Scotland rather than render it an abstract process based on money and machines in both rural and expanding urban settlements.

This was a theme Professor Smout returned to in an address at the launch of the Centre for Tayside and Fife Studies at the University of St Andrews in 1990, which included discussion of the 'interface between history and ethnography' in the study of farmtoun and fishing communities in the region, in which 'the study of man in relation to his use of work tools and the social organisation that surrounds work' was central. 'Ethnography has no purpose and little meaning,' he argued, 'except if it starts from the basis of careful study of a particular community, or at least a set of communities in a coherent regional context.'[5] One example Smout discussed was how material culture and economic and social history intersected in the study of the history of the use of tools, in which he had himself collaborated with Alexander Fenton on recovering 'the rationale of the older, more primitive tools'. In terms of folklore, Smout called for sustained efforts to collect (and publish) 'the lore of the agricultural communities, the coal mining areas and the textile towns' before oral testimony about them was no longer available.[6] One way to do this would be to build bridges between professional researchers based in universities (or museums, libraries and adult education) and those who were interested in local history.

NATIONAL ORGANISATION

Similar objectives were behind various attempts at forming a national organisation in Scotland that would encourage those interested in the history of Scottish communities and regions to exchange information about their activities and share examples of what now would be termed 'best practice'. A national exchange or forum would help to prevent duplication of effort while raising the quality and value of what could be achieved by local historians individually and collectively. In Scotland, the lead was taken by historians involved in adult education. The creation of a national organisation to promote the study of local history in Scotland, for example, was proposed at the aforementioned conference of 1965. Although much effort was expended in trying to achieve a genuinely national coalition, almost inevitably most of the organisational impetus came from central Scotland, and in particular Edinburgh. In the 1960s and 1970s, while Basil Skinner was Director of Extra-Mural Studies at the University of Edinburgh, efforts were made to form a Scottish Local History Congress and a Scottish Local History Council.[7] Later Ian MacDougall, at that time a lecturer at Newbattle Abbey adult education college in Midlothian, organised a conference on Scottish local history in 1981. He was not a local historian but a labour historian who served as Secretary of the Scottish Labour History Society from 1961 until 1996. Aware, however, that much labour history involved a degree of 'overlap', as he put it, with local history, MacDougall acted as Secretary to what was first the Scottish Local History Conference (SLHC) and from 1983 the Scottish Local History Forum (SLHF), initially with some assistance from the Wolfson Foundation in the shape of a small grant to cover postage and stationery expenses.[8]

Further institutional support for the SLHF, as it had become, was obtained when Professor Eric Forbes of the History of Medicine and Science unit at the University of Edinburgh agreed to become its Chairman. As Chairman of the History Department at the University of Edinburgh, he was able to provide modest but vital logistical support as the SLHF sought to expand its activities from organising two conferences per year to publishing a newsletter and embarking on a survey of local history societies in Scotland. An internationally known historian of science, Forbes was a native of St Andrews who genuinely embodied a Scottish tradition of international and national (rather than specifically local) scholarship. After his sudden and tragic death from a heart attack in late 1984, the committee of the SLHF was able to commission and publish a collection of essays in honour of Forbes that illustrated that the movement in Scotland, or at least Edinburgh, in the 1980s conceived of local history in Scotland as a discipline that should be practised in a national context. It was edited by Graeme Cruick-shank and published in 1988 under the title *A Sense of Place: Studies in Scottish Local History*, and its contributors included Alexander Fenton and Ian MacDougall.[9] It is telling, however, that the SLHF could not find a publisher for this work and had to meet the costs of publication and marketing the book itself. Commercial publishers felt that the collection lacked a coherent theme that justified publishing its contents collectively rather than individually – a common complaint of publishers regarding collections of essays, but nevertheless an indication of the challenges faced by a voluntary organisation devoted to the promotion of 'local history' in a Scottish national context.

One of the principal aims envisaged at the 1965 conference for a national organisation to promote the study of local history was to put local societies in contact (or perhaps under the influence of) 'national bodies'. They were identified at the conference by James McNaught, Director of Education for Banffshire, as the 'School of Scottish Studies [University of Edinburgh], Scottish History Society, Society of Antiquaries of Scotland, Ancient Monuments Commission, Ordnance Survey, Council for British Archaeology, museums including the Museums Council for Scotland, local authorities, universities, colleges, Colleges of Education and schools'.[10] Grant Simpson reported at the same conference that he knew of 'approximately 40 societies at present dealing with Scottish local history', of whom 'some 15 issued publications other than a mere annual report'.[11] Some societies that had published, such as the Orkney Record and Antiquarian Society and the Third Spalding Club (for north-east Scotland), had been unable to continue, whereas the Abertay Historical Society, based in Dundee and Perth, had begun the publication of a pamphlet series which was still ongoing in 2011.

In 1981 and 1982 the SLHC sent out questionnaires not only to local history societies but also to a miscellany of many additional Scottish societies that were thought in some way to pursue activities that related to local history in Scotland. Thirty-one societies had joined the SLHC by the autumn of 1982, as opposed to twelve university departments based in six universities, ten museums, eight archives, and two trade unions (the NUM and the Educational Institute of

Scotland).[12] The forms returned as part of this survey illustrate just how broadly local history in a Scottish context was defined by those organising the SLHC. Some of the less obvious groups contacted are listed in Appendix A.[13]

The survey resulted in a publication recording its results edited by Hilary Kirkland and published under the title *Scottish Local History*, with copyright claimed by the SLHF.[14] The dedication was to Sir John Sinclair of Ulbster, editor of the 'Old' or 'First' *Statistical Account of Scotland* in the 1790s, which raises a point regarding the influence of the Scottish 'Statistical Account' approach to local history. The tradition established in Scotland by the publication of the 'Old' and the 'New' *Statistical Account of Scotland* in the 1790s and the 1830s and 1840s respectively is still looked to by many local historians as a national template for the study of locality – an 'interface' (to use Professor Smout's expression) between historical, ethnological and sociological approaches to that study which is unique to Scotland, if not uniquely Scottish.[15] Whilst what was known in early modern Europe as 'political arithmetic' (the counting of people, their wealth and their work for the purposes of the state) was not solely the province of the Statistical Accounts, Scotland was perhaps unique in that this process was successfully carried out not only after political union with England rather than before it, but also because it was carried out under the auspices of the Church of Scotland as opposed to the state. Hilary Kirkland and her colleagues of the SLHC sent out over 500 questionnaires in 1981–82, not to parish ministers, as Sinclair had done, but to 'all organisations we could identify which were involved wholly or peripherally in Local History in Scotland'.[16] Those associated with the survey were disappointed that only a quarter of those who were sent questionnaires responded, which may have meant that some organisations were no longer active, or that 'some may not consider their interests fall within our categories'.[17] As with any census, there will always be those who prefer not to be recorded, even if those seeking the information are not directly associated with the state.

Similarly, we do not know the response to the SLHC note of guidance for those wishing to establish local history societies.[18] It was a document which conceived local history as part of the broader framework of community life and society, although beginning with the unattributed definition: 'Local History has been defined as "the study of the origins and rise, periods of stability and change, and possibly the decline and fall, of a Community".' It was acknowledged that 'this definition leaves a lot unsaid, and every Local History Society finds its own balance between Social events, Educational activities, Research projects, Publishing and the Conservation of the natural and built environment'. The author conceded that much depended on the committee that would be chosen to take responsibility for the activities of the society. It was argued that what was important about establishing a local history society was that it could 'quickly be of significant value in the community', and it was assumed that societies would work closely with salaried staff in local government. Readers were advised to approach their 'local Librarian, Regional Archivist or District Council Community Education Officer' before attempting to establish a society.[19] In practice, societies were established, or had been established and run long before the SLHC, in many different ways, with or without local government support. The SLHC also advocated that local history societies should do something more than meet to hear lectures; for example, identifying oral history projects, producing copies of primary sources for use in schools, indexing projects for local libraries and, of course, publishing. Conservation, including conservation of archaeological remains, was another area of activity identified. It is revealing that, in addition to advising local societies to affiliate with the SLHC, other 'national', yet voluntary, organisations were recommended as worth considering, including the Scottish Civic Trust, the Scottish Genealogy Society, the Scottish Labour History Society, the Scottish Society for Industrial Archaeology, the Society of Antiquaries of Scotland, the Scottish Records Association and the Scottish Oral History Group.

In short, the SLHC document was a forerunner of the national surveys of Scottish local history sources undertaken by Michael Cox at the end of the twentieth century, published in 1992 and 1999 under the title *Exploring Scottish History*, with the support of the Scottish Library Association as well as the SLHF. Cox's aim was to explore 'Scottish local history', which implicitly (again) looked back to the example of Sir John Sinclair's *Statistical Account of Scotland* as much as it reflected modern ideas of local or community history generated by the historical profession's movement away from political and diplomatic history, in favour of economic and social history, during the twentieth century. Sinclair and his successor editors of the *New Statistical Account of Scotland* did not define their work as history. Arguably, they reflected the 'modernism' of contemporary preoccupations of Scottish Enlightenment culture in the eighteenth century, determined to abandon national precedent in search of new solutions to the challenges of modern life that would 'improve' – to use the contemporary term – the lives and culture of everyone in modern society.[20]

Just as the original SLHC survey of 'local history' organisations had been exceedingly inclusive in its definition of just what was local history, or rather what related to Scottish history, *Exploring Scottish History* cast its net widely. Archives were listed, of course, both national and local. Local libraries were also included, often with a note of primary sources available for consultation. Many museums were listed, including the National Museums of Scotland, which housed the Scottish Ethnological Archive. As a work of reference, these books were more a directory of library services and research resources for both national and local Scottish history than a directory or survey of Scottish local history societies. Nevertheless some societies, including 'family history' societies, were included on the grounds that they had acquired collections that could interest researchers. Those listed in 1992 are given in Appendix B. Those listed in the second edition (1999) are given in Appendix C.

Although it has not yet been possible to organise the publication of a further edition of *Exploring Scottish History*, in 2004 and 2005 the SLHF cooperated with the Glasgow Caledonian University Heritage Futures initiative in attempting a survey of local history societies that reflected more the approach originally taken by the SLHC in 1981 than the 'directory' approach of the *Exploring Scottish History* volumes. The aim of the survey was ambitious: it was intended as 'a major study into how "the past" is used and perceived by local history/heritage groups in Scotland'.[21] Whether or not the membership of the SLHF adequately represented all local history/heritage groups in Scotland is more problematic. Nevertheless, sixty-seven such groups responded to the survey (with a total membership claimed as 'nearly 10,000'). It is striking that 72 per cent of these members were identified as retired, and 80 per cent as being over the age of 55. The survey made it clear that those in Scotland interested in 'local history' or 'heritage' pursued a wide variety of concerns: large numbers of groups reported interests in topics including labour/local industry (67 per cent), family history (59 per cent), archaeology (57 per cent) and agricultural or rural history (51 per cent), with one third of respondents also indicating substantial interest in 'maritime history or natural/horticultural themes'. Over two thirds of groups identified 'research' as a primary activity, and 58 per cent of respondents were involved in publishing.

Despite the fact that most, if not all, respondents to the Heritage Futures were contacted through the SLHF, most groups indicated a wish to develop further links with other local history and heritage groups. In the light of SLHC interest in encouraging societies to seek the help and support of relevant departments within local government, it is interesting that a quarter of the respondents surveyed 'reported partnerships with libraries, museums/galleries and local authority, whilst smaller numbers had ties to universities/colleges and schools'. A substantial number of groups (43 per cent) reported success in generating grant income, mostly from the Heritage Lottery Fund, which arguably substantiated the link between local history and heritage studies and community education, particularly for the retired, who had time to invest in research and further study. The accumulation of collections by some societies noted in a number of the entries in the *Exploring Scottish History* volumes was documented in greater detail in the Heritage Futures survey and raised the issue of ensuring that such collections were properly conserved and preserved.

The great diversity of activity in history and heritage at local level in Scotland illustrates the challenges posed in trying to adequately represent what this activity contributed culturally, or in terms of ethnology and folklore, on a national level. This is further demonstrated by material held in the Scottish Library Association Local Studies Database.[22] A significant level of resource is required to adequately record and support grass roots community history in Scotland. Whereas family history may be seen as primarily individualistic (and it attracts substantially more activity and people than local history), local history really is about communities. How these communities relate to the 'nation' is not a straightforward question, but posing that question raises issues about what constitutes a nation. It is instructive to note that there is a marked contrast in approach between the tradition of 'statistical accounts' in Scotland and that of the Victoria County Histories, a continuing project in England and Wales.

What has become apparent in the past century is that modern attempts to collate and present the 'local' at national level have not been achieved successfully in the same short period in which the 'Old' and the 'New' *Statistical Account of Scotland* were able to deliver in the eighteenth and early nineteenth centuries. This may be partly due to Scotland's small size, but in the twentieth century the attempt to produce a 'third statistical account of Scotland' through local government and the universities failed because these institutions manifestly did not have the national 'reach' to carry out such an ambitious undertaking within a limited period of time.[23] The Victoria County History suffered the same fate, although efforts continue to complete it, and considerable resources have been allocated to reviving what had been a moribund project as part of marking a new century and millennium.

The British Association for Local History takes an interest in Scottish local history. It is a charity that was founded at about the same time as the SLHC/SLHF with support from public funds in England and Wales, reflecting the platform of commitment to community services as well as community history that lies behind much of what defines 'local history'. This is much stronger in English national culture than in Scotland, Wales and Northern Ireland, where the contrast with 'national' (Scottish, Welsh and Irish history) is much more pronounced.[24]

Nevertheless, there are strong traditions of active scholarship in local history in many parts of Scotland, although the quality and nature of the activity varies greatly. The second edition of *Exploring Scottish History* recorded several new Highland historical societies, including the North Lochs Historical Society on Lewis, but not Comunn Eachdraidh Nis (Ness Historical Society), which now hosts a website that records its foundation in 1977, 'when a group of local history enthusiasts from north Lewis met informally to discuss how best to preserve the rich, but as yet largely undocumented, social and cultural heritage of their community'.[25] In 1977 Manpower Services Commission grants enabled seven workers to carry out 'a 20 week employment programme to record, document and archive aspects of Ness history'. In 1984 the society obtained a lease for its own premises, which 'enabled a further programme of activity and MSC sponsored employment' that resulted in the acquisition of additional collections; and in 1992 it was able to establish the Ness Heritage Centre in the village of Habost, which houses its collections of photographs, artefacts, and transcriptions and recordings of 'oral recollections of local history'. Another example of local history societies becoming involved in community initiatives and community education is the Ross of Mull Historical Centre, whose web pages invite visitors 'to explore these pages to learn more about this unique corner of the Hebrides, especially if your ancestors hail from here or you will be visiting the area'.[26] Amongst its projects has been the purchase of Bunessan Mill, built in the eighteenth century by the Argyll estate and enlarged in the 1830s, with the help of a grant from the Scottish Land Fund & Community Land Unit. This has been developed as a visitor and community centre that houses an archive of genealogical and other material relating to the Ross of Mull. Heritage Lottery Fund (HLF) grants have made possible a number of projects, including the installation of interpretation panels for walkers that give information about local plant and wildlife and that also attracted funding from the Argyll & Bute Local Biodiversity Partnership. Publications include an introduction to the social history, archaeology, wildlife and landscape of the Ross of Mull, as well as booklets relating to local burial grounds, including transcriptions of text on gravestones and plans of their layout. Although the name 'Ross of Mull Historical Centre' identifies it as a historical centre, clearly its work closely relates local and social history to ethnography.

Less 'local' in focus is the Gaelic Society of Inverness, whose *Transactions* have included papers that very much focus on the Highlands as a region rather than on specific localities within it. Volume LXIV (2004–06) included papers on Lochaber and North Uist that might be defined as 'local' interest, but also articles on medical practices in the Highlands and Islands at the time of the potato famine of 1845–53, and on the Harris Tweed industry in the nineteenth and twentieth centuries.

Some local history societies have a long history – in the case of the Hawick Archaeological Society, going back to 1856.[27] With roots in the public lectures associated with the Temperance Movement, the society moved into publishing its *Transactions* and has come to be associated with Hawick Museum. Similar publishing societies of some pedigree include the Dumfriesshire and Galloway Natural History and Antiquarian Society (DGNHAS) (founded 1862) and the East Lothian Antiquarian and Field Naturalists' Society (ELAFNS) (founded 1924), both of which publish *Transactions* similar in style to some of the long-established English county historical societies. Some of what is published in the transactions of these societies follows either an ethnological or ethnographical approach. The 2008 volume (Third Series Volume LXXXII) of the DGNHAS *Transactions* included an article on the laird and scholar Sir Herbert Maxwell, and another on the statistical accounts for Dumfries, Kirkcudbright and Wigtown, as well as an edition of the notebook of a Glencaple wildfowler kept from 1872 to 1947, and an article on Hoddam as a medieval estate in Annandale. Volume XXVI of the ELAFNS *Transactions* (2006) included an article by T C Smout on the woodlands of East Lothian, 1585–1765, while Volume XXVII (2008) published an article on the agrarian improver Sir George Buchan-Hepburn of Smeaton. Volume XXVIII (2010) included an piece on 'Leisure and the working class in East Lothian in the late Victorian age' by Jean Lindsay.

At the end of the twentieth century the ELAFNS was one of a federation of East Lothian societies that obtained funding from the HLF for a Fourth Statistical Account of East Lothian, with the aim of recording the economic, social and cultural life of the county parish by parish for the period 1945 to 2000, as well as its modern local history. This was published in seven volumes between 2003 and 2009.[28] A project with more of a 'community' than 'county' focus in East Lothian was the Prestongrange Community Archaeology Project of 2004–08. It raised financial support from the HLF and East Lothian Council, which led to a community archaeology conference in May 2009 built on the work at the harbour of Morrison's Haven on the former estate of Prestongrange near Prestonpans. The project was an ambitious exploration of a rich site for industrial archaeology specific to East Lothian but arguably of national 'Scottish' if not 'British' importance.[29]

In contrast to the *Transactions* of the ELAFNS and DGNHAS, the *Magazine* of the Kintyre Antiquarian & Natural History Society is more informal, as is *Kist*, the magazine of the Natural History & Antiquarian Society of Mid Argyll. The Abertay Historical Society publishes a pamphlet series rather than a journal, an example of which (No. 49) is by Ann Petrie, *1915 Rent Strikes: An East Coast Perspective* (2008), while for this part of Scotland archaeology is served separately in the *Tayside and Fife Archaeological Journal*, which began publication in 1995.

David Moody, in his essay on 'Scottish local and family history' in *The Oxford Companion to Local and Family History*, emphasised how different Scottish local history (and family history) was from English equivalents. 'In terms of population and affiliations,' he wrote, 'Scotland is no more and no less a region than, say, Lancashire. The dearth of local records has encouraged the tendency to plump for the national perspective.'[30] Yet he also acknowledged what he termed 'the ethnological impulse' in terms of 'the study of folk customs and music, material culture, social organization, and literature', as well as oral history.[31] Moody also noted the importance of the local and regional focus of economic and social historians which, together with ethnology, paradoxically unified a Scottish 'national' framework as a means of identifying distinctive aspects of Scottish ethnology and Scottish economic and social history. Much has changed since 1996; for example, parliamentary devolution has been put in place, although this has not yet led to 'national' Scottish funding for local history. Indeed, Westminster has allocated substantial sums to revive the Victoria County History of England under the slogan 'England's Past for Everyone',[32] with no reference to Scotland and Wales, on the grounds that this was a responsibility of the devolved governments.[33]

Local history in populous and wealthy countries such as England, France and Germany will always be different from the context in which local history is pursued in countries that are less well endowed. However, as the success of T C Smout's *History of the Scottish People* demonstrated – as, arguably, did the great Statistical Accounts of Scotland in the late eighteenth and early nineteenth centuries – the local and the national can be used to create a dynamic dialogue that is not possible in larger and wealthier societies. It is essential that this dialogue continues to take place.

APPENDIX A

Groups contacted in 1981–82 by the SLHC

Charles Rennie MacIntosh Society, the Costume Society of Scotland, the Conservation Bureau of the Scottish Development Agency, the Scottish Committee of the Garden History Society, the Fortress Study Group, the Heritage Co-ordination Group of Surrey (which declared its interest in 'encouraging local amenity and heritage preservation organisations'), the Mountaineering Council of Scotland, the North British Traction Society (which had an interest in tram transportation history), the Orkney Sound Archive, the Printed Ephemera Society, the Scottish Civic Trust, the Scottish Women's Rural Institutes (who acknowledged 'a worthwhile contribution to Local History in our Village History Books'), the Scottish Rights of Way Society, the Social History Curators Group (administered from Stockport museum in Lancashire) and The Stair Society. Overseas societies included the Royal Caledonian Society of South Australia (Inc.), Scottish Heritage USA (sponsors of the 'Grandfather Mountain Highland Games') and the Sons of Scotland Benevolent Association of Toronto (who listed one of their aims as preserving 'among the elements of Canadian culture the great traditions of Scottish history, music and literature').

Groups listed in *Exploring Scottish History*, 1992

Aberdeen and NE Scotland Family History Society, the Abertay Historical Society, Bridge of Weir History Society, Carluke Parish Historical Society, the Cathcart Society, Central Scotland Family History Society, Colinton Local History Society Library, the Costorphine Trust, Drymen and District Local History Society, Dumfries and Galloway Family History Society, the East Lothian Antiquarian and Field Naturalists' Society, the Fala Soutra & District History & Heritage Society, Fife Family History Society, Glasgow and West of Scotland Family History Society, Gullane Local History Society & Dirleton Local History Group, Hawick Archaeological Society, Kincardine Local History Group, the Lesmahagow Parish Historical Association Archive, the Liddesdale Heritage Association, the West Lyndedale Archive of the West Linton Historical Association, Milngavie and Bearsden Historical Society, Morningside Heritage Association, the Natural History & Antiquarian Society of Mid Argyll, the Sunart Archive in Ardnamurchan, and the Uig Historical Society.

Groups listed in *Exploring Scottish History*, 1999

Ayrshire Archaeological & Natural History Society, Blairgowrie Genealogy Centre & Blairgowrie, Rattray & District Local History Trust, Bonyrigg & Lasswade Local History Society, Kintyre Antiquarian & Natural History Society, Dalkeith History Society, Dunbar & District History Society, Tay Valley Family History Society, Dunning Parish Historical Society, Dunoon & Cowal Heritage Trust, Cramond Heritage Trust, the Edinburgh Archaeological Field Society, Galashiels & District Local History Association, Girvan & District Historical Society, Gorebridge & District Local History Society, Comunn Eachdraidh Bharraigh Agus Bhatarsaidh (Barra & Vatersay Historical Society), North Lochs (Isle of Lewis) Historical Society, Kirkliston Local History Archive Trust, Largs & District Historical Society, West Lothian History & Amenity Society Library, Comann Eiachdraidh Lios Mor (Lismore Heritage Society), Lorn Archaeological & Historical Society, the South Queensberry History Group, and the Forth Naturalist & Historian ('a Stirling University informal enterprise').

Under the heading 'societies without premises,' additional groups were listed: Borders Family History Society, Cawdor Heritage Group, Central Scotland Family History Society, Clackmannanshire Field Studies Society, Colinton Local History Society, Cullen Deskford & Portknockie Heritage Group, Currie & District History Society, East Ayrshire Family History Society, the Falkland Society, Ferryhill Heritage Society (Aberdeen), Friockheim & District (Angus) Historical Society, Glasgow Archaeological Society, Great North of Scotland Railway Association, Kinross Historical Society, Lanarkshire Family History Society (formerly Hamilton & District Family History Society), Largs & North Ayrshire Family History Society, Larkhall Heritage Group, Lothians Family History Society, Old Edinburgh Club, Pictish Arts Society, Prestwick History Group, Roslin Heritage Society and the Troon & District Family History Society.

1   Firth, 1920.
2   Alexander, 1877.
3   NAS, GD519/1/4/1: Barclay, 1966, 11–14. There is also a copy in the NLS.
4   Pratt Insh, 1932, 9–10, 39, 79–80.
5   Smout, 1990, 4.
6   Smout, 1990, 12 and 16.
7   See NAS, GD 519/1–2; also Dalzell, T. Obituary: Basil Skinner, *Independent*,
    10 April 1995; Skinner, 1965.
8   NAS, GD 519/3; also GD 519/4/1. Ian MacDougall has written and edited more than
    20 works relating to labour, oral and local history, including several published by the
    European Ethnological Research Centre founded by Alexander Fenton, in its
    'Flashbacks' series. He received an honorary doctorate from the University of
    Edinburgh for his work with the Scottish Working People's History Trust in 2004.
9   Meadows, A J. Forbes, Eric Gray (1933–1984). In *Oxford Dictionary of National Biography*,
    Oxford, 2004, available online at <http://www.oxforddnb.com/view/article/65707>
    [subscription databse, accessed June 2012]; NAS GD 519/4/12/1/1–44; Flamsteed,
    1995.
10 Barclay, 1966, 26.
11 Barclay, 1966, 6.
12 NAS, GD 519/3/1/1–3.
13 NAS, GD 519/3/7–13, including GD 519/3/13/35, letter from General Secretary of
    the Scottish WRI, 16 June 1982.
14 NAS GD 519/3/6/1. See also Kirkland, 1985.
15 Withers, 2006, 35–42.
16 NAS GD 519/3/6/1.
17 NAS GD 519/3/6/1.
18 National Library of Scotland. Scottish Local History Conference Newsletters and
    associated documentation shelved with the journal of the Scottish Local History
    Forum (*Scottish Local History*), shelfmark HP.la.120 PER.
19 Cox 1997, 27. Changes in local government are reflected in the job titles
    'Regional Archivist' and 'District Council Community Education Officer'.
20 Broadie, 1997 includes a translation of Immanuel Kant's famous essay 'What is
    Enlightenment', but this is the English translation of a work written and published
    in German. Anglophone writers in the eighteenth century wrote of 'Improvement'
    rather than of 'Enlightenment'; see Phillipson and Mitchison, 1970.
21 Garden, 2007, 49.
22 In progress 2009. My thanks to Sybil Cavanagh for information about this survey.
23 Cameron, 2007, 31–8.
24 See the BALH journal, *The Local Historian*, which has published articles by Scottish
    historians on aspects of Scottish local history, although not in recent years.
25 Comunn Eachdraidh Nis website, <http://cenonline.org/> [accessed June 2012].
26 <http://www.romhc.org.uk/> [accessed June 2012].
27 Muir, 2006.
28 *Fourth Statistical Account of East Lothian*, 2003–09.
29 Simpson and Johnson, 2009, 8–10.
30 Hey, 2002, 406.
31 Acknowledgement is also made of the important contribution to local history by
    the Scottish Life Archive.

32 Victoria County History project, 'England's Past for Everyone' pages, <www.englandspastforeveryone.org.uk> [accessed June 2012].

33 Also see the articles on 'Local History' and 'Community History' on the 'Making History' web pages, hosted by the Institute of Historical Research at the University of London, <www.history.ac.uk/makinghistory/resources/articles> [accessed June 2012].

BIBLIOGRAPHY AND FURTHER READING

Alexander, W. *Notes and Sketches Illustrative of Northern Rural Life in the Eighteenth Century*, Edinburgh, 1877.

Barclay, J B, ed. *Local history in Scotland. Report of residential Course at Carberry Tower, Musselburgh, Midlothian, 19th to 21st November, 1965*, Edinburgh, 1966.

Broadie, A, ed. *The Scottish Enlightenment: An Anthology*, Edinburgh, 1997.

Cameron, E. The idle dream of James G. Kyd: The *Third Statistical Account of Scotland, 1944–1992, Scottish Local History*, 69 (2007), 31–8.

Cox, M, ed. *Exploring Scottish History*, 2nd edn, Hamilton, 1999.

Fenton, A. Material culture as an aid to local history studies in Scotland, *Journal of the Folklore Institute*, 2:3 (1965), 326–39.

Firth, J. *Reminiscences of an Orkney Parish. Together with old Orkney Words, Riddles and Proverbs*, Stromness, 1920.

Flamsteed, J. *The Correspondence of John Flamsteed, the First Astronomer Royal / Compiled and Edited by Eric G. Forbes, and (for Maria Forbes) by Lesley Murdin and Frances Willmoth*, Bristol, 1995.

Fourth Statistical Account of East Lothian, 7 vols, ed. Sonia Baker, Haddington, 2003–09.

Garden, M-C. SLHF Report: Survey of local history groups, *Scottish Local History*, 69 (2007), 49.

Hey, D, ed. *The Oxford Companion to Local and Family History*, Oxford, 2002.

Kirkland, H. *Third Statistical Account of Scotland*, the County of Midlothian, vol. 22, Edinburgh, 1985.

Muir, J. '*Airchie Oliver's a hunder an' a half!': 150 years of Hawick Archaeological Society (1856–2006) and 100 years of Hawick Museum (1906–2006)*, Hawick, 2006.

Petrie, A. *1915 Rent Strikes: An East Coast Perspective*, Dundee, 2008.

Phillipson, N T and Mitchison, R, eds. *Scotland in the Age of Improvement. Essays in Scottish History in the Eighteenth Century*, Edinburgh, 1970, reissued Edinburgh, 1996.

Pratt Insh, G. *The Study of Local History and Other Essays*, Edinburgh, 1932.

Scottish Local History (journal of the Scottish Local History Forum).

Scottish Local History Forum. *Directory of Library Services for Local Historians*, Gullane, 1988.

Simpson, B and Johnson, M. Community archaeology at Prestongrange: Trying to leave an imprint, *History Scotland*, 9:2 (March/April 2009), 8–10.

Skinner, B C. *The Iron Mills at Crammond*, Edinburgh, 1965.

Smout, T C. *A History of the Scottish People, 1560–1830*, London, 1972.

Smout, T C. *The Cutting Edge: Prospects for Local History in Tayside and Fife*, St Andrews, 1990.

Withers, C. 'National Accountancy, Political Anatomy': The intellectual background to Scotland's Statistical Accounts, *Scottish Local History*, 68 (2006), 35–42.

ONLINE RESOURCES

Scottish Local History Forum: Information about its activities, member organisations and the journal *Scottish Local History* is available at, <http://www.slhf.org>.

9 Ethnology and the Heritage Industry

GARY J WEST

One of the key issues in modern approaches to ethnology as a discipline is the study of the relationship between the past and the present. While 'traditional' ethnological investigations based on folklore and folklife tended to be historically situated, more recent trends have begun to place increasing emphasis on contemporary cultural forms. And yet the concepts and phenomena which *unite* these two approaches continue to hold a deep fascination for ethnologists: *tradition* is one such, for it is often conceived as flowing through time, from past into present and on into the future. *Revivalism* is another, for the deliberate act of reinstating cultural forms which had previously disappeared can tell us a great deal about contemporary attitudes to culture and to our relationship to past creativity. A third strand is the selection, construction and packaging of elements of the past in order to serve certain functions within the present. The label which tends to be attached to this is *heritage*, and it is this which forms the focus of the present chapter. It begins with a brief examination of the various meanings and conceptualisations of the term 'heritage' which have emerged from within ethnology and neighbouring disciplines, before moving on to provide an overview of the current heritage sector within Scotland at both national and local levels. Issues relating to both tangible and intangible heritage are then discussed within the context of global approaches using the relevant UNESCO frameworks as a guide, and finally, some conclusions are drawn as to the ongoing importance of ethnology as a tool for both providing and understanding heritage in the modern world.

MEANINGS OF HERITAGE

While the literal meaning of 'heritage' is 'that which is inherited', scholars and practitioners have tended to impose a wider range of implications and associations on the term. If heritage involves *inheritance*, then by definition it must have a strong diachronic element, a 'passing on' of cultural forms between generations. However, in real terms heritage providers are not able to simply react passively to the arrival of this inheritance from the past, but must proactively seek it out. They do so according to an agenda, of course, determined by all manner of factors relating to their mission, aims, resources, abilities and interests. *Selectivity* is therefore a keyword of heritage, leading many scholars to point out the power which heritage managers and curators are able to exercise over our relationship with the past, and, indeed, in some cases to question the validity of their resulting versions. It is noticeable that there is a strong element of negativity in the academic literature on heritage, much of it centred on the issue of representation, and the question of whose heritage is being celebrated and whose is being ignored. Smith, for instance, goes so far as to question whether heritage actually exists as a valid 'thing' at all, asserting that it is 'ultimately a cultural practice, involved in the construction and regulation of a range of values and understandings'.[1] There is, she argues, 'an authorized heritage discourse' which is based on these values and which adheres to set attitudes towards nation, class, technical expertise and dominant aesthetic taste. For her, this discourse is hegemonic and all-embracing and is therefore exceptionally difficult to challenge.

Smith is not alone in giving voice to such a pessimistic view of the imbalances inherent in heritage provision. Lowenthal is even more negative in his analysis, especially when musing on the relationship between heritage and history. In everyday use, the two are often presented as synonyms, or at least their meanings are confused and intertwined, but as a professional historian himself, Lowenthal is rather disturbed at such unintentional distortion:

> History and heritage transmit different things to different audiences. History tells all who will listen what has happened and how things came to be as they are. Heritage passes on exclusive myths of origin and continuance, endowing a select group with prestige and common purpose. History is enlarged by being disseminated; heritage is diminished and despoiled by export.[2]

It is both the quality and the purpose of heritage that Lowenthal challenges, pointing out that it lacks the rigour of peer assessment which professional historians must meet, while being fuelled by a very different set of economic, political or cultural drivers to those of the academy. Research is often thin and partial, he argues, designed primarily for entertainment and display, and focusing on the spectacular or unusual rather than mundane realities or uncomfortable truths. It 'exaggerates and omits, candidly invents and frankly forgets', he warns us, and he spends a good deal of energy providing examples from throughout the Western world.[3] It is a depressing analysis, but it is not one generally shared by ethnologists, who tend, on the whole, to view the concept and practice of heritage in a rather more positive light.

While the task of the historian is primarily to make sense of the past and to produce a resulting diachronic narrative that can help to communicate that interpretation, ethnologists have slightly different concerns. Their project is to view the past and the present as a continuum, to reflect on our relationships with the past, and to consider the ways in which we use that past in order to inform our present. Myth and tradition are therefore of key importance, for they illustrate how as individuals, communities and nations, we often construct our own versions of our own pasts. Indeed, we sometimes refer to this as 'our heritage', casting doubt on Smith's insistence that all heritage adheres to a top-down, hegemonic grand narrative: people can and do create heritages for themselves. Ethnologists would never follow Lowenthal's lead by dismissing these creative or invented pasts, nor would we ever consider discarding the folklore and mythology that lies at their heart. As a discipline, therefore, ethnology can be a friend to heritage, not by blindly swallowing all that appears in its name, but by accepting its central validity as a practice and concept. I shall return to a discussion of how this is being approached towards the end of this chapter.

While many scholars offer robust challenges to the methods and purpose of heritage, most also see it as a product of the modern age, with roots in the late eighteenth century, but only reaching maturity from the 1970s.[4] To McCrone, Kiely and Morris (1995), for instance, it is a condition of the later twentieth century and should be seen as one element of a growing leisure and tourist market for the United Kingdom in general and for Scotland in particular.[5] In this respect, heritage is a commodity which can be created and traded, with scholars often invoking the language of commerce in their discussions: curators and heritage professionals are 'producers', while those who visit and engage with their 'products' are 'consumers'. The nature of the commercial relationship between the two may be direct, with payment being made at the point of entry, or it may be indirect and hidden within taxation. Such an emphasis results in a common assumption that heritage is an industry, and that it can therefore best be understood in economic as well as cultural terms.

This functional aspect of heritage has been noted and emphasised by most of the key scholars working in this field. Ashworth and Turnbridge link it to the regeneration of cities, viewing it as a vital although partial replacement for jobs that have disappeared through twentieth-century industrial decline.[6] Hewison is even more direct in making this link, the *Britain in a Climate of Decline* sub-title of his 1987 study demonstrating his belief that the rise of heritage within Britain was itself a direct product of an economy in trouble, and a symbol of the transition from an industry-based to service-centred economic infrastructure.[7] Walsh agrees, while also considering heritage as being heavily politicised, viewing the explosion of its provision in Britain from the late 1970s as being a direct product of the New Right policies of Margaret Thatcher's governments. Their aim, he argues, was to forge a renewed sense of Britishness through the construction of an idea of a shared past, a desire that could be achieved through a version of heritage that was politically steered yet highly marketable.[8]

MODERN HERITAGE IN SCOTLAND

If Walsh's thesis is indeed correct, the New Right manifesto for heritage did not work in Scotland, for it coincided with an increasing emphasis on Scottish rather than British identity. However, the other factors, outlined by Hewison in particular, do apply convincingly north of the border. Traditional trades in the industrialised lowlands were rapidly disappearing through this period, with heavy engineering, mining, shipbuilding and textile production all in their dying throes. It is not stretching the truth too far to conclude that the industrial heritage centres that now stand in their place serve as the tombstones of the industries they were created to represent. Examples of industrial heritage sites in Scotland include the New Lanark World Heritage site, a restored model cotton mill village founded by David Dale in 1785 and managed in an enlightened fashion by his son-in-law Robert Owen from 1800–25; the National Mining Museum Scotland at the Lady Victoria colliery, Newtongrange, Midlothian; and Summerlee, The Museum of Scottish Industrial Life incorporating early ironworks at Coatbridge, Lanarkshire.

On a more positive note, however, heritage in general, and its tourist-centred focus in particular, has certainly developed into a key player within the Scottish economy. Detailed research has shown that the estimated economic impact of the 'historic environment' sector is of considerable value, contributing around £2.3 billion to Scotland's economy and supporting around 60,000 jobs,[9] while natural heritage is also big business, with nature-based tourism in Scotland adding around £1.4 billion and 39,000 jobs.[10] The 455 museums and galleries within Scotland contribute around £750 million and just over 3,000 jobs.[11] Taken together, therefore, the various branches of the heritage sector play an increasingly important economic role within Scotland. However, for the ethnologist, it is not so much the economic value as the cultural implications of heritage that form the focus of our interest, and so let us turn our attention towards those now.

In their 1995 overview of the heritage industry in Scotland, McCrone, Kiely and Morris (1995) note the proliferation of museums and visitor centres that had appeared over the previous twenty years or so, and conclude that the nation seemed to be groaning under their weight:

> The power of heritage seems unduly onerous in Scotland. Indeed, it seems at times as if Scotland only exists as heritage: what singles it out for distinction is the trappings of its past while its modernity seems to make it little different from elsewhere . . . Heritage in Scotland seems to many to be too tainted, too heavy.[12]

In their suggestion that perhaps the past looms too large within our present, McCrone and his colleagues were implicitly situating heritage within the wider cultural debates which had been ongoing for nearly two decades by their time of writing. The key figure at the centre of these debates was Tom Nairn, one of the most outspoken critics of Scotland's cultural landscape which he believed had become 'deformed' due to the poisoning influence of tartanry and kailyardism. Tartanry refers to the conceptualisation of Scotland as a land of tartan, heather and whisky while, for him, the Kailyard School of literature of the early twentieth century portrayed Scotland as a bucolic paradise and ignored the harsh realities of urbanisation.[13] For Nairn, tartanry and the kailyard became a double-headed monster which represented a hegemonic influence which had overwhelmed all else. This influence was still present, he argued, in these final decades of the twentieth century, and the only solution was to wipe our cultural slate clean, and start again.[14]

Nairn's polemic was well received by many commentators at the time who accepted his arguments and formed a powerful anti-tartanry lobby, calling for a complete re-evaluation of Scotland's cultural landscape. Their cause was boosted by the reaction to an exhibition held in Edinburgh in 1981 entitled 'Scotch Myths'. Curated by Murray and Barbara Grigor, it brought together a substantial body of material culture, film and television output and literature that was displayed as a representative manifestation of tartanry and kailyard kitsch.[15] The impact was considerable and it spawned a new wave of reflexivity on a national scale as the followers of the Scotch Myths School began to see evidence of such false icons and invented traditions everywhere they looked. The result was a tendency towards 'the Scottish cringe' – an embarrassed rejection of any cultural form or policy that appeared on the surface to promote the mythical Scotland of tartan and kailyard. It was a viewpoint which was further fuelled by Hugh Trevor-Roper, whose exaggerated dismissal of Scotland's tradition and heritage as being almost entirely invented was received somewhat uncritically north of the border.[16]

Not everyone agreed with that point of view, however, rejecting the claim that tartanry and kailyard formed a hegemonic discourse, and seeing them as only one part of a much wider and richer cultural landscape. McCrone, for instance, prefers to see the residents of Scotland as having a 'pick and mix' identity, considering us able and willing to select different and even competing versions of our cultural output as we see fit.[17] Cairns Craig, too, is critical of the Nairn thesis while recognising some truths within it,[18] while the nationalist analysis of Beveridge and Turnbull sees too many contradictions in the cultural hegemony theory, and considers it to be another contribution to our generally 'inferiorist' approach to Scotland's history.[19]

It was against this background of debate that the modern heritage sector in Scotland took shape, and that the main players in the provision of heritage at the national level were established or reconstituted. With the foundation of Historic Scotland in 1985, its sister organisation, Scottish Natural Heritage, in 1992, the setting up of the Heritage Lottery Fund in 1994, and the long-standing vision of a new national Museum of Scotland eventually being realised in 1998, the final decade of the twentieth century saw a complete reordering of the nation's heritage landscape. And change has seldom been far from view in the new century either: the rebranding of the Scottish Museums Council as Museums Galleries Scotland in 2008, the complete organisational overhaul of the National Trust for Scotland (founded 1931) in 2011, new impetus for the Saltire Society in its seventy-fifth anniversary year (2011), and the proposed merger of the Royal Commission on the Ancient and Historical Monuments of Scotland (founded 1908) with Historic Scotland announced in 2012, all demonstrate that the heritage sector in Scotland continues to adapt and evolve today.

An ethnologically informed analysis of the ethos and work of these organisations reveals three main conclusions in relation to the various academic debates and viewpoints outlined above: 1) Lowenthal's criticisms are not valid in these cases, 2) Smith's probably are, and 3) they have all fought hard to consign Nairn's concerns to the past. Firstly, it is very hard to recognise the charges made by Lowenthal in his general critique of the heritage sector, for these are all highly sophisticated organisations, operating according to strict policies, performance indicators and professional standards which are every bit as rigorous as those of academic historians. All management and curatorial staff are highly trained, and each of these national-level organisations have designed their own research programmes which are implemented to professional standards based on methods and operating practices developed in academic settings. Their missions and objectives are clearly stated, and the establishing, promotion and sharing of good practice is central to their philosophies. Not one of these institutions 'exaggerates and omits, candidly invents and frankly forgets', and so Lowenthal's generalisations can be safely dismissed.

Smith's assertion that heritage tends to be centred around an authorised hegemonic discourse is perhaps worthy of deeper reflection, however, for with the exception of the National Trust for Scotland and the Saltire Society which are independent charities, the others are all instruments of government to a large extent, deriving most of their funding and support from the state. And while the 'arm's length principle' does apply, whereby the executives of each organisation are provided with the autonomy required to carry out their roles without direct interference from their paymasters, they nonetheless have to operate within the general context of political approval and adhere to national government policy guidelines and objectives.[20] And although each organisation has its own particular remits and priorities, there is a notable consistency in their mission statements and an agreed consensus on what heritage is and should be. All of them accept, for instance, that heritage can generally be divided into 'natural' and 'cultural' forms, and that both are primarily found in physical manifestations, through landscape in the case of natural heritage and through buildings, monuments and material artefacts in the case of cultural heritage. 'Protection' of these is highlighted as a key aim in all cases, underlining the viewpoint held by many that heritage is primarily about the preservation of the past, and that each generation has a moral duty to ensure its continued survival into the future. Heritage providers – especially those operating at a national level – are therefore seen as guardians and protectors of 'things' which are deemed to be of national value in the long term, physical manifestations of culture which somehow help to form the very character of the nation, providing a thread of continuity between past, present and future.

In this respect, Smith's analysis does have a degree of validity when applied to Scotland, for taken together, these large-scale national organisations do tend to present a united conceptualisation of what the key elements of the nation's heritage actually are. But what of Tom Nairn's charge? Are these heritage providers avoiding the dangers of 'Scotch Myths'? Do they appear conscious of that particular cultural debate, and are they actively avoiding these traps? Although these are subjective issues, it seems clear to this writer that the answer to each of these questions is 'yes'. Right from their early development or re-creation in the 1990s outlined above, these organisations seemed keen to distance themselves from these stereotypical versions of Scottishness. Even although the historic environment sector by definition deals with some of the same cultural icons that are associated with tartanry – castles, grand houses, ancient monuments, scenic beauty – it has been careful to contextualise these as belonging to a wider framework of social and cultural development within the nation. One way of doing this has been to place increasing emphasis on the role of heritage within education and lifelong learning, aiming its focus on the resident population rather than the tourist market in this regard. Such education programmes encourage participants to look beyond the iconic imagery of the buildings and landscapes themselves, to address their functions, and to bring new perspectives on the societies within which they have been set. Historic Scotland, Scottish Natural Heritage, National Museums Scotland and the National Trust for Scotland all have well-developed educational programmes aimed at providing the people of Scotland with the cultural capital to engage meaningfully with their heritage. And it is interesting to note that when the new Museum of Scotland was being planned in the early 1990s, one of its specific aims as set out within its exhibition ethos was to 'dispel myths'.[21]

THE LOCAL

While ethnology as a discipline has always concerned itself with issues relating to the national, it is perhaps more comfortable when dealing with the concept of *locality*. The local history movement in Scotland goes back to the description of the nation at parish level initiated by Sir John Sinclair in the Old Statistical Account (OSA) in the 1790s. Micro-level studies of specific communities have been central to the ethnological tradition throughout its history, and indeed it is that insistence on the empirical study of traditions and developments that are embedded within specific places that helps to set it apart from the social sciences which tend to look at the bigger picture of 'society'.[22] Heritage, too, can and must relate to the local as well as the 'imagined community' of the nation,[23] and it is this area that has seen the largest and fastest expansion of provision in Scotland over the last generation. New funding streams made available from the mid 1990s through the Heritage Lottery Fund have greatly improved access to resources for museums and heritage organisations at more localised levels, while the setting up of Museums Galleries Scotland as the body which offers developmental support to the non-national organisations in the sector has helped to bring an increasingly professional approach to heritage provision throughout the country, despite continued heavy reliance on voluntary staff amongst the smaller organisations.

The interface between ethnology and heritage at the local level can be a highly fruitful one, and perhaps one case study can serve to illustrate the ways in which this can be taken forward to their mutual benefit. The Ben Lawers Historic Landscape Project, run by Glasgow University Archaeological Research Division, now GUARD Archaeology Ltd, on behalf of the National Trust for Scotland, was established in 1996 and ran until 2005. Its aim was to provide a holistic, multidisciplinary interpretation of the Ben Lawers Estate on the north side of Loch Tay in Highland Perthshire. Field and underwater archaeologists, historians, woodland experts, geologists and soil analysis professionals came together to undertake a research programme relating to the changing nature of the landscape and the communities it supported over many centuries, with the major funding being provided by the Heritage Lottery Fund. In the final year of the project, a team of ethnologists from the University of Edinburgh's School of Scottish Studies, led by the present author, was commissioned to undertake a study of the oral history and tradition of these communities in order to complement and contextualise the other research strands of the project. The specific aims were as follows:[24]

- To carry out field collection of oral history and oral tradition from local informants relating to the north Lochtayside community;
- To increase our understanding of diachronic social and cultural change in the community within the span of living memory, with particular consideration to interaction with the landscape, with each other and with the environment as a whole.
- To collect such material which complements the research findings of the broader Ben Lawers Historic Landscape Project, e.g.:
  (a) history;
  (b) settlement; and
  (c) archaeology.
- To engage primary school children with their local heritage by training them in basic oral history recording techniques and facilitating interview sessions with local residents.

The methodology followed comprised a blend of archive and desk research together with a programme of fieldwork recording, with a strong level of engagement with the local community (as indeed was demanded by the funding agreement). This included engagement with a local heritage centre and its volunteers, a library, two primary schools, local businesses and a range of individual contributors. Archived fieldwork collected from the area in the 1960s and 1970s by the School of Scottish Studies allowed for a direct comparison to be made and the extent of change and scale of continuity within the area over the intervening period to be assessed. Information on a wide range of issues relating to local heritage was collected, including material on place names, oral narrative, custom and belief, music and song, social organisation, local trades and engagement with the land. The general conclusions drawn were that social and economic changes seen within the past two generations have had a direct impact on many people's construction of a sense of place, belonging and environment in the north Lochtayside community, and that their conceptualisation of their local heritage is a constantly shifting one. It serves to reinforce the idea that heritage is constructed according to the needs and views of the time from which it is viewed, and that, as such, it tells us as much about the present as it does the past. Also, it reminds us that heritage can indeed be forged locally and from the perspective of community, and that the 'grand narratives' of which Smith speaks are not the only versions which emerge and survive.

INTANGIBLE CULTURAL HERITAGE

While the main thrust of the wider Ben Lawers project related to material culture, the ethnological strand mainly dealt with oral tradition, and therefore with the 'imagined landscape' of the local area. Such non-corporeal culture has recently come to be recognised on the world stage, and it is closely allied to the discipline of ethnology. This is the idea of 'Intangible Cultural Heritage', or ICH. The 'intangible' qualification was devised by UNESCO in a way which would differentiate it from that organisation's long-accepted primary conceptualisation of heritage which was entirely limited to physical things. These might have belonged to the category of 'natural heritage' – landscape, flora and fauna – or to 'cultural heritage' – things which humans built, such as standing stones, monuments, buildings and artefacts. This was encapsulated in the World Heritage Convention, formalised in 1972, which encouraged all those participating nations to ensure the proper protection of their cultural and natural heritage, and invited them to nominate the best examples of their own for inclusion on the world heritage list.

Scotland has been awarded world heritage status for five sites: Edinburgh Old and New Towns, the Heart of Neolithic Orkney, New Lanark and the Antonine Wall, with St Kilda being one of very few places in the world to have double status, being recognised both for its cultural and natural value. Other sites which have been considered for future nomination include the Forth Bridge (which will be assessed in 2015), the Iron Age remains of Shetland, and the Caithness and Sutherland Flow Country. There are currently 962 sites listed across the world, most of them (745) given recognition under the 'cultural' banner, 188 as 'natural' heritage and 29 with dual status.[25]

Having world recognition like this is a major boon for a nation's cultural confidence and in many cases, Scotland included, for the positive impact it brings to tourism. However, some nations, or indeed peoples within and across nations, felt from the outset that the exclusive consideration given to physical sites within the world heritage framework was unfair, and that it only told part of the story of what heritage really is: the cultural inheritance which is passed on through each generation, and while this can certainly be physical, often it flows in other ways, shaped by mouths and ears rather than by hands. Thus, it is 'intangible' – spoken, sung, heard, acted – rather than physically built.

Some nations complained and the result was the foundation in 2003 of the Convention for the Safeguarding of Intangible Cultural Heritage, providing a framework for official international recognition of 'tradition':

> The 'intangible cultural heritage' means the practices, representations, expressions, knowledge, skills – as well as the instruments, objects, artefacts and cultural spaces associated therewith – that communities, groups and, in some cases, individuals recognise as part of their cultural heritage. This intangible cultural heritage, transmitted from generation to generation, is constantly recreated by communities and groups in response to their environment, their interaction with nature and their history, and provides them with a sense of identity and continuity, thus promoting respect for cultural diversity and human creativity. For the purposes of this Convention, consideration will be given solely to such intangible cultural heritage as is compatible with existing international human rights instruments, as well as with the requirements of mutual respect among communities, groups and individuals, and of sustainable development.[26]

Examples of ICH provided by UNESCO include:

- Oral traditions and expressions, including language as a vehicle of the intangible cultural heritage
- Performing arts
- Social practices, rituals and festive events
- Knowledge and practices concerning nature and the universe
- Traditional craftsmanship.

At present, 143 states have signed up to this convention, and 267 specific forms of ICH have been included on the official list, around 10 per cent of which are considered to be in need of urgent safeguarding.[27] The UK has not signed this treaty, considering it a low priority, and so our official contribution to the world's heritage must remain firmly tangible, for the time being at least. The Scottish Government is keen, certainly, but as Scotland does not have nation-state status in the eyes of UNESCO, its hands are tied. ICH is, therefore, in part a political issue, although not one which excites a great deal of public concern.

In reality there are a number of difficulties surrounding the development of ICH as a practical contributor to the wider heritage landscape, particularly in relation to determining just what exactly ICH actually is, to whom it belongs, to what extent it can or should be protected, and how to deal with the fact that a good deal of tradition transcends national boundaries. To its credit, UNESCO has recognised these issues and has tried to deal with at least some of them. It accepts that, unlike material heritage, the intangible version is not necessarily to be found in one particular place, and certainly not always within one single nation or state. It also leaves the decisions regarding precisely what should count as ICH to those to whom it belongs, although this is not straightforward either. However, it does have the potential to therefore bypass the concerns of Smith and others that heritage is by definition a top-down imposition of cultural values deriving from the authority of the ruling elite. In theory, at least, the ICH charter sets out to provide a mechanism and platform for specific individual communities to give voice to their own cultural traditions and to both protect these and share them with the wider world.

Although the UK has not signed the ICH convention, some embryonic work has been started in Scotland to move forward with the identification of just exactly what might constitute examples of our ICH. Under the leadership of Edinburgh Napier University, a list has been started, and the nationally funded body Museums Galleries Scotland is committed to developing the concept within its own remit.[28] These are welcome developments, although given the potential riches of Scotland's many and varied traditions, it is a very large task, and there is much work to be done. What we must remember, however, is that people and institutions have been collecting and studying ICH in Scotland for decades – even centuries – and as a nation we are very well advanced in understanding what it means and what its value is. It has been central to the business of ethnology. It is ethnologists, therefore, who are best placed to drive this initiative forward and to rise to the challenges set by UNESCO in helping to use heritage to forge a more positive form of globalisation whereby cultural difference is recognised and celebrated as a positive force.[29]

The main reason that Scotland is so well placed to contribute to the global ICH project is the creativity and richness of its cultural heritage combined with the long-standing tradition of collecting and studying it. Since the eighteenth century, key collectors and promoters of tradition such as Robert Burns, Sir Walter Scott, James Hogg, John Francis Campbell, John Lorne Campbell and three generations of staff within the School of Scottish Studies at the University of Edinburgh, have built up a representative corpus of material that adheres firmly to all of the UNESCO definitions of ICH, and which forms the central teaching and research data source for ethnologists in Scotland today. Since its foundation in 1951, The School of Scottish Studies Archives, recognised as 'the jewel in the crown' of the University of Edinburgh,[30] has built up a collection of around 30,000 recordings and images relating to the music, song, dance, oral narrative, custom, belief and place names of Scotland – the very stuff of ICH. That a solid proportion of this is now available online through the Tobar an Dualchais / Kist o Riches web resource[31] is a crucial step forward in its protection and dissemination, although the challenge now is to ensure that this is followed through proactively with its careful integration into education, further research and the wider heritage sector. It is ethnologists who are best placed to achieve this, and now that there are several hundred graduates in Scotland with a degree in Scottish Ethnology, this is entirely achievable.[32]

CONCLUSIONS

Heritage is a complex and varied phenomenon which, despite roots reaching back at least to the eighteenth century, is very much a product of the modern world. Scotland has not been alone in the rapid rate of expansion of its heritage provision since the 1970s, but there is no doubt that as an industry, it has grown into a major player in the nation's economic landscape. Yet its value and validity have certainly been questioned, especially by academics who have often reacted rather negatively, if somewhat unfairly, as I have attempted to show in this chapter, to the whole concept and enterprise of heritage. For ethnologists, though, heritage provides a fascinating laboratory, for in its need to construct selective versions of the past, often based on both material and oral culture, several of the central concerns of ethnology come into sharp focus as one. Representation, selection, cultural construction, identity, belonging, nation, locality – all these and more feed into the recipe of heritage provision and consumption in a way that few other aspects of modernity achieve. And in doing so, they capture a set of relationships between past, present and future that proves irresistible to scholars within the discipline. Ethnology has both learned from and contributed to the heritage cause in Scotland, and it is a relationship which looks set to continue in a positive manner in the years to come. Intangible Cultural Heritage, in particular, holds much promise as a key means of maintaining and developing this symbiosis, for it links the local, the national and the global in a manner that is wholly consistent with the ethnological ethos of the twenty-first century.

NOTES

1 Smith, 2006, 11.
2 Lowenthal, 2005, 128.
3 Lowenthal, 2005, 121.
4 The rise of the antiquarian movement in the second half of the eighteenth century is often identified as the birth of heritage, while the establishing of major museums and galleries from the mid nineteenth century is also considered a key milestone in its development.
5 McCrone, Kiely and and Morris, 1995, 1.
6 Ashworth and Tunbridge, 1990.
7 Hewison, 1987.
8 Walsh, 1992.
9 Historic Scotland, *Scotland's Historic Environment Audit*, 2012.
10 Bryden et al., 2010, i.
11 Museums Galleries Scotland, *Realising the True Impact of Museums and Galleries in Scottish Tourism*, 2010 Data.
12 McCrone, Kiely and and Morris, 1995, 6.
13 The principal kailyard writers were Ian Maclaren (1850–1907), S R Crockett (1860–1914) and J M Barrie (1860–1937). For a succinct account of the kailyard school, see Shepherd, 1988.
14 Nairn, 1977 and Nairn, 1988.
15 McArthur, 1983.
16 Trevor-Roper, 1983. For further discussion of this theme see McCrone, 1992 and West, 2012.
17 McCrone, 1992.
18 See, for example, Craig, 1982 and Craig, 1996.
19 Beveridge and Turnbull, 1989.
20 The Scottish Government, for example, has developed a *Scottish Historic Environment Policy* which provides direction for Historic Scotland and a policy framework for a range of other public sector organisations. See <www.historic-scotland.gov.uk/shep-dec2011.pdf>.
21 Private communication.
22 Examples include Glassie, 1995; Fenton, 1997; West, 2007.
23 The phrase was coined by Benedict Anderson, 2006.
24 Mackay, Dickson and West, 2005.
25 <whc.unesco.org/en/list>.
26 <www.unesco.org/culture/ich/>.
27 As of December 2012.
28 *Going Further: The National Strategy for Scotland's Museums and Galleries*, published by Museums Galleries Scotland in 2012, states that 'the sector is collectively responsible to current and future generations for safeguarding Scotland's tangible and intangible cultural heritage', 10.
29 For a more detailed discussion of these issues see West, 2012.
30 Ranft and Richmond, 2012.
31 <www.tobarandualchais.co.uk>
32 A degree programme in Scottish Ethnology has been delivered at the University of Edinburgh since 1986.

Anderson, B. *Imagined Communities: Reflections on the Origin and Spread of Nationalism*, London, 2006.

Ashworth, G and Tunbridge, J. *The Tourist-Historic City*, London and New York, 1990.

Bendix, R, Hemme, D and Tauschek, M, eds. *Prädikat 'Heritage': Perspektiven auf Westchopfungen aus Kultur*, Münster, 2007.

Beveridge, C and Turnbull, R. *The Eclipse of Scottish Culture*, Edinburgh, 1989.

Bryden, D M, Westbrook, S R, Burns, B, Taylor, W A, and Anderson, S. *Assessing the Economic Impacts of Nature Based Tourism in Scotland*, Scottish Natural Heritage Commissioned Report No. 398, 2010, available at <www.snh.gov.uk/docs/B726802.pdf> [accessed January 2013].

Cameron, F and Kenderdine, S, eds. *Theorizing Digital Cultural Heritage*, Cambridge, MA, 2007.

Corner, J and Harvey, S, eds. *Enterprise and Heritage*, London, 1991.

Craig, C. Myths against History: Tartanry and kailyard in nineteenth-century Scottish literature. In McArthur, C, ed., *Scotch Reels: Scotland in Cinema and Television*, London, 1982, 7–16.

Craig, C. *Out of History: Narrative Paradigms in Scottish and English Culture*, Edinburgh, 1996.

Glassie, H. Tradition, *Journal of American Folklore*, 108:430 (1995a), 395–412.

Glassie, H. *Passing the Time in Ballymenone: Culture and History of an Ulster Community*, Bloomington, IN, 1995b.

Gold, J and Gold, M. *Imagining Scotland*, Aldershot, 1995.

Hafstein, V. 'The making of intangible cultural heritage: Tradition and authenticity, community and humanity', PhD thesis, University of California, Berkeley, 2004a.

Hafstein, V. The politics of origins. Collective creation revisited, *Journal of American Folklore*, 117 (2004b), 300–15.

Hewison, R. *The Heritage Industry: Britain in a Climate of Decline*, London, 1987.

Historic Environment Advisory Council for Scotland. *Economic Impact of the Historic Environment of Scotland Report*, Edinburgh, 2008.

Historic Scotland. *Scotland's Historic Environment Audit*, Edinburgh, 2012.

Kirshenblatt-Gimblett, B. *Destination Culture: Tourism, Museums and Heritage*, Berkeley, CA, 1998.

Lowenthal, D. *The Heritage Crusade and the Spoils of History*, Cambridge, 2005.

Hobsbawm, E and Ranger, T, eds. *The Invention of Tradition*, Cambridge, 1983.

McArthur, C. 'Scotch Reels' and after, *Cencrastus*, 11 (New Year 1983), 2–3.

McCrone, D. *Understanding Scotland: The Sociology of a Stateless Nation*, London, 1992.

McCrone, D, Kiely, R and Morris, A. *Scotland the Brand: The Making of Scottish Heritage*, Edinburgh, 1995.

Mackay, S, Dickson, J and West, G. 'Voicing Ben Lawers: The oral history and tradition of North Lochtayside', unpublished report, Celtic and Scottish Studies, University of Edinburgh, 2005.

Museums Galleries Scotland. *Realising the True Impact of Museums and Galleries in Scottish Tourism*, Edinburgh, 2010.

Museums Galleries Scotland. *Going Further: The National Strategy for Scotland's Museums and Galleries*, Edinburgh, 2012.

Nairn, T. *The Break-up of Britain*, London, 1977.

Nairn, T. *The Enchanted Glass: Britain and its Monarchy*, London, 1988.

Ó Giolláin, D. *Locating Irish Folklore: Tradition, Modernity, Identity*, Cork, 2000.

Ranft, R and Richmond, L. Review of the School of Scottish Studies Archives. Report for the University of Edinburgh, 2012.

Shepherd, G. The kailyard. In Gifford, D, ed., *The History of Scottish Literature*, vol. 3, Aberdeen, 1988, 309–20.

Smith, L. *Uses of Heritage*, London, 2006.

Smith, L and Akagowa, N, eds. *Intangible Heritage*, London, 2008.

Stoklund, B. The role of the international exhibitions in the construction of national cultures in the 19th century, *Ethnologia Europaea*, 24 (1994), 35–44.

Urry, J. *The Tourist Gaze: Leisure and Travel in Contemporary Societies*, London, 1990.

Walsh, K. *The Representation of the Past: Museums and Heritage in the Post-Modern World*, London, 1992.

West, G. *An Historical Ethnography of Rural Perthshire, 1750–1950*, Lampeter, 2007.

West, G. *Voicing Scotland: Folk, Culture, Nation*, Edinburgh, 2012.

JOURNALS

Heritage & Society, 2008–present

Intangible Cultural Heritage Scotland Newsletter, 2009–present

International Journal of Heritage Studies, 1994–present

International Journal of Intangible Heritage, 2006–present

Theorizing Cultural Heritage, 2005–present

•

PART THREE

Select Ethnological Genres

10 Folk Narrative

LICIA MASONI

Folktales, fairytales, myths and legends: these are probably the first examples of stories that the expression 'folk narrative' brings to mind. Long stories performed aloud without a text or script, for the entertainment of young and old. But folk narrative is also storytelling in everyday life, a form of communication whose manifestations are prompted by life events and situations. Every time we describe an incident, thus giving it logical order, we create a narrative. End-of-the-day stories about things that happened at work, jokes exchanged among friends in a pub, alarming reports of what happened to a friend of a friend who went on a drastic diet, the long-rehearsed lie recited when one is shamefully late: these are only a few examples of our daily production of narratives, stories we tell each other with various intents and goals. The stories are passed on, crafted and re-crafted during transmission from person to person, generation to generation, place to place: they adapt according to the teller, the audience, and the situation. Stories exist to make sense of reality, of the environment and of puzzling events. Stories warn against danger, communicate standards, and allow us to experience a sense of identity. They do not exist, however, in a vacuum. They are adapted and used daily, and this is what the ethnologist is keen to study: their place in our lives. Indeed, although written, even urban legends that are spread through the web, as well as the making and updating of Facebook profiles, are of interest to the folk narrative scholar, given that they tell a story, a non-official one, that is constantly re-crafted to reflect the ideas and needs of those who tell and those who listen or read. In consideration of these new media, which make it even more difficult to draw a line between oral and written, the term 'folk narrative' is preferable to the near-cognate 'oral narrative'.

What defines folk narrative, however, is what distinguishes it from written literature; not in the sense that it is spoken as opposed to recorded on paper, but rather in terms of its fruition and dissemination. Unlike a written work, a folk narrative does not have a fixed or official version but instead a multiplicity of versions. An oral narrative text is fluid and variable by nature. The text of Jane Austen's novel *Sense and Sensibility* is unique, set as published, and that will persist, but the text of a story about a persecuted little girl helped by a magic creature, which we recognise as a Cinderella type of story, does not exist in only one version (unless we continually re-read Charles Perrault's): rather, it is the ensemble of all its possible versions. Somehow its text is as infinite as the possible versions a teller can conjure up. Folktales, legends and jokes take body at the moment of their performance, which is never a word-for-word recitation of a previous telling. No oral version is like the previous or the next. The storyteller works on an existing canvas, but then proceeds to tell the story differently each time. Each person who retells a story makes his/her own contributions to the story, altering it in some way.

'Variation' is the main characteristic of folklore and therefore of folk narrative.[1] The word 'variant' does not imply that there is a fixed text in comparison to which another is a deviation; it simply means that there are many ways of telling an existing story. Just as a folk narrative has no fixed and official text, it also has no single author that can declare ownership of it, but only artists, tellers, who elaborate stories through their creativity whenever they tell them in their own words, with their additions and variations. From the moment a story is told (even a personal narrative), it enters the folklore loop and from then onwards it will carry on through other people's voices.

The storyteller does not just carry a story, though: he re-delivers it, adapting it every time. In the process of transmission, the story mutates to fit audiences and social environments. The storyteller's action is vital. He adapts the story to the context, keeping it alive and relevant for those who listen. The changes he makes are on various levels and produce different kinds of variations with as many implications.

First of all there is adaptation to the immediate context of the performance. Most of the time changes are on the level of language (e.g. rephrasing, descriptions that allow people to visualise the scene, and asides to explain things or comment on facts), as well as on the extra-linguistic level (with gestures, mimicking of voices and so forth). The teller adapts to those who listen: he can decide to skip some parts or expand on others. While sometimes memory gaps can account for these changes, most of the time the teller makes a conscious decision to effect ad hoc changes, based on his understanding of the storytelling situation. The story that a woman tells to an exclusively female audience is very likely to differ from the 'same' tale when she tells it to a group of men. The all-female version may be shorter, as the common experience of the women may allow them to take much for granted, or longer, if the teller feels she can interpolate comments that somehow speak the audience's mind and voice the listener within the story. These ad hoc changes may just be temporary and disappear in the next telling. Some changes remain, however, and they become part of the story, adapting it, and allowing it to survive in a changing society. These changes are necessary for the survival of the story: to continue to make it relevant to the society in which it lives, to allow it to meet people's needs. For example, with time, certain stories have shed their elements of racism or gender discrimination. Initially the decision of one teller, these changes turned out to be what allowed the story to continue its journey in transmission.

As changed as a story could appear to us if we could record its journey from mouth to mouth over a long period of time, in the short term changes are limited. No matter how creative and imaginative the teller is, he will have to stick to a canvas, a structure, or the audience will not recognise the story. As Honko puts it: 'Flexibility rather than stability seems to be the key to the continuity of tradition, to the kind of "invariability" typical of oral tradition which prevents variation from going astray and distorting the song or the story completely.'[2] The audience takes part in the storytelling event by understanding the story and what it means. Somehow the meaning of a story is suspended in mid air, half way between teller and audience, where the two meet: one by communicating, the other by receiving and interpreting. This is the concept of the 'competent audience', as described by Foley, whereby those who listen can, through their 'implicit knowledge' of a story's nature, 'activate' the performance and become 'co-creators of the scene'.[3]

However, this does not mean that there are no new stories being cast into the folklore flux all the time. The experienced teller is able to create new combinations from the stories he has in his repertoire, playing with the building blocks of folk narrative material, and giving life to endless combinations. The master art of the teller is displayed in his great knowledge of narrative material.

Variation, adaptation, flexibility, and survival: these fundamental characteristics of oral narrative take us to another very important distinction between oral text and written text. A written text can be rejected by its first audience, but then welcomed by later generations that find it relevant after half a century. On the contrary, an oral text must be relevant in the present in order to survive. A folk narrative only exists if it is useful. Once it ceases to meet the needs of its group it dies out. An oral text must constantly adapt to be relevant for the present.

Sometimes narratives that cease to be relevant are not dropped, but rather recycled. This happens by transposing a narrative into another area of meaning, especially by changing its narrative genre. For example, a scary story that was believed as a true account in earlier times can be adapted to convey a different meaning once the element of belief is rejected by the following generation. The tale will no longer be perceived as a legend, but may circulate as a humorous narrative. As such, it is no longer useful as a way of discussing belief but has rather become a way of asserting one's superiority to past beliefs.[4] The texts of the two stories may be identical, if we look at the transcriptions, but what varies is the tone, the teasing voice of the narrator, the laughter of the audience, who now agree to receive such narrative as a joke, rather than as a cautionary legend. For this reason, definitions of genres in folk narrative are very difficult to formulate and always artificial. However, we do need general guidelines in order to facilitate cross-cultural communication and comparison. What follows is a broad and schematic classification of the main genres of folk narrative, according to their stylistic traits.[5]

- Stories perceived as fiction: Tales

  Under this category we can group long tales such as *märchen* or 'tales of magic' (also often known as 'fairytales'). They are set in an undefined time and space and perceived by the listener as fiction. Their opening formulas (such as 'In the days when animals could speak'), and codas ('and they lived happily ever after') enclose a narrative that follows a hero(ine) in his/her struggle and initiation, and ends with the restoration of a state of equilibrium coinciding with a social rise. In their adventures, heroes receive help from magic agents and creatures that often function to test their moral qualities. *Märchen* were told by experienced tellers, usually older members of the community, because the didactic content of the story (the hero succeeds only if he makes the right choices which reflect the community's set of values) called for an authoritative figure, be it a parent or an old fellow villager. These tales communicate gender and morality models.

The 'novella', or 'folktale', is normally very similar to a *märchen*, but it is set in a defined space and time, often that of the teller, and it contains no magic. Riddles are frequently a part of this kind of story, and the leading figure tends to succeed through cleverness and cunning rather than by magic.

Also perceived as fictional, but possessing didactic qualities, are 'animal tales' (where animals are allegories of human qualities and behaviours), fables, 'jocular tales', jokes, tall tales, and religious tales.[6]

• Stories believed as real

Myth: Because of their metaphorical and symbolic nature, myths are often impossible to distinguish from *märchen*. We can, by means of generalisation, say that myth is often a religious narrative, dealing with the origin of natural phenomena and elements of the world. Believed as true, and often connected with rituals, myths communicate values, standards and ways of interpreting the surrounding world.

Legend: The legend has a local character; it recounts something that happened to someone we know, or we know of. There are many kinds of legend, including narratives expressing religious beliefs and narratives connected with place-names, landscape features, and historical events. The legend is didactic, in that it warns against dangers and teaches lessons and facts that matter to the community. The legend as a genre is extremely fluid, however. It is reshaped in each telling, taking the audience's reaction into account, testing the boundaries of belief and thus adjusting the story so that it is more acceptable, therefore equipping it to continue its migration. It is migratory *par excellence*. In the modern world, so-called urban legends spread quickly on the internet. They deal with social phobias, changes imposed by technology and society, the fear of the unknown, the uncontrollable elements of our lives, and with death, diets, diseases and cures. Legends do not possess the stable, recognisable structures of fairy tales. As the prominent legend scholar Linda Dégh has written, a legend 'ranges from the simple communication of belief through various levels to the most intricate, multi-episodic narrative'.[7]

- True life accounts (or at least those presented as such)

> These include narratives exchanged in the workplace and humorous anecdotes that are meant to be believed. Such accounts are typically localised and feature people who are known to the audience (rather than generalised, as most jokes are). Also belonging to this category are gossip and life stories. Personal narratives count as folklore from the moment that they enter the folklore loop, for they are fed by the motifs of previous narratives (and most of all speak the mind of the group as well as that of the narrator). As Sandra Stahl puts it, each listener shares 'cultural clay' with the 'I' of the personal narrative.[8]

Genres not only merge and shift over time within the same culture, they also change across cultures. As Dan Ben-Amos explains:

> The same story may be myth for one group and *Märchen* for another. In that case the question of the actual generic classification of the tale is irrelevant, since it does not depend on any autonomous intrinsic features but rather on the cultural attitude toward it.[9]

Thus, genre definitions are highly dependent on context, and on matters such as belief patterns associated with the story, performance style and audience reception. What meaning and weight does the group/audience confer upon a story? How do those who listen to it perceive a story? Such questions can be explored through extensive fieldwork and through approaches that regard the story not purely as text, but also as community strategy. Scholars have been increasingly concerned with these extra-textual elements, asking themselves: what do community members think of their own stories? How do they classify them? What functions do they attach to them? What names do they use for the types of stories they tell? Such local classification is referred to as 'native or internal taxonomy'.

In early folk narrative scholarship, the fluidity of oral works was not recognised as an intrinsic element of folk narrative text, and neither was the importance of the social context from which texts derive their vital energy.

When a new subject area emerges, analytical tools and theoretical frameworks must be borrowed from already existing subjects. Scholars will eventually fashion their own disciplinary language, but this process takes time. At the beginning of folk narrative scholarship, the fields of linguistics, philology and literature furnished the analytical framework for those who approached orally collected narratives.

Arguably, the birth of folk narrative as a scholarly subject coincides with the work of the brothers Wilhelm and Jacob Grimm, and their monumental collection of tales, *Kinder- und Hausmärchen* (1812–15). However, interest in folk narratives had always been present, inspiring literary works across time and space (including the Greek and Latin fables attributed to Aesop, the Sanskrit *Panchatantra*, and the fourteenth-century masterpieces by Boccaccio – *Decamerone*

– and Chaucer – *Canterbury Tales*). The first written collections of fairytales as we think of them today are relatively recent: literary artists took tales from the oral tradition and rewrote them for the literate public. Giovan Francesco Straparola's *Le Piacevoli Notti* (1550–53) is the first instance, followed by Giambattista Basile's *Pentamerone* (1634–36). From Italy, the love of tales migrated to France, where possibly one of the most famous collections was created by Charles Perrault, *Histoires ou contes du temp passé avec des moralités* (1697). This collection marks the first appearance of the tale of Little Red Riding Hood, although we can easily theorise that it had been taken from the oral tradition, given the existence of many of the story's motifs in medieval documents.[10] This is a very important point. Printed tales that derived from oral tradition, once invested with new structure and motifs by literary artists, re-entered the loop of oral tradition. The ebb and flow between oral and written make the two intertwine so thoroughly that it is pointless to try to distinguish them. Oral tradition owes as much to written works as vice versa. It has been argued that the fairy tale as we think of it nowadays (the 'rise tale' of the rags-to-riches type, which implies a period of tribulations, followed by a social ascent) is no older than Straparola. This assertion is not accepted by most scholars, but it is a comment on how substantially the literary tradition has affected folk tradition.[11]

Learned writers of the seventeenth and eighteenth centuries made tales a respectable diversion for upper-class adults. Up to this point, as in oral tradition, literary tales were primarily addressed to adults, and not to children.

The Grimm brothers were among the first to adapt tales for children and to raise them to the state of object of study. The two brothers collected stories from oral tradition, but very few of their informants were 'peasants'. Most were literate people who had access to printed tales through texts, including Perrault's. While the brothers in their early work professed a commitment to presenting the printed texts exactly as they had been told by their sources, the language of the tales changed from edition to edition. Wilhelm Grimm was responsible for the later editions, and he altered the tales by creating collages from different versions of the same story until he reached the most complicated structure. Through these changes, the Grimms attempted to achieve a form that they considered more satisfying as well as closer to a hypothetical original, as if what they had received from their informants was a pale reflection of what the narrative could once have been. As interested as they were by some of their informants, in particular Frau Viehmann, they still felt that her versions could be improved upon.[12] The language of their stories was also often standardised. As a result, in the printed tales the vision of the two brothers often outweighs the spontaneity of the original performers.

Nevertheless, the importance of the Grimms' work cannot be overstated. First, they had the merit of drawing attention to folk narratives as objects worthy of study. Second, and most importantly, their work had widespread repercussions throughout the rest of Europe, inspiring many people to compile tale anthologies, such as Giuseppe Pitrè in Sicily, Aleksandr Afanasjev in Russia, Peter Buchan in Scotland and many others.

As it became clear that the stories collected in these other countries were often very similar in structure and theme to those collected by the Grimm brothers, scholars began to assert that the stories had to have a common origin. Influenced by emerging studies in Indo-European languages, the Grimm brothers put forward the theory that stories shared the same first home as the languages in which they were now found. They therefore hypothesised that tales were the remains of ancient myths of Indo-Germanic races, which had been spread through migratory movements of people.

Scholarship that followed built upon the Grimms' ideas and was also fed by the numerous new scientific and intellectual debates of the time. In 1846 William John Thoms coined the term 'folk-lore' in the hopes of inspiring British antiquarians to reconstruct the 'Mythology of the British Islands'. The idea grew that stories were the corrupted and faulty detritus of a once more developed form that had been slowly dying out; these stories were items to be salvaged and brought back to their original splendour by the scholar. Both the belief in the need for a mastermind who could draw together seemingly 'trifling and insignificant' details to reveal the nature of the earliest tales, and the idea that folklore is some construct that is lost in the past, were destined to accompany folk narrative studies for a long time, while many folklorists identified the need to look at the present before it was too late.[13]

Max Müller and other so-called 'mythologists' constituted another group that sought to discover the origin of tales. Müller postulated that myths originated as descriptions of natural phenomena; he developed the 'solar' interpretation of myth, according to which struggles between gods are interpreted as battles between light and darkness, dawn and dusk, thus finding a more acceptable explanation for the brutal and violent parts of myths and tales, from cannibalism to attempts to commit incest. As a result, the image of Cronus eating his children is only a metaphor for the Sun swallowing and then re-expelling the clouds. According to Müller, the *märchen* developed from myths, following the same evolutionary process.

Also concerned with origin was Theodor Benfey, founder of the Indic Theory. Through his studies of the *Panchatantra*, an ancient collection of Sanskrit tales, Benfey argued that the origin of all myths and tales was in India and that from there stories had migrated to Europe. The theory did not have much success or many followers, but it had the merit of attracting attention to the migratory nature of stories.

A new perspective on the origin of tales drew its inspiration from the publication, in 1859, of Darwin's *On the Origin of Species*, which inspired the idea that cultures, like organisms, had evolved over time. Edward B Tylor, a pioneer in the new field of anthropology, applied the Darwinian ideas of biological evolution to culture. According to Tylor, all cultures developed in the same path but at different rates, allowing 'civilised' people to learn about their past by studying the practices of 'savage' and 'barbarian' cultures that were stuck in the past.

The Scottish scholar Andrew Lang (1844–1912), a major exponent of the Anthropological School, applied its concepts to myth and tales. He argued that the traces of cannibalism and animal transformations displayed in folktales could be interpreted as vestiges of ancient ritualistic behaviours observed across many cultures. This implied that tales stemmed from primordial needs (and were therefore more archaic than myths), and as such they did not have a common origin; on the contrary, similar tales could have originated in different places at the same time, provided that the peoples inhabiting such places were at the same stage of cultural development, thus likely to possess the same needs. Tales were like fossils that could help in the reconstruction of the history of mankind.[14]

Although Lang shared many of the now-discarded ideas of the cultural evolutionists, he also advanced a more modern view by asserting that tales were conscious products of a society's needs, rather than degraded or 'diseased' forms of expression. Lang was paving the way for what would follow long after him: the debate about the function of narratives in relation to their specific communities.

The comparative method that was spreading across the sciences found its most successful expression, in folk narrative terms, in the Finnish School. It started with the philological and comparative work that Finnish scholar Julius Krohn (1835–1888) conducted on the *Kalevala*, the Finnish national epic. Krohn attempted to discover the archetype of the poem through a close comparison of existing variants. Later on, his son Kaarle (1863–1933) applied the method to a group of Norse magic tales. It is to him, along with the Swede Carl von Sydow (1878–1952) and the Dane Axel Olrik (1864–1917) that we owe the foundation of the Folklore Association (1907), which was to be the centre of folk narrative research for many decades to come. The 'Finnish Method', also referred to as historical–geographical, consisted of collecting as many variants of one tale as possible (across space and time) and then comparing them in order to find the original story, the 'Urform'. At the same time, historic–geographic scholars sought to discover the paths along which tales migrated. The Finnish School carried into the twentieth century the comparative perspectives that had dominated linguistic and evolutionary studies in the nineteenth. The comparative method culminated in 1928 with the publication of one of the most important instruments in folk narrative: *The Types of the Folktale: A Classification and Bibliography* (expanded in 1961). This was the work of the Finnish scholar Antti Aarne (1867–1925) and American scholar Stith Thompson, who classified according to 'types' the folk tales found in all the tale anthologies and archives to which they had access (in 2004, the index was revised and expanded into three volumes by Hans-Jörg Uther in *The Types of International Folktales: A Classification and Bibliography*). Such a resource was followed by an even more ambitious project, Stith Thompson's *Motif-Index of Folk-Literature: A Classification of Narrative Elements in Folktales, Ballads, Myths, Fables, Mediaeval Romances, Exempla, Fabliaux, Jest-Books, and Local Legends* (2nd edition 1955–58). This index itemised the narrative units, or motifs, contained in many narrative genres. Broadly speaking, a 'type' is the skeleton of a story, the main plot or series of narrative moves. 'Motifs' are the smaller units of action, character and setting that combine to create a narrative. Many other motif and tale type catalogues were created, each focusing more specifically on, for example, a single nation or genre such as Reidar Th Christiansen's *The Migratory Legends* (1958). Types were given numbers, and are now preceded by the acronym ATU (Aarne, Thompson, Uther), while motifs are given a letter and a number, according to their classification.

Despite their limitations (new variants are being discovered all the time, and clear boundaries between tales types are hard to draw, due to the fluidity of folk narrative), these indexes are undoubtedly a fundamental instrument for international communication and comparative work.

The Finnish School founded the *Folklore Fellows Communications*, a series of monographs; many of these were devoted to single tales and their variants, and each work aimed at establishing the tale's original form and geographical migration. The concern was with the tale as text, and with its contents taken as comparative units. However, even if the historical–geographical method recognised variation as its guiding paradigm, it relied upon what Honko called 'a haphazard collection of often incommensurable documents scattered widely in time and space and often of obscure origin . . . which practically never belonged to the same tradition community'. Also, 'there was no urge for more penetrating questions concerning the cultural context or performance of the oral text in question'. And there was no room for context, which reflected poorly on the reliability of the data: 'The lack of contextual information made it difficult to assess the cultural representativity of data. In short, the variation was artificial, visible only to the scholar, and certainly not representative of the real, organic variation of folklore to be observed through empirical research.'[15]

Carl von Sydow himself had become increasingly dissatisfied with the limitations of the historical–geographical method. In his essay 'On the Spread of Tradition' (1932), he argued that 'scholars have failed to study the biology of tradition'. He moved beyond the study of tale transmission as a simple geographic phenomenon. In introducing the concepts of 'active' and 'passive' bearers, he explored the process and means of transmission. In 1934 in 'Geography and Folk-Tale Ecotypes', he wrote:

> One of the most serious deficiencies in the study of folk tradition has been that investigators have . . . been content with extracts, instead of seeing their information as part of a natural, living whole . . . But it is not enough to study folk-tales as tales only. It is also necessary to make oneself familiar with the use of folk tales, their life in tradition, their transmission and spread.[16]

The study of tales had to be localised, and linked to the tellers, the artifices of transmission, to their style and creativity. And differences had to be studied within their context. With these ideas in mind von Sydow theorised the concept of 'ecotype':

> In the science of botany *ecotype* is a term used to denote a hereditary plant-variety adapted to a certain *milieu* (seashore, mountain-land, *etc.*) through natural selection amongst hereditarily dissimilar entities of the same species. When then in the field of traditions a widely spread tradition, such as a tale or legend, forms special types through isolation inside and suitably

for certain culture districts, the term ecotype can also be used in the science of ethnology and folklore. One can distinguish between ecotypes of a higher or lower order: (national, provincial, parochial, *etc.*).[17]

The concept of ecotype echoes and develops a most important argument in anthropology. Back in 1916, the anthropologist Franz Boas (1858–1942) argued that tales, although widely distributed across continents, 'have developed characteristic peculiarities in the restricted parts of the territory in which they occur'.[18] Boas, the main exponent of the concept of 'cultural relativism', was strongly opposed to the levelling action of comparative analysis in terms of cultural differences. On the contrary, items of folklore need to be looked at as expressions of their culture, specifically reflecting the society in which they exist.

These ideas had invaluable repercussions in the study of narrative. They were all moving toward a concept-related study of text, one that took the teller and his audience into consideration as well as, most importantly, the function that a story served for those who told and listened to it.

It was Bronislaw Malinowski, among other anthropologists, who drew attention to the concept of 'function'. His work was based on observation of narratives in context, far from the archival research of the text-comparative method. He called for attention to faithful transcriptions of texts, and for the need to record the context, thus keeping the text in its habitat. His focus on function translated into an 'attempt to grasp the natives' mental attitude towards the mythological aspect' of their narratives, trying to find out to what extent 'myths influence the native outlook'.[19]

He wrote:

> The question which presents itself first, in trying to grasp the native outlook on the subject is: what is myth to the natives? How do they conceive and define it? Have they any line of demarcation between the mythical and the actual reality, and if so, how do they draw this line?[20]

Later on he concludes that:

> Myth possesses the normative power of fixing customs, of sanctioning modes of behaviour, of giving dignity and importance to an institution. The Kula receives from these stories its stamp of extreme importance and value. The rules of commercial honour, of generosity and punctiliousness in all its operations, acquire through this their binding force. This is what we could call the normative influence of myth on custom.[21]

Malinowski observed that a strong link between the mythical and the actual existed in the community, whereby myths, although set in the distant past, were indispensable for the understanding of the present, both in terms of social organisation and worldview. Only in understanding the role it plays in the society in which it is told can we form an idea of what a narrative really is. And it has to be a local idea; it cannot be generalised for other cultures.

Such findings called for additional fieldwork. Scholars were inspired to collect more stories – and in more local contexts – through participant observation, with attention to recording the context as well as the performance situation itself. These are the ideas that formed the foundation for the study of folk narrative in the second part of the twentieth century, during the so-called 'performance period'.

Before moving on to performance, however, it is necessary to revert to text and its study, to look at two more important approaches to folk narrative texts: the structural and psychoanalytic approaches.

In addition to the idea of tale type, another important pattern emerged from the study of tales: specific narrative structures could be observed which crossed the boundaries of types and revealed that certain groups of tales tended to behave in the same way. Vladimir Propp pioneered the structural analysis of tales in 1928, with the publication of *The Morphology of the Folktale*. Propp studied a limited number of tales confined to a single genre (those included between ATU 300 and ATU 749, that is tales of magic) and observed that they possessed a shared structure, which he codified through a list of thirty-one functions; these were the basic components of the plot and followed a fixed chronological and logical order. He then identified a series of seven actors, or *dramatis personae*, among which the thirty-one functions are ideally distributed. As complicated and open to criticism as his method was, it was certainly groundbreaking.

However, *The Morphology* was not translated into English until 1958, and it was really through Levi-Strauss's critique of Propp that attention was drawn to the book. The 1960s and 1970s saw a renewed interest in the structure of folk narrative. Claude Bremond, Algirdes Julien Greimas and Alan Dundes conceived new structural models in the attempt to simplify Propp's classification, reducing the number of functions and trying to take the structural analysis to a more generalised level, which could be applied to other narratives beyond those that had formed the basis of Propp's analysis. Moving away from the syntagmatic (that is, the chronological structure of events) model elaborated by Propp, and building on studies such as those of Greimas, the Russian structuralists, and in particular Eleazar Meletinskij, concentrated on the so-called paradigmatic model: that is, the identification of couples of semantic oppositions that regulated and sustained the structure of tales, such as good/evil, high/low, own/foreign, which help to define the moral and social qualities of the hero, those of his antagonists, and the nature of his struggle. These efforts built upon Levi-Strauss' idea of deep structure, and the need to take meaning into account when trying to decode the structure of myths and tales. The French anthropologist had argued that tales were 'miniature myths' that were supported by lighter oppositions than those that sustained myths – no longer strong cosmological or natural oppositions, but more local, social and moral kinds of conflicts. It was therefore possible to argue that it was not the case that one had its origins in the other, but that the two co-existed and served different functions.

One structuralist concept that deserves special mention, as it was to inform future debates on meaning in narrative, was Dundes's notion of 'allomotifs': the diverse motifs that fill the same functional slot in different tales. For example, in a Scottish version of the story we usually know as 'Snow White', the queen who seeks the name of the most beautiful woman in the realm does not interrogate a mirror, but a trout! It does not follow, however, that the two motifs are identical in terms of meaning: when looking at variants across space and time, it is important to try to link differences to the specific cultural background. Therefore it will matter if we have a trout rather than a mirror. And such matters should be fundamental for understanding the relations between stories and their community.[22] In this respect, Bengt Holbek was able to build on the work of his predecessors and integrate the idea of community and the social roles of stories into his structural analysis. His masterpiece, *Interpretation of Fairytales*, is one of the most influential publications in folk narrative scholarship. While dealing with structure, he also attempted to explain metaphors and symbols in light of what they might have meant for the community in which they had been collected. Holbek's work also takes into account Dundes' psychoanalytical readings of tale motifs.

Dundes had applied the Freudian concept of 'projection' (in psychoanalysis, a defence mechanism whereby we transfer our feelings about something or someone onto another person) to the structure of a number of tales, with the intention of bringing *meaning* into structural analysis. Although not all of his readings are accepted, his contribution was invaluable in many ways. His work made it impossible from then onwards to divorce the study of structure from the meaning of the content. In addition to this, Dundes' work brought into folk narrative scholarship a voice which had many times tried to express itself, but with very little success: that of the psychological sciences. Freud had himself been interested in folklore, arguing that dreams and folklore were sustained by the same material. His study of jokes formed the basis for much modern theory on the function of humorous narratives in society. Jungian scholars were also attracted by tales. Among them, Marie-Louise Von Franz in particular has contributed numerous studies. However, it was almost always a case of psycho-analysts picking up a collection of tales – too often the Grimms' – and analysing it with very little attention to the knowledge that folklorists had accumulated. These studies were completely detached from the context of telling and from the community, in contrast with Holbeck's highly commendable analysis.

On the other hand, folklorists refused for a long time to take into consid-eration the analytical tools that psychoanalysis offered them: there was never a real interdisciplinary study of tales from the two points of view. Dundes brought the psychoanalytical study of folklore back into the hands of folklorists, arguing that a knowledge of folklore is essential to understand its implications, especially because of a real necessity to use as many versions of a story as possible. A story is the ensemble of all its variants, and not the one version we find printed in a book. All literal analysis, then, cannot be particularly enlightening. But one more problem in bringing folklore and psychoanalysis together is that the latter is a science of the individual, whereas folk narrative cannot be detached from its community. In analysing a story, one deals with a product that has neither only one author nor only one text. Psychoanalysts stress the unconscious aspects of the tales' contents and performance, but this approach fails to take the artistry of the performer, and the conscious response of the audience, into account. Rather than trying to uncover meaning in the text, the focus should be on how tales act upon people, and the exploration of meaning can start from there, from what people say about how stories make them feel.

And indeed, it was a performer-centred approach that paved the way for folklore studies from this point onwards. So far, the text has been the main object of study, but we have seen that there had been many attempts to direct the folklorists' attention to extra-textual dimensions such as meaning and context. Such voices became dominant in the second half of the twentieth century, in particular from the 1960s onwards with the advent of what came to be called 'Performance Studies'. Scholars had become more and more dissatisfied with the philological approach to the study of tales. What Dégh says about the 'biology of storytelling' (a term introduced by von Sydow) sums up the idea of a new direction in folk narrative scholarship:

> 'Biology' indicates a significant switch of focus in scholarship, from text to context. The term signals a change in concentration from the static view of artificially constructed and isolated oral narrative sequences, to the dynamics of telling and transmitting stories from person to person and from people to people, through the means of direct contact, interaction, and resulting processes responsible for the formation and continual recreation of narratives.[23]

This new approach posed a series of questions: How, when, on what occasion, by whom and to whom is a story told? What place does that story occupy in the repertoire of the storyteller? How does the story reflect the group's ideas and values? What are the uses of the story, what prompts its recitation, what comes before and after it? And, ideally, how does it change over time, and across different performances? How is a story learned, memorised, passed on?

Such questions could only be answered by the long neglected 'folk' and, as such, every answer was a good one. Fieldwork – that is, talking to people and voicing them – was seen as the way forward. Observant participation became the favourite method of collection and significant attention was paid to the performance and all its components. Transcriptions, which became dense and often complicated, reported on every element of the recitation of a tale, from gestures to audience reactions.[24] Studies of single storytellers and their repertoires replaced tale monographs.[25] The narrative corpuses under study were therefore forcibly 'thicker', as Honko put it.[26] Collecting material for performer-centred studies and repertoire analysis meant that the researcher was dealing with a number of different stories, or different versions of the same story, from a single teller. Such corpuses, which were likely to be collected over a relatively short period of time, could show the 'organic' variation of a folklore item much more effectively than the selections of scattered versions (in terms of time and space) that had been examined by the comparative school. And indeed, repertoire analysis offered the perfect chance to discuss uses of stories with their tellers.

The shift of focus onto performance resulted in an inevitable change in the narrative genres that were being studied. This was essentially due to social changes that lead to a rejection of certain genres of folk narrative, such as folktales. And although one of the best examples of performance-based studies, Dégh's *Folktales and Society* (2nd edn, 1989), is centred on folktales, it can be generally stated that, by the second half of the twentieth century, such long fictional narratives were very rarely performed in the Western world. Collecting them was often a case of trying to glean fragments of stories from inactive storytellers. Therefore, the folklorist who was willing to study narrative in context had to turn to those genres that were still being regularly and spontaneously performed in groups, i.e. shorter kinds of stories, such as anecdotes, jokes, tall tales and legends.

After all, stories are meant to be used. We can learn much more about a story's meaning when we look at how it is used in interaction. There is a story for every occasion; but why that story? How does it affect the listener? How does the teller choose it from amongst the tales in his repertoire? These became fundamental questions, and they still are. It is to the understanding of such questions that Carl Lindahl's study of Jane Muncy's storytelling practices,[27] and Barbara Kirshenblatt-Gimblett's view of a parable in context,[28] provide some of the most insightful and stimulating contributions. In her study, Kirshenblatt-Gimblett reported on a woman's use of parables in daily life, in order to communicate concepts that she would otherwise struggle to convey in direct ways. All this was done by engaging in conversation with the teller about her perceptions of her own stories. In the same way, Lindahl is able to convey the extent of Muncy's storytelling art by voicing her own views and reflections on how she used her stories, adapting them to different audiences and contexts.[29] The focus on voicing the tellers, rather than imposing the scholar's view on them, makes these works fundamental contributions to folk narrative scholarship. In addition, each has the merit of moving away from the study of performance as an isolated event, to open up the idea of storytelling as a life practice through which individuals construct their identities, as well as communicating and discussing their ideas with those around them.

Henry Glassie's celebrated *Passing the Time in Ballymenone* (1982), and more recently Ray Cashman's *Storytelling on the Northern Irish Border* (2008), were observations of storytelling as a way of life, but this time within the context of two communities. Through 'participant observation' (that is, getting involved with the community), both authors observed storytelling practice over an extended period of time. They were thus able to record all kinds of stories and – in the case of Cashman in particular – to present them in ways that clearly conveyed how everyday storytelling is used to articulate identity and a worldview within difficult realities, such as in Aghyaran (a mixed Catholic–Protestant border community), and how narratives play a vital role in the cohesion of the group. Cashman's contribution was particularly revealing, because he was able to let the voices and views of the storytellers be heard more than that of the academic.

When dealing with storytelling practice within a group or community, some important issues regarding ownership of stories arise. Studies such as Amy Shuman's *Storytelling Rights: The Uses of Oral and Written Texts by Urban Adolescents*

(1986) explored these matters in revealing ways. Her focus was on key questions, such as what can make material for a story (storiability) and who is allowed to tell a story (narrative rights). Her findings showed that the teller has knowledge of what he can and cannot tell and how much he can roam, within pre-set parameters, according to his audience. All this reinforces the idea that it is precisely in the encounter between the teller and his audience, i.e. the performance event, that stories take body and acquire sense. Therefore, any attempt to separate the story from its context would lead to an incomplete understanding of the story.

Each of the above approaches to stories has added enormously to the study of folk narrative by moving away from the story as pure text and looking at it as a rich and multi-dimensional report of a performance event that is unique in itself (because it will never happen again in the same way, under the same circumstances), but is at the same time part of a larger practice.

Amy Shuman's study dealt primarily with teenagers' diaries, which extended the concept of folk narrative to written representations. The spectrum of narratives under examination has become increasingly wider over the past sixty years, as folklorists have been concentrating on a much broader range of storytelling situations and communities, be they real or virtual. Indeed, the past decade has seen the number of studies on internet narratives grow exponentially:[30] virtual communities are gaining increasing importance in the study of folklore. But this is not all: a quick glance at the topics of the papers presented at the International Society of Folk Narrative Research congress in 2009 will be sufficient to provide an idea of the exciting variety of contemporary approaches to folk narrative and storytelling practice. They included the role of stories in connection with diaspora communities,[31] with the construction and conceptualisation of national and ethnic identity,[32] with the use of humour as a normative as well as a transformative agent,[33] with natural disasters,[34] and with psychological healing processes[35] and trauma recovery.[36] With reference to the last two examples, the 'Surviving Katrina and Rita in Houston' Project, created by Carl Lindahl and Pat Jasper, is one of the most important achievements in folk narrative studies, as well as in fieldwork practices. In this project, it was not folklorists but disaster survivors themselves who recorded their personal narratives from each other. The project deserves special mention for two main reasons: first, its approach to fieldwork and second, its people-based nature. Too often when we talk of narrative studies we lose sight of the narrators and, most of all, of the very tangible and physical nature of stories. This project was first of all a practical intervention through stories, that is to help the survivors of the hurricane elaborate their experiences and memories. It voiced these people on their own terms, by training them to interview each other rather than requiring them to submit to the questions of academics who did not experience the tragedy in the first place and could hardly find ways of asking about it. It was therefore a facilitating and enabling action on the part of the researcher, and those involved took the lead in the fieldwork process, which has in turn proved to be a healing journey for many of them. Most of all, they knew that their words would be recorded as they were spoken, and not filtered by strangers to fit the official narratives.

This synergy between folk narrative studies and community projects is most desirable for the future of folk narrative scholarship. The two cannot be detached. The physical dimension of folk narrative should not be overlooked, because it represents its very nature. Indeed, the therapeutic side of reminiscence and testimony deserves to be further explored through more such multidisciplinary efforts. In general, interdisciplinary collaboration is the direction that much folk narrative scholarship is currently taking, in an attempt to bring different disciplines together with folklore, to explore the uses of stories in an ever-growing number of dynamics. This kind of collaborative approach is bound to produce many inspiring works in the future.

FOLK NARRATIVE STUDY IN SCOTLAND

In the history of folklore theories and scholarship, Scotland deserves an individual mention. Scottish folklorists have tended to be their own masters, departing from mainstream approaches and carrying on with what has always been, even in the era of 'text above all', a strongly fieldwork-oriented approach. The Scottish scholars were first and above all fieldworkers, indefatigable collectors, with folk-oriented minds and ears.

While Peter Buchan (following the Grimms' example) heavily modified the language of the people in his collection *Ancient Scottish Tales* (1908), the major Scottish folklorists showed uncommon deference to the narrator. John Francis Campbell of Islay (1822–1885) set a new standard for folklore collectors by recording tales word-for-word as dictated by the narrators. In a famous passage from his introduction to *Popular Tales of the West Highlands* (1860), he wrote:

> The following collection is intended to be a contribution to this new science of 'Storyology'. It is a museum of curious rubbish about to perish, given as it was gathered in the rough, for it seemed to me as barbarous to 'polish' a genuine popular tale, as it would be to adorn the bones of a Megatherium with tinsel, or gild a rare copper coin. On this, however, opinions may vary, but I hold my own, that stories orally collected can only be valuable if given unaltered; besides, where is the model story to be found?[37]

Although convinced that he was just gleaning old remains of a dying art, he was nevertheless aware of the importance of the narrators' speech. So important were diction and style for Campbell that he even lamented the fact that, in taking down stories by hand, the collector altered the story: 'As often happens with aged reciters, when [Donald MacPhie] repeated it a second time slowly for transcribing, nearly all the curious . . . language was left out.'[38]

At a time when scholars were focusing only on the text and its migrations, Campbell paid attention to the tellers and dedicated entire pages to descriptions of them, men and women alike. For example, MacPhie 'had the manner of a practised narrator, and it is quite evident he is one; he chuckled at the interesting parts, and laid his withered finger on my knee as he gave out the terrible bits with due solemnity'. Campbell extends his descriptions, drawing the scene for us, both in words and in his sketches and beautiful watercolours.[39]

Another early compiler, Robert Chambers (1802–1871), published tales exactly as he received them, and frequently presented two versions of the 'same' tale side by side.[40] The respect for the storyteller and his art has always been at the centre of Scottish scholars' work. In the twentieth century, they were inspired by the collecting of Irish folklorists. In 1935, the Irish government established the Irish Folklore Commission 'for the purpose of collecting, cataloguing, and eventually publishing the best of what remained of Irish oral tradition'. Collectors were required not just to record stories with modern sound equipment, but also to keep fieldwork diaries for noting important details. Seán Ó Súilleabháin, the Commission's archivist, compiled for collectors an exhaustive *Handbook of Irish Folklore* (1942), which is useful for Scotland too.

Because Ireland possessed close linguistic and cultural ties with the west of Scotland,[41] the Commission appointed the Gaelic-speaking Scot Calum Maclean (1915–1960) to collect stories in Scotland. He became the first full-time collector in the School of Scottish Studies when it was founded in 1951. His work, which is also preserved in the School of Scottish Studies Archives, is invaluable. He discovered some of the most gifted Gaelic storytellers,[42] who delivered an unprecedented treasure of stories, many of which were international types,[43] and therefore opened up Scottish traditional narrative for comparative study across Europe.

Also of great importance was the work of the many other collectors who worked for the School: Alan Bruford (1937–1995), Donald Archie MacDonald (1929–1999), and Hamish Henderson (1919–2002), whose fieldwork built much of the School's tale archive. Henderson's work with the 'cairds', or Travellers, of Scotland was groundbreaking. Not only did it reveal a treasure of stories and gifted storytellers, such as Duncan Williamson and Betsy Whyte, but it also offered the unique opportunity to study stories in context, and most of all in a natural context, where stories were still used on a daily basis as a teaching and interactive tool. With their stories, most of which were collected in Scots, the Travellers had nurtured a tradition that had largely disappeared among the settled Scots-speaking population. In the second half of the twentieth century Duncan Williamson, Betsy Whyte, Stanley Robertson and other Travellers recorded dozens of international tale types that had not been recorded in the repertoires of other Scots speakers during the same period.

Collection work brought forward a surprising number of stories, many of which were unique to Scotland, while others turned out to be versions of international tales. These formed the basis for comparative work, such as Bruford's paper on versions of Snow White (1965), and drew much international attention to the archive of the School of Scottish Studies. A very important selection of such material is contained in the volume *Scottish Traditional Tales*, compiled by Bruford and MacDonald. In the 1960s Bruford also worked steadily at the compilation of two provisional type indexes based on School archive material: the first on fairy legend types (type numbers were prefixed by the letter F) and the second on Gaelic witch stories.[44] MacDonald added a number of Scottish variants to Christiansen's index of migratory legends.[45]

The Scottish input has been and continues to be fundamental to folklore studies. It has not only aided comparative studies by bringing forward many new versions of international tales, but also furthered the understanding of tale narration and function, with studies such as MacDonald's on the role of story-tellers' visual memory when remembering and reciting tales.[46]

John Shaw has continued this tradition, exploring the verbal art of Gaelic storytellers in particular, and extending his research to the Gaelic diaspora of Cape Breton. For example, in *Tales until Dawn: The World of a Cape Breton Gaelic Story-Teller* (1987) Shaw presents the oral autobiography and the narrative reper-toire of the formidable narrator Joe Neil MacNeil.[47]

CASE STUDY

This case study[48] is centred on ten Scottish versions, housed in the School of Scottish Studies Archives, of an international novella: type ATU 875 *The Clever Farmgirl* (also known as AT 875, *The Clever Peasant Girl*). The story has been documented all over the Western world and beyond,[49] and it belongs to a group of tales centred on the clever solving of riddles. What follows is a partial version of the type description given by Thompson in *The Types of the Folktale*.

> *The Clever Daughter*. A peasant finds a mortar in a field and against the advice of his clever daughter takes it to the king, who demands the pestle as well.

> *The Tasks*. The clever girl performs various tasks set by the king, answers questions, or solves riddles.

> *As King's Wife*. As a result she marries the king. He resolves a dispute over the possession of a calf with an unjust ruling; she advises the abused subject how to show the king the absurdity of his decision through an equally foolish act (this move often appears as a story on its own), for example trying to grow salt in a lake.

> *The Dearest Possession*. When the king casts her out and allows her to take with her only the one thing she holds dearest, she takes her sleeping husband along and moves him to forgive her.

The clever daughter is able to win the king's heart because of her intelligence, wisdom and wit, as the two engage in dialogues involving riddles, proverbs and humorous exchanges of ambiguous phrases. However, as soon as her intel-ligence is used to expose the lack of wisdom and practical sense of the king himself, he falls prey to fury and casts her out, and it is only when she proves to him how much she loves him that he is moved to forgive her.

The Scottish versions of this story display quite a few interesting differences from the international type. Collected in the Gaelic language between 1870 and 1979, mostly in South Uist,[50] the tales contain a series of narrative motifs that portray the Scottish clever girl as engaged in what appears more like a conflict between social classes, rather than the continental battle of sexes. The Scottish texts are so consistent in their differences from the international type that one could argue they constitute a unique Scottish ecotype. The Scottish motifs, taken as a whole, appear to be clear references to the reality of eighteenth- and nineteenth-century Scotland in terms of land distribution and management: as such, the tales offer a chance to explore variation in connection with historical and social change.

For reasons of clarity, here follows a summary of the typical Scottish version:

A landowner forbids crofters from hunting on his estate. One day, while he is out hunting, he calls at the house of his oldest crofter. Only his daughter is at home and the landowner asks her where her father is. She answers that he is out hunting. The landowner replies he should not be, for hunting is forbidden. The girl says the kind of hunting her father does is not going to make any difference to the landowner, because he leaves what he kills and brings home what he does not catch. The landowner eventually discovers what the girl means and appreciates her wit. Wishing to test the girl again, he tells her father that he has to answer three riddles or he will be evicted. The girl tells the father the answers to the riddles. The landowner discovers that the girl supplied the answers and asks to meet her. They meet and he tells her he would marry her, if she were a landowner's daughter. As a reward, though, he wants to give her some land. She has the land deeded to her father, instead. Now she is a landowner's daughter and she can marry the landowner. But she requires, and is granted, a prenuptial contract: in the event that the landowner throws her out, she will be allowed to take three armfuls of property from the house. They have a child and are happy together. One day, two crofters have a dispute over the possession of a foal and the landowner is called upon to solve it. He makes an unjust decision and gives the foal to the wrong man.

The real owner goes to the laird's wife and tells her what has happened. She advises him to go and throw salt in the loch, and tell the laird that he is hoping it will grow. The landowner remarks how strange a thing the man is doing, and the man answers that it is stranger that a gelding should bear a foal that is growing inside a mare. The landowner understands his wife has coached the man and he orders her to leave. She carries her three armfuls out of the house: the child, the title deeds, and the landowner himself, in his chair. He pleads to be forgiven and promises he will never bring anything against her again.

The difference in setting is clear from the beginning. In nine out of ten Scottish versions the male protagonist is not a king but a laird, or landowner. The landowner is depicted as unable to manage his land or his tenants' disputes, unlike his peasant wife. The gap between them is reinforced in some versions by the girl's answer to the laird: 'He leaves what he kills and brings home what he doesn't catch.' She means that her father is catching fleas on his own body, but the laird does not understand. However, we know from the sound-recording of one version that teller and audience used to laugh at this point, as if they all knew the answer. Thanks to the recording, which gives us an idea of the performance situation and of the interaction between teller and audience, we can assume that, back when the story was commonly told, people knew the meaning of the girl's answer, through which the laird's character was automatically isolated from the community for his lack of common sense. The sound-recording is essential in giving this added perspective on the story's meaning.

The laird's inability to interact with the people on his land is made explicit and somehow explained in one version in particular. In it, the storyteller, Donald MacIntyre from Loch Eynort, South Uist, describes the transfer of the land from the father to the son, who, having been educated in the south, has not been aware of the problems on the estate and proceeds to make some tragic changes to its management (suggested by his English friends, says Donald, 'who spent holidays on the estate and did not like to see crofters fishing and hunting on it').

The fact that five out of ten versions hint at the young laird's ineptitude and criticise his decision to forbid hunting on the land, suggests that the story was an efficient vehicle for airing a sense of frustration with the managerial methods adopted by some estate owners. One cannot help but think that motifs such as the laird being educated down south, the partial reorganisation of the estates as holiday destinations, and the prohibition of hunting and fishing in order to keep the land free from crofters and preserve its 'people-less'[51] beauty for the eyes of the visitors may represent realistic allusions to some concrete situations of discontent.

The realistic quality of the Scottish corpus is also reflected in its very 'down-to-earth' attitude to what should constitute a novella's romantic licence. Eight out of the ten Scottish versions bear the motif of the 'writing of the land',[52] an expedient that turns the clever daughter into a landowner herself, so that she can be deemed fit to marry the laird. As if to somehow prevent the suspension of disbelief, the tale seems to deny the possibility that cleverness in itself might be sufficient to overcome social barriers, and that rich and poor might be so easily united. To make matters even more sensible and practical, the Scottish clever daughter demands a prenuptial contract in all ten versions, which grants her the right to choose three things of her liking, should the laird tire of her. This demand may be connected with the practice of 'hand fasting' in Scotland, a trial marriage whereby

> a Man should take a Maid to his Wife and keep her the space of a Year without marrying her, and if she pleased him all the while, he married her at the end of the Year and legitimated these Children, but if he did not love Her, he return'd her to her Parents and her Portion also, and if there happened to be any Children, they were kept by the Father, but this unreasonable Custom was long ago brought in disuse.[53]

The woman's need to secure herself some compensation in case of rejection (after a year, as specified in many of the versions) might well evoke the memory of such trial marriages. In all ten versions, however, the clever daughter has given the laird a child – and maybe this is what saves the marriage. And it is the child that she takes as her first armful, followed by the chest containing the title deeds and, last, her husband. The title deeds seem to indicate that the land should go to the person who has proved able to manage it. This view is reinforced by the landowner's plea to be taken back into the house: 'I'll bring nothing, nothing against you for ever, neither will I make a judgement without finding from you that it's right.' The laird submits to his wife's wisdom, recognising the superiority of her judgement.

However, this does not appear to be a victory for the weak sex. Although two out of ten versions clearly point toward such emancipation – by humorously showing a clever daughter who shuts the door in the laird's face, saying 'you are now without land and I have it' – the final submission to the girl's wisdom on the landowner's part appears to be of a social nature. The fact that the finale with a pleading laird (who promises to adopt his wife's ways) was more popular than the one displaying a feminist revenge might indicate that the Scottish clever daughter is a symbol not so much of her sex as of her rank: the crofters. And it is not by chance that in a few versions, as if to de-feminise the daughter and focus attention on her wisdom, she is described as ugly – 'mingy, bold, bad-tempered, dark-skinned,' states Angus Maclellan.[54]

If we accept that the motif of the 'writing of the land' implied that marriage between different social classes is impossible, it seems unlikely that the story should now suggest that wisdom is as precious a quality as beauty for finding a husband. Rather, it seems more likely that the character of the weak sex has naturally turned into a symbol of the weak class. The laird does not submit to a 'woman', but to the people, to their moral values and common sense. The audience must have derived more satisfaction from seeing the landowner adopt their ways than from casting him out permanently. And seeing the people's common sense triumph, at a time when many believed that changes imposed by aristocratic outsiders were causing disastrous consequences, must have felt as a most cathartic ending for the story – much more so than the romantic (not to say sexist) conti-nental equivalent.[55]

When confronted with the ATU type description, we can state that the story has lost its romantic flair and that the power relationship has been subverted. It is no longer a case of women submitting to their men's authority, regardless of how much more clever than their husbands they prove to be. It is now a case of the man admitting that his wife can more shrewdly judge the very matters that he should master better than anyone else.

The battle of the sexes was indeed fertile ground for such themes of social protest. The character representing the weak sex was the most fitting to embody the socially weak, the unvoiced. Such social and historical motifs were woven into the story because the plot was already naturally predisposed to the discussion of class conflicts. And such changes were quite possibly what the story needed in nineteenth- and twentieth-century Scotland in order to remain relevant and survive up to the days when it was recorded.

To conclude, the analysis of the Scottish variants of 'the clever daughter' against the background of the European type illustrates some of the most important characteristics of folk narrative, as stated in the opening pages of this chapter. A story, in order to survive, must remain relevant to the lives of those who tell it. A folk narrative is never static: it is constantly adapted. Telling and adapting stories allow individuals and communities to redefine their identity in light of social changes, and to sustain themselves through potentially threatening times. Stories allow people to discuss, evaluate and criticise their social environment in safe ways, while at the same time reinforcing their social structure, worldview and shared beliefs.

As fictional as it might seem, a 'simple' folktale, and the way it is told, perceived and passed on, represents an invaluable window into the lives, history, values and sentiments of those who tell it and listen to it.

NOTES

1 Honko, 2000.
2 Honko, 2000, 4.
3 Foley, 1995, 42.
4 Cf. Dégh, 1972, 60.
5 See Dégh, 1972 for a more detailed discussion.
6 See Uther, 2004 for a full classification.
7 Dégh, 1972, 73.
8 Stahl, 1989.
9 Ben-Amos, 1971, 4–5.
10 For a comprehensive discussion of fairy tale motifs in medieval sources see Ziolkowski, 2009.
11 For an exhaustive and multilingual bibliography on fairy tale collections and studies see Gatto, 2006.
12 Dégh, 1995, 262–82.
13 Emrich, 1946.
14 These ideas were further developed by the Ritualistic Theory school, a major exponent of which was Pierre Saintyves (1870–1935), who analysed the initiatory character of tales; and later by Vladimir Propp in his *Historical Roots of the Magic Tale*, Leningrad, 1946.
15 Honko, 2000, 8.
16 Von Sydow, 1934, 344.
17 Von Sydow, 1934, 349, n7.
18 Boas, 1916, 397.
19 Malinowski, 2002, 326.
20 Malinowski, 2002, 298–9.
21 Malinowski, 2002, 328.
22 Simonsen, 1998.
23 Dégh, 1995, 47.
24 Finnegan, 1992.
25 Pentikäinen, 1977, 1978.
26 Honko, 2000.
27 Lindahl, 2001a.
28 Kirshenblatt-Gimblett, 1975.
29 Lindahl, 2001a.
30 Kropej, 2007.

31 Kirss, 2004.
32 Minton and Evans, 2001.
33 Fine and de Soucey, 2005; Masoni, 2011.
34 Narvaez, 2003; Lindahl, 2012.
35 Taylor, 2010; Goldstein, 2004.
36 Lindahl and Nash, 2008.
37 Campbell, 1983, ii–iii.
38 Campbell, 1983, 22.
39 Campbell, 1983, xxii.
40 Chambers, 1841.
41 Delargy, 1999.
42 For Gaelic storytelling, see the works of Shaw listed in the Bibliography.
43 Calum Maclean's recordings have recently been digitised and made available online at <www.celtscot.ed.ac.uk/calum-maclean/> [accessed November 2012].
44 MacDonald, 1994–95; Bruford, 1967.
45 MacDonald, 1994–95.
46 MacDonald, 1978 and 1981. This volume of *ARV* includes several articles on storytelling in Scotland.
47 See also Shaw, 2007a.
48 Part of an unpublished paper: Masoni, L. What does the clever girl have to say about history? Delivered at the international conference *The Deep History of Stories* organised by The International Association for Comparative Mythology, Edinburgh, 2007. A revised and expanded version will soon be published in article form in *Fabula*.
49 Thompson, 1946.
50 South Uist (five versions); North Uist (one version); Lewis (one version); Torloisk, Isle of Mull (one version); Argyll (one version); Port Charlotte, Islay (one version). Two are from printed sources and two from manuscript sources. See the Tale Archive of the School of Scottish Studies for details.
51 See McCrone, 2001.
52 Common also to an Irish version I have heard.
53 Martin, 1703, 114.
54 See also another version by the same storyteller in Campbell, 1997, 70–4.
55 Such realistic touches are accompanied by a number of detailed references to the reality of the rural society such as references to a rèiteach (pre-wedding ritual). In Donald MacIntyre's version (1959): 'The landowner and other people came with him to agree a betrothal (còrdadh) with the old man's daughter. [. . .] Then they came to the night of the rèiteach and a lot of people came with him.' See Martin, 2007 for detailed descriptions of Celtic marriage traditions. Another version bears what appears to be a reference to the 'bondager system', an old habit still present in nineteenth century Scotland, whereby a man was required to provide an able-bodied woman who could work in the house and in the fields. If he did not have a wife he was expected to 'hire' one. So, just before the girl's wedding the father says to her: 'It is all right for the two of us if you happen to go away. Maybe I could find somebody else to come in with me.'

BIBLIOGRAPHY AND FURTHER READING

Aarne, A and Thompson, S. *The Types of the Folktale*, 3rd edn, Helsinki, 1961.
Afanasjev, A. *Russian Fairytales* [1943], New York, 1973.
ARV: Scandinavian Yearbook of Folklore, 37 (1981).

Bascom, W. The forms of folklore: Prose narrative, *Journal of American Folklore*, 78 (1965), 5–29.

Bauman, R. *Verbal Art as Performance*, Rowley, 1977.

Bauman, R. *Story, Performance, and Event: Contextual Studies of Oral Narrative*, Cambridge, 1986.

Ben-Amos, D. Toward a definition of folklore in context, *Journal of American Folklore*, 84:331, Toward New Perspectives in Folklore (1971), 3–15.

Ben-Amos, D. *Folklore Genres*, Austin and London, 1976.

Boas, F. *Race, Language and Culture*, New York, 1940.

Boas, F. The development of folk-tales and myths. In Boas, 1940, 397–406.

Bruford, A. A Scottish Gaelic version of Snow-White, *Scottish Studies*, 9:2 (1965), 153–74.

Bruford, A. Scottish Gaelic witch stories: A provisional type-list, *Scottish Studies*, 11:1 (1967), 13–47.

Bruford, A. Recitation or re-creation? Examples from South Uist Storytelling, *Scottish Studies*, 22 (1978), 27–44.

Bruford, A. Memory, Performance and structure in traditional tales, *ARV: Scandinavian Yearbook of Folklore*, 37 (1981), 103–9.

Bruford, A and MacDonald, D A. *Scottish Traditional Tales*, Edinburgh, 1994.

Buchan, P. *Ancient Scottish Tales*, Peterhead, 1908.

Campbell, J F. *Popular Tales of the West Highlands*, 4 vols, Hounslow, 1983–4.

Campbell, J L. *Stories from South Uist Told by Angus MacLellan*, trans. from the Gaelic by John Lorne Campbell, Edinburgh, 1997.

Cashman, R. *Storytelling on the Northern Irish Border: Characters and Community*, Bloomington, IN, 2008.

Chambers, R. *Popular Rhymes of Scotland*, 2nd edn, Edinburgh, 1841.

Christiansen, R T. *The Migratory Legends: A Proposed List of Types with a Systematic Catalogue of Norwegian Variants*, Helsinki, 1958.

Dégh, L. Folk narrative. In Dorson, 1972, 53–83.

Dégh, L. *Folktales and Society: Story-Telling in a Hungarian Peasant Community*, 2nd edn, Bloomington, IN, 1989.

Dégh, L. *Narratives in Society: A Performer-Centered Study of Narration*, Helsinki, 1995.

Dorson, R M, ed. *Folklore and Folklife: An Introduction*, Chicago, IL, 1972.

Dundes, A. *The Study of Folklore*, Englewood Cliffs, NJ, 1965.

Dundes, A. *Analytic Essays in Folklore*, The Hague, 1975.

Dundes, A. *Interpreting Folklore*, Bloomington, IN, 1980.

Dundes, A. *Parsing through Customs: Essays by a Freudian Folklorist*, Madison and London, 1987.

Dundes, A, ed. *International Folkloristics: Classic Contributions by the Founders of Folklore*, Oxford, 1999.

Emrich, D. 'Folk-Lore': William John Thoms, *California Folklore Quarterly*, 5:4 (1946), 355–74.

Fine, G A and de Soucey, M. Joking cultures: Humor themes as social regulation in group life, *Humor: International Journal of Humor Research*, 18:1 (2005), 1–22.

Finnegan, R. *Oral Traditions and the Verbal Arts: A Guide to Research Practices*, London, 1992.

Foley, J M. *The Singer of Tales in Performance*, Bloomington, IN, 1995.

Freud, S. *The Interpretation of Dreams*, New York, 1961.

Gatto, G. *La Fiaba di Tradizione Orale*, Milan, 2006.

Glassie, H. *Passing the Time in Ballymenone: Folklore and History of an Ulster Community*, Dublin, 1982.

Holbek, B. *Interpretation of Fairy Tales. Danish Folklore in a European Perspective*, Helsinki, 1987.

Honko, L. Thick corpus and organic variation: An introduction. In Honko, L, ed., *Thick Corpus: Organic Variation and Textuality in Oral Tradition* (*Studia Fennica Folkloristica* 7), Helsinki, 2000, 3–28.

Kirss, T, Kõresaar, E and Lauristin, M, eds. *She who Remembers, Survives: Interpreting Estonian Women's Post-Soviet Life Stories*, Tartu, 2004.

Kirshenblatt-Gimblet, B. A parable in context. In Ben-Amos, D and Goldstein, K S, eds, *Folklore: Performance and Communication*, The Hague, 1975, 105–30.

Kropej, M. Folk narrative in the era of electronic media. A case study in Slovenia, *Fabula: Journal of Folklore Studies* 48 (2007), 1–15.

Lang, A. *Myth, Ritual and Religion*, London, 1887.

Lindahl, C. Two tellings of Merrywise, *Journal of Folklore Research*, 38 (2001a), 39–54.

Lindahl, C, ed. *Perspectives on the Jack Tales and Other North American Märchen*, Bloomington, IN, 2001b.

Lindahl, C and Jasper, P. The Houston survivor project: An introduction, *Callaloo*, 29:4 (2006), 1504–5.

Lindahl, C and Nash, S. Survivor-to-survivor storytelling and trauma recovery, *The Dialogue*, 5:1 (2008), 11–13.

Lindahl, C. Legends of Hurricane Katrina: The right to be wrong, survivor-to-survivor storytelling, and healing, *Journal of American Folklore*, 125 (2012), 139–76.

MacDonald, D A. Fieldwork: Collecting oral literature. In Dorson, 1972, 407–30.

MacDonald, D A. A visual memory, *Scottish Studies*, 22 (1978), 1–26.

MacDonald, D A. Migratory legends of the supernatural in Scotland: A general survey, *Béaloideas*, 62–63 (1994–95), 29–78.

MacDonald, D A. Some aspects of visual and verbal memory in Gaelic storytelling, *ARV: Scandinavian Yearbook of Folklore*, 37 (1981), 114–24.

MacDougall, I. *Bondagers: Personal Recollections by Eight Scots Women Farm Workers*, East Linton, 2000.

McCrone, D. *Understanding Scotland: The Sociology of a Nation*, 2nd edn, London, 2001.

Malinowski, B. *Argonauts of the Western Pacific (1922), with a Preface by Sir James George Frazer*, London and New York, 2002.

Martin, M. *A Description of the Western Islands of Scotland*, London, 1703.

Martin, N. *The Form and Function of Ritual Dialogue in the Marriage Traditions of Celtic-Language Cultures*, Lewiston, NY, 2007.

Masoni, L. Eliciting laughter in a changing community: Humorous narratives as coping tools and as narrative currency to buy reintegration, *Fabula: Journal of Folklore Studies*, 52:1 (2001), 17–31.

Minton, J and Evans, D. 'The Coon in the Box': A Global Folktale in African-American Tradition, Helsinki, 2001.

Müller, M. *Lectures on the Science of Language*, London, 1882.

Ó Duilearga, S. Irish tales and story-tellers. In Dundes, 1999, 153–76.

Ó Súilleabháin, S. *A Handbook of Irish Folklore*, Dublin, 1942.

Pentikäinen, J. Repertoire analysis, *Studia Fennica*, 20 (1977), 262–77.

Pentikäinen, J. *Oral Repertoire and World View*, Helsinki, 1978.

Perrault, C. *The Histories of Passed Times, or the Tales of Mother Goose, with Morals*, London and Brussels, 1785.

Pitrè, G. *Fiabe, novelle e racconti popolari siciliani*, Palermo, 1875.

Propp, V. *Morphology of the Folktale* (originally published in Russian as *Morfologiya skázki* in 1928), 2nd edn, revised and edited with a preface by Louis A. Wagner and a new introduction by Alan Dundes, Austin, TX, 1968.

Róheim, G. *The Gates of Dreams*, New York, 1953.

Shaw, J. *Tales until Dawn: The World of a Cape Breton Gaelic Story-Teller*, Edinburgh, 1987.

Shaw, J. Storytellers in Scotland: Context and function. In Beech, J, Hand, O, MacDonald, F, Mulhern, M A and Weston, J, eds, *Scottish Life and Society. A Compendium of Scottish*

Ethnology, Volume 10: Oral Literature and Performance Culture, Edinburgh, 2007a, 28–41.

Shaw, J. *The Blue Mountains and Other Gaelic Stories from Cape Breton*, Montreal, 2007b.

Shuman, A. *Storytelling Rights: The Uses of Oral and Written Texts by Urban Adolescents*, Cambridge, 1986.

Simonsen, M. Folktales and reality. Some remarks on the reflection theory as applied to folktales. In Chesnutt, M, ed., *Telling Reality. Folklore Studies in Memory of Bengt Holbek*, Copenhagen and Turku, 1993, 121–41.

Simonsen, M. Culture and symbols. Some thoughts about Bengt Holbek's *Interpretation of Fairy Tales, Estudos de Literatura Oral*, 4 (1998), 209–14.

Smith, D. *Storytelling Scotland: A Nation in Narrative*, Edinburgh, 2001.

Stahl, S D. The oral personal narrative in its generic context, *Fabula: Journal of Folklore Studies*, 8 (1977), 18–39.

Stahl, S D. *Literary Folkloristics and the Personal Narrative*, Bloomington and Indianapolis, IN, 1989.

Taylor, A. *The Black Ox: A Study in the History of a Folktale*, Helsinki, 1927.

Tylor, E B. *The Origin of Culture*, New York and London, 1958.

Thompson, S. *Motif-Index of Folk-Literature: A Classification of Narrative Elements in Folktales, Ballads, Myths, Fables, Mediaeval Romances, Exempla, Fabliaux, Jest-Books, and Local Legends*, 2nd edn, 6 vols, Bloomington, IN, 1955–58.

Thompson, S. *The Folktale*, Berkeley, CA, 1946.

Uther, H-J, ed. *The Types of International Folktales: A Classification and Bibliography*, 3 vols, Helsinki, 2004.

Von Sydow, C W. On the spread of tradition [1932]. In Von Sydow, C W. *Selected Papers on Folklore*, Copenhagen, 1948, 11–43.

Von Sydow, C W. Geography and folk-tale ecotypes, *Béaloideas*, 4:3 (1934), 344–55.

Von Sydow, C W. Folktale studies and philology: Some points of view [1948]. In Dundes, 1965, 219–42.

Ziolkowski, J M. *Fairy Tales from Before Fairy Tales: The Medieval Latin Past of Wonderful Lies*, Ann Arbor, MI, 2009.

11 Traditional Music

KATHERINE CAMPBELL

This chapter will look at the ways in which ethnomusicologists and others have researched traditional music, at some of the sources they have used, and at some future directions for research. It will not include a focus on song – Scots or Gaelic, partly because the two tend to be regarded as distinct in Scotland as far as special-isation in scholarship is concerned.[1] But of course there are many overlaps, and more work needs to be done on the relationship between the two, especially since many of our early instrumental tunes in Scotland are also songs and some of the pibroch repertoire, the most highly developed form of music for the Highland bagpipe, has been shown to have its roots in the Gaelic song tradition.[2]

People who play traditional music in Scotland often have no difficulty in telling the researcher what traditional music means to them. For academics the term is much harder to define, and there have been many debates over the years about what 'traditional' and 'folk' mean. In 1954 the International Folk Music Council (which changed its name to the International Council for Traditional Music – ICTM – in 1981) defined the music it studies as follows:

> Folk music is the product of a musical tradition that has evolved through the process of oral transmission. The factors that shape the tradition are: 1) continuity which links the present with the past; 2) variation which springs from the creative individual or the group; and 3) selection by the community, which determines the form or forms in which the music survives.
>
> The term can be applied to music that has been evolved from rudimentary beginnings by a community uninfluenced by popular and art music, and it can likewise be applied to music which has originated with an individual composer and has subsequently been absorbed into the unwritten living tradition of a community.
>
> The term does not cover composed popular music that has been taken over ready-made by a community and remains unchanged, for it is the re-fashioning and re-creation of the music by the community that gives it its folk character.[3]

Oral transmission, re-creation by the community, variation and the changes brought about by it, then, are key. Tunes do not exist in a static version on the page but are fluid entities in the oral tradition.[4]

Traditional music in Scotland is often studied through the discipline of ethnomusicology. Ethnomusicology generally used to be thought of as the study of music in culture but has more recently come to be commonly regarded as the study of music in and as culture.[5] It is a discipline whose roots can be traced to the end of the nineteenth century to comparative musicology, through to ethnomusicology, then ethnomusicology.[6] Alan Merriam's *The Anthropology of Music* was a landmark publication, and other major authors in the field include Jaap Kunst, John Blacking, Bruno Nettl and Philip Bohlman.[7] Central to it are fieldwork and transcription as ways of understanding a musical culture. Key to its development has been the ability of scholars to make high quality audio (and, later, video) recordings, which are commonly deposited in archives with associated cataloguing and field documentation. Ethnomusicology can be used to study all living musical traditions – classical music, popular music, jazz and so on, but it tends to be associated with the indigenous musical traditions of the world, and with music that has its base in an oral culture.[8] Ethnomusicology is not the only way of studying traditional music, however: studies have been undertaken by musicologists;[9] historians; sociologists interested, for example, in the demographics of audiences at folk clubs;[10] and folklorists and ethnologists, who tend to focus on aspects of tradition (e.g. tradition-bearers, transmission, variation), with perhaps less emphasis being given to the music.

With all historical research it is important to engage if possible with the primary source – e.g. the music collection, the instrument in the museum, the manuscript held in the library – and not to simply rely on secondary sources, i.e. the work that scholars have done based on these sources. Some of the earliest evidence we have about instruments relates to carvings of instruments on stones. John Graham Dalyell recognised this in his *Musical Memoirs of Scotland*, published in the nineteenth century, and he went to considerable lengths to include good quality illustrations in his book.[11] One of these was the hog-bagpiper gargoyle at Melrose Abbey,[12] which is the earliest representation we have of the bagpipe in Scotland. Representations of the harp are found on Pictish stones in Scotland, e.g. the Nigg Stone from Easter Ross.[13] Archaeological evidence can also shed light on instruments such as the Jew's Harp.[14] Extant instruments are valuable sources of information, such as the fiddles found on the Tudor ship, the *Mary Rose*,[15] and the bagpipe collections of National Museums Scotland.[16] The study of instruments is a field of investigation in its own right, termed 'organology'.[17]

Works of art, e.g. paintings and carvings, can often provide useful information, especially when used in conjunction with other sources. An important painting of the Lowland harp – about which we have little surviving evidence – is found on the ceiling of Crathes Castle.[18] In terms of social context, a number of artists such as Walter Geikie and Sir David Wilkie chose the topic of the blind fiddler for their paintings, and this relates to the fact that, historically, many such fiddlers existed in Scotland, supporting themselves financially through their music.[19] Our knowledge of this tradition can be supplemented by newspaper articles. Whilst these sometimes aim at entertaining readers rather than giving a factual account, and the accuracy and reliability may be questionable, newspapers were often the main (or perhaps only) forum through which local characters

Figure 11.1 The hog-bagpiper gargoyle at Melrose Abbey. Photograph: Mike Sutherland

and events, including musical parties and soirees, were documented.[20] In addition, they sometimes contain photographs that are helpful for research.

Manuscript sources of tunes are available from around the seventeenth century,[21] sometimes taking the form of personal tune books. Sometimes the music is in tablature rather than staff notation,[22] which can present problems for the reader. In the eighteenth century, many music collections were published, particularly for the fiddle. Quite often these contain subscription lists that tell scholars much about who was buying the volumes, where they lived, and what the market for the volumes was. Other information, apart from the music notation itself, typically includes tune titles, attributions to particular composers, a note of the publisher, and a dedication.

Written accounts in which musicians and instruments are sometimes mentioned include the *Statistical Accounts of Scotland*, which can now be searched online,[23] and Burgh Records.[24] The Treasurers' Accounts of the Royal Court[25] as well as household accounts are also useful. Two important early sources include the *Complaynt of Scotland*, c. 1550, by Robert Wedderburn, vicar of Dundee, which mentions instruments (including the Trump, or Jew's Harp) and tunes, and the 'Book of the Dean of Lismore' dating from the early sixteenth century, which contains Gaelic poetry (which mentions the harp) as well as historical material, including a 'list of 32 clarsairean from different parts of Scotland above the Forth-Clyde line'.[26] Music-making (and dancing) were often mentioned in letters, and those of Robert Burns, for example, contain many references to this.[27] Sometimes musicians feature in novels too, such as 'Wandering Willie' in Walter Scott's *Redgauntlet*, who is based on William ap Prichard, a blind harper and fiddler from Wales. Poetry was also written by and about Scottish musicians,[28] and tends to be particularly useful when employed in conjunction with other sources. Autobiographies are also found occasionally: James Scott Skinner (1843–1927), for example, penned a newspaper column entitled 'My Life and Adventures', which was aimed at amusing and entertaining the reader as much as talking about Scottish fiddling.[29]

In terms of the modern day and recent past, fieldwork, and fieldwork recordings held in archives, are important. Different types of questioning may be used in fieldwork interviews, such as unstructured (without a list of interview questions); semi-structured (using a list of interview questions but being prepared to deviate from it as interesting points in the interview arise); or structured (adhering to the list of questions and not deviating from it – particularly useful if the researcher is conducting the same interview with a number of different people and wishes to compare the material). Most interviews tend to be recorded if the interviewee is willing and, again, if permission is given, the material may be placed in an archive. Recording is particularly relevant and necessary in the case of music, especially if a transcription is to be made. Two types of transcription are commonly recognised: prescriptive and descriptive. The first gives an outline of the performance and can normally be easily read by other performers; the second is more detailed and describes the features of the performance.[30] Video recording is particularly useful for studying musical performance, as it also allows for repetition and thus close analysis of playing style. Again, permission to record will be required. It is important to bear fieldwork ethics in mind. This involves, for example, obtaining consent to make the recording, dealing with certain topics sensitively in the interview, checking that the interviewee is happy to have the interview lodged in an archive, if relevant (often archives have their own permission form for this purpose), and making sure that the information obtained is treated appropriately afterwards in any project or publication that may emerge.[31]

The following case study will attempt to show how methodologies for both historical and modern-day research can be brought together, and discusses the sources that were available for studying the topic. It will highlight the context of music-making, the music used in the past and at the present, and the theme of music in the community. The idea of undertaking a biography of a musician is also touched upon.

CASE STUDY – THE ROSEHEARTY FREEMASONS' WALK

The Freemasons' Walk at Rosehearty is an example of a procession that nowadays takes place on 2 January and has been going on continuously since the eighteenth century.[32] It involves the Masons of Lodge Forbes (pronounced Forbès) processing round the village, accompanied by a pipe band. Walk Day is more significant to the community than New Year's Day, and many people return to the village for the event. Although only the Masons (and children of Masons) may take part in the procession, local people will be involved in watching the event, hosting guests, and so on. The event thus provides community cohesion as well as marking the start of the new year.

Figure 11.2 George Riddell.
From Riddell, c. 1929, 2.

The writings of George Riddell, a shoemaker and fiddler who died in 1942, provide us with important historical details of the event.[33] As is often the case with musicians who were well known in their local areas, we have an obituary for Riddell, published in his local newspaper. Obituaries tend to cover a person's life chronologically, along with their significant achievements. Although they usually portray people in a flattering light, they often give us some sense of the character of the individual.

Rosehearty has lost its oldest inhabitant and one of its best-known residents by the death of Mr George Riddell, shoemaker . . .

He became famous early in life as a brilliant self-taught musician and his work for Scottish music was set on record in musical histories. As far back as 1872, when he was a shepherd lad, he spent hours lying on the grass trying to discover for himself which notes formed the many tunes he knew by ear. In 1890 he was successful in setting a song of Professor Blackie's to music out of 170 competitors. He composed melody and piano accompaniments and several hymn and psalm tunes – Exaltation, Cedron, Truth, Twilight, Myra, St Drostan, Kemuel, and Rathven. He contributed a number of part-songs to the National Choir.

Mr Riddell was a personal friend of the late Scott Skinner, and arranged a number of piano accompaniments for him . . .

Another of his musical friends was the late Sir Harold Boulton, and it was under his persuasion that Mr Riddell wrote new words for the old folk song 'The Tarrin' o' the Yoll.'

Mr Riddell has composed original fiddle music too. Strathspeys, reels, jigs, marches and hornpipes are all included in his works. He was a violinist of remarkable gifts and in his young days he had a dance band.

One famous pipe tune composed by him is 'The Gordons ha'e the guidin' o't.'[34]

Further biographical information can be obtained through a search of the birth, marriage and death records held either in the person's locality or in New Register House in Edinburgh, where they are held for Scotland as a whole (much of this material is now also available online).[35] Census records, which record who was living in or visiting an area at a particular time are useful too, particularly for identifying exactly where someone was living and the members of a household. In Riddell's case, a study of the records reveals that he was born in Pitsligo parish on 9 January 1853, that he married Margaret Lorimer, and that the couple had a daughter, Christian, and a son, Scott.[36]

Riddell collected music in his local area, and records survive of this through manuscript books held in the National Library of Scotland that were begun in 1903 and contain 108 tunes.[37] Although the size of this collection is somewhat exceptional, it was common in Scotland for literate musicians to compile their own tune books or manuscripts, and many of these are still in the possession of individual families,[38] though some have made their way into special collections and libraries. In addition, Riddell published tunes and short notes in a journal called *Miscellanea of the Rymour Club*,[39] and wrote a manuscript expressing his views on folksong.[40] These give important information on the place of folksong and instrumental music in society at the time.

The newspaper obituary stated that Riddell knew the fiddler James Scott Skinner, and he was also in touch with collectors such as Gavin Greig, who together with James Bruce Duncan amassed *The Greig–Duncan Folk Song Collection* in the early twentieth century. Riddell was in fact a contributor to it, and sent Greig sixty-four airs from his manuscript collection in 1905, and a further seven in 1907–8.[41] It is interesting to look at the networks that musicians and collectors belonged to.

One of the people that Riddell collected tunes from was the fife player Auld Jeck (or John Ritchie) of Rosehearty. Riddell noted:

The night previous to the 'walk' he used to take down his fife from the shelf where it had lain the whole year, and having oiled it, laid it down in readiness for the morrow, without playing a note. The 'walk' was the only occasion on which he played. I picked up the tunes from him when I was a boy.[42]

Figure 11.3 'I kissed my Love wi' his apron on'. From Greig and Duncan, 1981–2002, III, 471D.

Auld Jeck was the only musician who played for the Walk, and his repertoire included some Masonic tunes, including 'I kissed my Love wi' his apron on'.

Riddell was a Freemason who wrote a booklet about his local Lodge in Rosehearty, entitled *The Rise and Progress of Forbes Lodge*. The booklet contains several photographs, including one of Riddell himself, and the banners used on Walk Day. Localised publications such as this are often useful in providing a window on the past. For example, W C Henderson's publication celebrating the bicentenary of the Lodge in 1955 gives one account of the Walk:

> With pipes skirling and banners flying the walk commences and proceeds through the streets of the Burgh. The banners are of a size that on a windy day it takes members of considerable build and strength to bear them unfurled. During the procession the Senior and Junior Stewarts provide arches with their rods at the corner of each street. On return to the Lodge, the ranks are opened facing inwards and preceded by the Sword Bearer, the Master proceeds down the centre of the ranks followed by the Past Masters and Office Bearers and members in twos, and re-enters the Lodge while the pipe band plays 'O The Merry Masons'.[43]

Minute books of societies are another useful source. In the case of Rosehearty, the Lodge itself holds minutes of its meetings, dating back several centuries.[44]

Newspapers also cover significant events, and a study of these reports can reveal aspects of contemporary relevance. In the *Fraserburgh Herald* of 14 January 1908, for example, the focus was on the Freemasons' Conversazione and Ball:

> This annual event, under the auspices of the Forbes Lodge of Freemasons, was held on Tuesday. Headed by the Rifle Volunteer Pipe Band, the brethren marched to Pitullie and Sandhaven. After returning, the newly-elected office-bearers were installed . . . For the conversazione the lodge had

Figure 11.4 Banners from Masons' Walk. From Riddell, c. 1929, 6.

secured the services of Mr Dufton Scott's Company, Aberdeen, when an excellent programme was submitted and heartily appreciated by the audience. Rev. A. W. Stevenson, the chaplain, delivered an instructive address. On the motion of Brother George Riddell, cordial votes of thanks were accorded to the ladies who had presided at the table, the performers, and those who had in any way helped to make the day's proceedings a success, and to the chairman. The hall was then cleared for dancing, which was kept up to excellent music supplied by Messrs Sim and Riddell, the duties of M.C. being carried out by Brothers Kenneth Gerrard and James Simpson.[45]

In an account written during wartime (1943) the focus is on the Walk and on its continuity:

> Come weal, come woe, the Rosehearty Freemasons hold their annual 'walk'. Lodge Forbes (No. 67) is one of the oldest in Britain. It lost its charter for a time through Lord Pitsligo joining Prince Charlie in the Jacobite Rising. Up till comparatively recent years the brethren marched in procession to Sandhaven at the New Year; and one year, during a terrific snowstorm the outing looked liked an impossibility. But a few of the mystic stalwarts, determined that the chain should remain unbroken, donned their regalia, and after floundering about for hours among the snow-drifts, they accomplished their task and returned to their Lodge in triumph.[46]

The Walk has also been the subject of a poem, as is common in the case of calendar events in Scotland, and this poem gives us an insight into the feelings that local people had for the event. 'A Man at Rosehearty', published by Alexander Murison in 1925, stresses the importance of continuity since, even though its main character is the imaginary last survivor in the village, he has to ensure that the Walk goes on. The poem also relates to the question of identity, since it reveals the importance (and duty) for many male inhabitants of the village of taking part in the Walk. The final two verses run:

> Could he cairry a sword? could he cairry a book?
> Could he cairry a flag wavin' high?
> Could he rin wi' a stick an' be aye at the neuk
> To lat the procession gyang by?
>
> Could he spread 'imsel' oot, twa an' twa in a line,
> Fae the beach to the tap o' the Squaar?
> Could he play owre the aul' 'Merry Masons' sae fine?
> Could he dee't div ye think? would he daur?[47]

In order to try to understand the walk from a Masonic point of view, as well as its central role in the community, and which tunes were used and why, I interviewed Mr Alex Crawford, the secretary of the Lodge. An ethical question arose here, since I was dealing with Masonic material, which people often perceive to be of a 'secret' nature. However, as the focus of the interview was on the community procession – a public event – and its music, this proved to be less of an issue. Before publishing the material,[48] I engaged in what is sometimes called 'fieldback',[49] by sending Mr Crawford a draft of the article and asking him to comment on it.

Asking what music was used in the past revealed that a song called the 'Merry Masons' was the final piece used for the Walk, as mentioned in Henderson's account. Mr Crawford and Mr Thomson, whom I interviewed in 2006, could only recall part of it. A prescriptive transcription of their singing is given below (Fig. 11.5).

The song is no longer sung or played at Rosehearty. However, tunes that have been through the process of oral tradition typically exhibit variation and tend to be found under a number of different titles. This tune can be traced back to James Anderson's *The Constitutions of the Free-Masons* (1723), where it was called 'The Enter'd 'Prentice's Song'.[50] It was also used by Robert Burns for his 'No Churchman am I for to Rail and to Write', and is very well known by Freemasons.[51]

A video was also made of the 2007 Walk, at which I was an observer. The final part of the procession at Rosehearty is particularly significant, since this is when the ranks open up to the strains of the pipe band, and the Right Worshipful Master walks through the ranks and is the first to go back into the Lodge. One of the tunes used to accompany this is 'Highland Cathedral', a modern slow air. The video was particularly useful for understanding this part of the event, as well as for recording the tunes. Other tunes played at the 2007 walk included 'Shoals of Herring', 'Bonnie Gallowa', 'Rowan Tree', 'The Old Rustic Bridge', 'The Barren Rocks of Aden', 'Mairi's Wedding', 'The Barnyards of Delgaty', and 'Colin's Cattle'. 'We're no Awa tae Bide Awa' was the final tune played by the pipe band, symbolising the continuity of the event.[52]

Although elements of the Walk have remained static over time, the music has not. It has grown from one person performing on the flute in the nineteenth century and playing some Masonic repertoire for the Walk, to a large pipe band who are not necessarily Masons and who play non-Masonic repertoire for the event. The song 'Ho Ro the Merry Masons' fell out of use because the pipe band did not know the tune.

Figure 11.5 Transcription of 'Ho Ro the Merry Masons' by Katherine Campbell.

Figure 11.6 The ranks open up: Rosehearty Masons' Walk. Still from a video by Mike Sutherland. School of Scottish Studies Archive, University of Edinburgh, VA2007.01.

BIBLIOGRAPHICAL ESSAY

General studies on the music of Scotland, not confined to traditional music, include those by Purser, who begins with the earliest examples of music in Scotland and moves chronologically up to the present day; by Farmer, who begins with the Celtic period and ends with the nineteenth century; and by Thorpe Davie, who provides a introduction to the music of Scotland, including national music (vocal and instrumental), music of the church and classical music.[53] Collinson's book is concerned with exploring the musical characteristics of traditional music, and looks at genres of song as well as at the so-called 'national instruments' of pipes, fiddle and small harp (clarsach).[54] There are also sections on the music of Orkney and Shetland. Emmerson's *Rantin Pipe and Tremblin String* focuses on dance music in Scotland and includes useful appendix material, e.g. a list of the tune titles in the Gillespie Manuscript (1768). The entry on 'Scotland (II) Traditional Music' in Grove Music Online by Francis Collinson and Peggy Duesenberry provides a useful starting point for the scholar of Scottish music and song, especially in terms of the bibliography that accompanies it. Porter's *Traditional Music of Britain and Ireland* provides a guide as to the state of research up to the late 1980s.

Studies of seventeenth-century music include that of Stell, whose focus was on manuscripts of that period and who has constructed a website, Early Scottish Melodies Online, containing over 2,000 incipits of musical melodies; and the collection edited by Porter, which includes material on the harp and pipes.[55] For the eighteenth century, David Johnson has examined the music and society of Lowland Scotland, including the interplay between classical and folk traditions.[56] For those concerned with the music of these periods, the studies of Dauney – whose focus was the Skene MS – of Glen and of Chappell are of interest.[57] A wealth of tune collections exist that date from the eighteenth and nineteenth centuries; particularly significant are James Oswald's *Caledonian Pocket Companion* (now available on CD-ROM), and James Johnson and Robert Burns' *Scots Musical Museum* (600 songs with tunes).[58] The listing of tune titles in published fiddle collections of the eighteenth and nineteenth centuries by Charles Gore is invaluable not only for locating the sources of tunes but also for searching for tunes with particular openings (Gore includes a theme code index). For locating basic biographical information on significant musicians in Scotland up to the late nineteenth century, Baptie's *Musical Scotland* (1894) remains a useful starting point.[59] Biographies of many musicians, with useful bibliographies, can be found in the *Oxford Dictionary of National Biography*.[60]

The surveys of fiddle, pipes, harp, and free reed instruments available in volume 10 of this *Scottish Life and Society* series (*Oral Literature and Performance Culture*, 2007) give helpful bibliographies which reference the main books and articles on these particular instruments.[61] For basic facts about instruments, such as their range and typical repertoires, see their entries in Grove Music Online, as well as the 'Scotland (II) Traditional Music' entry. Peter Cooke's *The Fiddle Tradition of the Shetland Isles* is recommended as an example of an ethnomusicological field study in a particular community, and includes detailed music transcriptions.[62] Not included among the aforementioned bibliographies is Hugh Cheape's book *Bagpipes* (2008), which is based on the bagpipe collections held in National Museums Scotland and places the Highland bagpipe in its European context.[63] The collection edited by Joshua Dickson, *The Highland Bagpipe* (2009), discusses piping from an interdisciplinary perspective and gives a good indication as to current research trends. A recent teaching manual for the Lowland and Border tradition, *The Wind in the Bellows* (2010), gives an insight into issues of pedagogy.[64]

Recordings – archive and commercial – are clearly also important for the study of traditional music. One important collection is the Scottish Tradition Series, published by Greentrax Recordings and based on material in the School of Scottish Studies Archives.

FUTURE RESEARCH

Current issues of concern for researchers include identity,[65] in particular exploring the place of traditional music in modern Scotland following the inauguration of the Scottish parliament in 1999. An associated issue is music policy: to what extent are funding and sponsorship shaping the musical traditions of the country and having an impact on them?[66] The roles of organisations and societies receiving this funding, their structures, and the networks of people involved in traditional music in Scotland could be explored. Transmission and the teaching of musical traditions remains a central concern,[67] and the similarities between different instrumental traditions could be usefully looked at here, along with the role of singing in them. Both child and adult learners need to be considered. In the context of nursery, primary and secondary education it would be useful to look at the impact that introducing the teaching of Scottish music into the curricula (beginning with Standard Grade in the 1980s) has had and continues to exert.

Regarding instrumental traditions, particularly neglected have been the accordion and associated free-reed traditions in Scotland.[68] Other instruments to be considered might include, for example, the guitar, mandolin, bouzouki and the percussion family. The role of electronic instruments could be investigated: fiddles, harps, chanters and cellos, for example, are all available in this format. What impact is this having on the musical tradition? Along with work on instruments, research into present-day performers can be undertaken in terms of biography, styles of playing, aesthetic values and preferences, and repertoire (including issues of change and stability). Material of great value on performance styles and traditions exists in the School of Scottish Studies Archives[69] and in other archives – institutional and personal – in Scotland. Young musicians may be particularly interested in finding material relating to their own native areas and in learning new repertoire. It is important to remember that much of the material in archives only exists in an oral/aural form and will not be found in written sources.

The study of repertoire can shed light on issues such as tunes shared across instrumental traditions and on adaptations made to them according to the capacity of individual instruments. The extent to which the music is played 'by ear' and the interplay between the oral and written is of interest, as is the extent to which an oral culture is prevalent in terms of broad context. Whether the music is played for dancing or listening is something that is significant,[70] and much work is needed on the role of accompaniment in both contexts. The fusion of different instrumental genres in accompaniment, e.g. rock music or jazz, could be explored. Regional traditions are of particular interest (including the tunes common to that region and the instruments prevalent in it), and this can link with questions of identity. Allied to this is the issue of playing styles. Questions here include: What are the factors that influence a regional playing style? What has been the influence of technology on regional playing styles? Styles can be compared and contrasted across Scotland, and outside it, where emigration took place, e.g. the Gaelic-speaking areas of Cape Breton in Nova Scotia. Descriptive transcription can be used to good effect in terms of style analysis. The differences between the Highlands and Lowlands in terms of playing styles and repertoire and the role of music in assisting Gaelic language learning and maintenance[71] are important issues, as is the role of Scots language similarly.

A theme of concern to researchers not just in Scotland but elsewhere is that of music revivals.[72] The early twentieth century saw the revival of the clarsach, and in the late twentieth century it was the Lowland and Border piping tradition. In the 1950s and 1960s the folk music revival took place in Scotland,[73] and its ramifications were major. In the last few decades, the cello, used extensively with fiddle to accompany dance in the eighteenth century, has seen something of a revival. Reinvention of tradition has taken place in some locations, e.g. in the Shetland Isles through the teaching of the fiddle in schools.[74] Community is another important theme,[75] and here the concept of 'musical worlds' discussed by Ruth Finnegan – where musicians in effect create their own communities according to musical genre – may be useful.[76] Traditional music has been shown by researchers to have a major role in the community (e.g. integrating young and old),[77] and aspects of traditional music are often thought to foster a sense of community, e.g. group performance and sessions, where those of widely varying abilities can play music together. Seen by some as contrary to these egalitarian values, the theme of competition in fact runs through many aspects of Scottish traditional music and is worth investigating. Examples range from Strathspey and Reel societies, where groups compete against each other and soloists compete on an individual basis at fiddle festivals and are judged by adjudicators, to the recent Scots Trad Music Awards, where nominations are made online in different categories, such as Best Live Act or Pipe Band of the Year, and votes are cast by members of the public.

The role of technology – the internet, audio recordings, radio broadcasts, gramophone records in the earlier period, LPs, and so on – is a major topic that is also ripe for exploration. This links with the concept of globalisation that has preoccupied researchers,[78] and with the label of 'Celtic' music that is often attached to the tradition by outside forces such as record companies, but seldom by the musicians themselves to the music they play.[79] Commercialisation and authenticity are associated issues to consider here.[80]

For students seeking to understand events like sessions and folk clubs,[81] the DIY ethnography of performance proposed by Seeger[82] may be useful in the sense that it draws attention to the questions that ethnomusicologists would seek to cover, and for the need to take into account the views of performers, audience, organisers and so on, through a combination of informal interviews and observations. The topic of performance is a huge one, encompassing the performance practices of musicians, gender issues and repertoire selection. Significant questions include: How does performance change based on context (e.g. home[83] or stage[84])? What behaviour accompanies the playing of music, e.g. introductory narratives?

There are many sources available for the study of traditional music in Scotland, as outlined above. Finally, it is important not to neglect popular magazines, such as *Living Tradition*, and radio programmes, e.g. *Travelling Folk* and *Take the Floor* on BBC Radio Scotland, and to collect leaflets and other ephemera produced by organisations dealing with traditional music. Thinking about the sources available and planning a study around those is often a useful way to begin research.

NOTES

1 At the department of Celtic and Scottish Studies at the University of Edinburgh, for example, separate Honours courses are available in Scots song, Gaelic song, and traditional music.
2 Macdonald, 1996.
3 Bohlman, 1988, xiii.

4 For a recent discussion of the concept of oral tradition, see McLucas, 2010.
5 Nettl, 2005, 3.
6 Nettl, 2005.
7 Merriam, 1964; Kunst, 1955; Blacking, 1973; Nettl, 2005; and Bohlman, 1988. Nettl and Bohlman in particular have contributed numerous books to the field.
8 Myers, 1992, gives an introduction to the discipline.
9 See, for example, Johnson, 1972 and 1997.
10 See, for example, Mackinnon, 2003.
11 Dalyell, 1849.
12 Campbell, 2005.
13 Sanger and Kinnaird, 1992 and 2007; Boyd, 2005.
14 See Kolltveit, 2009, and for a more general discussion of music archaeology, see Both, 2009.
15 Alburger, 2000.
16 Cheape, 2008.
17 See the Galpin Society journals for studies of this nature.
18 Sanger and Kinnaird, 2007.
19 Campbell, 2007, Chapter 2.
20 Mackenzie, 1994.
21 See Stell and Stell, Early Scottish Melodies Online, <http://www.melody.celtscot.ed.ac.uk/about.php> [accessed January 2013].
22 Stell, 1993.
23 See <http://edina.ac.uk/stat-acc-scot/> [subscription site; accessed November 2012].
24 See the volumes produced by the Scottish Burgh Records Society.
25 See discussion in Sanger and Kinnaird, 2007, 276.
26 Bannerman, 1991, 7.
27 Roy, 1985.
28 See, for example, Matheson, 1970; and Campbell, 2007, for examples in connection with Scottish fiddle tradition.
29 Skinner, 1994.
30 Seeger, 1958.
31 See Barz and Cooley, 2008, for discussion of ethical considerations.
32 Campbell, 2008a.
33 For a short study where Riddell is paired with Scott Skinner, see Alburger, 2002.
34 *Fraserburgh Herald*, 1942, 4.
35 See the ScotlandsPeople website [subscription site], <http://www.scotlandspeople.gov.uk/> [accessed November 2012]. It is also possible by working with the records to trace descendants.
36 OPR 1853/233/3; census record, 1901/223/002; and death record, 1942/233/28. Another son was killed in World War I (*Fraserburgh Herald*, 1942, 4).
37 Campbell, 2008b.
38 See Miller, 2008, for an example from Galloway.
39 Riddell, 1906–11, 117.
40 Held in the National Library of Scotland, MS 3088/22.
41 Campbell, 2008b, 36.
42 Broadwood, 1915, 105.
43 Henderson, 1955, 48.
44 I was able to consult these with the kind permission of Mr Alex Crawford, the secretary of the Lodge, and Mr Charles Thomson.
45 *Fraserburgh Herald*, 1908, 5.

46 *Fraserburgh Herald*, 1943, 3. A special supplement was produced by the newspaper for the 250th anniversary of the Lodge on 5 August 2005.

47 Murison, 1925, 68–9, stanzas 7–9.

48 Campbell, 2008a.

49 Cooke, 1981.

50 Anderson, 1723, 90.

51 Campbell (forthcoming).

52 For understanding the event from the point of view of the musicians, members of the pipe band could be interviewed.

53 Purser, 1997; Farmer, 1970; Thorpe Davie, 1980. See the entry on 'Scotland (II) Traditional Music' in Grove Music Online for further bibliographical material, as well as chapters on music in volume 10 of the *Scottish Life and Society* series (see note 64 below).

54 Collinson, 1966.

55 Stell and Stell, <http://www.melody.celtscot.ed.ac.uk/about.php>; Porter, 2007.

56 Johnson, 1972.

57 Dauney, 1838; Glen, 1900; Chappell, 1855.

58 Purser and Parkes, 2006–7; Johnson and Burns, 1991.

59 Baptie's survey begins c. 1400.

60 Available in print or via subscription database, <http://www.oxforddnb.com/> [accessed November 2012].

61 See Alburger, 2007 (fiddle); MacInnes, 2007 (pipes); Sanger and Kinnaird, 2007 (harp); and Eydmann, 2007 (free-reed instruments).

62 Cooke, 1986.

63 The book includes a CD-ROM with sound clips.

64 Lowland and Border Pipers' Society, 2010. The society's website is also a good source of information on the tradition as a whole, <http://www.lbps.net/> [accessed November 2012].

65 The list of issues and concepts in ethnomusicology given by Nettl, 2005, may be a useful starting point.

66 See Olson, 2007, 390–6, for a discussion of the *Report of a Traditional and Folk Arts of Scotland Working Party* (1984) and the *Traditional Music in Scotland Report* (1999).

67 Miller, 2007.

68 Eydmann, 2007, provides useful suggestions as to future lines of research; see also his discussion of the concertina, 1995.

69 This archive has recently been the subject of a major digitisation project; see the Tobar an Dualchais/ Kist o Riches website, <http://www.tobarandualchais.co.uk/> [accessed November 2012].

70 See Shoupe, 2008.

71 For discussion of this in the context of Feisean nan Gaidheal, see Broad and France, n.d.

72 See Livingston, 1999.

73 See Munro, 1996 and, for the British Isles context, Brocken, 2003.

74 Swing, 1991; see Hobsbawm and Ranger, 1992, for the concept of invented tradition.

75 See Feintuch, 2001, for a discussion of this concept in a Northumberland context; NB the whole of *Western Folklore* (60, 2/3) is devoted to this concept.

76 Finnegan, 1989.

77 See, for example, Cooke, 1986.

78 Wade, 2009.

79 Reiss, 2003.

80 Wade, 2009; Bendix, 1997.

81 See Mackinnon, 2003.

82 Seeger, 1958; for a detailed discussion of transcription see Ellingson, 1992, and for a practical guide see Nettl, 1964, Chapter 4.

83 See West, 2006, for a discussion of this context.

84 The impact of the music hall tradition (see Maloney, 2003) on stage performance practices could be usefully explored.

BIBLIOGRAPHY AND FURTHER READING

Alburger, M A. The 'Fydill in Fist': Bowed string instruments from the Mary Rose, *Galpin Society Journal*, 53 (April, 2000), 12–24.

Alburger, M A. J Scott Skinner and George Riddell. In Greig and Duncan, 1981–2002, VIII, 588–9.

Alburger, M A. The fiddle. In Beech et al., 2007, 238–73.

Anderson, J. *The Constitutions of the Free-Masons. Containing the History, Charges, Regulations, &c. of that Most Ancient and Right Worshipful Fraternity. For the Use of the Lodges*, London, 1723.

Bannerman, J. The clàrsach and the clàrsair, *Scottish Studies*, 30 (1991), 1–17.

Baptie, D. *Musical Scotland, Past and Present: Being a Dictionary of Scottish Musicians from about 1400 till the Present Time*, Paisley, 1894.

Barz, G F and Cooley, T J. *Shadows in the Field: New Perspectives for Fieldwork*, 2nd edn, Oxford, 2008.

Beech, J, Hand, O, MacDonald, F, Mulhern, M A and Weston, J, eds. *Scottish Life and Society. A Compendium of Scottish Ethnology, Volume 10: Oral Literature and Performance Culture*, Edinburgh, 2007.

Bendix, R. *In Search of Authenticity: The Formation of Folklore Studies*, Madison, WI, 1997.

Blacking, J. *How Musical is Man?*, Washington, DC, 1973.

Bohlman, P V. *The Study of Folk Music in the Modern World*, Bloomington, IN, 1988.

Both, A A. Music archaeology: Some methodological and theoretical considerations, *Yearbook for Traditional Music*, 41 (2009), 1–11.

Boyd, M. The triangular frame-harp on the Pictish symbol stones, *Cosmos*, 21:2 (2005), 147–83.

Broad, S and France, J. *25 Years of the Fèisean – The Participants' Story*, Glasgow, n.d.

Broadwood, L. Songs from Scotland and the north country, *Journal of the Folk–Song Society*, 5:2 (19), 1915, 104–21.

Brocken, M. *The British Folk Revival, 1944–2002*, Aldershot, 2003.

Campbell, K. The hog-bagpiper gargoyle at Melrose Abbey, *Cosmos*, 21:2 (2005), 137–46.

Campbell, K. *The Fiddle in Scottish Culture: Aspects of the Tradition*, Edinburgh, 2007.

Campbell, K. The Masons' Walk at Rosehearty, *Review of Scottish Culture*, 20 (2008a), 127–32.

Campbell, K. George Riddell of Rosehearty: Fiddler and collector. In Russell, I and Alburger, M A, eds, *Driving the Bow: Fiddle and Dance Studies from around the North Atlantic 2*, Aberdeen, 2008b, 35–56.

Campbell, K. Scottish masonic songs and the stream of tradition, *Proceedings of the 38th International Ballad Conference, Cardiff, Wales* (2008), ed. E. Wyn James, (forthcoming).

Chappell, W. *Popular Music of the Olden Time*, vols 1–2, London, 1855.

Cheape, H. *Bagpipes: A National Collection of a National Instrument*, Edinburgh, 2008.

Collinson, F. *The Traditional and National Music of Scotland*, London, 1966.

Cooke, P. *The Fiddle Tradition of the Shetland Isles*, Cambridge, 1986.

Cooke, P. Experiments in fieldback in Shetland. In Cooke, P, ed., *Studies in Traditional Music and Dance, Proceedings of the 1980 Conference of the United Kingdom National Committee of the International Folk Music Council*, Edinburgh, 1981, 47–51.

Dalyell, J G. *Musical Memoirs of Scotland*, Edinburgh, 1849.

Dauney, W. *Ancient Scotish Melodies*, Edinburgh, 1838.

Dickson, J, ed. *The Highland Bagpipe: Music, History, Tradition*, Farnham, 2009.

Elliott, K, Collinson, F and Duesenberry, P. Scotland. In Sadie, S and Tyrrell, J, eds, *The New Grove Dictionary of Music and Musicians*, vol. 22, second edn, 908–22. London, 2001. (The full text of this dictionary is also available in Grove Music Online, *Oxford Music Online* database [subscription required], <http://www.oxfordmusiconline.com/subscriber/article/grove/music/40113> [accessed November 2012].)

Ellingson, T. Transcription. In Myers, H, ed., *Ethnomusicology: An Introduction*, London, 1992, 110–52.

Emmerson, G S. *Rantin' Pipe and Tremblin' String: A History of Scottish Dance Music*, London, 1971.

Eydmann, S. The concertina as an emblem of the folk music revival in the British Isles, *British Journal of Ethnomusicology*, 4 (1995), 41–9.

Eydmann, S. Diversity and diversification in Scottish music. In Beech et al., 2007, 193–212.

Farmer, H G. *A History of Music in Scotland*, New York, 1970.

Feintuch, B. Longing for community, *Western Folklore*, 60:2/3 (2001), 149–61.

Finnegan, R. *The Hidden Musicians: Music-Making in an English Town*, Cambridge, 1989.

Fraserburgh Herald. 'Rosehearty – Freemasons' Conversazione and Ball', *Fraserburgh Herald and Northern Counties' Advertiser*, 14 January 1908, 5, col. 2.

Fraserburgh Herald. 'Obituary: Mr George Riddell', *Fraserburgh Herald and Northern Counties' Advertiser*, 26 May 1942, 4, col. 3.

Fraserburgh Herald. 'The Rosehearty Walk', *Fraserburgh Herald and Northern Counties' Advertiser*, 12 January 1943, 3, col. 6.

Glen, J. *Early Scottish Melodies*, Edinburgh, 1900.

Gore, C, ed. *The Scottish Fiddle Music Index*, Musselburgh, 1994.

Greig, G and Duncan, J B. *The Greig–Duncan Folk Song Collection*, eds P Shuldham-Shaw, E B Lyle and K Campbell, 8 vols, Aberdeen and Edinburgh, 1981–2002.

Henderson, W C. *1755–1955: The Forbes Lodge of Rosehearty No. 67*, n.p., 1955.

Hobsbawm, E and Ranger, T. *The Invention of Tradition*, Cambridge, 1992.

Johnson, D. *Music and Society in Lowland Scotland in the Eighteenth Century*, London, 1972.

Johnson, D. *Scottish Fiddle Music in the 18th Century: A Music Collection and Historical Study*, 2nd edn, Edinburgh, 1997.

Johnson, J and Burns, R. *The Scots Musical Museum 1787–1803*, Intro. Donald A Low, Aldershot, 1991.

Kolltveit, G and Both, A A. The Jew's Harp in Western Europe: Trade, communication, and innovation, 1150–1500, *Yearbook for Traditional Music*, 41 (2009), 42–61.

Kunst, J. *Ethno-musicology*, The Hague, 1955.

Livingston, T. Music revivals: Towards a general theory, *Ethnomusicology*, 43:1 (1999), 66–85.

Lowland and Border Pipers' Society. *The Wind in the Bellows: A Handbook for Teachers and Students of Border Pipes and Scottish Smallpipes*, Edinburgh, 2010.

McLucas, A D. *The Musical Ear: Oral Tradition in the USA*, Burlington, VT, 2010.

Macdonald, A A. 'The relationship between pibroch and Gaelic songs: Its implications on the performance style of the pibroch urlar', MLitt thesis, University of Edinburgh, 1996.

MacInnes, I. Caus michtilie the weirlie nottis breike, on hieland pipes, scotts and hybernicke. In Beech et al., 2007, 225–37.

MacKenzie, A. *NEWSPLAN: Report of the NEWSPLAN Project in Scotland*, London, 1994.

Mackinnon, N. *The British Folk Scene: Musical Performance and Social Identity*, Buckingham, 2003.

Maloney, P. *Scotland and the Music Hall, 1850–1914*, Manchester, 2003.

Matheson, W, ed. *The Blind Harper: The Songs of Roderick Morison and his Music*, Edinburgh, 1970.

Merriam, A P. *The Anthropology of Music*, Evanston, IL, 1964.

Miller, J. The teaching and learning of traditional music. In Beech et al., 2007, 288–304.

Miller, J. A fiddle manuscript from eighteenth-century Galloway. In Elliott, K et al., eds, *Musica Scotica: 800 Years of Scottish Music: Proceedings from the 2005 and 2006 Conferences*, Glasgow, 2008, 7–17.

Munro, A. *The Democratic Muse: Folk Music Revival in Scotland*, 2nd edn, Aberdeen, 1996.

Murison, A. *Rosehearty Rhymes and Other Pieces*, Banff, 1925.

Myers, H. *Ethnomusicology: An Introduction*, New York, 1992.

Nettl, B. *Theory and Method in Ethnomusicology*, New York, 1964.

Nettl, B. *The Study of Ethnomusicology: Thirty-One Issues and Concepts*, new edn, Urbana, 2005.

Olson, I. Scottish contemporary traditional music and song. In Beech et al., 2007, 379–404.

Porter, J. *The Traditional Music of Britain and Ireland*, New York, 1989.

Porter, J, ed. *Defining Strains: The Musical Life of Scots in the Seventeenth Century*, Oxford, 2007.

Purser, J. *Scotland's Music*, new enl. edn, Edinburgh, 2007.

Purser, J and Parkes, N, eds, *The Caledonian Pocket Companion by James Oswald*, vol. 1 (books 1–6), vol. 2 (books 7–12), available on two CD-ROMs, self-published, 2006–7.

Reiss, S. Tradition and imaginary: Irish traditional music and the Celtic phenomenon. In Stokes, M and Bohlman, P V, eds, *Celtic Modern: Music at the Global Fringe*, Lanham, MD, 2003, 145–69.

Riddell, G. A set of six old airs, with notes. In Rymour Club, *Miscellanea of the Rymour Club*, 2 vols, Edinburgh, 1906–21, I, 116–21.

Riddell, G. *The Rise and Progress of Forbes Lodge of Freemasons, No. 67, Rosehearty, Aberdeenshire*, London, c. 1929.

Roy, G R, ed. *The Letters of Robert Burns*, 2nd edn, 2 vols, Oxford, 1985.

Sanger, K and Kinnaird, A. *Tree of Strings: A History of the Harp in Scotland*, Temple (Midlothian), 1992.

Sanger, K and Kinnaird, A. Harps in Scotland. In Beech et al., 2007, 274–87.

Seeger, C. Prescriptive and descriptive music-writing, *Musical Quarterly*, 44:2 (1958), 184–95.

Shoupe, C A. The 'problem' with Scottish dance music: Two paradigms. In Russell, I and Alburger, M A, eds, *Driving the Bow: Fiddle and Dance Studies from Around the North Atlantic 2*, Aberdeen, 2008, 105–20.

Skinner, J S. *My Life and Adventures*, Aberdeen, 1994.

Stell, E. Lady Jean Campbell's seventeenth-century music-book, *ROSC*, 8 (1993), 11–19.

Stokes, M, ed. *Ethnicity, Identity and Music: The Musical Construction of Place*, Oxford, 1994.

Swing, P S. 'Fiddle teaching in Shetland Isles schools, 1973–1985', PhD thesis, University of Texas at Austin, 1991.

Thorpe Davie, C. *Scotland's Music*, Edinburgh, 1980.

Wade, B C. *Thinking Musically: Experiencing Music, Expressing Culture*, Oxford, 2009.

West, G. Music. In Storrier, S, ed., *Scottish Life and Society. A Compendium of Scottish Ethnology, Volume 6: Domestic Life*, East Linton, 2006, 120–33.

ONLINE RESOURCES

Statistical Accounts of Scotland Online 1791–1845 [subscription site], <http://edina.ac.uk/stat-acc-scot/> [accessed November 2012].

Stell, E and Stell, A. Early Scottish Melodies Online website, <http://www.melody.celtscot.ed.ac.uk/about.php> [accessed January 2013].

12 Scots Songs

VALENTINA BOLD

> The Scots yield to none of their neighbours in a passionate attachment to
> their native music; in which, to say the truth, they seem to be justified by
> the unbiassed suffrage of foreigners of the best taste [. . .] Many ingenious
> reasons have been assigned [. . .] chiefly drawn from the romantic face of
> the country, and the vacant, pastoral life of a great part of its inhabitants;
> circumstances, no doubt, highly favourable to poetry and song.[1]

INTRODUCTION

This chapter attempts to define the rather fluid category of 'Scots song'. Aspects
considered include its historical development, collection and canonisation, as
well as the way the term has been understood by different audiences at different
times. Particular attention is paid to the key period for national song definition
starting in the mid seventeenth century and continuing until the present. Herd's
observations, quoted above, reflect the assumptions that tend to underpin the
adoption of a national canon. The chapter describes patterns in current research
and offers a list of possibilities for future research, together with resources to
encourage reflection and debate.

TOWARDS A DEFINITION OF SCOTS SONG

It should be said at the outset that the term 'Scots song' is highly resonant and
rather ambiguous. Loaded with 'national' connotations, it has various synonyms:
'Scottish song', 'the songs of Scotland', which are often (at least in the modern
period) mediated by the addition of 'traditional' or 'folk'. This group of terms
is both period- and context-specific, with various meanings for collectors,
performers and audiences. 'Scots song' can have strong geographical and/or
linguistic connotations or, at times, refer to very particular forms. Emic (from
the point of view of 'insiders' to the tradition and to Scotland) and etic (from the
perspective of external audiences, collectors and performers) understandings
vary considerably too.

Scots song, as a blanket term, covers the whole range of genres within
Scotland. The main genres in Scots song are outlined here; however, there is no
space to review these in detail in this chapter and, arguably, this kind of definition
is not particularly helpful. Probably the most studied genre, in terms of Scotland,
is ballad: a dramatic narrative form with distinctive structural and stylistic charac-

teristics. It is associated with a range of formulaic language and phrases and is not overtly emotional; emotions are expressed through performance and responses.[2] These features were determined by collectors and critics, working from the early nineteenth century, and combined scholarship from Scotland, Europe and North America in particular. Francis James Child (1825–1896) in his *The English and Scottish Popular Ballad* (1882–98) canonised – some would say ossified – notions of what constituted a ballad, which still shape definitions of the form today. In the Scottish context, in terms of ballad collecting, the dominant work is *The Minstrelsy of the Scottish Border* (1802–3), followed by a series of national and regional collections, some mentioned below. Lyric, too, is an almost equally dominant form, broadly speaking addressing topics around love, but ranging from the sentimental to the pragmatic to the bawdy (all are well represented in the pervasive work of Robert Burns within this genre).[3] Other significant genres include political (from the Jacobite form to the modern protest songs associated with songwriters like Mary Brooksbank (1897–1978)[4] and singers like Dick Gaughan and Brian McNeill), religious, work-related, urban-based (associated with song writers like Adam McNaughtan)[5] and children's song, along with particular types connected with temperance or sport – including football and the linked category of sectarian songs – in Scots. Apologies are given at this stage, too, for the omission of many collectors and performers who deserve mention here; readers who seek comprehensiveness are advised to start by browsing some of the web resources on song and music listed at the end of this chapter.

Scots song is, without question, a medium in which text and music are crucially related. As Emily Lyle has commented in relation to ballad as a sung form: 'to gain a full appreciation, every opportunity should be taken of listening to live or recorded performances'.[6] Developing a similar line of argument, of particular relevance to Scots song and, again, in relation to ballad, James Porter identified:

> a bifurcated existence in the modern world. They are read, in anthologies and scholarly editions, as literature; and they are sung, in homes, ceilidhs and folk clubs as performative genre [. . .] the function, communication, and nature of the audience are markedly different in these two modes of production and consumption.[7]

In drawing attention to the ways in which silent reading differs from the dynamic interaction between singer and audience in performance context, Porter privileges neither, but the distinction is well worth noting. Arguably, the last-mentioned way of receiving texts is significantly different from the others, particularly if listening is within communicative company. These points are highly relevant when approaching Scots song as a form.

So, too, the characteristics cited in Chapter 11 'Traditional Music', and defined by the International Folk Music Council, are as crucial to understanding Scots song now as they were in the past. 'Continuity' (the sustained existence of a traditional practice) determines the songs which survive within folk canons (whether based within narrow 'folk groups', to use Oring's term, like families, or regionally, nationally or internationally defined);[8] 'variation' (the changes which inform traditions over time) are hugely important to the development in particular song texts, written and sung; 'selection' (how the song survives in its performance contexts) is as crucial to Scots song and its evolutions, as they are to the music. 'Community', of course, is a contested term which can refer, in its 'traditional' sense, to a location-focused group, but also to contexts like family or even, in its modern usage, a community focused around YouTube. Performance is vitally important particularly to developing an understanding of particular textual 'events' at which Scots songs have been consumed (public or private, 'live' or 'passive'). Along with an appreciation of formal and structural elements, such observations are crucial to understanding the function and meanings of Scots songs. These are variable both for those who sing them and to those who listen.

Bearing this in mind, and turning now to more specific definitions, by far the commonest and earliest use of the term 'Scots song' is to indicate a song's point of origin within the physical nation. David Herd, for instance, uses 'Scots song' in this sense in his published collection of 1776, indicating subsets of 'heroic ballads or epic tales', 'sentimental, pastoral and love songs', 'comic, humorous and jovial songs'. 'Scots song', taken this way, refers solely to songs produced in Scotland, minus the Gaidhealtachd. This division entered into the critical discourse and, in general, has remained there; it was recognised, for instance, in a recording made as late as 1960 which brings together, yet distinguishes, Gaelic and Scots folk songs.[9] In a parallel way, in modern discussions, the term 'Scots song' usually excludes the traditions of, most recently, minority language groups living in Scotland – a rich area for musical cross fertilisation. Rich examples of recent culture exchanges range from the implicit notion of what can be considered 'Scots song', expressed in the growth of Scottish bhangra in bands like Gtown Desi, to the stated desire of the organisers of the Wickerman Festival of 2011, and documented in their then-current online publicity, to embrace the musical traditions of Poland. The area of Scots song and its travel, both within Scottish culture and to external audiences, would also reward further investigation.

The term 'Scots song' can also be used to refer to songs produced by Scotland's diaspora communities, past and present. However, in terms of collecting, the song traditions of the Gaelic-speaking diaspora have received a great deal more attention than those of the Lowland Scots, reflecting, arguably, a glamorisation of 'exotic' traditions of the Gaidhealtachd, and a 'Highlandisation' of emigrant communities. This process is evident in the tradition of holding Highland Games from the late nineteenth century onwards in 'Lowland' areas, as well as the assumption sometimes made by certain members of emigrant communities that Scotland equates with the Highlands. A similar process leads to a sometimes overriding interest in the past of the country, particularly in the periods of intense emigration.

Cross-fertilisations, through shared performance and transmission contexts (particularly in the digital age), are also to be taken in relation to diaspora Scots.[10] For instance, modern performers known for their 'Scottish' identity in the North

American context often blend Scots song with diverse items of repertoire. Glasgow-born Alex Beaton, for instance, who emigrated to the United States in the 1960s and had Scottish and Irish parents, not only records solely Scots material, like a CD of Robert Burns songs, but also mixes Irish and Scots-derived items in performance and recordings.[11] Counter-examples, of course, could be mentioned. The Aberdeen-born Norman Kennedy, for instance, who has lived in America since 1966, mixes expertise in craft performances (weaving) with an extensive repertoire of Scots songs from his home culture, from 'Drumdelgie' to the Byron-derived 'There was a Jolly Beggar'.[12]

Defining Scots song by place, then, while superficially simple and therefore appealing, is problematic. Songs – and more importantly singers – tend not to recognise national boundaries, or indeed even boundaries between Scots and non-Scots. Cecil Sharp, for instance, noted in 1905 that 'the Scottish ballad [. . .] is no other than the English ballad in Northern dress'.[13] Cross-cultural contacts have had indelible impacts on Scots songs in the case of particular items and as a corpus. In the case of South West Scotland, bordering England by land and Ireland by sea, as well as Ayrshire to the north, songs often reflect on connections. 'The Galloway Packman', collected by Phyllis Martin in the Isle of Whithorn in 1995 from Charlie McGuire, is about a young man who strays into England, 'I met wi' refusals in maisten ilk place, / They shook their heids at me, slammed doors in ma face', based on his being 'frae wild Gallowa'. To take two further examples from Martin's collecting, 'The Ayrshireman's Lilt' casts aspersions on the neighbours: 'Whaur ir ye ga'in tae? My bonnie Ayrshireman! / A'm gaun awa tae steel a wee coo'. 'The Irish Boy' explores linguistic confusions in an area where 'Galloway Irish' blurs accent and vocabulary: 'An Irish boy he may well be, / But he spake broad Scots when he coortit me'.[14] Traces of Irish-influenced performance styles – a peculiarly lilting delivery, a gentleness in the attack – can also be noted. This is a regional tradition which would merit more study.

There is sometimes a naturalisation process, rephrasing extraneous material into acceptable Scots idioms. International cross overs can lead to instances where prototypes generate songs perceived to be 'Scots'. Examples include the Scandinavian 'Death at Sea of John Remorsson', domesticated as 'Sir Patrick Spens' (Ch 58), with a reimagining of the original situation as a Scots-Norwegian experience: 'The king's dochter o Norrowa / It's thou must bring her hame'.[15] Subtle cross-overs include the adaptation of the Picardian New Year begging song 'aguillaneuf' within the Scots-language notion of appropriate behaviour at Hogmanay.[16]

Songs in the Scots tradition, too, are found in international forms: 'The Twa Sisters' was known by the late nineteenth century in versions from England, Scotland, Wales, Denmark, Iceland, Faroe, Sweden and Finland.[17] Singers too, are influenced by international pieces, in the past by face-to-face transmission, in the modern period through recordings and, latterly, new media, adapting the 'foreign' into acceptable local idioms. For instance Jane Turriff (b.1915) brings North East style, combined with influences from Western films, to country pieces like 'Empty Saddles'.[18] A parallel example would be the performance of the Newfoundland song by Ron Hynes, 'Sonny's Dream', by Scottish performers like Calcutta-born Hamish Imlach (1940–1996), or Jean Redpath (b.1937); both add a Scots inflection.[19]

Scots song generated among, or for consumption by, diaspora communities have particular characteristics. Like those within the parallel Gaelic-language tradition, they are often infused with a sense of exile and a nostalgia which is less obvious – although sometimes present – in songs generated by the physical nation. For instance, the Nithsdale-born stonemason and writer Allan Cunningham (1784–1842) expressed feelings he no doubt experienced as an exile in London in 'My Ain Countrie': here, the narrator is a Scot living in Bordeaux, who 'left my hert ahint me' in Galloway.[20] Similarly, 'The Canadian Boat-Song', probably by D M Moir and first published in 1829 in the 'Noctes Ambrosianae' series of *Blackwood's Edinburgh Magazine*, exemplifies the wistful exile lamenting what is left behind, as Christopher North (John Wilson) sings a piece supposedly transmitted and translated by a friend in Upper Canada, and typical of 'Highland oar-songs' in Gaelic:

> From the lone shieling of the misty island
> Mountains divide us and the waste of seas
> But still the heart is strong, the blood is Highland
> And we in dreams behold the Hebrides.[21]

The context here is important: 'Noctes Ambrosianae' is very much tongue-in-cheek and, it seems, Moir may be satirising a trend already in play.

Recent songwriters, among them first-generation diaspora Scots, often show (dark) humour, in engaging with traditional forms of exile discourse. For instance, the Peebles-born Eric Bogle (b.1944), who has lived in Australia since 1969, in 'The End of an Auld Song', references the alleged remark of the Earl of Seafield at the ratification of the Union of the Parliaments in 1707, placing the piece firmly in the line of descent for Scots song. He refreshes it in reflecting on his personal past in a Scotland at once 'a bonnie Border toon, / A grey and ugly housing scheme', combining 'Castlemilk and Brigadoon' into a whole which is 'a state o' mind'.[22] So too, Ed Miller, born in Edinburgh and living in Austin, Texas, since 1968, muses on his 'Home Away from Home', in the guise of *The Edinburgh Rambler*.[23] Scottish-based singers, too, have had success in producing Scots songs in this vein, focusing on the experience of exile. Take, for instance, the thoughtful responses of The Proclaimers, in their 'Letter from America' to the experience of 'the blood that flowed away / across the ocean to the second chance'. This piece, appreciated by Scots within the nation as much as by emigrants, is infused with a sense of exile from within, in their case from the former industrialised nation: 'Bathgate [. . .] Linwood [. . .] Methil no more'.[24]

What is considered 'Scots' outside of the physical nation can differ from domestic definitions. Scots, Gaelic and Irish materials are often considered together as 'Celtic' song (sometimes conjoined to the songs of 'Celtic' language areas, like Brittany) - in itself, a highly contestable term, linked to post-Romantic national definitions.[25] Similarly, in the context of communities with Ulster-Scots connections, the term 'Scotch-Irish' is used. Examples include the National Public

Radio (USA) show 'Thistle and the Shamrock', or the online station, 'Celtic Radio' (which also includes traditional English songs).[26] Sometimes the Scotch-Irish category is popularly associated with specific diaspora communities, such as those of the Appalachian area of North America, including eastern Tennessee, as well as North Carolina, and other areas including western Pennsylvania and northern New England.[27]

In short, 'Scots song' is a floating term internationally, with particular resonances that are absent for indigenous audiences although often, it has to be said, skilfully explored by Scottish performers on tour. Events from the Clear Lake Celtic Festival in Houston to the 'Celtic Colours' festival in Cape Breton offer opportunities for interactions within a broadly 'Celtic' area. To take the latter, the 2011 festival included Appalachian, Acadian, Irish and Scottish – from Scotland and Nova Scotia – performers, including well-known exponents of Scots song like Karine Polwart, Dougie Maclean and Archie Fisher.[28]

Songs generated in England, similarly, are often adapted using Scots language for performance within Scotland, or seen as representative of Scotland in the wider English-speaking world. From the eighteenth century onwards, there was a vogue for 'Scotch song', a lyric form with specific characteristics. As Matthew Gelbart noted:

> in England, the so-called 'Scotch songs,' whether [. . .] of Scottish origin or faked by English theater composers [. . .] came to be taken as lessons in simplicity and moral attitudes, or as pastoral satire. When Scots began to publish these songs, they had the same focus (though, with their own dignity at stake, the moral aspect was obviously stressed and the pastoral satire much rarer).[29]

Examples in England include those by Thomas D'Urfey (1653?–1723) in Henry Playford and John Young's *Wit and Mirth; or Pills to Purge Melancholy*. Many were his own compositions, such as "Twas within a furlong of Edinborough town', first published in 1696 in *Delicae Musicae,* in which 'Bonny Jocky blithe and gay' attempts to seduce 'Jenny making hay' on the premise that marriage is now no longer à la mode. [30]

The 'Scotch song' was just as influential in Scotland. Several of D'Urfey's publications, 'Gilderoy' for example, were included by the Leadhills-born Allan Ramsay (1686–1758), of whom more below, in his *Tea Table Miscellany* of 1726 as well as the *Orpheus Caledonius* of 1733. Drawing on broadsides (see Chapter 21), this is a lament from the foot of the gallows by an about-to-be-bereaved woman to her Perthshire freebooter husband who was hanged c.1638; it was later polished and published by Thomas Campbell. The Scotch song crossed the Atlantic with ease as can be seen in settlers' collections, such as that of the Charles Carroll family of Maryland; examples include 'Katherine Ogie' (known as a broadside, set by Burns, and included in *Pills to Purge Melancholy*) and Francis Sempill's 'Maggie Lauder'.[31]

The term 'Scots song', furthermore, can be broken down into pieces with specific regional connotations. For instance, Walter Scott (1771–1832)'s *Minstrelsy of the Scottish Border* (1802–3) suggests that the Border region – which, in this context, is centred on the historical Middle Marches around Eskdale and Liddesdale, with a focus, too, on Selkirkshire and Roxburghshire – had a distinctively martial national muse (volume I) with related interests in the supernatural. He does not use the term 'Scots song' explicitly in that collection, although 'Johnnie Armstrong' (Ch 169) is described as an 'Anglo-Scots ballad'. Indeed, his collection, taking account of a dividing line in its title, is based on the premise of a cross-border culture, although most of his examples are from the Scots' perspective.

Antiquarian collectors and their creative descendants were often interested in defining the region, with examples including [J Paterson's] *The Ballads and Songs of Ayrshire* (1846–), and Malcolm McLaren Harper's *The Bards of Galloway* (1889). Later critics, like David Buchan in *The Ballad and the Folk* (1972), pointed to North East Scotland as another border region (this time between Highland and Lowland culture) and, in responses to Walter Scott, as a focal point for song generation. Like Scott, Buchan privileged ballad as a significant national genre, and the people of the North East as 'a distinctive breed' with innately 'moderate spirit': 'they found their aesthetic form in the ballad, where emotions were objectified in near-ritualized terms and subordinated to the dramatic recounting of factual event [. . .] the ballads served a cathartic function'.[32]

Language usages, in addition, are crucial to determining what is understood as 'Scots song'. The term generally includes any song wholly in the Scots language or tempering Scots with English (often, during the editing or re-writing of orally-transmitted songs for publication, 'formalisations' into English occur; similarly, singers mediate Scots songs with English either because of aesthetic preferences or audience demands).[33] Using Scots in the modern period, and particularly after the Union of the Parliaments, as David Buchan points out, 'helped maintain a sense of native identity against the pervasive threat of alien anglicization'; Mrs Brown of Falkland, for instance, 'composed ballads in Scots because Scots was for her the language of *real* speech and *real* feeling'.[34] Thoughtful modern songwriters from Adam NcNaughtan to Brian McNeill also use Scots language as an integral part of their compositions, involving (often tongue-in-cheek) cultural definition and political protest.

However, a tight definition based around purely or largely Scots language pieces could be misleading. Take, for instance, songs composed in related language groups like that of Ulster Scots.[35] Audiences and critics often assume this is 'Scots song', transposed into an Irish context; this impression can be upheld by examples of shared repertoire. The Ulster Scots Agency features a selection of Ulster-Scots children's songs on its website, many of which would be equally familiar in Scotland, from 'Bobby Shaftoe' to 'Auld Lang Syne'. Others, however, would not be, like 'The Belfast Titanic Song' and 'The Big May Fair of Ballyclare'.[36] The situation is more complex, too, than that of locally based repertoires sharing language and musical features. As Willie Drennan explained in 2009, Ulster Scots music is not just 'Scottish music played in Ulster'; for one, it has been mediated by localisation over generations of performance; for another, much is self-generated and influenced by 'other parts of Ireland [. . .] England or [. . .] America' through exchange with the Ulster diaspora in these places. In short:

Ulster Scots folk music is the music that has been played by people who see themselves as being Ulster Scots. Some of the tunes that we play have been played all over the British Isles or played in North America for many generations [. . .] it's the music that has been played here traditionally.[37]

Similarly, notionally 'Scots' songs sometimes feature passages in the other languages of Scotland, mainland and island. There are traces of Norn, for instance, in the 'Unst Boat Song' from Shetland. Gaelic language elements can be found in, for instance, 'Erin go Bragh' and 'The Russian Jew'.[38] Indeed 'Scots' can be used, in one of its senses, to refer to the 'Gaelic language, supposedly spoken by the Scots before they arrived in Ireland, and then believed to survive as Basque'. Here, for reasons of space, the more commonly-held definition of Scots as 'the language of lowland Scots' is understood; historical and literary references to 'Scottis metir' and 'Scottish poesy', along with more contested examples such as 'Scots-jiggs' being sung to mock the Covenanters, make this a quite acceptable and precedented definition in the present context.[39] Such linguistic composites and resonances add depth and meaning to the corpus, although they are often ignored by all but specialist collectors.

Popular perceptions of what constitutes a 'Scots song' are, to complicate matters further, more inclusive. Audiences from furth of Scotland, from social groups who are unfamiliar with traditional-style source singers or prepared to suspend their own knowledge, often define Scots song in relation to performance conventions, by performers perceived to be particularly Scottish. From the late nineteenth century onwards, those familiar with music hall, later variety and film, stars like Harry Lauder (1870–1950) and Will Fyffe (1885–1947), would associate 'Scots song' with comical and sentimental pieces such as Lauder's 'Roamin through the Gloamin' and 'A wee Deoch-an-Doris' and Fyffe's 'I belong to Glasgow'.[40] Broadcasters associated with Scots songs include Robert Wilson (1907–1964), featured in the influential BBC television *The White Heather Club* (1958–68). Most of its cast members, incidentally, were formally trained either as singers – Kenneth McKellar (1927–2011), associated with pieces from 'Song of the Clyde' to 'The Bonnie Lass of Ballochmyle'; Bill McCue (1934–1999) and Moira Anderson (b.1938) – or as actors, like Andy Stewart (1933–1993), known for his compositions like 'Donald, Where's your Troosers' and 'Campbeltown Loch (I Wish You Were Whisky)'.[41]

More recently, there have been, arguably, more sophisticated media representations of Scots song through the BBC's *Hogmanay Show* and, in the past decade, *Hogmanay Live*. In this context, 'Scots song' would be associated with performers (often focusing on Burns songs) like Paolo Nutini and Karine Polwart (2006) and Amy Macdonald (2007). Radio, too, has been influential in constructing popular understandings of what Scots songs means. In this context, it is worth mentioning broadcasters with long careers, like Robbie Shepherd (b.1936) and Archie Fisher (b.1939), along with specific and thoughtful programmes, like Ewan MacColl (1915–1989)'s 'Singing the Fishing', part of his *Radio Ballad* BBC series. Scots song in its popular sense, then, encompasses a wide variety of popular, 'art', and cross-generic styles.

Another factor is the manner of generation and consumption of song, related to distinctions amongst audiences. In *Society and the Lyric*, Thomas Crawford distinguishes 'artificial song' and 'popular song'. The former is:

> a particularly insipid variety, often sung by professional singers [. . .] a peculiar sub-class of art-song [. . .] associated with a particular social group, the 'polite', and above all with the women of that group [. . .] their idea-content was often that of the mid-eighteenth-century cult of sentiment.

The latter is as:

> a generic term [. . .] (1) composed songs by popular writers of certain conventional types, sung to Scots or popular English tunes; (2) slip or chapbook songs [. . .] (3) 'Broadside' or 'stall' ballads [. . .] (4) folk-songs, subject to the laws that govern oral transmission.

Crawford suggests that these categories of songs 'appealed to all of lowlands Scotland', without the socio-economic biases one might assume between 'the "masses" and the "educated."'[42] If this categorisation is accepted, then the means of composition and preferences in consumption are elements to be considered too.

'Scots song', finally, is period-specific, as Hamish Henderson noted in 1964 – his article, featuring performances by Jeannie Robertson, Jean Redpath and Matt McGinn, is in itself a revealing snapshot of songs and singers in Scotland at that time.[43] Today, 'Scots song' tends to be understood in a somewhat inclusive sense, covering a variety of generic categories and musical styles. This can be seen by surveying current websites such as www.youtube.com, where a search for 'Scots Song' leads to hits from Gaelic mouth music to military pipe bands to songs by Robert Burns to Eurovision entries. In the case of retail platforms, such as www.Musicinscotland.com, the topic is defined simply as 'music from Scotland and its Celtic cousins'.[44] Other interactive sites, including the forum www.mudcat.org, take a similarly inclusive approach.

To summarise: 'Scots song' can reflect a point of geographical or ethnic origin, language, collectors' nation-building agendas, stylistic characteristics (the 'Scotch song') and popular understandings. It is understood differently in various historical contexts, and from varying geographical perspectives. For the rest of this chapter, for convenience, I use it primarily to refer to songs with significant Scots language elements which have been generated within Scotland.

COLLECTION AND CANONISATION

The corpus of Scots song, as it stands today, was shaped from notions of perceived necessity: to preserve what were seen as dying traditions, and to identify a national or regionally-based canon. From the seventeenth century onwards, collectors from Scotland and beyond sought to define the nation, often in the context of Enlightenment attitudes to Scots language materials: theirs was a counter movement to anglicisation. Richard Dorson in *The British Folklorists*, while addressing the phenomenon of national self-definition within Scotland, considers Walter Scott to have been the first national 'literary folklorist'.[45] In fact, although the term 'folklorist' is, of course, anachronistic, the study (or at least itemisation) of Scots song as a phenomenon began somewhat earlier than the nineteenth century.

While there is little direct evidence prior to the seventeenth century, the *Complaynte of Scotland* (1549) includes references to Scots songs from 'Tam Lin' to 'Froggy would a-wooing go', including the earliest mentions of several well known ballads, in the 'Monologue Recreative', 6th chapter. James Wedderburn (1495–1553)'s *Ane Compendious Booke of Godly and Spirituall Songs collected out of sundrie partes of the Scripture, with sundrie of other Ballates changed out of prophaine sanges, for avoyding of sinne and harlotrie, with augmentation of sundrie gude and godlie Ballates not contenit in the first editioun* (1567) –usually referred to as the *Gude and Godlie Ballads* – was a collection of Scots songs circulated in broadside form which had been reworked to ensure that they were religiously appropriate for the time. They suggest vibrant activity in Scots song at this period. There are examples, too, of Scots songs known as broadsides in the seventeenth century – Child notes a 'Blow ye winds blow' (Ch 2), for instance, of this type. However, it was not until the eighteenth century that collectors and editors – in particular, those who framed their collections as 'national' – started the process of delineating, in print, a tradition of poetry and song in Scots.

James Watson, in *A Choice Collection of Comic and Serious Scots Poems Both Ancient and Modern* (1706–1711), identified a burgeoning trend to publish collections of poetry in Scotland's 'Neighbouring Kingdoms and States' and claimed his was the first to be published in Scots dialect. Beginning with James V's 'Christis Kirk on the Green', the collection includes a number of Scots songs such as 'The Blithesome Wedding', William Clelland's 'Hollow My Fancy' and 'Old Long-Syne'. Watson's pioneering identification of a 'Scots' tradition' was closely followed by the work of Allan Ramsay (1686–1758). Ramsay's *Scots Songs* (1719) and *Tea Table Miscellany: A Collection of Scots Songs* in three volumes (1723, 1726 and 1727) with an additional volume in 1737, were hugely influential in asserting the significance of Scots language songs and in inspiring later collectors, as was his *Evergreen: being a Collection of Scots Poems, Wrote by the Ingenious before 1600* (1724). Linguistically, Ramsay played a vital role in invigorating interest in Scots language songs (as well as poetry), rehabilitating what was often seen as an inferior, vernacular means of expression. Neil Grobman notes that Ramsay's work 'gave actual folksong collecting in Scotland its initial influence' in an article which also draws attention to David Hume's important, if indirect, role in this respect.[46]

Account should also be taken of nominally 'external' influences, such as the Ossianic reconstructions of James Macpherson, *Fragments of Ancient Poetry*, *Fingal* (1761/2) and *Temora* (1765). Despite or perhaps because of their controversial provenance and Macpherson's precise level of reworking of collected sources, these undoubtedly inspired those interested in song to collect pieces in Scots. Macpherson certainly influenced the composition of national epics in Europe and the United States, and while his reception there has been considered in depth, it remains to be fully explored as to what his precise impact was on Scots song collectors and songwriters.[47]

The establishment of a Scots song canon has also to be seen in the British context. David Herd (1732–1810), in his *Ancient and Modern Scottish songs* (1769, revised and expanded 1776) produced his work at least partly in response to the English collector Thomas Percy's *Reliques of Ancient English Poetry* (1765), itself a response to Macpherson. Herd's collection of over three hundred items aimed to establish the seniority, and superiority, of the Scottish song tradition. The English antiquarian Joseph Ritson (1752–1803) should also be mentioned here. Dismissing John Pinkerton's *Select Scottish Ballads* (1783) in a letter to the *Gentleman's Magazine* of 1784, and having already produced *A Select Collection of English Songs* (1783), Ritson's Scottish works include *The Caledonian Muse: A Chronological Selection of Scottish Poetry*, 1785. Unfortunately, the introductory essay, in manuscript, was destroyed in a fire and the text itself was not published until 1821. Ritson's *Scotish Songs* [sic] (1794) proved influential and again refuted Pinkerton; in response to Pinkerton's notion that the Picts founded Scotland, Ritson's *Annals of the Caledonians, Picts, and Scots* offered a line of Celtic origin to the Scottish nation. As Janet Sorenson has established, both Herd and Ritson showed particular understandings of the relationship between orality and printed texts, and of the assumed musicality of Scottish texts.[48]

These undertakings and debates need to be understood in the context of European collecting and cultural transmissions, with the work of Johann Gottfried von Herder (1744–1803), for instance, playing an influential role. Herder's collection *Von Deutschen Art und Kunst* (1773), which included a piece by Goethe, was highly influential in the formation of ideas around national character for European nations including Scotland. The ballads of Gottfried Burger (1747–1794), too, were influential on Walter Scott's understanding of the ballad genre and, as Robert Crawford has noted, on the way he approached Scots language ballad texts.[49]

To return to material generated within Scotland by Scots, it is vital to consider the work of James Johnson (1753–1811), editor and compiler of the *Scots Musical Museum* (1787–1803). This is important both for its comprehensiveness, at around six hundred songs, and for the possibilities it gave Robert Burns as a platform for collecting and reworking traditional material in the Scots language. Donald Low described this as 'the most comprehensive and valuable of all Scottish song collections', partly because it includes unornamented music.[50] This is an opinion shared by many. Ellen J Stekert, for instance, noted, 'it is a collection of almost unparalleled scope in the eighteenth century, reflecting the early conscious recognition by the Scots of their cultural heritage'.[51] Parallels should be drawn with its contemporary musical collecting initiatives, such as that around James Oswald (1710–1769)'s *A Curious Collection of Scots Tunes* (1740) and the multi-volumed *Caledonian Pocket Companion* published from 1745 onwards and containing over 500 tunes, many setting well known Scots songs from 'The Mucking of Geordie's Byre' to 'The Bonny Earl of Murray'.[52] Burns used several of these airs – 'Go Fetch to me a pint of wine' and 'It is na Jean, thy bonny face', for instance, were both set to Oswald-published airs. Also worth mentioning is

George Thomson (1757–1851) and his *Select Collection of Original Scottish Airs* (1793); he played a major role in introducing Scots songs to composers from Haydn to Beethoven, whose settings gave international exposure to the songs of James Hogg and Robert Burns, for instance.

'Scots song', in the collections mentioned previously, is an inclusive term – songs are sometimes grouped by category (as outlined with Herd) but there is no concentration on one particular genre. One of the first genre-based sets was Walter Scott's *Minstrelsy of the Scottish Border* (1802–3), which marked a major shift in identifying ballad as the most characteristic and important of Scottish genres. Influenced by Percy's *Reliques of Ancient English Poetry* as well as by family song repertoires, Scott's work was, of course, in line with the post-Enlightenment drive towards epic and 'national' styles, shifting Scotland – with Scott playing a prominent role – towards a romantic conceptualisation of its past and its literature, oral and written. The *Minstrelsy*, in its first volume, focuses on the historical, on the 'military' characteristics of writers and audiences, and the 'valour' expressed, particularly on the territories of the Middle Marches of the Borders. The later multiple-edition volumes added more romantic texts and included 'imitations' by Scott and his circle. This began the process of defining the precise characteristics of ballad, later confirmed by Child. Scott has sometimes been accused, most spectacularly in the apocryphal remarks of Margaret Laidlaw, of undue tampering with texts but, as I have argued elsewhere, although sometimes 'heavy handed', he performed a valuable service in encouraging interest in and knowledge of ballad texts and, more generally, Scots songs.[53]

Other collections featuring Scots songs include Robert Cromek (1770–1812)'s *Remains of Nithsdale and Galloway song* (1810), which offered a contrasting interest in the lyrical, assisted by the zealous collecting – and re-writing – of Allan Cunningham. James Hogg (1770–1835)'s *The Jacobite Relics* (1819–21), commissioned by the Highland Society of London, was seminal in identifying a category of Jacobite song, some translated from the Gaelic, with Scots idioms. He sometimes includes 'amendments' alongside source texts – in some instances, as in 'Charlie is my Darling', this shows the robustness of the original song in Scots – for 'brawly weel he kend the way / To please a Highland lass' (II, L). Bawdy songs in Scots, incidentally, were vastly underrepresented in printed collections, with the exception of the privately circulated (Burns-related) *Merry Muses of Caledonia*, although, more recently, work like Peter Buchan's *Secret Songs of Silence* has gained new attention.[54]

Influenced by Scott, William Motherwell (1797–1835) produced the influential collection of *Minstrelsy Ancient and Modern* (1827) which is unusual for its period in advocating the minimum of editorial intervention in the presentation of texts. The Peebles-born Edinburgh publisher Robert Chambers (1802–1871) in *The Popular Rhymes of Scotland* (1826), *The Scottish Songs* (1829) and *The Songs of Scotland Prior to Burns* (1862), played an important role in preserving and transmitting repertoire. More recent collectors of Scots song include Gavin Greig (1856–1914) whose *Folk Songs of the North East* (Peterhead, 1914) and *Last Leaves of Traditional Ballads and Ballad Airs collected in Aberdeenshire* (Aberdeen, 1925) were seminal regional collections. The full extent of his work with James Bruce

Duncan (1848–1917) was brought to public attention more recently through the eight-volume *The Greig-Duncan Folk Song Collection* (1981–2002). John Ord's *Bothy Songs and Ballads* (1930)[55] cross-references well with this, foregrounding farm-related pieces in Scots.

The pioneering work of the School of Scottish Studies (f.1951) and their peers drew attention to a hitherto neglected tradition of Scottish Travellers' repertoires, anchored in the Scots language. *Travellers' Songs from England and Scotland* (1977) was highly praised for its scholarship, as was *Till Doomsday in the Afternoon, the Folklore of a Family of Scots Travellers*, and the *Scottish Tradition* series, featuring recordings from many of the finest Traveller singers, including (with apologies to those omitted from this necessarily truncated list) Jeannie Robertson (1908–1975), her daughter Lizzie Higgins (1929–1993) and Jimmy Macbeath (1894–1972). Hamish Henderson introduced the American collector Kenneth Goldstein (1927–1995) to Lucy Stewart; the latter's recordings feature on her eponymous release of 1975. More recently, Travellers have published their traditions, such as Sheila Stewart (b.1935)'s *From the Heart of the Tradition* (2000), Elizabeth Stewart (b.1939)'s *Binnorie* (2004) and the late Stanley Robertson (1940–2009)'s *The College Boy* (2009). Elizabeth Stewart has recently published *Up Yon Wide and Lonely Glen*, compiled and edited by Alison McMorland.

Recordings worth mentioning in this context include the entire *Scottish Tradition* series (Greentrax) which showcases material from the School of Scottish Studies Archive; the Serge Hovey collection of the songs of Robert Burns featuring Jean Redpath; and the monumental contribution of Fred Freeman, including the Linn twelve volume series of *The Complete Songs of Robert Burns* (1995–2002) and the current project to publish the works of Robert Tannahill (2006 ongoing), whose well known songs in Scots include 'The Braes o' Balquhidder' (also known as the 'Wild Mountain Thyme'). The Tobar an Dualchas / Kist o Riches website, too, integrates a range of archival recordings which form a searchable resource of great depth; the term 'Scots song', for instance, yields thirty pages worth of hits, ranging from field-captured material to radio recordings.

Genre-specific collections include recent work on children's songs in Scots. Pioneering work like James Ritchie's *The Singing Street* (1964), focusing on urban transmission contexts in Edinburgh and in the vein of the Opie's *Lore and Language of Children* (1959), and *The Singing Game* (1985) have been followed by Ewan McVicar's *Chokit on a Tattie* (2006) and *Doh Ray Me, When Ah Wis Wee* (2007). As defined by McVicar, in *Doh Ray Me . . .,* the distinctive characteristics of Scottish children's song and rhyme include 'vigour and bounce, direct language, the Scots voice, implied humour and the topics of childhood, home life, dance, parental actions that include an element of archaic control over women, courting, violent events and a surreal touch'.[56] He identifies a distinctively 'female' voice to this, too.

The current role of children's performers *The Singing Kettle*, deserves mention: they have played a vital role in introducing and reinforcing knowledge of traditional repertoire among the under-fives and their families; Cilla Fisher reflects on their active programme of recording and touring in a set of extracts accessible through the Tobar an Dualchas / Kist o Riches website. Modern transmission contexts outwith the playgrounds and family situations that have been studied in the past include input from the 'Book bug' (formerly 'Rhymetimes') weekly sessions run by the Scottish Book Trust, which teach traditional songs to parents and children through local libraries, with librarians often incorporating local repertoire preferences into this formal context.[57] This is a hitherto unstudied context which could yield interesting results: it is certainly a path to invigorating knowledge of children's songs and traditions.

CURRENT AND FUTURE RESEARCH

In terms of present activity, there are a number of active academic projects which encompass Scots song within their remit. Examples include the bringing together of the archival collection of the American folklorist James Madison Carpenter as a joint project between the Universities of Aberdeen and Sheffield and the American Folklife Center at the Library of Congress; these holdings contain substantial elements of Scots song. The Tobar an Dualchais / Kist o Riches project, mentioned above, makes accessible substantial amounts of material which will be immensely useful to students in this field, drawing on the archival materials of the School of Scottish Studies Archive at the University of Edinburgh and other collections. The Elphinstone Institute at the University of Aberdeen, too, has archival resources, and an ongoing collection and publication remit, and provides a platform for the study and performing of songs in Scots, from ballad to religious songs. The work of the Royal Conservatoire, formerly the Royal Scottish Academy of Music and Drama, through their BA (Scottish Music) and related programmes, is also providing a valuable service in educating a new generation of skilled performers of Scots songs and highly competent fieldworkers.

The University of Glasgow's Centre for Robert Burns Studies is engaged in a major reassessment of his songs in Scots and English as part of the Burns' *Songs for George Thomson* project. Similarly, the songs of James Hogg are currently undergoing reassessment as part of a joint project between the Universities of Glasgow and Stirling linked to the Stirling/South Carolina edition of the *Collected Works of James Hogg*. This will lead to a new publication of Hogg's songs, and has already yielded a searchable online index and CD. The University of Glasgow holds the substantial collection relating to political song made by Norman and Janey Buchan, which was formerly part of the Centre for Political Song at the Glasgow Caledonian University. Its new home makes it part of a project to promote an understanding of political song on the national and international arenas. The work of grassroots organisations like the Traditional Music and Song Association (TMSA) of Scotland plays a vital role in promoting Scots song in performance contexts, both during showcase festivals and through its network of active local branches throughout Scotland. Scottish Culture & Traditions (SC&T) is active in the North East of Scotland promoting song along with music and dance. Online resources which provide a comprehensive listing of performances and festivals where it is possible to hear Scots songs include www.scottish-folk-music.com.

The work of the ethnologist can have both beneficial and detrimental effects. Certain traditions are foregrounded to the near-exclusion of others. Ballad, for instance, is extremely well studied, with an International Ballad Commission (Kommission für Volksdichtung) ensuring sustained and detailed study of Scots balladry within a European context. These 'muckle sangs', which have rather macho and medieval associations at times, seem to appeal to the romantic side (as well as the aesthetic wonderment) of the modern collector, just as they did in the nineteenth century. Children's song, despite the sterling work of dedicated collectors, is somewhat denigrated except in the context of promoting literacy within the pre-school and school environment, despite the evident richness of this area for research. The cross-fertilisation with the popular, too, can be marginalised – the 'crossover' work of Eddi Reader in relation to Burns, for instance, frowned on by the purist academic; the lingering distaste at the likes of Harry Lauder interfering with the need to intelligently assess the impact of the music-hall Scot on Scots song and perceptions of the Scot (outside of popular cultural practitioners).

Traveller traditions have been brought to the fore, following on from the pioneering collecting work of Hamish Henderson and the fieldworkers of the 1950s, providing a rich national resource for Scots song. However, other areas, such as South West Scotland, have been neglected for reasons I have suggested elsewhere.[58] Equally, while the School of Scottish Studies archive collection is well promoted and well used, there are other significant collections of Scots song in manuscript and printed form which are much less well recognised: one of the best examples is Broughton House in Kirkcudbright, managed by the National Trust for Scotland, home of a substantial song-related collection, including the correspondence between William Macmath and Francis James Child, as well as many rare publications relating to Scots song. The Carnegie Library in Dunfermline has interesting material relating to bawdy song, including an annotated transcript of the first edition of *Merry Muses of Caledonia*. An audit of all such material, perhaps trawling, too, for material in private collections, would be immensely useful to future scholars of Scots song.

FUTURE PATHWAYS

Given the discussions above, future pathways for ethnological enquiry in relation to Scots song might include some of the following:

- The cross-fertilisation of Scots song with the songs of other language groups, whether of long-standing use in Scotland (Gaelic and English, for instance) or related to immigrant groups (often of long standing) including Asian, Polish and Italian Scots. This could include considering linguistic and cultural cross-overs and exchanges.
- The impact of areas of long-standing cultural contact on the growth and development of Scots song, e.g. Ireland and England, particularly in Border areas, and the impact of 'being Scottish' on first and later generation emigrants, in terms of repertoire and new compositions; what constitutes Scots-language 'Celtic' song

- Considering how the 'foreign' is adapted into the context of Scots songs, for instance, broadcast and related imports and exchanges from and into American and Canada
- The impact of collectors and performers of Gaelic song on collection and performance in Scots, and *vice versa*
- The notion of the 'regional' in relation to the 'national' to collecting in Scots, and the traditions of 'undercollected' areas, such as South West Scotland
- The meaning of popular song in Scots to Scots and non-Scots: how this defines the nation: beyond purism
- The usefulness of language or geographically based distinctions (and indeed distinctions based round academically-recognised genres) and their relationship to singers' definitions of what constitutes a Scots song
- Exploring under-appreciated genres, such as children's songs, and sporting songs, and examining their modern transmission, in a variety of public and private contexts
- Compiling an audit of material relating to Scots song, including manuscript and privately-held resources, in collections within Scotland and, ideally, beyond.

NOTES

1 Herd, 1776, vi.
2 See Hodgart, 1950; Buchan, 1997; Porter, 2009.
3 See Crawford, 1979.
4 See Livingstone, 1994.
5 See too McVicar, 2010.
6 Lyle, 1997, 12.
7 Porter, 2003, 24.
8 Oring, 1986.
9 *Gaelic and Scots Folk Songs*, 1960.
10 See Shapiro, 1990.
11 Beaton, 2008 and 2010.
12 Kennedy, 2010.
13 Quoted in Olson, 1998, 431.
14 I am extremely grateful to Phyllis Martin for allowing me access to her typescript collection. See too *Sangs Collected Frae Aw the Airts*, 2010 and Stravaig, 1994.
15 Cowan, 2000, 10.
16 Murison, 1964, 45.
17 See Philipose, 1990.
18 See Turriff, 1996.
19 Narvaez, 1992.
20 Recorded Stravaig, 1994.
21 Moir, 1829.
22 Bogle and Munro,1997.
23 Miller, 1998.
24 Proclaimers, 1987.
25 See Porter, 1998.

26 See <www.thistleradio.com> [accessed June 2012]; <www.celticradio.net> [accessed June 2012].

27 See Leyburn, 1962.

28 The Association of Highland Games includes a listing of Scottish festivals in the US, at <http://www.asgf.org/> [accessed June 2012]; parallel information online relating to Australian and Canadian festivals, for instance, is more ad hoc.

29 Gelbart, 2007, 45.

30 D'Urfey, 1791, 79–80.

31 Hildebrand and Hildebrand, 1991.

32 Buchan, 1972, 15–16.

33 *Dictionary of the Scots Language*, 2004 (online).

34 Buchan, 1972, 69.

35 *Ulster-Scots Agency*.

36 <http://www.ulsterscotsagency.com/weans//library/music/UlsterScotsSongs.pdf> [accessed June 2012].

37 Drennan, 2009.

38 Greig-Duncan, 1981–2002, VIII.

39 *Dictionary of the Scots Language*, 2004.

40 See Maloney, 2003; Irving, 1968.

41 *The White Heather Club*, 2005.

42 Crawford, 1979, 8–9.

43 Henderson, 1964.

44 <http://www.musicinscotland.com/acatalog/About_Us.html> [accessed June 2012].

45 Crawford, 2000; Dorson, 1968.

46 Grobman, 1975, 18.

47 See Stafford and Gaskill, 1998; Gaskill, 1996; Gaskill, 2004; Bold, 2001.

48 Sorenson, 2007.

49 Crawford, 2001, 140.

50 Stekert, 1991, I, 1.

51 Stekert, 1966, 33.

52 See Concerto Caledonia, 1999; Oswald, 2006–7.

53 Bold, 2000.

54 Barke et al., 2009.

55 Ord, 1995.

56 McVicar, 2007, 1–2.

57 *Scottish Book Trust*, 'Babies and Early Years'.

58 Bold, 2009.

BIBLIOGRAPHY AND FURTHER READING

Barke, J, Smith, S G and Bold, V, eds. *The Merry Muses of Caledonia by Robert Burns*, Edinburgh, 2009.

Bold, V. Scott, Child and the Hogg Family Ballads. In Cowan, E, ed., *The Ballad in Scottish History*, East Linton, 2000, 116–41.

Bold, V. Bard of the North: James Macpherson and the 'Folklore of Democracy', *Journal of American Folklore*, 114:454 (2001), 464–77.

Bold, V. "I wish I was whaur Helen lies" – collection, community and regeneration in modern South West Scotland, *Markings*, 28 (2009), 57–68.

Brown, M E. *Burns and Tradition*, London, 1984.

Brown, M E. Old Singing Women and the Canons of Scottish Balladry and Song. In Gifford, D and McMillan, D, eds, *A History of Scottish Women's Writing*, Edinburgh, 1997, 44–57.

Brown, M E. *William Motherwell's Cultural Politics*, Lexington, KY, 2001.

Buchan, D. *The Ballad and the Folk*, London, 1972.

Buchan, D. *The Ballad and the Folk*, 2nd edn, East Linton, 1997.

Buchan, D. Folk Tradition and Literature till 1603. In McClure, J D and Spiller, M R G, eds, *Bryght Lanternis*, Aberdeen, 1989, 1–14.

Buchan, D and Moriera, J. *The Glenbuchat Ballads*, Jackson, MS, 1997.

Buchan, P. *Secret Songs of Silence*, ed. I Spring, Edinburgh, 2010.

Campbell, K M, ed. *Songs from North-East Scotland: A Selection for Performers from the Greig-Duncan Folk Song Collection*, Edinburgh, 2009.

Cooper, D. On the Twelfth of July in the Morning . . . Or the Man who mistook his Sash for a Hat, *Folk Music Journal*, 8:1 (2001), 67–89.

Cowan, E J, ed. *The Ballad in Scottish History*, East Linton, 2000.

Crawford, R. *Devolving English Literature*, 2nd edn, Edinburgh, 2000.

Crawford, R. Walter Scott and European Union, *Studies in Romanticism*, 40:1 (2001), 137–52.

Crawford, T. *Society and the Lyric*, Edinburgh, 1979.

Dictionary of the Scots Language/Dictionar o the Scots Leid, (includes 12 vol *Dictionary of the Older Scottish Tongue*, and 10 vol *Scottish National Dictionary*, 1931–76, <http://www.dsl.ac.uk/dsl/> [accessed June 2012].

Dorson, R M. *The British Folklorists*, London, 1968.

Drennan, W. *Ulster Scots Music*, 2009, <http://www.culturenorthernireland.org/article/1047/ ulster-scots-music> [accessed June 2012].

D'Urfey, T. *Wit and Mirth; or Tom D'Urfey's Tales to Purge Melancholy: A Selection of his Best Songs into One Volume*, London, 1791.

Gaskill, H. *The Poems of Ossian and Related Work*, Edinburgh, 1996.

Gaskill, H, ed. *The Reception of Ossian in Europe*, London, New York, 2004.

Gelbart, M. *The Invention of 'Folk Music' and 'Art Music'*, Cambridge, 2007.

Greig, G and Duncan, J B. *The Greig–Duncan Folk Song Collection*, eds P Shuldam-Shaw, E B Lyle and K Campbell, 8 vols, Aberdeen and Edinburgh, 1981–2002.

Grobman, N. David Hume and the earliest scientific methodology for collecting balladry, *Western Folklore*, 34:1 (1975), 16–31.

Harper, M M. *The Bards of Galloway*, Dalbeattie, 1889.

Henderson, H. Scots Folk-Song Today, *Folklore*, 75:1 (1964), 48–58.

Henderson, H. *Alias MacAlias: Writings on Songs, Folk and Literature*, Edinburgh, 1992.

Herd, D. *Ancient and Modern Scottish Songs, Heroic Ballads, etc.*, 2 vols, first published 1776 anonymously, reprinted Glasgow, 1869.

Hodgart, M J C. *The Ballads*, London, 1950.

Hogg, J. *The Jacobite Relics of Scotland: Being the Songs, Airs and Legends of the Adherents of the House of Stuart*, 2 vols [first published 1819–21], ed. M G H Pittock, Edinburgh, 2002–3.

Irving, G. *Great Scot: The Life Story of Sir Harry Lauder, Legendary Laird of the Music Hall*, London, 1968.

Ives, E D. *The Bonny Earl of Murray: The Man, the Murder, The Ballad*, East Linton, 1997.

King, E. *Scotland Sober and Free: The Temperance Movement 1829–1979*, Glasgow, 1979.

Leyburn, J G. *The Scotch-Irish: A Social History*, Chapel Hill, NC, 1962.

Lyle, E. *Scottish Ballads*, 2nd edn, Edinburgh, 1997.

Lyle, E, McAlpine, K and McLucas, A D, eds. *The Song Repertoire of Amelia and Jane Harris*, Edinburgh, 2002.

McKean, T A. *The Flowering Thorn: International Ballad Studies*, Logan, UT, 2003.

McVicar, E. *One Singer, One Song: Songs of Glasgow Folk*, with illustrations by John Gahagan, Glasgow, 1990.

McVicar, E. *Doh Ray Me, When Ah Wis Wee*, Edinburgh, 2007.

McVicar, E. *The Eskimo Republic: Scots Political Song in Action*, Linlithgow, 2010.

Maloney, P. *Scotland and the Music Hall 1850–1914*, Manchester, 2003.

[Moir, D M]. The Canadian Boat-Song, *Blackwoods Edinburgh Magazine*, 26 (1829), 400.

Murison, D. The Scots tongue: The folk speech, *Folklore*, 75:1 (1964), 37–47.

Narvaez, P. Folkloristics, cultural studies and popular culture, *Canadian Folklore*, 14:1 (1992), 15–30.

Narvaez, P. 'I think I wrote a folksong': Popularity and regional vernacular anthems, *Journal of American Folklore*, 115:456 (2002), 269–82.

Olson, I. Scottish Song in the James Madison Carpenter Collection, *Folk Music Journal*, 7:1 (1998), 421–33.

Ord, J. *Ord's Bothy Songs and Ballads of Aberdeen, Banff and Moray, Angus and the Mearns*, Edinburgh, 1995.

Oring, E. *Folk Groups and Folklore Genres*, Logan, UT, 1986.

Paterson, J, ed. *The Ballads and Songs of Ayrshire*, Ayr and Edinburgh, 1846–47.

Philipose, L. The Twa Sisters: A Santal folktale variant of the ballad, *Folklore*, 101:2 (1990), 169–77.

Porter, J. Introduction: Locating Celtic Music (and Song), *Western Folklore*, 57:4 (1998), 205–24.

Porter, J. The traditional ballad: requickened text or performative genre? *Scottish Studies Review*, 4:1 (2003), 24–40.

Porter, J. *Genre, Conflict, Presence. Traditional Ballads in a Modernizing World*, Trier, 2009.

Ritchie, J T R. *The Singing Street*, Edinburgh, 1964.

Shapiro, A D. Sounds of Scotland, *American Music*, 8:1 (1990), 71–83.

Shephard, L. *The Broadside Ballad: The Development of the Street Ballad from Traditional Song to Popular Newspaper*, 2nd edn, Hatboro, PA, 1978.

Shoolbraid, M. *The High-Kilted Muse: Peter Buchan and his Secret Songs of Silence*, Jackson, MS, 2010.

Sorenson, J. Orality's silence: the other ballad revival, *International Journal of Scottish Literature*, 2 (Spring/Summer 2007), <http://www.ijsl.stir.ac.uk/issue2/sorensen.htm> [accessed June 2012].

Stafford, F. *The Sublime Savage: A Study of James Macpherson and the Poems of Ossian*, Edinburgh, 1988.

Stafford, F J and Gaskill, H, eds. *From Gaelic to Romantic: Ossianic Translations*, Amsterdam, 1998.

Stekert, E J. Review: The Scots Musical Museum, *Journal of American Folklore*, 79:312 (1966), 392–3.

Stewart, E. *Up Yon Wide and Lonely Glen*, compiled and edited by Alison McMorland, Jackson, MS, 2012.

Symon, P. Music and national identity in Scotland: A study of Jock Tamson's bairns, *Popular Music*, 16:2 (1997), 203–16.

Wannan, B, ed. *The Heather in the South:. Lore, Literature and Balladry of the Scots in Australia*, 2nd edn, Melbourne, 1967.

Wimberly, L C. *Folklore in the English & Scottish Ballads*, New York, 1965.

DISCOGRAPHY

Beaton, A. *The Songs of Robert Burns*, Franklin, TS, 2008.

Beaton, A. *From the Sea to the Shore*, Franklin, TS, 2010.

Bogle E and Munro, J. *The Emigrant and the Exile*, Cockenzie, East Lothian, 1997, CDTRAX121.

Bothy Ballads, Scottish Tradition Series, vol 1, Cockenzie, East Lothian, 1993, Greentrax Recordings Ltd CDTRAX 9001.

Chokit On A Tattie, Scottish Tradition Series, vol 22, Cockenzie, East Lothian, 2006, CDTRAX 9022.

Burns R. *The Complete Songs of Robert Burns*, prod F. Freeman, 12 vols. 2nd edn, Eaglesham, Glasgow, 2007, CKD 289

Concerto Caledonia. *Colin's Kisses. The Music of James Oswald*, Glasgow, 1999, CKD 101.

Duncan, J. *Ye Shine Whar Ye Stan*, Balmalcolm, Cupar, 1997, SPRCD 1039.

Fyffe, W. *Will Fyffe*, Glasgow, 2008, YCD09.

Gaelic and Scots Folk Songs, School of Scottish Studies, Edinburgh, 1960.

Gaughan, D. *Live! At the Trades Club*, Cockenzie, East Lothian, 1998, CDTRAX322.

Hildebrand, D and Hildebrand, G, *Over the Hills and Far Away. Being a Collection of Music from 18th-Century Annapolis*, Annapolis, 2006, CMI H103.

Hildebrand, D and Hildebrand, G. *Music of the Charles Carroll Family: From 1785–1832*, Annapolis, 1991, TROY056.

Hogg, J. *I'll Sing Ye a Wee Bit Sang: Selected Songs of James Hogg*, Stirling, 2007.

Kennedy, N. *Ballads and Songs of Scotland*, Sharon, CT, 2010, B003ZMDW14

Lauder, H. *Harry Lauder:. The First Knight of the Music Hall*, London, 2008, ACRCD170.

Livingstone, S. *Bonnie Fechters: Women in Scotland 1900–1950*, Motherwell, 1994.

McKellar, K. *The Very Best of Kenneth McKellar*, London, 1997.

McNaughtan, A. *The Words That I Used to Know*, Cockenzie, East Lothian, 2000, CDTRAX195D.

McNeill, B. *No Gods and Precious Few Heroes*, Cockenzie, East Lothian, 1995, CDTRAX098

McNeill. B. *From the Baltic tae Byzantium*, Cockenzie, East Lothian, 2009, CDTRAX341.

Martin, P. *O A the Airts: Sangs Collected in the Sooth*, Dalbeattie, 2011.

Miller, Ed. *The Edinburgh Rambler*, Austin, TX, 1998, CD 5018081016426.

The Muckle Sangs. Scottish Tradition Series, vol 5. Cockenzie, East Lothian, 1992, Greentrax Recordings Ltd CDTRAX 9005.

Oswald, J. *Caledonian Pocket Companion*, ed. John Purser. 2 vols, CD-rom, privately published, 2006–7.

Proclaimers, The. *This is the Story*, London, 1987. CHR 1602

Reader, E., *Eddie Reader Sings the Songs of Robert Burns*, London, 2003. YCD09.

Redpath, J. *The Songs of Robert Burns*, arr. Serge Hovey, vols 1–7, Cockenzie, East Lothian, 1996, CD TRAX 114, 115, 116, 129.

Rideout, Bonnie. *Harlaw: Scotland 1411*, Alexandria, VA, 2011, TM505.

Robertson, J. *The Queen Among the Heather*, Cambridge, MA, 1998, Rounder 1161-1720-2.

Robertson, S. *The College Boy*, Aberdeen, 2005, EI CD 005. (EIICD005(EICD005

Singing Kettle, The. *Greatest Hits*, vols 1–3, 1999–2002, Kingskettle, B000024J3V, B000V3S81Y, B00009QNTD.

Songs and Ballads from Perthshire Field Recordings of the 1950s, Scottish Tradition Series, vol 24, Cockenzie, East Lothian, 2011, Greentrax Recording Ltd CDTRAX 9024.

Stewart, B. *Queen Among the Heather*. First published 1976, Cockenzie, East Lothian, 1998, CDTRAX114.

Stewart, E. *Binnorie: Songs, Ballads, and Tunes*, Aberdeen, 2004, EICD002.

Stewart, L. *Lucy Stewart: Traditional Singer from Aberdeenshire*, Washington, 1961, FW03519.

Stewart, S. *From the Heart of the Tradition*, London, 2000, TSCD515.s

Stravaig. *Movin' On*, Cockenzie, East Lothian, 1994.

Tannahill R. *The Complete Songs of Robert Tannahill*, vol. I, Edinburgh, 2006, CDBAR003.

Turriff, J. *Singing is Ma Life*, Springthyme, 1996, CD SPRCD 1038

Wellington, S. *Hamely Fare*, Cockenzie, East Lothian, 2003, CDTRAX240.
The White Heather Club Party, vols I and II, Glasgow, 2005, Legacy 29CD, 30CD.
Wooed and Married And Aa, Scottish Tradition Series, vol 23, Cockenzie, East Lothian, 2008,
    Greentrax Recording Ltd CD TRAX 9023.

ONLINE RESOURCES

Celtic Radio, <www.celticradio.net> [accessed June 2012].
Centre for Robert Burns Studies,<http://www.gla.ac.uk/schools/critical/research/
    researchcentresandnetworks/robertburnsstudies> [accessed June 2012].
Dictionary of the Scots Language, ed Rennie, S et al. Dundee, 2004.
    <http://www.dsl.ac.uk/dsl/> [accessed June 2012].
Francis J. Child Ballads, <http://www.contemplator.com/child/> [accessed June 2012].
Giving Voice Workshops,
    <http://www.givingvoiceworkshops.co.uk/> [accessed June 2012].
Glasgow Broadside Ballads: The Murray Collection,
    <http://www.gla.ac.uk/t4/dumfries/files/layer2/glasgow_broadside_ballads/>
    [accessed June 2012].
James Hogg: Research, <http://www.jameshogg.stir.ac.uk/> [accessed June 2012].
James Madison Carpenter Collection On-Line Catalogue,
    <http://www.hrionline.ac.uk/carpenter/> [accessed June 2012].
The Mudcat Discussion Forum, <http://www.mudcat.org/> [accessed June 2012].
Music in Scotland: A Gateway to Scotland's Music,
    <http://www.musicinscotland.com/> [accessed June 2012].
Janey Buchan Political Song Collection,
    <http://www.gla.ac.uk/schools/cca/research/music/ projectsandnetworks/jbpsc
Scottish Book Trust,
    <http://www.scottishbooktrust.com/node/70936> [accessed June 2012].
Scottish Culture & Traditions, <http://www.scottishculture.org> [accessed June 2012].
Scottish Folk Music.com, <http://www.scottish-folk-music.com> [accessed June 2012].
The Singing Kettle, <http://www.singingkettle.com/> [accessed June 2012].
Traditional Music and Song Association of Scotland, <http://www.tmsa.org.uk/>
    [accessed June 2012].
Ulster-Scots Agency, <http://www.ulsterscotsagency.com/> [accessed June 2012].
Thistleradio (The Thistle and the Shamrock),
    <www.thistleradio.com> [accessed June 2012].
Tobar an Dualchais / Kist o Riches,
    <http://www.tobarandualchais.co.uk/> [accessed June 2012].

13 Gaelic Song

MORAG MACLEOD

The impression of Gaelic song held by a majority of Scots has been formed through listening to singing competitions at the National Mod[1] and to translated versions sung by Scots performers, especially those taken from the repertoire available in Mrs Kennedy-Fraser's *Songs of the Hebrides*. Singers begin to achieve a working knowledge through membership of Gaelic choirs, through various media such as sound recordings accessible in different forms as technology has advanced over the years, and radio and television. In this century, mostly because of the development of sound technology, knowledge has widened, but there is still much more to the genre than many admirers realise. Part of an ancient linguistic heritage, Gaelic song has retained influences of a complex system of poetic composition through what can only be described as a people's extraordinary facility in recalling words, melodies and styles which go back many centuries. This facility is particularly crucial in the retention of melodies, which were hardly ever written down.

FEATURES OF GAELIC SONG

An article by James Ross in the first issue of *Scottish Studies*, and others before that in the Irish journal *Eigse*, attempted to categorise Gaelic Song,[2] coming very late in the history of the genre. The lack of such a study amongst native speakers of the Gaelic language must be acknowledged as a sign of lasting good health, as it was only when an awareness arose of a general dilution of the culture that studies about Gaelic song were deemed necessary. An Comunn Gàidhealach, a society founded in 1891 that takes an interest in things to do with the language, various societies which brought together exiles from different Gaelic areas (such as the Lewis and Harris Association, the Skye Association, the Uist and Barra Association) in Scotland's main cities and in London, and the Folklore Institute of Scotland all arose out of a feeling that the indigenous culture was liable to disappear. Such bodies became more common at the turn of the nineteenth to the twentieth century.

The School of Scottish Studies at the University of Edinburgh, where James Ross was based when he wrote those articles, was started by a group of academics who feared for the survival of our traditions, both Scots and Gaelic. The Folklore Institute of Scotland (FIOS) was a short-lived forerunner of the School, and both owed much of their philosophical outlook to the Irish Folklore Commission. An Comunn Gàidhealach developed with its main shop window for Gaeldom being its annual musical competitive festival, the National Mod. The set pieces for the singing competitions gradually became the responsibility of outsiders who did not know the language and whose judgement was based on a very sparse knowledge of the Gaelic musical idiom. Little was known initially of those competitions within the areas where the language was strongest, but the appearance of gramophone records and the introduction of a few minutes of Gaelic broadcasting by the BBC[3] brought the competition winners into focus, and gradually those who appeared on records and sang on radio – generally chosen from the lists of winners – set the standard of taste amongst Gaelic speakers. After a time it seemed as if the traditional way of singing – unaccompanied and free of the imposition of note-for-note accuracy from a prescribed written form – was seldom to be heard, and the pioneers of the Folklore Institute of Scotland and the School of Scottish Studies thought it was time to restore the balance towards the indigenous product.

It is important to know the background of the British education system and its influence on Gaelic culture in order to appreciate the necessity of oral transmission for our knowledge of Gaelic song. Very briefly, education in the Highlands from the nineteenth century onwards did not consider the teaching of Gaelic in any way comparable with the teaching of English. The emphasis on English literacy, seen as crucial to every child, invariably placed literacy in Gaelic in an inferior position. Much depended on the individual teacher (quite often they did not speak Gaelic in any case), and, while some may have seen the benefits of learning to read and write in one's native language, there are many tales of dire punishment for speaking Gaelic in the classroom. Some went so far as to forbid it in the playground. It is only since the 1960s that literacy in Gaelic began to be taken seriously for primary school pupils, and for senior pupils who did not go on to higher education. It has to be understood, therefore, that 'well-educated', intelligent, very articulate Gaelic speakers of the age of fifty upwards may not be literate in the language. It is ironic that in the mid 1980s Gaelic-medium teaching started when the use of Gaelic in the home had declined radically, and it is also ironic that there are more employment opportunities for Gaelic speakers now than there ever were, but the psychological damage done by teachers over many years causes those whose home language it should be to reject it. But the oral transmission of songs is to this day part of the psyche of older Gaelic speakers. It has a respectable history. As Anne Lorne Gillies says:

> Gaelic oral tradition was rooted deep in an ancient, essentially non-literate society (common to both Ireland an Scotland), in which the arts were held in the highest reverence, and history, law, medicine, music, poetry and story were preserved and reproduced, not in books, but in the highly-trained memories of the bardic orders.[4]

Professor Derick Thomson, in an article in *The Companion to Gaelic Scotland*, quotes a description of a Bardic School:

> A snug, low hut, and beds in it at convenient distances, each within a small

apartment . . . No windows to let in the day, nor any light at all us'd but that of candles, and these brought in at a proper season only.' The students were given appropriate subjects and went to their cubicles to work at them, 'each by himself upon his own bed, the whole next day in the dark, till at a certain hour in the night, lights being brought in, they committed it to writing'; this work was afterwards discussed and corrected, and fresh tasks were allocated for next day. The session lasted from Michaelmas to 25 March.[5]

This information came from the memoirs of the Marquis of Clanricarde, a seventeenth-century Lord Deputy General of Ireland, but Professor Thomson goes on to quote the Scottish writer Martin Martin:

> They shut their doors and windows for a day's time, and lie on their backs, with a stone upon their belly, and plaids about their heads, and their eyes being covered, they pump their brains for rhetorical encomium or panegyric; and indeed they furnish such a style from this dark cell, as is understood by very few.[6]

The poets had to learn a complicated system of rhyme, assonance and alliteration in an archaic form of the language, Classical Common Gaelic. Their training provided them with assured entry to guild membership of a professional elite – surely their right, given the hardships they had to endure to become experts in their craft.

DÀN – SYLLABIC QUATRAINS

The compositions of the highest-trained member in the school of poetry were called *Dàn*, and the composer was a *filidh*. One of the characteristics of *Dàn* is the organisation of a specified number of syllables for each line. This created an irregularity in the stress pattern of the line, and it may be compared with blank verse in English poetry – in a Shakespearean soliloquy, for example. Most of the Gaelic material exists only in writing, but there is a corpus of syllabic poetry which has come to us through oral transmission, via poetry connected with a group of Scoto-Irish heroes including Fionn MacColla and Cu-Chulainn. Unfortunately the poems of Ossian gained notoriety through the attentions of James Macpherson (1736–1796) who 'discovered' poems in Gaelic about those heroes and published them in English translation. Their provenance was more Scottish than the originals, and he gave them names like Fingal and Temora. His purpose was to claim that Scotland and Scottish Gaelic had their own claim to epic poetry which could compete with *The Iliad* and *The Odyssey*. They were very well received amongst scholars throughout Europe, but were eventually found to be false, although some authentic ballads were used within the corpus of his poems. For a detailed account of the man and his writings, see Professor Thomson's article on the subject in *The Companion to Gaelic Scotland*.[7]

Those poems have been labelled Fenian ballads and Ossianic ballads, but we can use Heroic ballads as an inclusive term. On what occasions they were sung, and how they came to last so long in the oral tradition, we cannot tell; we can surmise that the attractive narrative element in them gave them a lasting power amongst tradition-bearers. They may indeed have once been sung as part of the folktales, although in more modern times the two genres seem to have become separated. There are obvious difficulties with the language occasionally, and words are used now which happen to be familiar, even when they do not make sense in the context of the poem. The poems of which the Heroic ballads are examples seem to have been in quatrains.

DÀN – LONGER STANZAS

Another type of syllabic verse was referred to as being in stanzas of eight lines, although a musical criterion might label them differently. No sung examples of that type – with all the strictness attached to the classical genre – remain, but a modification of it was used and could still be heard in the repertory of vernacular bards until recently. All songs in its metre are sung to the same basic tune, the prototype for them being Julia MacDonnell's lament for Alasdair of Glengarry. Both kinds of syllabic verse were sung in a recitative manner, with no regularity of musical stress. Here are two examples:

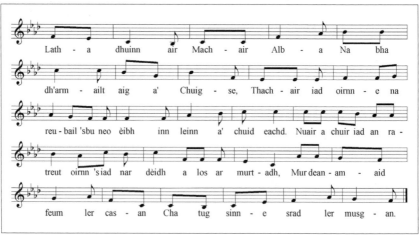

Figure 13.1 Music for 'Blàr na h-Eaglaise Brice'. Music transcription by Morag MacLeod, keyed by Katherine Campbell.

Figure 13.2 Music for 'Laoidh a' Choin Duibh'. Music transcription by Morag MacLeod, keyed by Katherine Campbell.

As well as the requirement of regular numbers of syllables, the old classical poetry required internal rhyme (that is, a word at the end of one line rhyming with a word in the middle of the following line) and end-rhyme. It may be that concern with the rhythms of words, which is typical of the best traditional Gaelic singers, is a legacy from syllabic verse. Even where the accented notes in a melody could come at regular intervals, there is a tendency to use the rhythm of speech, as would be the case in the older classical songs.

IORRAM OR BARDIC VERSE

There was another degree of classical poet, usually named bard, who composed in a different type of metre called *Iorram*. In *Dàn* the performer should take the responsibility of placing a musical stress where the sense of the text requires it; in *Iorram* it seems to have been already decided by the poet. The shortness of the line helps in this, and the stress is so regular it is difficult to vary the rhythm from the way the poet has initiated it.

There is end-rhyme within the stanza, and a rhyme between the last words of each stanza. The shortest verse in this type is three lines, with two stressed syllables in the first two lines and an extra stress in the final line. In English it would be a little like 'Old King Cole / Was a merry old soul / And a merry old soul was he'.[8] There may be a greater number of lines, up to seven, and some poems have a different number in each verse. However long or short the verse, the system of end-rhyme has to be adhered to.

> 'S i fhras nach *ciùin*
> Thàinig as *ùr*
> A shrac ar *siùil*
> 'Sa bhrist ar *stiùir*
> 'S ar cairt mhath *iùil*
> 'S ar taice *cùil*
> 'S ar caidreabh *ciùil*
> Bhiodh againn 'nad thùr èibhinn.
> Bhiodh againn 'nad thùr èibhinn.
>
> 'S mòr an ionndrain tha *bhuainn*
> Air a dùnadh san *uaigh*
> Ar cùinneadh 's ar *buaidh*
> Ar cùram 's ar n-*uaill*
> 'S ar sùgradh gun *ghruaim*
> 'S fad' air chuimhne na fhuair mi fèin deth.
> 'S fad' air chuimhne na fhuair mi fèin deth.[9]

We have to rely largely on oral tradition to know how such verses were treated. With the three-line verse, the last line only or the whole verse might be repeated. The verse repeated may be to the same melody or to a different melody. Where the verse is longer, the most popular device is to repeat the last line, usually as the first line of the next verse. (In the above example the repeated line is the end of the verse, i.e. has a closed cadence.) The Rev. William Matheson, a noted scholar and exponent of Gaelic song, thought that the repeated line or phrase may have been a reflection of a 'bridge passage' on the harp. In his edition of *Mairghread nighean Lachlainn: Song-maker of Mull*,[10] Professor Colm Ó Baoill has given several tunes for a particular song. This clarifies the system to some extent, but not where the lengths of stanza are irregular. When the verses are of a different length within the song, then the singer has to ensure that he/she finishes the melody with the right kind of cadence, either a complete one or one that directs him/her to the next verse, and that the preceding phrases blend well with each other and with the final phrase. Professor Ó Baoill's examples are among a very few published versions that exist.[11] Most often, only the melody for one verse is given, and when the lengths of verses are irregular it is almost impossible to know how to sing other verses. Matheson made a special study of it, and it was he who concluded that the metre was *Iorram*. Examples appear on the Greentrax Recordings CD *William Matheson – Gaelic Bards and Minstrels*. The type more or less disappeared from the Gaelic singers' repertory, both private and public, but Greentrax's Scottish Tradition series has already stimulated a renewed interest in it among singers. On the other hand, it has virtually gone out of fashion among poets, but Donald John MacDonald of South Uist has used it more than once, to the extent of incorporating irregular lengths of stanzas in one of his poems.[12]

AMHRÁN

Within the same regime there was a minstrel who performed the works of the poets but also composed his own particular form of poem and song, accompanying himself on the clarsach. In a similar way to the other members of the poetic hierarchy, he reported his and his patron's exploits, his family's births, marriages and deaths and, at appropriate times, the clan's genealogy. A strong esoteric feeling of pride and loyalty existed as a result of the compositions commissioned by the laird. Professor William J Watson, in the introduction to his anthology of Gaelic poetry *Bàrdachd Ghàidhlig*, maintains that at the beginning of the sixteenth century classical poetry 'was in full vigour from Lewis to Kintyre, and to a considerable extent, doubtless, on the eastern side of Gaelic Scotland'.[13] By the end of the fifteenth century, however, Gaelic society had received the first in a series of blows with the destruction of the Lordship of the Isles. The Statutes of Iona (1609) stipulated, among other rules, that the younger sons of chiefs should be educated in the Lowlands, and then the aftermath of the Jacobite risings of 1715 and 1745 accelerated the general decline of Gaelic society *vis-à-vis* its role as the background to the Gaelic poetry we have been discussing. The status of the gentry diminished, and with that the poets who could be described as professional gradually disappeared. John Maclean (1787–1848), the poet to the Laird of Coll, is given the honour of being the last professional bard, but see Margaret Lobban's reference to the role of Lachlan Livingstone in her book *Lachann Dubh a' Chrògain*.[14]

Meantime, however, there were the bards who were deemed slightly lower within the hierarchy in the aristocratic households, and they were permitted to compose the simpler form with regular stress. Performances by the minstrels of such poems were heard by the ordinary members of the household, and imitated by them. Those who admired the form used by the *filidh* did not – could not – adhere to the strict rules of *Dàn*, of course. The main composers of *Iorram* were John MacDonald (Iain Lom, c.1624–1707) and Mary MacLeod (Màiri Nighean Alasdair Ruaidh, c.1615–1707), but we cannot imagine that the type emerged suddenly within their lifetimes.

THE FOLLOWING PERIOD

Professor Watson refers to the time between 1640 and about 1830 as 'a period truly remarkable for the number of composers and the quantity and excellence of their output'.[15] We should perhaps note that this was the time when non-professional poets came into their own. Bards and minstrels certainly came more to the fore during this period. Watson maintained that poets were born, not made, and that contention is a common one to this day, even amongst poets themselves. Watson mentions 'the charm of the language itself, so copious, so flexible, and so adequate, possessing also a vocalic system difficult to match for compass and melody'.[16] This partly becomes apparent in the use of rhyme, where the same word may be used in different mutations according to its grammatical purpose and even according to its dialectic ambience. A poet will often use a pronunciation of a word that is not his or her own, but which will be recognised by the hearer because of his or her familiarity with all kinds of poetry.

The minstrels were well-travelled, not only in connection with their training, and Scottish harpers learned melodies from their contemporaries in France and Ireland. The tunes of this type are known internationally (see Fig. 13.3). The stanza is usually of four lines, although the lengths of some lines cause them to be divided and written as eight. Musically, however, the stanza is almost invariably in four phrases. If we call each musical phrase by a letter, the shape of the tune may be expressed in the formula AABA, ABBA, ABAB, or variations of those. It is not inconceivable to have a melody with no phrase repeated, but there is always a feeling of symmetry between the lines. To a listener who does not know the language, tedium is a danger in this type of structure. If you imagine, for instance, a song of five stanzas of AABA, only five of the phrases in the song are different from the other fifteen. Unfortunately, in Gaelic many songs have the same tune, and this detracts from the song if the tune is well known to a different – sometimes better – text. Add to this nowadays the strong influence of the waltz rhythm that some singers favour, and tedium is inevitable. Variety can be achieved in Gaelic by paying attention to the differing lengths of syllables, and for the song to be sung in the rhythm in which it would be spoken, but it is essential that the words are understood. The best traditional singers demonstrate that, as Anne Lorne Gillies states, 'however beautiful, haunting or dramatic the melodies are, they are almost always of secondary importance to the lyrics'.[17]

A structure that does not fit into any scheme which I have mentioned so far is where the poem is written in continuous lines, with end-rhyme throughout. There are not many of them, and they usually involve a narrative. Two in particular

Figure 13.3 Music for 'A' Fagail Bhornais'. Music transcription by Morag MacLeod, keyed by Katherine Campbell.

have been recorded by the School of Scottish Studies, and a version of one appears in its Scottish Tradition series released by Greentrax recordings, sung by Angus Kenneth MacIver. Gaelic narrative songs are different from English and Scottish ballads in that the stories are told in the first person, and the metre favoured for ballads is not popular in Gaelic.

It is logical to write the poem in lines of four stresses, in consideration of the end-rhyme. Angus Kenneth MacIver's version of the song begins:

> Tha thìd' agam **èirigh** ach a **lèir** dhomh mo **bhrògan**
> Ach a lèir dhomh mo **bhata** 's gun toir e **tacan** an **ròid** mi[18]

The other song has:

> A Mhic Dhùghaill 'ic **Ruairi** chuir am **buaireadh** am **chèill-sa**
> Dh'fhàg thu tana mo **ghruaidhean** 's chuir mo **ghruag** air dhroch
> **ghrèidheadh**.

The most common way of singing these songs is to repeat the last line as the first line of the next 'verse' or melodic unit, and that is one reason why the persistence of the end-rhyme throughout the song is important. There are several different versions of each song, and all the remaining examples of the genre are probably quite old. The structure is reminiscent of some waulking songs which, if written in the same way, would look like the above, with the internal rhymes and the end-rhymes indicated in bold, even if the choral part were to intrude after every line or half-line.

As mentioned before, the poets in the chief's hall were obliged to compose songs about the chief, much as poets laureate do for royalty. Good things would be said about the chief's family, his wife, kin from generations back, looks, prowess in sailing, hunting and fishing, and his generosity with drink whilst never collapsing under its influence. The *filidh* and the bard generally chose little else, but they did compose love poems, as Thomson points out:

> They present love as a sickness or derangement, from which only the (unattainable) desired one's kiss can liberate the sufferer. The poets revel in the paradoxes implicit in this fatal yet life-giving condition, and tantalise with anagrams and acrostics concealing the lady's name.[19]

There are many examples of such themes, especially the latter, right down to the present day, although of course the classical poetry was dependent on the regime of the laird and his followers. Women hardly came into the equation, but aristocratic women were allowed to dabble in what was the prerogative of men. There are poems from the classical period in print by Isabel, the Countess of Argyll, for example.[20] The themes used by the harper were varied and freer, but still very much concerned with eulogy and elegy as well as love and satire.

WORK SONGS, LULLABIES, DANCE SONGS

Function is a very important form of classification, and acting as accompaniment to work is one of the most important functions. Manual labour is now virtually part of rural history, but singing used to be involved in milking, churning, reaping, grinding, rowing, spinning and weaving – any activity that was best done with a steady rhythm. Most of those tasks had songs allocated to them within the tradition. I personally doubt the existence of spinning songs or weaving songs, since the rhythm of the work tends to be spasmodic, but spinners and weavers would certainly sing while they worked. A cow was believed to give a better milk yield if sung to. Live music has now been replaced with recorded, but belief in the efficacy of music in the milking parlour is still very strong! Some work songs contained references to the work in their texts, but there are so few examples of some types that we cannot infer that this was generally the case. I can think of only one churning song, and it goes:

> Mary's churning at the bottom of the glen, increasing the butter,
>   reducing the milk.
> Come, churn (bucket), come; buttermilk to fist, butter to elbow.

> There's a 'glug' here, there's a 'glag' here, there's something better than
>   we deserve here, something better than wine.

There's a glug here, there's a glag here; there's a great snail immersed
here. We have Christina's cog full of lovely yellow butter.[21]

The grinding song I can recall also has reference to the work, but it is a tease for
a spinster. She is asked to grind, with the promise of various unenticing rewards
such as the bannock the meal would produce, or a piece of hard cheese. She
replies that she will not grind, because it is not her job. Then she is promised the
son of the man of the house. The work speeds up and she says 'Yes! Yes!'

Churning required only one person, as did milking, although there was
also the cow to consider. Grinding could also be solitary, but there were sometimes
two handles in the grinding stone so that two could do it – and an illustration
in Pennant's *A Tour of Scotland* seems to show two women sharing the one long
handle. Where only one person was involved, the rhythm and speed of the song
were up to the individual. Even with the pair involved in grinding, another
element appears: the song helps the operators keep in time with each other. This
would certainly be crucial in rowing songs, and in waulking.

I do not know how song and rhythm interacted in rowing songs. For
example, in what is called 'An Iorram Niseach' (The Ness Rowing Song),
presumed to be a rowing song from some internal evidence, I do not know where
the movement of the oars came. Did it depend on the weight of the boat and the
number of the oarsmen? We have absolutely no examples of rowing to music,
though a rowing song was collected from Alasdair MacNeill of Tiree in the 1970s
and has been performed since by groups of male singers.[22] Here is how 'An
Iorram Niseach' is usually sung:

Figure 13.4 Music for 'Iomair Thusa'. Music transcription by Morag MacLeod, keyed by
Katherine Campbell.

The dips of the oars could come at a slow pace at the junction of each bar here,
but much would depend on the speed. It is, of course, an activity which is not
confined to Gaelic-speaking communities.

Rowing songs can be recognised from internal evidence within the
waulking song repertory. In Scotland there are two words to describe the finishing
of hand-woven cloth by rubbing it on to a board: waulking and fulling. In Nova
Scotia, Canada, it is referred to as milling. For a comprehensive account of all
aspects of waulking, see the three volumes of *Hebridean Folksongs*, edited by
Campbell and Collinson, especially volume 1.

Accounts of waulking from early in the eighteenth century describe it as
communal, and as women's work. John Ramsay of Ochtertyre states that women
sang 'not only at their diversions, but also during almost every kind of work
where more than one person is employed'.[23] The songs that go with waulking

are said to originate from before the seventeenth century. There are songs which have always been labelled waulking songs, and they have generally remained as the necessary accompaniment for the work in Scotland. In the areas of Gaelic diaspora in Canada, more songs of the *Amhrán* type were used as milling songs.

The main necessity for a waulking song is provision for a solo singer and a group. In general the soloist sings the meaningful text whilst the choral group sings vocables. Sometimes the choral part is made up of words and vocables, or of words only. The nature of the vocables is unique to Scottish Gaelic, consisting of sounds like *Ho, Ro, Hoireann* (approx. ho-run), *He O Ail-uh,* and so on. A cursory appraisal of the melodies would make one think that the soloist gets the simpler part, with the group able to show their vocal skills in the more easily memorised vocables.

Figure 13.5 Music for "'S muladach mi 's mi air m'aineoil'. Music transcription by Morag MacLeod, keyed by Katherine Campbell.

The words of waulking songs are varied, and more than one theme may appear in one song. Not only are they usually sung by women, but they cover themes which are of concern to women, such as praise of some young man. It is apparent that the composers of such songs follow the formulae of the classical poetry: the same terms are used of the admired heroes that the poets would use to describe their patrons – good at hunting and fishing, handsome, generous and of good lineage. The meat they ate was venison, the fish they ate was salmon, they drank wine from France and Spain. But some have the atmosphere of a discussion among young girls that would not have taken place if men were present:

> Margaret of the tricks, you have boldly slandered me. You told of me that I should be wearing the *bréid* [a head-cover which signified married status], that there was a baby concealed below my ribs. Why would you not tell the truth, as I would of you? You said spitefully that my father was in want. My father cannot be compared with yours.[24]

The song goes on in that vein. Some texts complain of being tied to an old man; some tell of sad deaths and tragic events.

Rowing songs had the same kind of structure as waulking songs, and one suspects that songs used in the waulking that seem to be from a man's point of view may have been rowing songs first.

The purpose of waulking was not just to wash the tweed but to thicken it. Any number from about six women would take part, and they sat around a board, specially made or just a door taken off its hinges. The tweed would be spread out on the board for each woman to have a piece and, having maintained a rhythm, they would beat it onto the board in unison. Waulking with the feet was practised in some island communities as late as hand-waulking – until about the 1950s – but the process was the same. In some places it was thought unlucky to have any part of the tweed with no song attached to it; in others, a lot of gossip was often incorporated into the singing and exchanged as they worked. The participants would mainly be the young women of the village.

THE TEXT CONSTRUCTION

The longest solo section is a couplet, usually interspersed with a three-line refrain. Other possibilities are: one line followed by a refrain, with sometimes the line repeated to a different refrain, and a half-line followed by a short refrain. A line has four beats. The actual work is seldom mentioned, although there is one song with the refrain:

> The lads' cloth, work on it!

And a verse says:

> What spoiled my tweed on the young woman was the tightness of the fists and the slowness of the mouths (tongues).

Famous poets, such as Duncan Ban Macintyre (1724–1812) and Alexander MacDonald (c.1695–c.1770) made waulking songs in which the work is mentioned. Duncan Ban made a long song lamenting a pet sheep. After about forty-six couplets praising her, he tells of his efforts to find another source of wool:

> Since I have now lost my ewe my raiment is like to be threadbare.

But he has high hopes of getting wool, getting it woven and waulked:

> Many a dame can make a sumptuous cloth, but, without a quartet, cannot waulk it.
> I should want the damsels of Glen Etive all to come into the township.
> When I set them well a-going, then will the tweed be shrunken.
> . . .
>
> When they sing the songs, they drive the birds into the trees.
> . . .

Each of them takes her task in hand, while her mouth will sing the
    music.
One sees to water, one to peats, another keeps the fire well trimmed;
One tramps it in a tub, one steeps it and one rinses it;
A couple pound it with vigour, and a couple wring it with strong grasp.
But before they hand it over, I'm sure it will become firm-textured.[25]

Alexander Macdonald was well known as a Jacobite poet, and he composed a
song in which the metaphor of women being invited to a waulking is maintained
through about forty couplets. The 'maidens' are the clans who, he hopes, will
come to get the Prince back to Scotland and fight for him:

O noble youth with the long hair, I hate it that you are wanting
    clothing.
Europe has put cloth in the loom for you, and until it comes out, there
    will be no peace.
But it will be woven, shaped, and waulked before the harvest of
    Michaelmas comes.
Scotland will help the waulking, if there are maidens in the kingdom.

LULLABIES

To lull a child to sleep only requires someone singing, and it does not matter
what they sing. Songs labelled 'lullabies' do also have characteristics which make
them more than just any song. The typical lullaby has repetition, say a quatrain
consisting of lines with two strong beats, repeated twice, and a final line that is
different. The tunes are very simple, pentatonic usually, but not distinctively
Gaelic. They do not in general have a lot of verses. The child is addressed,
promised pleasant pursuits tomorrow, and promised prosperity when he grows
up:

You and I will go tomorrow to the sheep's shieling.
. . . Sleep, little one, I am your granny's sister.

Oh my child will have, oh, a little piece of land hey an ha
Rum and Canna ho an ho, Oh Islay and Kintyre, ha.

Sweet as birdsong is (sung 3 times) in the early morning
More lovely is my darling (3 times) fast asleep.[26]

Songs which were previously used as milking songs are perpetuated as lullabies,
and so are songs connected with bagpipe music. There is a small number of
longer lullabies, the most famous being the lament for Gregor MacGregor of
Glenstrae, supposed to have been composed by his wife, whose father, a Campbell,
killed Gregor. Whether it was intended as a lullaby, we cannot tell, but it developed
into one with the addition of a refrain. The term for Hush! Hush! in Gaelic is *Bà*

bà – close to hush-a bye? – and these are snippets of refrain that go with different versions of the lament for Gregor:

> Bà bà bà my baby / Bà my baby, bà / Bà bà bà my baby / You are but tender.

> Ba-hoo, ba-hoo, little forlorn one / You are still only weak / and I fear the day will never come / when you will avenge your father.

> Hovan, hovan hovan eerie / Hovan eerie oh / Hovan, hovan, hovan eerie / Great, great is my sorrow.[27]

Another longer lullaby has a grave-robber theme, and as is the case with many songs in Gaelic, the story is known to anyone who sings the song, but not included in the song text. A young mother has died. Her husband sings desperately to an infant: 'Mòr, my wife, will not come home / My dear wife, Mòr, will not come / My child's mother will not come / She will not lie beside me tonight.'[28]

The story goes that she is actually listening to this lullaby. When robbers dug up her grave and tried to remove her ring, she wakened and made her way home, because she had just gone into a coma and had been buried alive!

PUIRT À BEUL

Vocal dance music has been developed to a really fine art in Gaelic, but you have to know the language to appreciate it. No translations can deal with the play on words and the dependence on the sounds of words as much as on their sense. It has similarities with the lullaby, and dandling songs, which are intended to entertain a child rather than put it to sleep, are included in the *port à beul* repertory. My heading translates 'tunes out of a mouth' and is the plural of *port à beul*. One assumes the term implies that it or they first came from somewhere else, when 'out of a mouth' is so specified. An instrumental origin can almost always be found for the tune, and a lot of different texts exist to the same tune. Themes in *puirt à beul* are varied and they are sometimes a vehicle for bawdy verse. I think inventive people saw a situation; a few words would bring a tune to mind and it was a simple matter to finish the song with a similar form to that of a lullaby; that is, a line of perhaps four beats repeated twice with a slight modification, followed by a fourth slightly different line. For dancing, this is all sung twice, and another 'verse' of the same structure is sung twice to another section of the tune. They were used for dancing when there was no instrument available. A simple example will clarify:

> 'S ann an Ile 'n Ile 'n Ile
> 'S ann an Ile rugadh mi
> 'S ann an Ile 'n Ile 'n Ile
> 'S ann an Ile bha mi.

Figure 13.6 Music for "'S ann an Ile'. Music transcription by Morag MacLeod, keyed by
Katherine Campbell.

'S ann an Ile bhòidheach
A rugadh mi 's a thogadh mi
'S ann an Ile bhòidheach
A rugadh mi 's a bha mi.[29]

RHYTHMS

I mentioned above that the performance of songs in syllabic verse has apparently
influenced singing to other kinds of verse. Syllabic verse was sung to the rhythm
of speech, and songs in the *Amhrán* metre are sung as close to speech rhythm as
is possible by singers who know the tradition well. A good rule is to keep long
syllables long and short ones short, and to place a strong beat on a syllable that
would be important in speech.

Waulking songs are different. The emphasis with all work songs is the
rhythm of the work, so that sometimes the speech rhythm could go against what
is required for the work. For example, in a song which appears in *Music from the
Western Isles* in the Scottish Tradition CD series (an example, perhaps, of a rowing
song which was incorporated into the waulking repertory, as it is in praise of a
boat), if this line was to be spoken, it would go like this (the vertical line precedes
a strong beat):

Di |luain an |dèidh Di-|Dòmhn-aich
|Dh'fhalbh sinn le |Seòn-aid à |Arc-aibh.

When sung, it is done like this:

Di |luain |an de -|idh Di |Dòmhn-aich
|Dh'fhalbh sinn |le Seòn- |aid à |Arcaibh.

This phenomenon is present in *puirt à beul* too, but it is interesting to find that it
is present in any song which has a strong rhythm, not necessarily connected
with work. Listen to Calum Johnston on the CD *Calum and Annie Johnston –
Songs, Stories and Piping from Barra* singing 'Oran don Mhusg'. This is just one
example of an *Amhrán-* type song – it is in an ABA'C structure, with A' only

slightly different from A – where stresses are placed where we would not place them in speech, in order to maintain the overall rhythm of the song.[30]

What is distinctive about Gaelic song? The language itself, obviously, but what would tell you that a song is Gaelic in origin if you did not know? Without benefit of the words, certain songs we can hear in Scotland could equally belong to the Isle of Man, Lowland Scotland or even parts of continental Europe. Many anthologies of Gaelic songs have names of tunes written at the tops of pages, the names not always being Gaelic names. 'The Lass of Patie's Mill' is suggested for Alexander MacDonald's 'Allt an t-Siùcair' (The Sugar Brook). He composed several of his poems to Lowland and English airs. For more instances of tunes from outside the Gaelic world, see *The Blind Harper* and *Songs of John MacCodrum* by the Rev. William Matheson. 'Loch Lomond', 'Spancil Hill', 'Woo'd and Married an' Aa' and 'The Flowers of Edinburgh' are among the tunes that are used for Gaelic songs perpetually, and they are thus named because that is the tune most likely to be known to the reader, not because it is the first-known example of it. They are not always sung exactly the same to each song. What the songs have in common is their four-square structure, as I have outlined regarding *Amhrán* metre. The same tune is sung to Duncan Ban Macintyre's 'Coire Cheathaich' (The Misty Corry) and to John Maclean of Tiree's song of complaint on arriving in Canada, 'A' Choille Ghruamach' (The Gloomy Forest), and to a song of regret for leaving a place called Bornish in South Uist (see Fig. 13.3).

The remnants of syllabic metre as depicted in the Heroic ballads and in songs which have their prototype in Julia MacDonnell's lament for Alasdair of Glengarry, along with the *Iorrams* – in which one verse may contain a different number of lines or musical phrases from another – work songs, lullabies and *puirt à beul*, however distinctive the non-Gaelic speaker may find them for other reasons, all have in common that the Gaels have a predilection for the pentatonic scale, and for modes which are not just major and minor. *Amhrán* metre songs have this characteristic too, as can be seen in the above example. It was not, and perhaps is not, unique to Gaelic within Scotland, but our isolation has caused it to become more established here than elsewhere.

A custom which began in the south of England in the wake of the Reformation, created then because church singing had previously been the prerogative of a trained choir, came to be called 'putting-out-the-line'. This was so that a congregation could take part in the sung worship, and that consisted of the Psalms of David, from the Old Testament, which had been translated into a metrical form. Because many could not read, and there were not enough copies available anyway, a person was elected to read a line at a time, to be repeated by the congregation. The metre chosen was ballad or common metre, and folk tunes from Britain and Europe were adapted for the singing. Chanting the line and ornamenting the congregational melody were developments that spread throughout and into Scotland, and it eventually spread into Gaelic Protestant churches. The metre used in Gaelic Psalms is also ballad metre. Putting-out-the-line was used in English-speaking congregations until fairly recently, and may still be heard occasionally in the Free Presbyterian church, but it is really now a distinguishing feature of Gaelic worship. Only about twenty-three tunes are used and, in spite of Psalmody classes, where the written tunes would be taught, they were learned with a more lasting effect through oral transmission. Thus there came about a modifying of any major, in particular, but also straightforward minor elements in the written versions of the tunes. Were an interval to be introduced which was not familiar in the tradition, a note would be changed to conform to the indigenous idiom.

There are only two songs in Gaelic in ballad metre. One uses the tune of 'Barbara Allan', which many of my generation learned – in English of course – in school. Two of the tunes for 'Barbara Allan' have been adopted for Gaelic songs. One is a song of lament for the deserted countryside in Argyll where Dr MacLachlan of Rahoy (1804–1874) lived. Another was composed by John Maclennan in Tolsta in Lewis as the reminiscences of a sailor about the good things he misses when away from home. My additional bar of music gives a little indication of the traditional way of singing Barbara Allan, but over the years the tune we learned in school has become more and more the norm.

Figure 13.7 Music for 'Barbara Allan'. Music transcription by Morag MacLeod, keyed by Katherine Campbell.

HYMNS

The singing of hymns in public worship in Gaelic was until recently virtually confined to islands in Argyllshire where, early in the nineteenth century, Baptist congregations were formed in places like Tiree, Coll, Colonsay and Mull. Hymns were composed with original tunes or given melodies already known for secular songs or for the pipes, and were used in those congregations. In other Gaelic areas hymns are confined to private performance within the home. Published anthologies are available, and many households have their own handwritten collections. Familiar secular tunes to suit are chosen by the singer and the hymns are read rather than known by heart.

In 1970, when Catholic congregations were permitted to use vernacular languages for worship, there was a scarcity of Gaelic hymns, and steps were taken by the diocese of Argyll and the Isles to rectify this. A book of hymns, *Seinnibh dhan Tighearna* (Sing to the Lord), suitable for use in Catholic churches was produced in 1986. It features new texts with new melodies, but English-language hymns in translation were also included with their original tunes.

WHERE ARE WE NOW?

There is far more attention paid now to the traditional versions of songs, and there are far more of them available. The School of Scottish Studies holds a rich treasury of traditional material in both Scots and Gaelic, but while the best tradition-bearers were alive there were slight reservations about releasing that material to the general public. The role of the Royal National Mod competition for singing a song in the traditional manner became more important in 1971, when better prizes were offered. The prescribed songs began to be written in a more authentic way, and the stipulation that 'Gaelic stresses and vowel values take precedence' began to be better understood by non-Gaelic-speaking adjudicators, so that they began to consult their fellow language adjudicators more. But gradually the line between traditional and modern has become blurred so that singers enter for both of the two important adult competitions, the Gold Medal and the medal for traditional singing. The prescribed songs for the Gold Medal are more traditional, and the singers do not necessarily have the highly trained voices that used to be a requirement. In the traditional song competition few adjudicators will be bold enough to choose a singer who does not have a fairly sophisticated voice, and many do not know what the difference between the two norms is.

Many singers learn well what is required for the competition and, if they win, very quickly go into a studio to record a CD. What I said at the beginning of this chapter about standards of taste then comes into play, and singers who are on CD – or albums – become the approved standard.

On the other hand, winning a medal at the Mod is not necessary now for success. The *Fèisean* movement began in 1991, and there are now forty-three events every year at which young people can get tuition in instrumental music and Gaelic. An important festival began in South Uist in 1998, called Ceòlas (difficult to translate, but something like 'musicness'), mainly for adult students. It attracts large numbers from the UK and abroad, who learn Gaelic songs amongst other music skills. At secondary level, the School for Excellence in Music in Plockton, Ross-shire includes Gaelic song in its curriculum. The Royal Conservatoire of Scotland, formerly the Royal Scottish Academy of Music and Drama in Glasgow, has Gaelic Song as part of its BA degree in Scottish Music, and Gaelic song is taught in degrees offered by the University of the Highlands and Islands. All of these breed talented performers, and they are much more familiar with the singing of genuine tradition-bearers than used to be the case. The accompaniments to Gaelic songs are much more acceptable to Gaelic speakers now, because more instrumentalists are familiar with the songs and they do not mould them into conventional Western European modes, as was the tendency previously. They are all to be heard and seen on radio and television. Television programmes have also given scope for more use of original and translated hymns.

The digitisation of the archives at the School of Scottish Studies, the BBC and John Lorne and Margaret Fay Campbell's collection in Canna, makes a wonderful selection of Gaelic songs available online through Tobar an Dualchais / Kist o Riches. The only cloud on the horizon for the song tradition is that so few young fluent Gaelic speakers are interested, and those who are interested do not always care about the language. Young singers who do not speak Gaelic have an incredible command of the sounds and give convincing performances of the most tender of songs, but it is a pity that there are not more singers who are native speakers. One cannot help but feel that the latter would appreciate better the subtle nuances of the language and its connections with the history and music. But there are fine examples in both categories, and Tobar an Dualchais/Kist o Riches has placed the traditional material into a secure and accessible state for their inspiration and use.

NOTES

1 Since the early 1980s known as the Royal National Mod, it is a yearly Gaelic-language competitive festival with a strong emphasis on singing competitions.

2 *Scottish Studies*, (1957), 95–151.

3 The BBC began sporadic Gaelic broadcasting in 1923, but a Gaelic producer was appointed in 1935. Output expanded gradually, until now Gaelic programmes may be heard from 7.30 a.m. until 11.30 p.m., with a lesser schedule on Sundays. For more details of the history of the network, see Thomson, 1983, 26, 27.

4 Gillies, 2005, xxi.

5 Marquis of Clanricarde, *Memoirs* (Dublin, 1744), cviii–cvix, quoted in Thomson, 1983, 258–9.

6 Thomson, 1983, 258, quoting from *Martin's Description of the Western Isles* [1703]; *Martin's Voyage to St Kilda* [1698]; *Monro's Description of the Western Isles In 1549*, ed. D J MacLeod, Stirling, 1934, 176–7.

7 Thomson, 1983, 189–90.

8 Bruford, A. Gaelic Bards and their themes, *Folk Review* (January 1979), 5.

9 Mary MacLeod. *A Lament for Sir Norman MacLeod*, CDTRAX 9016D (see booklet accompanying CD) 'An ungentle shower came anew which tore our sails and broke our helm and our good compass, and our support, and the friendship in music that we enjoyed in your delightful house.
'Our loss is great, enclosed in the grave, our wealth, our success, our care and our pride, and our sport with no gloom. The amount I received of it is well remembered.' Translation from Scottish Tradition 16, Iorram, Track 14.

10 Ó Baoill, 2009.

11 Ó Baoill, 2009, 224–8.

12 Innes, 1998, 204, 206 and 302–3.

13 Watson, 1976, xviii.

14 Lobban, M D. *Lachann Dubh a' Chrògain* (*Lachlan Livingstone and his grandsons*), Iona, 2004.

15 Watson, 1976, xix.

16 Watson, 1976, xix.

17 Gillies, 2005, xx.

18 See *Music from the Western Isles*, CDTRAX 9002.

19 Thomson, 1983, 293.
20 Watson, 1934, 234–5, 307–8.
21 *Clò Dubh, Clò Donn* (Gaelic songs by various singers), Greentrax CD.
22 'Alla Bharra Bò Choisinn Cò-Bheag', sung by Alasdair MacNeill, recorded for the School of Scottish Studies Archives by Margaret Mackay, SA1977/77/B7.
23 MacInnes, J. *Music from the Western Isles*, CDTRAX 9002, CD notes.
24 This song comes from the oral (sung) tradition and takes its title from the first few words, which are in Gaelic 'Och, a Mhaighread nan cuiread'.
25 MacLeod, 1952, 140.
26 My translation.
27 My translations, with an attempt at anglicisation of vocables.
28 My translation.
29 'Twas in Islay, Islay, Islay / Twas in Islay I was born and lived. Twas in bonny Islay that I was born and raised', etc.
30 MacLeod, M. An Ceangal a tha Eadar Ceòl is Faclan ann an Orain Ghàidhlig (The connection between music and words in Gaelic songs). In Ó Baoill and McGuire, 2002, 35–44.

BIBLIOGRAPHY AND FURTHER READING

Cameron, H, ed. *Na Bàird Thirisdeach*, Glasgow, 1932.
Campbell, J C and Collinson, F. *Hebridean Folksongs: A Collection of Waulking Songs*, 3 vols, Oxford, 1969–81.
Gillies, A L. *Songs of Gaelic Scotland*, Edinburgh, 2005.
Innes, B, ed. *Chi mi: Bardachd Dhomhnaill Iain Dhonnchaidh*, Edinburgh, 1998.
Kennedy-Fraser, M. *Songs of the Hebrides*, 3 vols, London, 1909–22.
MacDonald, A. *Story and Song from Loch Ness-Side*, Inverness, 1914.
MacDonald, K N. *The Gesto Collection of Highland Music*, reprint, Wales, 1997.
MacDonald, K M. *Puirt-à-Beul: The Vocal Dance Music of the Scottish Gaels*, ed. W Lamb, Upper Breakish, 2012.
MacLeod, D J. *Donnchadh Bàn Mac an t-Saoir*, Inverness, n.d.
Macpherson, J. *Fragments of Ancient Poetry*, Edinburgh, 1760.
Macpherson, J. *Fingal: An Epic Poem*, London, 1761 and 1762.
Macpherson, J. *Temora: An Epic Poem*, London, 1763.
Martin, C. *Orain an Eilein, Gaelic Songs of Skye*, Isle of Skye, 2001.
Ó Baoill, C, ed. *Duanaire Colach 1537–1757*, Aberdeen, 1997.
Ó Baoill, C, ed. *Gàir nan Clàrsach – The Harp's Cry*, Edinburgh, 1994.
Ó Baoill, C, ed. *Iain Dubh*, Aberdeen, 1994.
Ó Baoill, C, ed. *Mairghread nighean Lachlainn: Song-maker of Mull*, Scottish Gaelic Texts Society, n.p., 2009.
Ó Baoill, C and McGuire, N R, eds. *Rannsachadh na Gàidhlig, Papers Read at the Conference, Scottish Gaelic Studies, 2000*, Aberdeen, 2002.
Patrick, M. *Four Centuries of Scottish Psalmody*, London, 1949.
Pennant, T. *A Tour in Scotland*, London, 1772.
Ramsay, J, (of Ochtertyre). *Scotland and Scotsmen in the Eighteenth Century*, ed. A Allardyce, Edinburgh and London, 1888.
Ross, J. A Classification of Gaelic Folk-Song, *Scottish Studies*, 1 (1957), 95–151.
Thomson, D, ed. *The Companion to Gaelic Scotland*, Oxford, 1983.
Watson, J. Carmichael, *Gaelic songs of Mary MacLeod*, London and Glasgow, 1934.
Watson, W J. *Bàrdachd Ghàidhlig (Gaelic Poetry 1550–1900)*, Inverness, 4th edn, 1976.

Watson, W J. *Scottish Verse from the Book of the Dean of Lismore*, Edinburgh, 1937.

SCOTTISH GAELIC TEXTS SOCIETY VOLUMES, CONTAINING ENGLISH TRANSLATIONS AND MUSIC EXAMPLES

Campbell, J L, ed. *Highland Songs of the Forty-Five*, Edinburgh, 1983.
MacLeod, A, ed. *Orain Dhonnchaidh Bhàin, The Songs of Duncan Ban Macintyre*, Edinburgh, 1952.
Matheson, W, ed. *The Songs of John MacCodrum*, Edinburgh, 1938.
Matheson, W, ed. *The Blind Harper*, Edinburgh, 1970.
Ó Baoill, C, ed. *Mairghread nighean Lachlainn*, Edinburgh, 2009.

JOURNALS

Eigse, 1939–present
Eilean Fraoich, first published 1938, revised and expanded, 1982
Scottish Studies, 1957–present
Tocher, 1971–present

DISCOGRAPHY

All of the following are in the Greentrax Recordings 'Scottish Tradition' series

Music from the Western Isles, CDTRAX 9002.
Waulking Songs from Barra, CDTRAX 9003.
Gaelic Psalms from Lewis, CDTRAX 9006.
Calum Ruadh, Bard of Skye, CDTRAX 9007.
James Campbell of Kintail – Gaelic Songs, CDTRAX 9008.
Calum and Annie Johnston – Songs, Stories and Piping from Barra, CDTRAX 9013D.
William Matheson – Gaelic Bards and Minstrels, CDTRAX 9016D.
Clò Dubh, Clò Donn (Gaelic songs by various singers), CDTRAX 9018.
Joan MacKenzie –Seonag NicCoinnich, CDTRAX 9019.
The Carrying Stream (Gaelic and Scots songs, instrumental music, compilation), CDTRAX 9020.
Wooed and Married and Aa (Scots and Gaelic songs, tunes and customs), CDTRAX 9023.

14 Custom, Belief and Folk Drama

NEILL MARTIN

This chapter explores two interrelated areas of ethnological enquiry, those of custom and belief and traditional drama. A case study combines both.

In the field of ethnology in the Scottish context, the study of custom and belief is taken to mean the analysis of traditional cultural forms of the secular kind such as those associated with the calendar and lifecycle, and of traditional belief such as the evil eye or supernatural entities. The study of the nature of belief in the context of mainstream religion is usually considered a separate strand of ethnological discourse, designated 'the ethnology of religious expression' or similar. However, the study of lifecycle traditions of Christian origin, such as baptism and marriage, has formed and still forms an important strand of ethnological enquiry. A distinction may be drawn between ethnological work which seeks to understand popular usages and conceptions of lifecycle customs and those which focus on these rituals in the context of Christianity or other faiths. The distinction may be seen today as rather arbitrary, but likely stems from the desire to separate indigenous folk belief and Christian tradition in the minds of early ethnologists, who approached their craft in the context of an intellectual climate characterised by widespread Christian observance. Even today, the ethnologist espousing an interest in custom and belief is more likely to be found investigating local festivals or sightings of trows than collecting descriptions of the physical appearance of angels or contemporary Jewish festivals. Indeed, one of the thorniest areas of ethnological enquiry in this area is where indigenous belief and Christian observance collide, such as in second sight (where the Christian dimension may loom large) or in divinatory traditions, of which, on paper at least, mainstream religions generally disapprove, but which many adherents to Christian teachings practise.

We may say that topics such as the investigation of the nature of religious belief, its rituals as practised among active believers and practitioners, and the day-to-day influence and integration of religious teachings in the lives of individuals and groups fall under the heading of the ethnology or anthropology of religion. The ethnologist of custom and belief is more likely to focus on secular tradition, such as the preparatory phases leading to marriage, or the marriage rituals themselves where those taking part are not active members of a particular religion following the 'script' but rather espouse popular conceptions and create customised iterations of this ritual event. The emphasis of the ethnologist will be on questions such as the nature, function and symbolic content of customary tradition and patterns of (largely secular) belief. The exploration and understanding of the event or belief itself is central, as opposed to using these to provide the springboard for the analysis of wider societal topics such as gender relations, church membership, demographic change in communities, and studies of class or taste, which fall more naturally under the headings of sociology and social anthropology.

In the context of Scottish ethnology, by 'traditional drama' we chiefly refer to a tradition which takes the form of a play with script and characters performed in front of onlookers. The example for which we have the best evidence is the folk play usually termed 'Galoshins', a 'death and revival' drama formerly performed around the year beginnings of Hallowe'en or Hogmanay.[1] Brian Hayward argues that Kirk Session records point to its being performed as early as 1701, but we are perhaps on safer ground to say that there is good evidence to suggest Galoshins was a popular seasonal tradition in the nineteenth and early twentieth centuries.[2]

Walter Scott describes the arrival of the guisers at Abbotsford on the first of January 1825:

> Yesterday being Hogmanay, there was a constant succession of Guisards – i.e., boys dressed up in fantastic caps, with their shirts over their jackets, and with wooden swords in their hands. These players acted a sort of Scene before us, of which the hero was one Goloshin, who gets killed in a 'battle for love,' but is presently brought to life again by a doctor of the party.[3]

This kind of seasonal drama, in which two adversaries fight, then one is killed and revived, is still found in many locations in England along with several other related dramatic traditions, such as sword-dance plays. The rude health of these dramas in England is amply demonstrated by the hundreds of texts of contemporary accounts available on the folk play website maintained by the University of Sheffield. In Scotland, Galoshins appears not to have survived as an adult tradition beyond World War II, although it continued in a revived form among schoolchildren in the town of Biggar until relatively recently, where the play was taught by a local museum director who had performed it as a boy.[4] Galoshins was a tradition of southern Scotland.

Scholars continue to work on collecting and analysing this play. In 2002 I was fortunate enough to film a solo rendition of Galoshins, given from memory by a gentleman in his nineties.[5] A fuller discussion of the Galoshins play is given in volume 10 of this *Scottish Life and Society* series.[6]

In a diary entry of 1814, Walter Scott recalls a visit to Shetland that year, where he was told of a sword-dance drama involving seven 'warriors':

> At Scalloway my curiosity was gratified by an account of the sword-dance, now almost lost, but still practiced in the Island of Papa . . . There are eight performers, seven of whom represent the Seven Champions of Christendom, who enter one by one with their swords drawn, and are presented to the eighth personage, who is not named. Some rude couplets are spoken (in *English*, not *Norse*), containing a sort of panegyric upon each champion

as he is presented. They then dance a sort of cotillion, as the ladies described it, going through a number of evolutions with their swords. One of my three Mrs. Scotts readily promised to procure me the lines, the rhymes, and the form of the dance. I regret much that young Mr. Scott was absent during this visit . . . probably I might have interested him in preserving this dance, by causing young persons to learn it. A few years since a party of Papa-men came to dance the sword-dance at Lerwick as a public exhibition with great applause. The warlike dances of the northern people, of which I conceive this to be the only remnant in the British dominions, are repeatedly alluded to by their poets and historians.[7]

Scott includes a romanticised version of the above description in his novel *The Pirate* (1822). Aside from a brief allusion that Scott makes to a chapbook describing a sword dance performed by fishermen in Buckhaven in Fife, there is little evidence that this was a tradition found outside Shetland.[8] The Papa Stour sword dance is flourishing, as confirmed by the many performances available to view on the internet.[9] It is important to note that these modern versions are dances, as opposed to a play with words incorporating dance, which is what Scott and his contemporaries were describing. The text of the Papa Stour play is discussed below.

This is not to say that these are our only examples of traditions with a performative aspect. Seasonal guising traditions involve dressing up, adopting a persona, following a particular pre-determined sequence of actions and using space in a marked kind of way (such as the threshold to the home) which distinguishes it from the usual. Indeed much the same could be said of rituals that have a dramatic aspect, such as those connected with marriage, which feature costume, an inherited traditional script and performers with 'lines' which are to be said in the right order, this all taking place in a defined performance space. The Gaelic *Oidhche Challain* or Hogmanay features a guising tradition of house-visiting, which in the past was highly ritualised, involving the use of animal disguise, chanting, special rhymes and the passing round of the *caisean-uchd*, the singed neck-part of a sheep.[10] The tradition is still to be found in various locations, including South Uist and Eriskay.[11] I noted a ritual dramatic dimension to the Gaelic betrothal ritual *rèiteach* where, in a re-run of an earlier meeting between the two families about to be joined, a 'false bride' motif is acted out. The meeting is the *rèiteach mòr* at which, the union of the young couple having been agreed at the *rèiteach beag*, a replaying of this latter, private meeting is arranged for the benefit of a wider group of people. At this, instead of the young woman being presented to her prospective family-in-law straight away, a succession of 'false brides' is brought in for comic effect. These typically feature the young woman's elderly or married relatives, who are decorously rejected by the groom's side in a humorous and witty manner. Several fundamental elements suggestive of drama may be identified: the women to be 'rejected' wait their turn 'off-stage'; they are cued by someone who has taken charge of the timing of the event; the play-space is prepared in advance; a heightened form of speaking is expected (the performance often relies heavily on the ability to use allegory); and onlookers have gathered for the purposes of entertainment.[12]

We may observe that these dramatic forms – including the folk play proper with its main and supporting cast, and sometimes music and song – may be seen as more redolent of rituals which contain dramatic elements, rather than being akin to anything we might call a play in a theatrical context. The ritual dimension is discussed in more detail below, but suffice it to say that there is little agreement on what 'folk drama' or 'traditional drama' is. Here is how the *Concise Oxford Companion to the Theatre* defines the folk play:

> Folk Play, rough-and-ready dramatic entertainments given at village festivals by the villagers themselves. They were derived from the dramatic tendencies inherent in primitive folk festivals, and were given on May-Day, at Harvest Home, or at Christmas, when to the central theme of a symbolic death and resurrection, which comes from remotest antiquity, were added the names and feats of local worthies. Later, though not before 1596, these were replaced by the Seven Champions of Christendom or other heroes, probably under the influence of the village schoolmaster (cf. Holofernes in *Love's Labour's Lost*). As patron saint of England, St George may have figured among them from the earliest times. With some dramatic action went a good deal of song and dance. Practically no written records of the folk play survive, and it contributed very little to the main current of modern drama, but its early influence should not on that account be entirely disregarded.[13]

One scarcely knows where to begin with the demolition of this text, published not fifty years ago but in 1996. The online version dates from 2012. Even if we still have 'villagers' in our midst, with their primitive tendencies to dramatic expression, we know such plays were not always performed at village festivals, but many – perhaps most – were visiting customs. The past tense is used throughout, but of course these plays were being performed in 1996 and still are today.[14] That the plays are mobile is true of the English tradition, which is clearly referred to here, as well as our Scottish Galoshins, and Welsh and Irish tradition too. 'Some dramatic action' is grudgingly acknowledged, but this is seen as a dead form, a minor historical footnote.

The Golden Bough: A Study in Magic and Religion by Sir James George Frazer (1854–1941) was the origin of the thesis that folk drama is a survival of a pre-Christian fertility ritual, with the slain-then-revived hero at the centre of Galoshins and its English analogues illustrating the 'dying god' thesis. This had considerable traction among early theatre historians. The most eminent scholars of traditional drama were still holding to this theory of origins in 1967 when they noted that 'the necessity for a physically fit king, and the need to kill him before he weakens, is still a living belief', referring to an article in the *Radio Times* from four years before. This is confidently developed to reach the conclusion: 'Thus, we can carry back the themes of our Play to the earliest periods of history and say that they most probably have their roots in pre-history.'[15] This reading continued into the next decade, notably with Alan Brody's *The English Mummers and their Plays: Traces of Ancient Mystery* (1970).

Considering drama as text is another problem area, and a cursory glance at the material gathered on the folk play website mentioned above reveals that even today far more effort goes into the comparative analysis of versions of a particular play than into the context in which they are performed, performance features, the motivations which drive individuals to get involved, and so on. A computer programme has been developed to assist in the comparison of large numbers of play texts, although we may note that the author of this ingenious tool cites the discovery of a 'proto text' from which all others are apparently derived as one of the chief discoveries, demonstrating a continuing fascination with origins.[16] I am not certain this takes us very far in understanding the nature and role of these cultural phenomena. It seems that just as we learn to read drama at school as text, so it is with many who study the dramatic form under discussion. As an ethnologist, I believe that in order to reveal what these plays are actually doing in the lives of people and why they are perpetuated, what meanings individuals attach to them and how they are understood, we must go out and ask questions of those who perform them and those who observe them. There really is no alternative, unless we are to consider them as mere text, as performed text, where the textual has primacy and the rest of this complex, three-dimensional, ephemeral event which takes place in front of our eyes is of little import. In contrast, it seems to me that the scholarly community who work with traditional narrative have long since given up the search for the origins and proto-text of, say, Rumplestiltskin.

KEY THINKERS

In this section, I offer a highly personal selection of a few scholars whose work in my view has had the greatest influence on the study of custom, belief and traditional drama, seeking a balance between historical and contemporary scholarship.

From the very beginning of our discipline, it was 'popular religion', 'popular mythology' and the 'curious customs' of the rural population that were uppermost in the minds of folklorists. In the celebrated 1846 letter to the *Athenaeum* by William John Thoms (1803–1885) in which the term 'folk-lore' was first used, he observes:

> No one who has made the manners, customs, observances, superstitions, ballads, proverbs, &c., of the olden time his study, but must have arrived at two conclusions:– the first, how much that is curious and interesting in these matters is now entirely lost – the second, how much may be rescued by timely exertion.

He goes on to exhort the readership to set about collecting then forwarding to the magazine 'some record of old Time – some recollection of a now neglected custom – some fading legend, local tradition or fragmentary ballad'.[17]

This emphasis on collecting in the field – inspired by the model presented by the Grimms – makes Thoms a key thinker in the history of the discipline. It is not enough, he seems to say, to note down examples of nursery rhymes as mere text, as was done by earlier scholars of 'popular literature'; we must also know *how* they are used in context, through the observation of tradition as action. He describes a divinatory rhyme given by the Grimms, which connects the cuckoo and cherries. Thoms knows of a similar rhyme which also has a divinatory function:

> A friend has communicated to me that children in Yorkshire were formerly (and may be still) accustomed to sing round a cherry-tree the following invocation:
>
> Cuckoo, Cherry-tree,
> Come down and tell me
> How many years I have to live.
>
> Each child then shook the tree, – and the number of cherries which fell betokened the years of its future life. The nursery rhyme I have quoted, is, I am aware, well-known. But the manner in which it was applied is not recorded by Hone, Brand or Ellis:– and is one of those facts which, trifling in themselves, become of importance when they form links in a great chain.[18]

This is important; unlike earlier scholars, Thoms is advocating the wholesale collection of not just text but living traditional forms which may not be complete or seem particularly important in isolation but which have value when placed into a larger interpretative model – the 'bigger picture'. The text alone would give us the divinatory function and the key information: that cuckoos and cherries are linked in this tradition. However, through observation of the tradition as a living form, we get confirmation that this was something which belonged to the world of children, that it was sung rather than spoken and that it was a group activity. The extra information imparted by means of observation is classically ethnological; we want to collect and understand not just the surface form, but the impulse which generates it, the context in which it is performed and used, and how it fits into the wider tradition of comparable forms. We note Thom's remark 'may be still' – this issue cannot be settled by 'armchair scholarship', only by going to the location mentioned.

'Armchair scholarship' is of course the easy criticism commonly levelled at Frazer's monumental *The Golden Bough: A Study of Magic and Religion*, a vast comparative study first published in two volumes in 1890 and expanded twenty years later into twelve volumes plus a supplement. It had an enormous and lasting impact on many areas of scholarship, notably the fledgling field of anthropology. We cannot enter into a detailed summary or critical appreciation of the work here, but it is necessary to reflect on its contribution to the development of our discipline, notably the academic study of the areas of ethnological enquiry under discussion. Frazer shows that the study of myth is of profound importance to understanding not just religion past and present, but secular tradition. His central thesis – that society evolves in a natural progression from magic to religion to science – may not be accepted in our day, but there is still much of value in Frazer's work. On a basic level, the sheer volume of comparative material on ritual, magical beliefs and recurrent motifs is astonishing. His 'two laws' of magic, the sympathetic and the homeopathic, are still entirely relevant today, and frequent reference may be found to them. However, the real achievement of his work is to discuss culture, religion and myth objectively, avoiding a theological interpretation. Controversial at the time (for example, the life of Jesus is essentially discussed in a comparative light) Frazer laid the ground for the disciplines of anthropology and ethnology. From a methodological standpoint, his observations were drawn from the comparison of material collected from printed studies dealing with widely disparate societies and time periods, an approach which differs greatly from the ethnographic norms of today, which stress collection and observation in the field.[19] Crucially, Frazer provides very little context for the items of cultural practice he selects, which is a major failing from the modern standpoint. He collects together, for instance, many examples of fire-festivals from all over the world and seeks to marshal them together in support of his emerging thesis. In addition, modern ethnologists are alert to the hazards of what we might term 'non-genetic' comparison: we are comfortable with working with Scottish, Irish and Welsh material side by side; less so with Scottish, Inuit and Polynesian. However, cross-cultural studies are by no means outdated. Frazer blazed a trail in comparative scholarship and the relevance of the study of mythological systems to contemporary society.

A major theme in the area of custom and belief is the study of calendar customs, many examples of which Frazer detailed and sought to place in his overarching system. By calendar customs we mean those rituals and traditions associated with key points in the year such as New Year or harvest. In Scotland, several calendars – or systems of ordering time – may be seen to have operated. For example, in Yule and midsummer traditions we see a reflection of a calendar based on equinoxes and solstices, temporal junctures which many magnificent monuments such as the Ring of Brodgar in Orkney were likely created to predict. In our Samhain (or Hallowe'en) and Beltane traditions we see evidence of a calendar more geared to an agricultural context, for example in traditions associated with transhumance. Samhain was the eve of the New Year, and Beltane the eve of summer; in the former, animals were taken from their winter pastures, and at Beltane to their summer grazing ground. The liturgical calendar, based on the life of Jesus Christ, sees a clustering of important days between His birth and resurrection, coinciding with the crucial growing season. Pope Gregory's innovations in 1582, where ten days were removed from the calendar and the 'new style' Gregorian replaced the Julian, completes the list of calendrical systems known to have operated in the Scottish context.[20] The interface between these temporal systems gives rise to many interesting areas of enquiry. Many hundreds of pages in folklore collections have been devoted to detailing the rituals associated with the marking of important points in, or units of, time. Ploughing traditions, hiring fairs, guising, bonfires, processions – the list is long, and early scholarship is replete with detailed summaries that can be put to good use by modern ethnologists. What these old studies lack in critical or theoretical sophistication they more than make up for in providing us with what are often first-hand accounts of how individuals and communities managed and marked time, information on the symbolic world in which they lived and insights into how they understood their environment.

The analysis of the structural underpinning to rituals and other traditions associated with social time had its origins in the work of pioneering scholar Arnold van Gennep (1873–1957). In his seminal study *The Rites of Passage* (1909) he describes lifecycle rituals as being characterised by a sequential tripartite structure of separation, transition and incorporation. The initiate, or person undergoing the ritual, is first separated from their initial state. This need not mean a physical separation, but the notional ending of a prior state, examples of which might be a baby leaving the womb or a woman her family home and single status. A period of transition follows, in which the individual is 'betwixt and between' – they are no longer connected to the prior state, nor have they yet joined the group or state to which they will progress. Ritual exists to manage this transition, and during this phase they do not fit into the accepted categories of social status. This in-between state explains the historical anxiety surrounding the risk to children who are born but not yet baptised and named, as well as the ridicule and teasing associated with hen and stag nights, still observable in contemporary wedding customs. In the latter example, the individual is marked because they are neither bachelor nor married. This chaotic state of affairs may be linked with ideas of being 'unclean', hence our Scottish traditions of washing the feet of brides- and grooms-to-be and 'blackening', where popular substances like boot polish, tar and porridge may be combined to striking effect.[21] The incongruity and lack of status indicated by the transitional phase is resolved by means of the final ritual stage, that of incorporation, where the individual is accepted as a new member of the social group. The child is baptised and named and thus, in the Christian tradition, known to God and protected. The bride joins the ranks of married women, with a symbol of her new status – the ring – and usually a change of name as well.

Van Gennep's model allows us to see the common structural relationship between rites of passage. As Alan Dundes observes, in the past folklorists tended to consider different rituals separately – van Gennep's work anticipated structuralism by several decades.[22]

Researching traditional cultural forms such as marriage traditions may seem the ultimate in 'old hat' ethnology, but it remains the case that these rituals persist, and must do so for a reason, this alone justifying their investigation.[23] In our modern, atomised society, we rarely feel what we might call 'the weight of tradition', the sense of colliding with society's expectations of us as we move through social time. The number of apprentices likely to be mercilessly teased or sent 'for a long stand' (a workplace initiation rite) has dwindled, and the significance of 'coming of age' or having 'a key to the door' is scarcely discernible. However, highly charged rituals such as those connected with marriage and death continue to function to make sense of these transitional phases in our lives and the lives of others, and are replete with symbolic content, little of which is understood by those taking part. One thing that the individual at the centre of ritual activity in our era does recognise, however, is that something out of the ordinary is expected of them. Friends and relatives will have strong ideas about what is acceptable or not as regards behaviour and dress, normal time is somehow suspended for the duration, and the ritual makes its demands regardless of social status. For every couple deciding on a service on the beach at Tahiti, in a chapel in Las Vegas, underwater, or as they plunge to earth from a light aircraft there will be many, many others choosing the 'traditional' route, emulating generations who have come before in movement, dress and speech. All those about to be married will sense the weight of tradition and what it means to be part of a wider group with clear social norms. It is not just that we replicate the cultural script of marriage ritual generation after generation because it has 'aye been', but that in so doing we demonstrate its utility in providing a mechanism which harmonises that which was formerly separate and which proclaims the creation of a new family and, with it, its fertile promise.

Although van Gennep is known in the English-language world chiefly for his *Rites of Passage*, it should be remembered that he is considered to be the father of French ethnology, producing several masterly and comprehensive studies of the folk traditions of that country.[24]

The Scottish anthropologist Victor Turner found van Gennep's ideas to be of great use in his own work in African tribal society, further developing this structural model and placing special emphasis on the exploration of the transitional (or in Turner's term 'liminal') phase. Turner belongs in our 'key thinkers' section because of the contribution he makes to understanding the function of these rituals in engineering social change and solving social disharmony. He believed that social rituals had a role to play in changing attitudes and might have therapeutic value for both individuals and communities. Rituals make individuals aware of the structure of their society and therefore more able to comment on and change or challenge this structure. The performative and dramatic aspects of ritual were of great importance to Turner, and his emphasis was on the liminal phase, since this is where individual's role in the existing structure is in flux, indicating the potential for change that can emerge from this period of disorder.[25] There are links here to a comparable function that Bakhtin argued for in discussing the liminal period we call carnival, when 'normal time' and the usual hierarchical structure is suspended and new potentialities revealed through a period of licence and disorder. Individuals, he argued, could engage in a kind of dialogue with the authorities during this period of temporal flux.[26]

The study of calendars and related cultural forms moved to a new level of sophistication and significance in 1990 with the publication of Emily Lyle's *Archaic Cosmos*. Lyle, a pioneering scholar in the area of cosmology, has done much to reveal the deep structure and symbolic significance of the calendar, her exploration into archaic calendrical systems and associated cognitive patternings bringing new insights into the Celtic year.[27] Earlier scholarship such as Alwyn and Brinley Rees' *Celtic Heritage* undertook an exploration of the archaic cosmological system evidenced through early Irish sources, but it is Lyle who has broken new ground by demonstrating a wider Indo-European system in which temporal schema and their ritual expression are shown to be linked to social time in the lives of human beings. Whilst we cannot know for certain how our ancestors thought, how they ordered their world or read their environment, that which we can grasp is integrated, amplified and improved immeasurably by Lyle's work.[28]

Lyle has also made a major contribution to the understanding of traditional drama. In recent years she has produced a full-length volume dealing with our Galoshins play, as well as an influential essay on the topic.[29]

Much of modern ethnology is predicated on the use of material gathered through fieldwork. In practice, university-based researchers can rarely 'embed' themselves in the life of an entire community for an extended period of time, although many, including the present writer, would very much wish to. One who did is Henry Glassie, whose magnificent study of the Irish village of Bally-menone was the product of seven years spent in the community. It remains hugely influential and for many represents the gold standard in ethnographic fieldwork-based scholarship of recent times.[30] Glassie's book contains material useful for any scholar of traditional culture, songs, tales, and material culture among many other topics, but this is not why I have selected it here. Rather, Glassie's work takes the reading of a particular worldview, conceptual system and symbolic system to a new level. He tries to understand his chosen community's way of seeing, their relationship with the land and their interaction with space, with one another, with their history and how they understand the structure of their lives. The book is replete with examples of cultural traditions; we can trawl through his book and collect the items, just as our scholarly ancestors did, but this would miss the point of his work, which is nothing less than to characterise a mental world, a lived reality. The study of custom and belief must have value beyond the curatorial, and through integrating such material into a larger schema Glassie demonstrates how revealing and powerful this area of ethnology can be, providing an eloquent meditation on the business of living.[31]

I mentioned in passing that a ritual event such as a marriage ceremony was inherently dramatic, as are the visits of the seasonal guisers. Quite where we draw the line as to what is considered 'performance' or 'drama' is beyond the scope of this chapter, but the utility of performance theory in understanding the nature of the cultural form we are looking at is undeniable. We have chosen to focus most of our attention on Galoshins, because this is demonstrably a play, predicated on the creation of a 'make-believe' frame; no one watching thinks it is the real William Wallace who has entered the room. In its formal features, Galoshins resembles a play in that is reminiscent of other theatrical performances. Beyond this, when we consider forms such as rituals, house-visiting customs and the like, we are obliged to tackle the complex question of what kind of performance we are looking at. In this we can enlist the aid of pioneering perform-ance scholar Erving Goffman, a sociologist who saw the term 'performance' as being 'all the activity of a given participant on a given occasion which serves to influence in any way any of the other participants', which opens the way for a very broad conception indeed.[32] Goffman finds performance in many spheres of human activity, such as greetings, gesture and other face-to-face interactions.

He sees a connection between theatrical performance and the kind of role-playing and acting that people engage in as part of their daily lives. This kind of material is helpful to us in understanding 'let's pretend', of 'being' someone else, which is highly relevant to the analysis of performed traditions, such as what traditional drama is doing in the lives of others, what it feels like to engage in this kind of activity, and why individuals get involved. His groundbreaking work paved the way for later scholars such as Schechner and Bauman to develop ideas surrounding the nature of the self-reflexive, heightened awareness that characterises performance.[33]

Finally, mention must be made of Irish scholars who have provided us with some of the most influential studies of traditional culture in recent years and which have a direct connection to our area of ethnological enquiry. Gearóid Ó Crualaoich's study of the Cailleach, the wise-woman/hag figure familiar to Gaelic scholars here, examines not just this figure as evidenced through oral narrative, but develops also a rich and complex discussion to show that such narratives are embedded in the life of individuals and can resonate with how they approach significant life events such as childbirth, death and marriage. It is a masterclass in demonstrating how a traditional form can be interrogated to reveal something of the worldview subscribed to by those who have incorporated it into their day-to-day existence. Séamas Ó Catháin's study of the festival of Brigit offers a highly interesting variation on the straightforward analysis of an extant folk tradition. The material on the tradition in Ireland is wonderfully detailed and explored with great subtlety, drawing upon some impressive resources. What makes the book unusual is that the author expands his analysis to link Irish tradition with, for example, shamanistic traditions of Siberian and Finnish culture. Although the reader may baulk at such connections, the overall achievement is nevertheless very thought-provoking and a long way from more traditional studies of seasonal custom. Ó Catháin acknowledges his debt to Máire MacNeill's majestic *Festival of Lughnasa* which, whilst now rather elderly, is still in my view required reading for any ethnologist with an interest in understanding seasonal tradition.[34]

SOURCES

In this section, the major sources for ethnological work in the area of custom, belief and traditional drama will be discussed, developing themes such as the challenges presented by historical material and the potential inherent in modern technological advances in the field.

Early travelogues, in which observers move from location to location noting cultural practices which strike them as interesting, form an important resource for ethnologists of custom and belief. Of course, we cannot expect of, say, an eighteenth-century account the participant-observer values of our times, and the usefulness of some studies may be questionable. However, in my view all are interesting for the sense of place they impart, and there is much valuable detail on lives lived in remote parts of the country contained among the mass of information on flora and fauna that many, indeed most, travelogues feel obliged to provide. Here, to my mind, are the intrepid early ethnologists we would recognise as colleagues. They are in the field, asking questions, adjusting their co-ordinates to the unfamiliar, communicating their delight or bafflement, perhaps all the time cognisant of their metropolitan bias. Scholars of ethnographic photography and film will agree that the culture behind the lens is as important as that depicted, and so it is with early travelogues. Samuel Johnson, or the Wordsworths, offer us the truly alien eye on rural Scotland of centuries past, whilst the likes of Martin Martin (a native Gaelic speaker from Skye) might be expected to reflect the point of view of those closer to the culture under examination.[35] However, these were books written for a literate urban audience, and the tone is often that of the educated eye startled by backwardness. It is nevertheless in these descriptions of a society 'behind the times' that much of the gold in these publications can be mined, such as in this description of a supernatural belief from South Uist from Martin Martin, a scholar whose interview technique is perhaps on the robust side:

> There are several big Kairnes of Stone on the East side [of] this island, and the Vulgar retain the ancient Custom of making a Religious Tour round them on Sundays, and Holidays. There is a Valley between two Mountains on the East side . . . The natives who Farm it come thither with their Cattle in the Summer time, and are possessed with a firm belief that this Valley is haunted by Spirits, who by the Inhabitants are called the great Men; and that whatsoever Man or Woman enters the Valley without making first an entire resignation of themselves to the Conduct of the Great men will infallibly grow Mad . . . I told the natives that this was a piece of silly Credulity as ever was imposed in the most ignorant Ages, and that their imaginary Protectors deserved no such Invocation. They answer'd, That there had hapened a late instance of a Woman who went into that *glen* without resigning herself to the Conduct of these Men and immediately after she became Mad, which confirmed them in their unreasonable fancy.[36]

Martin Martin, we might assume, would be similarly withering as regards other supernatural beliefs – but this is not the case, notably with his material on second sight. Not only does Martin give marvellously detailed descriptions of the phenomenon and those who possess it, but offers eye-witness testimony:

> I was present in a House where a child cried out of a suddain, and being ask'd the reason of it, he answer'd that he had seen a great white thing lying on the Board which was in the Corner; but he was not believ'd, until a Seer who was present told them that the Child was in the right; for, said he, I saw a Corpse and the shroud about it, and the Board will be us'd as part of a Coffin, or some way imploy'd about a Corpse; and accordingly, it was made into a Coffin, for one who was in perfect health at the time of the Vision.[37]

So convinced is Martin of the veracity of this belief he goes on to 'answer the

Objections that have recently been made against the reality of it'. To the assertion that 'there is none among the Learn'd able to oblige the World with a satisfying account of those visions, therefore it is not to be believed' he counters:

> If every thing for which the Learned are not able to give a satisfying account be condemn'd as impossible, we may find many other things generally believed, that must be rejected as false by this rule. For instance, Yawning, & its influence; & that the Load-stone attracts Iron, and yet these are true as well as harmless, tho' we can give no satisfying account of their Causes. And if we know so little of Natural Causes, how much less can we pretend to things which are supernatural.[38]

Here we have evidence of both the value and the difficulties inherent in this material. The key is to understand as far as possible the intellectual context in which the material was produced and the worldview of the collector. What do we know about the author? Who was he writing for? What were his motivations in writing? If we can achieve this, we can go some way to approaching this wonderful resource with our critical faculties more attuned to its complexity and so receptive to the resolution of apparent inconsistencies as illustrated above. Perhaps Martin Martin's objection in the first example is that only God can provide the protection the farmers seek, and to call down the blessing of some other entity is redolent of what he terms 'the most ignorant ages'. He bluntly discounts this belief; it is not valid and has no bearing on reality. The people are mistaken. However, the second example is also a supernatural belief – indeed he uses the term. He evidently sees no contradiction with religion here; only sensible, sane, respectable individuals possessing a capacity to predict future events. There are things supernatural which, like other unexplained phenomena, must wait for science to unravel. For Martin, there are clearly beliefs and practices which do not fit into the category of what we might call 'respectable supernatural', but second sight is not one of them. As what we would now term an 'insider' researcher, he cannot stand outside his subject. He is a native Gael, and it is very likely he had grown up with this traditional belief. He anticipates objections, but mounts a strong defence, effectively a strong defence of the culture in which the belief is found.

Our task is to refine our critical analytical skills, then endeavour to make sense of such material as best we can. The same applies to the many other splendid travelogues which exist, rich in vivid encounters with landscapes and people, their joys and fears and ways of understanding their world.[39] Modern editions of these can be helpful in preparing the reader; Ronald Black's critical introduction to his *To the Hebrides*, which combines Johnson's and Boswell's accounts is excellent. There are also valuable studies exploring the background to travelogues from this period which greatly assist the researcher's understanding of their intentions, methods and reception.[40]

The observations we have made regarding the importance of understanding the context in which early ethnological material is composed is of course true of the many studies of customary traditions which appeared in the nineteenth and early twentieth centuries. Again, these contain much of great value to us; strong indications of the actual circumstances of people's lives, in the main the rural population, whose experiences and voices would scarcely have made it into the historical record in any other way. In the work of major early folklorists such as Alexander Carmichael (1832–1912), Robert Craig Maclagan (1839–1919), John Gregorson Campbell (1834–1891) and Walter Gregor (1825–1897), we have a significant corpus of material on custom and belief which remains of incalculable value to the researcher.[41] To these we should add the many, many studies of local tradition which exist that cover particular counties, towns and parishes, and the published diaries and memoirs of people of note.[42] Vivid and detailed descriptions of seasonal traditions, fairs and festivals, supernatural beliefs such as the evil eye, and aspects of traditional medicine abound in these sources, and again we get a real sense of how people went about their lives, the rhythms of their days and years, and the life of the wider community. Efforts have been made in recent times to tackle the question of the reliability and by extension the utility of such material, the Pròiseact MhicGilleMhìcheil MhicBhatair/Carmichael Watson Project at the University of Edinburgh being a conspicuous example.[43] Carmichael is chiefly noted for his famous collection of charms, prayers and incantations, *Carmina Gadelica*, published from 1900. These are tremendous, intoxicating productions, even in translation, containing charms for everything from countering the evil eye to curing toothache and jaundice. However, one is often struck by examples of where the material somehow does not feel quite right; for example in the juxta-position of Christian imagery and references amidst what appear as reflections of a worldview more indigenous in its character. Carmichael has earned himself the reputation for being something of an 'improver' of his material, manipulating the data he collected to suit the *mores* of the time. As the project's website notes:

> Niggling doubts remained, however, concerning just how much Carmichael had edited and polished the original texts he had collected in order to present them in print. During the mid-1970s these doubts came to the fore in a heated scholarly debate over *Carmina*'s authenticity: the fiercest debate in Gaelic scholarship since Macpherson's 'Ossian'.[44]

The project seeks to better understand Carmichael's methods by digitising and analysing his notebooks, a highly valuable undertaking, allowing us to bring to bear on his work a more modern and nuanced understanding of how it was put together and the nature of the intellectual climate of the day.

Mention was made earlier of a sword-dance play, described to Walter Scott by his hosts on a visit to Shetland in 1814. The description which appears in his novel *The Pirate* (1822) is very likely based solely on the information he gleaned from this initial encounter and noted in his diary. Scott sets his novel in 1689. As Paul Smith points out, Scott's field notes have morphed somewhat in the process:

> A cursory comparison of Scott's 1814 diary entry, and the related passages in *The Pirate* (1822) is sufficient to see the novelist at work. For example, in the diary he describes the dancers as

'eight performers, seven of whom represent the Seven Champions of Christendom, who enter one by one with their swords drawn, and are presented to the eighth personage, who is not named.'

In *The Pirate* (1822), however, the dancers have suddenly become eighteen in number: 'A dozen cutlasses . . . armed the same number of young Zetlanders, with whom mingled six maidens.'[45]

We cannot criticise Scott for exercising some artistic licence here; that he used his ethnographic material in this way is well known. In 1822 Samuel Hibbert publishes a text of the play in his *Description of the Shetland Islands*. He begins:

We shall suppose Yule to be arrived . . . as the evening approaches, piles of turf are lighted up in the apartment where wassail is to be kept; young and old of each sex make their appearance, and, after the whisky has gone liberally around, it is announced that the sword-dancers are making their appearance;

'The actors are at hand, and, by their show,
You shall know all that you are like to know.'

The company then seat themselves on the forms, tubs, beds, and benches which serve the place of chairs, leaving a large space in the middle of the room for the exhibition. The fiddle strikes up a Norn melody, and at the sound of it a warrior enters in the character of St George, or the master of the Seven Champions of Christendom, a white hempen shirt being thrown over his clothes, intended to represent the ancient shirt of mail that the Northman wore, and a formidable-looking sword being girt to his side, constructed from the iron-hoop of a barrel. St George then stalks forward and makes his bow, the music ceasing while he delivers his

PROLOGUE

'Brave gentles all within this bow'r, if ye delight in any sport,
Come see me dance upon this floor:– you, minstrel man, play me a porte.'

The Minstrel strikes up: the master bows and dances.

'Now I have dance with heart and hand, brave gentles all, as you may see;
For I've been tried in many a land, in Britain, France, Spain, Italy.
I have been tried with this good sword of steel, yet never did a man yet make me yield.'

Draws his sword, flourishes it, and returns it to his side.[46]

A series of six further warriors then present themselves, each with their own boastful challenge 'their respective names and deeds being announced in well set verse'.[47] Individual sword dances follow, this being the verse given by the Scots hero:

> 'Thou kindly Scotsman come thou here; Andrew's thy name of
>   Scottish land!
> Draw out thy sword that is most clear, and by the strength of thy
>   right hand,
> Fight for thy king with all thy heart, fight to confirm his loyal band,
> Make all his enemies to smart, and leave them dead upon the land.'

Andrew draws and dances.[48]

The complex, interlocking sword dance featuring all the participants follows, and at the conclusion there is a parting verse which finishes: 'Farewell, farewell, brave gentles all, that herein do remain,/ We wish you health and happiness, till we return again.'[49] It is not unusual, notes Hibbert, to have the event brought to a conclusion by the arrival of the guisers:

> A number of men enter the room, dressed in a fantastic manner, their inner clothes being concealed by a white shirt as a surtout, which is confined, at the waistband, by a short petticoat formed of loose straw, that reaches to the knee. The whole are under the controul [sic] of a director named a *skudler*, who is distinguished from his comrades by a very high straw cap, the top of which is ornamented with ribbons. He is the proper *arbiter elegentiarum* of his party, regulating their movements, and the order in which they should alternately dance with the females assembled. The amusement thus afforded is the same that may be found in any politer masquerade, since it depends on the guisards being able to conceal from the company who they are.[50]

This description of the play and dance by Hibbert gives us a great deal of information. We know something of the space in which it takes place, the costumes worn, how props like swords were handled, the lines delivered by the combatants and a highly detailed account of the interlocking sword dance. The guisers' appearance, organisation and behaviour is also nicely documented, including the detail that they tried to conceal their identity. The whole account is consonant with later descriptions of seasonal dramas from elsewhere, which also often end with the guisers getting the ladies up to dance.[51] As to how accurate it is as a rendering of something which actually took place we cannot tell, and Hibbert himself acknowledges some 'improvements': 'The words of this drama are taken from an official prompt-book, for which I am indebted to a lady of the island; a few glaring interpolations have been omitted and the words have been corrected according to other recitations.'[52]

Another text of the play, promised at dinner in 1814, is eventually sent to

Walter Scott by the 'young Mr Scott', now James Scott, a gentleman of some note. Acknowledging that Walter Scott must have seen Hibbert's account, on 11 December 1829 James Scott writes:

> On hearing . . . that you wished to have a Copy, it immediately occurred to me that, as the Doctor [Hibbert] had thought it necessary to expunge certain passages, which he considered glaring interpolations, and to give a description of the evolutions of the Ballet from his own pen, you were desirous of obtaining a verbatim et literatim Copy of the only authentic M.S now extant. I, therefore, beg your acceptance of such a Copy.[53]

James Scott makes a robust claim for the provenance of his 'authentic' and 'verbatim' text:

> The Manuscript from which the above was copied was transcribed from a very old one, by Mr. Wm. Henderson, Junr, of Papa Stour, in Shetland. Mr. Henderson's Copy is not dated, but bears his own signature, and, from various circumstances, it is known to have been written about the year 1788.[54]

We are not privy to these 'various circumstances', but this was more than enough for Walter Scott, who incorporates the text in a later edition of his novel, noting:

> This dramatic curiosity was most kindly procured for my use by Dr Scott . . . Dr Hibbert has, in his Description of the Zetland Islands, given an account of the sword-dance, but somewhat less full than the following:
> 'Words Used as a Prelude to the Sword-Dance, a Danish or Norwegian Ballet, Composed Some Centuries Ago, and Preserved in Papa Stour, Zetland.'[55]

What follows is a more full and elaborated text of the verses, but with far less contextual information. The dance itself is not as clearly described, there is no sense of place or occasion and no mention at all of the guisers.

I have chosen to focus on this text because it demonstrates how difficult it is to work with sources of this kind. We have seen spurious claims to authenticity, edited and 'improved' manuscripts, great store set by elderly providers of undated information, and more. Our knowledge of the form, content and context of other dramas leads us to see in Hibbert's text something we recognise, but we shall never know for certain what lines were exchanged between those champions at Yule. Certainly, despite the lack of corroborating evidence, the date of 1788 so confidently offered by James Scott as the year his manuscript was composed was deemed plausible enough for E K Chambers to use it in his *Mediaeval Stage* (1903), and indeed it is also used to date the text reproduced on the Folk Play Research website referred to above, which simply states at the top of the page 'Scott's Papa Stour Sword-Dance – 1788'.[56]

Returning to the present day, modern editions of some of the classic early folklore texts exist, and the critical eye of the contemporary editor can aid in their utility by adding modern references, explaining arcane or archaic terms, outlining the context of their creation, and much more. Easily the best in many years is the magnificent *The Gaelic Otherworld* edited by Ronald Black, which brings together John Gregorson Campbell's *Superstitions of the Highlands and Islands of Scotland* (1900) and *Second Sight in the Highlands and Islands* (1902). Black's introduction and commentary amount to around 350 pages, almost half the entire volume, and the author also provides a full biography of Campbell. Black's masterful grasp of the subject area combined with his extraordinarily detailed and comprehensive notes make this undoubtedly the most important work of its kind published in our field in recent times.[57]

In addition to the published studies noted above, there exist large manuscript collections from around the same period – such as those held by the School of Scottish Studies Archives – which present another important resource for scholars of custom and belief. To give one example held by the archives, the Maclagan Manuscripts amount to many hundreds of pages of Victorian handwriting, and the category of 'superstitions and beliefs' is probably the largest of them all.[58] The manuscripts are immensely rich in material amassed by collectors from their informants and are a true treasure trove for scholars interested in this area of enquiry. However, until resources can be found to digitise this material it is likely to remain underused.

Film and sound archive sources are of great importance to our study. Reading accounts of supernatural entities or of gala days gone by is one thing, but listening to someone describing things that happened to them, or what they saw, is a very different proposition. The vividness and immediacy of the spoken voice can be electrifying, and this kind of data, responsibly collected, can form the basis of new understanding of the meaning and significance of a particular cultural tradition. The School of Scottish Studies Archives has an enormous wealth of material on traditional custom and folk beliefs, which can be used alongside conventional academic sources to remarkable effect. The Scottish Screen Archive hosted by the National Library of Scotland is a wonderful resource, searchable by keyword or subject headings; for example, 'Celebrations, Traditions and Customs' and 'Ceremonies'.[59] Short clips are visible for many, although access to the full-length versions may require payment. Visual resources obviously bring a whole new dimension to the reading of customary tradition, rituals and the like, and being able to see the space in which events occur, costumes, action, gesture, facial expressions and other paralinguistic information is clearly of significant value to our field. The importance of visual records to the critical analysis of traditional drama is self-evident.

Returning to old technology, another rich resource for scholars of custom and belief is Kirk Session minutes, which provide detail on miscreants brought before the authorities for anti-social behaviour. The kinds of activities which caused individuals to fall foul of the Kirk's beady eye are often exactly those we have an interest in. In this example from Newbattle, dated 6 February 1620, a number of individuals have been hauled up after what sounds like rather a fun night out guising:

Givin vp be Iohnne Fleck Iames goudie helene foster Margaret Corsser. The said helene fouster bad on mens clais Andro bowie A wyfs busk and a wemens cot Iohnne porteous helen porteous having ladis clais on Catie h< > had hir gudmans clais on : Thomas tait Ionet wadie vnder ye sclander of furnicatioun The said Iohnne ludgit a pyper be his awin confessio< > quha went with the gyssers being conducit be yaim . . .[60]

The *Statistical Accounts of Scotland* (1791–1845) are searchable by keyword, and can quickly direct the researcher to examples of customary tradition and other material of interest. From here, the researcher can cross-reference with local historical material to begin building a more detailed picture.[61]

Margaret Bennett's collection *Scottish Customs: From the Cradle to the Grave* (1992) is a most useful book which skilfully combines contemporary oral testimony with historical accounts. The oral material (much of it from the School of Scottish Studies Archives) is placed alongside the kind of resources described above: local and regional studies, well-known travelogues and much more. The range of written material deployed here is enormous, and forms a convenient and highly valuable handbook of key sources, to say nothing of the value inherent in the data on custom and belief itself.

Emily Lyle has achieved something similar for traditional drama with her *Galoshins Remembered* (2011), which uses the archives to bring together recollections of the play recorded by the author and others. Having these often highly detailed accounts transcribed and placed in a logical sequence, interwoven with the author's commentary, makes for a tremendously useful resource. The songs which often feature in the play are here rendered in notation, another bonus.

CONDUCTING RESEARCH

The analysis of customary tradition, and traditional belief and drama, is much reliant upon observation and even participation in the tradition being studied, in addition to the personal interview, audio and video recording, and still photography. In the study of festivals, rituals and games, for example, the use of space is often highly marked, and the ethnologist needs to be physically present to be able to 'read' the environment, which may be quite transformed from its workaday format. When seeking to understand the nature of traditional belief, skilful and sensitive interviewing skills are necessary to engage with experiences and worldviews that may be difficult for the interviewee to describe or that may leave them feeling exposed or uncomfortable. Personal interviews are invaluable in allowing the researcher to collect first-hand accounts of traditions which are no longer practised, with multiple interviews in one locality being the most obvious and effective way of building a corpus of data for analysis. The use of video is preferred over audio by researchers, in order to collect that which is lost in the encounter using audio alone. However, this may not be the view of the interviewee; a small recording device placed discreetly on the table may be a lesser cause of anxiety than a video camera on a tripod. We cannot here develop an extensive discussion on fieldwork methods, but suffice it to say that with every step we take away from the real-life encounter between individuals we lose something precious, and the nature, quality and status of the information imparted changes, usually for the worse. Mention was made earlier of a video recording I made of a solo performance of Galoshins, the result, more or less, of a serendipitous encounter. If I had only made an audio recording, I would still have been delighted to have a rendition of the play, with all the spoken parts rendered in different character voices, the song at the end and the commentary my interviewee included. However, instead I have film of this extraordinary encounter, and I can see how my interviewee uses the space; gestures to his right and left, indicating where the characters are placed; I see the stooped figure of Old Doctor Brown; I see the meta-dramatic figure who separates the 'warriors' like a boxing referee. In short, I can imaginatively reconstruct far more of the complex, multi-sensory event this individual took part in perhaps seventy to eighty years before, and which he had committed to memory.

The ultimate in remote collecting is the questionnaire, used to great effect by the Irish Folklore Commission. One would think it had fallen out of vogue completely, but demonstrably it still has its uses. In my experience, ours is not a country much enamoured of the questionnaire, perhaps being too closely associated with the periodic intrusion of the census or some other instrument of

Figure 14.1 Sandy Robertson of Biggar giving a solo performance of Galoshins in 2002. Still from a video by Neill Martin, 2002.

officialdom. Although many of my students have attempted to use this method, it has yet to produce sufficient responses to render the data usable. For this reason, I look on with envy at the study conducted in 2006 by my friend and colleague Professor Terry Gunnell at the University of Iceland, who undertook a large-scale survey, *by post*, in order to assess contemporary belief in the super-natural. Six hundred and thirty-nine people answered a question on whether they could distinguish between 'elves' and 'hidden people' – now, this is usable data.[62] It may be that some future scholar in our area will have better luck than I or my students have had. There are, of course, modern alternatives in the form of social media, which can be used to post requests for information, forming virtual spaces in which people can share reminiscences and the like. Emily Lyle has successfully used an appeal for information published in a widely read magazine, and print media could still be of use in this regard, especially since the older generation, who may often be our focus, are less likely to be found on social networking forums.[63]

Assuming that the personal interview is the basis of modern ethnographic enquiry – and this is what I teach – we encounter first the question of who to talk to. The scholar of custom and belief has an advantage over the colleague who is setting out to explore, say, music or material culture, in that knowledge of and participation in such traditions is likely to be more widespread among the chosen group or community. One effective way of generating a list of individ-uals to interview is to approach local historians, local museum staff, oral history groups and community organisations and ask to be pointed in the right direction. In an age where communities often have their own websites, placing a request for information on a noticeboard or emailing the webmaster can be very effective.[64]

Internet resources are, of course, indispensable for scholars in our area of enquiry. Many out-of-print folklore books are available online, some of them searchable.[65] The multimedia site Scottish Cultural Resources Access Network (SCRAN) gives access to photographs, video and audio, with a wealth of material including many examples of traditional customs and drama.[66] Tobar an Dualchais/Kist o Riches is the largest of several digitisation projects which are proving to be of increasing value to researchers in our field. The Calum Maclean Project is another vast digital resource of great interest to scholars of custom and belief.[67]

CASE STUDY

The intention here is to demonstrate how some of the principles, practical consid-erations and scholarly resources were brought together to produce a modern ethnological study in our area. I hope I will be forgiven for selecting one of my own works, although in truth I think it more likely that I can offer an in-depth analysis by referring to my own study rather than second-guessing the method-ology and intentions of another. I will focus on the background to my article 'A Game of Two Halves'.[68]

Almost as soon as I took up my post as Lecturer at the University of Edinburgh, I was made aware of the handball games that take place at various locations in the Borders in the period around Lent. Colleagues had been documenting them for several years, especially the game at Jedburgh, and there existed a good collection of photographs, interviews and some film in the School of Scottish Studies Archives. A better-documented game is played in Kirkwall on Christmas Day and New Year's Day.[69]

In brief, the games in the Borders see a ball thrown up from a central location. The two teams then battle to take the ball back to their own 'hail' or 'goal'. Balls, made locally and stitched from leather and moss, are typically sponsored by a newly married couple, those celebrating an anniversary, or by the local hotel or pub, and an amount of money is settled on each. Whoever hails the ball gets to keep the money. Handball or 'street football' is also found in various locations in England.[70]

On observing the game for the first time in Jedburgh, I was struck by several things. First, there was no visual distinction between the players, despite their being two teams – the 'Uppies' on one side and 'Doonies' on the other. Second, it was very challenging as a spectator sport. For one thing, it was hazardous, as large numbers of men raced through the narrow streets in pursuit of a leather ball with ribbons attached. The pace was alternately painfully slow, as the knot of players remained locked together for long periods, or frighteningly fast. There was no referee. Another factor was that the goals, or 'hails' were very far apart, too far to see both simultaneously. Indeed, depending on location in these Borders games, the hails can be miles apart. It was thus impossible to follow the action except if one was actually part of it, which I confess did not appeal. The assembled crowd waited in the town centre as the ball and men disappeared from view, lingering in expectation of the ball again returning to the central area. What looked like cheating was not only tolerated, but expected. The game also lasted a very long time – many, many hours, often late into the night. Several balls are played throughout the day, and each must be played out to a conclusion; that is, they must be hailed. Confusingly, there was no limit on where the players could go; no boundaries. The play-space was everywhere and anywhere the ball was, including private property, main roads and shop entrances. The playground extended into infinity. This explained the strange sight of an attractive market town boarded up as if in anticipation of repelling invaders – breakages and injuries are expected. From time to time someone in the crowd would call out 'come on the Uppies'. I wondered about the nature of allegiance to the direction notionally 'up'. Given the potential for damage to life and limb, as well as to property, I was struck by how light a touch was being exerted by the authorities, who were not much in evidence at all. Despite the large crowds and holiday atmosphere (the schools are closed for the day) there were no special arrangements in evidence for controlling the traffic, with unwary drivers attempting to negotiate the streets whilst the game played on, and people going in and out to banks and bakers as if nothing out of the ordinary was happening.

Every second year my students and I returned to collect more data. We decided on some themes: the business of winning and losing, and what, if anything, it meant; the nature of the distinction between Uppie and Doonie, and whether this distinction was one which held throughout the rest of the year;

Figure 14.2 Players reach for the ba at the boys' game in Jedburgh, March 2012.
Photograph: Neill Martin, 2012.

local traditions as to the origins of the game; how exclusive the game was – that is, if it was only for those from the town; what money was settled on each ball and how it was spent; gender aspects – this is a male-only tradition, but teenage girls seemed to play a role too, encouraging the younger lads to show off as well as being interested in collecting ribbons; at what age or according to what criteria a boy graduates from the boys' game (played earlier in the day) to the men's.

As to the selection of interviewees, it had been immediately apparent that we were invariably sent to an individual who played a prominent role in overseeing the proceedings, who was said to 'know everything' we needed to know. He was often to be seen being interviewed by media, with tourists and locals alike listening in to learn the definitive history of the event. In my experience, this is a common occurrence in fieldwork; there are those who feel that there is little point in their making a contribution when a reputed oracle on the subject is available. True, this is often someone who has made an enthusiastic personal study of a particular phenomenon, and such individuals can be highly useful. They may already have a list of contacts known to be willing to talk, for example, or have tracked down rare materials in parish records or local libraries that they are willing to share. However, for our purposes, we have to regard the local expert's narrative not as privileged but as just another version among many, to be considered along with the less polished, less emphatic responses of others. Factors such as age and gender in the sample are important, unless of course our enquiry is focusing only on one stratum of the population. We should also not forget that we are not only interested in those who have left the comfort of their home and gathered in a chilly square to watch a local tradition. For every one person motivated to turn out, there will be several others who do not wish to take part, for whatever reason. They may support the tradition and feel part of the community impetus which sustains it, but having seen it once they see no need to go again. They may, however, have strong negative opinions, and as settled non-combatants see the event as anachronistic and embarrassing. Whatever their reasons, we must gather these responses too if we are to gain a proper understanding of the tradition under examination.

As I have suggested above, the collection and examination of comparative data plays an important part in our work. Easiest to access was material from Orkney where, fortunately for me, an Orcadian postgraduate student of mine had her family home. Apart from the time of year it was played the tradition there was very similar, although with one major extra dimension, which was very well-known – a divinatory function. In Kirkwall, the Uppies' hail is inland; if they win, a good harvest is predicted. The Doonies' hail is the harbour, the sea; if they win, a good year's fishing is expected.

The distinction to be made is between those contests which take place between two groups or communities, and those which feature a single entity that has been divided in two for the purpose: inter- as opposed to intra-community contest.[71] Emily Lyle published an important article in an edition of the journal *Cosmos* devoted to contests, which noted essentially that intra-community contests had a 'win–win' outcome: it did not matter which side triumphed since, as is the case of the game in Orkney, the outcome was either a good harvest, which was in everyone's interests, or plenty of fish, which was also a good thing for all.[72] Although the outcome of the game was random – either side may win – according to the logic of the game in Orkney it did not matter who won. This was different from other examples of seasonal contests we can find in the historical record, such as summer versus winter, where a battle between the two dramatises the passing of one season to another and where the outcome is necessarily fixed; after all, we cannot have the forces of winter triumphing on the eve of the main growing season.

Aside from the game in Orkney, there was material to look at from England, Ireland and France. To my surprise, I also found examples from much further afield of the same kind of seasonal contest, performing the same function as in Orkney. In Okinawa and Korea enormous tugs-of-war are played at key points in the rice-growing season. The ropes may be 200 metres long and weigh more than 40 tons. There, we see the teams are typically east playing west, with the rope initially in two separate pieces termed both north/south and male/female. The two halves of the rope are brought to the centre of the town, where they are joined, one piece interlocking with the other, suggestive of the symbolising of sexual union. Again, the two sides represent agriculture and fishing, and a divinatory function is clear, with a win for either side being desirable. I was very struck by the similarity of these contests to those I have described, and notwithstanding the limitations of comparative study between two distant cultures I remain fascinated by this.[73]

As the data built up from our recordings, we were able to obtain corroboration of our evidence. We discovered that players from surrounding villages came to play at Jedburgh, just as the Jedburgh men travelled to their games. As with Orkney, anyone could play, and indeed those in town for the day were automatically included in the underlying logic of the event. Those who arrive by sea to Kirkwall are Doonies, those by air Uppies. My students and I approach Jedburgh from the north, and as a result we are Uppies for the day. Were we to approach the town from the south, we would become Doonies. It was as if, for the duration of this special time, the event was functioning as a total system, where everyone was included and which incorporated all space; it was, well, *cosmological*. Several people in Jedburgh told us that as the hospital was south of the town, and so all newborns were by default Doonies, some infants were brought by a circuitous route so as to undo the deleterious effects of 'Doonieness' and seal the child on the desired side of Uppie. Directional status could be hereditary or based on one's current place of residence. These accounts notwithstanding, it was evident that the allegiance to up or down did not persist beyond the day of the game. Some young girls considered the ribbons lucky. It was often unclear what happened to the money settled on each ba. A surprising number of people asserted that the game in Jedburgh began in antiquity with the kicking around of a captured Englishman's head.[74]

Our fieldwork over the years, asking the same questions time and time again of more and more people, allowed us to gain a firm working knowledge of this local tradition. We were able to gauge a sense of the level of popular support for it, how it was used and understood, the challenges that faced it in the future, and how it had changed in living memory. Although we had answered many of our original questions as regards the context of the game, there were larger issues that had not been dealt with.

The first was, is this a game at all? Everyone calls it a game. It looked like one, but demonstrably it had few or even none of the formal features of a game other than an agonistic character. To summarise:

- No limit on numbers on either side (so concept of 'fairness', equally matched teams, equal opportunity to win, etc., irrelevant).
- No visual distinction between players (uncertainty as to who was playing, especially given strangers can play).
- No limit on play-space.
- No discernible rules (so, smuggling the ball or taking it to the hail in a car is acceptable – concept of 'cheating' and 'spoilsport' absent).
- No referee.
- No limit on time allowed.
- Aim is take the ball back to one's own territory (inverse of normal, which removes the core idea of prestige reflected on the side who make a

successful incursion into the space of the opponent, i.e. the diminishing effect of overwhelming or overcoming the resistance normally predicated on ownership of space).
- Limited scope as a spectator sport (near-impossible to follow the action; outside of the central area, the players are most often alone; therefore the purpose is not entertainment – they play for themselves).
- Evidence from Orkney and analogues suggested concept of winning and losing problematic, given divinatory function.

In my ruminations on the above I was inspired by the superb study *Homo Ludens* by Johan Huizinga (1872–1945), truly one of the most influential studies I have ever read. Huizinga's theme is the instinct for play in human culture – what is 'play'? He has much to say on the special conditions we attach to the zone marked out for play and the rules that obtain within it, on the special qualities of play-time, on what he calls the 'play-mood' and the 'differentness' of play, and many other subjects besides. Importantly, he notes the connection between spaces marked out for play and those for ritual, and how play differs from 'ordinary' life.

> Play begins, and then at a certain moment it is 'over'. It plays itself to an end. While it is in progress all is movement, change, alternation, succession, association, separation . . . Into an imperfect world and into the confusion of life it brings a temporary, a limited perfection.[75]

His work is also valuable for the insight we gain into the characteristics of carnival, the name we give to a special period of time inserted into the normal temporal flow where certain kinds of behaviours are permitted and where there is a temporary suspension of the normal rules, perhaps accompanied by a flat or inverted hierarchy. As I remarked above, Bakhtin is the pre-eminent early scholar in this area, and his concept of the 'carnivalesque' is highly valuable to this particular study. Material on medieval carnival and popular festivals proves very useful in order to better understand the phenomenon of seasonal traditions that feature the population taking over the central space of a settlement for the purposes of what we can broadly define as play.[76]

In addition to the difficulty I faced in trying to categorise this event, there was the question of winning and losing; it seemed to matter on the ground, but the evidence from Orkney was pointing to this not being a zero-sum outcome where one side actually 'lost' in the conventional sporting sense. Conceptually, it made no sense for a single community to engage in an activity that saw the diminishing of one of its halves, even temporarily. However, there was no firm divinatory evidence from the Borders.

I went on to explore other seasonal contests, notably one in Biggar where, as noted above, there is also found rich evidence for the play Galoshins. The contest lay in fire-building, and took place between the two 'halves' of Biggar, which are separated by a burn. When the tradition was active, it took place between what we might consider the more prosperous half associated with the town's mercantile and residential areas, and the half composed of those who lived in the West Row, rows of farming cottages next to the fields in which they worked, many of them Irish labourers. Each side competed to build the bigger fire of Biggar. It struck me that judging such a thing would not be easy. Crucially for my emerging argument, the way that money was collected to buy coal, tar, paraffin and wood for these fires was through each team's performing the Galoshins play around their respective territories. This data was collected through interviews conducted in the town itself.[77] It suggested that, although rivalry was real enough, there was also co-operation, such as when the location of the West Row fire was temporarily moved and their rivals assisted in moving it back to the original spot. This was highly suggestive of a conception of a 'whole' composed of two interrelated and interdependent parts. After all, the split here was not 'up versus down', but rather looked like 'producers versus processors'. Those who toil on the land have their produce made edible, and it generates an income; whilst the processors rely on the raw material produced by the labourers for their livelihood.[78] The spatial aspect was still evident, however, in the demarcation offered by the burn. Similarly, I learned of a tradition of tug-of-war in Stromness, Orkney – the 'Yule-tree game' – between the Northenders and Southenders, where a burn also separated the two halves. Our evidence from Biggar suggested that the event offered the opportunity for each side to cross into the other's territory, something that was rare or unwise at other times. In other words, there was rivalry underpinned by mutual dependency and co-operation, and at the end of the event the two sides intermingled.

I began to develop the idea that these contests and the traditional drama actually have very similar structures. In Galoshins, we have two warriors who challenge each other to a fight. One kills the other, who is revived by a comic figure called Dr Brown. In very many of the examples of Galoshins we have, the combatant who does the killing laments his actions, and following the cure there is a promise to fight no more. In some, he identifies his slain counterpart as his brother, or 'father's son', or similar: 'We'll all shake hands and gree/ And never fight no more./ But we will be like brothers,/ As we were once before.'[79] Examination of the texts we have (and those collected in England and elsewhere) reveals that there is no consistency as to which warrior will do the slaying and which will be killed; as either can be the victor, it appears not to be an important aspect of the play. I formed the view that it was the theme of reconciliation following temporary division (rather than the theme of resurrection, so seized upon by other commentators) which was important.

In the ball games, the single entity is temporarily divided for the purposes of a contest. This division is not important at other times of year.[80] We might say temporary prestige is at stake, since there is money and brief celebrity status accorded to those who hail the balls. But if we zoom out from this picture we see that the essential logic cannot be one where the aim is to diminish the other half, since each is half of the same whole, and each implies the other and is part of the other. In the same way, I have argued elsewhere that traditions surrounding marriage that have a contestual element are designed to articulate rivalry and difference but are constructed with a view to engineering harmony and resolution.[81] The 'wedding ba' at Melrose furnishes us with a good example of this, where guests from either side competed. Clearly, a zero-sum outcome of such a contest at a wedding would not be in anyone's interests, and I see this as another example of a ritual designed to dramatise the resolution of opposites, of polarities. In that context, we cannot have male without female, and the two individuals and their families are brought together to create a new, interrelated and inter-dependent whole. The wedding day is a liminal in-between time, where these polarities enter a state of flux, resolved through ritual.

In our ball games, the New Year fires at Biggar and other analogues, it is also a matter of temporal flux. In Jedburgh the event is connected with the period around Lent, in the liturgical calendar the period of approximately six weeks leading up to Easter. These forty or so days are inserted into the normal flow of time. The prohibitions of Lent give rise to carnival time, a period of liminality or in-betweenness which precedes the days of abstinence from all that is fleshly. The opposition between these two units of time, expressed as a contest, is splen-didly illustrated by the painting *The Battle between Carnival and Lent* by Brueghel the Elder (1559). On the left we see a portly gentleman astride a beer barrel, with a pie for a helmet and a lance strung with sausages and other meat. He is engaging an emaciated nun, whose lance is dotted with fish. On her side of the painting there is dry bread, self-denial and sobriety. On the carnival side, there is feasting, dancing, drinking and the performing of plays and music.

The contests in Orkney are at the year beginning and at Christmas. This invites a similar reading, in that there is again a connection with a perceived juncture in time. At particular times of year where temporal flux is identified, we find traditions designed to articulate and resolve such spatio-temporal uncer-tainty. In the same way as common ridings in the Borders are initiated to redefine and restate the borders of the community, so these 'games' dramatise the transition between two units of time. This play imposes order, just as Huizinga remarked in the quotation above.

What was formerly one enters a state of flux. One becomes two by means of a fairly arbitrary division; it could be up/down, east/west, north/south, processor/producer, or even married/bachelor as it is with the game at Duns. The contest between the two halves dramatises a process – a process which sees chaos rendered as cosmos again, the two elements recombining into the inter-related whole. That the division is arbitrary and temporary is demonstrated through our evidence (although the two halves of Biggar appear to have retained a degree of separateness throughout the year).

It does not matter who wins the sword fight in Galoshins – the point is the reconciliation between the two related entities, formerly separate. In the same way it does not matter who wins in these seasonal contests, since either the outcome is demonstrably win–win, as with the divinatory aspect in Kirkwall, or else the division has no meaning beyond the day of the event.

Figure 14.3 (overleaf) *The Battle between Carnival and Lent* by Peter Brueghel, 1559. Reproduced by kind permission of Kunsthistorisches Museum, Vienna.

This kind of structural analysis, inspired by some of the scholars I have discussed above, allowed me to move beyond the social context and expand my thinking to develop an interpretative model that I could use as a template to overlay on other examples of traditional cultural forms which employ contest. My research in this area is far from over, and I may not be correct in my ideas. There are many leftover questions unanswered, the absence of a divinatory function from our Borders evidence being but one. I freely admit that my musing on liminal spatio-temporal phenomena is a long way from the thundering boots of the Jeddart hand ba; however, for me, it is in the developing and application of theoretical models to apply to our cultural traditions that the utility of our discipline in exploring custom, belief and traditional drama lies.

Ours has to be a modern discipline unafraid to range widely into related fields, picking up and borrowing critical approaches and models if they prove useful. I have argued that understanding what these traditions are doing in the lives of individuals is a central concern, as is discerning something of their history and development and the challenges they face in the future. This analysis of the surface form is entirely necessary and highly rewarding. The ethnographic work on which it is based brings us out of our books and into the world of real events and connects us to people, communities and our cultural history. The expressive forms we see on the surface, however, are given shape and motion and symbolic charge by the deeper structures from which they are derived, which lie beneath the visible culture, which stem from cosmology, shared symbolic and conceptual systems, evolutionary psychological inheritances and myriad other factors.

This in my view is our challenge as scholars of traditional culture in the area under discussion: to remain devoted to understanding the form, function, nature, use and creation of traditional forms at the level of their performance and practice, whilst ensuring we bring to bear on them all the insights we can gain from modern, theory-based scholarship, from whichever scholarly area we judge best for our purposes. Ours is a fluid kind of discipline, a dynamic mixture of anthropology, literary history, sociology, psychology and many others. We should celebrate the fact that we do not have to remain in a field, turning up material to show others who are standing next to us in the same field. We can vault fences and climb walls to reach the scholarly domains of others, without sanction. Our craft is to remain invigorated by scholarship and the world of ideas, whilst remaining umbilically connected to the expressive culture of our country.

Or, as Norman MacCaig put it in his poem 'The Academic':

Tidiness is decent. Trains
have to reach their destinations.
But yours, that should be
clattering and singing,
through villages and landscapes.[82]

1 See Hayward, 1992, 13. He plots known locations for the play's performance, revealing an east–west split. The play was performed at Hallowe'en chiefly in the west of Scotland, and at Christmas or New Year in the east.

2 Hayward places great importance on a reference in the Falkirk Kirk Sessions to seven young men or boys who went about 'in disguise acting something unseemly' at Hogmanay in 1701.

3 Lockhart, 1838, V, 292.

4 <http://www.folkplay.info/>. A history of the tradition and collected texts of Galoshins may be found in Hayward, 1992. For the revival of the play in Biggar see Lyle, 2011, 75, and interview from 2002 in the School of Scottish Archives ref. J02.192.1.

5 Sandy Robertson, Biggar, performed the entire play, including all the major characters. He had no prior warning of my visit to his home. The film is in the School of Scottish Studies Archives. The most important recent study is Lyle, 2011.

6 Beech et al., 2007, 556–70.

7 Lockhart, 1838, III, 130.

8 Discussed by Smith, 2002, 57.

9 See for example http://www.youtube.com/watch?v=BiLNytj76qo [accessed April 2013]

10 See Carmichael, 1928, I, 149–55. The tradition was also described by Samuel Johnson in his *Journey to the Western Islands of Scotland* (1775).

11 See Martin, 2008.

12 Martin, 2007, especially 237–55.

13 Hartnoll and Found, 1996, entry for 'Folk Play', <http://www.oxfordreference.com/views/ENTRY.html?subview=Main&entry=t79.e1135>.

14 See <http:www.folkplay.info/>. The Master Mummers website is another useful resource for the contemporary performance of traditional drama: <http://www.mastermummers.org/>.

15 Cawte et al., 1967, 30. The source used as evidence for the living tradition of executing a weak king is Harry Hastings, 'The King Who Can't Grow Old', *Radio Times*, vol. 161, no. 2089 (21 November 1963), 21b.

16 Millington, 2002, 102.

17 Thoms, 1846, 862–3. In the letter, Thoms uses the pseudonym 'Ambrose Merton'.

18 Thoms, 1846, 862–3. Although he does not make it explicit, the earlier studies he refers to here are most likely Brand, 1777, Hone, 1826–27 and Ellis, 1841. The material in all three of these studies has its origin in Bourne, 1725, each representing a successive reworking and expansion of this early study.

19 Frazer was not entirely static; he visited the location of the temple at Nemi in 1901. For an excellent commentary on scholarly opinion of Frazer, see Beard, 1992.

20 In some parts of Gaelic Scotland, New Year is still celebrated on 12 January, demonstrating adherence to the Julian calendar.

21 See Bennett, 1992, 103–113 for examples of feet-washing and blackenings.

22 Dundes, 1999, 101.

23 Modern studies of rites of passage include Holm, 1994, offering a very useful comparative analysis across the major world religions; Garces-Foley, 2006; Padilla, 1999; and Cox, 1998. Two excellent and highly readable works on the theory and function of ritual are Bell, 1992 and 1997. On the specific question of the continuity observable in rites of passage, see Pickering, 1974. A comparative analysis of

betrothal customs may be found in Martin, 2007.

24 See for example his *Le Manuel de Folklore Contemporain*, 1946.

25 See especially Turner, 1969.

26 See Bakhtin, 1941.

27 Lyle's first major study in the area was *Archaic Cosmos*, 1990.

28 The Irish scholar Gearóid Ó Crualaoich has also made a notable contribution to the field of calendar and ritual; see Ó Crualaoich, 2008.

29 Lyle, 2007 and 2011.

30 Glassie, 1982.

31 Glassie, 1982, also contains many valuable observations on mumming; see especially 141–9. See also Glassie, 2007 for an interesting discussion of mumming in a divided community.

32 Goffman, 1959, 15.

33 See especially Schechner, 2003; Bauman, 1984a and 1984b,

34 Ó Crualaoich, 2003; Ó Catháin, 1995; MacNeill, 1962.

35 I refer here to Boswell's *Journey of a Tour to the Hebrides with Samuel Johnson LLD* (1785), Johnson's *A Journey to the Western Islands of Scotland in 1773* (1775) and Dorothy Wordsworth's *Recollections of a Tour Made in Scotland AD 1803* (1874). Dorothy Wordsworth made the trip accompanied by her brother William and the poet Samuel Taylor Coleridge.

36 Martin, 1703, 85–6. I have modernised the typography.

37 Martin, 1703, 306.

38 Martin, 1703, 307–9. The load-stone (in modern spelling 'lodestone') is a stone or rock which is naturally magnetic, being composed of the mineral magnetite.

39 Other celebrated travelogues include Pennant, 1774; Buchanan, 1793; Necker de Saussure, 1822; Hibbert, 1822; Low, 1879; Monro, 1594.

40 For example Rackwitz, 2007 and Glendening, 1997.

41 Major works by these folklorists include Carmichael, 1900; Maclagan, 1901 and 1902; Campbell, 1900 and 1902; and Gregor, 1874 and 1881.

42 I here offer a representative selection of the kind of material to which I refer: Scott, 1831; Penny, 1836; Burt, 1754 and 1815; Barry, 1808; Wood, 1887.

43 The project's website is <www.carmichaelwatson.lib.ed.ac.uk/cwatson/>.

44 'Carmichael's Legacy', <www.carmichaelwatson.lib.ed.ac.uk/cwatson/>.

45 Smith, 2003, 51.

46 Hibbert, 1822, 253–4.

47 Hibbert, 1822, 255.

48 Hibbert, 1822, 256.

49 Hibbert, 1822, 257.

50 Hibbert, 1822, 257.

51 For notes on the fiddle music relating to this play, see Cooke, 1986, 5.

52 Hibbert, 1822, 257.

53 Scott, James. 'Letter to Walter Scott, 11th December 1829', National Library of Scotland, MSS 3911, ff. 137–9. Quoted in Smith, 2003, 53.

54 Chambers, 1903, II, 276.

55 Chambers, 1903, II, 272.

56 Chambers, 1903, II, x; see the Folk Play Research website, <www.folkplay.info/Texts/78hu16sw.htm>

57 Black, 2005.

58 The Maclagan MSS contain material on a very wide range of subjects, including legends and tales, proverbs, traditional medicine, local history, place-names and

descriptions of daily life and work. It is perhaps worth mentioning here that the term 'superstition' is not one now used in scholarly discourse, the pejorative implication being inescapable.

59 <http://ssa.nls.uk/>.

60 Newbattle Kirk Session Minutes, NAS, CH2/276/1. The angle brackets indicate where the text could not be deciphered.

61 The Statistical Accounts are accessible at <http://stat–acc–scot.edina.ac.uk/sas/sas.asp?action=public>, a subscription site with some free access to unregistered users.

62 A 1975 survey on psychic experiences by the psychology department at the University of Reykjavik used questionnaires and yielded 902 responses, 80% of the sample size.

63 See Lyle, 2011, 19. In 1982 an appeal for information on Galoshins was made to the *Scots Magazine*.

64 Many examples could be cited here, but see for example the website for Kirk and Town Yetholm, villages around a mile from the English border: <www.yetholmonline.org.uk/>.

65 See, for example, Internet Sacred Text Archive, <www.sacred-texts.com/neu/celt/index.htm>; Scottish Chapbook Project, list of online catalogues, <library.sc.edu/spcoll/britlit/cbooks/cbook4.html>; Gutenberg Project, <www.gutenberg.org/>; Folklore and Mythology Electronic Texts (University of Pittsburgh), <www.pitt.edu/~dash/folktexts.html>; The Internet Archive: Canadian Libraries, <https://archive.org/details/toronto>.

66 <www.scran.ac.uk/>. A subscription is required for full access to content. Material dealing with early drama in Scotland, including folk drama, has been collected as part of the Records of Early English Drama project hosted by the University of Toronto. Once the Scottish material has been added to this digital resource it will be a very valuable asset to researchers in the field. The project may be consulted at <www.reed.utoronto.ca/>.

67 Tobar an Dualchais / Kist o Riches, <www.tobarandualchais.co.uk/>; Calum Maclean Project, <www.celtscot.ed.ac.uk/calum-maclean/>.

68 Martin, 2007.

69 For details on the Kirkwall ba see Robertson, 1967 and Gibson, ?1984.

70 For a comprehensive survey of these games throughout the UK, see Hornby, 2008. For the Scottish context as regards games and sport pre-1860 see Burnett, 2000.

71 Chambers, 1903, vol. 1, 149–51. He mentions both kinds of contest and the detail of a side seeking to return the ball etc. back to their own territory.

72 Lyle, 1990b.

73 'The 42nd Naha Great Tug of War Festival', Okinawa Story website, <www.okinawastory.jp/en/event/event_111008-10.html>; 'Gijisijuldarigi, A Tug-Of-War Held to Pray for A Bountiful Harvest', Arirang website, <www.arirang.co.kr/Tv2/ALegacy_Archive.asp?PROG_CODE=tvcr0301&view _cont_seq=25&code=St1&sys_lang=Eng>.

74 See Chambers, 1903, I, 149, where he identifies sacrificial elements in seasonal contests. He also believes both the golf club and the hockey stick are derived from the shepherd's crook.

75 Huizinga, 1980, 9–10.

76 See for example, Muir, 1997; Burke, 1994; Thompson, 1991; Bushaway, 1982.

77 Reference has already been made to interviews conducted with Brian Lambie and film of Sandy Robertson. Emily Lyle reprints her interview with Peter Thomson of

Biggar in Lyle, 2011, 74–98.
78 The division 'town v country' was found at the game in Sedgefield until 1920 and is found in that of St Columb Major in Cornwall. See Hornby, 2008, 86 and 142.
79 Hayward, 1992, 196–97.
80 My former student from Stromness, Helga Tulloch, noted that her schoolteacher used to divide up the class into northender and southender for the purpose of playing games.
81 Martin, 2007, 363–8.
82 MacCaig, 1990, 233.

BIBLIOGRAPHY AND FURTHER READING

Adair, J. Calendar Customs. In Beech, J, et al., eds, *Scottish Life and Society. A Compendium of Scottish Ethnology, Volume 9: The Individual and Community Life*, 2006, 118–29.
Bakhtin, M. *Rabelais and his World*, Cambridge, Mass., 1968.
Barry, G. *History of the Orkney Islands, Including a View of the Manners, and Customs of their Ancient and Modern Inhabitants*, 2nd edn, London 1808.
Bauman, R. *Verbal Art as Performance*, Prospect Heights, 1984a.
Bauman, R. *Explorations in the Ethnography of Speaking*, London, 1984b.
Beard, M. Frazer, Leach, and Virgil: The popularity (and unpopularity) of *The Golden Bough, Comparative Studies in Society and History*, 34 (1992), 203–24.
Bell, C M. *Ritual Theory, Ritual Practice*, Oxford, 1992.
Bell, C M. *Ritual: Perspectives and Dimensions*, Oxford, 1997.
Bennett, M. *Scottish Customs from the Cradle to the Grave*, Edinburgh, 1992.
Black, R. *The Gaelic Otherworld*, Edinburgh, 2005.
Black, R, ed. *To the Hebrides*, Edinburgh, 2011.
Bourne, H. *Antiquitates Vulgares, or, The Antiquities of the Common People*, Newcastle, 1725.
Brand, J. *Observations on the Popular Antiquities of Great Britain*, Newcastle, 1777.
Brody, A. *The English Mummers and their Plays: Traces of Ancient Mystery*, 1st edn, London, 1970.
Buchanan, J L. *Travels in the Western Hebrides: from 1782–1790*, London, 1793.
Buckley, A, Mac Cárthaigh, C, Ó Catháin, S and Mac Mathúna, S, eds. *Border Crossing: Mumming in Cross-Border and Cross-Community Contexts*, Dundalk, 2007.
Burke, P. *Popular Culture in Early Modern Europe*, Aldershot, 1994.
Burnett, J. *Riot, Revelry and Rout: Sport in Lowland Scotland before 1860*, East Linton, 2000.
Burt, E. *Letters from a Gentleman in the North of Scotland to his Friend in London*, 2 vols, London, 1754.
Bushaway, B. *By Rite: Custom, Ceremony and Community in England 1700–1880*, London, 1982.
Campbell, J G. *Superstitions of the Highlands and Islands of Scotland*, Glasgow, 1900.
Campbell, J G. *Witchcraft and Second Sight in the Highlands and Islands of Scotland*, Glasgow, 1902.
Carmichael, A. *Carmina Gadelica*, 6 vols, 2nd edn, Edinburgh and London, 1928.
Cawte, E, Helm, A and Peacock, N. *English Ritual Drama: a Geographical Index*, London, 1967.
Chambers, E K. *The Medieval Stage*, 2 vols, Oxford, 1903.
Cooke, P. *The Fiddle Tradition of the Shetland Isles*, Cambridge, 1986.
Cox, J. *Rites of Passage in Contemporary Africa: Interaction between Christian and African Traditional Religions*, Cardiff, 1998.
Croker, J. *Boswell's Life of Johnson: Including their Tour to the Hebrides*, London, 1853.
Dundes, A, ed. *Folkloristics: Classic Contributions by the Founders of Folklore*, Oxford, 1999.
Ellis, H. *Observations on Popular Antiquities*, 3 vols, London, 1841.

Frazer, J G. *The Golden Bough: A Study in Magic and Religion*, 12 vols, 3rd edn, London, 1906–15.

Garces-Foley, K, ed. *Death and Religion in a Changing World*, London, 2006.

van Gennep, A. *The Rites of Passage* [1909], London, 1960.

van Gennep, A. *Le Manuel de Folklore Contemporain*, Paris, 1946.

Gibson, G. *The Ba', 1945–59*, Kirkwall, ?1984.

Glassie, H. *Passing the Time in Ballymenone: Culture and History of an Ulster Community*, Philadelphia and Dublin, 1982.

Glassie, H. Mumming in Ballymenone. In Buckley et al., 2007, 1–18.

Glendening, J. *The High Road: Romantic Tourism, Scotland and Literature 1720–1820*, Basingstoke, 1997.

Goffman, E. *The Presentation of Self in Everyday Life*, New York, 1959.

Gregor, W. *An Echo of Olden Time*, Edinburgh and Glasgow, 1874.

Gregor, W. *Notes on the Folk-Lore of the North-East*, London, 1881.

Gunnell, T. *The Origins of Drama in Scandinavia*, Cambridge, 1995.

Gunnell, T. *Masks and Mumming in the Nordic Area*, Uppsala, 2007.

Hartnoll, P and Found, P. *The Concise Oxford Companion to the Theatre*, 2nd edn, Oxford, 1996. Also available from Oxford Reference Online [subscription database], <www.oxford reference.com/views/ENTRY.html?subview=Main&entry=t79.e1135>

Hayward, B. *Galoshins: The Scottish Folk Play*, Edinburgh, 1992.

Hayward, B. The seasonal folk-drama *Galoshins* in southern Scotland. In Beech, J, Hand, O, MacDonald, F, Mulhern, M A and Weston, J, eds, *Scottish Life and Society. A Compendium of Scottish Ethnology, Volume 10: Oral Literature and Performance Culture*, Edinburgh, 2007, 556–70.

Hibbert, S. *A Description of the Shetland Islands, Geology, Scenery, Antiquities, and Superstitions*, Edinburgh, 1822.

Holm, J, ed. *Rites of Passage*, London, 1994.

Hone, W. *The Every-day Book*, London, 1826.

Hornby, H. *Uppies and Downies: The Extraordinary Football Games of Britain*, Swindon, 2008.

Huizinga, J. *Homo Ludens* [1944], Oxford, 1980.

Johnson, S. *A Journey to the Western Islands of Scotland in 1773*, London, 1876.

Lindahl, C et al., eds. *Medieval Folklore: An Encyclopedia of Myths, Legends, Tales, Beliefs and Customs*, 2 vols, Santa Barbara and Oxford, 2000.

Lockhart, J G. *Memoirs of the Life of Sir Walter Scott*, 7 vols, Philadelphia, PA, 1838.

Low, G. *A Tour through the Islands of Orkney and Shetland in 1774*, Kirkwall, 1879.

Lyle, E. *Archaic Cosmos: Polarity, Space and Time*, Edinburgh, 1990a.

Lyle, E. Winning and losing in seasonal contests, *Cosmos* ('Contests' edition), 6 (1990b), 161–71.

Lyle, E. *Galoshins*: The Scottish death and revival play performed by boys at Yule and Hallowe'en. In Gunnell, T, ed., *Masks and Mumming in the Nordic Area*, Uppsala, 2007, 733–41.

Lyle, E. *Galoshins Remembered, 'A Penny Was a Lot in these Days'*, Edinburgh, 2011.

MacCaig, N. *Collected Poems*, London, 1990.

McGavin, J. *Theatricality and Narrative in Medieval and Early Modern Scotland*, Aldershot, 2007.

Maclagan, R C. *Evil Eye in the Western Highlands*, London, 1902.

Maclagan, R C. *Games and Diversions of Argyllshire*, London, 1901.

McNeill, F M. *The Silver Bough: A Four Volume Study of the National and Local Festivals of Scotland*, Glasgow, 1957–68.

MacNeill, M. *The Festival of Lughnasa: A Study of the Survival of the Celtic Festival of the Beginning of Harvest*, London, 1962.

Martin, M. *A Description of the Western Isles of Scotland circa 1695*, London, 1703; 2nd edn, London, 1716.

Martin, N. *The Form and Function of Ritual Dialogue in the Marriage Traditions of Celtic-Language Cultures*, New York, 2007.

Martin, N. Ritualised entry in seasonal and marriage custom, *Folklife*, 46 (2007–08), 73–95.

Martin, N. A game of two halves: Guising and contest in Scotland. In Buckley et al., 2007, 171–201.

Millington, P. Textual analysis of English quack doctor plays: Some new discoveries. In Cass, E and Millington, P, eds, *Folk Drama Studies Today: The International Traditional Drama Conference 2002*, Sheffield, 2003, 97–132.

Monro, D. *Description of the Western Isles of Scotland called Hybrides* [1594], Glasgow, 1774, 1884, 1934.

Muir, E. *Ritual in Early Modern Europe*, Cambridge, 2003.

Murphy, A, ed. *The Works of Samuel Johnson*, volume 8, London, 1797.

Necker de Saussure, L. *A Voyage to the Hebrides, or Western Isles of Scotland; With Observations on the Manners and Customs of the Highlanders*, London, 1822.

Newton, M. Folk drama in Gaelic Scotland. In Brown, I, ed., *The Edinburgh Companion to Scottish Drama*, Edinburgh, 2011, 41–6.

Ó Catháin, S. *The Festival of Brigit: Celtic Goddess and Holy Woman*, Dublin, 1995.

Ó Crualaoich, G. Gender aspects of traditional calendar, *Béascna*, 4 (2008), 1–14.

Ó Crualaoich, G. *The Book of the Cailleach, Stories of the Wise-Woman Healer*, Cork, 2003.

Padilla, M, ed. *Rites of Passage in Ancient Greece: Literature, Religion, Society*, London, 1999.

Pennant, T. *A Tour in Scotland and Voyage to the Hebrides*, 2 vols, Chester, 1774.

Penny, G. *Traditions of Perth, Containing Sketches of the Manners and Customs of the Highlanders*, London, 1822.

Pickering, W. The persistence of rites of passage: Towards an explanation, *British Journal of Sociology*, 25:1 (1974), 63–78.

Rackwitz, M. *Travels to Terra Incognita: The Scottish Highlands and Hebrides in Early Modern Travellers' Accounts, c. 1600 to 1800*, Münster, 2007.

Rees, A and B. *Celtic Heritage: Ancient Tradition in Ireland and Wales*, London, 1961.

Robertson, J. *The Story of the Kirkwall Ba' Game*, Aberdeen, 1967.

Schechner, R. *Performance Theory*, revised edition, London, 2003.

Scott, W. *Letters on Demonology and Witchcraft*, London, 1831.

Shaw, M F. *Folksongs and Folklore of South Uist*, London, 1955.

Smith, P. Sir Walter Scott and the sword dance from Papa Stour, Shetland: Some observations. In Cass, E and Millington, P, eds, *Folk Drama Studies Today: Papers Given at the International Traditional Drama Conference, 19–21 July 2002*, Sheffield, 2003, 47–66.

Stiùbhart, D U, ed. *The Life and Legacy of Alexander Carmichael*, Port of Ness, 2008.

Thompson, E P. *Customs in Common*, London, 1993.

Thoms, W J. Folk-Lore, *Athenaeum*, 982 (1846), 862–3.

Turner, V. *The Ritual Process: Structure and Anti-Structure*, London, 1969.

Wood, W. *The East Neuk of Fife. Its History and Antiquities*, 2nd edn, Edinburgh, 1887.

Wordsworth, D. *Recollections of a Tour Made in Scotland AD 1803*, Edinburgh, 1874.

ONLINE RESOURCES

All websites last accessed November 2012.

Calum Maclean Project, <www.celtscot.ed.ac.uk/calum-maclean/>
Carmichael Watson Project, the, <www.carmichaelwatson.lib.ed.ac.uk/cwatson/>
Canadian Libraries page, Internet Archive, the, <https://archive.org/details/toronto>
Folklore and Mythology Electronic Texts (University of Pittsburgh),
<www.pitt.edu/~dash/folktexts.html>
Gijisijuldarigi, A Tug-Of-War Held to Pray for A Bountiful Harvest, Arirang website (Korea),
    <www.arirang.co.kr/Tv2/ALegacy_Archive.asp?PROG_CODE=tvcr0301&view_cont_
    seq=25&code=St1&sys_lang=Eng>
Internet Sacred Text Archive, <www.sacred-texts.com/neu/celt/index.htm>
Master Mummers, <http://www.mastermummers.org/>
Project Gutenberg,
Records of Early English Drama project (University of Toronto),
Scottish Chapbook Project, list of online catalogues, Scottish Screen Archive [requires
    regstration], <library.sc.edu/spcoll/britlit/cbooks/cbook4.html>
Scottish Cultural Resources Access Network (SCRAN) [subscription site],
Scottish Screen Archive [requires registration], <http://ssa.nls.uk/>
Statistical Accounts of Scotland 1791–1845, <http://stat-acc-scot.edina.ac.uk/sas/sas.asp?
    action=public>
The 42nd Naha Great Tug of War Festival, Okinawa Story website, <www.okinawastory.jp/
    en/event/event_111008-10.html>
Tobar an Dualchais/Kist o Riches,
Traditional Drama Research Group, Folk Play Research website,

15 Social Organisation

MARGARET A MACKAY

Of all the genres of ethnology represented in this volume, social organisation is the one which should send the reader to each and all of the other volumes in the *Compendium* as a whole. This is as it should be in any case, for the study of ethnology is an integrated and interconnected matter and the understandable need to create categories and topics for teaching and research should never be allowed to suggest that human life can actually be segmented in this way.

In particular, Volume 9 of the Compendium, which has as its theme *The Individual and Community Life*, is a textbook and a source-book for the subject in the Scottish context, providing a wealth of research-based material in thirty-five chapters. The volume is organised in four broad sections: the human life cycle and the family; diet and health, including sport and other uses of leisure time; communities of many different types; and those Scots from other lands who have made their homes here in recent centuries and up to the present day. These and the accompanying bibliographies are essential for gaining an understanding of the relationships between, among and within the people of Scotland past and present. Volumes 11, 12 and 13, on *Education, Religion* and *The Law* respectively, offer further essential insights on distinctive institutions with which the individual interacts throughout life, while Volumes 3, 5, 6 and 10, on *Scotland's Buildings, The Food of the Scots, Scotland's Domestic Life* and *Oral Literature and Performance Culture*, furnish data on the material context and the forms of communication which characterise the life of home and community. Volumes 2, 4, 7 and 8 – *Farming and Rural Life; Boats, Fishing and the Sea; The Working Life of the Scots* and *Transport and Communications* – focus on resources and work on the land, at sea and in manufacturing, engineering, the extractive industries and other places of employment. All of these have contents which are directly relevant to social organisation, including studies of the regulation of work, those associations which have campaigned for better conditions, and social activities connected with the world of work.

Sigurd Erixon's foundation stones for ethnology – time, space/place and social milieu – allow us to study those links which connect the individual to other individuals, singly or in groups. Other disciplines focus on society and its constituent parts – sociology, human geography, social anthropology, history – and these have evolved in perspective, scope and methods. Ethnology has taken on some of their methodologies and analytical approaches. But how does the ethnological approach differ from that of disciplines such as these? How has it been studied and taught in Scotland? This chapter looks briefly at the place of social organisation as a theme of research and collecting in the School of Scottish Studies, with a short account of the value and use of comparative material in this work and in the teaching of the subject since the 1980s.

The subject was integral to the work of the School of Scottish Studies from the first decade of its existence. The social sciences were also developing at the University of Edinburgh, and social anthropology and sociology were to set their own paths, but it is useful to look at how the School fostered such studies. For English-speaking scholars, work such as that found in the 1956 publication *The Little Community* by Robert Redfield (1897–1958) was influential. The School drew scholars from beyond Scotland for much of this early research. Among its fellows on short research contracts were the Canadian Frank Vallee (1918–1999), who undertook studies of the lives of Scottish Travellers, Farnham Rehfisch, who also studied the Travellers, and the Welsh ethnologist Trefor Owen, who studied both religious life and the Hebridean township as a social and economic unit, publishing articles on both in the journal *Gwerin*, edited by Iorwerth C Peate, which preceded *Folk Life*.[1]

Calum Maclean, the first full-time collector on the staff, was also interested in this subject, as is evidenced by his book *The Highlands* published in 1959, and it is correct to say that all the early collectors were highly aware of the social context of transmission and performance, and the role of the family and neighbourhood, as interviews in the sound archive reveal. Ian Whitaker, who was to go on to a career in social anthropology in Canada in the 1960s, was appointed to the staff in 1952 with a material culture remit but combined this with interests in social organisation. He had previously worked amongst the Sami in northern Scandinavia. With Basil Megaw, the School's Director from 1957, and Calum Maclean he undertook fieldwork in Smearisary in western Inverness-shire, to take one example, examining domestic life, land division and allocation, and other features of community life.

It is also interesting to note that the social scientist Erving Goffman, a Canadian whose career was USA-based, was in the Department of Social Anthropology at the University of Edinburgh during this period, when he incorporated findings from the fieldwork carried out in Shetland for his 1953 Chicago PhD in preparing his book *The Presentation of Self in Everyday Life* (1959). Shetland was also of interest to the pioneering Norwegian ethnologist Rigmor Frimannslund (later Holmsen) (1911–2006), who was the first student to gain a degree in ethnology in a Norwegian university.[2] She was a specialist in the subject of social organisation in rural Norway, carrying out extensive research for the Institute for Comparative Research in Human Culture in Oslo. In 1951 she visited mainland Shetland and carried out some fieldwork there, hoping to return and undertake more. This was not to be, but her field notebooks and photographs, now in the National Archives of Norway, represent a small but nonetheless important piece of documentation from a time of considerable changes there, such as the introduction of the tractor.

In 1963 James Littlejohn at the University of Edinburgh published his study *Westrigg: The Sociology of a Cheviot Parish*. From the 1970s Shetland, and in particular the island of Whalsay, was the focus of research and subsequent publication by the Edinburgh anthropologist Anthony Cohen, and in the 1980s by Reginald Byron, among others from the UK and further afield. John Stephenson, a sociologist of Appalachia, studied the community of Ford in Argyll in the 1980s, and the role and contribution of geographers such as James Caird (1928–2012) to our knowledge of community life and its environment should be acknowledged as well.

When Eric Cregeen (1921–1983) was appointed to the School of Scottish Studies in 1966 the subject of social organisation came again to the fore. Of Manx background himself, he had worked in the Manx Museum on its survey of folk life, which was modelled on Irish precedents, and his first appointment in Scotland was as Extra-Mural Tutor in Argyll for the University of Glasgow. There he had given support to several local history organisations, delivered and arranged lectures throughout the Argyll mainland and islands, and had become acquainted with the muniments of the Argyll estate, a very extensive archive relating to land management in the Campbell territories of Argyll.

In relation to one of these, the island of Tiree, outermost of the Inner Hebrides, he became acquainted with a rich vein of oral tradition, including family and township history, providing detailed information on the cultural, religious, economic and social life in this community of some thirty townships, extending back many generations. Importantly, a further source of evidence was to be found in the Gaelic songs composed by local bards, often conveying eyewitness accounts of people or events, and commentary upon these, encapsulating local *mores* and values. From the mid-1970s Cregeen directed a series of collecting and research projects about Tiree in the eighteenth and nineteenth centuries, including its emigrant offshoots in Canada, using a combination of oral, written and visual sources. Collectively known as The Tiree Project, and funded by the Social Science Research Council, this innovative study used a diachronic approach to examine the life and history of a Hebridean community during a period of great change, for the Campbell Dukes of Argyll were advocates of agricultural improvement, and Tiree was one of the early sites for the experimental introduction of crofting.

In the context of this project it was useful to look at studies in other cultures which offered comparisons with some of the phenomena detected in Tiree. Amongst these was the work of Rigmor Frimannslund Holmsen on three Norwegian institutions, the *bedlag*, the neighbourhood group invited for ceremonial events, the *dugnad*, the group gathered for collective work, and the *bytesarbeid*, the group who would exchange work.[3] Memoirs from Brittany and from Hungary such as *The Horse of Pride: Life in a Breton Village* by Pierre Jakez Hélias (1914–1995), originally published as *Le Cheval d'Orgueil*, and *People of the Puszta* by Gyula Illyés (1902–1983), first published in 1936 as *Puszták Népe*, provided useful insights. The longitudinal study of the life of the Danish island of Laesø over many centuries, conducted by Bjarne Stoklund, was also highly influential.[4]

Closer to home, and closely relevant to Scotland, was the work of the Irish ethnologist Anne O'Dowd on the concepts of shared and exchanged labour, published in her study *Meitheal: A Study of Co-operative Labour in Rural Ireland* in 1981. It and the work of Frimannslund Holmsen and those who worked with her in Norway, such as Per Hvamstad on the *bedlag* and Asbjørn Klepp on the *dugnad*, had an influence on the research later undertaken by Gary West on similar institutions in rural Perthshire.[5]

It was not until the launch of the full four-year honours degree in Scottish Ethnology in the 1980s that teaching of the subject was offered as part of the honours undergraduate programme, although postgraduate research on topics with a strong social organisation focus had already begun. The approach to the subject was one which aimed initially to ground the subject in the experience of the individual student, to identify and use those sources of evidence most pertinent to the study of social organisation in Scotland, to examine elements in society with which the individual interacts from his or her youngest days onwards, and to draw on case studies, synchronic or diachronic, of individual communities. Opportunities for fieldwork were provided as part of the course assessments.

Students of social organisation will remember the instruction to bring to the first meeting of the class an invitation list for an event at which they would be the central focus – a special birthday perhaps – and to be prepared to account for the presence of each person on it. Who would you wish to share a time of celebration with you? Each person's circumstances will differ, and convention might come into play, but the exercise draws out a useful representation of people in different categories and a sense of diachronicity through those relationships which last through time, such as friendships from schooldays and perhaps several generations of relatives. In this way the nature of social organisation, a very intangible concept, can be made tangible, just as a *love-darg*, a day's work given freely to assist a household where there was illness or other need, made manifest the connections in a small rural community. Students may also recall a simple diagram (Figure 15.1) devised to illustrate the expanding contacts which the child makes through the process of acculturation, the institutions which are gradually encountered and the adult groupings and affiliations which may or may not overlap with family and neighbourhood links.

In the 1980s honours degree programme there was a strong emphasis on resources for the study of social organisation, and their critical appraisal. Visual resources from different periods were examined and ranged from medieval woodcuts showing the stages of childhood development from the swaddled child to the crawling, walking and running child, to depictions from several cultures of the seven or ten 'ages of man', including a scene painted on the front of a Slovenian beehive, and a range of paintings showing family members in a variety of settings from the National Gallery of Scotland. Pictorial sources for depictions of work groups, religious bodies, leisure activities, self-help, charitable and similar organisations were identified. Films showing rites of passage were analysed.

Dictionary and thesaurus sources were of particular importance and were examined at the start of the course. The word 'neighbourhood', for example, is a spatial as well as a societal concept and over time it, and 'neighbour', have acquired a range of specific meanings in the Scottish context, as exemplified in *A Dictionary of the Older Scottish Tongue* and the *Scottish National Dictionary*. The expression of good relations might be informal, spontaneous or reciprocal, or formality might be involved. To *kepe, hald, schaw* or *use gude nichbourheid* was to

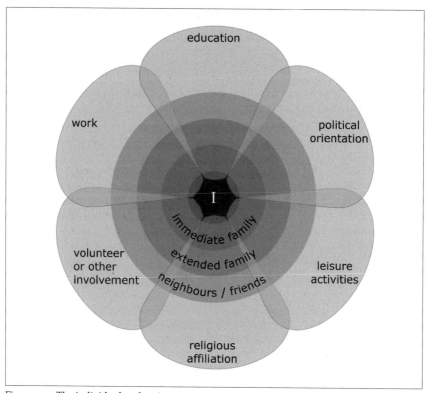

education

work

political
orientation

volunteer
or other
involvement

immediate family

extended family

neighbours / friends

leisure
activities

religious
affiliation

I

Figure 15.1 The individual and society

observe agreed rules for carrying out common duties and obligations, and such phrases might be incorporated into the leases of tenants on an estate. *To neibour* or *to neibour wi* meant to co-operate with someone nearby, generally in agricultural tasks. The term 'friend' can imply both kin and non-kin relationships in Scots and in Gaelic (*càirde*), while the roots of the word 'gossip' reveal relationships arising from the practice of godparenting.[6] Several of the categories outlined in *The Scots Thesaurus* deal with relationships, phases of life, modes of behaviour and membership. Informal naming usages and forms of address within families were also explored in class.

An understanding of those groupings which are familiar to insiders but have not always been well documented or studied in Scotland was assisted by the examination of studies of comparable institutions from other cultures. For example, in the past wedding and funeral protocol called for a formal message or invitation to be delivered by word of mouth. In Scots the term most often used for this is *bid*, both as a noun and a verb. This 'invitation group' corresponds to the Norwegian *bedlag*, the members of which were *bedt* (bidden). In Gaelic-speaking communities, the group who because of kinship ties or other associations and obligations were part of the funeral invitation group were said to share *càirdeas fios tòrraidh*, 'the relationship of the funeral invitation'. In Shetland the *leek* (Old Norse *lik*) was the term for the district whose inhabitants were responsible for the funeral and burial rites of their neighbours. On a happier note, a traditional wedding song in a Shetland district accompanied a women's dance in which the bride's move from one family to another was portrayed symbolically by incorporating one *fremd* or 'non-kin' person, the mother of the groom.[7]

Urban settings as well as rural communities provide instances of the creation of institutions with their own governing principles. One of these is the *menodge* (the Scots term may relate to the French *ménage* or 'housekeeping', 'thrift', 'economy'), a locally organised savings club.

Autobiographies and memoirs, in written or oral form, are a vital source of evidence for aspects of social organisation, and these were consulted. Such resources are included in the bibliography and in Chapter 18. Importantly, those illustrating different experiences within a group which might from the outside look homogeneous were purposely sought, such as four autobiographies reflecting Jewish life in Scotland: that of David Daiches, son of Edinburgh rabbi Rev. Dr Salis Daiches; that of Howard Denton, from the working class Jewish community in Edinburgh's Pleasance; that of Evelyn Cowan, a working widow's daughter in Glasgow; and that of Ralph Glasser, whose family circumstances propelled him into self-education from an early age.[8]

Institutions which form elements of society were explored, the household, the extended family, the neighbourhood, education, religious affiliation, the world of work, leisure and other types of association. Case studies of individual communities, such as that of an oil rig or an army regiment, those based on farming, crofting or fishing, mining or manufacturing, a range of urban entities and those where sense of place is no less potent than in a firmly rooted settlement, such as a Scottish Traveller site, provided the focus for a holistic treatment involving all or many of these elements, looking critically at the very idea of 'community', at insider–outsider perceptions, the means by which society is regulated, and concepts of identity and belonging.

Students were encouraged to generate new primary material by under-taking interviews on one of the weekly themes. One element of source criticism evident early on was the fact that recollections of childhood are generally the product of an adult mind and memory, and that childhood experience as it is lived can be difficult to find or to document. Quite properly, there are strict rules and regulations governing research conducted with children in the setting of a playgroup or class, but some students were able to interview family members or friends in suitable circumstances and gather interesting insights into themes of interest to children themselves.

Several students of social organisation went on to produce postgraduate dissertations of high quality on associated themes and to make contributions to several volumes of the *Compendium*, including Volume 9, *The Individual and Community Life*, and Volume 1, this *Introduction to Scottish Ethnology*.

1 Owen,1956–57, 1958–59.
2 Horgen, Jones and Olsen, 2011.
3 Frimannslund, 1956.
4 Stoklund, 1988.
5 West, 1999, 2007.
6 Mackay, 1987; Dawson, 2005.
7 Mackay, 1987.
8 Daiches, 2001; Denton and Wilson, 1991; Cowan, 1974; Glasser, 1986.

BIBLIOGRAPHY AND FURTHER READING

Beech, J, Hand, O, Mulhern, M and Weston, J, eds. *Scottish Life and Society. A Compendium of Scottish Ethnology, Volume 9: The Individual and Society*, Edinburgh, 2005.

Brown, C. *A Social History of Religion in Scotland since 1730*, London, 1987.

Byron, R. *Burra Fishermen: Social and Economic Change in a Shetland Community*, SSRC Publication, n.d.

Byron, R. *Oil and Changing Concepts of Community in Burra Isle, Shetland*, Barmarick, 1983.

Cohen, A P, ed. *Belonging: Identity and Social Organisation in British Rural Cultures*, Manchester, 1982.

Cohen, A P, ed. *Symbolising Boundaries: Identity and Diversity in British Cultures*, Manchester, 1986.

Cohen, A P. *Whalsay; Symbol, Segment and Boundary in a Shetland Island Community*, Manchester, 1987.

Collins, K E. *Second City Jewry*, Glasgow, 1990.

Cowan, E. *Spring Remembered: A Scottish Jewish Childhood*, Edinburgh, 1974.

Cregeen, E R. *Recollections of an Argyllshire Drover: And Other Selected Papers*, ed. M Bennett, Edinburgh, 2004.

Daiches, D. *Two Worlds: An Edinburgh Jewish Childhood*, Edinburgh, 2001.

Daiches, D. *Was: A Pastime from Time Past*, Edinburgh, 1975.

Dawson, J E A. 'There is nothing like a good gossip': baptism, kinship and alliance in early modern Scotland. In Kay, C J and Mackay, M A, eds, *Perspectives on the Older Scottish Tongue*, Edinburgh, 2005, 38–47.

Denton, H and Wilson, J C. *The Happy Land*, Edinburgh, 1991.

Docherty, M. *A Miner's Lass*, Preston, 1992.

Dorian, N C. *The Tyranny of Tide: An Oral History of East Sutherland Fisherfolk* (with Preface by E R Cregeen), Ann Arbor, MI, 1984.

Flashbacks Series, published by the EERC and NMSE Publishing.

Frimannslund, R. Farm community and neighbourhood community, *Scandinavian Economic History Review*, 4:1 (1956), 62–81.

Frimannslund Holmsen, R. The traditional rural community in Norway: Institutional network and social groupings, *Scottish Studies*, 32 (1993–98), 107–18.

Glasser, R. *Growing up in the Gorbals*, London, 1986.

Gordon, E and Breitenbach, E, eds. *The World is Ill Divided*, Edinburgh, 1990.

Hélias, P J. *The Horse of Pride: Life in a Breton Village*, New Haven, CT, 1978.

Holmes, H. *As Good as a Holiday: Potato Harvesting in the Lothians from 1870 to the Present*, Edinburgh, 2000.

Horgen, J E, Jones, M and Olsen, V, eds. *"Studenten som kom før faget": Etnolog Rigmor Frimannslund Holmsen (1911–2006) – et minneskrift*, Oslo, 2011.

Jamieson, L and Toynbee, C. *Country Bairns: Growing Up 1900–1930*, Edinburgh, 1992.

Kay, B, ed. *The Complete Odyssey: Voices from Scotland's Recent Past*, Edinburgh, 1996.

Kay, C J. Footprints from the past: The survival of Scots kinship terms. In Anderson, W, ed., *Language in Scotland: Corpus-based Studies*, Amsterdam, 2013, 145–65

Kydd, R and N, eds. *Growing Up in Scotland: An Anthology*, Edinburgh, 1998.

Leitch, R, ed. *The Book of Sandy Stewart*, Edinburgh, 1988.

MacArthur, E M. *Iona: The Living Memory of a Crofting Community, 1750–1914*, Edinburgh, 1990.

Mackay, M A. 'Kinship and community in northern districts of Argyll', unpublished report for the SSRC, 1984. Copies lodged in the British Library and the National Library of Scotland.

Mackay, M A. Heard, seen, told: The oral record in Shetland. In Crawford, B E, ed. *Essays in Shetland History*, Lerwick, 1984, 234–42.

Mackay, M A. 'The Sib and the Fremd': Community life in the dictionaries. In Macafee, C and Macleod, I, eds, *The Nuttis Schell: Essays on the Scots Language*, Aberdeen, 1987, 211–18.

Maclean, C I. *The Highlands*, London, 1959.

Macleod, I with Cairns, P, Macafee, C and Martin, R, eds. *The Scots Thesaurus*, Edinburgh, 1990.

Marshall, C W and Sutherland, G, ed. *A Stranger on the Bars*, Macduff, 1994.

Neville, G K. *The Mother Town*, Oxford, 1994.

Norddølum, H. The 'Dugnad' in the pre-industrial peasant community, *Ethnologia Scandinavica*, (1980), 102–12.

O'Dowd, A. *Meitheal: A Study of Co-operative Labour in Rural Ireland*, Dublin, 1981.

Owen, T M. The 'Communion season' and Presbyterianism in a Hebridean community, *Gwerin*, 1:2 (1956–57), 53–66.

Owen, T M. The role of the township in a Hebridean crofting economy, *Gwerin*, 2:4 (1958–59), 147–61.

Redfield, R. *The Little Community*, Chicago, IL, 1956.

Smout, T C and Wood, S, eds. *Scottish Voices 1745–1960*, London, 1990.

Stephenson, J. *Ford: A Village in the West Highlands*, Edinburgh, 1984.

Stoklund, B. *Arbejde og kønsroller på Læsø*, Læsø, 1988.

Ugolini, W. *Experiencing War as the 'Enemy Other': Italian Scottish Experience in World War II*, Manchester, 2011.

West, G J. Conceptualising neighbourhood: Charity labour gatherings in rural Perthshire 1850–1950, *Scottish Studies*, 33 (1999), 132–45.

West, G J. *An Historical Ethnography of Rural Perthshire, 1750–1950: Farm, Family and Neighbourhood*, Lampeter, 2007.

16 Onomastics

IAN FRASER AND DOREEN WAUGH

WHAT IS ONOMASTICS?

The term 'onomastics' comes from the Greek *onoma* 'a name', so onomastics can be defined as the study or science of names. In recent times, the bulk of scholarly research in the field of name studies has focused on place-names and personal names, but the subject can encompass any group of names which form a distinct corpus – including analysis of named objects of all kinds, such as plants, animals, houses, motor vehicles, ships, and so on. Literary onomastics, for example, investigates the significance of, say, personal names or place-names in fiction, and literature in general.[1] Many of these studies are ethnological or sociological in nature, while others may have religious, medical, or psychological significance.[2]

Indeed, a collection of names, no matter how trivial they may seem to the academic observer, can be regarded as grist to the mill of some researcher, in onomastic terms. The student of name studies, or the onomastician, can therefore use a wide range of material for analysis, depending on the field of study in which the onomastician specialises. The use of names in research is therefore dependent upon the role of the onomastician, and the view that he or she takes of the material selected for study.

It is easy to forget that names are lexical items, i.e. words which have or had a meaning to those who coined them and, as such, they are usually approached by the researcher as linguistic features which have special qualities of interest to others. So although many of the earlier researchers in name studies were themselves linguists, the field of study has expanded to include historians,[3] geographers, lexicographers[4] and archaeologists, as well as those concerned with many aspects of cultural studies,[5] demography, ethnology[6] and sociology. Indeed, few disciplines within the humanities can or should ignore onomastics.

ONOMASTICS AND THE ETHNOLOGIST

One of the most important features of human activity is the way in which there has been a constant process of naming features in the landscape.[7] This is a practice which must have been a prime feature of life from the earliest times. The practice of human naming is one that is a basic feature of life, and it continues to be a highly relevant subject for ethnological research. The ethnologist will find these two fields – place-names and personal names – to be the most fruitful for ethnological investigation, but they are not exclusively so. Other types of naming, such as naming of boats in a fishing community, can also be revealing. One researcher has even written about names of oil fields in the North Sea in a most amusing and thought-provoking way.[8]

The study of place-names itself is wide-ranging. For historians, the investigation of settlement names, their origins and their linguistic development, is a key activity. Any British historian will acknowledge the role that onomastics has played in the reconstruction of the historic past, especially if the region under study has been subjected to settlement by several peoples who spoke different languages. The death of a spoken language in a given area will be a major drawback to a historian who is attempting to provide a full account of the area's history, but the survival of place-names in the 'dead' language may well provide considerable usable data, as in the case of Norn, the name for the Scandinavian language formerly spoken in Caithness and the Northern Isles. The trained onomastician can often provide the linguistic expertise, given the appropriate source material.

The same can be said of the onomastician's role in the service of the ethnologist. As far as place-names are concerned, they can speak when all other ethnological sources are silent. A good example of this is the corpus of minor names in parts of Scotland where fluent Gaelic speakers died out in the twentieth century. A collection of minor names accurately recorded on tape by these last survivors of Gaelic speech and culture could provide the ethnologist with all kinds of relevant cultural material. The example of Eilean nan Ròn off the north coast of Sutherland, whose place-name record was investigated,[9] provided some useful insights into the life of a community whose settlement history lasted for just over a century. A survey of a Shetland settlement, in the same way, demonstrated the value of oral tradition in the survival of the place-names of a local community.[10]

In both of these studies, and in many more of a similar nature, the ethnologist has available much useful data. Some of this is linguistic or dialectal, some sociological, some relating to agricultural activity, animal husbandry, fishing lore, or similar fields. All of these minor names were important to those who coined them. These people were intimately concerned with the landscape and their relationships with it. Therefore, the names they gave to their environment reflected their lifestyles, often in very basic ways, but sometimes in more subtle terms. It is in the nature of place-names to vary in the amount and detail of information that they readily provide, and it is sometimes a laborious process to elucidate the wider ethnological value of a collection of local names, but it is nevertheless very worthwhile.

The study of personal names has long been a major feature of onomastics. Surnames do, of course, provide data for genealogical studies but their derivations can, in addition, provide a fascinating insight into the structure of society.[11] In Europe, we use a number of surname categories, with patronymic, occupational and locational being the most common.[12] A survey of these names can provide ethnologists with a range of data that will help them to assess the very nature of society. Occupational surnames, as Nicolaisen shows in his article on 'Surnames and medieval popular culture', provide a great deal of information on the range of human activities during specific periods of history, while locational surnames sometimes give a good idea of the nature of population movement in society. As Professor W F H Nicolaisen has also pointed out in one of his many articles of relevance to ethnological research: 'We survive because we can structure the world around us through identifying naming and also not less because we can create true chunks of the past through narration. My old friends *homo nominans* and *homo narrans* turn out to be not just twins but one and the same.'[13] David Sellar, Lord Lyon King of Arms of Scotland, is another researcher who has contributed much to the study of personal names in Scotland.[14]

W F H Nicolaisen's comment also applies to first names or given names, which are likewise key indicators of human behaviour for the ethnologist. Choice of these is usually very dependent on current cultural forces, reflecting as they do the preferences of parents in selecting children's names. Some societies have very strict rules governing the naming of children, and may even have lists of 'approved' names, which can only be breached in exceptional circumstances. Most of Western society, however, is much more relaxed in such matters, leaving the choice up to the parents. Onomasticians who have studied the subject of given names are able to identify trends which reflect society's popular culture in the choice of names. This is a key reflection of the cultural forces at work in the naming process.[15]

Although these are the most important aspects of name studies of use to the ethnologist, we should never discount other aspects of the subject which afford valuable insights into the human condition. A glance at the journal of the American Name Society – *NAMES* – for example, will give a good idea of the range of material studied by researchers outwith the United Kingdom. For instance, in the issue of *NAMES* which celebrated the 50th anniversary of the American Name Society, there were articles on topics ranging from 'Toponymy in Missouri' to 'A fancy for the fantastic: Reflections on names in fantasy literature', 'Research on first names by two psychologists', 'Toponymy and technology' and 'Linguistic approaches to names', to list but a few.[16]

ETHNOLOGICALLY USEFUL MATERIAL

Theoretically, the majority of onomastic data is of use to the ethnologist. While certain collections of, say, technical and scientific names, medical names and some of the more esoteric collections may be of marginal interest, there are many onomastic studies which are of significant value to the ethnological investigation of a particular genre, or a particular geographical region. These studies include such branches as traditional music and song, for example, where a comprehensive list of Scottish pipe-tunes containing place-names or personal names could well provide a significant insight into the range of a composer of such music. Gary West's recently published book *Voicing Scotland* has a chapter aptly entitled 'Voicing place', which draws attention to the importance of place and the identifying of it in everything we do.[17] In the context of awareness of place, we should also mention the list of place-names included in volume 8 of the *Greig–Duncan Folk Song Collection*.[18] To give an example from another area of research, an investigation into traditional practices might find a list of local names of plants useful in building a picture of the kind of techniques involved in traditional medicine, dyeing and handcraft. Such onomastic collections are usually established by specialists in their own fields.[19]

The best illustration of onomastic material which is of use to the ethnologist, however, is a collection of place-names. A particularly vivid example concerns a group of sea-lochs in the Sound of Harris, their names and their derivations, as well as historical incidents connected with them.[20] The information associated with these minor names naturally includes many personal names of individuals who had close contact (sometimes literally!) with the rock in question; terms for animals, fish and birds with a maritime link; weather and tidal times; names of vessels which came to grief on individual rocks;[21] names associated with fishing techniques, fish preservation, curing, and landing of catches; sea-marks which were established as good places to catch fish (*meids*); historical incidents, some of which may only be revealed in the place-name concerned, and knowledge of the incidents at a very local level. An excellent book by Charles Simpson on sea-marks or *meids* was published in Shetland in 2011. Simpson uses the technique of interviews with local fishermen in Shetland, recorded in the local dialect, to identify these *meids* and establish their names, along with a wealth of information about the period in which they were employed as fishermen, prior to the electronic age.[22]

Such onomastic investigations are part and parcel of the full ethnological history of a given area. It is not always possible to provide a complete place-name record of an area – place-names are subject to change in the natural process of language development and cultural change – and in some areas, the complete loss of population can prevent useful collection from oral sources, especially in the lightly populated Highlands of Scotland. But the role of the tradition bearer as an onomastic source should not be underestimated. Most place-name scholars place great store on the accumulation of the lore of a community as having preserved traditional cultural features like storytelling, traditional crafts, husbandry, agriculture, fishing and general life techniques, as well as the more obvious songs and music.

Any ethnologist studying the traditional culture of an area will find the record of personal names significant. Some communities have had, traditionally, limited numbers of surnames, especially those that have retained a conservative, inward-looking culture, independent of outside influence. Fishing communities, whose survival depended on these independent qualities, are typical of this, and not only featured few surnames, but few given names as well. This conversation between a stranger, seeking someone named Alexander White in a Buchan fishing village, and a local girl is worth quoting in full here to exemplify the point:

'Cou'd you tell me fa'r Sanny Fite lives?'
'Filk Sanny Fite?'
'Muckle Sanny Fite.'
'Filk Muckle Sanny Fite?'
'Muckle lang Sanny Fite.'
'Filk muckle lang Sanny Fite?'

'Muckle lang gleyed Sanny Fite,' shouted the stranger.
'Oh! It's "Goup-the-lift" ye're seeking,' cried the girl, 'an fat the deevil
for dinna ye speer for the man by his richt name at ance?'[23]

Many of these aspects of naming are now obsolete, at least in this country, since
the general influence of the media has tended to provide a range of given names
which are almost universal. However, the old system of given names survives
in some communities, and in some families, even if such traditional practices
are much less prevalent today. The terminology of kinship in Scotland is also a
subject for study.[24]

The agricultural landscape has been a major source of interest to ethnologists. The nomenclature of the farm environment, expressed in the names of
farm fields, has been an important aspect of onomastics, since it offers a great
deal of evidence for the ethnologist on agricultural change and human development of the landscape. The categorisation of field names provides a good idea
of the various forces which have combined to give us the rural landscape of
today. Again, many of these names reflect an earlier lifestyle, and now-obsolete
farming techniques.[25] Field names are liable to change more rapidly than
topographic names or settlement names, yet many survive as indicators of an
agricultural past. The earliest names will contain terminology that has passed
out of present speech, even in rural areas which traditionally preserve archaic
terms in dialect, and because of this they are of interest not only to ethnologists
but also to dialectologists and lexicographers.

OUTLINE OF ONOMASTICS RESEARCH IN SCOTLAND

As far as the study of onomastics in Scotland is concerned, the major interest of
early scholars was in place-names rather than other types of name. James A
Robertson's *The Gaelic Topography of Scotland* was published in 1869 but it was
another 1869 publication by the Irish scholar P W Joyce, entitled *Irish Names of
Places,* which was more highly regarded in Scotland, where contemporary scholars
saw much material for which they could provide parallels.[26] Stimulated and
encouraged by Joyce's work and his sound academic approach, a number of
Scottish onomasticians produced important works over the next few decades.
Among these, Professor Donald Mackinnon's 'Place-names and personal names
in Argyle' appeared as a weekly serial in the *Scotsman* in 1887 and 1888, one of
the first popular, but scholarly, treatises on onomastics in this medium.[27] Other
scholars, like Dr Alexander Cameron and Sir Herbert Maxwell were influenced
by Joyce.[28]

It was, however, the publication of W J Watson's *Place-Names of Ross and
Cromarty* in 1904 that provided the first systematic and scholarly study of the
place-names of an entire Scottish county, although unfortunately lacking in grid
references to help in locating the place-names. Not only had Watson investigated
and recorded early documentary forms of the names, but he had consulted local
Gaelic speakers in order to ascertain the current pronunciation. This eminent
Celtic scholar provided the framework for detailed research into Celtic place-

names in Scotland, and established firm ground rules for virtually every serious onomastic researcher in the twentieth century.

Personal name studies in Scotland were provided with a major piece of scholarship in the form of G F Black's *Surnames of Scotland* (1946). This was an alphabetical list of the majority of Scottish surnames, with plentiful documentary forms, and a systematic lexicographic approach to the subject. Black's training as a librarian was a major factor in the production of what was for its time a highly comprehensive volume, running as it did to over 800 pages.

Watson's seminal work entitled *History of the Celtic Place-Names of Scotland* (1926) and Black's dictionary formed the basis for much further research, but it was not until the establishment of the School of Scottish Studies at the University of Edinburgh in 1951 that a dedicated organisation, in the form of the Scottish Place-Name Survey, came into being (see below), followed, in 1996, by the Scottish Place-Name Society, which has connections with most Scottish universities.

The English Place-Name Society, founded in 1921 had, by 1950, published a number of volumes in a county-by-county series which has become well established.[29] In addition, there has been a substantial amount of collaboration between scholars from the UK and Ireland in the activities of the Society for Name Studies in Britain and Ireland, which was founded in 1963 to promote onomastic research in all the home countries, as well as Ireland. This organisation provides an annual forum for onomasticians, attracting young scholars and private researchers. Its annual journal, *NOMINA*, has now become a well-established publication containing many articles with an ethnological angle, some of which are included in the bibliography.

The interest in Scandinavian studies, especially from the 1960s onwards, with Professor Hermann Pálsson, the first President of the Scottish Society for Northern Studies, in the vanguard, gave name studies connected with the Atlantic seaboards a major boost. Increased cooperation between Scandinavian and British scholars resulted in a number of place-name publications which were of key interest to archaeologists and historians attempting to understand the relationship between Scandinavia and these islands during the periods of Viking settlement. This stimulated much onomastic research not only in Scotland but also in Faroe, Iceland and Norway, which were the closest geographically and culturally.[30] A scholarly response to this Scandinavian interest came in 1968 with the foundation of the Scottish Society for Northern Studies, originally conceived as a northern offshoot of the London-based Viking Society. The society produced the first issue of its journal, *Northern Studies*, in 1972, and many onomasticians have contributed to this over the years.[31]

Today, onomastic research is carried on by a number of Scottish-based scholars, covering a wide range of areas and topics. Probably the most significant (and popular) work in general Scottish place-name studies remains W F H Nicolaisen's *Scottish Place-Names: Their Study and Significance*, first published in 1976 but revised in a second edition in 2001 and reprinted in 2011. By any standards, this was a major breakthrough in the field, as it provided a clear and scholarly survey of the whole range of Scottish place-names by an established expert. Ian Fraser joined Professor Nicolaisen in the Scottish Place-Name Survey in 1965 and continued in post until his retirement in 2000, publishing many works on place-names during his time in the Survey.[32] Professor Carole Hough, Scotland's only professor of onomastics, should be mentioned here as well. She is very active in the field and has published several articles, one of which, entitled 'The role of onomastics in historical linguistics', is particularly useful as an introduction to aspects of the subject.[33] Other recent writers have concentrated on more specialised studies, or on specific areas of the country. These have included Eileen Brooke-Freeman, Thomas Clancy, Richard Cox, Peder Gammeltoft, Arne Kruse, Alan Macniven, Berit Sandnes and Doreen Waugh on aspects of Scandinavian names in Scotland, and Jake King's unpublished PhD thesis on the topic of river names.[34] The Scottish Place-Name Society produces a regular *Newsletter* which contains updates of research in progress, as well as reviews of current onomastic literature. The *Journal of Scottish Name Studies*, jointly edited by Richard Cox and Simon Taylor, is an important vehicle for the dissemination of articles on name studies relating to Scotland.[35] In addition, the volumes covering the place-names of Fife, produced by Simon Taylor with Gilbert Márkus, are impressively thorough.[36] Gilbert Márkus has also recently produced a book on the place-names of Bute in similar format.[37]

RESEARCH MATERIALS IN ONOMASTICS

There is a wide range of material available for onomastic study. For place-name studies, the most important sources are those which can help to elucidate the derivation of the place-name in question. The most systematic approach to this is the collection of early forms of the name which may appear in early writings or on historic maps. These may well be different from current forms, but may provide the skilled researcher with clues which can reveal the true meaning of the name. Pronunciation and spelling are likewise useful in reconstructing the derivation of 'difficult' names. Folk etymology is also a fascinating branch of the subject because, although local tales told to 'elucidate' the meaning of a name may not always succeed in arriving at an accurate etymology, linguistically speaking, they have much to reveal about the lives of the people who created the tales.

The written materials that are the focus of most academic research are usually documents which provide references to place-names at an official or administrative level. An early land grant, royal charter, rental or legal document will provide a form which may well be dateable, and may even give some information on historical data such as land value, status or ownership. All of these factors may help the researcher to understand the significance of a place-name, the linguistic origins of which may be obscure to the modern user of the name. Changes in language or dialect may well have occurred which make the derivation of individual place-names opaque. Scotland's linguistic history is complex, and many of its place-names were coined in languages which are not now spoken in their original settlement areas. A good example of this is found in Fife, where names of Pictish, Gaelic, Norse, Scots, French and Scottish Standard English have survived in the place-name coverage.

Important sources for place-names are early maps.[38] The spelling forms on these are usually dateable, and provide a location as well, even if the accuracy of maps before 1700 tends to be low compared with their modern equivalents. In Scotland, important maps such as those of Timothy Pont (c. 1590–1600) and General William Roy's Military Survey (1748–55) contain many names which are of key significance in onomastics.[39]

Personal name studies can use source material of similar origins, but they obviously find more relevant data in such records as census data, genealogical works and other collections of personal names. These could include not only documentary material but also such esoteric sources as tombstones in churchyards and ecclesiastical buildings. Lists of names appear in commissariat records, burgh and county records, accounts of workers' guilds and societies, and innumerable sources of this kind.[40]

Onomastic material relating to topics other than place and personal names can be found in many different sources, too numerous to list in this survey, although an attempt has been made to include a representative selection of articles by current researchers in the bibliography. Specialist publications on all aspects of the humanities, technical and scientific works, dictionaries, handbooks and general reference works can all provide data for research. These days, the internet will also supply an enormous resource for listings of all kinds, many of which will prove relevant research material for onomasticians.

ONOMASTIC STUDIES IN SCOTLAND

Up till the 1950s, as has been pointed out, much of the significant research into place-names on mainland Scotland had been in the field of Celtic studies, with the aforementioned publications by Mackinnon and Watson being among the most important. Scholars like Kenneth H Jackson, working in the complex areas of Celtic language, found the distribution of certain key Celtic generics, and the presence of early Celtic river names, to have important significance in their researches.[41] There were, in addition, two seminal PhD theses produced in the 1940s that covered areas where Celtic place-names were in the minority. May Williamson's 'Non-Celtic Place-Names of the Scottish Border Counties' (1942) and Norman Dixon's 'Place-Names of Midlothian' (1947)[42] owe much to the scholarly legacy of W J Watson, and to the influence of the English Place-Name Society. *The Place-Names of West Lothian* by Angus MacDonald (1941) was one of the first sound academic volumes to cover a single Scottish county since W J Watson's *Place-names of Ross and Cromarty* (1906). The other major work to appear in print was William M Alexander's *The Place-Names of Aberdeenshire*, which appeared in the Third Spalding Club series in 1952. All of these studies were substantial, well-researched and well-documented pieces of work.

The place-names of the Northern and Western Isles were the focus of eminent scholars who had a particular interest in Norse language and settlement. Among these were Jakob Jakobsen, whose work on *The Place-Names of Shetland* was published in English in 1936 (reprinted 1993, with an introduction by Gillian Fellows-Jensen of the University of Copenhagen), having first been published in

Danish in 1901; and Hugh Marwick, who produced *Orkney Farm-Names* in 1952. There were also some significant journal articles published in this period, including such important studies as Magne Oftedal's 'The village names of Lewis in the Outer Hebrides', which appeared in *Norsk Tidsskrift for Sprogvidenskap* in 1954. Unfortunately, as with this paper by Oftedal, some of the research papers were published in academic journals which had a limited readership and, in addition, many parts of Scotland were scantily researched, while other areas enjoyed more attention from the academic community, not only in place-name studies but in other disciplines. This was particularly true of the Scandinavian north and west, which came under much closer scrutiny from the mid-1960s onwards, as mentioned above. On the positive side, one project which has recently attracted significant funding is 'The Shetland Place-Name Project'. Initially funded for three years by a locally matched lottery grant but now part of the Shetland Amenity Trust, Lerwick, the project has been instrumental in collecting and collating place-names from both printed sources and oral tradition for the entire island group.

The Scottish Place-Name Survey, at Edinburgh University, was given the role of a body which would collect, collate and analyse all of the forms of Scottish place-names from documents, maps, and oral tradition. This latter function was very much in keeping with the remit of the School of Scottish Studies, which was to record on tape and photograph the traditional culture of Scotland, and to disseminate this material by whatever means available. As part of an institution which was primarily formed for the collection, recording and analysing of Scotland's oral tradition, there was also a strong emphasis on the process of recording place-name data from informants in the field. With Gaelic in rapid decline during the period 1950–90, the main thrust of this recording programme was aimed at those areas of Scotland where the language was on the verge of extinction.

The School's journal *Scottish Studies*, which provided a forum for a wide range of articles in ethnology, also proved an important vehicle for a series of articles by W F H Nicolaisen and others working in onomastic fields. Among these was Professor G W S Barrow, whose historical researches used place-names and personal names in particularly significant ways, attempting to shed light on early Christian activity in Scotland.[43]

A wide range of studies relating to place-names continued in the last few decades. Many of these were at a local level, involving individuals who had an interest in particular aspects of the discipline which were relevant to local historical studies.[44] A number of these emerged in print, such as Professor John MacQueen's *Place-Names in the Rhinns of Galloway and Luce Valley* (2002) and Catriona Niclain's *Ainmean-Aiteachan Sgire Sholais* (1999). MacQueen's work was the result of scholarly research in documentary sources, while Niclain's, in Gaelic, published a list of place-names largely drawn from oral tradition and early maps. Both of these studies successfully drew upon the various sources available to the authors. Peter Drummond, a former MSc student in Celtic and Scottish Studies, produced a very popular and well-researched book on Scottish hill names which has sold widely to the hill-walking community and to many others who share his interest in naming the landscape.[45]

The University of Glasgow has recently been particularly successful in attracting awards for name research and their current project, entitled 'Scottish Toponymy in Transition', is to run from 2011 to 2014 and is jointly managed by staff in the departments of Celtic and English Language. In 2007, the Scottish Place-Name Society funded a project to digitise a database entitled 'Brittonic Language in the Old North' (BLITON), the fruit of ongoing research by Dr Alan James on this important, but little-investigated subject.[46]

COMPARATIVE STUDIES

The process of onomastic research continues in many directions, with comparative studies being among the more important. The most obvious country to take as a comparator, at least as far as scholarship is concerned, is Ireland. There are many parallels to observe here, since the Irish Folklore Commission, the Irish Ordnance Survey and, in the north, the Ulster Place-Name Society have all been major contributors to the study of names. There are, of course, important bodies of onomastic material common to both Scotland and Ireland, especially in Gaelic and Irish toponymy, but also in the rich and varied range of surnames that have crossed the Irish Sea in both directions. No scholar of personal names can ignore the links between Galloway and Northern Ireland, for example.

Similarly, the English Place-Name Society's production of material is of much relevance to Scotland as far as English place-name elements are concerned. An examination of place-name generics in the Scottish Border counties will produce many parallels with, say, Northumbrian material. The study of place-name elements relating to the expansion of Scandinavian influence in the British Isles has seen much cooperation between Nordic scholars and their Scottish counterparts.[47] There has been a long tradition of comparative study in England of Scandinavian onomastics, and much interplay of ideas, research and publication – and not just on place-names. Numbers of originally English surnames have become established in Scotland as well, and vice versa, and should provide much material for the cross-border researcher.

CASE STUDY METHODOLOGY

There are innumerable situations that the onomastician can use as case studies. The availability of suitable data is the usual criterion in case selection. In general, place-names and personal names are the most fruitful areas for studies of this kind, but this should not deter the researcher from attempting to deal with collections of names outwith these.

Any case study should have definite limits. In the example of place-names, investigation should concentrate on a specific, well-defined geographical area, a well-considered time period, or a particular place-name element. There are many such studies which have been successful, as in the case of the investigation of p-Celtic place-names in *pit-*, which suggested a genuine homeland area for the historical people known as the Picts.[48] A dot-distribution map, comparing the extent of *pit*-names with Pictish Class II symbol stones, provides a vivid example of the way in which onomastic data and archaeological material can be utilised to the benefit of both disciplines.

The development of Scottish surnames can be traced back to the twelfth century, probably due to Norman influence in Scotland, which reflected the appearance of 'fixed' surnames or descriptive surnames from about 1000 in France.[49] But a useful case study could examine Scottish surnames in the mediaeval period that were associated with occupations rather than patronymics. The period from 1100 onwards saw the development of a number of specialised occupations. There was an emergence of organisations such as crafts guilds in a period which experienced an increased European trade and therefore an expansion of urban life. This spawned a wide range of crafts, specialised techniques and improvements in agriculture and animal husbandry, as well as a substantial amount of sophistication in the royal court and the houses of the aristocracy in Scotland. All of this activity generated specialised terms that were adopted by the individuals involved, so that by the later mediaeval period most specialists called themselves after the crafts or offices which identified them in their community. Within the feudal system of tenure and relations, many of these occupations and offices were hereditary, with a powerful motive for the lord to retain the services of his servants. Other surnames, however, are associated with occupations which reflect increasing specialisation in industry, agriculture, food processing or general technology, and thus reflect change rather than continuity.

The sources for investigating these names are extensive, and cover a long period, from c. 1100 to the present day. Among the most important of these, as far as Scottish material is concerned, are the great collections of registers which form the mass of royal and legal documents, many available online, freely available to researchers. These include:

1. Thomson, J M, Paul, J B, Stevenson, J H and Dickson, W K, eds. *Registrum Magni Sigilli Regum Scotorum. The Register of the Great Seal of Scotland, A.D. 1306–1424 [–1660 –1668]* [RMS], 11 vols, Edinburgh, 1882–1914.
2. Burton, J H, Masson, D and Hume Brown, P, eds. *The Register of the Privy Council of Scotland [1545–1689]* [RPC], 36 vols, Edinburgh, 1877–1970.
3. Livingstone, M, Fleming, D H, Beveridge, J and Donaldson, G, eds. *Registrum Secreti Sigilli Regum Scotorum. The Register of the Privy Seal of Scotland. A.D. 1488–1529 [– A.D. 1581–1584]* [RSS], 8 vols, Edinburgh, 1908–82.
4. Thomson, T, ed. *Inquisitionum ad Capellam Domini Regis retornatarum, quae in publicis archivis Scotiae adhuc servantur, abbreviation* [Retours], 3 vols, Edinburgh, 1811–1816.
5. Innes, C and Thomson, T, eds. *The Acts of the Parliament of Scotland. A.D. M.C.XXIV[–M.DCC.VII]* [APS], 12 vols, Edinburgh, 1814–75. See also the online resource <http://www.rps.ac.uk/> [accessed March 2011].

These are valuable for the broad sweep of surnames which are fully indexed and therefore easily accessed. But there are many other collections that will provide suitable examples. The census returns, dating from the 1755 analysis of population by the Rev. Alexander Webster to the present day, contain much important data.[50] A search of church records, such as birth, marriage and death records, will yield much material, and the wide range of rentals, legal records, trade and excise documents will supply similar results.

A collection of occupational surnames can then be divided into distinct categories, and it is the researcher's decision to choose these. However, a general categorisation may emerge as follows:

1. Surnames associated with 'officials' or those involved in administration. This would include surnames like Sargeant, Baillie, Stewart and Marshall.
2. Surnames associated with service to the king or an important member of the aristocracy, such as Cook, Butler, Hunter, Forrester, Dorward (door-keeper), Baxter, Warrender (in charge of a rabbit warren originally), Napier (in charge of napery), etc.
3. Names of specific crafts, such as Cooper, Smith, Lorimer, Cordiner, Fuller, Fletcher, Carpenter, Turner, Taylor, Glover and names ending in -wright, including Cartwright, Wheelwright, Silverwright, etc.
4. Names of trade occupations, such as Merchant, Goldsmith, Naysmith (knife-maker), Peutherer (pewter-maker) and Miller.
5. Agricultural names, such as Hind, Herd, Shepherd, Calvert (calves), Coward (cows), Stoddart (stots), Hoggart (hoggs) and Colthart (colts).
6. Others include Fisher, Skinner, Slater and Sawyer.

Such a categorisation is clearly subjective. The majority of these surnames are still in current use, although the links between name and the actual occupation have long since dissolved. Nevertheless, one may still find a man named Gardener who will specialise as a gardener.

The more recent sources for comparative material will be the censuses of the twentieth and the present centuries. Even telephone directories can give an idea of the regional variation of occupational surnames.

As already noted, the case study requires to be strictly limited in terms of period, geography and choice of material. A study of occupational surnames may be limited to, say, a specific Scottish county, such as Fife, Berwickshire or Banff, where one would find distinct patterns of examples emerging over time. Since few studies have been undertaken in this field, we can speculate that we might find agricultural names predominating in Berwick and names of trades and crafts in Fife, which had a number of urban centres such as Dumfermline and St Andrews that attracted substantial populations. Banff, on the other hand, with both agricultural and maritime populations, might have names which reflect these activities. Yet it could be that occupational surnames in some areas are relatively rare, and very much less common than patronymic names.

In a case study such as this, much depends on the nature of the source material, and the examples of the population which the record displays. The majority of earlier records, such as *RMS* and *RSS*, will feature the names of important individuals in society in medieval times.[51] It is only when census information, after 1801, becomes available, that it is possible to gain access to the complete range of surnames in Britain.

The majority of place-names require analysis in different ways. Much will depend on the nature of the name in question. Is it composed of elements which the user understands? Is it in a dead language? Does it contain linguistic items which are in dialect, or obsolete in common use? These are all relevant questions which can be answered, fully or in part, by an assessment of the written (and spoken) forms of the name as revealed in documentary evidence.

Most settlement names have a written history. They are usually recorded in early documents, maps and similar material. Some names, usually minor in nature, have never appeared in text, and remain in the oral tradition of their particular area, so analysis of settlement names tends to reveal much more about the history of the area in all its aspects.

There are many reasons for the process of derivation of place-names. Some names have a history of more than one language, while others reveal aspects of language that the documentary evidence helps to elucidate and unravel. Many contain personal names, which can themselves tell us about the nature of human society when the name was coined, and so on.

To illustrate this process, we can select a well-known Scottish place-name, and list the known documentary forms:

> *Prestwick*, Ayrshire, is a well-established parish, and now the site of a famous international airport. The early forms are as follows:
>
> - *Prestwic, 1165–1293, Paisley Registrum; 1227, Glasgow Registrum*
> - *Prestwyc, c. 1272, Paisley Registrum*
> - *Prestwyk, 1335–7, Calendar of Documents Relating to Scotland (CDS)*
> - *Prestwik, 1330, Exchequer Rolls; 1504–1551, Register of the Great Seal (RMS)*
> - *Prestvik, 1468, RMS*
> - *Prestuik, 1609, 1629, RMS*
> - *Presticke, 1621, Retours*
> - *Prestinck, 1654, Blaeu Atlas*
> - *Prestrick, 1658, RMS*

The consistent appearance of *prest* in most of these early spellings clearly points to Old English *prēost* 'priest' as the specific element in the name, while Old English *wīc* 'dwelling', 'farm' is the generic, giving 'priest's dwelling or farm' as the full derivation. There are, of course, parallels which are found in England, such as *Prestwich* in Lancashire, and *Prestwick* in Northumberland. And there are many *Preston* 'priest's farm' examples throughout England.

When dealing with a name like *Prestwick*, one should always be aware of other place-names which contain the *-wīc* generic. In Scotland, we have *Hawick* and *Fenwick* in Roxburghshire, *Fishwick* in Berwickshire, *Dawick* in Peebles, *North*

Berwick in East Lothian and four *Borthwicks* (Roxburgh, Midlothian, Berwickshire and Selkirkshire). This Old English farm term is widespread in England, so the presence of these names clearly indicates the spread of English settlement into Southern Scotland from the eighth century AD onwards.

This kind of investigation is crucial to any study of place-names, as it is only this process which, in many cases, can reveal the name's true meaning and significance.

CONCLUSION

It is most encouraging that current research is more extensive than at any time in the past and involves a number of scholars and students, part-time workers, local historians and amateur enthusiasts, most of whom are members of the Scottish Place-Name Society (SPNS) and who keep in touch with current research through the Society, its publications and its regular conferences. The Society has proved a real benefit to research in the field of Scottish place-names in that it provides a regular forum for discussion on the many complex issues involved. The Society's website is also an excellent resource for all serious name researchers. A newcomer to the digital landscape is Onomastics.co.uk, a website established in October 2012 by two postgraduate students at Glasgow University, Alice Crook and Leonie Dunlop, with help from IT specialist Scott McGready. It complements research tools available on the SPNS website.

The process of producing an all-embracing and comprehensive work on place-names is complex and time-consuming. Not only does it depend on a rigorous standard of scholarship, but there is often an element of research that simply requires the dogged investigation of written matter, in the form of records, maps and charters, which is enormously dependent on volunteers who are experienced in the process. Members of local history societies, who have the necessary background for local studies of this nature and who have access to a wide range of source material, can be enormously helpful, but the future of onomastics depends on healthy university funding. It is good to see that university departments are currently giving their support to onomastic research at the postgraduate level, and it is to be hoped that this will make the publication of name research increasingly possible.

Scholars such as Simon Taylor and Gilbert Márkus, with their five published volumes of *The Place-Names of Fife*,[52] have clearly demonstrated that such comprehensive county surveys require dedicated teamwork, not only by the academics involved in the leadership of the process but also by a supporting group of volunteers with specific skills. The experience of those working on the Shetland Place-Names Project is very similar. Here, the contribution of local people, who know the local landscape and its history, is a vital ingredient in the success of the project. Ethnology and onomastics can and should go hand in hand, to the benefit of both.

1 For example, Nicolaisen, 2011, 324–44.
2 Meek, 1998, 147–68.
3 For example, Crawford, 1987, 92–115.
4 For example, Scott, 2008 and Grant, 2010.
5 For example, Ray, 1995, 3–28; Ridinger, 1998, 97–111.
6 For example, the ethnological approach taken in Bramwell, 2007, 35–56.
7 Stewart, 1975, 3–19.
8 Young, 2009, 75–112.
9 Fraser, 1978, 83–90.
10 Waugh, 1996, 242–54.
11 McKinley, 1990, 51–71.
12 Black, 1946.
13 Nicolaisen, 2011, 156.
14 For example, Sellar, 2005, 199–208.
15 Hanks and Hodges, 1990.
16 See *NAMES*, 2001, 228–30; 248–53; 259–62; 288–92; 304–8.
17 West, 2012, 76–103.
18 Shuldham-Shaw, Lyle and Campbell, 2002, 526–29.
19 For example, Clyne, 1989 and Walker, 2003.
20 MacKillop, 1986–90, 428–502.
21 See also Macleod, 2005.
22 Simpson, 2011.
23 Black, 1946, xxxi.
24 Kay, 2013.
25 Field, 1972.
26 For a valuable analysis of Joyce's publication, see Nicolaisen, 1982, 72–89.
27 MacKinnon, D. Place-names and personal names in Argyle, *Scotsman*, 9 November 1887 to 18 January 1888.
28 Cameron, 1890, 122–39; Maxwell, 1894.
29 English Place-Name Society (EPNS), vols. 1–89, 1924–2012.
30 See Crawford, 1987, especially 92–115. Also Crawford, 1995.
31 See, for example, Pálsson, 1996, 7–24; Grant, 2004, 97–123; and Kruse, 2011, 17–40.
32 These publications include his book on the place-names of Arran, 1999.
33 Hough, 2009, 29–46.
34 See also King, 2010 and 2009.
35 *Journal of Scottish Name Studies* volumes have been produced annually since 2007.
36 Taylor, with Márkus, 2006–13.
37 Márkus, 2012.
38 Royal Scottish Geographical Society, 1973, 1983.
39 See also Fleet, Wilkes and Withers, 2011.
40 Black, 1946, lix–lxxi gives a good list of sources for Scottish surnames.
41 Jackson, 1953.
42 Both of these University of Edinburgh theses are available digitally on the website of the Scottish Place-Name Society, <http://www.spns.org.uk>. The Society has also reprinted the Dixon thesis (Edinburgh, 2011).
43 See, for example, Barrow, 1983, 1–15.
44 A good example is Reid, 2010.

45 Drummond, 2007.
46 The database can be found at <www.spns.org.uk/bliton/Aindex.html> [accessed November 2012].
47 See, for example, Fellows-Jensen, 1985, 65–82.
48 Nicolaisen, 2011, 198.
49 Black, 1946, xiii.
50 Kyd, 1975.
51 A good example is Taylor, 1994, 99–118.
52 Taylor with Márkus, 2006–13.

BIBLIOGRAPHY AND FURTHER READING

Barrow, G W S. The childhood of Scottish christianity, *Scottish Studies*, 27 (1983), 1–15.
Black, G F. *The Surnames of Scotland*, New York, 1946.
Bramwell, E. Names in multicultural Scotland, *ONOMA*, 23 (2009), 158–63.
Bramwell, E. Community bynames in the Western Isles, *NOMINA*, 30 (2007), 35–56.
Brooke-Freeman, E. Memories, meids and maps: The Shetland Place-Names Project, *Journal of SNS*, 4 (2011), 43–60.
Brooke-Freeman, E. Putting Jakobsen on the map: Collecting Shetland place-names in the 21st century. In Sigurðardóttir, T and Smith, B, eds, *Jakob Jakobsen in Shetland and the Faroes*, Lerwick 2010, 99–109.
Cameron, A. Arran place names, *TGSI*, 17 (1890), 122–39.
Clyne, D. *Gaelic Names for Flowers and Plants*, Cornwall, 1989.
Crawford, B E. *Scandinavian Scotland*, Leicester, 1987.
Crawford, B E, ed. *Scandinavian Settlement in Northern Britain*, London, 1995.
Curtis, L. Tarbat or not Tarbat? Was there a portage on the Tarbat peninsula, *Journal of Scottish Name Studies*, 5 (2011), 1–34.
Drummond, P. *Scottish Hill Names*, Glasgow, 2007.
Drummond, P. Place-name losses and changes – a study in Peeblesshire: A comparative study of hill-names and other toponyms, *Nomina*, 32 (2010), 5–17.
Fellows-Jensen, G. Viking settlement in the Northern and Western Isles – the place-name evidence as seen from Denmark and the Danelaw. In Fenton, A and Pálsson, H, eds, *The Northern and Western Isles in the Viking World*, Glasgow, 1984, 148–68.
Fellows-Jensen, G. Scandinavian settlement in Cumbria and Dumfriesshire: The place-name evidence. In Baldwin, J R and Whyte, I D, eds, *Scandinavians in Cumbria*, Edinburgh, 1985, 65–82.
Field, J. *English Field Names*, Newton Abbot, 1972.
Fleet, C, Wilkes, M and Withers, C W J. *Scotland: Mapping the Nation*, Edinburgh, 2011.
Fraser, I A. The place-names of a deserted island: Eilean nan Ròn, *Scottish Studies*, 22 (1978), 83–90.
Fraser, I A. *The Place-Names of Arran*, Glasgow, 1999.
Gammeltoft, P, Hough, C and Waugh, D, eds. *Cultural Contacts in the North Atlantic Region: The Evidence of Names*, Shetland, 2005.
Gilbert, J M. Place-names and managed woods in medieval Scotland, *Journal of Scottish Name Studies*, 5 (2011), 35–56.
Grant, A. A reconsideration of the *kirk*-names in south-west Scotland, *Northern Studies*, 38 (2004), 97–123.
Grant, A. *The Pocket Guide to Scottish Place-Names*, Glasgow, 2010.
Greig, G and Duncan, J B. *The Greig–Duncan Folk Song Collection*, eds, P Shuldham-Shaw, E B Lyle and K Campbell, 8 vols, Aberdeen and Edinburgh, 1981–2002.

Hanks, P, Hodges, F, Mills, A D and Room, A. *The Oxford Names Companion*, Oxford, 2002.

Hanks, P and Hodges, F. *A Dictionary of First Names*, Oxford, 1990.

Hough, C. The role of onomastics in historical linguistics, *Journal of Scottish Name Studies*, 3 (2009), 29–46.

Jackson, K H. *Language and History of Early Britain*, Edinburgh, 1953.

Jakobsen, J. *The Place-Names of Shetland*, Copenhagen, 1936 (reprinted Orkney, 1993).

Joyce, P W. *The Origin and History of Irish Names and Places*, Dublin, 1869.

Kay, C J. Footprints from the past: The survival of Scots kinship terms. In Anderson, W, ed., *Language in Scotland: Corpus-based Studies*, Amsterdam, 2013, 145–65.

King, J. Haberberui: An aberration, *Journal of Scottish Name Studies*, 3 (2009), 127–34.

King, J. Aberkarf, *Journal of Scottish Name Studies*, 4 (2010), 159–68.

Kruse, A. Fair Isle, *Northern Studies*, 42 (2011), 17–40.

Kyd, J G, ed. *Scottish Population Statistics, Including Webster's Analysis of Population 1755*, Edinburgh, 1975.

MacKillop, D. Rocks, skerries, shoals and islands in the sounds of Harris and Uist and around the Island of Berneray, *TGSI*, 56 (1988–90), 428–502.

Macleod, G. *Muir is Tír*, Stornoway, 2005.

MacQueen, J. *Place-Names in the Rhinns of Galloway and Luce Valley*, Stranraer, 2002

MacQueen, J. *Place-Names of the Wigtownshire Moors and Machars*, Stranraer, 2008.

Márkus, G. *The Place-Names of Bute*, Stamford, 2012.

Marwick, H. *Orkney Farm-Names*, Kirkwall, 1952.

Maxwell, H. *Scottish Land-Names*, Edinburgh, 1894.

McKinley, R. *A History of British Surnames*, London and New York, 1990.

Meek, D E. Place-names and literature: Evidence from the Gaelic ballads. In Taylor, S, ed., *The Uses of Place-Names*, Edinburgh, 1998, 147–68.

Miles, J. *Owl's Hoot: How People Name Their Houses*, London, 2000.

Muhr, K. Place-names and Scottish clan traditions in north-east County Antrim. In McClure, J D, Kirk, J and Storrie, M, eds, *A Land that Lies Westward: Language and Culture in Islay and Argyll*, Edinburgh, 79–102.

Nicolaisen, W F H. P.W. Joyce and Scotland. In MacAodha, B S, ed., *Topothesia: Essays in honour of T.S. Ó Maille*, Galway, 1982, 72–89.

Nicolaisen, W F H. *Scottish Place-Names: Their Study and Significance*, 2nd edn, Edinburgh, 2011.

Nicolaisen, W F H. *In the Beginning was the Name: Selected Essays by Professor W F H Nicolaisen*, Lerwick, 2011.

Oftedal, M. The village names of Lewis in the Outer Hebrides, *Norsk Tidsskrift for Sprogvidenskap*, 17 (1954), 363–408.

Pálsson, H. Aspects of Norse place-names in the Western Isles, *Northern Studies*, 31 (1996), 7–24.

Ray, A G. Calling the dog: The sources of AKC [American Kennel Club] breed names, *NAMES*, 43:1 (March 1995), 3–28.

Reid, J. *The Place-Names of Falkirk and East Stirlingshire*, Falkirk, 2010.

Ridinger, R B M. Children of the satyrs: Naming patterns of leather and Levi clubs, *NAMES*, 46:2 (June 1998), 97–111.

Robertson, J A. *The Gaelic Topography of Scotland and What it Proves Explained, with much Historical, Antiquarian and Descriptive Information*, Edinburgh, 1869.

Royal Scottish Geographical Society. *The Early Maps of Scotland*, vols 1 and 2, Edinburgh, 1973, 1983.

Scott, M. *Say it in Scots: Scottish Place-Names*, Edinburgh, 2008.

Scott, M. Words, names and culture: Place-names and the Scots language, *Journal of Scottish Name Studies*, 2 (2008), 85–98.

Sellar, D. The significance of names: Scandinavian personal names in the Northern and Western Isles. In Gammeltoft, P, Hough, C and Waugh, D, eds, *Cultural Contacts in the North Atlantic Region: The Evidence of Names*, Lerwick, 2005, 199–208.

Simpson, C H. *Water in Burgidale: Shetland Fisheries in a Pre-Electronic Age (Includes Names of Fishing Meids or Marks)*, Lerwick, 2011.

Stewart, G R. *Names on the Globe*, Oxford, 1975, 3–19.

Taylor, S. Babbet and bridin pudding, or polyglot Fife in the Middle Ages, *NOMINA*, 17 (1994), 99–118.

Taylor, S, ed. *The Uses of Place-Names*, St John's House Papers No. 7, St Andrews, Edinburgh, 1998.

Taylor, S, with Márkus, G. *The Place Names of Fife*, 5 vols, Donington, 2006–13.

Walker, A. *A Garden of Herbs*, Argyll, 2003.

Watson, W J. *The Place-Names of Ross and Cromarty*, Inverness, 1904.

Watson, W J. *The History of the Celtic Place-Names of Scotland*, Edinburgh, 1926.

Waugh, D. Neglected topographic names: *Ness*-names in Orkney and Shetland, *New Orkney Antiquarian Journal*, 4 (2009), 17–28.

Waugh, D. *Drongs, hjogelbens, pobis* and *skoreks*: Jakobsen recorded them all. In Sigurðardóttir, T and Smith, B, eds, *Jakob Jakobsen in Shetland and the Faroes*, Lerwick, 2010, 14–32.

Waugh, D J. Sand, Innersand and Garderhouse: Place-names in use. In Waugh, D, ed., *Shetland's Northern Links, Language and History*, Edinburgh, 1996, 242–54.

West, G. *Voicing Scotland: Folk, Culture, Nation*, Edinburgh, 2012.

Young, S. Oil and gas field names in the central and northern sectors of the North Sea: Their provenance, cultural influence, longevity and onshore migration, *Nomina*, 32 (2009), 75–112.

JOURNALS

Journal of the English Place-Name Society, 1924–present
Journal of Scottish Name Studies, 2007–present
NAMES: A Journal of Onomastics (journal of the American Name Society), 1953–present
NOMINA (journal of the Society for Name Studies in Britain and Ireland), 1977–present
ONOMA (journal of the International Council of Onomastic Sciences (ICOS)), 1950–present

PART FOUR

●

Sources and Resources

17 Oral Testimony

GARY J WEST

The use of oral sources has been central to the discipline of ethnology throughout much of its history, although only from the middle of the twentieth century did portable audio technology develop fully enough to allow for the widespread capture of the sound of speech itself.[1] Up until then, the spoken word of those 'fellows who cut the hay'[2] had to be transcribed onto the page by hand, thus immediately altering its character to that of a partial representation that engaged eyes rather than ears. And yet this preoccupation with the written word has proved to be a stubborn habit to break, for transcription of the sound into text has remained a central practice for most scholars down to the present day. Only now, in the digital age, have we begun to question the wisdom of this and, through increasing use of websites and other electronic media, actual voices are once again coming to the fore.

That journey has been a long and complex one, with a plethora of ideas, theories, attitudes and concerns emerging along the way. This chapter attempts to present a synthesis of these issues, especially as they relate to Scotland, discussing both oral history and oral tradition, with some illustrative case study examples drawn largely from my own research. Volume 10 of this series[3] serves as an illuminating insight into some of the many manifestations of the creative use and power of oral culture, but it should be remembered that oral sources are relevant to the entire spectrum of ethnology in general, and of this series in particular.

THE PROGRESS OF ORAL HISTORY

Oral history is usually considered to be first-hand testimony reported retrospectively by someone 'who was there' and who therefore personally witnessed the event or process being described. The term is used to refer to both the research activity, involving the recording of verbally delivered information, and to that information itself. It is therefore a product of 'memory' and, in many respects, the mid twentieth-century move towards its inclusion within the toolkit of historians represented revival rather than innovation, for before the nineteenth-century preoccupation with the written document, scholars of both folklore and history were quite happy to rely on individual and collective 'remembering' for the construction of their narratives of the past.[4]

However, what we now term oral history is a modern activity, and in his analysis of its development as a discipline since the middle of the twentieth century, Alistair Thomson identifies what he terms 'four paradigm transforma-tions'.[5] The initial shift was towards the use of memory at all, as left-leaning historians began to borrow ideas from neighbouring disciplines, especially folklore and ethnology, in order to tell the story of the past 'from below'. In this respect, the use of oral sources was in itself a politicised issue, challenging not only *how* history should be uncovered, but also *whose* history should be addressed in the first place.[6] The underlying philosophy was to give literal voice to those whose stories were seldom told: the masses, the minorities and the dispossessed. The authoritative voice of the all-seeing professional historian could be challenged in the process, with ordinary people now able to serve as narrators of their own lives. In this respect, the development of oral history represented much more than a new methodology: it was, at its best, a deep-seated challenge to the historical establishment *per se*.

As might have been expected, the course of such a fundamental challenge to orthodoxy did not run entirely smoothly, and the pioneers of oral history found themselves facing penetrating questions as to the validity of their work. The fallibility of the human memory, the subjective nature of opinion-based reflection and the temptation of outright invention were all issues that were highlighted by the movement's critics and which had to be faced full-on by its proponents. Leading the way for the latter was Paul Thompson, whose work, especially his *Voice of the Past*, first published in 1978, went a long way towards placing oral history on a professional footing. Indeed, it can be viewed as the marker for the move into the second transformative phase, which Alistair Thomson characterises as a 'post-positivist' attitude to memory and subjectivity, whereby oral historians issued a counter-challenge to their critics:

> In the late 1970s imaginative oral historians turned these criticisms on their head and argued that the so-called unreliability of memory was also its strength, and that the subjectivity of memory provided clues not only about the meanings of historical experience, but also about the relationships between past and present, between memory and personal identity, and between individual and collective memory.[7]

History is not only about facts, they argued, but also about opinions, feelings, aspirations and experiences. How people reflect on their own past, and why they choose to voice some aspects and not others came to be seen as being just as valid a line of enquiry as 'what actually happened'. In this claim they were pre-empting the new attitudes that emerged within the ethnographic sciences in the following decade, especially amongst anthropologists, who began to be much more self-reflexive in their methods of representing the cultures they studied.[8] Even through their 'participant-observation' approach of living within the communities they were investigating, all that could ever be provided, they admitted, was a 'version' of that way of life, as refracted through their own experience and personalities. Some went as far as to vociferously denounce the use of any oral recording in ethnographic fieldwork at all, considering it a poor substitute for the observation of 'speech in action'. Stephen Tyler, in particular, was scathing of those who had moved towards this method of data gathering:

> For even as they think to have returned to 'oral performance' or 'dialogue', in order that the native have a place in the text, they exercise total control over her discourse and steal the only thing she has left – her voice.[9]

While oral historians would clearly reject Tyler's accusation that to record a voice is also to steal it, the next key phase of their discipline was certainly marked by a similar preoccupation with the role and power of the interviewer. While the second period had highlighted the subjectivity of the memories of 'the observed', the third shifted the focus to the actions and personality of 'the observer', and to the importance of recognising that any given oral history interview is the direct product of the engagement between at least two people. Which questions are asked, how they are framed, how the agenda is set, what biases and ideologies are held by the interrogator and the prevailing attitudes and wisdom of the day must influence the collected narrative in ways which had not hitherto been considered. Interviewer and interviewee now became 'interview partners', as the final product – the interview transcription – was now seen to be a collective production, and not simply a record of the respondent's unfiltered memories alone.

All this has led to a movement away from treating the use of oral testimony as simply a means of filling in factual gaps that have been left by reliance upon documentary sources. Oral sources can, of course, fulfil this role in many circumstances, particularly in cases where the topic of enquiry relates to the 'everyday', but the influence of anthropologists, folklorists and ethnologists has brought a marked revisionist attitude which challenges the idea held by many that the oral interview, once transcribed, represents a source document which is no different in essence from any other. The oral history practitioner can never be detached from the results of the collecting process, for the interviewer plays such a central role in the creation of the transcript document that it cannot therefore be treated in the same manner as written evidence consulted passively in a library or archive.[10]

The use of orally sourced material adheres to what Lindqvist categorises as 'history as experience',[11] for the life story or biographical approach provides a projection of the worldview of the individual informant, relying heavily on personal interpretations of the past: it is micro-history through the eyes and indeed memories of those whose lives helped to shape it. The emphasis, then, is upon the *experience* of living in a past context rather than on the wider political, economic and social framework that can in turn be provided through use of complementary sources of a documentary form. As Portelli notes, the importance of oral testimony 'may lie not in its adherence to fact, but rather in its departure from it, as imagination, symbolism, and desire emerge'.[12]

All this may seem proof to the general reader that academics are wont to make life much more complicated than it need be! However, it is important to realise that the use of oral sources is *not* a straightforward issue, and is seldom simply a matter of 'asking the fellow who cuts the hay'. Rather, it has become a highly theorised and sophisticated activity, as rigorously debated and deconstructed as any other scholarly methodology in the humanities and social sciences, and one which has now earned itself widespread (if not unanimous) acceptance in the academy.

Thomson's final paradigm transformation has brought us to the phase in which we currently find ourselves, as marked by the digital revolution of the early twenty-first century. Both the capturing and dissemination of oral sources has entered an entirely new context that has the potential to be as revolutionary to their impact as was the introduction of the portable tape recorder in the mid twentieth century. The implications of this are as yet unclear, but Michael Frisch's prediction in 2004 that digitisation would end our preoccupation with transcription and return actual sound to the centre of oral history is already showing signs of truth.[13] As highlighted below, Scotland is at the forefront of the digital revolution, and is very well placed to lead from the front in the return to aurality. The ways in which we use this technology may also substantially reshape the process of oral history, offering new approaches that might break the traditional linear model of preparation, interview, editing and dissemination. One leading folklorists agrees:

> These textual and archival tools have great promise: they will help us identify the contours of oral tradition in older texts, they will help us discern previously unrecognized patterns in the archives, and they will help us shape new research questions.[14]

As is clear from this short passage, Tangherlini's focus is not so much on 'history', but rather on another related concept that relies on both voice and memory for its lifeblood. Let us turn, therefore, to 'oral tradition' in general, and to its influence on ethnology in Scotland in particular.

SCOTLAND AND ORAL TRADITION

If ethnology is a discipline that sits at the intersection between history and anthropology, as argued by Stoklund amongst others,[15] then it is natural that we consider the use of oral *history* as central to its activities. And yet *tradition*, too, lies at the heart of ethnological investigation.[16] Jan Vansina, a leading historian of Africa, was one of the first to produce an extended discussion of the connections and differences between oral history and oral tradition, and his 1985 book on the subject remains a central text for any discussion of oral sources in general. For Vansina,

> the expression 'oral tradition' applies to both a process and to its products. The products are oral messages based on previous oral messages, at least a generation old. The process is the transmission of such messages by word of mouth over time until the disappearance of the message. Hence any given oral tradition is but a rendering at one moment, an element in a process of oral development that began with the original communication.[17]

These 'oral messages' can take many different forms: news, anecdotes, reports, proverbs and gossip, but also what are often termed 'the verbal arts', such as songs, tales, legends and myths. Oral tradition thus differs from oral history both in terms of the variety of subject matter it contains and, critically, also in its character, purpose, provenance and longevity. And it too has been the focus of a good deal of theoretical debate, much of it coming to maturity in the twentieth century, but with strong antecedents stretching back to at least the eighteenth century.[18]

Scotland has served as a key focus of this, for the use of oral sources in attempts to understand the past has very deep roots here. This story has been told elsewhere,[19] but one only has to consider the approaches of a handful of key cultural figures in order to appreciate the strength of orality within the nation's past. The controversy surrounding the Ossianic publications of James Macpherson in the early 1760s brought into sharp focus the debate which continues to this day concerning *authenticity*, and in particular the role of the collector in the re-presentation and onward transmission of the traditions themselves. Encouraged by various key figures of the Scottish Enlightenment, especially Hugh Blair, Macpherson used his knowledge of the oral tradition of the Highlands and the Gaelic language that conveyed it to supply a growing demand for what we might term the exotic otherness of home. With Jacobitism safely out of the way, Highland society could now become repackaged as a noble survival of an ancient culture on the fringes of European civilisation, and any manifestation of this had the potential to capture the imagination not just of Scotland but of the entire continent. In 1760, Macpherson anonymously published *Fragments of Ancient Poetry, Collected in the Highlands of Scotland, and Translated from the Gaelic or Erse Language*, and claimed that these fragments of prose-poems were composed by a single ancient Scottish bard called Ossian. The project was an immediate success, causing great excitement amongst the literati of Europe who believed that the north now boasted its own Homer, and so Macpherson followed up with two further collections: *Fingal* in 1761 and *Temora* two years later. A two-volume edition of all of this material, *The Works of Ossian, Son of Fingal*, followed in 1765.

The resulting controversy related to the perceived gap between the claims and the reality of the provenance and authorship of this material, and the whole episode highlighted a fundamental misunderstanding of the nature of oral tradition. Dr Samuel Johnson was the most critical sceptic at the time, refusing to believe that oral tradition could support narratives of that complexity and degree of development over such a long period, and demanded to see manuscript proof. That none was forthcoming, and that Johnson therefore dismissed Macpherson as a fraud, has had lasting implications down to the present day. As James Porter has shown, there has since been two centuries of 'Macpherson-baiting', accompanied by a strong and lasting mistrust of oral tradition in general within some sectors of academia. Porter, McKean and other contributors to a themed volume of the *Journal of American Folklore* in 2001 have done a good deal to begin to rescue Macpherson's reputation, however, demonstrating how influential his fieldwork methods were, and detailing the extent to which his creative and polished narratives did indeed rely on oral traditions still extant during his lifetime.[20]

Despite the heat of the Ossian controversy, a steady stream of key figures in the collection and study of oral tradition emerged within Scotland, all of them fully conversant with similar activities amongst their European contemporaries. Robert Burns (1759–1796), Walter Scott (1771–1832), John Francis Campbell (1822–1885), Alexander Carmichael (1832–1912), Gavin Greig (1856–1914), James Bruce Duncan (1848–1917) and John Lorne Campbell (1906–1996) all made extensive and lasting contributions to the known corpus of traditional tales and songs.[21] And so, when the School of Scottish Studies was founded at the University of Edinburgh in 1951, there already existed a very strong foundation on which to build.

The School's initial remit was wide-ranging and interdisciplinary in nature, including linguistic, historical, archaeological, musical, legal and geographical interests. However, Scotland's oral traditions were especially emphasised as a pre-eminent focus for collection and study, as the nation was recognised internationally as having one of the richest legacies of folklore and folksong anywhere within the Western world. These developments were part of a wider northern European movement that encouraged the establishment of national collections of cultural tradition, building on earlier work in the likes of Germany, France, Finland, Sweden, England and Ireland. The modus operandi and the archival system employed was closely modelled in focus and form on the Irish Folklore Commission, founded in 1935, which in turn had been heavily influenced by earlier Swedish initiatives, especially the archives of folk culture and dialects at Uppsala. Colleagues from both of these nations offered considerable support to the nascent development in Scotland.

While the contributions of the first two fieldworkers at the School of Scottish Studies, Calum Maclean and Hamish Henderson, have rightly received a reasonable amount of attention, another key figure on the early staff deserves recognition for his work in uniting the sister fields of history and ethnology. Through forensic empirical investigation of all forms of historical source material, Eric Cregeen demonstrated how the study of oral history, oral tradition, language, material culture and documentary evidence could be combined to provide deep and penetrating insights into the social and cultural pasts of specific communities. From his appointment in 1966 until his untimely death in 1983, Cregeen developed a particular interest in the Western Highlands, and especially the island of Tiree. His work provides convincing evidence of the reliability of oral tradition in those areas where it played a significant role in society and where both individual and collective memory formed a keystone of people's understanding of their place in the world:

> Family tradition in the Gaelic areas is remarkable for its depth and accuracy
> . . . This family lore opens up tremendous possibilities to the historian.
> One's informant's grasp of the patronymics of his ancestors and of those
> of his neighbours frequently gives easy access to very early data indeed,
> enables one to identify individuals who are named in 17th and 18th century

records and vastly reduces the labour of investigating written records. Indeed it is an indispensable research tool in Highland areas where parish records may not be available until the end of the 18th century . . . One of these same informants, asked to comment on the names of sixty seven heads of households listed in the 1851 census of his township, had information about sixty two of them, knew the name of the individual's father in thirty two cases, and was able to give a great deal more detail for a considerable number: e.g., the names and occupations of grandparents and great grandparents; details of their children, their occupations, appearances and abilities (whether for example they had the second sight or composed songs – and frequently he could sing their songs, which were otherwise unknown).[22]

These sentiments were delivered in 1973 to an audience comprising many of the key figures of both oral history and tradition within Britain and Ireland, and were very well received. T C Smout considered it 'the very best of the marriage between oral history and folk-life studies' and, while recognising the enormous scope and value of the School's work, was keen to make the point that it could not be expected to shoulder the full burden of oral source development on behalf of the nation.[23] 'Folklorists' and oral historians' interests only partly overlap,' he believed, and so other routes must be followed alongside that of the School.[24] His pleas were noted and indeed acted upon, with the founding of the UK-wide Oral History Society the following year (1974) and the Scottish Oral History Group, with Cregeen as its first chairman, in 1978.[25]

During the six decades of the School of Scottish Studies' life so far, an immense collection of oral, visual and documentary sources has been amassed and serves as the central resource for the delivery of both undergraduate and postgraduate teaching to well over 200 students per year, as well as fuelling the research activities of a wide range of national and international scholars. The audio collections comprise over 30,000 items of sound recordings of song and verse, instrumental music, oral narrative, custom and belief, traditional knowledge, material culture and contemporary ethnology in Scots, Gaelic and English. This includes around 13,000 fieldwork recordings undertaken by staff and students, as well as donated material from individual collectors and Scottish oral history projects, such as the Scottish Labour History project (394 recordings); the Ian MacDougall Collection of work and wartime experience (556); the Calum Maclean wax cylinder collection made in the 1940s (236) and the John Levy Collection of original fieldwork of mainly religious music from Taiwan, Hong Kong, India, Sri Lanka, Bhutan, Iceland and Britain (694). Published items include commercial discs, LPs and 78s of folk and traditional music donated by individuals (4,870).[26]

The new century has seen the beginnings of a digitisation programme within the School, in partnership with other institutions holding key oral source collections, such as BBC Scotland and the National Trust for Scotland. Under the umbrella organisation set up for this purpose, Tobar an Dualchais/Kist o Riches, around 80 per cent of the fieldwork recordings have been digitised, with around 50 per cent having been catalogued.[27] Although there remains much work to be done, this represents a major advancement in the dissemination of oral source material for the study of Scotland's culture and tradition, with free worldwide access now available to these sound recordings which span sixty years.[28] In this respect, Scotland has begun to embrace Thomson's fourth 'paradigm transformation' and as such is well placed to take full advantage of the digitisation phase by seeking new audiences and applications for orally collected and transmitted materials.

Smout's warning that Scotland must develop a tradition of oral enquiry that was in keeping with the aims of social history as well as those of folklore and ethnology has indeed been heeded, with several scholars having made notable contributions to 'the memorable immediate life experience, the study of work and class relationships, the typical rather than the extraordinary (and) certainly the city as well as the countryside'.[29] Ian MacDougall has been one of the most energetic and prolific, his focus having been mainly on the working-class experience of the industrial heartlands of Scotland. Extensive interviewing of miners, female agricultural workers, hunger marchers, war veterans and representatives of a wide range of occupational communities has made the same kind of contribution to our understanding of the recent past as has the work of Studs Terkel in the USA.[30] Others who have contributed significantly to Smout's vision include Graeme Smith, Hugh Hagan, Arthur MacIvor, Wendy Ugolini and Billy Kay.

CASE STUDY ONE: NEIGHBOURHOOD AND BELONGING

My own research has benefited a good deal from the use of oral sources, often employed in conjunction with documentary evidence, and I would now like to reflect on some brief examples of the ways in which this relationship has worked. The first relates to my investigation of informal economies in early twentieth-century rural Perthshire, and especially the use of reciprocal farm labour carried out on an exchange, rather than a paid, basis.[31] I was particularly interested in the micro-level detail of daily and seasonal routines, of the influence of changing technologies and of the functional relationships between the individual and the wider communities to which they belonged. While documentary sources – estate records and local newspapers primarily – were useful in setting the wider context of the agricultural and economic systems within which these relationships were set, it was only through the use of oral testimony that I was able to access the minutiae of the processes and activities I needed for a fuller understanding of how it all worked. Crucially, oral sources also revealed the deeper meanings of such activities to those who took part and, by extension, to the wider neighbourhoods of which they formed a part. The result was a much fuller appreciation of the importance of these labour-based functional relationships to the construction of a sense of belonging and to the building and maintenance of social cohesion.

One example of this relates to the use of mobile steam-driven threshing mills, and the need for inter-farm cooperation in order to make the process possible. These first appeared in Britain in the mid nineteenth century, having developed from static farm-based steam mills that had begun to appear by the end of the Napoleonic Wars. These, in turn, were an advanced variation of stationary horse- and water-powered mills which were an innovation rapidly gaining popularity on some arable farms in the final decade of the eighteenth century.[32] Perthshire, represented in particular by the Carse of Gowrie, had been at the forefront of the adoption of this new technology, which could make great savings in time, effort and therefore money when compared with the use of the traditional flail. By the 1860s, the services of travelling mills were being regularly advertised in the local press in Perthshire. One such announcement read:

> The Portable Steam Thrashing Machine, by Roley and Co, well known in the Coupar Angus district of Strathmore, is now under the superintendence of Robert Watt, Engineer, Coupar Angus. Orders sent to him, or Mr Patterson, saddler, will receive prompt attention.[33]

This method of threshing grain remained highly popular in Lowland Perthshire for the best part of a century, although for the final couple of decades of their lifespan they tended to be diesel-driven rather than relying on steam. In both cases, however, their operation remained much the same, and required a large workforce of around fourteen to run smoothly. Few farm units could muster these numbers by themselves, and so reciprocal arrangements took shape in order to avoid the extra expense of hiring day-labourers. Thus, typically four or five farms tended to pool their resources for this purpose, creating an informal but essential cooperative unit that could be relied upon when the need arose:

> Aye, that was an understanding. Everybody understood that. You needit anything – for a thrashin mill coming in, you needit anything from fourteen to sixteen men to keep everything going like clockwork. So it was understood, they'd just let you know two days before the mill, 'we're getting the mill in on Wednesday I'll maybe need three men'.[34]

A highly detailed description of a typical event was provided orally by my late uncle, Will West, of Aberfeldy, who attended many such occasions between the 1920s and 1950s. Delivered in a rich Perthshire Scots dialect, it brought the entire process to life for me, demonstrating his intimate familiarity with the organisation and techniques required, detailing the gender roles and key tasks with no hesitation or vague generalisations:

> One o the millmen stood in the hole in the mill; one louser stood there and the other stood there (points to either side of himself) and the men forked off the stacks onto these boards. And they had a knife – the women had a knife in their hand, and they liftit the sheaf, cut the string and handit to the millmen and he stood there and riddled it into the trough. All the one way – no time aboot – but heads all the one way. And then they just kept goin. They'd draw the mill in atween two rows o stacks you see. Which would maybe be aboot fourteen, sixteen feet wide, tae let the mill in, cause when the mill was travellin forward they let the boards doon,

you see Gary? And each board was close to the stack – two stacks, one man on each stack, forkin to each o his lousers – that side and then that side. The result would be that maybe that two stacks would maybe be done before ten o'clock. And the other two would maybe be done – depends on the size o them – by denner time. That'd maybe be eicht to ten stacks in the day. Depends what size they were. And you've maybe – depends where the grain was goin – it was usually weighed up into hunderweight-and-a-half bags. And maybe be . . . two or three men on there weighin them up and carryin them on yer back, usually up to a bloody granary up the stair so's it was easier loaded onto lorries or carts. It was mostly carts tae the station at that time. You'd hae somebody, the two men on the stacks, maybe another one heavin ower the sheaves, and then there'd be a man buildin the straw – the straw stack, and there'd be folk trailin the bunches fae the back o the mill tae the stack for the man tae fork them onto the stack. And then a casual worker or a women at the chaff that cam oot the end o the mill, carryin it away in a caff sheet or rakin it back into a heap . . . And the other millman just went roond aboot to see everything was goin aright you know. And then he would go up and have a shot o the feedin for maybe half an hour or an hour if he was the foreman on the mill.[35]

My fieldnotes from the interview indicate that Will looked to me as if he had been transported back to the time and place of which he spoke: in his mind's eye he was 'back there', I noted. This is oral history at its most basic and raw: it is 'history from below', recounted almost literally by the fellow who cuts the hay, and who presents a narrative that comprises a series of factual descriptions but that is largely devoid of subjectivity or emotion. On other occasions, and indeed in others parts of this same interview, Will could certainly be emotional, but in this particular passage it is the detail of the process that counts.

It is the kind of oral history which the pioneers in the first of Thomson's phases were looking for, largely objective and filling gaps which more conventional historical sources had left, for I have found no other non-oral sources which provide anything approaching this level of detail. However, for another of my interviewees, John Menzies, from twenty miles to the east and a generation younger than Will, the memory of these threshing days seemed to spark a rather more emotive response:

Well that was wi the travellin mills that came in. But that was a different – see at that time it was a different sort o a life, you know. I think we've lost a lot o that. You know, there was far mair pride in your work. You know at night you would walk the district to see somebody else's stacks. You know, when it came to thrashin, the thrashin mill came in and you see well we would have – I think it was five other farms, and we all worked together. When you had the mill everybody came to you, and there was never any money changed hands, nothing like that. I don't even, well there's a big farm down there, lower down than us, now they were a big farm; they employed far more staff than we had here. But they still sent their staff up just the same, and when they were thrashin we sent our staff down. It didnae matter if they were sendin four men up and we were only sendin two back – that was never – there was never anything like that taken into account. If he had four days at the thrashin mill and we only had three, you know, it balanced itself out. But money never entered it at all. These were good days in that . . . well, I was younger, right enough, as well, but you went to the mills and there was great rivalry and plenty fun at the thrashin mill days, you know. Hard work, a lot o it right enough, when you think about it now, but you never thought that at the time. We never knew anything else, that was the way it was done.[36]

Clearly, John was judging 'thae days' very positively, and lamented their passing, for his narrative was peppered with highly charged asides: 'I think we've lost a lot o that'; 'there was far mair pride in yer work'; 'these were good days'; 'there was great rivalry and plenty fun'. John's testimony was therefore of the kind that fuelled the second phase of oral history development as identified by Thomson and discussed above. It is steeped in his *feelings* about a time now gone and, perhaps more starkly, of his attitudes to his present. There is a strong flavour of regret, and his narrative is both a lament for the passing of his earlier days in farming, and of dissatisfaction with the very different demands and emphasis of modern agriculture. Unlike Will, who left farming in the 1950s and who therefore did not experience the same degree of change, John lived through the revolution of the widespread introduction of the combine harvester within Lowland Scottish arable farming, which elsewhere in the interview he identifies as the key element of radical change within his lifetime. The contrast in these two differing tones within the accounts of the same process, then, illustrates a point that became recognised within Thomson's second phase and has been regularly emphasised since: interpretation of any given narrative must take into account the subsequent experience of the teller. Memory is always filtered through the process of *remembering*, and the resulting account will always therefore be influenced by the full life story of the narrator.[37]

But was John viewing his past through an overly positive lens? Is this an example of the unreliability of memory, and the alleged tendency to remember the good times and filter out the bad? In this case, he himself seems aware of the possibility of such a tendency, and briefly checks himself when commenting, 'These were good days in that . . . well, I was younger, right enough, as well.' He seems to realise that he is possibly not taking the enthusiasm of youth into account, but after a moment's reflection rejects this and reiterates the very positive memories that these gatherings hold for him. But what was it about them that make their memory so positive for John? Implicit in some of these remarks is the suggestion that they were linked to, or indeed indicative of, an entire way of farming life that was somehow *better* and more enjoyable than that of today. All of the short statements outlined above show that he compares 'those days' favourably to 'now'. These appear to be closely linked to the idea of communality or working together: this was what brought the 'fun' and also the 'rivalry' (which is portrayed in a very positive sense here, and indeed elsewhere in the interview). 'Rivalry' is linked here to 'skill' and 'pride in your work', but the context is clearly that this was measured in relation to the wider community:

> You know, there was far mair pride in your work. You know at night you would walk the district to see somebody else's stacks.

This tends to suggest (and is widely corroborated in other interviews completed for this research) that to this individual at least, the local farming community as opposed to the individual farm unit was perceived as being the main arena within which workers were judged and with which they identified themselves. The arrival of the threshing mill and the workers from neighbouring farms was therefore one opportunity for such rivalries to be given an outlet. This rivalry or spirit of competition extended to the support network attached to these gatherings in the form of food provision, again emphasising the fact that people's behaviour and aspirations were closely bound up with their attitudes towards the community at large, or indeed with their own perceptions of the community's attitudes towards them:

> The farmer's wife provided the meals. You got a piece in the mornin, your dinner, and then a piece in the afternoon. And then there was a lot of rivalry as well, you know. How good a meal you got here – you knew where all the best meals were, by the time you were goin roond.

This rivalry tendency should of course be seen in context, however. The basic principle underpinning the existence of this form of exchange labour was mutual aid, not mutual competition. Rivalries could certainly operate to improve performances, and indeed this is a phenomenon which was extremely common amongst the farm labouring population of Perthshire and far beyond. In this case, the standard of food provision at these gatherings was presumably kept high because of the judgmental attitudes of those attending and the resultant effect on the reputations of the providers. However, it was not only the channels of rivalry that disappeared with the passing of this tradition, for neighbours were also denied an important opportunity simply to *be* together – a situation again obviously viewed unfavourably by John Menzies when asserting that 'now you never – very seldom – you see yer neighbours the same as ye did in those times'. This contact through work appears to have been cherished by John, not only because of the fun it brought through rivalry, but because of the feeling of common purpose that was engendered as a result of the communal labour process. The egalitarian nature of the concept, for instance, is obviously strong in his mind:

> Well there's a big farm down there, lower down than us, now they were a big farm; they employed far more staff than we had here. But they still sent their staff up just the same, and when they were thrashin we sent our staff down. It didnae matter if they were sendin four men up and we were only sendin two back – that was never – there was never anything like

that taken into account. If he had four days at the thrashin mill and we only had three, you know, it balanced itself out.

John seems impressed by the fact that neighbours were prepared to cooperate even if they operated on different scales in terms of production and size of labour force. Exact reciprocity in arithmetic terms was not important: the arrangement was fair in his eyes, and the concept behind it was sound, and so these factors were further positive markers for him in his recollection of these events.

Another notable feature of this form of exchange labour was that no money changed hands. This information was volunteered by John as opposed to being offered in response to a specific question, and he seems to identify this as being both important and, again, a very positive feature of these arrangements:

When you had the mill everybody came to you, and there was never any money changed hands, nothing like that.

But money never entered it at all.

At a later stage in the interview, John is discussing the fact that, in general, neigh-bours are much less prepared to help one another out nowadays, and this he again links to the greater reliance on 'money':

If the boy was needin help, you went and gave him help, it didnae matter what it was. But now, you see, it's difficult. You wouldnie go and offer: if he asked, fair enough. That has gone in the thing as well. But I think that's only the way the whole thing's gone – financially, and – money's the biggest involvement in the whole thing . . . And that has done away with a lot of the comradeship and what not in the area I think. Everybody's that committed now.

Here John overtly claims a direct relationship exists between the increased emphasis on money and the loss of 'comradeship' that he perceives to have occurred within his local community. There is a strong link being made here between communality, fun and absence of cash on one hand, and individuality, lack of fun and reliance upon cash on the other. Indeed, this is a connection that was made by a number of informants in relation to all forms of exchange (and charity) labour:

There wis more neighbourliness in these days than what there is now. Folk weren't livin just for money entirely. It was more community spirit ye know . . . which you don't get nowadays. Money's done all that out.[38]

Thus we see that in the case of John Menzies at least, the reasons behind his very positive attitude towards his early years in farming are clearly expressed within his comments, and they are certainly linked in this case to the existence of communal labour arrangements. There *are* explanations encoded in his testimony which serve to back up his enthusiasm for 'the old days', and he is thus sheltered from accusations of blind sentimentality. His evidence is valid, as it is intrinsically consistent and appears to be representative of his perceptions of his past. This is a point which requires emphasis, as this examination is ethnological rather than purely historical: communal labour must be viewed as having been an important aspect of local life in John's view *because he signposts it as such* in his testimony.

While this is just one small example from this Perthshire research, it illustrates the importance of oral sources to my own understanding of the deep subtleties of social organisation within my native county during a period of great change. Serious consideration of the spoken word, alongside a range of other sources, led me towards the identification of key differences in labour organisation within different parts of the county, and of the complex layers of interdependency that existed between households. Only oral testimony led me towards recognition of the social mechanisms that were forged and shaped by tradition in order to facilitate mutual survival and maximise the potential of the available environmental and human resources. But beyond those largely functional issues, it was also the voices of those who lived through these periods that brought the subject to life, that added colour and vibrancy, and indeed that reminded me that nostalgia *is* a key element in our relationship with our past. Although I was dealing largely with history rather than tradition, Eric Cregeen's template was a fine one to follow.

CASE STUDY TWO: THE COCKENZIE PROJECT

While the case study above took the form of a thematically focused individual research project in which I had a large degree of control over the agenda, use of oral sources can bring rich rewards within other organisational contexts too. Increasing emphasis on the 'impact' of research on the world beyond the academy has been encouraging more innovative work in community settings, whereby the process of the research is seen to be of equal value to the findings which emerge from it. 'Applied ethnology' is therefore increasing in popularity, and I would like now to discuss one such project that used oral interviews in a variety of different ways to help bring a greater degree of inter-generational understanding to its participants, but which also served as a rich ethnographic data source in its own right.

In 2000–01, a project was set up in the neighbouring villages of Cockenzie and Port Seton in East Lothian, the aim of which was to use oral history and storytelling to bring together children aged 10–11 from Cockenzie Primary School and clients of the John Bellany Day Centre for the elderly in Port Seton. The initiators of the project felt that 'these two groups have an enormous amount to give one another', and that meaningful exchanges between the young and the elderly within the context of a rapidly changing local community could produce a rich learning experience for both groups.[39] The project was steered by the East Lothian Library Service, and was one part of a larger literacy programme entitled *Book Now!*, funded by a grant from the National Lottery New Directions Scheme.

My own involvement was as a member of a small team from the department of Celtic and Scottish Studies at the University of Edinburgh which helped to design and facilitate the sessions, provide the recording equipment, and process and archive the resulting audio recordings.

Initially a team of three storytellers[40] was employed to begin visiting the day centre to gather and record memories and stories from around thirty of the elderly clients, most of whom were born during the first two decades of the twentieth century and who had resided within the local area for most or all of their lives. The sessions took place in small groups of around six clients, each group being facilitated by one of the storytellers. The idea was to encourage the clients to 'tell their stories' – to share their own memories and experiences of life in the local area with their fellow clients and the storytellers acting as willing and interested listeners. In this respect, this part of the methodology took a similar form to other reminiscence projects, many of which had been set up as a popular form of 'therapy' for the elderly in Britain during the final quarter of the twentieth century.[41] After several sessions, the facilitators began to encourage the participants to organise some of their reminiscences into 'stories', still retained within their minds rather than being written down but arranged into slightly more formalised narratives dealing with specific events, people or processes. The aim of this step was not to constrict the creative process, nor indeed to 'correct' their rich local dialect and replace it with standard English (both of these would have been anathema to all of us who were involved in running this project), but rather to sort their life narratives into themes that were succinct and focused enough for successful delivery to primary school children within a limited time slot.

The first involvement of the children was as 'audience', when they were brought to the day centre in a large group to hear a selection of the stories. The three storytellers acted as facilitators, encouraging the clients to get started:

> Lizzie, tell the boys and girls about your work on the buses during the war. They're studying World War 2 just now.
>
> Well, Marion used to help her mum papering. Do you want to tell the boys and girls about when you started?
>
> Now the person that really had to work hard was Jeannie. Go on Jeannie, tell the children about your work.
>
> Now someone who did something different than the others is Rita. Tell us about your work, Rita.[42]

The children started out as listeners and learners, therefore, and several asked the clients questions about the people and events in their stories, obviously keen to know more. In this way, the lines of intergenerational communication were opened, and a framework for a developing relationship to emerge between the two groups was now in place. It seems likely that the initial stage of refining the tellers' narratives into short, themed stories was indeed helpful in presenting the children with material that was focused enough to capture and retain their attention. Now the seed of interest was sown, and this provided a solid base upon which to build the rest of the programme. The 'thank you' letters sent by the children to the day centre clients following this first session reveal a genuine enthusiasm for the experience:

> Thanks a lot for your super stories. It made me think what life was like back then. It's a lot different now. I like writing, what about you? I'm half way through my own version of Harry Potter. I would really like to go back in time and see what it was like. Thanks to all of you. My favourite story was about the Nickum twins (they were nasty). My Granda was a fisherman, his name was Akie Coull, I wonder if you knew him? Hope to see you again . . . Ps You were stars.[43]

This extract from one of these letters is most revealing in terms of the way this particular child reacted to the storytelling session and how the experience seems to have been processed in her mind afterwards. Both time and place are strongly emphasised, with an awareness of diachronic change (it was different then to now) sitting happily alongside an expectation of common knowledge and personal links bridging the generational divide (did you know my grandfather?). Indeed, as became clear later in the project, individuals and family contacts were very important markers in the exchange of narratives between the young and the elderly. Occupation too, remained a popular theme throughout. The children seemed to be well aware that commercial fishing had once been the mainstay of the local economy, and it appeared to hold a fascination for many of them, while their interest was willingly embraced by the elderly participants, many of whom had worked within the industry themselves.

The next stage of the project involved setting up group sessions in which the children interviewed the day centre clients, asking questions that they had previously prepared in class. Once again the initial storytelling session proved to be a very useful foundation, for the questions raised tended to reflect many of the themes touched on earlier. The groups comprised around five to six children and three to four clients, as well as a facilitator whose task was to operate the recording equipment and keep the communication flowing if possible, encouraging the children to ask follow-up questions that had not been pre-scripted.[44]

Listening back to the recordings of these sessions now and reading the accompanying transcripts, it seems clear that the participation of the children influenced the shape of the clients' responses, and that the resulting narratives are markedly different in flavour to any I have worked with before in more 'conventional' oral history work. The most conspicuous difference is that those telling their life stories had a much stronger tendency to compare aspects of their own past with modern equivalents. Their stories are peppered with references to 'nowadays', often in the form of returning questions to the children about 'how it is for you'. In this respect, the relationship between the interviewer and interviewee was arguably more balanced and the flow of narratives less unidirectional than is usually the case with 'trained' collectors conducting the interviews. This was enhanced at the next stage of the project outlined below.

It seems almost axiomatic that oral history should involve younger people interviewing the elderly and that the flow of information tends therefore to be in one direction only. The older generation is thus considered to be a historical resource, a human archive from which much can be learned about the past. This is true, of course, but why should the relationship always be that way round? Don't members of younger generations have the right to share their voices too? It was partly in response to this question that we decided to introduce an unusual practice into the Cockenzie Project, whereby in one of the sessions we invited the day centre clients to interview the school children about *their* lives. The older generation would now become listeners and learners, the children speakers and teachers. We felt that this would bring several positive elements to the overall project. First of all, it would help to encourage a more balanced exchange between the participants than is normal in oral history situations, and both groups would feel like equal partners. The children would also gain experience as 'storytellers', and might, we hoped, feel more empowered within the project, as their own lives and their own stories would be seen to be as important and as valuable as those of the day centre clients. The skills the children had been developing as interviewers in earlier sessions would surely be enhanced by the experience too, as they would now appreciate the position of the interviewee. Finally, such an approach might well help to bring the past and the present together into the same frame, bringing into sharper focus continuities and changes in local life experience for both generations. We were, after all, aiming to facilitate a learning experience for both groups, and not only for the children. We were also committed to the idea of recording 'the history of the present' and not just 'the history of the past', an idea that was enthusiastically advocated by the influential Popular Memory Group at the Centre for Contemporary Cultural Studies at the University of Birmingham.[45] Although our sessions would only produce a small sample of such material, we felt that the children involved might begin to appreciate that their lives today represent tomorrow's history, and that history is therefore an ongoing process and not just something hidden in the past.

This initiative was only partly successful. We decided to base the session around a classic 'show and tell' format, in which the children brought with them an object which had meaning to them – a toy, a photograph, a book, perhaps – with these acting as catalysts for the day centre clients' line of questioning. The children responded well to this; indeed, they were obviously used to conducting this exercise (from earlier experience in school, it seems) and many did not even wait for an opening question before launching into an account of what their object was and what it represented to them. The clients seemed to adapt less well to their new role as interviewers, however, perhaps not surprisingly given the fact they had by now been involved in several sessions in which the children had been asking the questions. Given their earlier readiness to throw questions back to the children in the original sessions, we felt that this approach would work well, but it seems that the formality of this reversal left them confused. In hindsight, we could have done more to initiate a more successful transition of roles by working with the clients in advance, and discussing their new roles more overtly with them beforehand: it may simply have been the case that we failed to explain our plans adequately. As it turned out, those of us acting as facilitators asked most of the questions, and despite attempts to bring the clients back into the exchanges, they tended to remain as passive listeners. Nonetheless, we felt that the exercise was certainly worth doing, and it served as a foundation for one of the final exercises undertaken by the children in relation to this project, in which each wrote short autobiographical accounts for inclusion in the final book publication.

We felt from the outset that it was important for there to be a tangible product emerging from the project, and a decision was made to produce a book that could be sold commercially. This could serve several functions. First of all, in the course of the sessions a significant body of data relating to local life and history had been gathered, and while this was archived in the School of Scottish Studies, we felt that it was important to make this material readily accessible as a worthwhile contribution to the local history literature. It could, for example, provide a central text for the local schools to use in their history lessons, a reinforcement of the notion that history is accessible to all. Second, and perhaps more important, the book has provided a way to give the participants in the project 'something back' – tangible proof that their efforts and their stories are worthwhile and valued.

The book is entitled *Tell Us A Story: Memories of East Lothian*, and runs to 167 pages. It is published jointly by the East Lothian Museums Service and the University of Edinburgh. The costs of production were built into the Heritage Lottery Fund award that supported the whole project. It is illustrated with coloured paintings produced by the day centre clients under the guidance of a visual art tutor who was brought into the centre for several sessions as part of the project. These images are visual representations of some of the events and places mentioned in the collected narratives. Individual photographic portraits of each client, class photographs of the children and 'action' photographs taken at some of the sessions are also included.[46] The main section of the book is based on the clients' testimonies contained within the transcriptions of the initial interviews undertaken by the storytellers, the second-stage 'storytelling' sessions, and the interviews conducted by the children. These chapters include such themes as 'Home and Family', 'Schooldays', 'Jobs', 'Courtship, Dancing and Marriage', 'Fishing and the Box Meeting' and 'Local Legends'. The narratives are divided into short sections, ranging from two or three lines to two pages, each quotation being attributed to the named respondent.

The second part of the book comprises work written by the children in follow-up sessions in their classroom, supervised by their class teachers. This falls into three groupings: 'Retelling the Past', 'Children's Lives Today' and 'Special Memories'. 'Retelling the Past' relates to creative writing in which the children used the stories they heard at the day centre as inspiration. Most adopted the persona of an elderly man or woman relating some aspect of their past, very much in the manner of the clients' storytelling sessions, and many focused on a particular incident or memory they had heard about in earlier sessions:

> One day a long time ago when I was finishing school and getting a job, my first job was making fishing nets . . .

When the war was on, I used to play chap-door run. It was a funny game. Once a lady caught me . . .

My name is Anne and I'm going to tell you a story about when I got a job at Duncan's Chocolate Factory.[47]

The retelling of these stories serves to reinforce the themes within the children's minds, and helps them internalise the events they have heard about in a creative way. In terms of intergenerational sharing of narratives, however, it raises some interesting points of debate. Mindful of the ethical questions relating to ownership and representation of memory, and in particular of the 'dispossession' worries articulated by Stephen Tyler and Gillian Elinor referred to above, I wondered whether this 'borrowing' and reshaping of the clients' stories by the children would be viewed as ill-conceived. That may yet prove to be so, but the clients themselves appeared to be delighted when I chatted with several of them at the launch of the book. They were pleased when able to trace a child's story to one of their own, and on that evidence at least, I believe that this initiative was successful.

Following the retelling of the past, the children's short autobiographies are included. These are based loosely on the 'role reversal' sessions, although as these did not produce adequate transcription material on this theme, the material was again produced by the children as creative writing in follow-up classroom sessions. This provided the children with a chance to reflect on their own 'stories', encouraging them (and the readers of the book) to appreciate that their experiences and the daily goings-on of their own lives are just as much a part of the story of their community as those of the older generation. The inclusion of these texts within the final book was vital if the publication was to accurately reflect the emphasis placed upon the *exchange* of narratives as opposed to the more standard, uni-dimensional 'collection' approach.

This, indeed, was enhanced within the final section entitled 'Special Memories'. Just as the day centre clients' stories recalled both daily processes and one-off events, the children too were able to differentiate on a similar basis. Whether recalling their excitement at the arrival of a baby sister, being picked to sing in the school concert, or being asked to be a bridesmaid at a wedding, the children proved that special memories are not the preserve only of the older generation. Nostalgia can form early and, as Lowenthal reminds us, nostalgia is a vital ingredient in our sense of place and in our mental blueprint of our place in the world.[48] It was there for John Menzies when recounting communal labour gatherings, and it was there for the children of a very different time and place.

No claims are being made that the methodology employed within the Cockenzie Project is in any way unique.[49] Participative oral history has been embraced by many schools within Britain over the last two decades. In England in particular, the advent of a centralised national curriculum for the teaching of history in the early 1990s provided an official sanctioning of the use of oral history as a valid method of investigation at all key stages. As Tim Lomas points out, this was only made possible through the prior work of several individual schools who had already demonstrated the potential power and penetration of well-planned oral projects as adjuncts to more 'conventional' approaches to the teaching of history.[50] Lomas demonstrates how the possibilities for the use of oral history within the national curriculum are considerable, and asserts that it can contribute in several ways: a. as a source of content; b. as a vehicle for developing historical skills and concepts; c. as a way of developing skills valid across and beyond the institution; d. as an element of teaching providing interest and motivation; and e. as a form of assessment.[51]

Although in Scotland this national curriculum does not apply, these aims are certainly laudable, and I believe that the Cockenzie Project provides a template that can be adapted to fulfil them all. For the purposes of this chapter, Lomas' third category of skills is highly relevant, for I strongly believe that the nurturing of a sense of locality is one aim that should go across and beyond the institutions involved, and also that this requires to be emphasised within the context of the ongoing debates concerning the teaching of 'national' history in Scotland's schools. In Scotland, the contextual foundation for teaching in primary schools during the period when this research took place was the 5–14 Guidelines: non-statutory guidelines that covered structure, content and assessment of the curriculum in primary schools and the first two years of secondary education. There were five broad curricular areas: language, mathematics, environmental studies, expressive arts, and religious and moral education. Environmental Studies was subdivided into the three key themes of social subjects, science and technology, and the stated attainment outcomes in social subjects neatly encompass the rationale underpinning the Cockenzie sessions: 'people in the past', 'people and place', and 'people in society'. In conventional labelling, this tends to cover history, geography and modern studies, but an attempt is made to treat these together in a holistic manner, with pupils being encouraged to explore the symbiosis between them. The teaching of place and locality, then, has certainly been explicitly advocated within the primary sector in Scotland, and I believe that the Cockenzie Project provides a template for one approach that might be further explored in order to make these aims manifest. The replacement for the 5–14 Guidelines, Curriculum for Excellence, also encourages and supports work of this kind, and so the framework does exist for oral history to be further developed within the primary and secondary education systems of modern Scotland.[52]

The mutual exchange of narratives between the young and elderly, publicly celebrated in published form, constitute a document that is deeply rooted in the local, and is free in the most part from the constraining stereotypes of the national. In this respect the findings serve as a counter to those of Ewan Hague, whose research amongst children of a similar age within two schools in Edinburgh revealed that their conceptualisation of Scotland was already dominated by stereotypical images of castles, kilts and bagpipes.[53] But as the Cockenzie data show, when left to articulate their own stories, locality appears to play a much more significant role in the partcipants' worldview than nation. 'Place' is emphasised constantly within these narratives, and names of local areas, streets, businesses, landmarks and buildings provide a common map of understanding for both generations. The themes themselves are varied – home and family, work, schooldays, holidays, wartime, courtship and marriage – yet all are grounded in a sense of locality that seems to underpin every stage of the interaction.

The key message from the Cockenzie research, for me, is that within the discipline of ethnology, oral sources can be used to improve our understanding of the present as well as the past, and indeed as a means of bridging the gap between the two. Increasingly, this is becoming a key task for the ethnologist, as the relationship between past and present begins to take centre stage within the discipline internationally. Bringing the youngest and oldest of a local community together through the medium of voice, in a controlled and facilitated way, and providing the opportunity for them to *exchange* narratives, looks to be a promising methodology for the ethnologist to consider developing further in the future.

CONCLUSIONS

Within the discipline of ethnology, the principle of 'collection' has always been a cornerstone of teaching and research and it remains one of the key defining features that sets it apart from sister disciplines. The recording and archiving of oral sources in particular has been central to the modes of enquiry favoured by ethnologists, and within this chapter I have attempted to illustrate a few examples of ways in which this can be approached. Both oral history and oral tradition remain key components of the discipline, and while the two overlap to some extent, we must always be aware of the key differences between them. Of course, these are categorisations imposed on oral material by academics, and essential as we consider this division to be it is seldom one recognised by interviewees themselves. I have never encountered any who have signposted their narratives in this way, and so it is up to the interviewer to tease out the meanings, implications and transmission routes of the spoken testimony, both during the interview itself and through subsequent analysis.

Oral sources have contributed in some degree to the contents of all fourteen volumes within this *Scottish Life and Society* series, and each one would be the poorer for their absence. They can bring information to light which might not be discovered through any other source types; they can, as Eric Cregeen demonstrated so well, serve to complement and corroborate the written record; and they can bring colour, subtlety, emotion and vibrancy to our record of both the past and the present. They can also help to challenge our perceptions of the process of history, and remind us that as individuals we experience both continuity and change in our lives in different ways. And yet there are certainly warnings to heed too. Memory *is* subjective, and the stories that emerge from oral interviews are, of course, filtered through the life experiences of the teller. The behaviour and personality of the interviewer does influence the resulting narrative to some extent, and we must be aware of this when considering the ways in which we use and make sense of the results.

Nonetheless, oral sources can and should play a key role in the ethnological study of any given community, region or nation. When used wisely, and often in conjunction with the other source types discussed in this volume, our understanding of Scotland's life and society, past and present, can be greatly enriched.

1 Although audio recording technology had been developed by the late nineteenth century, its expense and cumbersome nature rendered it impractical for widespread use within this field.

2 The phrase was that of George Ewart Evans in his pioneering book of that name (1956).

3 Beech et al., 2007.

4 A full account of the 'pre-history' of oral history is provided in Thompson, 2000, 25–82.

5 Thomson, 2006.

6 However, not all early oral history took this position: several early projects, especially within the USA, concentrated on the lives of white social elites, including the first organised project to rely mainly on oral interviews which was undertaken by Allan Nevins of Columbia University in 1948. See Thomson, 2006, 51.

7 Thomson, 2006, 54.

8 This position is fully explained in Clifford and Marcus, 1986.

9 Tyler, 1986, 128.

10 See for instance Thompson, 2000; Grele, 1991; Lummis, 1987.

11 Lindqvist, 1992.

12 Portelli, 1998, 68.

13 Frisch, 2004.

14 Tangherlini, 2003, 137.

15 Stoklund, a highly respected Danish ethnologist, made this point consistently throughout his career, but see in particular Stoklund, 1983.

16 For a discussion of the meaning of tradition (with or without the 'oral' qualifier), see Glassie, 1995; Noyes, 2009; West, 2012.

17 Vansina, 1985, 3.

18 The other key text for a detailed discussion of oral tradition within a Western context is Finnegan, 1991.

19 See, for example West, 2012; Bruford and MacDonald, 2003.

20 Porter, 2001; McKean, 2001. See also Gaskill, 1996 and 2004.

21 For a succinct account of the key collectors of oral narrative in Scotland see MacDonald, 2007.

22 Cregeen, 1974, 25–6.

23 Smout, 1974, 12. Those in attendance included Paul Thompson, George Ewart Evans, Charles Parker (a pioneer of the broadcasting of oral history through the BBC), Sean O'Sullivan of the Irish Folklore Commission, R Page Arnott and several staff members at the School of Scottish Studies.

24 Smout, 1974, 11.

25 For a discussion of the early development of the Scottish Oral History Group and of Eric Cregeen's role in particular, see 'Dr Margaret Mackay reflects on the SOHG's genesis', the 'About Us' page of the Scottish Oral History Group's website: <www.thesohg.org/about-us>.

26 Ranft and Richmond, 2012, 6–7. Many prolific collectors of oral history and tradition amongst the staff of the department have contributed to this corpus. In addition to those mentioned in the text, these include Alan Bruford, Margaret Bennett, Peter Cooke, Ian Fraser, Emily Lyle, Donald-Archie MacDonald, John MacInnes, Margaret Mackay and Morag MacLeod.

27 Ranft and Richmond, 2012, 13. See also Macaulay, 2012.

28 Readers are encouraged to engage with this resource in order to experience the power of this material at first hand. See the Tobar an Dualchais/ Kist o Riches website, <www.tobaranualchais.co.uk>.

29 Smout, 1974, 11.

30 Examples include MacDougall, 1986, 1990, 1991 and 2000.

31 See West, 2000 and 2007.

32 Collins, 1972, 17.

33 *Perthshire Courier*, 6 September 1860.

34 Author's interview with Dave West, Crieff, School of Scottish Studies Archives, SA1988.21.

35 School of Scottish Studies Archives, SA 1988.19.

36 School of Scottish Studies Archives, SA 1998.23.

37 See Anderson, 2001; Barber, 2005; Chandler, 2005.

38 John Fisher, School of Scottish Studies Archives, SA 1988.20.

39 Dale, 2002, xiii. The original idea for this initiative came from Sophie Dale, a project officer with East Lothian Council, and Ann Anderson, co-ordinator of the John Bellany Centre.

40 A major revival in oral storytelling has been ongoing in Scotland over the last decade. Revival tellers draw on the rich source of traditional tales preserved in archives, such as those at the University of Edinburgh's School of Scottish Studies, although many are creating their own material relating to modern life. For a penetrative account of the revival see Smith, 2001. The storytellers involved in the Cockenzie project were Barbara McDermitt, Heather Yule and Bea Ferguson.

41 A critical discussion of the reminiscence phenomenon is provided in Bornat, 1989.

42 Transcript of session, Thursday 30 November 2000. School of Scottish Studies Archive, University of Edinburgh.

43 As published in Dale, 2002, xi.

44 My own direct role in the project began as a facilitator within these particular sessions.

45 See, for example, Popular Memory Group, 1998.

46 Permission slips had to be signed by the parents of each child before any photographs were taken. This is standard policy within many local education authorities in Scotland.

47 Dale, 2002, 149–53.

48 Lowenthal, 1985, 4–13.

49 I am not aware, however, of any other projects that have used the 'role reversal' methodology, whereby the older participants become interviewers and the children interviewees.

50 Lomas, 1992. Examples cited include a Shropshire secondary school which built in, as part of a local history unit, a visit to an elderly person in the town for each Year 7 pupil (aged 11–12); four rural schools in Cumbria which used oral sources with Year 5 and 6 pupils (aged 8–11) as part of a local case study, and a Lincolnshire primary school that traced and interviewed a number of World War II evacuees who had been moved to their village from Grimsby. A detailed account of an oral history project that was carried out in a London primary school is provided in Ross, 1984.

51 Lomas, 1992, 35.

52 See <www.curriculum-for-excellence.co.uk>.

53 Hague, 2001.

Anderson, W. Oral history and migrant wage labor: Sources of narrative distortion, *Oral History Review*, 28:2 (2001), 1–20.

Barber, M. Hearing women's voices: Female migration to Canada in the early twentieth century, *Oral History*, 33:1 (2005), 68–76.

Beech, J, Hand, O, MacDonald, F, Mulhern, M, and Weston, J, eds. *Scottish Life and Society. A Compendium of Scottish Ethnology, Volume 10: Oral Literature and Performance Culture*, Edinburgh, 2007.

Bornat, J. Oral history as a social movement: Reminiscence and older people, *Oral History*, 17:2 (1989), 16–20.

Bruford, A and MacDonald, D A, eds. *Traditional Scottish Tales*, Edinburgh, 2003.

Chandler, S. Oral history across generations: Age, generational identity and oral testimony, *Oral History*, 33:2 (2005), 48–56.

Clifford, J and Marcus, G E, eds. *Writing Culture: The Poetics and Politics of Ethnography*, Berkeley and London, 1986.

Collins, E J T. The diffusion of the threshing machine in Britain 1790–1880, *Tools and Tillage*, 2:1 (1972), 16–33.

Cregeen, E. Oral sources for the social history of the Scottish Highlands and Islands, *Oral History*, 2:2 (Autumn 1974), 23–36.

Dale, S, ed. *Tell us a Story: Memories of East Lothian*, Edinburgh, 2002.

Evans, G E. *Ask the Fellows who Cut the Hay*, London, 1956.

Finnegan, R. *Oral Tradition and the Verbal Arts*, London, 1991.

Frisch, M. Towards a post-documentary sensibility: Theoretical and political implications of new information technologies in oral history. Paper presented to the 13th International Oral History Conference, Rome, June 2004, and published in Perks, R and Thomson, A, eds, *The Oral History Reader*, 2nd edn, London, 2006, 102–14.

Gaskill, H (Intro. Fiona Stafford). *The Poems of Ossian and Related Works*, Edinburgh, 1996.

Gaskill, H. *The Reception of Ossian in Europe*, London, 2004.

Georges, R and Jones, M. *People Studying People: The Human Element in Fieldwork*, Berkeley, CA, 1980.

Glassie, H. Tradition, *Journal of American Folklore*, 108:430 (1995), 395–412.

Grele, R, ed. *Envelopes of Sound: The Art of Oral History*, New York, 1991.

Grills, S. *Doing Ethnographic Research: Fieldwork Settings*, London, 1998.

Hague, E. Nationality and children's drawings – pictures 'about Scotland' by primary school children in Edinburgh, Scotland and Syracuse, New York State, *Scottish Geographical Journal*, 117:2 (2001), 77–99.

Lindqvist, M. Between realism and relativism: A consideration of history in modern ethnology, *Ethnologia Scandinavica*, 22 (1992), 3–16.

Lomas, T. Oral history and the National Curriculum, *Oral History*, 20:1 (1992), 34–40.

Lowenthal, D. *The Past is a Foreign Country*, Oxford, 1985.

Lummis, T. *Listening to History: The Authenticity of Oral Evidence*, London, 1987.

Macaulay, C. Dipping into the well: Scottish oral tradition online, *Oral Tradition*, 27:1 (2012), 171–86.

MacDonald, F. Narrative collection and scholarship. In Beech et al., 2007, 9–27.

MacDougall, I. *Voices from the Spanish Civil War: Personal Recollections of Scottish Volunteers in Republican Spain, 1936–39*, Edinburgh, 1986.

MacDougall, I. *Voices From War: and Some Labour Struggles; Personal Recollections of War in our Century by Scottish Men and Women*, Edinburgh, 1990.

MacDougall, I. *Voices From the Hunger Marches: Personal Recollections by Scottish Hunger Marchers of the 1920s and 1930s*, Edinburgh, 1991.

MacDougall, I. *Voices From Work and Home: Personal Recollections of Working Life and Labour Struggles in the Twentieth Century by Scots Men and Women*, Edinburgh, 2000.

Maclean, C. *The Highlands*, Edinburgh, 2006.

McKean, T. The fieldwork legacy of James Macpherson, *Journal of American Folklore*, 144:454 (Fall 2001), 447–63.

Newton, M, ed. *Duthchas nan Gaidheal: Selected Essays of John MacInnes*, Edinburgh, 2006.

Noyes, D. Tradition: Three traditions, *Journal of Folklore Research*, 46:30 (2009), 233–68.

Passerini, L. Women's personal narratives: Myths, experiences and emotions. In The Personal Narratives Group, eds, *Interpreting Women's Lives: Feminist Theory and Personal Narratives*, Bloomington, IN, 1989, 189–97.

Perks, R. *Oral History: An Annotated Bibliography*, London, 1990a.

Perks, R. *Oral History: Talking about the Past*, London, 1990b.

Perks, R and Thomson, A. *The Oral History Reader*, London, 1998.

Popular Memory Group. Popular memory: Theory, politics, method. In Perks and Thomson, 1998, 75–86.

Portelli, A. What makes oral history different. In Perks and Thomson, 1998, 32–42.

Porter, J. 'Bring me the head of James Macpherson': The execution of Ossian and the wellsprings of folkloristic discourse, *Journal of American Folklore*, 144:454 (2001), 396–435.

Ranft, R and Richmond, L. *Review of the School of Scottish Studies Archives, University of Edinburgh*, Edinburgh, 2012.

Ross, A. Children becoming historians: An oral history project in a primary school, *Oral History*, 12:2 (1984), 21–31.

Smith, D. *Storytelling Scotland: A Nation in Narrative*, Edinburgh, 2001.

Smith, R. Popular memory as oral narratives: Luisa Passerini's reading of oral history interviews, *Oral History Review*, 16:2 (1988), 95–107.

Smout, T C. Scotland: The state of oral history, *Oral History*, 2:1 (1974), 11–14.

Stoeltje, B, Fox, C and Olbrys, S. The self in 'fieldwork': A methodological concern, *Journal of American Folklore*, 112:444 (1999), 158–82.

Stoklund, B. *Folklife Research: Between History and Anthropology*, Cardiff, 1983.

Tangherlini, T. 'Oral tradition' in a technologically advanced world, *Oral Tradition*, 18:1 (2003), 136–38.

Thomson, A. Four paradigm transformations in oral history, *Oral History Review*, 34:1 (2006), 49–70.

Thompson, P. *The Voice of the Past: Oral History*, 3rd edn, Oxford, 2000.

Tonkin, E. *Narrating Our Pasts: The Social Construction of Oral History*, Cambridge, 1992.

Tyler, S A. Post-modern ethnology: From document of the occult to occult document. In Clifford and Marcus, 1986, 122–40.

Ugolini, W. *Experiencing War as the 'Enemy Other': Italian Scottish Experience in World War II*, Manchester, 2011.

Vansina, J. *Oral Tradition as History*, Nairobi, 1985.

West, G. Conceptualising neighbourhood: Charity labour gatherings in rural Perthshire, 1850–1950, *Scottish Studies*, 33 (2000), 132–44.

West, G. *An Historical Ethnography of Rural Perthshire, 1750–1950: Farm, Family and Neighbourhood*, Lampeter, 2007.

West, G. *Voicing Scotland: Folk, Culture, Nation*, Edinburgh, 2012.

JOURNALS

Béaloideas, 1927–present
By Word of Mouth, 1980–present
Oral History, 1972–present
Oral Tradition, 1986–present
Tocher, 1971–present
Words and Silences, 1997–present

ONLINE RESOURCES

Oral History Society,
Scottish Oral History Centre, University of Strathclyde, <www.strath.ac.uk/humanities/
    research/history/sohc/>
Scottish Oral History Group,

18 Private Accounts

HEATHER HOLMES

INTRODUCTION

Dictionary definitions are useful in defining the scope of 'private accounts'. *Chambers 20th Century Dictionary* defines 'private' as being:

> apart from the state; not in public office . . . peculiar to oneself; belonging to, or concerning, an individual person or company . . . relating to personal affairs; in an unofficial capacity; not public; not open to the public; not made known generally; confidential; retired from observation.[1]

Private accounts may be intended to be read only by the individual who wrote them or their immediate family, groups of friends or like-minded readers, and not for wider circulation or publication, though some accounts have been published.[2] Historians and archivists have also defined 'private accounts' and 'private papers'. The online guide 'Private papers', published by the National Archives of Scotland (NAS), states that they 'include the family and estate papers of landowners from all over Scotland, records of businesses, societies and institutions'.[3]

This chapter explores the range of private accounts – as primary and secondary sources – available for ethnological research, their use and future lines of ethnological enquiry.

THE RANGE OF PRIVATE ACCOUNTS AND THEIR EVIDENCE

Karina Williamson suggests that 'despite their heterogeneity in character and form, Scottish private writings [personal diaries, journals, letters, personal reminiscences, autobiographies and memoirs] constitute a loosely coherent whole united by common social and cultural roots'.[4] They appear in increasing numbers in the eighteenth century, though at that time most were written by members of the upper and middle classes. Some accounts, such as autobiographies, became more widely written by other groups, especially in the nineteenth century. Writing on the eighteenth and nineteenth centuries, Williamson suggests that these 'private' accounts were 'virtually never "private" in an absolute sense; that is, intended for closet reading by the author or recipient alone'. Rather, they were to be circulated among family members.[5] The analysis and interpretation of the different types of private sources also raises similar issues. These relate to the personal idiosyncrasies and the representativeness of the authors and their experiences, the wider contextualisation of the personal experience, the authenticity of the accounts, and the survival of particular accounts though not others.

Diaries

Arthur Ponsonby observes that 'the Scot may be regarded as specially addicted to diary writing'. He suggests that the 'religious motive instilled by the Covenanters was responsible for producing many diaries',[6] a fact also noted by Karina Williamson.[7] William Matthews provides a helpful definition of a 'diary'. He suggests that it is 'a personal record of what interested the diarist, usually kept day by day, each day's record being self-contained and written soon after the events occurred, the style usually being free from organized exposition'.[8]

Farmers' diaries have received some attention in Scotland and further afield. Few survive from the seventeenth century, they increase in number in the eighteenth century, but most are from the nineteenth century and later. Alexander Fenton suggests that diary writing is being replaced by other methods of recording information. As he notes: 'the precedence of legislation and regulation has meant that for many purposes, official forms to be ticked, or computerised records, have largely replaced diary keeping, other than for purely personal purposes'.[9] Diaries were written by private individuals for their own purposes, and not for other people, including other members of their family. They can reveal information that cannot be found in other sources. As Fenton observes, they 'show rhythms of work and patterns of social and economic interaction which have rarely come under review'.[10] M E Turner, J V Beckett and B Afton note that they can also 'provide insights into the focus, concerns, and strategies of the farmers who kept them as they planned, undertook, and finally examined the results both of their routine practices and of the introduction of changes and innovations'.[11] In his analysis of the diary of J Badenach, a Stonehaven farmer, written between 1789 and 1799, Mowbray Pearson notes how the author refers to the weather ('details of the weather were given every day throughout the Diary'), agricultural practices, livestock, servants (though 'it was hard to tell exactly how many regular workers were employed on the farm'), markets, trysts and fairs (including activities at the markets and the specialist nature of some of the markets), mills and distilleries, prices of a range of farm commodities ('usually at the middle and end of the month'), building and construction, planting, work in the garden, and the transport of commodities (wood, coal, building stone, slates and lime).[12]

Ponsonby suggests that the best diaries were written by people who were either young or very old. He believes that 'uncomfortable mannerism, self-consciousness, and perhaps a desire to publish make their writing in the middle period less spontaneous'.[13] Social class and public stature also had an impact on their quality. As he observes:

> few celebrities are good diarists. Many obscure people, otherwise unknown, are excellent diarists. Neither the quality nor the magnitude of a person's

work and occupation has anything whatever to do with his inclination for diary writing or the nature of his diary.[14]

The analysis of diaries raises a number of issues. Diaries do not always reveal a great deal of evidence about their author. As Ponsonby notes: 'in some cases it may be difficult from their diary to learn what their occupation was'.[15] Helen and Keith Kelsall point out that George Home's diary of 1694 to 1696, was 'written for himself alone, so that he did not feel it necessary to explain anything. All that was needed was to put it on record what he would otherwise inevitably forget'.[16] When editing his diary, they had to insert a substantial number of explanatory notes to assist readers. Authors do not always state why they kept their diary. Some are clear on their reasons: for example, John Sturrock, a millwright in Dundee, and Adam Mackie of Fyvie, farmer, merchant and innkeeper.[17]

Diary writers are selective in what they chose to write about. They present information that they considered to be important to them. Fenton notes that the information in farmers' diaries focuses 'almost solely on daily work and who did what, on the weather which could affect annual work rhythms, and on journeys, visits, and personal and public occasions'.[18] The diaries are selective about the people to whom they refer. They present a particular view of the world, generally a masculine one in the case of farmers' diaries. The outside world rarely appears: major political or other events, or their impact on the author, may not be recorded. The diary writer's experience may not be typical of a particular social or occupational group; it should be viewed as a personal experience. Not all diaries are reflective. Fenton notes that most of the farmers who wrote their diaries 'are not visibly philosophers or thinkers' but observers.[19] However, like the diary writers who recorded weather details, they can provide very detailed observations.

A number of diaries have been published. Societies such as the Scottish History Society have played an important role in making some older diaries, especially of prominent persons (at a local or even a national level), more widely accessible (see also the section on sponsors in this chapter). J G Fyfe's edited collections *Scottish Diaries and Memoirs, 1550–1746* (1927) and *Scottish Diaries and Memoirs, 1746–1843* (1942) provide extracts from a number of diaries whose authors came from a wide range of occupational groups, notably members of the landed classes and ministers, and biographical accounts of their authors. Ponsonby's *Scottish and Irish Diaries from the Sixteenth to the Nineteenth Centuries* (1927) also employs the same format. Fenton points out that there have been 'sporadic publications of or about farmers' diaries for half a century, but in each case primarily for their local interest'.[20] They have also received attention in other countries such as Denmark, England, Germany, Norway and Sweden, and through the International Association for Research on Peasant Diaries, which has published a newsletter *Research on Peasant Diaries* since 1989.[21] A number of farmers' diaries and other rural diaries have been published with extensive analyses of their contents. They include those of Mr Smith, farmer at Maisondieu, Brechin, Angus (1794–1801) and Dr James Badenach, Balmakewan, Stonehaven (1779–1786); and the diaries of gardeners, such as one at Skail in Orkney for 1801. Tom Barry has used the diaries of John Spottiswoode to observe life and labour on a Berwickshire estate between 1753 and 1793. Although diaries and account books kept by day labourers 'are in any case rare', Fenton has identified and examined two day labourers' books from Glenesk, Angus, from 1826–56 and 1866–73.[22]

Bibliographies are available to locate and analyse diaries. William Matthews has compiled *British Diaries: an Annotated Bibliography of British Diaries Written Between 1442 and 1942* (1950). This provides a chronological list of diaries, together with some biographical details of their authors, and their provenance. Matthews excludes parliamentary diaries and explorers' journals as well as other types of accounts which he does not strictly consider to be 'diaries'.[23]

Accounts of travellers in Scotland

Although Arthur Ponsonby includes the accounts of travellers as a specific category of diary, Matthews suggests that not all travel accounts were 'diaries' as some were not day-to-day records or accounts of travel. Travel accounts thus embrace diaries and other forms of observational writing. Accounts of travels, tours, journeys, voyages, cruises, excursions, wanderings, rambles, and visits to Scotland, or parts of the country, have been written from ancient times. However, they were not written or published in significant numbers until 1770–1820, a period of increasing growth in travel and travel literature. After that date tourism became increasingly common. Accounts of travels were written for a variety of purposes: political, military/diplomatic, ecclesiastical, commercial/economic, sport, tourism and literary ('to impress their readers with their literary skills as well as their travel experience').[24] Some travel accounts have become well known and extensively reprinted, even over a number of centuries. They include: Martin Martin's *A Voyage to St Kilda; the Remotest of all the Hebrides. Or, Western Isles of Scotland* (1698) and his *A Description of the Western Isles of Scotland circa 1695* (1703); Daniel Defoe's *A Tour Through the Whole Island of Great Britain* (1724–26); Edward Burt's *Letters from a Gentleman in the North of Scotland to his friend in London* (1754); and Thomas Pennant's *A Tour in Scotland, 1769* (1771), and his *Tour in Scotland and Voyage to the Hebrides, 1772* (1774).

The value of traveller accounts has been assessed by a number of writers. Denis Rixon suggests that the accounts relating to the Hebrides reflect 'the interests and preferences of the writers . . . They have brought with them their own prejudices and preconceptions and often what they tell us is more about themselves than the culture or people they are visiting.'[25] Arthur Mitchell was critical of the authors of travel accounts. He observes that many 'appear either to have had eyes which did not see, or not to have known what they should look for and what ought to be described or recorded in view of its ultimate value'. However, he acknowledges that 'the narratives, as a whole, contain a large amount of accurate and well-recorded observation, which is of value to the historian, and of value also to the student of pre-history'.[26] Denis Rixon believes that they 'supply a kind of material of which ordinary histories make a meagre use': they are 'often the only records we have . . . so few early documents survive which can be said to be native'.[27]

There have been numerous studies on travellers' accounts. These fall into six categories: general studies (including bibliographies); studies on specific types of accounts; studies on accounts in specific periods of time; studies on accounts describing particular geographical areas; studies on particular travellers and their accounts; and studies of accounts held in particular libraries or archives. Extensive bibliographical lists have been compiled. Mitchell has a bibliography and critical analysis of travel accounts until the early twentieth century.[28] Mitchell and C G Cash provide another bibliography of accounts up to the early twentieth century in *A Contribution to the Bibliography of Scottish Topography* (1917). The *Bibliography* (2003) volume of the Scottish Life and Society series includes a comprehensive section on early travellers' accounts. Alastair J Durie outlines the sources for the study of tourism in nineteenth-century Scotland. Among the other categories of studies, P Hume Brown has brought together and published twenty-four accounts of travellers before 1700; Christopher Smout has surveyed the tours in the Scottish Highlands from the eighteenth to the twentieth centuries; E Mairi MacArthur gives further insights into this geographical area and the Western Isles; Alison Hiley examines German travellers in Scotland (1800–60); and Peter G Vasay describes a selection of travel diaries held in the NAS.[29]

Letters

Letters started to be more frequently written in the late sixteenth century. Karina Williamson observes that by 1707 they 'were already ensconced in the emergent bourgeois public sphere'.[30] The extension of the Post Office to Scotland in 1711 created 'a communications revolution'. It has been estimated that in London prior to 1730 the postage rates brought the letter carriage within the reach of the gentry, merchants and professional classes but also a number of members of the lower classes, notably small shopkeepers, artisans and domestic servants. By the mid eighteenth century these beneficiaries also included journeyman notaries, engravers, builders and watchmakers, and also 'ordinary people'. Although postage rates facilitated the spread of correspondence, literacy levels (reading being a different activity to writing) continued to vary greatly between the different social classes and occupational groups, thus also had an impact on the practice of writing and receiving letters.[31]

The increasing practice of letter writing in the seventeenth and eighteenth centuries gave rise to a number of letter-writing manuals which provided guidance on the codes, conventions and practices of letter writing, and on 'the proper conduct of conversation and of familial, social, sexual, professional and commercial life'.[32] They also set out the different purposes for which letters could be used. In Scotland these manuals included W H Dilworth's *Complete Letter-writer, Or Young's Secretary's Instructor* (1783), which was also available in New York in the mid 1790s. Their content varied in the different editions throughout Britain and the United States, thus reflecting social conventions and the social and economic need of letter writing. The Glasgow edition of W H Dilworth's *Complete Letter-writer* generally offered 'fewer business letters, fewer courtship letters, and less focus on gentility than American ones did, but included letters of recommendation for servants, and letters on the subject of local elections that American versions often cut out'.[33]

Although some significant collections of letters have survived and are available in libraries and archives, they have not survived to the same extent in all social classes or occupational groups. The largest collections of letters have survived amongst family papers from the landed or upper classes and some members of the professions. Thus, the Duff of Braco and Wharton-Duff of Orton papers (1665 to 1869), held in the University of Aberdeen, consist primarily of correspondence between Lord Braco, first earl Fife (William Duff), his wife and children, and members of the family of Wharton-Duff of Orton.[34]

Extensive collections of letters have been published. Most of these relate to members of the upper classes, the professions and literary figures such as Lord Cockburn and Robert Burns, but they also include other classes and occupational groups such as farmers like Gavin Scott from Lanarkshire.[35] A number of studies have focused on the correspondence between one correspondent and one or a close network of correspondees, or on correspondence at a particular time.

Studies have also analysed the correspondence of particular groups of people. David A Gerber considers that letters from British immigrants who went to North America in the nineteenth century are very important: 'probably the largest single body of the writings of ordinary people to which historians have access'.[36] He has examined their letter-writing practices and analysed a selection of their letters. He suggests that they are characterised by their:

> significant diversity of subject matter . . . there was so much in their lives that was new and, they believed, unimaginable to others at home, alongside many unanticipated sources of continuity, immigrants often seem to have been compelled to discuss a wide range of phenomena, events, and experiences in the same text.[37]

Gerber identifies four issues in analysing the letters of nineteenth-century British immigrants. First, it is difficult to learn anything beyond the most basic biographical information about either the letter-writers or those to whom they wrote. Second, the letters are selective in the subject matter and experiences their authors choose to write about or not to write about (despite the fact that they cover a significant range of subjects), and they do not always reveal their motivations for writing about certain experiences or subjects. Third, he finds it difficult to assess the accuracy and authorial authenticity of the letters. This is important as some were written with publication in mind or as propaganda, rather than for personal purposes. Fourth, the survival of the letters is patchy: some collections have survived but others have not.[38]

Autobiographies

Autobiographies have been written in increasing numbers since the eighteenth century. Throughout Britain in the nineteenth century the most numerous authors were politicians and statesmen, followed by the clergy, missionaries, doctors and soldiers. Accounts written by working people started to appear in increasing numbers from the late eighteenth century. Their development was shaped by two factors: growing educational opportunities and shorter working hours, which gave people 'more leisure and more opportunity to think of things other than the daily struggle to survive'.[39] David Vincent also suggests that 'their contents were the product of a new and much-more self-confident attitude towards the development of the working man's personality'.[40]

Working class autobiographies have been written by a disparate group of individuals, including beggars and hawkers such as Hawkie, a 'gangrel'. Some occupational groups were more inclined to write accounts than others. John Burnett concludes that 'there are more memoirs of skilled workers than of unskilled, more of upper domestic servants than of lower, more of school-teachers than of farm labourers'. Most of the authors were males; there were few women authors, especially in the nineteenth century.[41] Vincent identifies three factors which contributed to the paucity of women writers. First, women did not have the self-confidence 'required to undertake the unusual act of writing an autobiography'. Second, they were excluded from most forms of working-class organisations, 'especially self-improvement societies, which provided the training and stimulus for self-expression for so many of the male autobiographers'. Third, they had a subordinate position within the family.[42]

The authors of the working-class autobiographies were set apart from other members of their class and occupational groups. Vincent, who has analysed their personal characteristics and values, suggests that 'most, but not all [the authors], led honest and fairly sober lives, and a great many read books and attempted to improve themselves'.[43] All the authors had their own reasons for writing an account of their lives.

Working-class autobiographies share a number of characteristics. They were written after a significant event or a series of events in an author's life. They recount select aspects of their life and episodes that shaped its course and their personal beliefs. Vincent believes that 'more than any other form of source material . . . [they have] the potential to tell us not merely what happened but the impact of an event or situation upon an actor in the past'. They reveal their attitudes, values and beliefs. For Vincent, 'it is precisely the element of subjectivity which is of the greatest value'.[44]

The autobiographies pay limited attention to the experience of work. Some authors consider that their association with organisations, trade unions and political campaigns was a central part of their life experience. Accounts of struggles in the workplace generally focus on those with their fellow workers rather than those with their employers. Accounts of the occupational and residential history of the author's family are usually very short. The role of women is under-represented, and where it is recorded it is confined to the home or kitchen. Accounts of childhood are presented as a 'series of disconnected fragments whose meaning is unclear' even to their author. For Vincent, they offer 'a particular freedom of selection and interpretation'.[45] Almost all the autobiographies provide an account of their author's education, no matter how short or fragmentary it was.

A number of studies have focused on aspects of working-class autobiographies. Indeed, some working-class autobiographies have come to be regarded as classic accounts of specific occupational groups.[46] Most studies have a British-wide focus, but also refer to Scottish autobiographical accounts. John Burnett's edited collection *Useful Toil: Autobiographies of Working People from the 1820s to the 1920s* (1994) provides extracts of autobiographies from the labouring classes, domestic servants and skilled workers. David Vincent's *Bread, Knowledge and Freedom: A Study of Nineteenth-Century Working Class Autobiography* (1981) analyses how working-class authors wrote their autobiographies and, through them, how they understood their lives during the period 1790 to 1850. He includes a comprehensive bibliography that includes some Scottish examples. Meg Bateman has assessed the characteristics of Gaelic autobiographies.[47]

Family records

Family records or papers survive for many of the great families in Scotland. Some of their collections are extensive and contain papers that extend over a number of centuries. For example, the papers in the Castle Fraser collection (MS 3470) in the University of Aberdeen, which relate to the Frasers of Fraser Castle and Muchalls, a strongly military family, extend over 500 years.[48] There are also papers relating to the lesser families who may have been important locally within their communities. The spread of literacy, especially in the nineteenth century, allowed an increasing number of families to keep and maintain their own family records.

Family records include legal papers, papers relating to family settlement, inventories, accounts, rentals, household books, correspondence, diaries, notebooks, sketches, printed books (and even libraries), and miscellaneous papers. The records of land-owning families usually contain estate papers. These may form a significant part of their papers, especially if their estates were extensive or located in different parts of the country, or they were especially interested in estate matters. Collections of family papers have been regarded as 'an important supplement to the archives of the great estates'.[49]

Estate papers

As noted, the papers of families who owned an estate or estates may include estate papers. These are business records that detail the business and management of an estate or estates. As Ian Whyte so succinctly notes, they are largely 'dry, factual records of estate management'.[50] They relate to the work, preoccupations and management of the estate officials and the aspirations of the landowner.

The NAS observes that 'although the most useful records from different estates follow general patterns, the wide variety in the geographical and chronological coverage makes generalisation difficult'.[51] Estate papers include the following types of documents:

- Legal documents. These concern ownership, succession, marriage and genealogical information.

- Rentals (rent rolls). These record the rents paid for the farms on the estate. They may simply comprise an account of the annual income of an estate, but can also include the names of tenants, the name of the farm and other areas of land, acreage and value of the land leased, the year in which the lease began and its duration, and payments made.
- Tacks or leases of holdings. These include information on the rent (in money or kind) paid by a tenant, the amount and nature of services on the estate, such as harvesting activities and carting specific goods. If the lease is an improving one, it also records the steps that the tenant was required to take to improve the holding.
- Estate accounts and vouchers (receipts from which the accounts are compiled) kept by the proprietor's estate manager and agent (sometimes known as 'the factor's accounts'). These give details of the management of the estate (such as information on crops, livestock, activities on the home farm or farms run directly by the estate, forestry, quarrying and mills), life and work on it.
- Inventories (lists of goods and materials).
- Correspondence.
- Estate maps and plans. These refer to the estate boundaries, parts of the estate or the estate as a whole, the estate farm or tenanted farms, as well as the estate buildings.
- Household accounts.
- Local administration. These records refer to the erection and running of churches and schools and the building of roads and bridges.

Collections of estate papers, like family records, vary in extent and scope. Some are extensive and include papers created over a number of centuries. For example, the Duff House/Montcoffer papers (Aberdeen University, MS 3175) comprise 1,300 volumes and 1,300 boxes of material, together with over 500 estate plans.[52] Collections may contain extensive papers for particular periods but have few or none at other times. They may be strongest for particular periods of the eighteenth and early nineteenth centuries when estates were making fundamental changes to the way the land was managed and tenanted and farms and estate buildings were being rebuilt, but have few papers thereafter. A number of the largest estates that have transmitted their papers to archives have insignificant collections for the twentieth century. There may be gaps in the availability of particular types of record, either in a collection as a whole, or for specific periods. Thus, the Rubislaw Estate papers, held in the University of Aberdeen, are considered to be 'fragmentary and one-sided'. The Cushnie Estate papers, which extend from 1464 to 1956, and are also in the University of Aberdeen, are 'large but uneven in scope'. Writing on that collection, Colin A McLaren notes that 'the lack of complete sets of rentals or systematically-compiled accounts over a long period, however, makes the collection less satisfactory as a source of economic data'.[53] Another collection, the Duff of Meldrum Estate papers (Aberdeen University, MS 2778), extending from 1456 to 1916, has an incomplete series of rentals 'for the entire period covered by the collection but domestic and other estate accounts are abundant'. The collection 'contains a substantial group of correspondence covering the period 1669–1861, but this is less comprehensive than might have been expected in a deposit which is otherwise so full; and it includes little of special interest beyond the day-to-day business of estate management and litigation'.[54]

Estate papers have been extensively used in a number of studies on rural Scotland from the seventeenth century onwards. As they present the views of the landowners and their land managers, they have been primarily used to research the changes (including its mechanism and speed) in the way the land and rural society and estate communities were re-organised during the Agricultural Revolution. T M Devine has charted the rate and progress of agricultural change on a number of estates in Lowland Scotland between 1660 and 1815. Ian Whyte has used such papers as a central source of evidence in his survey of agriculture and society in the seventeenth century. He has used them to focus on the land and the people, the estate and the rural community, the farm, the country house and enclosure, the tenant and his holding, transport, communications and marketing, developments in arable farming, and the grain and droving trades. Susanna Wade Martins has charted the farming activities on the Sutherland Estate between 1790 and 1890. Leah Leneman has investigated the social history of the Atholl estates between 1685 and 1785, and James Mair has focused on the social history of the Cessnock Estate in Ayrshire during the Agricultural Revolution. Collections also contain evidence on material culture on the estates. Ian D Whyte analyses the papers as a source of evidence for rural housing in the seventeenth century. Studies have also focused on particular types of papers. Peter Clapham has analysed rentals and tacks in Angus during the period 1760 to 1850 to assess agricultural change and its impact on the tenancy.[55]

Business records

All businesses create and preserve records on their management and activities. Their records are available especially from the mid nineteenth century, though there are exceptions: the records of the Carron Company held in the NAS (GD58), are available from 1478 to 1982.

Business records are generally factual documents. They may include account books (including general ledger, day books, journals), production, stock and sales records, purchase and receiving records, letter books, labour records (including wage books, time books, minute books), travellers' and agents' expenses and commissions, technical records and miscellaneous papers. The scope of the records held by a business may vary from business to business. For example, businesses may have created and maintained their own documentation systems to manage their activities. Business size has a significant impact on record management systems. Those in joint partnership require a significantly greater amount of documentation than businesses run by a sole proprietor actively involved in all aspects of the business. Their systems also reflect changing methods of record keeping and the development and use of new record-creation and storage technologies. Business records also reflect the activities of a business: if it did not employ travelling salesmen, for example, the records would not indicate that such an activity took place. However, businesses may not have kept particular records as they were not required to do so by legislation.

Legislation has played an important role in shaping the records that businesses have been required to keep for administrative purposes. John Armstrong and Stephanie Jones state that company law 'has had a great impact on the preservation of business documents'.[56] The Joint Stock Companies (Registration) Act 1844, its consolidating Act of 1862, the Companies Act 1907 and the successive Companies Acts have made provision for the keeping of specific records. They have ensured that there is 'a rich deposit of information about business that might otherwise not have survived'.[57] Journals and ledgers that record the finances of a business have largely been preserved as a result of legislative requirements. Indeed, for some businesses the financial records may cover an extensive period of time. The 'Registers of Directors' in a business is also likely to have survived, especially where it was lodged with the Registrar of Companies, responsible for ensuring its preservation. The Register of Members is also frequently preserved as a result of legislative requirements. Minutes of meetings of board directors for joint stock companies exist for some businesses. Although there was no legislative requirement for joint stock companies to keep these minutes until 1809, most companies nevertheless kept them, thereby indicating their importance. Their quality varies, with small businesses having less need for detailed minutes than larger ones.

Some categories of records have not survived to any great extent. Documents intended for internal use only, and not to be more widely circulated, for example to shareholders, had not legislative requirement to be kept. They include letter books, which record the correspondence – in-going or out-going – relating to a business, and business diaries, a private record usually kept by the director or owner. However, some business diaries have survived, such as those of Sir Alexander Grant and William Finnie, a Kilmarnock merchant.[58]

Each of these categories of business record provides particular types of information on the management and activities of a business. In *Business Documents: Their Origins, Sources and Uses in Historical Research* (1987), Armstrong and Jones detail the source and function of the different categories of business records, as well as the range of information they contain. Letter books provide a wide range of information about the range and nature of activities undertaken by a business and its relations with suppliers and customers. They are 'absolutely invaluable to anyone investigating the history of a specific company, for the light they throw on the firm's activities and personnel; more importantly, the reasoning of the directors may be given so explaining why certain policies or actions were adopted. They are similarly valuable for research on firms that might have had relationships with the originator firm'.[59] Wages books recording the wage rates and earnings of employees, and their names, can be analysed to gather evidence on the sex ratio, and changes in employment patterns and conditions, for example over a season or a longer period. Sales ledgers, recording activities on sales, may be analysed to show the extent of the geographical influence of a business, changes to sales patterns over time, and the social class and occupation of the customers either at one point in time or over a longer period. The Register of Directors records some biographical information on the directors, including their addresses. Analysis of a series of registers may show the influence of directors within the business community and changes in the character of the leadership of a firm over time. The Register of Members gives a list of the names of shareholders, their address, occupation and status (aristocratic, military or naval rank is normally fully specified) and the number of shares owned. Analysis may reveal the social and geographical patterns of investment of a business, its sphere of influence and any patterns of links between the investors.

Sources are available to identify collections of business records. The Business Archives Council publishes the journal *Scottish Industrial History*, which includes studies on specific businesses and their activities. The Scottish History Society has published *Scottish Industrial History: A Miscellany of Documents* (1978), edited by R H Campbell. There are extensive bibliographies on specific businesses. Brewing is covered in Lesley M Richmond's and Alison Turnton's *The Brewing Industry: A Guide to Historical Records* (1990); shipbuilding in L A Ritchie's *The Shipbuilding Industry: A Guide to Historical Records* (1992); and banking in Leslie Sedden Pressnell and John Orbell's *A Guide to the Historical Records of British Banking* (1985). John Imrie has compiled a list of sources in the Scottish Record Office (the National Records of Scotland) (2006) and A M Broom and A Anderson have undertaken a complementary survey of records held in private hands surveyed by the National Register of Archives for Scotland (NRAS), published in 2006.

Numerous studies, largely written by social and economic historians and business historians, have made extensive use of business records. They include the work of Ian Donnachie on the brewing industry, Alastair J Durie on the linen industry in the eighteenth century, Clifford Gulvin on the Scottish hosiery and knitwear industry between 1680 and 1980, and John Butt and Kenneth Ponting's edited work on the textile industry. There are also regional business histories such as those of the west of Scotland for the period 1750 to 1960 by Anthony Slaven, and the development of Aberdeenshire in the nineteenth century by Sydney Wood.[60]

Farm account books

Account books are an important category of business records, which had growing importance for farmers during the nineteenth and twentieth centuries. Accounting textbooks suitable for estate factors and other estate managers were available earlier than those for farmers.[61] Although the noted English agricultural writer Arthur Young promoted farm accounting methods to farmers in the early 1770s in his *Rural Oeconomy* (1770), and *Farmer's Kalendar* (1771), there were few account books for farmers in following decades. Robert Hamilton included a chapter on 'farm accompts' in *An Introduction to Merchandize* (1777–79). John Rose offered a more extensive account in *The Transactions of the British Farmer Accountant Adapted to the Four Seasons of the Year Wherein the Gentleman Farmers Gave a Plan of Books, Entirely new, and Suitable to their Occupation* (1780). In 1790, David Young, a merchant in Perth and former farmer in that area, published *The Farmer's Account Book*, an analysed account book in which farmers could record a year's agricultural activity and which provided them with a management accounting system to show the profit and loss accrued from a range of farming activities. Young's book was a forerunner of the specialist account book and the pre-printed annual account book for farmers which started to appear in large numbers in the early nineteenth century.[62]

By the late eighteenth century and the first decades of the nineteenth century, some of the surveyors employed by the Board of Agriculture and Internal Improvement found it difficult to provide examples of farm accounts and statements of 'expense and profit', which were to be included in the chapter on 'Mode of Occupation' in their county agricultural surveys. Writing on this period, M E Turner, J V Beckett and B Afton suggest that there were good reasons why some farmers did not keep accounts: formalised accounts were of limited use to farmers who ran their own their farms. There was generally no obvious reason why tenant farmers and owner-occupiers should keep accounts. The keeping of such records was a personal activity, undertaken by choice: 'for the most part, those farmers who kept records did so for their own information and recorded data because they thought it might be useful to them'.[63]

Farm account books, including cash books (an account of the money outlay and income), are highly individualistic. Turner et al. observe that farmers recorded 'what they found useful rather than what they were told by experts to note. Their understanding of modern accountancy methods was weak, and so, like all other farm records, accounts were individualistic, sometimes to the point of being idiosyncratic.' Accounts reflect the particular economic activities on a specific farm or farms. They record a wide range of information such as the daily and monthly in-goings and outgoings on a farm, the sales of the various crops and livestock, details of the size and activities of the labour force, their wages (both in cash and in kind; and the different rates paid to men, women and children), the purchase of new implements and changes in farming practice over time, the seasonal activities and transactions for crops and livestock sold from the farm and purchases made. Turner et al. suggest that 'their value lies in what they reveal about the mentality of the farmer, his farming, and his relationship to his environment'. However, they conclude that 'in general [farm account books] do not offer much by way of deep insights into [the farmer's] financial solvency'.[64]

Farm account books have received greater attention in England than in Scotland, where agricultural historians, who are largely from departments of social and economic history and history departments, have made a number of extended surveys of them. In Scotland, for the mid eighteenth century, Alexander Fenton has published an analysis of an account from Begbie, East Lothian (1729–70). A larger number of accounts have been analysed for the nineteenth century. They include cash books from Glenesk, Angus (1885–98), and South Knapdale, Argyll (1843–54).[65]

Records of clubs, societies and trade unions

Clubs, societies and trades unions have been important organisations in Scotland for a number of centuries. They have undertaken and promoted a range of activities: philanthropic activities such as mutual benefit of their members, the promotion of entertainment and sporting activities (such as curling, football and golf), cultural activities and education in its widest sense. They have operated at a number of geographical levels: throughout Scotland (or even the United Kingdom), a district, a parish, or a settlement such as a city, town or village. Some national organisations, such as the Scottish Women's Rural Institute, friendly societies, trades unions and co-operative societies (such as the Scottish Co-operative Wholesale Society), have developed and used extensive networks throughout the country to undertake and promote their activities.

These organisations have created and maintained a range of records of their activities, including rules and regulations for their governance and the behaviour of their members, minute books, lists of members and records to fulfil statutory requirements (such as the Charities Acts etc). Minute books, for example, are a widely noted form of record in surviving trade unions' records.[66] As for business records, their character and extent vary according to a number of factors such as the nature of their organisation, its size, activities, record-keeping practices and statutory requirements.

The records of a wide range of organisations have survived. The records and activities of agricultural societies, farmers' clubs and societies which had a number of roles in rural society and agricultural and rural improvement, have received a great deal of attention in England, but not in Scotland. R C Boud outlines their development and role in Scotland during 1723 to 1835.[67] Most studies have focused on specific societies, from national societies such as the Royal Highland and Agricultural Society of Scotland to local societies such as the Gordon's Mill Farming Club (1758–64), the Lesmahagow Farmers' Club (for 1803), and the Easter Ross Farmers' Club (1811–98).[68] A number of county and district societies, which have celebrated centenaries or other historical landmarks, have published commemorative histories: Marcus W T Wood describes 150 years of the South Ronaldsay and Burray Agricultural Society, and Turriff and District Junior Agricultural Club examines fifty years of activities between 1932 and 1982.[69]

These records provide information on the societies' membership, organi-sation, activities, their role and influence on the areas where they had jurisdiction. For example, the minute book of the Lesmahagow Farmers' Club, which runs from 1803 when the Club was instituted, reveal the reasons for its establishment ('to promote improvements'), its regulations and activities (and changes over time) such as ploughing matches, discussion meetings (including the questions to be debated), and formal dinners.[70] These can be compared with the activities of other societies so that comparative studies can be developed, giving a wider understanding of their influence.

Records relating to trade unions and co-operative societies form part of the wider body of records relating to labour history and are discussed by Ian MacDougall in his *Labour Records in Scotland* (1978). Trade union records cover a very broad range of occupational groups, mainly industrial, such as boiler-makers, shipwrights, brewery works coachmakers, carters, coopers, dockers, foundry workers, mineworkers, postal workers, railwaymen, shop workers, slaters, weavers and woodworkers. Their records largely date from the nineteenth century onwards, as do the records of co-operative societies, though their survival can be patchy. In some cases they have only survived for a few years (sometimes reflecting the short-lived nature of these organisations), though some have survived for a number of decades. Earlier occupational records are to be found in the records of the craft guilds and trades formed in the Middle Ages and in more recent times.[71]

Records of hospitals, charitable schools and other philanthropic institutions

Philanthropic institutions have played an important role in Scotland for a number of centuries, but especially in the mid nineteenth century, the 'golden age of middle-class philanthropy'.[72] They had a wide range of motivations for undertaking charitable work: to display their affluence and status; to provide assistance to the poorer classes who lived in close proximity to themselves (philanthropy declined when better transport made it possible for people to live in the suburbs); to express professional concerns; or for political reasons. Philanthropic activities were various and multi-faceted. Some of them had been traditionally undertaken by the family or church, including the provision for hospitals and schooling. It was in these last two areas that philanthropists are considered to have made their greatest contributions in Victorian Scotland.[73] Other activities included securing better environmental health, temperance, remedial activities (such as the provision of orphanages and remedial homes for the disabled), and better housing, model housing and lodging houses.

The records of philanthropic organisations include categories already mentioned in this chapter: minute books, annual reports, lists of members, and accounts. Legislation, such as the Charity Acts, also shaped the records that were to be created and maintained. Olive Checkland has extensively researched the welfare provision by philanthropists in the nineteenth century in *Philanthropy in Victorian Scotland: Social Welfare and the Voluntary Principle* (1980). She finds that their annual reports and minute books are particularly important for researching their activities. Their annual reports include the name of the society, the date of its foundation (and Biblical motto if appropriate), a treasurers' report and annual statement of funds, and a list of contributors which includes their addresses and the size of their contributions; this can be used to provide evidence of a society's status and its geographical influence. Checkland finds that the records are more useful when they can be cross-checked with other contemporary records such as newspapers and Government reports.[74]

There have been a number of significant histories of philanthropic and charitable institutions, including those relating to the Chalmers Hospital in Edinburgh, Allan Glen's School (1855–1953), and the Dick Bequest. There are also studies on more minor ones such as the Navvy Mission Society.[75]

Maps and plans

Maps and plans form part of the private as well as the public record. They include plans made by businesses to show proposed activities such as the building of railways and canals, and plans of estates. Estate maps and plans were drawn up for a range of purposes. Many were drawn up as boundary plans to help resolve disputes between landowners. Others were used to record the division of commonties, or common land, a legal procedure that became more common from the mid eighteenth century. They have been inextricably linked with agricultural and estate improvement in the eighteenth and nineteenth centuries, though they continued to be used after this date. The increasing agricultural changes brought with them the need to map estates and thus the rise in the professional surveyor. Although there are few estate plans and maps in the late sixteenth century, they were being used in increasing numbers in the early nineteenth century; by the middle of the century when the changes to the rural landscape were at their most extensive, the number of maps and plans continued to increase. Ian H Adams suggests that between 1700 and 1850 more than 30,000 such plans were produced in Scotland. Surveyors could be required to make a number of plans of an estate, at different times: for example, to assess the potential of the land to be improved and laid out and the 'improved landscape' created, and also after the land had been 'improved'. The quality of plans varies: Adams observes that some 'were crude but serviceable, many were merely competent, and on rare occasions they were cartographic masterpieces'.[76]

Tristram Clarke provides an introduction to estate maps and plans and their value for historical research. He considers that they are a 'visual record of landed rights and the relationship between landlord and tenant, and even as statements of privilege and power'.[77] They have been used to show the process and progress of agricultural and landscape change in the eighteenth and early nineteenth centuries. Studies by Betty Third, A Geddes and J H G Lebon are well-known and classic accounts.[78] More recently, Rosemary Gibson has used estate and other private maps and plans in her *The Scottish Countryside: Its Changing Face, 1700–2000* (2007) to examine a range of aspects of the countryside and changes to it during the course of the last 300 years. She provides detailed analyses of particular maps, demonstrates how to analyse them, and shows the information they can provide on the countryside.

SPONSORSHIP AND PROMOTION OF PRIVATE ACCOUNTS

The European Ethnological Research Centre (EERC) has sponsored two series of publications which promote the testimony and experiences of 'those holding lowlier positions in the world – in other words, the great majority'. The first of these, the 'Sources in Local History' series, was inspired by 'the current international interest in the diaries and account books of farmers and tradesmen, as well as their personal papers'.[79] It is concerned with the publication and promotion of 'ego-documents': documents 'written by individuals for their own purposes, and not for the wide world to stare at'.[80] The sources relate to a specific household, or a single economic unit (such as a farm), or activities within a parish; they may also include numerous districts throughout Scotland (as in travellers' accounts). They had, according to Alexander Fenton, 'more to do with their own localities than with overviews of wider regions'.[81] They document both rural and urban areas, though the former is more widely represented.

The series has a range of personal accounts, largely from members of the working classes. They include a cashbook from Buskhead Farm, Glenesk, written between 1885 and 1898. This provides 'a record of the money outlay and income of a small farm which was working, as most did, at the lower margins of profitability, but also producing food, the value of which was not taken into the equation and is not easy to assess'.[82] Personal diaries have also been published. A thematic selection of material has been taken from the diaries of Robert and Elsie Thomson, schoolteachers in Nairn, and prominent local figures and natural history enthusiasts, in the late nineteenth century. Another publication in the series, that of John Sturrock, a millwright in Dundee, written in 1864 and 1865, provides an annotated text of his diary, which recalls, in daily entries, how he spent his leisure time. It records his habits and interests, his voracious reading of particular types of books and magazines, his social networks with friends and family, and relationships with his work colleagues outwith the workplace. It notes the relation between his working hours and his leisure time, and the impact of long hours on his leisure activities. Most of the entries in the diary are short, up to a few lines of text, though those detailing his activities on a Sunday are much more extensive. The series also includes the account of an early traveller, Sir William Burrell, an English aristocrat who toured Scotland, England and Ireland in 1758. It reveals 'a great deal of light on the various localities' which he visited. According to Fenton, it also 'helps to fill in gaps in the record of history'.[83]

The second series sponsored by the EERC is 'Flashbacks'. Fenton suggests that 'every single individual, every family has a story to tell. Everyone can add a quota to the total sum of knowledge of human history'.[84] The series publishes personal accounts based on three methodologies. The first is oral recollection from a particular social or occupational group, including: bondagers or women farmworkers in south-east Scotland; Midlothian women farmworkers; women potato workers in Midlothian; miners in Newtongrange; and employees of Thomas Nelson and Sons, the Edinburgh-based printing and publishing firm.[85] The second is the autobiographical recollection of one's own experiences. These include the reminiscences of a Border shepherd, a woman in the fishing community of Nairn in the twentieth century, a journalist in Aberdeen, and a schoolteacher and journalist on the Isle of Lewis.[86] The third is the use of letters, diaries and memoirs written by members of one's own family to recount the experience of a family or particular members of it. Colin MacLean draws on the letters of his mother, Isabella MacLean, in *Your Father and I: A Family's Story* (1998). Evelyn Wright edited a manuscript written by Thomas Wyld Pairman (a relation), of episodes and aspects of the life of his father, Robert Pairman, a doctor in Biggar, Lanarkshire between 1818 and 1873 (2003). The daughter of Frances Rimington edited her mother's reminiscences of life in Perth, in *That's Fourpence You're Eating! A Childhoood in Perth* (2006).

The Flashbacks series has published material from a range of districts throughout Scotland, especially the east. In William Kenefick's review of the first eight volumes, he observes that 'the reader is thus left more with a sense of what country life was like in the twentieth century, as opposed to that in the city or the more familiar industrial landscape in the west of Scotland'. For him, the series has played an important role in shifting the emphasis on research away from the west central industrial belt which 'defined much of recent historical research of modern twentieth century Scotland': it 'gives a greater sense of balance to Scotland's more recent historical development'.[87]

The journal *Review of Scottish Culture* publishes a range of material on diaries, largely from members of the working classes. They include shorter notes, full texts where they are available, and analyses of their contents. They include the diaries of a cattle dealer, James Fyffe, a gardener at Skaill, and a farmer at Balmakewan, Kincardineshire. A farm manager's cashbook from Kilberry Argyll has also been analysed.[88]

The Scottish History Society (SHS) sponsors the publication of private accounts. These primarily focus on the writings of members of the landed and upper classes, the professions and prominent public figures. Most of the accounts are from earlier periods than for the publications of the EERC, largely the sixteenth to the eighteenth centuries. Diaries include those of landowners such as Patrick, the first earl of Strathmore, and Andrew Hay of Craignethan 1659 to 1660.[89] There are diaries of ministers, such as the Reverend George Ridpath, minister of Stitchel for the period 1755 to 1761, and the Reverend John Mill, minister of the parishes of Dunrossness, Sandwick and Cunningsburgh in Shetland (1740–1805).[90] Other personal records include published memoirs, such as the one on the life of Sir John Clerk of Penicuik, Bart, 1675–1755.[91] There are journals, one of which was written by John Erskine of Carnock between 1683 and 1687.[92] Collections of letters have been edited and published. They include those from John Cockburn of Ormistoun to his gardener from 1727 to 1744, and John Ramsay of Ochtertyre from 1799 to 1812.[93]

The Scottish History Society has edited and published collections of household account books. They include the household book of Lady Griselle Baillie from 1692 to 1732, and the Ochtertyre house book of accompts from 1737 to 1739. The SHS has also edited and published some business records relating to a Scottish cloth manufactory at New Mills, East Lothian, 1681–1708, the British Linen Company 1745–75, and Peter Carmichael of Arthurstone and the Dundee textile industry 1790–1885.[94]

Archives and professional archival bodies have promoted the use of private accounts. The National Records of Scotland (formerly National Archives of Scotland) has published guides to a number of categories of private records on its website,[95] including records relating to crafts and trades, industries such as shipbuilding and coal mining, and estates. The Society of Archivists in its *Journal of the Society of Archivists* and the Scottish Records Association in its *Scottish Archives: The Journal of the Scottish Records Association* publish articles on the use of sources for research, especially historical research. Although the majority of these relate to public accounts, there are some studies on private ones. The Scottish Local History Forum promotes the use of historical sources of evidence for local history research and its journal *Scottish Local History* publishes a range of articles on sources, including private accounts, and their use for local history research.

Private accounts are located in a number of archives, libraries and other reposi-tories throughout Scotland. Michael Cox's *Exploring Scottish History: With a Directory of Resource Centres for Scottish Local and National History in Scotland* (1999) provides a list of the contact details, access, holdings, finding aids and reprographic facilities of 384 facilities throughout Scotland. Although these details are now outdated, his work demonstrates the diversity of institutions where records (private and public) are kept and also the difficulty in identifying where particular records are held.

A number of professional organisations and societies have outlined and described the holdings of particular archives and libraries. *Scottish Archives* includes a section 'Around the Archives' that focuses on the holdings of specific archives, usually ones that hold private records, such as those of Blair and Glamis castles, Mount Stuart, Traquair House, and the Royal College of Physicians and Surgeons of Glasgow.[96] *Northern Scotland* has published 'Reports and surveys of archives in northern Scotland', short accounts that focus on particular archives and their holdings, collections (including key ones), and specific types of documents.[97] The journal *Scottish Industrial History* includes surveys of archives that hold records that can be used for researching industrial history and an annual summary list of acquisitions to archives.

The paragraphs that follow outline the main types of repositories and private records held in them. The NRS (formerly NAS), an agency of the Scottish Government, 'holds historical records created by businesses, landed estates, families, churches and other corporate bodies' from throughout Scotland as well as records of the activities of Scottish emigrants.[98] It holds over 500 large collections of private papers which have been gifted to the nation, deposited on long-term loan or purchased; these are known as 'Gifts and Deposits'. They include family papers relating to some of the ancient families and major landowning families, their estates and business activities throughout Scotland until recent times, such as that of the dukes of Buccleuch (1165–1947) (GD224), the dukes of Hamilton (1543–1858) (GD406), the earls of Cromartie (1257–1960) (GD305), and the earls of Seafield (1215–1939) (GD248). It also holds over 1,400 smaller collections of private papers. There are records of a number of philanthropic organisations which have made an important contribution to social and welfare provision sometimes over a number of centuries: Dean Orphanage and Cauvin Trust (1641–1959) (GD417); Edinburgh Children's Holiday Fund (1887–1959) (GD1/909); George Heriot's Trust (from the sixteenth to the twentieth centuries) (GD421); and Dr Guthrie's Schools (1854–1986) (GD425). A broad outline of the contents of a number of these collections (GD4 to GD96) is contained in the two-volume *List of Gifts and Deposits in the Scottish Record Office* (1971, 1976). It also has an online catalogue (see later in the chapter).

The NRS also holds the 'Register House Plans', comprising over 150,000 maps and plans (including significant collections relating to estates) and archi-tectural and engineering drawings. The first 4,999 maps and plans in the collection are listed in Ian H Adams and Loretta R Timperley's *Descriptive List of Plans in the Scottish Record Office* (1966–88).

The focus of the manuscripts and archive collections in the National Library of Scotland (NLS) is on private rather than public records. It 'has extensive holdings of manuscripts and archives relating to Scottish history and culture and Scots men and women at home and abroad, dating mainly from the seventeenth century to the present day'. These 'include papers of major politicians or military leaders, and other public figures of international significance, including writers, philosophers and historians, scientists, engineers, missionaries and explorers'. Its collections also comprise 'large contemporary institutional archives from a wide range of modern Scottish cultural, political, scientific, sporting and trade union organisations'.[99] The John Murray Archive relating to the London-based publishing house John Murray embraces the business and family records of seven generations of the Murray family, descended from the Edinburgh-born publisher John Murray. The NLS has significant collections of estate papers from all parts of Scotland; these are especially strong for south and east-central counties. Noted collections include the Sutherland Papers (Sutherland), Lynedoch Papers (Perthshire), Minto Papers (Roxburghshire, Selkirkshire, Fife and Angus) and the Yester and Saltoun Papers (East Lothian).

University Archives throughout Scotland have significant holdings of private papers. For example, Edinburgh University Archives maintain the historical records of the University of Edinburgh (particularly post 1858 but many records date from earlier periods), its predecessors and affiliated bodies. Its website states that its collections are diverse, largely reflecting the university's strengths in the areas of medical and scientific history, Scottish literature, Middle Eastern studies, architecture, music, Gaelic & Celtic studies and theology.[100] The Special Libraries and Archives of the University of Aberdeen hold over 4,000 collections of manuscripts and archives relating to the institutional history of King's College, Marischal College and the University of Aberdeen, as well as family, estate and business papers relating to the north-east of Scotland, records relating to Jacobitism, nineteenth-century literature, Scottish balladry and folksong, the Scottish Enlightenment, philosophy and theology.[101] The University of Glasgow holds the records of the history of the university and its management, staff and students from its foundation in 1451 to the present day.[102] These include university-related records deposited by staff, alumni, associated organisations and predecessor institutions. It also hosts the Scottish Business Archive, whose collections were inaugurated in 1959, and have been managed by the university since 1975. It is one of the largest collections of historical business records in Europe. It holds over 500 archive collections relating to individuals and families of entrepreneurs, businesses and organisations. These focus on many types of business and industrial activity in Scotland and the UK, from banking, distilling and brewing to retail and undertaking. Its holdings are especially extensive for west-of-Scotland industries such as shipbuilding, locomotive manufacture, textiles and mining. The Scottish Brewing Archive is also located in the University of Glasgow and is managed by its Archive Services.[103]

Local authority archives are another source for private accounts. These include the archives of Glasgow City – Glasgow Life – and Edinburgh City

Archives.[104] Although they principally hold the records relating to their local authority and its administrative structures (see Chapter 19, Public Accounts), their holdings also include private records, the strength, nature and character of which vary greatly. Writing about the Highland Regional Archive (now the Highland Archive Service) in 1986, Alan B Lawson analyses the strength of particular collections of private records. He observes that the Archive holds 'a range of estate papers, some for individual farms and a few for farming societies'. The holdings of records on commerce, trade and industry are 'not large, as might be expected from a rural area'. There are limited banking records in the archive. Nevertheless, there are significant papers of Highland families and persons. There are also records of groups concerned with charitable organisations such as hospitals and welfare societies, and other organisations of a recreational or social nature.[105]

There are specialist archives located throughout the country. These focus on a range of industries, businesses and the activities of various professions and their societies. They include the Scottish Brewing Archive, the archives of the Halifax and Bank of Scotland Group and the Royal Bank of Scotland Group, professions such as the Royal College of Physicians of Edinburgh, and professional societies such as the Royal Scottish Geographical Society and the Royal Highland and Agricultural Society of Scotland. Archives are also attached to museums, such as the Savings Bank Museum, the Regimental Museum of the Highlanders, the Highland Folk Museum and the Strathclyde Police Museum.

Some of the landed and professional families, and businesses and organisations, still retain their own papers. Some collections are significant in extent and content and have papers of historical and ethnological significance. If they have been identified and catalogued by the NRAS (see later in the chapter), access can be made by application to the NRAS. Some collections have restricted access, for example, to non-genealogical researchers.

ELECTRONIC RESOURCES: BIBLIOGRAPHIES OR
CATALOGUES AND DIGITISED TEXTS

Technological advances have enabled a wide range of electronic resources to be developed which can be used to identify and research private papers. In recent decades, as the electronic revolution has gained momentum, these resources have become available in increasing numbers and now can have advanced technical capabilities, including advanced searching mechanisms. Two main types of resources can be identified: (1) electronic bibliographies or catalogues relating to the holdings of specific libraries or archives or particular categories of archival or published accounts, sometimes from particular periods; (2) electronic facsimile copies of published or archival material on a particular topic (and/or time period) which are fully searchable. Some of these resources focus on particular categories of private accounts, while others do not distinguish between private and public accounts and include both. They may be freely available for consultation; some are only available by means of subscription, for example through libraries and archives.

Bibliographies or catalogues

Electronic library and archive catalogues are now widely available. Copac is an integrated catalogue of the online catalogues of over seventy major university and national libraries in the United Kingdom and Ireland.[106] It includes the catalogues of the NLS, the legal deposit library in Scotland. It is able to identify the holdings of books, reports, periodicals and conference papers. The catalogue has some gaps; the administrators note that many libraries do not have all or part of their holdings in an electronic format. The catalogue also includes a substantial amount of older material, especially before 1900. The standard of the individual record entries also varies, especially between the different library catalogues. Some records include the full imprint details of the publications while others do not.

The Archives Hub is 'gateway to many of the UK's richest historical archives'.[107] It provides a single point of access to the archives in over 220 institutions mostly in the Higher Education sector in the UK, and forms part of the United Kingdom's National Archives Network, alongside related network projects. The Scottish Archive Network (SCAN) 'aims to revolutionise access to Scotland's archives by providing a single electronic catalogue to the holdings of more than 50 Scottish archives'.[108] It is a unified online catalogue of Scottish archives, including the archives of local authorities, universities and those that focus on collections of private records such as Mount Stuart Trust Archives, the Scottish Brewing Archive, the National Trust for Scotland, and the Royal College of Surgeons of Edinburgh. SCAN has also started to digitise and index Scottish historical records on an extensive scale – including surviving wills and testaments registered in Scottish commissary courts and sheriff courts between 1500 and 1901 and kirk session and presbytery records – so that the original records can be preserved and digital surrogates made more widely available.

The NRAS has an online register recording information relating to over 4,300 surveys of private papers, such as landed estates, private individuals, businesses, law firms and societies, held in private hands throughout Scotland.[109] As the register was started in 1946, not all the surveys are available electronically, but are available in the NRS. New surveys entered in the register are also published in the *Annual Report of the Keeper of the Records of Scotland*, also available electronically.

The NRS (NAS) website has an online public access catalogue which embraces all its catalogued holdings (including private accounts).[110] The level of detail in each catalogue record varies greatly, some being described in the briefest of terms. Catalogues for series of records do not contain specific information on every item. The catalogue, which has made the records more accessible and easier to search, makes links across collections and different categories of records. The NRS also holds paper catalogues in its search rooms; some collections such as business records in private collections and a source list for games, sports and gambling are only listed in this form.

The NLS has a number of online manuscript catalogues and guides on its website.[111] It has a 'Guide to Manuscript Collections', an alphabetical list of all significant manuscripts and archives (together with detailed inventories of many of the larger collections) held by its Manuscript collections. It has electronic descriptions of special and named printed collections, such as the John Francis Campbell Collection and the Crawford Ballads Collection.[112] The majority of the records continue to be identified by paper and published catalogues.

A number of specialised bibliographies are available to research private (and public) accounts. The NLS has a 'Scottish Bibliographies Online' resource.[113] This has three separate components. The first is the 'Bibliography of Scotland', described as 'Scotland's national bibliography'. It is a bibliography of books, periodicals and major articles of Scottish interest published all over the world. It provides easy access to articles in journals and contributed essays and chapters in books that are not traditionally made available on library catalogues (see also JSTOR as a resource for providing access to this type of material). It has a contemporary focus and includes material published since 1987; its origins, however, are in an annual bibliography first published in 1976. It has some gaps. Although it draws on a comprehensive list of journals to identify suitable articles, not all of the articles are included even if they fall within its collection statement. The second component is the 'Bibliography of Scottish Gaelic' (BOSG), a bibliographical list of books and periodicals published in Gaelic, or which contain substantial Gaelic text, from the beginning of Gaelic publishing. The third component is the 'Bibliography of the Scottish Book Trade' (BSBT), a research tool which brings together secondary materials on the fields of publishing, printing, bookselling, broadcasting, journalism, graphic design, illustration, binding, libraries and library history and the transmission of Scottish culture overseas.

Bibliographies also focus on publications from a specific period of time. The English Short Title Catalogue (ESTC) provides bibliographical information of letterpress books, pamphlets, newspapers, serials and a variety of ephemera that were published mainly in the English language, in the British Isles and North America before 1801.[114] It also identifies the provenance for each of these items in libraries and other institutions. ESTC draws on the collections of the British Library and over 2,000 other libraries including the NLS. A number of books and other items are omitted from the resource, but are included in other library catalogues such as that of the NLS. While it has been important in assisting the work of book historians in their rapidly expanding discipline, ESTC can be used to identify additional sources for ethnological study, such as further Scottish agricultural and rural books between 1697 and 1790.[115]

Digitised texts

A number of electronic resources contain facsimile images, usually of particular types of documents that can be searched by means of free-text searches. These resources can make it easier to access a range of private (and public) accounts that previously required extensive and laborious work to access and use. They can widen access to books, especially rare ones. This is especially important where such books are only available in a few specialist libraries and archives and where existing hard copies are in a poor condition, and access to them would make their condition worse. Digitised texts also allow the books to be brought within easier reach of researchers, especially where the books are located some distance away, and a trip to view them would be an expensive undertaking. Searching tools, which enable searches to be made within a publication and between publications, may allow researchers to make connections that might not have been possible using other finding aids. The paragraphs that follow provide a guide to some of the electronic resources available for researching private accounts.

Large collections of books and periodicals have been digitised and made available through a number of resources. These focus on particular genres of books or books published in specific periods. In the former category is 'Making of the Modern World: The Goldsmiths'-Kress Library of Economic Literature 1450–1850', which offers new ways to understand the emergence of modern economics and other social sciences. Despite its name, it includes a wide range of books with an inter-disciplinary focus that can be used for ethnological research. In the latter category is Early English Books Online (EEBO), which has digitised versions of some 100,000 books printed in England, Ireland, Scotland, Wales and British North America and works in English printed elsewhere from 1473 to 1700. Eighteenth Century Collections Online (ECCO) has digitised virtually every work printed in England, Ireland, Scotland, Wales, and British North American, and words in English printed elsewhere.

Some resources specifically focus on private accounts, and particular categories of them. The NLS's resource on emigrants' letters and the activities of the Scots overseas, drawn from its manuscript collections from 1685, and especially the nineteenth and twentieth centuries, is found in the 'Emigration from Scotland: Emigrants' Correspondence' database.[116] It gives details of material relating to the lives of Scots and their experiences overseas.

Electronic resources also focus on specific maps and plans or categories of them. The 'Maps of Scotland' resource on the NLS's website provides access to high-resolution images of over 48,000 maps in Scotland. Although most of the maps were drawn up and used by public rather than private organisations and institutions, there are some estate maps. There are also digitised copies of some of the earliest mapping of Scotland such as the late sixteenth-century maps of Timothy Pont and Blaeu in 1654.[117] The 'Charting the Nation, 1590–1740' resource on the University of Edinburgh website includes a wide variety of published maps, and maps in atlases and other bound books, together with important manuscript and published texts relating to the geography and mapping of Scotland from 1550 to 1740 and beyond.[118]

PRIVATE ACCOUNTS THAT ARE NOT BEING WIDELY USED

Private accounts have been widely used within ethnological research. The focus on the individual and their personal experiences, and their relationships with their family and wider communities, has ensured that personal accounts are also important sources for ethnological research. However, not all types of personal accounts have been used to the same extent.

Some private accounts have not survived in any great numbers. Some may also be difficult to locate because of their nature as private documents that are personal to families. Alexander Fenton suggests that farmers' diaries 'are scattered, and not readily available'. He also notes that the day-books of labourers, such as those he analyses for the nineteenth century, are scarce and difficult to find copies of.[119] Matthew Williamson's work suggests that diaries from the eighteenth century are scattered throughout archives and archival collections. There are also diaries and other personal correspondence which are not held in archives or other repositories and are not available for wider consultation. Some accounts may simply not have survived. Not every family has kept their correspondence between different members. This was noted by Colin MacLean in his introduction to *Your Father and I: A Family's Story* (1998).[120]

Some private accounts have not been fully used as they may be difficult to access or the character of the records may require researchers to wade through several volumes of papers before they can find relevant material or draw up a broader picture of the papers and events recorded in them. Eighteenth-century estate papers and business records may contain extensive quantities of very detailed information, and a significant volume have to be read in order to cover a short period of time. They may be frustrating to use for research and may not always reveal evidence which a researcher is looking for. Ian Whyte observes that seventeenth-century estate papers:

> were designed for purposes other than the conveying of direct information about agriculture and rural society. Indeed, the most useful information in them is often provided by chance and was not strictly relevant to the purpose for which the document was written, providing a valuable bonus.[121]

The same statement could also be apply to business records and the wider communities in which they were located.

Some private records are also very specialised; they may require some knowledge of how to access and interpret them. For example, business records and estate papers require a basic understanding of business practice, as well as the form and function of the records to be consulted. Some types of accounts may only be of interest to researchers working in a specific business area. Thus, business records, such as those of larger companies and industries, have largely been neglected for ethnological research purposes. Research into the ethnology of work or particular trades and industries has not been widely carried out as research has focused on other subjects. Likewise, the family records, especially of the landed classes and professions, have not received widespread attention, as ethnologists have traditionally focused on the experiences of the 'ordinary folk', though there is recognition that the experiences of the upper classes are important in revealing the dissemination of material culture, such as that of drinking tea and coffee, and growing and eating potatoes.

There is a need to more fully understand the different types of private accounts, the links between them, their development over time and geographically, and their use, for example among the different social classes or occupational groups, and in rural and urban areas. Some studies have been undertaken which have brought these different types of private accounts together. For example, Karina Williamson has focused on letters, journals and domestic writing.[122] That work could be more fully developed. Our understanding of the characteristics of the different types of private accounts varies considerably. There has been significant work on the defining characteristics of working-class autobiography, the letters of British immigrants to the United States in the nineteenth century, business records and some work on diaries, including farmers' diaries. There are also other types of private accounts which need to be researched and analysed in order to more fully understand their characteristics. Thus, while studies on working-class autobiographies largely focus on accounts written by males, the accounts of women could be studied to analyse their generic structure and patterns of creation. There have been a number of studies into farmers' diaries, but there have been few studies of the diaries of businessmen and tradesmen, and other occupational groups, and these should also receive attention. These could also bring out any distinctions in the characteristics of these accounts between rural and urban areas and occupations. Methodological approaches could be developed further, especially for types of private accounts that have received little attention. Methodological approaches from a range of disciplines could also be utilised to develop further these ethnological methodologies. For example, methodologies used by literary historians to study letters could also be used in ethnological research. Studies could also focus more closely on the idiosyncrasies of the accounts and their authors, as well as analyse the strengths and weaknesses of their evidence.

Private accounts could also be used to reveal more fully the personal experiences of individuals, their family and family networks, members of their communities. They could be used to reveal any regional differences in people's experiences and their ways of life, at one time or over a longer period. Accounts from different social and occupational groups could show the rich diversity of experiences in Scotland. They could be more extensively used to analyse the day-to-day experiences of people, how people arranged their day, and how their daily routines and experiences altered over the course of the year or over a period of years. Private accounts could also be analysed to provide evidence on material culture and the use of particular objects. There is a need to focus on the lives of the 'ordinary' people whom historians have neglected until recent decades, although there is an increasing number of accounts of reminiscences, diaries and letters that are now being published.

Personal papers are important for showing the relationships between people and revealing what people thought, felt and their reactions to particular episodes in their lives and the wider world around them. Collections of letters could be more fully researched. Indeed, there are few published collections of letters from 'ordinary people'. These letters are also important for exploring the work activities of people and their interests. There are significant collections of correspondence relating to a number of the most important ethnologists and collectors from the eighteenth century onwards. These include the papers of Peter Buchan, the ballad collector, and author of *Ancient Ballads and Songs of the North of Scotland*, the papers of Gavin Greig and James B Duncan, folksong collectors in north-east Scotland, held in the University of Aberdeen, and the papers of I F Grant, founder of the Highland Folk Museum, the first open air museum in Scotland, held in that museum's archives.[123] The correspondence of the Gaelic scholar John Francis Campbell of Islay is held in the J. F. Campbell Collection in the NLS, as is that of Francis Collinson.[124] Selected letters of Hamish Henderson were published in 1996, as *The Armstrong Nose: Selected Letters of Hamish Henderson*; further letters were published in *Chapman*. Some of his papers are also held in the NLS.[125] The papers of Sir Arthur Mitchell (1826–1909) are held in the NRS.[126] The private papers of individuals could be examined to more fully understand their activities, influences and how they shaped ethnological inquiry. Indeed, few studies have surveyed the development of ethnological research in Scotland.

Private accounts can also be used to develop research into a range of subjects that use other ethnological approaches. Business records could be more widely used within oral history research to provide detailed research material and also to augment the oral record. Records of some businesses survive until recently, and former employees can be identified and interviewed. This approach has been used in some recent oral histories, and the approach could be more widely developed. It has been particularly employed for researching aspects of life in the printing and papermaking industries in Edinburgh and surrounding districts. The papers of Thomas Nelson and Sons of Parkside Works, Edinburgh, held in the University of Edinburgh, were used to provide research materials for a series of reminiscences of former employees of Thomas Nelson and Sons, while the papers of John Galloway and Sons, and those of Henry Bruce and Sons Ltd, both in the NRS, provided material for a collection of reminiscences on papermaking on the Water of Leith.[127] The papers of the various paper mills in the Esk valley could also be used to develop further studies on that industry following the publication of an extensive oral history of the experiences of former workers in the Penicuik mills.[128] There are significant collections of records relating to particular businesses throughout Scotland. These could also be used to understand the work experiences in a particular business, or in different firms in the same area or provide a comparison between different areas or regions.

The development of electronic online resources (such as finding aids and facsimile collections of particular sources) is transforming research and the character of research. These resources have enabled records to be more easily identified and links to be made between different collections of records or the different types of public accounts. Thus, electronic finding aids, such as SCAN or NRAS, may be able to identify other examples of particular types of private papers. They may also identify particular types of personal accounts – such as diaries, cash books, travel accounts, or particular types of estate records – so that systematic studies can be made into these different types of accounts. Thus a search for 'diary' on the online catalogue of the NRS (NAS website) shows the diversity of accounts that are classed as 'diaries'. These resources may provide connections between different collections of records that would not have been possible using paper file lists. They will also enable the texts of documents to be searched both internally and between the different documents, thus enabling a more systematic investigation into particular subjects recorded in personal accounts.

NOTES

1 Kirkpatrick, 1983, 1023.
2 Williamson, 2007, 58.
3 NAS, Guides, Private Papers, <www.nas.gov.uk/guides/privatePapers.asp> [accessed 6 February 2013].
4 Williamson, 2007, 58.
5 Williamson, 2007, 58.
6 Ponsonby, 1927, 2.
7 Williamson, 2007, 57.
8 Matthews, 1950, xv.
9 Fenton, 1997, 22.
10 Fenton, 1988b, 123–30.
11 Turner, Beckett and Afton, 2001, 55.
12 Pearson, 1992, 5, 25, 28.
13 Ponsonby, 1930, 60.
14 Ponsonby, 1930, 9.
15 Ponsonby, 1930, 42.
16 Kelsall and Kelsall, 1990, 16.
17 Stevenson, 1991; Whatley, 1996.
18 Fenton, 1988b, 125.
19 Fenton, 1988b, 125.
20 Fenton, 1988b, 124.
21 See Fenton, 1997, 22–3; Turner, Beckett and Afton, 2001, 55.
22 Fenton, 1998–9, 78–88; Hall, 1997; Hewison, 1993, 35–42; Pearson, 1995–6, 76–97; Pearson, 1992.
23 Matthews, 1950, xv.
24 Rixson, 2004, 3–6.
25 Rixson, 2004, 3.
26 Mitchell, 1900–01, 431.
27 Rixson, 2004, 1.
28 Mitchell, 1900–01, 431–626.
29 Durie, 1996b, 13–23; Hume Brown, 1978; Smout, 1982–3, 99–121; MacArthur, 1993, 23–31; Hiley, 1996, 24–38; Vasey, 1996, 39–46.
30 Moody, 1988, 26; Williamson, 2007, 59.
31 Tavor Bannet, 2005, 9, 12, 171.
32 Tavor Bannet, 2005, ix.
33 Tavor Bannet, 2005, 171.
34 McLaren and Stephen, 1974–77, 86.
35 Bell, 2005; O'Rourke, 2000; Richens, 1981–92.
36 Gerber, 2006, 5.

37 Gerber, 2006, 6.

38 Gerber, 2006, 7–9.

39 Burnett, 1994 [1974], 12.

40 Vincent, 1982 [1981], 36.

41 Strathesk, 1888; Burnett, 1994 [1974], 12; Vincent, 1982 [1981], 8–9.

42 Vincent, 1982 [1981], 9.

43 Vincent, 1982 [1981].

44 Vincent, 1982 [1981], 4, 6.

45 Fraser, 2000, 48–55; Vincent, 1982 [1981], 87.

46 Smout, 1986, 285.

47 Bateman, 2007, 225–30.

48 Chavez, 2002, 153–7.

49 Johnston, 1984–5, 71.

50 Whyte, 1979, 5.

51 NAS, Guides, Estate Records, <www.nas.gov.uk/guides/estateRecords.asp> [accessed 6 February 2013].

52 Hart, 1991, 73.

53 McLaren and Stephen, 1972–73, 224; McLaren, 1972–73, 117, 118.

54 McLaren, Stephen and Tough, 1977–80, 95.

55 Devine, 1994; Whyte, 1979; Wade Martins, 1996–7, 33–54; Leneman, 1986; Mair, 1996; Whyte, 1979; Clapham, 1994, 144–63.

56 Armstrong and Jones, 1987, 3–12.

57 Armstrong and Jones, 1987, 8.

58 Adam, 1992; Close, 1994, 12–14.

59 Armstrong and Jones, 1987, 64.

60 Donnachie, 1979; Durie, 1979; Gulvin, 1984; Butt and Ponting, 1987; Slaven, 2006; Wood, 1985.

61 See Mepham, 1988, chapter 14. Chapter 15 provides an examination of farm account books.

62 Holmes, 2004–5, 22–56; Mepham, 1988, 502; Turner, Beckett and Afton, 2001, 39.

63 Turner, Beckett and Afton, 2001, 38, 50, 57.

64 Turner, Beckett and Afton, 2001, 51.

65 Campbell, 1989, 41–50; Fenton, 1966, 1–23; Fenton, 1988a, 10–6; Turner, Beckett and Afton, 2001.

66 See, for example, NLS, Scottish Labour History Collections, <www.nls.uk/collections/manuscripts/collections/scottish–labour> [accessed 6 February 2013].

67 Boud, 1984, 70–90.

68 Fenton, 2003–4, 115–30; Fenton, 2004–5, 110–12; Ramsay, 1879; Smith, 1962.

69 Wood, 1996; Turriff and District Junior Agricultural Club, 1982.

70 Fenton, 2004–5, 112.

71 NAS, Guides, Crafts and Trades Records, <www.nas.gov.uk/guides/crafts.asp> [accessed 6 February 2013].

72 Moody, 1988, 121.

73 Checkland, 1980, 231.

74 Checkland, 1980, 365.

75 Laurie, 1904; Rae, 1953; Watson, 1964.

76 Adams, 1968, 249; Third, 1957, 39.

77 Clarke, 2003, 27–31.

78 Third, 1955, 83–93; Third, 1957, 39–64; Geddes, 1938, 124–43.

79 Fenton, 1997, 22.

80 Fenton, 1994, vii.

81 Dunbar, 1997, vii.

82 Fenton, 1994, vii.

83 Love and McMullen, 1994; Whatley, 1996; Dunbar, 1997; Fenton, in Dunbar, 1997, vii, viii.

84 Fenton, in Slee, 1993, vii.

85 Holmes and Finkelstein, 2001; MacDougall, 1993, 1995a, 1995b, 2000.

86 Bochel, 2004; Macdonald, 2003; Purves, 2001.

87 Kenefick, 2001, 38.

88 Campbell, 1989, 41–50; Dundas, 1988, 125–30; Hewison, 1993, 35–42; Pearson, 1995–6, 76–97.

89 Miller, 1890; Reid, 1901.

90 Paul, 1922.

91 Gray, 1892.

92 MacLeod, 1893.

93 Colville, 1904; Horn, 1996; Szechi, 1989.

94 Durie, 1996a; Colville, 1907; Gauldie, 1969; Scott, 1905; Scott-Moncrieff, 1911.

95 NAS, Guides, <www.nas.gov.uk/guides/> [accessed 6 February 2013].

96 Anderson, 2003, 99–106; Fox, 1997, 89–94; Mclean, 2002, 121–30; Parry, 2001, 78–88.

97 For example, Johnston, 1982–3, 71–9; Donaldson, 2000, 167–78; Anderson-Smith, 1997, 129–33.

98 NAS, About the National Archives of Scotland, <www.nas.gov.uk/about/default.asp> [accessed 6 February 2013].

99 NAS, Guide to Manuscripts Collections, <www.nls.uk/catalogues/online/cnmi/> [accessed 6 February 2013].

100 The University of Edinburgh, Information Services, Special Collections, Edinburgh University Archives, <www.ed.ac.uk/schools-departments/information-services/services/library-museum-gallery/crc/collections/special-collections/eua> [accessed 6 February 2013].

101 University of Aberdeen, Special Libraries and Archives, <www.abdn.ac.uk/historic/Intro.shtml> [accessed 21 January 2013]

102 University of Glasgow, Archive Services, <www.gla.ac.uk/services/archives/> [accessed 21 January 2013]

103 University of Glasgow, Archive Services, <www.archives.gla.ac.uk/sba/default.html> [accessed 21 January 2013]; University of Glasgow, Archive Services, Scottish Business Archive, <www.gla.ac.uk/services/archives/collect/business/> [accessed 21 January 2013]; University of Glasgow, Archive Services, Scottish Brewing Archive, <www.archives.gla.ac.uk/sba/default.html> [accessed 21 January 2013].

104 Glasgow Libraries, Archives, <www.glasgowlife.org.uk/libraries/the-mitchell-library/archives/Pages/home.aspx> [accessed 21 January 2013]; The City of Edinburgh Council, Archives, <www.edinburgh.gov.uk/info/428/archives> [accessed 21 January 2013].

105 Highland Archive Service, <www.highlandarchives.org.uk/> [accessed 21 January 2013]; Lawson, 1986, 160–61.

106 Copac, <www.copac.ac.uk/> [accessed 21 January 2013].

107 Archives Hub, <www.archiveshub.ac.uk/> [accessed 21 January 2013].

108 Scottish Archive Network, <www.scan.org.uk/> [accessed 21 January 2013]. See also Barnes, 2000, 13–16.

109 NAS, The National Register of Archives for Scotland, <www.nas.gov.uk/nras/register.asp> [accessed 21 January 2013].

110 NAS, Catalogues and Indexes, <www.nas.gov.uk/catalogues/default.asp> [accessed 21 January 2013].

111 NLS, Manuscript Catalogues and Guides, <www.nls.uk/catalogues/manuscripts> [accessed 21 January 2013].

112 NLS, Special and Named Printed Collections in the National Library of Scotland, J. F. Campbell Collection, <www.nls.uk/catalogues/online/snpc/list.cfm?letter=J> [accessed 21 January 2013]; NLS, Special and Named Printed Collections in the National Library of Scotland, Crawford Ballads Collection, <www.nls.uk/catalogues/online/snpc/list.cfm?letter=C> [accessed 21 January 2013].

113 NLS, Resources Online, <www.nls.uk/collections/newspapers/online> [accessed 21 January 2013].

114 English Short Title Catalogue, <http://estc.bl.uk/> [accessed 21 January 2013].

115 Holmes, 2007, 98–137.

116 NLS, Catalogues Overview, <www.nls.uk/catalogues> [accessed 21 January 2013].

117 NLS, Maps of Scotland, <www.maps.nls.uk/> [accessed 21 January 2013]; NLS, Estate maps, 1772–1878, <http://maps.nls.uk/estates/index.html> [accessed 21 January 2013]; NLS, Pont Maps Website, <www.maps.nls.uk/pont/>; NLS, Blaeu Atlas of Scotland, 1654, <www.maps.nls.uk/atlas/blaeu/> [accessed 21 January 2013].

118 Charting the Nation: Maps of Scotland and Associated Archives 1550–1740 website, <www.chartingthenation.lib.ed.ac.uk/> [accessed 21 January 2013].

119 Fenton, 1988b, 123–30.

120 Matthews, 1950, 1980; MacLean, 1998.

121 Whyte, 1979, 5.

122 Williamson, 2007.

123 McLaren, 1972–3, 116–25; McLaren and Stephen, 1972–3, 223–33.

124 NLS, Acc.11745, 4705, 6650, 7857, 8650, 8985, 9003, 9975.

125 Finlay, 1996; Henderson, 1995, 47–57; NLS, Acc.10157, 10327, 10528, 10552, 10616, 10627, 10788, 12643, 12643, 4526.

126 NAS, GD192, 1597–1909.

127 Holmes and Finkelstein, 2001; McCleery, Finkelstein and Bromage, 2006.

128 Macdougall, 2009.

BIBLIOGRAPHY AND FURTHER READING

Adam, J S, ed. *The Business Diaries of Sir Alexander Grant*, Edinburgh, 1992.

Adams, I H. The land surveyor and his influence on the Scottish rural landscape, *Scottish Geographical Magazine*, 84 (1968), 248–55.

Adams, I H and Timperley, L. *Descriptive List of Plans in the Scottish Record Office*, 4 vols, Edinburgh, 1966–88.

Anderson, J. The archives at Blair and Glamis castles, *Scottish Archives*, 9 (2003), 99–106.

Anderson-Smith, M. Local pamphlets, *Northern Scotland*, 17 (1997), 129–33.

Armstrong, J and Jones, S. *Business Documents: Their Origins, Sources and Uses in Historical Research*, London, 1987.

Bateman, M. The autobiography in Scottish Gaelic. In Brown, I, ed., *The Edinburgh History of Scottish Literature, volume 3: Modern Transformations: New Identities (from 1918)*, Edinburgh, 2007, 225–30.

Bell, A, ed. *Lord Cockburn: Selected Letters*, Edinburgh, 2005.

Bochel, M M. *Salt Herring on Saturday: The Fishertown of Nairn Last Century*, Flashbacks no 18, East Linton, 2004.

Boud, R C. Scottish agricultural improvement societies, 1723–1835, *Review of Scottish Culture*, 1 (1984), 70–90.

Broom, A M and Anderson, A. Historical business records in private hands surveyed by the National Register of Archives (Scotland). In Payne, P L, ed. *Studies in Scottish Business History* [1967], London, 2006, 30–41.

Burnett, J, ed. *Useful Toil. Autobiographies of Working People from the 1820s to the 1920s* [1974], London, 1994.

Burt, E. *Letters from a Gentleman in the North of Scotland to his friend in London*, London, 1754.

Butt, J and Ponting, K, eds. *Scottish Textile History*, Aberdeen, 1987.

Campbell, M. A farm manager's cashbook, 1843–1854, *Review of Scottish Culture*, 5 (1989), 41–50.

Campbell, R H, ed. *Scottish Industrial History: A Miscellany of Documents*, Scottish History Society, fourth series no 14, Edinburgh, 1978.

Catalogue of Manuscripts Acquired Since 1925, 8 vols, Edinburgh, 1938–92.

Chavez, H R. Reports and surveys of archives in Northern Scotland: the Frasers of Castle Fraser (1550–1976), *Northern Scotland*, 22 (2002), 153–7.

Checkland, O. *Philanthropy in Victorian Scotland: Social Welfare and the Voluntary Principle*, Edinburgh, 1980.

Clapham, P. Agricultural change and its impact on tenancy: the evidence of Angus rentals and tacks, c. 1760–1850. In Cummings, A J G and Devine, T M, eds, *Industry, Business and Society in Scotland since 1700: Essays Presented to Professor John Butt*, Edinburgh, 1994, 144–63.

Clarke, T. Estate plans hold appeal for historians, *Scottish Local History*, 37 (2003), 27–31.

Close, R. Work in progress: the diary of William Finnie, 1818–1820, *Scottish Local History*, 32 (1994), 12–14.

Colville, J, ed. *Letters of John Cockburn of Ormistoun to His Gardener, 1727–1744*, Scottish History Society, first series no 45, Edinburgh, 1904.

Colville, J, ed. *Ochtertyre House Book of Accompts, 1737–1739*, Scottish History Society, 1st series no 55, Edinburgh, 1907.

Cox, M. *Exploring Scottish History: With a Directory of Resource Centres for Scottish Local and National History in Scotland* [1992], 2nd edn, Edinburgh, 1999.

Defoe, D. *A Tour Through the Whole Island of Great Britain*, London, 1724–26.

Devine, T M. *The Transformation of Rural Scotland: Social Change and the Agrarian Economy, 1660–1815*, Edinburgh, 1994.

Donaldson, W. Manuscript material in the University of Aberdeen for the study of piping, *Northern Scotland*, 20 (2000), 167–78.

Donnachie, I. *A History of the Brewing Industry in Scotland*, Edinburgh, 1979.

Dunbar, J G, ed. *Sir William Burrell's Northern Tour 1758*, Sources in Local History no 6, Edinburgh, 1997.

Dundas, J. The diary of James Fyffe, *Review of Scottish Culture*, 4 (1988), 125–30.

Durie, A J. *The Scottish Linen Industry in the Eighteenth Century*, Edinburgh, 1979.

Durie, A J, ed. *The British Linen Company, 1745–1775*, Scottish History Society, 5th series no 9, Edinburgh, 1996a.

Durie, A J. Sources for the study of tourism in nineteenth-century Scotland, *Scottish Archives*, 2 (1996b), 13–23.

Durie, A J. 'Notes very much chattered with mice'. Banking records as a source for the study of Scottish local history, *Scottish Archives*, 3 (1997), 20–9.

Fenton, A. The Begbie farm account book 1729–70, *Transactions of the East Lothian Antiquarian and Field Naturalists' Society*, 10 (1966), 1–23.

Fenton, A. A farm cash book from Glenesk in Angus, 1885–1898, *Journal of the Edinburgh Agricultural Association*, 62 (1988a), 10–16.

Fenton, A. Farmers' diaries and their interpretation. In Gailey, A, ed., *The Use of Tradition. Essays Presented to G B Thompson*, Cultra, Holywood, Co Down, 1988b, 123–30.

Fenton, A, ed. *At Brechin with Stirks. A Farm Cash Book from Buskhead, Glenesk, Angus, 1885–1898*, Sources in Local History no 1, Edinburgh, 1994.

Fenton, A. Two nineteenth-century day labourers' day-books from Glenesk in Angus, *Scottish Local History*, 33 (1995), 16–18.

Fenton, A. The European Ethnological Research Centre, *Scottish Local History*, 40 (1997), 21–4.

Fenton, A. The diary of Mr Smith, farmer at Maisondieu, Brechin, Angus, 1794–1801, *Review of Scottish Culture*, 11 (1998–9), 78–88.

Fenton, A. The Easter Ross Farmers' Club, 1811–1898, *Review of Scottish Culture*, 16 (2003–4), 115–30.

Fenton, A. The Lesmahagow Farmers' Club, *Review of Scottish Culture*, 17 (2004–5), 110–12.

Finlay, A, ed. *The Armstrong Nose: Selected Letters of Hamish Henderson*, Edinburgh, 1996.

Fox, M. The Traquair House Archives, *Scottish Archives*, 3 (1997), 89–94.

Fraser, W H. Remembering work. In Mays, D C, Moss, M S and Oglethorpe, M K, eds, *Visions of Scotland's Past Looking to the Future. Essays in Honour of John R Hume*, East Linton, 2000, 48–55.

Fyfe, J G, ed. *Scottish Diaries and Memoirs, 1550–1746*, Stirling, 1927.

Fyfe, J G, ed. *Scottish Diaries and Memoirs, 1746–1843* [1928], Stirling, 1942.

Gauldie, E, ed. *The Dundee Textile industry, 1790–1885, From the Papers of Peter Carmichael of Arthurstone*, Scottish History Society, 4th series no 6, Edinburgh, 1969.

Geddes, A. The changing landscape of the Lothians, 1600–1800, as revealed by old estate plans, *Scottish Geographical Magazine*, 54 (1938), 129–43.

Gerber, D A. *Authors of their Lives: The Personal Correspondence of British Immigrants to North America in the Nineteenth Century*, New York, 2006.

Gibson, R. *The Scottish Countryside: Its Changing Face, 1700–2000*, Edinburgh, 2007.

Gray, J M, ed. *Memoirs of the Life of Sir John Clerk of Penicuik, Bart, Baron of the Exchequer, Extracted by Himself from His own Journals, 1675–1755*, Scottish History Society, 1st series vol 13, Edinburgh, 1892.

Gulvin, C. *The Scottish Hosiery and Knitwear Industry 1680–1980*, Edinburgh, 1984.

Hall, D, introduction, commentary by T Barry. *Spottiswoode: Life and Labour on a Berwickshire Estate, 1753–1793*, East Linton, 1997.

Hamilton, R. *An Introduction to Merchandize*, Edinburgh, 1777–79.

Hancock, P D. *A Bibliography of Works Relating to Scotland, 1916–1950*, Edinburgh, 1959.

Hart, R M. Reports and surveys of archives in northern Scotland, Duff House/Montcotter Papers, MS 3175, *Northern Scotland*, 11 (1991), 73–6.

Hart, R M. Burnett of Leys Papers, MS 3361, *Northern Scotland*, 12 (1992), 133–4.

Henderson, H. Selected letters, *Chapman*, 82 (1995), 47–57.

Hewison, N. The diary of a gardener at Skaill, Orkney: 3 January–7 May 1801, *Review of Scottish Culture*, 8 (1993), 35–42.

Hiley, A. 'Scotland's name is poetry to our ears': German travellers in Scotland, c1800–1860, *Scottish Archives*, 2 (1996), 24–38.

Holmes, H. For the encouragement of agricultural improvement in Scotland in the 1780s: subscribers to the agricultural books of David Young, *Review of Scottish Culture*, 17 (2004–5), 22–56.

Holmes, H. A bibliography of Scottish agricultural books to 1790, *The Journal of the Edinburgh Bibliographical Society*, 2 (2007), 98–137.

Holmes, H and Finkelstein, D, eds. *Thomas Nelson and Sons: Memories of an Edinburgh Publishing House*, Flashbacks no 14, East Linton, 2001.

Holmes, H and MacDonald, F, eds. *Scottish Life and Society. A Compendium of Scottish Ethnology, Volume 14: Bibliography*, East Linton, 2003.

Horn, B L, ed. *Letters of John Ramsay of Ochtertyre, 1799–1812*, Scottish History Society, 4th series no 3, Edinburgh, 1996.

Hume Brown, P, ed. *Early Travellers in Scotland*, Edinburgh, 1978.

Imrie, J. National Archive sources for business history. In Payne, P L, ed., *Studies in Scottish Business History* [1967], Oxford, 2006, 3–29.

Johnston, D B. Letters and papers of the Setons of Mounie, Aberdeenshire, including the papers of Dr James Anderson (1739–1808), AUL MS 27787, *Northern Scotland*, 5 (1982–3), 71–9.

Johnston, D B. Reports and surveys of archives in northern Scotland, *Northern Scotland*, 6:1 (1984–5), 71–80.

Journal of the Society of Archivists 1955–.

Keeper of the Records of Scotland. *Annual Report of the Keeper of the Records of Scotland*, Edinburgh (1950–).

Kelsall, H and Kelsall, K. *An Album of Scottish Families 1694–96. Being the First Instalment of George Home's Diary. Supplemented by Much Further Research into the Edinburgh and Border Families Forming his Extensive Social network*, Aberdeen, 1990.

Kenefick, W. An overview of the 'Flashbacks' Oral History Series, *Scottish Local History*, 51 (2001), 37–42.

Kirkpatrick, E M. *Chambers 20th Century Dictionary*, Edinburgh, 1983.

Laurie, S S. *The Dick Bequest*, Edinburgh, 1904.

Lawson, A B. Highland Regional Archive, *Northern Scotland*, 7 (1986), 160–1.

Lebon, J H G. The face of the countryside in central Ayrshire during the eighteenth and nineteenth centuries, *Scottish Geographical Magazine*, 62:1 (1946a), 7–15.

Lebon, J H G. The process of enclosure in the Western lowlands, *Scottish Geographical Magazine*, 62:3 (1946b), 100–10.

Leneman, L. *Living in Atholl A Social History of the Estates, 1685–1785*, Edinburgh, 1986.

Love, J and McMullen, B, eds. *A Salmon for the Schoolhouse. A Nairnshire Parish in the Nineteenth Century from the Diaries of Robert and Elsie Thomson*, Sources in Local History no 3, Edinburgh, 1994.

MacArthur, E M. Blasted heaths and hills of mist: the Highlands and Islands through travellers' eyes, *Scottish Affairs*, 3 (1993), 23–31.

McCleery, A, Finkelstein, D and Bromage, S, eds. *Papermaking on the Water of Leith*, Edinburgh, 2006.

Macdonald, I S. Alexander Macdonald, Esq of Glencoe: Insights into early Highland sheep-farming, *Review of Scottish Culture*, 10 (1996–7), 55–66.

Macdonald, K. *Peat Fire Memories: Life in Lewis in the Early Twentieth Century*, Flashbacks no 16, East Linton, 2003.

McDonald, S. Bank of Scotland Archives: past, present and future, *Scottish Archives*, 3 (1997), 30–6.

MacDougall, I. *Labour Records in Scotland*, Edinburgh, 1978.

MacDougall, I, ed. *'Hard work, ye ken' Midlothian Women Farmworkers*, Flashbacks no 2, East Linton, 1993.

MacDougall, I, ed. *Hoggie's Angels: Tattie Howkers Remember*, Flashbacks no 3, East Linton, 1995a.

MacDougall, I, ed. *Mungo Mackay and the Green Table: Newtongrange Miners Remember*, Flashbacks no 4, East Lothian, 1995b.

MacDougall, I, ed. *Bondagers*, Flashbacks no 10, East Linton, 2000.

MacDougall, I, ed. *Through the Mill; Personal Recollections by Veteran Men and Women Penicuik Paper Mill Workers*, Falkirk, 2009.

McLaren, C A. Reports and surveys of archives in northern Scotland, *Northern Scotland*, 1:1 (1972–3), 116–25.

McLaren, C A and Stephen, M A. Reports and surveys of archives in northern Scotland, *Northern Scotland*, 1:2 (1972–3), 223–33.

McLaren, C A and Stephen, M A. Reports and surveys of archives in northern Scotland, *Northern Scotland*, 2 (1974–77), 85–93.

McLaren, C A, Stephen, M A and Tough, A. Reports and surveys of archives in northern Scotland, *Northern Scotland*, 3 (1977–80), 87–100.

McLean, A. The Mount Stuart Archives, *Scottish Archives*, 8 (2002), 121–30.

MacLean, C. *Monkeys, Bears and Gutta Percha: Memories of Manse, Hospital and War*, Flashbacks no 11, East Linton, 2002.

MacLean, I G. *Your Father and I: A Family's Story*, ed. C MacLean, Flashbacks no 6, East Linton, 1998.

MacLeod, W, ed. *Journal of the Hon John Erskine of Carnock, 1683–1687*, Scottish History Society, 1st series no 14, Edinburgh, 1893.

Mair, J. *Cessnock: An Ayrshire Estate in the Age of Improvement*, Ayr, 1996.

Martin, M. *A Voyage to St Kilda; the Remotest of all the Hebrides. Or, Western Isles of Scotland*, London, 1698.

Martin, M. *A Description of the Western Isles of Scotland circa 1695*, London, 1703.

Matthews, W, comp. *British Diaries: An Annotated Bibliography of British Diaries Written Between 1442 and 1980*, Cambridge, 1950.

Mepham, M J. *Accounting in Eighteenth-Century Scotland*, New York, 1988.

Miller, A H, ed. *The Book of Record: A Diary Written by Patrick, First Earl of Strathmore, and Other Documents Relating to Glamis Castle, 1684–1689*, Scottish History Society, 1st series no 9, Edinburgh, 1890.

Mitchell, A. A list of travels, tours, journals, voyages, cruises, excursions, wanderings, rambles, visits, etc, relating to Scotland, *Proceedings of the Society of Antiquaries of Scotland*, 35 (1900–01), 431–626.

Mitchell, A and Cash, C G. *A Contribution to the Bibliography of Scottish Topography*, 2 vols, Scottish History Society, Edinburgh, 1917.

Moody, D. *Scottish Family History*, London, 1988.

Moody, D. *Scottish Towns. A Guide for Local Historians*, London, 1992.

Northern Scotland 1972–.

NAS. *Tracing Your Scottish Ancestors: The Official Guide*, 5th edn, Edinburgh, 2009.

O'Rourke, D. *Ae Fond Kiss; The Love Letters of Robert Burns and Clarinda*, Edinburgh, 2000.

Pairman, T W. *A Scottish Country Doctor 1818–1873 Robert Pairman of Biggar. Recalled by his Son Thomas Wyld Pairman*, ed. E Wright, Flashbacks no 17, East Linton, 2003.

Parry, C. Royal College of Physicians and Surgeons of Glasgow, *Scottish Archives*, 7 (2001), 78–88.

Paul, J B, ed. *Diary of George Ridpath, Minister of Stitchel, 1755–1761*, Scottish History Society, 3rd series no 2, Edinburgh, 1922.

Pearson, M, ed. *Flitting the Flakes: The Diary of J. Badenach a Stonehaven Farmer 1789–1979*, Aberdeen, 1992.

Pearson, M. Aspects of farming in Kincardineshire 1779 to 1786, from the diary of Dr James Badenach, Balmakewan, *Review of Scottish Culture*, 9 (1995–6), 76–97.

Pennant, T. *A Tour in Scotland, 1769*, Chester, 1771.

Pennant, T. *Tour in Scotland and Voyage to the Hebrides, 1772*, 2 vols, London, 1774.

Ponsonby, A. *Scottish and Irish Diaries from the Sixteenth to the Nineteenth Centuries*, London, 1927.

Ponsonby, A. *British Diarists*, London, 1930.

Pressnell, L S and Orbell, J. *A Guide to the Historical Records of British Banking*, Aldershot, 1985.

Purves, A. *A Shepherd Remembers*, Flashbacks no 13, East Linton, 2001.

Rae, J A. *The History of Allan Glen's School 1855–1953*, Glasgow, 1953.

Ramsay, A. *History of the Highland and Agricultural Society of Scotland*, Edinburgh, 1879.

Reid, A G, ed. *The Diary of Andrew Hay of Craignethan, 1659–1660*, Scottish History Society, 1st series no 39, Edinburgh, 1901.

Reid, L. *Scottish Midwives, Twentieth Century Voices*, Flashbacks no 12, Edinburgh, 2000.

Richens, R, ed. *Letters from Your Loving Father, Gavin Scott, a Lanarkshire Farmer Written in 1811–17*, Cambridge, 1981–92.

Richmond, L M and Turnton, A. *The Brewing Industry: A Guide to Historical Records*, Manchester, 1990.

Rimington, F, ed. *That's Fourpence You're Eating! A Childhoood in Perth*, Flashbacks, Edinburgh, 2006.

Ritchie, L A. *The Shipbuilding Industry: A Guide to Historical Records*, Manchester, 1992.

Rixson, D. *The Hebridean Traveller*, Edinburgh, 2004.

Rose, J. *The Transactions of the British Farmer Accountant Adapted to the Four Seasons of the Year Wherein the Gentleman Farmers Gave a Plan of Books, Entirely new, and Suitable to their Occupation*, Edinburgh, 1780.

Scott, W R, ed. *The Records of a Scottish Cloth Manufactory at New Mills, Haddington-shire, 1681–1708*, Scottish History Society, 1st series no 46, Edinburgh, 1905.

Scott-Moncrieff, R, ed. *The Household Book of Lady Griselle Baillie, 1792–1732*, Scottish History Society, 2nd series no 1, Edinburgh, 1911.

Scottish Archives: The Journal of the Scottish Records Association 1995–.

Scottish Industrial History (Scottish Industrial Heritage Society and Business Archives Council of Scotland) 1984–.

Scottish Local History (Scottish Local History Forum) 1983–.

Scottish Record Office. *List of Gifts and Deposits in the Scottish Record Office*, Edinburgh, 2 vols, 1971 and 1976.

Slaven, A. *The Development of the West of Scotland, 1750–1960* [1975], London, 2006.

Slee, D, ed. *Two Generations of Edinburgh Folk*, Flashbacks no 1, East Linton, 1993.

Smith, J H. *Gordon's Mill Farming Club 1758–1764*, Aberdeen, 1962.

Smout, C. Tours in the Scottish Highlands from the eighteenth to the twentieth centuries, *Northern Scotland*, 5 (1982–3), 99–121.

Smout, T C. *A Century of the Scottish People 1830–1950*, London, 1986.

Strathesk, J, ed. *Hawkie; The Autobiography of a Gangrel*, Glasgow, 1888.

Stevenson, D, ed. *The Diary of a Canny Man, 1818–28: Adam Mackie, Farmer, Merchant and Innkeeper in Fyvie. Compiled by William Mackie*, Aberdeen, 1991.

Summary Catalogue of the Advocates' Manuscripts, Edinburgh, 1971.

Szcechi, D, ed. *Letters of George Lockhart of Carnwath, 1698–1732*, Scottish History Society, 5th series no 2, Edinburgh, 1989.

Tavor Bannet, E. *Empire of Letters: Letter Manuals and Transatlantic Correspondence, 1688–1820*, Cambridge, 2005.

Third, B M W. The changing landscape and social structure in the Scottish Lowlands as revealed by eighteenth century estate plans, *Scottish Geographical Magazine*, 71 (1955), 83–93.

Third, B M W. The significance of Scottish estate plans and their associated documents, *Scottish Studies*, 1 (1957), 39–64.

Topen, A. The Scottish Brewing Archive, *Scottish Archives*, 4 (1998), 97–103.

Turner, M E, Beckett, J V and Afton, B. *Farm Production in England 1700–1914*, Oxford, 2001.

Turriff and District Junior Agricultural Club. *Turriff and District Junior Agricultural Club: 50th Anniversary 1932–1982*, Turriff, 1982.

Vasey, P G. 'Visitors and voyages': a personal selection of travel diaries and related material in the Scottish Record Office, *Scottish Archives*, 2 (1996), 39–46.

Vincent, D. *Bread, Knowledge and Freedom. A Study of Nineteenth-Century Working Class Autobiography* [1981], London, 1982.

Wade Martins, S. A century of farms and farming on the Sutherland Estate, 1790–1890, *Review of Scottish Culture*, 10 (1996–7), 33–54.

Watson, W N B. *A Short History of Chalmers Hospital*, Edinburgh, 1964.

Whatley, C W, ed. *The Diary of John Sturrock, Millwright, Dundee 1864–5*, Sources in Local History no 4, East Linton, 1996.

Whyte, I D. *Agriculture and Society in Seventeenth-Century Scotland*, Edinburgh, 1979.

Williamson, K. The emergency of privacy: letters, journals and domestic writing. In Manning, S, ed. *The Edinburgh History of Scottish Literature, volume 2: Enlightenment, Britain and Empire (1707–1918)*, Edinburgh, 2007, 57–70.

Wood, M W T. *The South Ronaldsay and Burray Agricultural Society 150th Anniversary: A History and Celebration*, Orkney, 1996.

Wood, S. The *Shaping of Nineteenth Century Aberdeenshire*, Stevenage, 1985.

Young, A. *Rural Oeconomy*, London, 1770.

Young, A. *Farmer's Kalendar*, London, 1771.

Young, D. *The Farmer's Account Book of Expenditure and Produce for Each Day, Month and Year, Stating the Profit and Loss per Year upon Each Article in the Farm, Containing A Register of the Whole Work and Transactions Done Upon the Farm Each Day*, Edinburgh, 1790.

ONLINE RESOURCES

Archives Hub, <www.archiveshub.ac.uk> [accessed 6 February 2013].

Charting the Nation: Maps of Scotland and Associated Archives 1550–1740, <www.chartingthenation.lib.ed.ac.uk/> [accessed 6 February 2013].

Copac, <www.copac.ac.uk/> [accessed 6 February 2013].

Early English Books Online, <http://eebo.chadwyck.com/home> [accessed 21 January 2013].

The City of Edinburgh Council, Archives, <www.edinburgh.gov.uk/info/428/archives> [accessed 21 January 2013].

The University of Edinburgh, Information Services, Edinburgh University Archives, Special Collections, <www.ed.ac.uk/schools-departments/information-services/services/library-museum-gallery/crc/collections/special-collections/eua> [accessed 21 January 2013].

English Short Title Catalogue, <www.estc.bl.uk/> [accessed 6 February 2013].

Glasgow Libraries, Archives, <www.glasgowlife.org.uk/libraries/the-mitchell-library/archives/Pages/home.aspx> [accessed 21 January 2013].

Highland Archive Service, <www.highlandarchives.org.uk/> [accessed 21 January 2013].

National Archives of Scotland, <www.nas.gov.uk/> [accessed 6 February 2013].

National Library of Scotland, <www.nls.uk/> [accessed 6 February 2013].

Scottish Archive Network, <www.scan.org.uk/> [accessed 6 February 2013].

University of Aberdeen, Special Libraries and Archives, <www.abdn.ac.uk/historic/Intro.shtml> [accessed 6 February 2013].

University of Glasgow, Archive Services, <www.gla.ac.uk/services/archives/> [accessed 6 February 2013].

19 Public Accounts

HEATHER HOLMES

INTRODUCTION

Dictionary definitions are helpful in defining the scope of 'public accounts'. *Chambers 20th Century Dictionary* defines 'public' as being:

> of or belonging to the people: pertaining to a community or a nation: general: common to, shared in by, or open to, all: generally known: in open view, unconcealed, not private: engaged in, or concerning the affairs of the community.[1]

Public accounts are thus created by government, local government, parliament, the legal institutions, the church and other public organisations. Not all of the public accounts are, however, published, and may be in the form of unpublished manuscript accounts. This chapter explores the range of public accounts available to the ethnologist as primary and secondary sources for research, and their current and future use in ethnology.

THE RANGE OF PUBLIC ACCOUNTS AND THE
ETHNOLOGICAL EVIDENCE THEY PROVIDE

The following sections cover the different types of public accounts available for ethnological research.

The Statistical Accounts of Scotland

The most widely known statistical surveys are the *Statistical Accounts of Scotland* comprising the *(Old) Statistical Account of Scotland (OSA)* (1791–99), the *New Statistical Account of Scotland (NSA)* (1834–45) and the *Third Statistical Account of Scotland (TSA)* (1944–92). A *Fourth Statistical Account* has been compiled for two counties: the account of East Lothian covers the period 1945 to 2000 and that of Midlothian provides a snapshot of the county in 2000 with some historical information.[2]

    The *OSA*, published in twenty-one volumes, is a survey of the 938 parishes of Scotland which aims to 'elucidate "the Natural History and Political State of Scotland"'. It collected data from each parish in the country 'for the purpose of ascertaining the quantum of happiness enjoyed by its inhabitants and the means of its future improvement'. The former was especially important. As Donald J

Withrington and I R Grant state, Sir John Sinclair, the director of the project, was aware that 'there were changes taking place in society which were demanding government action . . . without any effective forward planning or monitoring or control which could help determine whether that precise form of action had been the most appropriate'. Sinclair believed that the project would provide 'important hints for the improvement of agriculture, for the extension of commercial industry, for regulating the conduct of individuals, or for extending the prosperity of the state' and to 'promote the general happiness of the species'. At the time he devised the project he had seen the results of 'statistical' enquiries in Germany that sought to measure political strength. He wanted to 'adapt these procedures to his own purpose; while using the word "statistical", he would extend its meaning to include the estimating of the general state of the nation at large'.[3] Sinclair provides an account of the progress of undertaking statistical inquiries in Europe before 1791 in his *Analysis of the Statistical Account of Scotland*.[4]

Sinclair devised a comprehensive list of topics that were to be included in his enquiry. This was to form the basis for the parish accounts. Initially there were 160 questions. These were followed with another six questions which Sinclair included in a circular to ministers of 25 May 1790; a further five were also included in his circular letter in January 1791. The 160 questions were divided into four sections: questions 1 to 40 were concerned with the geography, climate, natural resources of land and sea and the natural history of the parish; questions 41 to 100 focused on population and related matters; questions 101 to 116 dealt with the 'productions' of the parish, and questions 117 to 160 on miscellaneous matters such as land rents, language, the poor and poor relief, wages and prices, industrial and fishing developments, and social conditions.[5]

The parish accounts were written by ministers and other people who 'generally knew their parishes very well. In particular areas, perhaps in them all, a majority – even a large majority – of the ministers had been in post for a long time in the localities about which they were writing'.[6] They also had long-standing positions in their communities. Their accounts vary in length, style and content, with the longest (and also the best) ones being published in the later volumes. Donald J Withrington considers that the reports of Kilsyth in Stirlingshire, Sorn in Ayrshire, Marykirk in Kincardineshire, Kilmadock in Perthshire, Wick and Thurso in Caithness, and the Isle of Harris were particularly noteworthy. Arthur Geddes regards the account of the Isle of Harris as 'a classic'. Withrington observes that the ministers generally provided a response 'to most if not all' of Sinclair's questions. Grant and Withrington, were 'uniformly impressed by the extent and depth of treatment which his [Sinclair's] correspondents generally gave to the enquiry'.[7] Some also wrote extensive accounts on subjects that were of particular interest to them, such as antiquities or plant and bird species.

The parish accounts were published in the order in which they were completed and sent to Sinclair. This mode of publication meant that the accounts of a particular county were scattered throughout the twenty-one volumes, or a significant number of them. Maisie Steven notes 'the sheer exasperation these 21 higgledy-piggledy volumes must have caused to users throughout the years'. (Sinclair commented that the arrangement of publishing the accounts as they were given in 'has its peculiar advantages').[8] Recognising the difficulties of accessing the accounts, Grant and Withrington reorganised the parish accounts into their respective counties and published them in county volumes with introductory essays that provided overviews of the counties.

The *NSA* and the *TSA* shared similar features to the *OSA*. The parish accounts continued to be largely researched and written by ministers. They also included contributions by, or assistance from, local doctors, schoolmasters and landowners who also had specialist knowledge of their parishes. Again, a detailed questionnaire was sent to the ministers and other researchers. Indeed, the Superintending Committee of the Society Instituted in Scotland for the Benefit of the Sons and Daughters of the Clergy, which sponsored the *NSA*, wanted to 'achieve a high degree of uniformity' and 'follow certain standard lines'.[9] The *NSA* was published in three formats. The first edition was published in fifty-two quarterly parts between 1834 and 1845; in the first reissue, thirty-three separate county volumes were published between 1841 and 1845; a second re-issue published in 1845 comprised fifteen collected county volumes.

The *TSA* departs from the form used in the *OSA* and the *NSA*. Although parish accounts, also largely written by ministers, continued to be central to the *TSA*, each volume also includes an account of its respective county and detailed introductory essays on a range of topics, such as population, settlement, and farming. This model was also adopted for the *East Lothian Fourth Statistical Account*. By the time the *TSA* was being written, there had been significant administrative changes that meant that it was important that the parish accounts were located within the wider context of their counties. As Henry Hamilton, the editor of Aberdeenshire volume of the *TSA*, observed: 'an account of the county as a whole was to be included, since to-day it now overshadows the parish as an economic and administrative unit'. The *TSA* was published in thirty-one volumes, issued at 'very irregular intervals, and not in sequence according to the volume numbering'.[10]

The *TSA* took even longer to complete than the *OSA* or the *NSA*. J A Gibson comments that 'it is very unfortunate that publication of the entire series took over 40 years, thus precluding uniformity'. By the time the last volumes were published they were out of date. They include parish accounts which were written some years earlier and had to be updated with postscripts giving an impression of life in the 1980s. They also did not contain the extensive introductory material and thematic essays of the earlier volumes. The expansion of government departments and their role in Scotland during the period when the accounts were published meant that they were, according to Ewen A Cameron, 'quickly superseded as a source of information on many of the topics with which it was originally concerned'.[11]

Researchers from a wide range of disciplines have testified to the value of the parish accounts, especially in the *OSA*. Gibson observes that 'nothing quite like them exists for any other country in the world' while F A Leeming considers that it is 'a standard source of local information'. Gibson suggests that 'taken together they provide a matchless comparable record of all aspects of Scotland and Scottish life over the past two centuries'. Maisie Steven considers that 'the sheer diversity of the *Old Statistical Account* is nevertheless, to my mind, its most attractive feature'. Assessing their value, Withrington concludes that 'used with due care, there is much dependence to be placed on the returns in the Statistical Account. It is in many respects, and for many topics, a uniquely important source for the social historian'.[12]

Researchers have not made as widespread use of the *TSA* as of the *OSA* or the *NSA*. Cameron notes that 'it is rarely used by scholars of 20th-century Scotland despite the growth of interdisciplinary activity on that topic'. Nevertheless, the *TSA* can be used to research issues that cannot be revealed through other sources. Murray Watson, for example, notes its importance as a source for examining the role of English migrants to Scotland.[13]

Board of Agriculture's County Agricultural Reports

The *OSA* provided Sir John Sinclair with the first stage of his three stage 'pyramid of statistical inquiry'. As noted, the *OSA* brought together a great mass of information on the level of the parish. The second stage was to focus on the level of a county. Sinclair was to produce reports which focused on the level of the county through the newly established Board of Agriculture and Internal Improvement (sometimes called the 'Old Board of Agriculture'), based in London, of which he was founder and first president. He proposed and oversaw a series of county agricultural reports or surveys for each county in Britain which were published in volumes with the title *'General View of the Agriculture of the county of x'*, *'x'* being a specific county. This was a British project rather than a Scottish one, and it should be viewed within this context, even though Sinclair had specific responsibility for the Scottish reports or surveys. The surveyors would point out 'in what respects there is room for improvement'.[14]

The Board undertook two series of county agricultural surveys or reports. The first was published between 1793 and 1797. The surveyors were to gather information on thirty-five points that covered aspects of agriculture, agricultural practices, land use and agricultural improvements. They were also to gather information on any produce, breeds of livestock, crops, or activities 'in which it [the county] may excel'.[15]

The surveyors included 'some very intelligent' individuals and 'persons skilled in husbandry'.[16] In Scotland, they included eminent agriculturists and economists, such as James Anderson, the author of the Aberdeen survey. Others were agricultural writers such as the noted English writer William Marshall (Central Highlands), major landowners such as John Francis Erskine (Clackmannanshire), factors such as James Donaldson (Banff, Elgin or Moray, Nairn, and the Carse of Gowrie), and farmers such as George Robertson (Midlothian). There were also ministers such as the Reverend Mr Roger (Angus or Forfar), the Reverend Bryce Johnston (Dumfriesshire), and the Reverend James Robertson (southern districts of Perth). Sinclair conducted the extensive survey of the Northern Counties of Scotland.

The Board printed this first series of reports as 'manuscripts'. They were printed in the form of quartos, with wide margins, to be circulated in the counties to which they related. This method of publication was intended to collect 'a great mass of additional valuable information' and enable readers to make observations, additional remarks and any amendments to the reports to ensure their accuracy. Sinclair suggests that some 80,000 papers were circulated for comment throughout Britain.[17] The Scottish reports were of varying length and detail. Most were less than a hundred pages, though those of Aberdeen, Berwick, Dunbartonshire and the southern districts of the county of Perth were longer; few had maps or plates.

The reports as a whole were criticised. Although Sinclair considered that they were 'manuscripts' and had not been finalised (their imprints note that they were printed rather than published), critics of the Board insisted that they were definitive works. The Board recognised that they should be finalised, and resolved to reprint the Survey of each County as soon as they appeared to be suitable for publication. It started to publish the 'revised reports' or the second series in 1795; the first series became known as the 'original reports'.

These revised reports, which were published as soon as they were finished, took much longer to complete. The last Scottish survey, Bute, was not published until 1816, and the last report of all, the third volume of the Derbyshire survey, was published in 1817. As editions of reports sold out, the Board requested a number of its surveyors to provide revised second or even third editions. Three revised Scottish reports – Argyll, Clydesdale, and Perth (which were among some of the earliest ones to be published) – had a second edition.

Most of the revised reports were in fact recommissioned, and were surveyed and written by different surveyors. In Scotland, only four surveyors were re-employed: James Naismith (Clydesdale), George Robertson (Midlothian), James Robertson (Perth), and James Trotter (West Lothian); this trend was also noted in England. The Board also rearranged some of the areas to be surveyed into new surveying areas. The Northern counties and islands of Scotland, which had been one survey area, was divided into six districts. The county of Perth, which had been covered by three surveys (southern Perth, Carse of Gowrie and central Highlands), was covered by one. For the first time a survey was conducted for Inverness-shire; it had been dealt with in four surveying districts: Argyll, Elgin, the Hebrides and Nairn. The counties of Roxburgh and Selkirk and also those of Moray and Nairn were surveyed as separate counties but were published in two volumes.

The Board exercised more control over its surveyors and their activities. It gave them guidance on how to undertake their survey and write their obser-vations. The 'Plan for re-printing the agricultural surveys. By the President of the Board of Agriculture', which was inserted into a number of the surveys, set out a uniform model which they were to follow. Their surveys were to have seventeen subject headings or chapters and a conclusion. Their subject matter was to be more extensive than that of the 'original reports'. It included additional topics such as buildings, the mode of occupation, and rural economy and political economy as connected with or affecting agriculture. This plan, issued in 1795, was revised in 1806 with a number of minor amendments to include subjects that had been erroneously omitted or others that had received only cursory attention and which were to be treated in more detail.

The 'revised reports' bore little resemblance to the original reports. They were much longer and more rigorous, with some having over 600 pages. The Board's extensive 'Plan' ensured that even if the surveyors treated all the headings as briefly as possible they still had to write a substantial volume. Surveyors generally investigated and wrote on all headings of the 'Plan'. This included subjects for which they had a great deal of knowledge, but also others for which they had little. They found it difficult to gather information on some of the headings. They could not always calculate the acreage of land in a county, the expense and profit of farmers, or ascertain the rainfall or other meteorological data, a topic that was especially problematic for many surveyors. They were not always able to obtain information or ensure its accuracy or obtain documents that they knew existed.

The county agricultural reports have received some attention by researchers. Writing critically on them, Rosalind Mitchison observes that 'some of the early reports were useful, for instance Marshall's report on the Central Highlands'. Alexander Fenton has made extensive use of them in his work on material culture and rural society, such as his *Country Life in Scotland: Our Rural Past*, and *Scottish Country Life*. He notes that they are an 'invaluable resource' but that they also record 'the prejudices of ardent improvers against what was old'.[18]

Statistical Analysis of Scotland as One District

The third stage of Sinclair's 'pyramid of statistical inquiry' is a statistical analysis of Scotland as one area. Sinclair achieved this in two ways. The first was through his *General Report of the Agricultural State, and Political Circumstances, of Scotland*, published in three volumes in 1813. Having amassed a great volume of information in the county reports, Sinclair recognised that the Board of Agriculture and Internal Improvement should 'compress, within moderate limits, the results of all these various publications, so as to render, at least the substance of the whole, accessible to every proprietor and farmer in the kingdom'. This would help to diffuse information on the agricultural state and the political circumstances of Scotland. Sinclair hoped that 'useful knowledge will be rapidly diffused, and that by the union of public encouragement, and private exertion, this part of the United Kingdom, will be raised to an unexampled degree of happiness and prosperity'.[19]

The *General Report* was another ambitious project. Sinclair did not undertake the *General Report* on his own. He commissioned the work to 'over a dozen of the ablest men in Scotland . . . and every one of them has got the material for his own Department'.[20] Sinclair notes that 'the report itself, independent of the Appendixes, has been condensed into three volumes octavo, of a size similar to the larger county reports, or the statistical volumes'. The *General Report* was also organised under the same topic headings and subdivisions as the county agricultural reports. Sinclair remarks that 'it appeared highly expedient, to follow the comprehensive system adopted, in preparing the enlarged County Reports for publication'.[21] Not only did this make it easier to arrange the large volume of information, but it also enabled the county reports to be located within the wider national framework of the *General Report*.

Sinclair published a further analysis of Scotland: his *Analysis of the Statistical Account of Scotland: With a General View of the History of that Country: and Discussions on Some Important Branches of Political Economy* of 1826. Sinclair was conscious that the *Analysis* should be as widely accessible as possible, and 'produce so much public benefit'.[22] Like the *General Report*, this meant that the information should be compressed as far as possible. He suggests that 'the Author had always intended to restrict the work, to *one volume*, that the information it contained might be more generally accessible, and more widely diffused'.[23] This would bring its cost within the reach of the wider public, thereby allowing it to be as widely circulated as possible. Sinclair described the work as 'properly speaking, an Analysis of the "*Statistical Account*" as originally drawn up in 1791–8, except in so far as respects the population of the kingdom'. As information on the population had been superseded since that time, he brought it up to date with information from several parliamentary enumerations. He recognised that there had been changes in the agricultural 'and other circumstances of Scotland', but that to bring these up to date would require a significant amount of work.[24] He did not therefore include an up to date account of these subjects in his *Analysis*.

The *Analysis* was divided into eleven chapters with numerous subheadings (including ones on the general divisions of Scotland, the climate, the healthiness and the longevity of the people of Scotland, population, the various classes of inhabitants, agriculture, manufactures, and commerce) and extensive appendices and errata (on the ecclesiastical establishment of Scotland, education, and the poor), a conclusion and appendix.

Both the *General Report* and the *Analysis* have received little attention by researchers. Rosalind Mitchison considers that the *General Report* is a 'solid piece of work: it surveyed the country throughout and for the most part it was written by competent people'. However, she criticises it for its 'ambivalence of aim', as it contains 'both a survey of the country and proposals for the future', and for its focus on Lowland rather than Highland agriculture.[25]

The Work and the Record of Activities of Modern Government Departments

Iain G Hutchison observes that 'state involvement in many aspects of British life has grown throughout most of the twentieth century'. The Scottish Office (subsequently the Scottish Executive and now the Scottish Government) created in 1885, has been the heart of the State's expansion in Scotland. By 1953 the Balfour Report could argue 'that wherever practicable, the Scottish Office should handle Scottish matters'.[26] Following consideration of that report, the Scottish Office was given further responsibilities, including the administration of transport and energy. By 1985 it had five departments (Agriculture and Fisheries Department, Industry Department, Environment Department, Education Department, and Home and Health Department) and a group of central services divisions (Central Services). These were abolished in 2007.

There have been a number of histories of the Scottish Office such as those written by Sir David Milne and John S Gibson which provide general accounts of their development and work until recent times.[27] Specific departments and agencies have also received some attention, with those having responsibility for the development of the Highlands and Islands receiving the most. Donald Mackay has examined the activities of the Congested Districts Boards of Ireland and Scotland and Scotland's rural land use agencies. Alexander Mather focused on government agencies and land development in the Scottish Highlands, James Shaw Grant on government agencies in the Highlands since 1945, and James Grassie on the history of the Highlands and Islands Development Board (HIDB).[28]

Official publications

Publications which are 'produced by organisations associated with Government in its widest sense' are referred to as 'official publications'. David Butcher has suggested that they are a 'very diverse group' of publications.[29] A number of handbooks are available to guide researchers and other users through this wide array of publications. The first category of handbooks outlines the types of government publications. Butcher's *Official Publications in Britain* covers the scope and structure of official publishing in Britain, including parliamentary publications, the publications of Government and national office departments, and local government. James G Ollé's *An Introduction to British Government Publications* outlines the scope and classes of publications and how to acquire them.[30] The second category is guides which arrange Government publications according to their subject matter. These are usually printed in the form of lists. The most important are compiled by Percy Ford and Grace Ford, whose work has been continued by Diana Marshallsay and J H Smith.[31] The third category is lists of statutes and associated papers published by the government. They include lists of the legislation made by Parliament as in *Public General Statutes Affecting Scotland 1707–1847*, which is continued in annual volumes for later years.[32] Local and personal acts are covered in the *Index to Local and Personal Acts 1808–1947*, which has been updated to cover the years 1948 to 1966.[33]

Government publications can be divided into two classes: (1) parliamentary publications; (2) non-parliamentary publications. Ollé suggests that the first class, published by Her Majesty's Stationery Office (HMSO), comprises a number of distinct serials and series: House of Lords Publications (such as the official Report of the Parliamentary Debates – Lords Hansard), House of Commons publications (such as the official report of the Parliamentary debates – Commons Hansard); papers presented to parliament by Command (Command papers); and acts and measures (including public general acts and local and personal acts). As their name suggests, they are 'intimately connected with the activities of Parliament'.[34]

Publications in the second class were formerly known as 'Stationery Office publications'. These papers are not 'intimately connected' with the activities of parliament. They comprise three broad classes: statutory instruments (secondary legislation not directly enacted by Parliament), reports (annual reports of government institutions and various standing commissions and committees and the reports of *ad hoc* investigating committees and working parties) and information publications which 'include a wide variety of books, pamphlets, leaflets, periodicals and other forms of literature providing the public with information and advice, most of which is derived from experts employed in government departments and institutions'.[35]

Some of these classes of publications are particularly valuable resources for ethnological research. They include command papers, 'papers presented to Parliament by a Minister on his own initiative, not in pursuance of an Act of Parliament'. These comprise: state papers; policy papers (White Papers providing statements of government policy); annual reports (including those of departments); reports of Royal Commissions (appointed by Royal Warrant 'to investigate and report on some matter on which new legislation seems desirable'); reports of Departmental Committees (committees appointed by ministers); reports of Tribunals (the reports of investigating judges and Tribunals of inquiry appointed to investigate matters of public concern such as alleged breaches of security); and Commissions of Inquiry and statistical reports.[36]

Royal Commissions, usually referred to by the name of their chairman, have published extensive reports ('blue books') and their associated evidence from a wide range of witnesses. Some of them have been heavily utilised by researchers from a range of disciplines. They include the Royal Commission of Inquiry into the Condition of the Crofters and Cottars in the Highlands and Islands of Scotland, popularly known as the Napier Commission after its chairman, Lord Francis Napier, ninth baronet of Napier and Ettrick. The Commission was sanctioned by Queen Victoria on 17 March 1883 in response to crofter and cotter agitation on high rents, lack of security of tenure and deprivation of de facto rights of access to land. It was appointed on 22 March 1883 'to inquire into the condition of the crofters and cottars in the Highlands and Islands of Scotland, and all matters affecting the same or relating thereto'. It gathered its evidence by means of public invitation. It heard evidence in eight counties, in which seventy-one meetings were held at sixty-one stations in buildings such as churches (the Established Church or the Free Church), schools, Sheriff court houses, volunteer drill halls, a hotel and even a temperance hall.[37] The Commissioners received testimony from 775 persons, including crofters (many of whom gave their evidence in Gaelic, though not without difficulty as some landowners took steps to ensure that giving evidence in this way was not easy), proprietors (though few made a personal appearance, preferring to submit statements or be represented by their factors or chamberlains), tacksmen, farmers, ministers, fish curers, shopkeepers and merchants, and sympathisers in the towns. They also received written returns from proprietors. This provided statistical information relating to crofters, such as their stock, acreage and rents. This was published in an appendix to their report.

The Commissioners were aware of the biases in the evidence they heard and gathered. Their report observes that it was 'in many cases delivered by illiterate persons speaking from early memory, or from hearsay, or from popular tradition, fleeting and fallacious sources even when not tinged by ancient regrets and resentments, or by the passions of the hour'. However, they also point out that 'the depositions of the superior order of witnesses, embracing proprietors, factors, farmers, clergymen, and members of the other learned professions, contain much that is valuable in connection with the industrial history and moral and physical condition of the population'. They had difficulty securing comprehensive information in the statistical returns on the crofters. They found that it was not 'solicited with entire fullness and accuracy'.[38]

The Commission's report and its written evidence, published on 28 April 1884, extends to four substantial volumes of 4,070 pages. It includes 3,375 pages of oral answers to 46,750 questions. The subject matter included in these pages is extensive. MacPhail observes that the report and its evidence 'has provided a great number of writers on crofting with a rich variety of source material. Indeed, the Report and its accompanying evidence have been called the "Domesday Book" of the Highlands and Islands.'[39] Ewen Cameron refers to it as a 'uniquely precious body of evidence about crofting as a way of life which deserves to be better known'. It has been used as evidence in a number of studies such as those of MacPhail, James Hunter and A D Cameron in his *Go Listen to the Crofters: The Napier Commission and Crofting a Century Ago*, an account of the Commission's work and biographies of some of its informants, together with their testimony.[40]

Unpublished government records

Readers will be interested in the records of the United Kingdom Government in Scotland as well as the Scottish Government. Most of the activities of Scottish Government departments are not published and are recorded in files (paper and now electronic). All records are covered by the Freedom of Information (Scotland) Act 2002 which sets out that a record of a public authority becomes a 'historical record' at the end of a period of thirty years, when it is made public. 'Closed' records of less than thirty years old can be accessed by making a formal 'freedom of information request' to the National Archives of Scotland (NAS) (if they are held there), or if they have not been transmitted or destroyed, to the respective directorate of the Scottish Government. Certain classes of records are 'closed' for longer periods. For example, the census records (enumerators' books) and Health Board records are closed for 100 years as they contain personal information.

The records of the Scottish Office (and its successors) are arranged by department, and the work of the various divisions within each one. They can be divided into a number of types of records:

- Cabinet Committee papers.
- Papers relating to ministerial activity such as ministerial tours and meetings.
- Correspondence between ministers and other parties such as MPs/MSPs and members of the public, other ministers and government departments. These may provide information on the individual, their personal circumstances, problems with policies or the need to reform legislation.
- Papers relating to bills and their passage through the Westminster/ United Kingdom Parliament (and also the Scottish Parliament). These include briefing, amendments to clauses and records of debates (which can also be found in *Hansard*).
- Annual reports and accounts of departments and agencies. These outline

their activities and work in developing policies and administrating schemes.

- Papers relating to departmental committees, inter-departmental committees, advisory committees and statutory bodies. These include minutes of meetings, administrative papers, evidence, and reports (and their drafts) (such as those of the Committee on Farm Workers on Scotland and the various reports of the Advisory Committee on Scotland's Travelling People).
- Surveys and reports on social and economic conditions. Some studies were instigated as a result of complaints brought to the attention of the Scottish Office. Others include specially commissioned research and research reports.
- Papers relating to disputes between members of the public and departments and agencies.
- Departmental management papers. These describe management of their assets (such as the Scottish Office's crofting estates) and statutory reviews of schemes and organisations (such as the Scottish Seed Potato Development Council).
- Circulars, memoranda and minutes from government departments. These were issued to provide guidance.
- General policy documents. These provide an over-arching view on specific subjects.
- Casework files relating to particular legislation.
- Papers relating to the set up and administration of departmental schemes.
- Papers relating to projects such as housing schemes or public works construction.
- Statistics.

Although a large volume of papers is created through the daily work of Scottish Government departments (and now directorates), much of that record is destroyed by the time it is made publicly available. Only files which cover significant subjects are retained and are transmitted to the NRS. Records on particular subjects may therefore not have survived or only certain files been retained. Particular subjects may have received attention by departments at particular periods of time but not at others, so that there is not a continuous record. Files vary greatly in character and in the different types of records contained in them. They may provide a very full record of activities and evidence from individuals and organisations which cannot be obtained from other sources, or receive only cursory attention in the printed record. Others may only contain core papers which do not appear to be connected, and it may be difficult to work out the relationship between the different papers.

Local government papers

Just as central government departments have played an important role in shaping Scotland and the experiences of the people who live in the country, so too has the work of local government. Anne E Whetstone's *Scottish County Government in the Eighteenth and Nineteenth Centuries* describes the role and work of the four county authorities before 1890: the sheriffs, the commissioners of supply, the justices of the peace and the lieutenancy and militia.[41] In 1889 county councils were established and inherited many of the jurisdictions and records of their predecessors. Further changes were made to local authorities in 1929. For example, parish councils were replaced by district councils and different categories of burghs were established (county councils, large burghs and small burghs) which were to change in 1974 and then again in 1995.

The powers and duties of local authorities are derived from parliament and are set out in legislation. This may place statutory duties on them to provide a service or a permissive duty which allows them to provide a service if they want to. They may also act as enforcement agencies for national legislation. Their varied functions include education, planning, roads, traffic planning and transport, social services, fire services and police, housing and environmental services and leisure services.

Their records can be grouped into two classes. According to David Butcher, in his *Official Publications in Britain*, the first group comprises council and committee documents and publications. These are:

- Agendas (for committees and sub-committees).
- Minutes (of committees and sub-committees such as those of public buildings, burgh ground, epidemic hospitals, cottage hospitals, parks, arts, public baths, watching, lighting and fire engines).
- Byelaws (made under powers given by parliament).
- Reports (such as annual reports which record the activities of a local authority and its departments such as sanitary inspectors, medical officers of health and chief constables over the course of a year).
- Yearbooks and statistics.[42]

The second group consists of departmental documents and publications. These include:

- Reports and statistics.
- Technical and research studies (which provide evidence on which policy decisions may be based).
- Planning documents (the single largest group of local government publications).
- Publicity and information material (which outlines the activities and services of local authorities, and may seek to attract industry to an area).
- Tourist literature (local guidebooks which detail the facilities in an area).
- Local studies publications (published by the public library service, local museums, art galleries and local authority archives) to support the teaching of environmental and historical studies in schools.
- Bibliographical sources (such as pamphlets and articles about an area, guides to the records of local archives).

Church Records

Few of the records of the pre-Reformation Church survive in Scotland. Most of them have been published by societies such as the Scottish History Society. The Reformation established a new Church of Scotland; further Churches emerged after the Disruption of 1843 such as the United Free Church and the Congregational Union. In 1929 a number of the Presbyterian Churches were reunited by the Church of Scotland (such as the Reformed Presbyterian). The history and the influence of these Churches are examined in a number of studies. These include Callum G Brown's *The Social History of Religion in Scotland since 1739* (1987) and his *Religion and Society in Scotland since 1707* (1997). Volume 12 of the *Scottish Life and Society* series provides a study of the cultural and social history of religion. There are also histories of specific Churches such as Andrew L Drummond and James Bulloch's *The Scottish Church 1688–1843: The Age of the Moderates* (1973) and *The Church in Victorian Scotland, 1843–1874* (1973). Journals are published by societies interested in the history and culture of the churches in Scotland. The Scottish Church History Society, which promotes the study of the history of all branches of the Church in Scotland, issues its *Records of the Scottish Church History Society*. The Scottish Catholic Historical Association focuses on the part played by the Catholic Church in Scottish history and culture, and publishes the *Innes Review*.

The records of the Church of Scotland relate to the hierarchical structure of the church and its courts:

- Records of administrative bodies and courts: the General Assembly, synod, presbytery and kirk session.
- Kirk session records. These include minutes and accounts into investigations into the moral behaviour of parishioners and payments to the sick and disabled.
- Records of heritors (local landowners and property owners), responsible for building and maintaining the parish church, its manse and school (including the appointment of the schoolmaster and his salary) until 1925.
- Poor relief records. These document the provision of poor relief which was jointly held by heritors and the kirk session of each parish until 1845.
- Teind records relating to the annual salary paid to a parish minister who had ownership of the teinds of the parish. These records include information on the value of the stipend, the ownership and valuation of lands and teinds within a parish, the size of the parish and its population.
- The records of Commissary Courts which, until their abolition in 1823 when their business was transferred to the Sheriff Courts, had exclusive jurisdiction in cases of a strictly consistorial nature, such as marriage, divorce, separation and legitimacy and the confirmation of testaments of all persons dying outside Scotland who had moveable estate in the country.

- The Old Parish Registers. These record births, marriages (the name of the marrying couple), and deaths before statutory registration began in 1855. Records of baptisms usually provide the names of the child and father, and sometimes that of the mother, and some additional information.

Legal Papers

The Scottish legal system has well defined branches and aspects: private and public law; administrative, criminal and civil law; civil law and commercial law; common law and equity; common law and statute law; and substantive and adjective law. Court records are created and held by a number of courts in Scotland:

- The High Court of Justiciary, Scotland's supreme criminal court. It has exclusive jurisdiction over serious crimes, in particular murder, treason, heresy, counterfeiting, rape and crimes of a sexual nature, prisoners who were to be sentenced to be transported. It acts as a court of appeal for criminal proceedings in the sheriff (or inferior) courts. Its records also include cases relating to witchcraft trials.
- The Lord Advocate's department. It has had jurisdiction over serious crimes tried at the High Court from the nineteenth century onwards.
- The Privy Council (abolished in 1708). It heard cases relating to people accused of witchcraft and seditious practices.
- The Admiralty Court (from 1557 until its abolition in 1830). It dealt with crimes committed on the high seas or in harbours, including smuggling, piracy and 'trading with the enemy'.
- The Commissary Courts, which were re-established between 1564 and 1566, had exclusive jurisdiction in cases which had a strictly consistorial nature, such as marriage, divorce and separation. In 1823 all inferior Commissary Courts were established and their business transferred to the Sheriff Courts; the Commissary Court of Edinburgh was abolished in 1836 and its powers and jurisdiction were transferred to the Sheriff Court. These courts were completely abolished and their functions taken over by the Sheriff Courts in 1876.
- The Sheriff Courts. These deal with lesser crimes, both criminal and civil, such as theft and assault. They hold sequestration records (bankruptcy), criminal records, registers of deeds and protests, commissary records, records on services of heirs (inquests to determine a claimants' right to heritable property), the register of improvements to entailed estates (from 1770 owners of entailed estates were allowed to charge their estates with three-quarters of the cost of improvements made), fiars' courts (on the official prices of grain fixed by the sheriffs), corn law returns, annual accounts of public utilities, freeholders' records, electoral records (after 1832), records of the commissioners of supply, lieutenancy and militia records, records of heritable jurisdictions, and

plans. They also hold records relating to workmen's compensation for employees injured in the course of their employment, fatal accident inquiries into fatal accidents in the workplace and cases of sudden death where the public interest is involved.

- The burgh courts. These deal with minor offences in the royal burghs including disputes between inhabitants, such as small debts, the removal of tenants, and any physical and verbal assault.
- The justice of the peace courts. These deal with minor offences such as criminal trials for assault, disorderly conduct, being drunk and incapable, poaching, or small debt cases. From 1934 they included juvenile court cases.
- The franchise courts (until their abolition in 1747). These were local courts where a person, usually a local landowner, held a franchise from the crown to administer justice (both criminal and civil) in his area. The records include disputes between tenants, physical violence, cases of defamation, theft, financial claims and damages to property.

Not all court records have survived. Current legislation allows for the selective destruction of some types of Sheriff Court records. There can be large gaps within individual series of Sheriff Court cases, especially for earlier periods. Records may also be located with other types of records for a different period, therefore making them difficult to locate. There are also restrictions on access to some court records. Precognitions in the Lord Advocate's department which are less than seventy-five years old are closed to public access. The records of the Sheriff Courts are not normally transmitted to the NRS until they are more than twenty-five years old; more recent records are to be found at the court where a particular trial took place. Adoption records are closed for 100 years.

A number of studies have aimed to make the wide range of legal records more accessible and provide guides to them. Patrick Rayner, Bruce Lenman and Geoffrey Parker have compiled the *Handlist of Records for the Study of Crime in Early Modern Scotland (to 1747)* (1982). There are printed lists of cases such as the Scottish History Society's *The Records of the Proceedings of the Justiciary Court, Edinburgh, 1661–1678* (1905), Henry Home Kames and A F Tytler's *The Decisions of the Court of Session from its first Institution to the Present Time* (1791–7), and the 35 volume *The Register of the Privy Council* [for 1545–1689] (1877–1970). A report on the records of the Court of Session is published in the *Annual Report of the Keeper of the Records of Scotland* from 1972. There are also a number of guides to Scots law, including its structure and terminology. David Walker's *The Scottish Legal System* (2001) sets out the development of Scots law and outlines the different types of legal sources. The Stair Society has an introductory survey of the sources and literature of Scots law.[43] A G M Duncan's *Green's Glossary of Scottish Legal Terms* (1992) is a useful guide to legal terms and their definitions. Volume 13 of *Scottish Life and Society* (2012) focuses on the institution of the Law.

Studies have also focused on particular types of legal records and the range of evidence they can provide. These include records of the various courts such as the High Court of Justiciary, the Lord Advocate's department, the Sheriff

Court, Commissary Court testaments, as well as the records of courts in particular areas of Scotland for specific periods, and types of records including testamentary inventories (probate inventories), testaments, and police records.[44] The NRS has information sheets on the NAS website. These include five sheets on the Court of Session; others focus on crime and criminals, Sheriff Court records, justice of the peace records, and High Court criminal trials.[45] Court records relating to witchcraft for the period 1563 to 1736 are found in the online resource 'The Survey of Scottish Witchcraft'.[46] It is a database of people accused of witchcraft in Scotland that enables researchers to 'examine biographical and social information about accused witches; cultural and sociological patterns of witchcraft belief and accusation; community, ecclesiastical and legal procedures of investigation and trial, national and regional variations; and the chronology and geography of witchcraft accusation and prosecution.'

Newspapers

Newspapers are daily or weekly publications which are not the organ of a particular party or group and carry general news relating to a town and its surrounding districts, a county, the country as a whole, or a particular topic. They evolved in Scotland in the middle of the seventeenth century. Until the end of the second decade of the nineteenth century they were relatively short lived. The Edinburgh-based, national newspapers the *Edinburgh Evening Courant* (1817–73) and the *Caledonian Mercury* (1800–59) were the first successful newspapers to be published for many decades. The provincial or regional press became established through the *Glasgow Journal* (established in 1741) and the *Aberdeen Journal* (established in 1748). The 'first substantial local news coverage' appeared in the *Glasgow Mercury* (established in 1778). It was not until the mid nineteenth century that local newspapers evolved their modern form by including reports and comments on local events, obituaries of local people, and providing less focus on national and international news. Even the earliest agricultural newspapers from the mid 1840s such as *The Ayrshire Agriculturist* carried national and international news.[47]

There are several histories on the Scottish newspaper press. Their early development is covered by R M W Cowan in *The Newspaper in Scotland: A Study of its First Expansion 1815–1860* (1946). J S Ferguson's *Directory of Scottish Newspapers* (1984) provides a helpful guide to the newspapers that have been published. The National Library of Scotland (NLS) lists a number of resources on Scottish newspapers.[48] There are histories on specific newspapers. These include Norman Harper's *Press and Journal: The First 250 Years 1748–1998* (1997) and Albert Morris's *Scotland's Paper: The Scotsman 1817–1992* (1992).

The value of newspapers as a source of evidence has been widely recognised. They have been regarded as 'a vital part of the country's heritage' and as the 'life-blood of local history'.[49] They have been used to research a wide range of subjects. Henry W Noble has examined the role of newspaper advertisements in the spread of the availability of dental treatment in Scotland and Sebastian Pryke has analysed them to develop a picture of the Edinburgh furnishing trade between 1708 and 1790. Douglas Lockhart has also drawn on the provincial press to provide evidence on planned villages in Aberdeenshire, and on migration to estate villages in north-east Scotland. Sarah Pedersen has explored the writing of women correspondents to Aberdeen daily newspapers between 1900 and 1914. Heather Holmes has used news articles and editorials in local and national Scottish and Irish newspapers to construct identities of Irish migratory potato workers in Scotland.[50]

Maps and Plans

Maps and plans form part of the official public as well as the private record. They range from extensive surveys specially commissioned by United Kingdom Government and Scottish Government departments to map the entire country, to maps concerned with a specific aspect of a locale or locales, such as the location of planned train and road communications or the boundaries of the Scottish Office crofting estates.[51]

Some maps, such as General William Roy's Military Survey of Scotland undertaken following the Jacobite risings of 1715 and 1745, are especially important. The military engineers thoroughly explored and laid open the country and established military posts in parts of the country that were considered to be remote. Such mapping was 'paralleled in other extensive operations, on similar scales, by military engineers in the same century; by the British in North America, by the Hanoverians, by the Austrians and French in the Low Countries'. Roy's map is significant for the extensive area that it covers: the entire mainland of Scotland. It only excludes the islands. It also gives a 'uniform synoptic view – or historical cross-section – of the entire country at a single point in time, and serves as a basis for comparative geographical or statistical studies'.[52] R A Skelton and, more recently, Graeme Whittington and A J S Wilson have analysed it as a source of evidence. [53] From 1843 Ordnance Survey maps, which have been variously resurveyed and published, have mapped the country to a standard scale. They are able to provide comparative material throughout time.

A number of printed maps of Scotland have been available from at least 1630. County maps were published by map makers such as Dorret (1750), Ainslie (1789) and Arrowsmith (1807). M L Parry has investigated a range of county maps to demonstrate developments in mapping and changes in the landscape.[54] Complete atlases have also been published. Notable ones include those of Thomas Brown (1807), John Lothian (1827) and John Thomson (1820s and 1830s).[55]

Directories and Almanacs

Directories were developed in the early nineteenth century to record basic information about settlements and the people in them: the names of farms and their occupiers, the location of the nearest post office, the availability of hotels and inns, and the names of local officials such as chairmen of school boards, registrars, ministers, bank agents, provosts, town clerks and so forth. They could focus on a county, as in the county directories, or cover the whole of Scotland. They included *Pigot and Co's National Commercial Directory* (1820, 1825–7, 1837), the

County Directory of Scotland (1842–1912), and *Slater's Directory Ltd, Royal National Commercial Directory and Topography of Scotland* (1852–1915). Post Office Directories became available for the largest cities – Aberdeen, Edinburgh, Glasgow and Perth – from the early nineteenth century (many of which are digitised).[56]

As directories comprise a diverse body of publications, a number of bibliographies have attempted to make them more accessible. The most important is Gareth Shaw and Allison Tipper's *British Directories: A Bibliography and Guide to Directories Published in England and Wales (1850–1950) and Scotland, (1773–1950)* (1997). Others refer to other types of public accounts as well as directories: James H Tierney's *Early Glasgow Newspapers, Periodicals and Directories* (1934), and D Richard Torrance's *Scottish Trades & Professions: A Selected Bibliography [Including a Summary of Scottish Directories]* (1991).

Almanacs, cheap and ephemeral publications published in Scotland from 1623, were of two types. The first was the 'annual' almanac, to be used for a year and then discarded. They include information on tide tables, mathematical and scientific information, and lists of fairs. From the mid to late eighteenth century they also included peer lists, lists of members in the House of Commons, the universities, and the army and navy. The second were 'everlasting' or 'prognostications'. Despite the amount of biographical matter contained in them, they have received cursory attention, though Kaye McAlpine has examined them as a source of evidence on fairs.[57]

SPONSORSHIP AND PROMOTION OF PUBLIC ACCOUNTS

A number of organisations have promoted the wide range of public accounts. Archives have published guides in order to make their collections and the public accounts in them accessible. The NAS has published a number of guides on different types of public accounts, the information contained in them and suggestions on how to use that evidence. These include its *Guide to the National Archives of Scotland* (1996), and its *Tracing your Scottish Ancestors: A Guide to Ancestry Research in the Scottish Record Office* which has been revised a number of times since its first publication in 1990. Cecil Sinclair's *Tracing Scottish Local History: A Guide to Local History Research in the Scottish Record Office* (1994) provides a guide to researching local history and the records (public and also private) that are available to investigate subjects such as houses and streets, householders and buildings, estates and farms, parishes, districts, communications, business and recreation. The *Annual Report of the Keeper of the Records of Scotland* provides details of the latest records accessioned and catalogued. Its website includes guides to public records held by it such as adoption records, divorce records, military records, Scottish Parliament records, wills and testaments and the records of various courts. It published (as the Scottish Record Office) guides on a range of subjects such as emigrants, the Scots in Canada, education, crofters, military history, and poor relief.[58] These included a historical background on the subject, a list of documents (including a number of public accounts), extracts and facsimiles.

Professional archive organisations such as the Society of Archivists (in their *Journal of the Society of Archivists*) and the Scottish Records Association (in their *Scottish Archives: The Journal of the Scottish Records Association*) publish articles on the use of particular sources for research, especially historical research. Some of these have brought attention to little known sources or shed new light on well used ones.[59] For example, Craig Young has described the evidence of Scottish sequestrations to examine the role of women in the small firm. Bill Inglis has considered the use of testamentary inventories as 'a neglected source' for the study of Scottish agriculture.[60]

A number of other types of organisation provide guides to particular types of public accounts for researching a range of subjects. Family history societies have been especially active in this work. Their publications analyse the use of public (as well as private) sources for personal, family and community history research. Among the published books is David Moody's *Scottish Family History* (1992). Local history societies and local historians have also been active. Moody has compiled sources for the study of towns in his *Scottish Towns: A Guide for Local Historians* (1992).

Researchers from a range of disciplines have turned their attention to the use of public sources to research a range of subjects. These include rural land occupancy in Scotland, settlement in the Highlands between 1750 and 1950, the 'traditional history' of the Highlands and Western Isles, sources for planned villages, labour history and education. Iain Flett and Judith Cripps have also documented the sources for studying the Scottish medieval town.[61]

The Scottish History Society has published some public accounts, though the focus of its work is to promote private accounts. Its public accounts include the Court books of the Barony of Urie in Kincardineshire, 1604 to 1747, and Carnwath, 1523 to 1542: records of the presbyteries of Inverness and Dingwall, 1643 to 1688; and records of the Baron Court of Stitchill, 1655 to 1807. It has also published the minutes of the justices of the peace for Lanarkshire from 1707 to 1723. Though much of its focus is on pre-eighteenth century material, it has also given some attention to government and social conditions in Scotland between 1845 and 1919 and the Scottish Office between 1919 and 1959.[62]

THE LOCATION OF PUBLIC ACCOUNTS

Public accounts are held by a wide range of institutions and organisations located throughout Scotland. Michael Cox's *Exploring Scottish History. With a Directory of Resource Centres for Scottish Local and National History in Scotland* (1999) is a list which includes the contact details, information on holdings, search tools and reprographic facilities and access of 384 facilities. These include libraries, archives, special collections, museums and galleries, local history societies, family history societies and societies which do not have any premises. Though now outdated, his resource list not only demonstrates the diversity of libraries and archives, but also suggests the difficulty faced by the researcher in locating particular records. This difficulty has been partly alleviated by the development of the Scottish Archive Network's (SCAN) unified online catalogue which provides access to the records of archives throughout Scotland.[63]

The NAS, an agency of the Scottish Government, exists 'to preserve, protect and promote the nation's records; to provide the best possible inclusive and accessible archive that educates, informs and engages the people of Scotland and the world'. It has responsibility for the custody and preservation of the records of the government of Scotland, including government departments and agencies, which have been transmitted to it (it is also a major repository for private records).[64] Its collections also include 'Register House Plans', over 150,000 maps and plans and architectural and engineering drawings. Its website provides a broad outline of its holdings together with its searchable Online Public Access Catalogue (OPAC). Its four-volume *Descriptive List of Plans in the Scottish Records Office* (1966–88), edited by Ian H Adams and Loretta R Timperley, is a detailed list of the first 4,999 plans in its maps and plan collection. These include maps and plans produced and used by government departments and public bodies.

The NLS is a national archive repository. It 'has extensive holdings of manuscripts and archives relating to Scottish history and culture and Scots men and women at home and abroad, dating mainly from the seventeenth century to the present day'.[65] It does not, as a rule, hold the long consecutive runs of records that can be found in the NAS. Its holdings focus on private rather than public records, though it has some holdings. These include the records relating to Banff Town Council (MSS.8130–8169; Ch.7677–7697), and Kelso Burgh Court books (Mss.847–848).

The NLS has extensive map collections, both hard copy (located in its Causewayside Building in Edinburgh), and electronic. Its holdings include atlases, gazetteers, guidebooks, journals, and mapmaking books relating to Scotland and the rest of the world. Its hardcopy maps include the Board of Ordnance plans (MSS.1645–1651). Its website has thousands of digitised map images. These include county maps, town plans (such as those of the Great Reform Act Plan and Reports 1832 and the Ordnance Survey large-scale town plans from 1847 to 1895), sea charts, and eighteenth-century military maps (Roy's Military survey of 1747 to 1755). It also has extensive holdings of Ordnance Survey maps. The Ordnance Survey also has a large archive of historic maps, including maps from the nineteenth century for Scotland, England and Wales.

There are extensive holdings of local, regional and national newspapers held throughout Scotland. *NEWSPLAN: Report of the NEWSPLAN Project in Scotland* (1994) records the existence of approximately 1,750 Scottish newspapers from the date of their first publication until 1994. John S North provides a directory of Scottish newspapers and periodicals between 1800 and 1900. The NLS is the main repository for Scottish newspapers and has significant holdings. The microfilming of newspapers has enabled copies of many titles to be held in other libraries close to the place where they were originally printed and for copies of hard copies of newspapers that were only held in the British Library's Newspaper Library to be available in Scottish libraries. Online resources such as the British Newspaper Archive are making them further available.[66]

As most newspapers still require a significant amount of time and effort to research, a number of indexes have been developed to identify their contents.

The NLS website has a 'Guide to Scottish Newspaper Indexes', a searchable list of 183 Scottish newspaper titles that have an index.[67] It provides details of the type of list, its format (some lists, such as that of the *Press and Journal*, are electronic), the dates covered in it and its location. Their coverage is variable and some are only available for short periods of time or have significant gaps in their coverage. Some cover only certain geographical areas within a newspaper's circulation area.

The records of local authorities – and also records created by the burgh and county authority bodies – are divided between the NAS and local authority archives. The statutory provision for local authority archives has changed in recent decades. Peter D Anderson outlines their evolution between 1960 and 1990.[68] The Local Government etc (Scotland) Act 1994 makes provisions for local authorities to preserve and manage any records which are created or acquired by them during the exercise of their functions, or are transferred to them or have otherwise been placed in their custody by other means. Local authorities may also dispose of any records which they do not consider to be worthy of preservation. There are a number of studies that focus on their holdings. Robert Steward and Alan B Lawson describe the range of records held by Highland Regional Archive (now the Highland Council Archives Service). Kevin Wilbraham undertakes that activity for the scope of records in Ayrshire Archives. The websites of local authority archives provide information on their holdings and access; collectively they can be accessed through SCAN.[69]

Local studies centres, sometimes attached to local authority library headquarters, hold a wide range of materials relating to the county in which they are located. These include local authority records (and sometimes school log books), valuation rolls, copies of census returns (these are held centrally by the General Registers of Scotland in New Register House), copies of old parish registers, local newspapers, and other papers and locally published books.

A number of public bodies also have their own archives. These include health boards. The Royal Commission on the Ancient and Historical Monuments of Scotland (RCAHMS) has its own archive. Some religious groups have their own archives. They include the Scottish Jewish Archives Centre and the Scottish Catholic Archives. The records of the Church of Scotland are largely held in the NAS.

University Archives are important repositories for archival material, though their collections focus on their own institutional records and those of their predecessors and other private records, rather than public records.

ELECTRONIC RESOURCES: BIBLIOGRAPHIES
OR CATALOGUES AND DIGITISED TEXTS

Technological advances have enabled the development of electronic resources that have advanced searching capabilities. A number of resources described in the chapter 'private accounts' can also be used to research public accounts, and the reader should also consult that chapter. There are some resources that focus on public accounts. These are described in the following sections.

Bibliographies or Catalogues

Electronic library and archive catalogues of major libraries and archives can be used to research public as well as private records. These include 'Copac', the integrated catalogue of the online catalogues of seventy major university and national libraries in the UK and Ireland.[70] The NAS Online Public Access Catalogue (OPAC), published on its website, includes catalogued holdings; it does not include uncatalogued material.[71] The 'Scottish Bibliographies Online' resource, described as 'Scotland's Bibliography', is available on the NLS website, with older volumes being available in published volumes.[72] It excludes some public accounts such as maps, departmental circulars, parliamentary proceedings and statutory instruments. The English Century Short Title Catalogue (ESTC) provides bibliographical information on a wide range of printed matter – books, pamphlets, newspapers and other serials – published mainly in the English language, in the British Isles and North America between 1473 and 1800.[73] SCAN is the unified online catalogue of the holdings of Scottish archives. For researching public accounts, it has digitised all wills and testaments in Scottish commissary and Sheriff Court registers for the years 1514 to 1901, and there are kirk session and presbytery records.[74]

Digitised Texts

A number of electronic resources provide facsimile images of documents, usually of particular types of document, which can be searched by means of free-text searches. Some of these do not distinguish between public and private accounts. Some are specifically available for researching public accounts. The latter resources are described in this section.

The full text of the parish accounts in the *OSA* and the *NSA* have been digitised and are fully searchable.[75] Keyword and subject searches mean that the researcher no longer has to read through all the volumes if they want to undertake a survey of a particular topic throughout Scotland. Newspapers have also become available in a number of electronic formats. Some newspapers that were available on microfilm have been converted to a digital format and their past issues have been made available. Every edition of the *Scotsman* published between 1817 and 1950 is digitally available while there are also searchable copies of the *Caledonian Mercury*, the *Glasgow Herald* and the *Aberdeen Journal*.[76] A large number of current Scottish newspapers, especially provincial ones, are now published online, but also continue to be published by conventional means. Their websites may not always provide all their news online unless a reader takes out a subscription. Scottish newspaper websites, especially provincial ones, are available through the 'Online newspapers' portal.[77]

Parliamentary Papers have been digitised and made available in a number of electronic resources. The 'Records of the Parliaments of Scotland to 1707' provides full facsimiles of the original text and modern translations of the Scottish Parliament from 1235 to the Union of 1707.[78] That resource describes itself as 'the most comprehensive record of Scottish parliamentary proceedings ever available'. The 'British Official Publications Collaborative Reader Information Service' (BOPCRIS) is the official portal for eighteenth-century parliamentary publications (1688–1834).[79] It is a bibliographic database of selected British official publications to recent times. It includes journals of the House of Commons and House of Lords, parliamentary registers, sessional papers of the House of Commons, Acts, bills and Local and Personal Acts. The 'House of Commons Parliamentary Papers' provides full text access and a search facility for these papers between 1801 and 2000; it also has an index of papers to 2004.[80] The Scottish Parliament website provides a fully searchable record of the Parliament's proceedings, committees, petitions, bills and Acts passed by the Parliament from 1999 onwards.[81] The Scottish Government website has access to full-text electronic versions of publications (including consultations, consultation responses, research reports, annual reports, press releases, bills and Acts) from 1997 onwards.[82] Recent legislation (including Acts, local Acts, Explanatory Notes, Statutory Instruments, and Church measures) is available for Scotland and the rest of the United Kingdom from 1987 on the website of the Office of Public Sector Information (OPSI).[83] The UK Statute Law Database provides an online revised edition of the primary legislation of the United Kingdom.[84] It contains full texts of primary and secondary legislation. Most of the primary legislation is held in 'revised form' with amendments being incorporated into the text.

'ScotlandsPeople' is the Scottish Government source for the 'official records of Scotland's people'. It holds digitised records from the 'Old Parish Registers' (1553 to 1854); the statutory registers of births, marriages and deaths (from 1855 onwards); banns and marriages (from 1538 to 1854) and deaths and burials (from 1538 to 1854); the census records (1841 to 1901); wills and testaments (1513 to 1901); and Coats of Arms (1672 to 1902). 'Scottish Documents' has a searchable index of Scottish wills and testaments in Scottish commissary and Sheriff Court registers from 1515 to 1901.[85] It is, in partnership with the NAS, the Church of Scotland and the Genealogical Society of Utah, making digital copies of the records of kirk sessions, presbyteries, synods and the General Assembly of the Church of Scotland from the sixteenth century to 1901. The NAS is also digitising the valuation rolls, first published from 1855, and the rolls for 1905 have recently been made available.

Large collections of books and periodicals have been digitised and made available through electronic resources. These focus on particular genres of publications or manuscripts from specific periods. As they do not distinguish between public accounts and private accounts, the reader should consult the chapter 'Private accounts'. Such resources include 'Making of the Modern World: Goldsmiths'-Kress Library of Economic Literature 1450–1850' which contains facsimile copies of economic and social science books. 'Early English Books Online' (EEBO) has facsimile images of books printed between 1473 and 1700.[86] For the period 1701 to 1800, there is the Eighteenth Century Collections Online (ECCO).[87] Over 700 directories, including Post Office Directories in the largest towns and cities, have been made available digitally by the National Library of Scotland through an extensive collaborative project and can be found on the Library's website.

A range of public accounts have been used to examine the migration and employment conditions of squads or groups of Irish migratory potato workers employed to harvest the potato crop in south-western and central districts of Scotland from the late nineteenth century until the 1980s.[88] These squads, employed by Scottish potato merchants, largely comprised women and teenagers recruited in the west and north-west of Ireland, notably the counties of Mayo and Donegal. During their employment, which extended from June until November each year (some workers remained over the winter months to dress or sort the crop), the workers were employed for short periods on a number of farms. While this period could be as long as six weeks in Ayrshire, where the workers started their employment, in other districts it was much shorter, from a few days to a few weeks. They were housed on the farms where they were employed in existing buildings made habitable for the workers before their arrival or in specially erected dwellings.

The workers and their migration are recorded in a wide range of government papers. They include departmental reports. The two reports of Mr Wilson Fox, employed by the Labour Department of the Board of Trade, focus on the wages, earnings and conditions of employment of agricultural labourers in the United Kingdom, including migrant agricultural workers such as the potato workers.[89] They were published in 1900 and 1905. The mode of housing the workers on the farms where they were employed and the condition of their accommodation are considered as part of one Royal Commission, the Ballantyne Commission, set up in 1912. The evidence the Commissioners gathered and published largely focuses on Ayrshire, but also includes other districts. It provides the most detailed published account until that time (1917). It also gives invaluable evidence of their working conditions and aspects of the history of their migration which is not recorded in other sources.

Scottish Office departmental papers provide detailed information on a wide range of aspects of the migrants' work and accommodation, especially from the first decade of the twentieth century, largely in the records of the former agriculture, development, and health departments, which, at various times, took an interest in them. Their papers include specially commissioned reports on the accommodation for the workers and their living conditions. One such report is a systematically undertaken survey by the Local Government Board for Scotland in 1907. Another is a special inspection of their housing in response to a series of reports submitted by an Irish Committee, the Bishops' (Gresham) Committee, which operated between 1920 and 1923 to secure better accommodation for the workers.[90] The latter records the provision, nature and condition of the housing on individual farms in the most important employment districts. After legislation was introduced in 1919 to provide a specific standard of accommodation for the workers, papers document the work of the Home and Health Department in making model byelaws, and the work of local authorities in using or adapting these to form the basis for their own byelaws. Records are also available for the making of other byelaws after legislation was revised in 1925, 1938, 1951 and 1966. These reveal the difficulties of securing better accommodation for the workers and attitudes by local authorities and farmers (who provided their accommodation) towards these legislative changes. Correspondence also survives between individuals, such as parish priests in Ireland and Scotland, and the Scottish Office departments. This reveals the interest and work of the Churches and their officers to secure better accommodation for the workers, and a wide range of evidence on their migration.[91]

As the workers were recruited in one country and employed in another, public records on them can also be found in Ireland. From the end of the World War I onwards, the Department of Taoiseach and the Department of Foreign Affairs took a periodical interest in the workers; their papers are held in the National Archives of Ireland. Some of their files hold documents that have not survived as part of the official record in Scottish Office files. These include some papers relating to the activities of the aforementioned Bishops' (Gresham) Committee, and full sets of correspondence from Irish priests, especially from the worker-recruiting districts, who attempted to put pressure on the Scottish Office to secure improvements to their accommodation.[92]

The British and Irish governments were especially concerned at the extent of migration, including seasonal migration, from Ireland, and its impact on their respective economies and societies. They commissioned, and sometimes published, a range of statistical evidence on the extent of that migration. Statistics of the numbers of Irish migratory agricultural workers in Britain and Ireland were collected and published by the Department of Agriculture and Technical Instruction for Ireland between 1880 and 1915. The Department reveals that the collection of these statistics was not without its difficulties and that the gathered statistics are not fully accurate.[93] They nevertheless provide a guide to the extent of their employment and changes to it throughout time. Parliamentary questions in both parliaments also provide further information.

Sheriff Court papers provide evidence on the potato workers and aspects of their migration at critical points in its history. The papers of a fatal accident inquiry into the deaths of ten male workers in a bothy at 37 Eastside, Kirkintilloch, on 16 September 1937 are held in the papers of Dumbarton Sheriff Court. Not only do they give an account of the tragedy, but they provide evidence on the individual workers in the squad concerned and on their social organisation and work patterns. As that inquiry made recommendations which would improve their housing provision and standards, the resultant action taken by the Scottish Office and local authorities can be charted through further files in the Home and Health Department and parliamentary debates in *Hansard*.[94]

Aspects of the employment and housing of the workers are recorded in the papers of Scottish local authorities in their main employment districts: Ayrshire, Wigtownshire, Midlothian and East Lothian. These include papers that record their work in administering the various Housing (Scotland) Acts and byelaws made under them. The annual reports of the County Medical Officer of Health provide evidence on the work of their departments and their attitudes towards the accommodation for the workers and the need to reform it, improvements to the accommodation over time, as well as information on their migration such as changes to its extent, the number of workers employed and their characters. These officials visited the accommodation each year before the workers arrived, and after they were in attendance, they gave first hand accounts of it. Their reports can be used to provide comparative evidence on their accommodation and living conditions and the migration in the different employment areas. The standard of their annual reports varies from county to county depending on the enthusiasm of the officials and their departments to improve the accommodation and their concern for the workers. The early reports of Dr John McVail, the County Medical Officer of Health for Western Stirling and Dumbarton, who had a particular interest in the workers following an outbreak of enteric fever on a farm in his area in 1897, are among the most detailed and extensive for the late nineteenth and early twentieth centuries. They give an extensive account of the accommodation at each farm where the workers were employed, together with the character of the squads that were accommodated at them.[95] An analysis of the annual reports of the local authority sanitary departments from 1945 to the early 1970s counters the view that few improvements were made to their accommodation.[96] Other records include minutes of meetings of the county council and specialist committees such as the Housing Committee. These give evidence of compliance with the Housing (Scotland) Acts and byelaws made under them and the work of a local authority in ensuring compliance. They detail their work in developing new byelaws, the difficulties of doing so, and pressure on the Scottish Office to press for legislative reform.

The workers and their migration are recorded in a wide range of newspapers, both national and provincial, in Ireland and Scotland. In Ireland, they were often featured when they left their homes, from early June onwards, to travel to Scotland, and when they arrived home after they completed their work, usually at the end of October or later if the season was a poor one. They also commented on their employment conditions. In Ayrshire, where the workers appeared as a distinct community for a period of around six to eight weeks, local newspapers such as the *Ayr Advertiser* and the *Ayrshire Post* record their arrival and presence in the area, together with any activities such as their attendance at mass. Provincial newspapers, both in Ireland and Scotland, are the most important sources for recording the largely unsuccessful attempts to unionise the workers in the early twentieth century and until 1938. National newspapers in both Ireland and Scotland also took an interest in the workers, especially at times of tragedy, such as the Kirkintilloch tragedy in September 1937, or when attention was directed to them and their accommodation at a national level. They have played an important role in developing and presenting identities for the workers.[97]

PUBLIC ACCOUNTS THAT ARE NOT BEING WIDELY UTILISED

In general, ethnological research has not made extensive use of public accounts, though other disciplines, especially those relating to general, social and economic history, have made widespread use of the wide range of public and also specific accounts (especially parliamentary papers). They have also developed their own methodologies for analysing them. Where public accounts have been used for ethnological research they have been utilised to varying extents. Some have received very little attention (such as the records of central and local government, parliamentary papers, including Royal Commissions, the Church and the various courts), while others (such as the *Statistical Accounts of Scotland*) have received a significant amount, and are regarded as standard works for particular periods. Even particular series of accounts have received varying amounts of attention. Thus, while the *OSA* and *NSA* are widely used and are regarded as standard works, little use has been made of the *TSA*. Likewise, neither Sir John Sinclair's *Analysis* of the *OSA* nor his *General Report* has been widely consulted. The county agricultural reports have also received less attention than the *OSA*. Indeed, the Scottish county surveys have been ignored by comparison to the English ones which have been widely used. Yet, the Scottish reports include some of the best ones to be produced, with many also being published at a later date than those on the English counties.

Limited use has been made of some public accounts because they are difficult to understand without a knowledge of the workings of central and local government and the institutions in Scotland. Some of their papers are written in a specialist manner and language, and training may be required to understand their function or the terminology in them. They may also be difficult to work with, either as a result of the volume of papers or the way they have been organised. Thus, many of the criminal records are not indexed and are therefore difficult to access.[98]

The evidence which public accounts can provide has not always been recognised as being valuable for ethnological research and may be thought to be of value only to other disciplines. This is especially noted for some specialist records, such as those created by the Church and the courts. Blair-Imrie suggests that eighteenth-century Sheriff Court records are 'wonderful' documents for local history research. They can also be successfully used for ethnological research. The NRS has recognised the value of a wide range of records of the courts in Scotland for research on individuals, their communities and values. It recognises that 'the records of the Commissary courts ... and sheriff courts ... contain a vast amount of material on all aspects of local history'. It observes that precognitions in the Lord Advocate's department 'provide a snapshot of the local community': 'they are a wonderfully rich source of information about individuals, economic conditions, contemporary attitudes and even language'.[99] The Commissary Court records, especially testaments, are:

> an extremely valuable source for family history, but also for local, social and economic history ... For the early modern period there is no other record group which gives such an all round picture of the lives of ordinary Scots, their standard of living, business and personal contacts and patterns of agriculture.[100]

Public accounts have not been used to a great extent for ethnological research as researchers have not always been aware that they use a wide range of methodologies and types of evidence that are used and found in other sources that are more traditionally associated with ethnological research. Central and local government departments have gathered a wide range of evidence to enable them to develop their policies, administrative schemes and legislation to deal with a range of social, cultural and economic issues and problems. This includes oral evidence collected during the course of meetings, consultations and also as part of the work of Royal Commissions, especially in the nineteenth and early twentieth centuries. As has been demonstrated in this chapter, commissioners drew much of their evidence from specially organised evidence sessions in which they sometimes also used questionnaires. Questionnaires are widely used for gathering evidence in countries such as Ireland and Sweden, and this type of approach could be developed to analyse the evidence gathered by commissioners. In their work, civil servants and other officials have undertaken field investigations, sometimes as part of their routine work, or to investigate particular concerns. If they were assessing compliance with particular legislation, or investigating particular points, they may provide systematic evidence which is also available from a number of different geographical areas.

FUTURE DIRECTIONS FOR RESEARCH

Public accounts have great potential to provide a great deal of evidence for ethnological research and to shape future directions and should therefore be more fully exploited. There is a need to recognise the value of these accounts for research and the types of information that they can provide. Researchers also need to appreciate that some of the public accounts use methodologies such as questionnaires, oral evidence and field observation that are already used by ethnologists.

Public accounts could be used within existing ethnological approaches. They include material collected systematically, often over an extended period of time, and frequently at all administrative areas throughout Scotland, as well as more detailed studies in particular areas. Therefore they provide a useful resource for comparative research, and can be used to highlight differences in social, economic and cultural circumstances between parishes, counties and regions. They can allow the researcher to focus on the traditional areas of ethnological investigation, the rural areas and also the outlying areas such as the Western Isles and the Northern Isles. But they also enable the researcher to investigate urban communities, a more recent focus for ethnological research in Scotland.

Public accounts can be used to study a very broad range of subjects, many of which are considered traditional areas for ethnological examination. Such subjects include settlement and dwelling, livelihood and household support, communications and trade, the community, social control, historical tradition, religious tradition, and sports and pastimes. They can be used to broaden and deepen our understanding of these areas. For example, an examination of divorce court records may be used to 'reveal the lives, loves, and lusts of men and women of every social class during a period when frankness rather than reticence was the rule'.[101]

Public records could be used to help to explain a fundamental concept of ethnology: 'explaining not only tradition but also change, since the one cannot be understood without the other'.[102] Indeed, such records have not always been considered as being of use for ethnological research, a significant omission, especially for undertaking research that focuses on the late nineteenth and twentieth centuries. Thus, although James Porter lists a number of factors which bring about change to traditions – such as emigration and immigration, economic upheaval, the impinging of the global on the local, demand for easier and quicker communication, the expansion of mental horizons by technological means – he does not mention the role of central or local governments, which can have a significant impact.[103] The increased use of the records of Scottish Government departments – also other administrative units – which have shaped many aspects of Scottish life, will provide an increased understanding for the rationale behind the changes they have made and may be able to chart how, when, and at what rate, they took place.

Public records could also be used to develop a number of areas of ethnological research relating to the individual and the world they inhabit. These include: the experience of the individual or aspects of their life, values and material world; the existence of 'subcultures, with standards and goals quite different from the established consensus';[104] the psychological values of subcultures; the place and role of the individual and their community, together with the values and attitudes and particular forms of behaviour; the personal and group identities of particular occupational groups or classes, as revealed in official papers; the creation and presentation of personal testimony to official investigations; the interface between the individual and official rules and regulations.

The increasing availability of online resources (such as search tools and facsimile collections of particular sources) is already transforming research. These have enabled research projects to be developed which would not have been possible, or which would have been extremely laborious in the past without these resources. They have already made it easier to identify sources for investigation and to suggest records which may not have in the past been considered as means of evidence. They have made specific types of records more accessible. Thus, whereas a researcher had to have some knowledge of the Scottish Office to identify where to search for relevant papers in guides to official documents, a search on the NAS (NRS) website for a particular topic will identify and bring up all records, irrespective of their provenance and their type. They may be able to provide a fuller understanding of particular subjects which have already received some attention or to suggest areas of research which have not been previously considered. Electronic resources which enable the text of documents, either published or archival, to be searched across a wide number of books, can make links to other ones. Such resources will also make it easier to undertake the systematic collection and also analysis of material, and to provide a greater understanding of local, regional and national patterns throughout Scotland. For example, the digitisation of the *OSA* and the *NSA* enables research to be undertaken on a particular topic within a particular geographical area, or have more extensive examination to show regional differences.

NOTES

1 Kirkpatrick, 1983, 1041.
2 *Fourth Statistical Account of East Lothian*, 2003–09; Cox, 2004, 19–20; Midlothian Council, Midlothian Library Service, 2001.
3 Withrington and Grant, 1983, xiii, xiv, xv.
4 Sinclair, 1831, I, 64–70.
5 Withrington and Grant, 1983, xviii.
6 Withrington and Grant, 1983, xxv.
7 Withrington and Grant, 1983, xii, xxi, xxiv.
8 Sinclair, 1831, I, 1; Steven, 1995, 18.
9 Gibson, 1995, 3.
10 Gibson, 1995, 6; Hamilton, 1960, 13.
11 Cameron, 2007, 37; Gibson, 1995, 3.
12 Gibson, 1995, 3; Leeming, 1963, 34; Steven, 1995, 14; Withrington and Grant, 1983, xxvi.
13 Cameron, 2007, 31; Watson, 2004, 100–22.
14 Sinclair, 1796, 47; Withrington and Grant, 1983, xlvi.
15 Sinclair, 1796, 47–49.
16 Sinclair, 1796, 47.
17 Naismith, 1806, vi; Sinclair, 1796, 54.
18 Fenton, 1999, xii, 18; Mitchison, 1962, 153.
19 Sinclair, I, 1813, 3, 9.
20 Mitchison, 1962, 210.
21 Sinclair, I, 1813, vi, 4.
22 Sinclair, 1831, 3.
23 Sinclair, 1831, 2.
24 Sinclair, 1831, 1, 2.
25 Mitchison, 1962, 210.
26 Hutchison, 1996, 46, 50.
27 Milne, 1957; Gibson, 1985.
28 Grassie, 1983; Grant, 1987, 95–9; Mackay, 1995; Mackay, 1996, 141–73; Mather, 1988, 39–50.
29 Butcher, 1991, 11, 13.
30 Butcher, 1991; Ollé, 1973.
31 Ford and Ford, 1953; Ford and Ford, III, 1951-61; Ford, 1970; Marshallsay and Smith, 1979.
32 HMSO, 1948.
33 HMSO, 1967.
34 Ollé, 1973, 21.
35 Ollé, 1973, 21, 54.
36 Ollé, 1973, 37, 41.
37 Cameron, 1986, 127–9.
38 *PP*, 1884, XXXIII–XXXVI, C.3980, I, 2, 3.
39 MacPhail, 1972–4, 454.
40 Cameron, 1986, xi; Hunter, 2000, especially chapter 7; MacPhail, 1972–4, 435–72.
41 Whetstone, 1981.
42 Butcher, 1983, 1991.
43 Stair Society, 1936.

44 Bigwood, 2004, 27–38; Donnachie, 1995, 85-92; Blair-Imrie, 2002, 23–30; Inglis, 2004, 55–68; Longmore, 2004, 39–54; Sanderson, 2008, 15–26; Stewart, 2001, 25–35; Whyte and Whyte, 1986, 4–10.

45 NAS, Guides, <www.nas.gov.uk/guides/default.asp> [accessed 7 February 2013].

46 Survey of Scottish Witchcraft, <www.shc.ed.ac.uk/Research/witches/> [accessed 7 February 2013].

47 Holmes, 2001–2, 25–38; Moody, 1986, 24.

48 NLS, Newspapers Collections, <www.nls.uk/collections/newspapers/ resources.html> [accessed 7 February 2013].

49 Cox, 1999, 12; Mackenzie, 1994, 18.

50 Holmes, 2004–5, 32–55; Lockhart, 1978, 96–102; Lockhart, 1980, 35–43; Noble, 2004–5, 103–5; Pedersen, 2002, 159–66; Pryke, 1989, 52–67.

51 For example, Gibson, 2007, 149–53, 162–3.

52 Skelton, 1967, 3.

53 Skelton, 1967, 3–16; Whittington and Gibson, 1986.

54 Parry, 1975, 15–26.

55 Cox, 1999, 10.

56 <http://digital.nls.uk/directories/> [accessed 7 February 2013].

57 McAlpine, 1999–2000, 69–84; McAlpine, 1999, 76–88.

58 Scottish Record Office, 1994a, b; Scottish Record Office, 1995a, b; Scottish Record Office, 1996.

59 Society of Archivists, <www.archives.org.uk/> [accessed 7 February 2013]; Scottish Records Association, <www.scottishrecordsassociation.org/> [accessed 7 February 2013].

60 Inglis, 2004, 55–68; Young, 1992, 143–51.

61 Bell, 2002, 72–84; Dorson, 1971, 147–82; Flett and Cripps, 1988, 18–35; Gray, 1962, 145–77; Lindsay, 1997, 61–8; Lockhart, 1997, 34–9; Mather, 1995, 127–31.

62 Barron, 1892; Dickinson, 1937; Levitt, 1988; Levitt, 1992; Mackay, 1896; Malcolm, 1931.

63 SCAN, <www.scan.org.uk> [accessed 7 February 2013].

64 NAS, About the National Archives of Scotland, <www.nas.gov.uk/about/ default.asp> [accessed 7 February 2013].

65 NLS, Guide to Manuscript Collections, <www.nls.uk/catalogues/online/cnmi/ index.cfm> [accessed 7 February 2013].

66 The British Newspaper Archive, <www.britishnewspaperarchive.co.uk/> [accessed 7 February 2013]; North, 1989.

67 NLS, Newspapers Collections, <www.nls.uk/collections/newspapers/indexes/ index.cfm> [accessed 7 February 2013].

68 Anderson, 1997, 9–15.

69 SCAN, <www.scan.org.uk> [accessed 7 February 2013]; Steward, 1996, 90–7; Lawson, 1986, 159–61; Highland Archive Services, <www.highlandarchives.org.uk/> [accessed 7 February 2013]; Wilbraham, 2000, 83–93.

70 Copac, <http://copac.ac.uk/> [accessed 7 February 2013].

71 NAS, <www.nas.gov.uk/> [accessed 7 February 2013].

72 NLS, Online Resources, <www.nls.uk/catalogues/resources> [accessed 7 February 2013].

73 English Short Title Catalogue website, <http://estc.bl.uk/> [accessed 7 February 2013].

74 SCAN website, <www.scan.org.uk> [accessed 7 February 2013]; ScotlandsPeople: <www.scotlandspeople.gov.uk/> [accessed 7 February 2013]

75 Statistical Accounts of Scotland, <www.//edina.ac.uk/statacc/> [accessed 7 February 2013].

76 The British Newspaper Archive, <http://www.britishnewspaperarchive.co.uk/> [accessed 7 February 2013].

77 Onlinenewspapers.com, <www.onlinenewspapers.com/scotland.htm> [accessed 7 February 2013]; The Scotsman Digital Archive, <www.archive.scotsman.com> [accessed 7 February 2013].

78 Records of the Parliaments of Scotland to 1707, <www.rps.ac.uk> [accessed 7 February 2013].

79 British Official Publications Collaborative Reader Information Service (BOPCRIS), <www.southampton.ac.uk/library/ldu/parl18c.html> [accessed 7 February 2013].

80 House of Commons Parliamentary Papers, <http://parlipapers.chadwyck.co.uk/marketing/index.jsp> [accessed 7 February 2013].

81 Scottish Parliament, < www.scottish.parliament.uk/> [accessed 7 February 2013].

82 Scottish Government, <www.//home.scotland.gov.uk/home> [accessed 7 February 2013].

83 Office of Public Sector Information, <www.opsi.gov.uk/> [accessed 7 February 2013].

84 The UK Statute Law Database, <www.statutelaw.gov.uk/> [accessed 7 February 2013].

85 Scottish Documents, <www.scottishdocuments.com/> [accessed 7 February 2013]; ScotlandsPeople, <www.scotlandspeople.gov.uk/> [accessed 7 February 2013].

86 Early English Books Online, available by subscription at: <www.eebo.chadwyck.com/home> [accessed 7 February 2013].

87 ECCO, <www.gale.cengage.co.uk/product-highlights/history/eighteenth-century-collections-online.aspx> [accessed 7 February 2013].

88 For example, Holmes, 2005; Holmes, 2000, 71–82.

89 Fox, 1900; Fox, 1905.

90 Holmes, 1998a, 57–74.

91 Holmes, 2000b, 31–57.

92 Holmes, 1998a, 57–74.

93 Holmes, 2005, 50.

94 Holmes, 1995–6, 57–75.

95 Holmes, 1998b, 1–16.

96 Holmes, 1999, 45–58.

97 Holmes, 2000a, 207–29; Holmes, 2004–5, 32–55.

98 NAS, Guides, Crime and Criminals, <www.nas.gov.uk/guides/crime.asp> [accessed 7 February 2013]

99 NAS, 2008; NAS, Guides, Sheriff Court Records, <www.nas.gov.uk/guides/sheriffCourt.asp> [accessed 7 February 2013]

100 NAS, Guides, Commissary Court, <www.nas.gov.uk/guides/commissaryCourt.asp> [accessed 7 February 2013].

101 Leneman, 1998, 2.

102 Porter, 1999, 11–12.

103 Porter, 1999, 12.

104 Moody, 1986, 43.

BIBLIOGRAPHY AND FURTHER READING

Adams, I H and Timperly, L R. *Descriptive List of Plans in the Scottish Record Office*, 4 vols, Edinburgh, 1966–88.

Anderson, P D. The evolution of local authority archives 1960–90, *Scottish Local History*, 39 (1997), 9–15.

Annual Report of the Keeper of the Records of Scotland, Edinburgh, 1999–.

Annual Report of the Keeper of the Records of Scotland for 1972, Edinburgh, 1972 (list of Court of Session papers).

Archives (British Records Association), 1949–.

Barron, D G, ed. *The Court Book of the Barony of Urie in Kincardineshire 1604–1747*, Scottish History Society, 1st series, no. 12, Edinburgh, 1892.

Bell, A R. Sources for Scottish labour history in the Manuscripts Division of the National Library of Scotland, *Scottish Labour History*, 37 (2002), 72–84.

Bigwood, F. The courts of Argyll, 1664–1825, *Scottish Archives*, 10 (2004), 27–38.

Blair-Imrie, H. Sheriff court files, *Scottish Local History*, 54 (2002), 23–30.

Brown, C G. *Religion and Society in Scotland Since 1707*, Edinburgh, 1997.

Brown, C G. *The Social History of Religion in Scotland since 1739*, London, 1987.

Butcher, D. *Official Publications in Britain* [1983], 2nd edn, London, 1991.

Cameron, A C. *Go Listen to the Crofters: The Napier Commission and Crofting a Century Ago*, Stornoway, 1986.

Cameron, E A. The idle dream of James G Kyd: The Third Statistical Account of Scotland, 1944–1992, *Scottish Local History*, 69 (2007), 31–8.

Coventry, A. *Discourses on Agriculture and Rural Economy*, Edinburgh, 1808.

Cowan, E. *The Newspaper in Scotland: A Study of its Expansion, 1815–60*, Glasgow, 1946.

Cox, M. The East Lothian Fourth Statistical Account from 1945 to 2000, *Scottish Local History*, 60 (2004), 19–20.

Cox, M. *Exploring Scottish History. With a Directory of Resource Centres for Scottish Local and National History in Scotland*, 2nd edn, Edinburgh, 1999.

Dickinson, W C, ed. *Barony Court Book of Carnwath, 1523–1542*, Scottish History Society, 3rd series, no. 29, Edinburgh, 1937.

Donnachie, I. Profiling criminal offences: the evidence of the Lord Advocate's papers during the first half of the nineteenth century in Scotland, *Scottish Archives*, 1 (1995), 85–92.

Dorson, R M. Sources for the traditional history of the Scottish Highlands and Western Isles, *Journal of the Folklore Institute*, 8:2–3 (1971), 147–82.

Drummond, A L and Bulloch, J. *The Scottish Church 1688–1843: The Age of the Moderates*, Edinburgh, 1973a.

Drummond, A L and Bulloch, J. *The Church in Victorian Scotland, 1843–1874*, Edinburgh, 1973b.

Duncan, A G M. *Green's Glossary of Scottish Legal Terms*, 3rd edn, Edinburgh, 1992.

Fenton, A. *Scottish Country Life*, East Linton, 1999.

Ferguson, J P S. *Directory of Scottish Newspapers*, Edinburgh, 1984.

Flett, I and Cripps, J. Documentary sources. In Lynch, M, Spearman, M and Stell, G, eds, *The Scottish Medieval Town*, Edinburgh, 1988, 18–35.

Ford, P and Ford, G. *Select List of British Parliamentary Papers 1900–1954*, 3 vols, Oxford, 1951–61.

Ford, P and Ford, G. *Select List of British Parliamentary Papers 1833–1899*, Oxford, 1953.

Ford, P J and Ford, P. *Select List of British Parliamentary Papers 1955–1964*, Dublin, 1970.

Fourth Statistical Account of East Lothian, 7 vols, ed. S Baker, Haddington, 2003–09.

Geddes, A. Scotland's 'Statistical accounts' of parish, county and nation: c.1790–1825 and 1835–1845, *Scottish Studies*, 3 (1959), 17–38.

Gibson, J A. *The New Statistical Account of Scotland, 1834–45: correct publication dates of the parish accounts, *The Scottish Naturalist*, 107 (1995), 3–52.

Gibson, J S. *The Thistle and the Crown: A History of the Scottish Office*, Edinburgh, 1985.

Gibson, R. *The Scottish Countryside: Its Changing Face, 1700–2000*, Edinburgh, 2007.

Grant, J S. Government agencies and the Highlands since 1945, *Scottish Geographical Magazine*, 103:2 (1987), 95–9.

Grassie, J. *Highland Experiment: The Story of the Highlands and Islands Development Board*, Aberdeen, 1983.

Gray, M. Settlement in the Highlands, 1750–1950: the documentary and the written record, *Scottish Studies*, 6 (1962), 145–77.

Hamilton, H. *The Third Statistical Account of Scotland: Aberdeenshire*, Glasgow, 1960.

Hancock, P D. *A Bibliography of Works Relating to Scotland, 1916–1950*, Edinburgh, 1959.

Harper, N. *Press and Journal: The First 250 Years 1748–1998*, Aberdeen, 1997.

HMSO. *Index to Local and Personal Acts 1808–1947*, London, 1967.

HMSO. *Public General Statutes Affecting Scotland 1707–1847*, 3 vols, London, 1848.

Holmes, H. The Kirkintilloch bothy fire tragedy of September 16, 1937: an examination of the incident and the resulting legislation, *Review of Scottish Culture*, 9 (1995–6), 57–75.

Holmes, H. Improving the housing conditions of the Irish migratory potato workers in Scotland: the work of the Bishops' (Gresham) Committee, 1920–1923, *Rural History, Economy, Society, Culture*, 9:1 (1998a), 57–74.

Holmes, H. Dr John McVail and the improvement of the housing of Irish migratory potato harvesters in Scotland, 1897–c1913, *Ulster Folklife*, 44 (1998b), 1–16.

Holmes, H. Sanitary inspectors and the reform of housing conditions for Irish migratory potato workers in Scotland from 1945 to the 1970s, *Saothar: Journal of the Irish Labour History Society*, 24 (1999), 45–58.

Holmes, H. Organising the Irish migratory potato workers: the efforts in the early twentieth century, *Rural History, Economy, Society, Culture*, 11:2 (2000a), 207–29.

Holmes, H. 'Unwearied investigations and interminable correspondence': the Churches and clerical work in improving housing conditions for Irish migratory potato workers in Scotland, *Scottish Economic and Social History*, 20:1 (2000b), 31–57.

Holmes, H. Viewing an 'Underworld': sources of evidence for Irish migratory potato workers in early twentieth century Scotland, *Scottish Archives*, 6 (2000c), 71–82.

Holmes, H. *'As Good as a Holiday': Potato Harvesting in the Lothians from 1870 to the Present*, East Linton, 2000d.

Holmes, H. Scottish agricultural newspapers and journals and the industrialisation of agriculture, 1800–1880, *Folk Life: Journal of Ethnological Studies*, 40 (2001–02), 25–38.

Holmes, H. Constructing identities of the Irish migratory potato workers in Scotland, *Folk Life: Journal of Ethnological Studies*, 43 (2004–5), 32–55.

Holmes, H. *Tattie Howkers: Irish Potato Workers in Ayrshire*, Ayrshire Monographs 31, Ayrshire Archaeological and Natural History Society, Ayr, 2005.

Holmes, H and MacDonald, F, eds. *Scottish Life and Society. A Compendium of Scottish Ethnology, Volume 14: Bibliography*, East Linton, 2003.

Hutchison, I G. Government. In Devine, T M and Finlay, R J, eds, *Scotland in the 20th Century*, Edinburgh, 1996, 46–63.

Hunter, J. *The Making of the Crofting Community*, Edinburgh, 2000.

Index to Local and Personal Acts 1808–1947, Edinburgh, 1949.

Index to Local and Personal Acts 1948–1966, Edinburgh, 1967.

Inglis, B. Scottish testamentary inventories: a neglected source for the study of Scottish agriculture – illustrated by the case of Dunblane, 1660–1740, *Scottish Archives*, 10 (2004), 55–68.

Kames, H H and Tytler, A F. *The Decisions of the Court of Session from its First Institution to the Present Time*, 4 vols, Edinburgh, 1791–7.

Kirkpatrick, E M. *Chambers 20th Century Dictionary*, Edinburgh, 1983.

Lawson, A B. Highland Regional Archive, *Northern Scotland*, 7 (1986), 159–61.

Leeming, F A. Social accounting and the old statistical account, *Scottish Geographical Magazine*, 79:1 (1963), 34–48.

Leneman, L. *Fit for Heroes? Land Settlement in Scotland after World War 1*, Aberdeen, 1989.

Leneman, L. *Alienated Affections. The Scottish Experience of Divorce and Separation, 1684–1830*, Edinburgh, 1998.

Levitt, I, ed. *Government and Social Conditions in Scotland, 1845–1919*, Scottish History Society, 5th series, no. 1, Edinburgh, 1988.

Levitt, I, ed. *The Scottish Office: Depression and Reconstruction 1919–1959*, Scottish History Society, 5th series, no. 5, Edinburgh, 1992.

Levitt, I. Scottish papers submitted to the cabinet, 1917–45: a guide to records held at the Public Record Office and National Archives of Scotland, *Scottish Economic and Social History*, 19:1 (1999), 18–54.

Lindsay, A J. Sources for the study of education in the Scottish Record Office, *Scottish Archives*, 3 (1997), 61–8.

Lockhart, D. The planned villages of Aberdeenshire: the evidence from newspaper advertisements, *Scottish Geographical Magazine*, 94 (1978), 96–102.

Lockhart, D. Sources for studies of migration to estate villages in north east Scotland, *Local Historian*, 14 (1980), 35–43.

Lockhart, D. Nuts and bolts: planned villages – a review of sources, *Scottish Local History*, 39 (1997), 34–9.

Longmore, B. High Court of Justiciary databases: a 'solemn path' through crime, *Scottish Archives*, 10 (2004), 39–54.

McAlpine, K. 'Those having business there': fairs in Scottish almanac lists, *Scottish Studies*, 33 (1999), 76–88.

McAlpine, K. Fair lists in Scottish almanacs, *Review of Scottish Culture*, 12 (1999–2000), 69–84.

Mackay, D. The Congested Districts Board of Ireland and Scotland, *Northern Scotland*, 16 (1996), 141–73.

Mackay, D. *Scotland's Rural Land Use Agencies*, Edinburgh, 1995.

Mackay, W, ed. *Extracts from the Presbytery Records of Inverness and Dingwall, 1638–88*, Scottish History Society, 1st series, no. 24, Edinburgh, 1896

MacKenzie, A. *NEWSPLAN: Report of the NEWSPLAN Project in Scotland*, London, 1994.

MacPhail, I M M. The Napier Commission, *Transactions of the Gaelic Society of Inverness*, 48 (1972–4), 435–72.

Malcolm, C A, ed. *The Minutes of the Justices of the Peace for Lanarkshire, 1707–1723*, Scottish History Society, 3rd series, no. 16, Edinburgh, 1931.

Marshallsay, D and Smith, J H. *Ford List of British Parliamentary Papers, 1965–1974*, London, 1979.

Mason, A K. Explorations in the use of sources. The importance of sasines for Scottish history: an analysis of a register from the Royal Burgh of Banff, 1768–1784, *Northern Scotland*, 14 (1994), 113–33.

Mather, A S. Government agencies and land development in the Scottish Highlands: a centenary survey, *Northern Scotland*, 8 (1988), 39–50.

Mather, A S. Rural land occupancy in Scotland: resources for research, *Scottish Geographical Magazine*, 111:2 (1995), 127–31.

Midlothian Council, Midlothian Library Service. *The Midlothian 2000 CD-ROM: A Fourth Statistical Account of Midlothian*, Loanhead, 2001.

Milne, D. *The Scottish Office, and Other Scottish Government Departments*, London, 1957.

Mitchell, A and Cash, C G. *A Contribution to the Bibliography of Scottish Topography*, 2 vols, Edinburgh, 1917.

Mitchison, R. *Agricultural Sir John: The Life of Sir John Sinclair of Ulbster 1754–1835*, London, 1962.

Moody, D. *Scottish Family History*, London, 1988.

Moody, D. *Scottish Local History: An Introductory Guide*, London, 1986.

Moody, D. *Scottish Towns: A Guide for Local Historians*, London, 1992.

Moore, J N. *The Historical Cartography of Scotland: A Guide to the Literature of Scottish Maps and Mapping Prior to the Ordnance Survey*, 2nd rev edn, Aberdeen, 1991.

Morris, A. *Scotland's Paper: The Scotsman 1817–1992*, Edinburgh, 1992.

Naismith, J. *General View of the Agriculture of Clydesdale*, London, 1806.

NAS. *Guide to the National Archives of Scotland*, Edinburgh, 1996.

NAS. *Local History*, 2008 (leaflet).

NAS. *Tracing your Scottish Ancestors: A Guide to Ancestry Research in the National Archives of Scotland*, 5th edn, Edinburgh, 2009.

New Statistical Account of Scotland, Edinburgh, 1835–1845.

Noble, H W. The role of newspaper advertisements in the spread of the availability of dental treatment in Scotland, *Review of Scottish Culture*, 17 (2004–5), 103–5.

North, J S, ed. *The Waterloo Directory of Scottish Newspapers and periodicals, 1800–1900*, 2 vols, Waterloo, Ontario, 1989.

Northern Scotland (Centre for Scottish Studies, University of Aberdeen), 1972–

Ollé, J G. *An Introduction to British Government Publications*, 2nd edn, London, 1973.

Ó Súilleabháin, S. *Handbook of Irish Folklore*, Hatbro, Pa, 1963.

PP, 1870, XIII, C.221: *Commission on the Employment of Children, Young Persons, and Women in Agriculture*.

PP, 1884, XXXIII–XXXVI, C.3980: *Report of the Commissioners of Inquiry into the Conditions of the Crofters and Cottars in the Highlands and Islands of Scotland* [Napier Commission].

PP, 1900, Cd.346: *Report by Mr Wilson Fox on the Wages and Earnings of Agricultural Labourers in the United Kingdom*.

PP, 1905, XCVII, Cd.2376: *Board of Trade, Labour Department, Second Report by Mr Wilson Fox on the Wages, Earnings, and Conditions of Employment of Agricultural Labourers in the United Kingdom, with Statistical Tables and Charts*.

Parry, M L. County maps as historical sources: a sequence of surveys in south-east Scotland, *Scottish Studies*, 19 (1975), 15–26.

Pedersen, S. Within their sphere? Women correspondents to Aberdeen daily newspapers 1900–1914, *Northern Scotland*, 22 (2002), 159–66.

Porter, J. Aims, theory and method in the ethnology of Northern Scotland, *Northern Scotland*, 18 (1999), 1–25.

Powell, W R. *Local History from Blue Books. A Select List of the Sessional Papers of the House of Commons*, London, 1962.

Pryke, S. A study of the Edinburgh furnishing trade taken from contemporary press notices, 1708–1790, *Regional Furniture*, 3 (1989), 52–67.

Public General Statutes Affecting Scotland 1707–1847, 3 vols, Edinburgh, 1848.

Rayner, P, Leneman, B and Parker, G. *Handlist of Records for the Study of Crime in Early Modern Scotland (to 1747)*, London, 1982.

Records of the Scottish Church History Society (Scottish Church History Society), 1926–.

The Register of the Privy Council [1545–1689], 36 vols, Edinburgh, 1877–1970.

Review of George Robertson's A General View of the Agriculture of the County of Midlothian, 1795, *The Farmer's Magazine*, 3 (1802), 86–96.

Review of James Robertson's A General View of the Agriculture of the County of Perth, 1799, *The Monthly Review*, 33 (1800), 134–40.

Richmond, L and Turnton, A. *The Brewing Industry: A Guide to Historical Records*, Manchester, 1990.

Ritchie, L A. *The Shipbuilding Industry: A Guide to Historical Records*, Manchester, 1992.

Robertson, G. *General View of the Agriculture of Kincardine*, London, 1810.

Sanderson, M H B. Lives of the Scottish cottars, 1585–1620: the evidence of their testaments, *Review of Scottish Culture*, 20 (2008), 15–26.

Scott-Moncreiff, W G, ed. *The Records of the Proceedings of the Justiciary Court, Edinburgh, 1661–1678*, 2 vols, Scottish History Society, 1st series, 48 and 49, Edinburgh, 1905.

Scottish Archives: The Journal of the Scottish Records Association (Scottish Records Association), 1995–.

Scottish Record Office. *The Emigrants: Historical Background, List of Documents, Extracts and Facsimiles*, Edinburgh, 1994a.

Scottish Record Office. *The Scots in Canada: Historical Background, List of Documents, Extracts and Facsimiles*, Edinburgh, 1994b.

Scottish Record Office. *Poor Relief in Scotland: Historical Background, List of Documents, Extracts and Facsimiles*, Edinburgh, 1995a.

Scottish Record Office. *Crofters: Historical Background, List of Documents, Extracts and Facsimiles*, Edinburgh, 1995b.

Scottish Record Office. *Guide to the National Archives of Scotland*, Edinburgh, 1996.

Shaw, G and Tipper, A. *British Directories: A Bibliography and Guide to Directories Published in England and Wales (1850–1950) and Scotland (1773–1950)*, Leicester, 1997.

Sinclair, C. *Tracing Scottish Local History: A Guide to Local History Research in the Scottish Record Office*, Edinburgh, 1994.

Sinclair, J. *Account of the Origin of the Board of Agriculture, and its Progress for Three Years After its Establishment*, London, 1796.

Sinclair, J. *History of the Origin and Progress of the Statistical Account of Scotland*, n.p., 1798.

Sinclair, J. Address to the Board of Agriculture, by Sir John Sinclair, Baronet, the President, at the conclusion of the session, on the 7th of June, 1808, *The Farmer's Magazine*, 9 (1808), 336–46.

Sinclair, J. Address to the Board of Agriculture, on the progress made by that institution in promoting the improvement of the county, on Tuesday the 12th of June, 1810, by Sir John Sinclair, Bart, the President, *The Farmer's Magazine*, 11 (1810), 337–47.

Sinclair, J. *General Report of the Agricultural State, and Political Circumstances of Scotland*, 3 vols, Edinburgh, 1813.

Sinclair, J. *Analysis of the Statistical Account of Scotland; With a General View of the History of that Country, and Discussions on Some Important Branches of Political Economy*, 2 vols, Edinburgh, 1831.

Sinclair, W M. Sir John Sinclair, founder and President of the First Board of Agriculture, *Journal of the Royal Agricultural Society of England*, 3rd series, 7 (1896), 1–21.

Skelton, R A. The military survey of Scotland 1747–1755, *Scottish Geographical Magazine*, 83 (1967), 3–16.

Stair Society. *An Introductory Survey of the Sources and Literature of Scots Law*, Edinburgh, 1936.

(Old) Statistical Account of Scotland, Edinburgh, 1791–99.

Steven, M. *Parish Life in Eighteenth-Century Scotland: A Review of the Old Statistical Account*, Dalkeith, 1995.

Steward, R. Highland Regional Archive: the first five years, *Scottish Archives*, 2 (1996), 90–7.

Stewart, M M. 'A policeman's lot': Police records in Dumfries and Galloway, 1856–1950, *Scottish Archives*, 7 (2001), 25–35.

Stevenson, D and Stevenson, W B. *Scottish Texts and Calendars: An Analytical Guide to Serial Publications*, London and Edinburgh, 1987.

Third Statistical Account of Scotland, Edinburgh, 1944–92.

Tierney, J H. *Early Glasgow Newspapers, Periodicals and Directories*, Glasgow, 1934.

Torrance, D R. *Scottish Trades and Professions: A Selected Bibliography [Including a Summary of Scottish Directories]*, Scottish Association of Family History Societies, 1991.

Walker, D M. *The Scottish Legal System*, 8th revised edn, Edinburgh, 2001.

Watson, M. Using the Third Statistical Account of Scotland to expose a major gap in Scottish historiography, *Contemporary British History*, 18 (2004), 100–22.

Whetstone, A E. *Scottish County Government in the Eighteenth and Nineteenth Centuries*, Edinburgh, 1981.

Whyte, I D and Whyte, K A. Commissary court testaments: a neglected source for Scottish local history, *Local Historian*, 17 (1986), 4–10.

Whittington, G and Gibson, A J S. *The Military Survey of Scotland, 1747–1755: A Critique*, Norwich, 1986.

Wilbraham, K. Ayrshire Archives, *Scottish Archives: The Journal of the Scottish Records Association*, 6 (2000), 83–93.

Withrington, D J, with additional introductory material by Grant, I R. *The Statistical Account of Scotland 1791–1799*, Wakefield, 1983.

Young, C. Scottish sequestrations and the role of women in the small firm: an assessment of a new source for women's history, *Journal of Society of Archivists*, 13:2 (1992), 143–51.

ONLINE RESOURCES

The British Newspaper Archive,

18C British Official Parliamentary Publications, <www.southampton.ac.uk/library/ldu/parl18c.html>

Copac Library Catalogue, <http://copac.ac.uk/>

Early English Books Online, <www.eebo.chadwyck.com/home>

English Short Title Catalogue, <http://estc.bl.uk/>

House of Commons Parliamentary Papers, <http://parlipapers.chadwyck.co.uk/marketing/index.jsp>

National Archives of Scotland,

National Library of Scotland,

Nineteenth-Century Short Title Catalogue, <http://nstc.chadwyck.com/>

RCAHMS, <www.rcahms.gov.uk/search.html>

Records of the Parliaments of Scotland to 1707, <http://www.rps.ac.uk/>

ScotlandsPeople,

Scotsman Digital Archive, <www.archive.scotsman.com>

Scottish Archive Network, <www.scan.org.uk>

Scottish Documents,

Scottish Government, <www.//home.scotland.gov.uk/home>

Scottish Parliament,

Scottish Post Office Directories, <http://digital.nls.uk/directories/>

Statistical Accounts of Scotland, <www.//edina.ac.uk/statacc/>

20 Literary Sources

VALENTINA BOLD

Being little conversant in books, and far less in men and manners, the local circumstances on which some of my pieces are founded, may not be unentertaining to you. It was from a conversation that I had with an old woman, from Lochaber, of the name of Cameron, on which I founded the story of *Glengyle*, a ballad; and likewise the ground-plot of *The Happy Swains*, a pastoral, in four parts.[1]

INTRODUCTION

As James Hogg's statement suggests, folklore is a key agent in the making of Scottish literature, and 'written evidence' of the traditional – whether in poetry, novels or short stories – is the product of external and internal acts of dialogue. Memories of personal and communal experiences are translated into print through creative acts; the reader plays an active role, too, in receiving and interpreting these. Using written evidence, then, should be seen as a dynamic process, as evidence shifts between oral and literary contexts (in a way analogous to perform-ance), showing the same processes of continuity, variation and selection found in oral transmission.

In the past, ideas around 'authenticity' led to anxieties as to whether writers could be trusted as transmitters of the traditional (a classic example being responses to James Macpherson's Ossianic translations); whether, in effect, they were primary or secondary sources. This was due, no doubt, to readers' difficulty in telling whether creative writers reflect tradition in a 'photographic' way, or reimagine it for fictitious or poetic ends. This debate is, from a twenty-first century perspective, pointless, leading to frustrations rather than illumination and ignoring the valuable material that written evidence can offer the folklorist. It also neglects the related point (perhaps reflecting a reaction, from those studying oral tradition, against the traditional written-text scholars' assumption that oral transmission is less reliable than written) that oral accounts also involve reimagining information – even if received first hand – just as written evidence does. Having said that, the relationship between written evidence and folklore is of course complicated by the peculiar subjectivity of creative presentation – even if no more so, as I have suggested, than evidence in documentary or documented sources.

The open-minded ethnologist has a great deal to gain from utilising written evidence. Arguably, the folklorist may be more biographically focused than the literary critic, sensitive to how the experience of the writer's sociocultural background is reflected in the text. However, being aware of the interplay between written and oral conventions of structure and style can lead to a better understanding of both. The folklorist, to some extent, has to catch up with literary scholarship which – certainly in the Scottish context – has long been aware of the fact that written texts are cultural and often politicised constructions, as well as potentially entertaining. It would be overly reductive to say that critics explore style and content and folklorists seek for 'facts' within written texts; both groups have much to gain in looking at texts holistically, and imaginatively. In terms of their chosen genres, for instance, creative writers are also often skilled at revealing experienced 'truth'. Their work by its nature can be singularly engaging, particularly for those who lack first-hand experience of certain forms of the traditional; in short, it can provide an access point to the deep meanings in orally based texts. In the overview that follows, I make one main point: written evidence is a rich resource for the modern folklorist to approach, in ways that go beyond the (archaic) recognition of traditional 'sources' within creative work to offer imaginative insights into the reception, and making, of traditional culture.

The relationship between orality and text, in Scotland as elsewhere, goes far beyond source and its reworking, of incorporated type and motif, or social history in action. As long ago as 1940, Stith Thompson demanded a detailed study of 'the relation of written and oral tales'.[2] Thompson particularly noted (predictably) the historic–geographic method as a tool for classification and identification, and drew attention to the necessity of awareness of the full range, characteristics and interactions among transmission contexts.[3] Similarly, in 1975 H R Ellis Davidson pleaded for a paradigm shift from 'dredging our literature to search for nuggets of folklore lurking in the depths' to a more holistic approach in which 'knowledge of folklore motifs can help literary scholars and folklorists alike to understand and interpret'. She highlighted the 'two-way traffic between written literature and oral folk tradition', identifying a resonant relationship between literary and orality from structural underpinnings to the use of beliefs to support literary themes. Davidson noted: 'Folklore is an integral part of literature, not an intrusive element in it, something which may affect the language, structure and themes of outstanding works in both poetry and prose.'[4]

Such manifestos and concerns have fostered imaginative approaches to written evidence in international contexts. Critics including Zipes, Bettelheim, Warner and Bacchilega have analysed interactions between the oral and the literary, helping to identify changing perspectives and engagements in written contexts over time. International treatments of specific oral/literary interactions include Leo Tak-hung Chang's discussion of the ways in which classical Chinese literary tales reflect amateur oral storytelling and 'conversational narrative' in elite circles. Ray Cashman has profiled interactions between chapbook literature, nationalist periodicals and orally transmitted attitudes of resistance, noting that outlaw lore was 'a cultural script that sanctioned, and possibly inspired, action'.[5] Here, approaching popular literature becomes an important means of understanding attitudes and even actions.

Equally imaginative approaches have not as yet been closely developed in Scotland. Here, on the whole, written evidence is used as contextual, historical or parallel, rather than complementary, forms of information about traditional material. Storytelling and written narrative are approached as separate sources that occasionally meet. There are of course exceptions, such as considerations of oral and written intersections in the work of Burns, or recent treatments of the way that poetry, ballads and chapbook literature inform Scottish Romanticism, particularly that of Scott.[6] This leaves some leeway for the development of new approaches to writers hitherto neglected by folklorists.

For reasons of space, my focus here is on authors working within the physical nation, writing in Scots and English but excluding Gaelic writing except where – as in the Ossianic translations of James Macpherson – there are crossovers. Non-fictional contexts, including memoirs and purpose-made collections, are excluded, along with evidence in song, theatre and film scripts. Another area not discussed is the verbal aspects of interactive storytelling in new media contexts – a new way of communicating and creating traditions.[7]

POETRY

From the Middle Ages onwards, poetry in Scots and English has provided an extremely rich resource for ethnological investigation. 'The Dream of the Rood', carved in runic script on the Ruthwell Cross in Dumfries and Galloway in the eighth century is the earliest written example of the ancestral (to Scots) Northern Anglo-Saxon that was then spoken.[8] As the rood speaks, there is an indication of very vividly held Christian beliefs at the period of its generation, framed within contemporary social structures. Christ is envisaged as a king, dethroned and mocked by misguided warriors and nobles; the cross stands firm to support Christ in his misery. Eighteen feet tall, it incorporates visual images from the life of Christ alongside decorative elements that suggest a mingling with indigenous traditions, reminiscent of those on Pictish crosses, and implying cultural intersections at least in art and possibly in other areas.[9] These would repay further ethnological investigation.

Other early texts include *The Brus* by John Barbour (c.1320–1395), Archdeacon of Aberdeen. Responding to the Wars of Independence, fifty years after its hero's death, this is written evidence of near-contemporary tales, combining oral storytelling styles and techniques in formal couplets. Hero-tales are also combined with dramatic accounts, over half a century afterwards, of events such the battle of Bannockburn (1314), presumably based on oral accounts known to Barbour. The patriotic tenor gives a sense of attitudes to the near-historical during Barbour's lifetime – often a useful aspect of traditionally anchored texts. The *Orygynale Chronicle of Scotland* of Andrew Wyntoun (c.1355–1422), prior of St Serf's Inch, similarly encapsulates ideas of Scotland's formation which reflect contemporary attitudes among the religious establishment that are otherwise difficult to access. A third text of this type is Hector Boece's *Chronicle of Scotland* (1527), which includes an adaptation of Geoffrey of Monmouth's *Historia*, in the process investing Scotland with Arthurian associations: Guanora (Guinevere), for instance, is buried in Meigle, close to Boece's childhood home in Dundee, arguably beginning an association between Arthur's queen's last resting place and a sculptured stone there, which was accepted by the later eighteenth century in this area.[10] *The Wallace* (c.1477) by Blind Harry (c.1440–1492) draws on oral traditions that were vibrant and in transmission a century after the patriot was active. An overview source for the oral and written narrative of this period is *The Complaynte of Scotland* (1549), probably by Robert Wedderburn (d.1557), who was also a compiler, with his brothers James and John, of *The Gude and Godlie Ballatis*.

Probably the richest poetic period, from the folklorist's perspective, begins in the fifteenth and sixteenth centuries.[11] This period, which was also and more than coincidentally a time of prime ballad generation, is one of poetic renaissance that culminates in the work of the 'Makars', who were in the past sometimes called, slightly misleadingly, Scottish Chaucerians. Their work features in collected form in the *Bannatyne Manuscript*, compiled by George Bannatyne from 1568.[12] Folk lives, experiences and forms of speech – from those of the higher echelons of society to those from 'humbler' backgrounds – are encapsulated in the work of some of Scotland's most accomplished medieval poets. The work of the court poet and diplomat William Dunbar (c.1450–c.1520) offers vivid pictures of contemporary social life, particularly among the higher echelons of society, in pieces such as 'To the Merchants of Edinburgh' (directed at those who have allowed, through their greed, the city to become, in effect, a slum) and 'Of a Dance in the Quenis Chalmer'. Linguistically, too, Dunbar offers insights into contemporary and developing forms of Scots language. He appears for instance to draw directly on orally based tradition (particularly in Gaelic poetry) in works such as 'The Flyting of Dunbar and Kennedy', where mutual abuse is an alliterative art form.[13] His habitual use of Scots in Boccaccio-esque pieces such as 'The Tua Mariit Wemen and the Wedo' exemplifies the language at its peak of literary usage and suggests too its oral characteristics, highlighting the possibilities of Scots as a creative form of expression and arguably presenting written evidence of lively oral traditions, albeit in a particularly accomplished way. The work of Dunfermline schoolmaster Robert Henryson (c.1420–1490) is worth noting in this context. His *Morall Fabillis of Esope the Phrygian* (c.1480s) explores animal tales in confident Scots, including 'The Taill of the Uponlandis Mous and the Burges Mous', which alludes to contemporary shifts towards urban living.

For information on traditions of Scottish conviviality, the scholar of folklore must be acquainted with the work of Allan Ramsay (1684–1758). While his drama in verse *The Gentle Shepherd* (1725) is notable for its attempt to engage with rural life, albeit from a romantic perspective, the use of Scots language elements is intriguing, as it is in his earthy portrayals of Scottish life and characters in works such as the *Elegies on Maggy Jonston, John Cowper and Lucky Wood* (1718) and the Edinburgh bawd of *Lucky Spence's Last Advice* (1718).[14] In a similar vein, Robert Fergusson (1750–1774) captures the convivial experiences of Scottish folk life in his 'Leith Races', 'The Daft Days' (on the festivities of winter), 'Caller Oysters' (a celebration of tavern culture) and 'Hallow Fair'. The last of these offers particular insights into adult customs in the eighteenth century, which were later to be adapted and sanitised into those of childhood, as I have discussed elsewhere.[15] Fergusson's work, which is stylistically accomplished in both English and Scots, deserves detailed attention from folklorists for the evidence it contains of folklife and practices and the reductive affection in which this citizen of Edinburgh held them.

Although this chapter does not include work in Gaelic, it is worth mentioning at this point the hugely influential reconstructions of the matter of *Ossian* by James Macpherson. In *Fragments of Ancient Poetry, Fingal* and *Temora* Macpherson introduced poetic models based on oral tradition (as Derick Thomson usefully established, in a postponed coda to the 1805 *Enquiry*) and on his own fieldwork; and, arguably, a remembered mood from his childhood in Badenoch. Extending his influence from France to Germany, America and beyond,[16] Macpherson's work fostered new romantic, melancholic and sentimental idioms with which to approach Scottish culture, which would feed into the growth of common-sense-influenced poetry and prose works, such as Henry Mackenzie's *The Man of Feeling* (1771). Whatever the level of intervention by Macpherson himself, he played a crucial role in providing models for the treatment of orally grounded material in new, written contexts, and on an international basis.

The Ossianic poems were a major influence on later writers, with their admirers including Robert Burns (1759–1796). The way in which Burns utilises and creates oral traditions, particularly in song, has been well documented and I do not want to dwell on it here. However, it is worth reiterating how *Poems, Chiefly in the Scottish Dialect* (1786) and Burns' subsequent work both draw on supernatural traditions and employ Scots vernacular spectactularly well, in ways that indicate a fusion between his understanding of the folkloric and his literary skill. Burns' poetry is at once resonant, engaging and revealing. Examples include 'Tam o' Shanter', provided as part of written evidence illuminating traditional beliefs to Francis Grose and published in volume 2 of the London-based writer and antiquarian's *The Antiquities of Scotland* (1797). Anchored in wry reflections on alehouse life, on one level it could be viewed as a repository of contemporary witchcraft beliefs and on another as a wry response to notions which, even in Burns' lifetime, were viewed as antique, at least in the Enlightenment circles he frequented. Burns adopts a range of approaches to the traditional. There is the near-documentary and highly humorous approach to contemporary folklife, and supernaturally anchored predictions of future partners, of 'Halloween', which builds on Fergusson's masterly piece on this topic. There are reflections on the nuances of religious life and (nominal) beliefs in 'Holy Willie's Prayer' and the supernaturally adept 'Address to the Deil'. At one extreme there is the raucous atmosphere of minority cultural lives in 'The Jolly Beggars'; on the other there is the moving, sentimental and religious atmosphere of 'The Cotter's Saturday Night'.[17] I have argued elsewhere that working-class writers provide particular insights into the traditional culture they knew, an element that limits their critical acceptability.

To return to the influence of *Ossian* – and with the observation that, in approaching creative work for 'written evidence', readers should be alert to chains of literary influence as well as personal creativity – it is worth noting the forays of Walter Scott (1771–1832) into the 'bardic'. The southern poet of *The Lay of the Last Minstrel* (1805), for instance, presents an idiosyncratic equivalent to

Macpherson's Highland bards, drawing on Scott's experience too as collector and editor of *The Minstrelsy of the Scottish Border* (1802–03). The dark atmosphere of *Marmion* (1808) draws on a similar force, and *The Lady of the Lake* (1810) draws on Lowland and Highland stereotypes to present influential images of each – the literature, in this sense, providing written evidence of future popular notions of different types of Scots, and a precedent in terms of treatments for Scott's contemporaries and later poets.

There are also traces of Macpherson's influence in the work of the self-styled 'Mountain Bard' James Hogg (1770–1835), whose poetry seems always infused with an atmosphere of loss. Hogg combines this with a deep knowledge of traditional matter and styles. In *Scottish Pastorals* (1801), he explores the creative potential primarily of traditional lyric and ballad forms, but without musical accompaniment in most cases. *The Mountain Bard* (1807) engages in similarly formal and thematic exercises, while the longer narrative poems interweave mythology from the Scottish tradition, with indigenous spirits greeting George IV in the *Royal Jubilee* (1832), to the Norse and the Celtic in *Queen Hynde* (1825). Equally, he creates new tradition-based fantasies, as in *Pilgrims of the Sun* (1815), which uses the premise of vision to create an imagined and imaginative journey through space and time.[18] In *The Witch of Fife* (1813), Hogg engages with traditional matter on several levels. There are the humorous accounts in 'The Witch of Fife' of the night raids of witches, reflecting already vanishing traditional beliefs. In a more sophisticated way the fairy beliefs of 'Kilmeny' are integrated within the plot. The eponymous heroine, as pure as pure can be, has first-hand experience of a realm that may be fairyland or heaven. All this is integrated within a structure which at a deep level draws on tradition, from ballad stylistics to the episodic, overarching structure reminiscent of traditional tale-telling sessions over several nights. This is no surprise, perhaps – James Porter, for instance, building on David Buchan's work and that of previous scholars, has drawn attention to the ways in which singers perceive songs as more than merely 'story'; similarly, writers use the traditional as a means to a creative end rather than as scholarly 'text'.[19] Written evidence, as here, can be a dynamic part of the creative whole – for the folklorist, it is possible to both see engagement with the traditional and observe creative processes of reinventing these in literary contexts, an aspect of Hogg's work which still deserves full recognition and study.

A rich vein of engagement with the oral comes in poetry by working-class writers. Hogg's contemporaries include Allan Cunningham (1784–1842), known of course for his songs but also of interest for his longer poems, which incorporate highly personal responses to the oral traditions of Dumfriesshire and Galloway: *Sir Marmaduke Maxwell* (1822) focuses on the period around Comyne power in the area; and *The Maid of Elvar* (1832) draws on traditional tales of the high masquerading as low. Both offer local resonances, as Cunningham combines knowledge of his contemporary folk culture with musings on the past. Later, the *Whistlebinkie* collections provide evidence of a more sentimental stream of responses to Scottish folk culture; these contrast with examples of more industrial landscapes in the work of poets like 'Surfaceman' (Alexander Anderson, 1845–1909), reflecting his deep psychological bond (ambiguously presented) to the engine in works such as his collection entitled *A Song of Labour* (1873). The writers represented in Henry Shanks' *The Peasant Poets of Scotland* (1881), including William Laidlaw (1780–1845) and Henry Scott Riddell (1798–1870), are often primarily concerned with reflecting on day-to-day experiences and their meaning, and as such provide wonderful resources. Other poets of this type include William Nicholson (1782–1849), the Galloway packman whose 'Aikin Drum' and *Brownie of Bludnock* reflect local traditions and local idioms in an engaging and revealing way.

The poets of Scotland's early twentieth-century 'renaissance' offer real insights into intellectual life during this period. Hugh MacDiarmid (Christopher Murray Grieve, 1892–1978), often engages directly with the traditional, and his early work in particular draws on traditional tale and idioms. These are augmented in the process of creating 'synthetic Scots', such as the collections *Sangschaw* (1925) and *Penny Wheep* (1926). *A Drunk Man Looks at the Thistle* (1926) his chef-d'oeuvre, includes memorable sections around customs and beliefs, including the common riding section based on practices in Langholm, or the 'crying of the fair' and allusions to the witch beliefs of 'Tam o' Shanter'.[20] The work of Edwin Muir (1887–1959), particularly his early poetry, reflects on the innocent experiences of childhood and, later, exile within the bounds of Scotland. In *First Poems* (1925) 'Childhood' is an insightful response to the shift from rural to urban; the darker 'Horses' mourns the lost 'rapture' of watching horses at work. Elsewhere, in *The Narrow Place* (1941), Muir reflects on the sorry condition of 'Scotland 1941'; and in *One Foot in Eden* (1956) 'Scotland's Winter' continues this vein of thought, set in a hero-less nation.[21]

Several poets engage specifically with the experience of childhood. William Soutar (1898–1943) in his 'bairnrhymes' reflects memories of traditional verse and singing games, and their styles. They are reimagined engagingly, with compassion and humour. *Seeds in the Wind* (1933, enlarged 1943) uses ballad forms, and Soutar explores fable too in works such as 'The Whale' and 'The Herryin o Jenny Wren'. In a more adult vein, reading 'Ballad' can only enhance the understanding of the form for folklorists: it is a masterclass in economy, expertly using dialogue. Allusions to the notion of revenant as the question 'O! Shairly ye hae seen my love / Doun whaur the waters wind' elicits a tragic, deadpan, response; the lover found in 'dreepin nets', localised 'No far frae Walnut Grove'.[22] Later writers who adopt similar techniques include J K Annand, whose traditionally modelled *Bairn Rhymes* (1998) engage children and their parents. While being a creative act, such poems can also be used in an educational context, to help those lacking a background of tradition bearers to engage with traditional idioms and appreciate them.

Studying the work of certain poets, as well as oral song and story, allows the scholar to form an innate appreciation of vernacular idioms and standard usages. For instance, the work of the New Zealand-born Edinburgh poet Sydney Goodsir Smith (1915–1975) pays homage to story and song in several titles, such as *Under the Eildon Tree* (1948), which alludes to 'Thomas the Rhymer'. Smith's work is often compared to Fergusson's for the insights it offers into Edinburgh life, most notably in *Kynd Kittock's Land* (1965). Similar observations could be made about Norman MacCaig (1910–1996), who celebrates life in Edinburgh and the natural environment of Sutherland, in resonant English verse. Poetry is a rich resource for specifically regional varieties of the languages of Scotland. The works of 'Vagaland' (the pseudonym of T A Robertson, 1909–1973) include *Laeves fae Vagaland* (1952) and, co-edited with his wife Martha, *Sangs at A'll Sing ta Dee* (1973). Showing a deep engagement with Shetland life, Vagaland offers real insights into lived experience, sounds and smells in pieces such as 'Hjalta'. A selection of his best-known work can be heard on the Shetland Dialect website, along with that of many of Shetland's finest and most culturally evocative writers past and present, from Billy Tait (1918–1992) to the expatriate Christine De Luca (b.1947).[23]

It is only possible to mention other writers whose work should be consulted for their insights into folklife and language. They include Violet Jacob (1863–1945), Marion Angus (1866–1946), George Bruce (1902–2002) and Sheena Blackhall (b.1947) from the north-east of Scotland; the Lanarkshire poet Janet Hamilton (1795–1873) for her politicised portrayals of the travails of working people's lives; the visionary and precisely located poetry of Orcadian George Mackay Brown (1921–1996); the Edinburgh voices of Robert Garioch (1909–1981); the mountaineering culture of Andrew Greig (b.1951); and the current Scottish makar, Liz Lochhead (b.1947), for her collaborations with songwriter Michael Marra (1952–2012). Liz Niven (b.1952) celebrates the traditions of Scotland's rural south-west. Modern ecologically engaged poets such as John Burnside (b.1955), who is worth mentioning for his fiction also, Kathleen Jamie (b.1962) and Valerie Gillies (b.1948) engage with the environment in a way that directly reflects on experiences within Scottish landscapes. In short, the topic is vast, but the writers mentioned above might prove a starting point towards a reading list.

FICTION

Fiction is an important source from the later eighteenth century onwards. While the novel is relatively new – early Scottish examples include the sentimental *The Man of Feeling* (1771) by Henry Mackenzie (1745–1831) and the historically driven *The Scottish Chiefs* (1810) by Jane Porter (1776–1850) – it plays a vital role in transmitting traditional cultural idioms: language, practices, experiences and beliefs. For instance, the work of Susan Ferrier (1782–1854) – *Marriage* (1818), *The Inheritance* (1824) and *Destiny* (1831) – offers a vivid picture of the economic pressures on young, marriageable girls of a certain class, as well as of their social milieu, in her lifetime. In the nineteenth century, the relationship between orality and writing becomes particularly complex, as can be seen in a corpus dominated by the influence of Walter Scott and his coterie.[24] As a whole, his work offers carefully crafted pictures of specific folk groups and folk lives at all levels. The hero of 'Wandering Willie's Tale' in *Redgauntlet* (1824), for instance, is a travelling fiddler with hidden depths. The antiquarian approach of *Tales of a Grandfather* (1828–30) with its vividly realised and imaginatively used portrayal of 'The Two Drovers', for instance, draws attention to real and perceived national and cross-border attitudinal divides, as well as to the cattle-based culture it describes. *The Heart of Midlothian* (1818), although historically based, reflects Scott's deep knowledge of legal culture, an aspect of many of the *Waverley Novels*.

John Galt (1779–1839) deserves attention for his humorous, realistic portrayals of Scottish life and characters. *Annals of the Parish* (1821) draws on the conventions of the *Old Statistical Account* to show the quiet existence of the rural minister, oblivious to the wider issues of the world in his concern for the minutiae of village life. Galt's *Ringan Gilhaize* (1823), like Hogg's *The Brownie of Bodsbeck* (1818), draws on oral traditions and written accounts to portray the Covenanting period. In Hogg's case, the work also offers insights into supernatural belief around fairies and their associates, and both of these novels are more illuminating, in terms of folk responses to major political events, than Scott's (arguably) less partisan work. All these novelists are of interest, too, for the way in which they document beliefs in transition as, from the Enlightenment period onwards, attitudes to the supernatural became rather more sceptical.

James Hogg, in *The Private Memoirs and Confessions of a Justified Sinner* (1824), offers evidence of Scottish belief culture in transition. Gilmartin, the central character, can be understood to be the devil as a real entity or a psychological delusion. This is a novel of verisimilitude, and the pictures it offers of seventeenth-century Edinburgh (from a nineteenth-century perspective) are highly revealing; at least for the gentry, the town operates like a village – a place of physical exercise as well as tavern life and law courts. *The Brownie of Bodsbeck* (1818) also explores Borders cultural beliefs at a time of historical crisis; through the Covenanting culture, based on oral traditions, it explores and commemorates seventeenth and eighteenth century memories. The belief culture around supernatural beings, which acts as a plot device, is also revealing in terms of contemporary, changing attitudes. Hogg's shorter fiction, such as his 'Shepherd's Calendar' sketches, originally published in *Blackwood's Edinburgh Magazine*, also offers observations on contemporary working practices and beliefs.[25]

In his short stories, like 'Thrawn Janet', Robert Louis Stevenson (1850–1894) also explores supernatural traditions.[26] The adventure novels, such as *Treasure Island* (1883) and *Kidnapped* (1886), are anchored in Scottish tradition, in the case of the latter in the post-1745 climate that seems so resonant for Scottish writers. *The Master of Ballantrae* (1888) deals with this period too, evoking real landscapes and Scottish 'types' in a way that is integral to the novel's plot. On an even darker note, *The Strange Case of Dr Jeckyll and Mr Hyde* (1886) explores the doubling motif so resonant in Scottish literature from Hogg's work onwards, which resurfaces in the novels of Muriel Spark – discussed below – and Emma Tennant (b.1937) in *The Bad Sister* (1978).

Notions of Scottish community life – whether idealised or otherwise – can also be explored through Scottish fiction. The novels previously dismissed as sentimental 'kailyard' – a myth which Andrew Nash has shown bears traces of ethnic stereotyping and class biases – are useful on folk life in the late nineteenth onwards.[27] Their nostalgic bent aside, there are intriguing pictures of community life and of real bonds within folk groups that it would be intriguing to compare with the oral recollections of a 'golden age' that the folklorist often encounters. Examples include the kind of communities that feature in the novels of Ian

Maclaren (John Watson, 1850–1907), *A Window in Thrums* by J M Barrie (1860–1937), or *The Lilac Sunbonnet* (1894) by S R Crockett (1859–1914). Of course these writers also wrote in other genres. Maclaren, as well as considering village life and religiosity in his collected sketches *Beside the Bonnie Brier Bush* (1894), considered Glasgow life in *St Jude's* (1907). Barrie's dramatic career is well known. Crockett wrote adventure fiction, including *The Raiders* (1894) and *The Men of the Moss Haggs* (1895), which reflect on his own experience of life in south-west Scotland as much as its historical past. The reaction to the perception of 'kailyard' should also be mentioned – most spectacularly, the alternative depiction of fractured communities and families in *The House with the Green Shutters* by George Douglas Brown (1869–1902) and, later, John Macdougall Hay's *Gillespie* (1914).

Pictures of functional and dysfunctional communities feature in many Scottish works. Margaret Oliphant (1828–1897) wrote novels of middle-class life that include *Effie Ogilvie* (1886) and *Kirsteen* (1890). Her shorter fiction includes 'The Open Door', a wonderful study of the supernatural, from the perspective of children and adults.[28] Later, John Buchan (1875–1940) contrasts evocative images of rural Scottish life in *The Thirty-Nine Steps* (1915) with the alienating experiences residing in the London and exciting South African pasts of its hero Richard Hannay. Hannay features in five additional works (in four as the central character). *The Island of Sheep* (1936) is particularly intriguing, as it draws on a (short) period of research in the Faroes in 1935.

In terms of regional perspectives, many works could be cited. Neil M. Gunn (1891–1973), a Caithness fisherman's son, reflects early experiences in *Grey Coast* (1926) and *Morning Tide* (1930). He portrays northern coastal culture at key periods from the Viking *Sun Circle* (1933) to the post-Clearances *Butcher's Broom* (1934) and *The Silver Darlings* (1941). Combining personal knowledge with metaphysical musings – notably in *Highland River* (1937) – his work offers insights into the experience of living in the Highlands. The work of Fionn MacColla (Thomas Douglas Macdonald, 1906–1975) can be approached in a similar way: *The Albannach* (1932), *And the Cock Crew* (1945) and *The Ministers* (1979) vividly portray Highland life past and present, and its religious elements (often from a hostile perspective). The work of Eric Linklater (1899–1974), from *White Maa's Saga* (1929) onwards, explores northern Scotland and on occasion other areas: *Magnus Merriman* (1934) reflects on political culture of Scotland at this time, while *The Merry Muse* (1959) includes humorous profiles of literary culture. George Mackay Brown (1921–1996), in his prose just as in poetry, offers real insights into the historical and contemporary folklife of Orkney. *Greenvoe* (1972), although based on an imagined community, is highly revealing, as is *Hawkfall* (1974) and *The Sun's Net* (1976).

On farming, and particularly its north-eastern context, the folklorist must consult Lewis Grassic Gibbon (James Leslie Mitchell, 1901–1935), still best known for his trilogy *A Scots Quair* (1934) comprising *Sunset Song* (1932), *Cloud Howe* (1933) and *Grey Granite* (1934). His short stories in a similar vein, 'Clay', 'Smeddum' and 'Greenden', for instance, illustrate the hold of the land on the people of Scotland past and, arguably, present, along with its inspiration and tragedies. Reflecting on the farm life he knew first-hand, in contrast with the urban, Gibbon is too self-aware to be nostalgic but does give a sense of the loss of a way of life after World War I. William Alexander (1826–1894), earlier than Gibbon, writes from a similar perspective: *Johnny Gibb of Gushetneuk*, serialised in the *Aberdeen Free Press* between 1869 and 1870, is remarkable for its prolonged use of Scots language alongside English, and its believable country life. The work of Nan Shepherd (1893–1981), including *The Quarry Wood* (1928) and *The Weatherhouse* (1930), and of Jessie Kesson (1916–1994), such as *The White Bird Passes* (1958) and *The Glitter of Mica* (1960), all reflect on the regional specificity of north-east life in revealing ways; Kesson's work in particular offers synergies with orally collected reminiscences of the disadvantaged, past and present.

Other regionally adept writers include the dramatist Robert McLellan (1907–1985), whose Clyde valley childhood features in *Linmill and Other Stories* (1977). Muriel Spark (1918–2006) is best known for *The Prime of Miss Jean Brodie* (1961), usually seen as reflecting her Edinburgh schooldays. Its verisimilitude should not distract from the way in which here, as elsewhere, Spark draws on Scottish traditions – from the demonic elements in the central character and her (unknown) adversary Sandy to the supernatural undertones of *Memento Mori* (1959) and *The Ballad of Peckham Rye* (1960), the last of these experimenting with structures and forms drawn from the traditional ballad and filtered through a deep knowledge of fiction that runs from Hogg to Stevenson.

South-west Scotland features in the work of James Barke (1905–1958), known for his fictionalised biography of Burns, *The Immortal Memory* (1946–54). For the folklorist, his most perceptive work is *The Land of the Leal* (1939), which moves from the Galloway he knew well into the Borders, Fife and Glasgow. *The Wigtown Ploughman* (1938) by John Macneillie (Ian Niall, 1916–2002) is a dark response to the south-west; he remembered the area more favourably in *A Galloway Childhood* (1967). R B Cunningham Graham (1852–1936) goes beyond the regional in 'Beattock to Moffat', reflecting on the identity tensions of Scots living (and dying) in exile. The artistic life of this region is humorously realised from an outsiders' perspective in Dorothy L Sayers' *Five Red Herrings* (1931), which captures the painting and angling culture of well-to-do residents and visitors.

An interest in mythology, not always in Scottish contexts but often reflecting Scottish perspectives, features in the works of many writers from Naomi Mitchison (1897–1999) to Margaret Elphinstone (b.1948). Mitchison's *The Corn King to the Spring Queen* (1931) draws on her knowledge of international customs; *The Bull Calves* (1947) includes vivid and convincing portrayals of rural life in Scotland post-1745 and draws on the history of her own aristocratic family, the Haldanes. Elphinstone – building on early work, such as her short story 'The Green Man' – goes even further in reimagining Mesolithic culture in *The Gathering Night* (2009), based on her knowledge of the archaeological and the anthropological.

Different varieties of working life – or the lack of it – is a particular concern for modern writers. George Friel (1910–1976) provides a disturbing, but sympathetic, account of teaching in *Mr Alfred M.A.* (1972), while James Kelman (b.1946) offers provocative and revealing accounts of the socially disenfranchised in, for example, *A Disaffection* (1989) and *How Late It Was, How Late* (1994). Irvine Welsh (b.1958) could also be mentioned in this context, and his accounts of drug culture in Edinburgh and beyond have become synonymous with this cultural field; *Trainspotting* (1993) is probably his best known novel of this kind.[29]

The darker sides of Scottish life are represented too in contemporary crime fiction, exemplified by the series of *Rebus* novels by Ian Rankin (b.1960). *The Falls* (2001), for example, uses the device of wooden dolls from a museum, found on Arthur's Seat in 1836, to reflect on beliefs past and present. Rankin's fictionalised Edinburgh continues the tradition of Hogg and Stevenson in this respect, and parallels that of James Robertson (b.1958). Robertson's *The Fanatic* (2000) combines religious history and witchcraft accounts and, like his *The Testament of Gideon Mack* (2008), it is an imaginative responses to the real which reads as anchored in oral tradition. As reflections on key aspects of Scottish identity, which is a major theme in modern Scottish writing, they could also be compared to a variety of material from other orally collected sources.

The evidence offered by diaspora writers is particularly rich for understanding identity as Scots engage with the traditions of their past and their experience of the present. For instance, in Canada the poetry of Tiree-born John Maclean (Am Bàrd MacGilleathain, 1787–1848) reflects the emigrant experience in all its moods, from 'A'Choille Ghruamach' (The Gloomy Forest) to more positive, later reflections. Alistair Macleod's *No Great Mischief* (1999) addresses similar topics from a modern perspective, arguably influencing modern-day notions of this historical period. The New South Wales poet Andrew Barton 'Banjo' Paterson (1864–1941), whose father was born in Lanarkshire and his mother in Australia, is known for helping to define the Australian identity with 'Waltzing Matilda', but he also explores the emigrant experience directly in the pragmatic 'We're All Australians Now' (1915). More recent exiles, like Mick Imlah (1952–2009) who was born in Glasgow, raised in Kent and educated in Oxford, have drawn attention to complex engagements between homeland and place of residence. In his 'Elegy for Stephen Boyd', Imlah notes how 'a Southern education . . . trimmed my Scottishness to a tartan phrase / Brought out on match days and Remembrance Days'.[30]

New Scots offer a rich vein of material through which to understand the experience and lives of immigrants, whether first or later generations, and bring new perspectives and input to Scotland's traditional culture. Bashabi Fraser (b.1954), for instance, explores cultural contacts around migration, from the voluntary to the forced, between Scotland and India in works such as *From the Ganges to the Tay: An Epic Poem* (2009) and, more recently, with the photographer Hermann Rodrigues, *Ragas and Reels* (2012). Her work offers creative insights which are at once unique and yet typify the migrant experience. The work of Jackie Kay is equally resonant in engaging with cultural identity from her *Adoption Papers* (1991) to *Red Dust Road* (2010). Readers interested in pursuing this strand of written evidence could consult Kevin MacNeil and Alec Finlay's multicultural anthology *Wish I was Here* (Edinburgh 2000) as a starting point.

Children's literature is another rich yet often neglected source. Some manipulate tradition into purely literary forms, from George Macdonald Fraser in *The Princess and Curdie* (1872) to the best-selling works of J K Rowling (b.1965). Others include observations on community life in child-friendly contexts – R M Ballantyne's Arbroath-based *The Lighthouse* (1865), for instance, or J J Macgregor's *Wee Macregor* (1901) sketches, bringing the domestic into an urban context. Neil Munro's *Para Handy Tales,* from 1905 onwards, are enjoyable accounts of 'puffer' culture that can be read by adults or older children.[31] It is hoped that the new Centre for Children's Literature, in development by the Peter Pan Moat Brae Trust in Dumfries, will prove to be a revealing and educational source of information on this rich vein of material for folklorists to explore.[32]

Finally, I would like to mention broadside texts, which are made available by a number of good websites. Broadsides offer particular information on social life and its conventions, the folkloric material that was popular in other contexts, and particularly on attitudes among the so-called lower social echelons, particularly from the mid nineteenth century onwards, as popular printed works became more inexpensive.[33]

CONCLUSION

Written evidence, drawn from fictional contexts, covers a variety of topics, regional perspectives and experiences that can be used in conjunction with oral literature collected by folklorists to build up a comprehensive picture of folklife, experiences and attitudes. Whether the writer is seen as a single voice of experience, as can many of those cited above, or representative of their community and people, the dialogues implied by their creative acts can offer valuable sources and insights into orally expressed ideas and sentiments. The folklorist ignores the literary at her or his peril; an open mind is essential to move beyond context into explorations of the implications and reworkings of fiction.

NOTES

1   Hogg, 1807, xii.
2   Aarne, 1964; Thompson 1955–58; Thompson, 1940, 874.
3   Thompson, 1940, 869.
4   Davidson, 1975, 74, 80, 91–2.
5   Zipes, 2008; Warner, 1994, 2001; Bacchilega, 1997; Chang, 1997; Cashman, 2000, 209.
6   Smith, 2001; Brown, 1984; Newman, 2011; McCue, 2011.
7   Aylett, 2010.
8   See the Scots Language Centre website, <www.scotslanguage.com/books/view/69/2068> [accessed November 2012]; Swanton, 1996; Cassidy, 1992.
9   Fraser, 2008; Henderson and Henderson, 2004.
10   Loomis, 1958.
11   Jack and Rozendaal, 1997.
12   Aitken, McDiarmid and Thomson, 1977.
13   Bawcutt, 1983.
14   Ramsay, 1945–74.
15   Fergusson, 2000.
16   Thomson, 1952; Mackenzie, 1805; Stafford, 1998; Gaskill, 1991, 2004; McKean, 2001; Bold, 2001; Nagy, 2001.
17   Bold, 2009; Burns, 1968.

18 Bold, 2007.
19 Porter, 1980.
20 MacDiarmid, 1985.
21 Muir, 2008.
22 Soutar, 1988.
23 See Shetland ForWirds, <www.shetlanddialect.org.uk/> [accessed November 2012].
24 Hart, 1978; Craig, 1999; Duncan, 2007.
25 Bold and Gilbert, 2012; Hogg, 2008.
26 Murray, 1983; Reid, 1989.
27 Nash, 2007.
28 Murray, 1983, 56–96.
29 Schoene, 2007.
30 Imlah, 2008.
31 Alison, 2010.
32 <http://peterpanmoatbrae.org/> [accessed November 2012].
33 Glasgow Broadside Ballads, <http://digital.nls.uk/broadsides/>; The Word on
   the Street, <www.gla.ac.uk/t4/~dumfries/files/layer2/glasgow_broadside_
   ballads/> [both accessed November 2012].

BIBLIOGRAPHY AND FURTHER READING

Aarne, A. *The Types of the Folktale*, trans. and enlarged S Thompson, 2nd revision, Helsinki,
   1964.
Alison, J. Towards an overview of Scottish children's literature from 1823 to 2010, *The Bottle
   Imp*, 7 (May 2010), <www.arts.gla.ac.uk/ScotLit/ASLS/SWE/TBI/TBIIssue7/
   Alison.pdf> [accessed February 2012].
Aitken, A J, McDiarmid, M P and Thomson, D S, eds. *Bards and Makars*, Glasgow, 1977.
Aylett, R et al., *Interactive Storytelling* [electronic resource], Berlin, 2010.
Bacchilega, C. *Postmodern Fairy Tales*, Philadelphia, PA, 1997.
Bannatyne, G. *The Bannatyne Manuscript: National Library of Scotland, Advocates' MS.1.1.6 / with
   an Introduction by Denton Fox and William A. Ringler*, London, 1980.
Barbour, *The Bruce*, ed. A A M Duncan, Edinburgh, 2000.
Bawcutt, P. The art of flyting, *Scottish Literary Journal*, 10:2 (1983), 5–24.
Bawcutt, P and Riddy, F. *Selected Poems of Henryson and Dunbar*, Edinburgh, 1992.
Bettelheim, B. *The Uses of Enchantment*, London, 1991.
Bold, A. *George Mackay Brown*, Edinburgh, 1978.
Bold, A. *Modern Scottish Literature*, London, 1983.
Bold, V. 'Rude Bard of the North': James Macpherson and the folklore of democracy, *Journal of
   American Folklore*, 113:454 (2001), 464–77.
Bold, V. *James Hogg*, Bern, 2007.
Bold, V. 'The Apple at the Glass'. In Foley, M and O'Donnell, H, eds, *Treat or Trick?*,
   Newcastle, 2009, 56–65.
Bold, V and Gilbert, S. Hogg, Ettrick and oral tradition. In Duncan, I, ed., *The Edinburgh
   Companion to James Hogg*, Edinburgh, 2012, 10–20.
Brown, M E. *Burns and Tradition*, London, 1984.
Burns, R. *The Poems and Songs of Robert Burns*, ed. J Kinsley, Oxford, 1968.
Carrick, J D, Rodgers, A and Robertson, J. *Whistlebinkie*, Glasgow, 1848.
Cassidy, B, ed. *The Ruthwell Cross*, Princeton, 1989.
Cashman, R. The heroic outlaw in Irish folklore and popular literature, *Folklore*, 111:2 (2000),
   191–215.

Chang, L T. Text and talk: Classical literary tales in traditional China and the context of casual oral storytelling, *Asian Folklore Studies*, 56:1 (1997), 33–63.

Craig, C. *Scottish Literature and the Scottish People 1680–1830*, London, 1961.

Craig, C. *The Modern Scottish Novel: Narrative and the National Imagination*, Edinburgh, 1999.

Craig, C, ed. *The History of Scottish Literature*, 4 vols, Aberdeen, 1987–88.

Crawford, R. *Scotland's Books: The Penguin History of Scottish Literature*, London, 2007.

Davidson, H R. Folklore and literature, *Folklore*, 86:2 (1975), 73–93.

Dorson, R M. *The British Folklorists. A History*, London, 1968.

Dunbar, W. *The Poetry of William Dunbar*, ed. P Bawcutt, 2 vols, Aberdeen, 1999.

Duncan, I. *Scott's Shadow: The Novel in Romantic Edinburgh*, Princeton, NJ, 2007.

Fergusson, R. *Selected Poems*, ed. J Robertson, Edinburgh, 2000.

Fox, D. *The Poems of Robert Henryson*, Oxford, 1980.

Fraser, B. *From the Ganges to the Tay: An Epic Poem*, Edinburgh, 2009.

Fraser, B and Rodrigues, H. *Ragas and Reels: Visions and Poetic Stories of Migration and Diaspora*, Edinburgh, 2012.

Fraser, I, ed. *The Pictish Symbol Stones of Scotland*, Edinburgh, 2008.

Gaskill, H. *Ossian Revisited*, Edinburgh, 1991.

Gaskill, H. *The Reception of Ossian in Europe*, London; New York, 2004.

Gibbon, L G. *Smeddum: A Lewis Grassic Gibbon Anthology*, ed. V Bold, Edinburgh, 2001.

Gifford, D and McMillan, D. *A History of Scottish Women's Writing*, Edinburgh, 1997.

Gifford, D and Riach, A. *Scotlands Poets and the Nation*, Manchester, 2004.

Gray, D. *Selected poems of Robert Henryson and William Dunbar*, London, 1998.

Hart, F R. *The Scottish Novel: A Critical Survey*, London, 1978.

Henderson, G and Henderson, I. *The Art of the Picts*, London, 2004.

Hogg, J. *The Mountain Bard*, Edinburgh, 1807.

Hogg, J. *Contributions to Blackwood's Edinburgh Magazine. Volume 1: 1817–1828*, ed. Thomas C Richardson, Edinburgh, 2008.

Imlah, M. *Selected Poems*, London, 2008.

Jack, R D S and Rozendaal, P A T, eds. *The Mercat Anthology of Early Scottish Literature*, Edinburgh, 1997.

Kerrigan, C, ed. *An Anthology of Scottish Women Poets*, Edinburgh, 1991.

Loomis, R S. Arthurian tradition and folklore, *Folklore*, 69:1 (1958), 1–25.

McCue, K. Scottish song, lyric poetry and the romantic composer. In Pittock, M, ed., *Edinburgh Companion to Scottish Romanticism*, Edinburgh, 2011, 39–48.

McKean, T. The fieldwork legacy of James Macpherson, *Journal of American Folklore*, 114 (2001), 447–63.

McNeil, K and Finlay, A. *Wish I was Here*, Edinburgh, 2001.

MacDiarmid, H. *The Complete Poems of Hugh MacDiarmid*, eds M Grieve and W R Aitken, Harmondsworth, 1985.

Mackenzie, H. *Report of the Committee of the Highland Society of Scotland*, Edinburgh, 1805.

Macpherson, J. *The Poems of Ossian and Related Works*, ed. H Gaskill, Edinburgh, 1996.

Muir, E. *Selected Poems*, ed. M Imlah, London, 2008.

Murray, I. *The New Penguin Book of Short Stories*, Harmondsworth, 1983.

Nagy, J. Observations on the Ossianesque in medieval Irish literature and modern Irish folklore, *Journal of American Folklore*, 114:454 (2001), 436–46.

Nash, A. *Kailyard and Scottish Literature*, Amsterdam, 2007.

Newman, S. Ballads and chapbooks. In Pittock, M, ed., *Edinburgh Companion to Scottish Romanticism*, Edinburgh, 2011, 13–26.

Porter, J. Principles of ballad classification, *Jahrbuch für Volksliedforschung*, 25 (1980), 11–26.

Ramsay, A. *The Works of Allan Ramsay*, vols 1 and 2 eds B Martin and J W Oliver, vols 3–6 eds A M Kinghorn and A Law, Scottish Text Society, Edinburgh, 1945–74.

Reid, J M. *Classic Scottish Short Stories*, Oxford, 1989.

Royle, T. *The Macmillan Companion to Scottish Literature*, London, 1983; revised as *The Mainstream Companion to Scottish Literature*, Edinburgh, 1994.

Schoene, B. *The Edinburgh Companion to Contemporary Scottish Literature*, Edinburgh, 2007.

Smith, D. *Storytelling Scotland*, Edinburgh, 2001.

Soutar, W. *Poems of William Soutar. A New Selection*, ed. W R Aitken, Edinburgh, 1988.

Stafford, F. *The Sublime Savage*, Edinburgh, 1988.

Swanton, M, ed. *Dream of the Rood*, Exeter, 1996.

Tasioulas, J A, ed. *The Makars: The Poems of Henryson, Dunbar and Douglas*, Edinburgh, 1999.

Thomson, D S. *The Gaelic Sources of Macpherson's Ossian*, Edinburgh, 1952.

Thompson, S. Folklore and literature, *PMLA*, 55:3 (1940), 866–74.

Thompson, S. *Motif-Index of Folk-Literature*, 6 vols, rev. edn, Bloomington, 1955–58.

Warner, M. *From the Beast to the Blonde*, London, 1994.

Warner, M. *Stranger Magic*, London 2011.

Zipes, J. *Relentless Progress*, New York, 2008.

ONLINE RESOURCES

All of the listed websites were last accessed February 2012 or later.

Association for Scottish Literary Studies, <www.arts.gla.ac.uk/ScotLit/ASLS/>

Glasgow Broadside Ballads, <www.gla.ac.uk/t4/~dumfries/files/layer2/glasgow_ broadside_ ballads/>

Itchy Coo,

The National Libary of Scotland, <www.nls.uk>

Peter Pan Moat Brae Trust, <http://peterpanmoatbrae.org/>

Scots Language Centre,

Scottish Pen,

The Scottish Poetry Library,

The Scottish Storytelling Centre,

Shetland ForWirds: Promoting Shetland Dialect,

STELLA (Software for teaching English Language and Literature and its assessment), <www.arts.gla.ac.uk/STELLA/>

The Word on the Street (National Library of Scotland digital broadsides), <http:// digital.nls.uk/broadsides/>

21 Broadsides, Chapbooks, Popular Periodicals and Newspapers

EDWARD J COWAN WITH JOHN BURNETT

Their houses in auld times they were na' sa braw;
The kitchen was dining-room, parlour, and a'.
Among them, at meal-times, it was aye the rule
To sup their drap kail at the auld buffet-stool.

But the auld buffet-stool is now thrown awa',
And they have got rooms and a table full braw;
And nane dare draw near it but them and their ain,
But the servants they still in the kitchen remain.

When the farmer comes in, he will never sit doon
Till he puts on his slippers and ben to the room,
Where it's furnished wi' sofas and stuff-bottomed chairs,
And fanciful carpets spread over the floors.

When the servants langsyne to the plough did gang out.
Their masters gaed wi' them, and ploughed rig about;
But now about that they ken naething ava,
And they make their sons merchants and limbs o' the law.

But now they are gentlemen, and they work nane,
But rides in their gig when a wee bit frae hame,
And me night and day never out o' the drudge,
And when I seek my siller they gie't wi' a grudge.

A central concern of ethnology is the theme of change over time and popular perceptions about the same, about the relationship between the reality of the present and memory – actual, imposed or imagined. The above verses are quoted from a broadside, *The Laird o' Loanhead's Description of the Farmers*,[1] which mentions the latter growing fat on the Corn Laws and so must date from before the abolition of the legislation in 1846. The 'laird' is the village blacksmith, nicely placed for social observation, who is finding the farmers tighter with their cash, presumably because they were spending it on conspicuous consumption. The growing gap between farmer and workforce is noted by many contemporary commentators who bemoan the destruction of agricultural communities in which people worked, and supped, together, irrespective of status.[2] Broadsides offer much of value to ethnologists as do their sibling publications, chapbooks. Both can be supplemented with periodical literature including newspapers, journals, magazines and collections of tales. In some cases the folk-voice is preserved, coming through loud and clear, but more often that voice is moderated by reporters, *literati* or editors more concerned with issues of supposed morality, decency and middle-class manners than they are with accurate transmission of the oral narrative.

BROADSIDES AND CHAPBOOKS

Broadsides comprised single sheets, generally retailing by the mid nineteenth century for one penny. Overwhelmingly they contained songs and sometimes verses, often of current interest and reflecting the news or buzz of the day, but old favourites were also available such as ballads and the songs of Robert Burns. Some legislation was issued as broadsides, as were proclamations, accounts of battles, protests, political squibs and, a perennial favourite, the alleged final thoughts of those about to be executed, frequently invented but always cautionary. Some of the poems printed by Scotland's first publishers, Chepman and Myllar, in 1508 may have circulated as broadsides, a stratagem also employed somewhat later in 1721 by Allan Ramsay in retailing his original verse as well as earlier material which he culled from manuscripts.

On the eve of the Reformation, 1 January 1559, an iconic broadside known as *The Beggars' Summons*, a 'ticket of warning, at the instance of the whole poor people of this realm', was attached to the yetts (doors) of friaries throughout the country, claiming that the friars, for their own selfish purposes, had diverted the alms intended for poor relief. Framed in terms of a summons of removal, the poor, the blind, and the sick, as well as widows and orphans, demanded restitution and reformation. Friars were given notice to quit their occupation of almshouses by Whitsunday next otherwise the deprived would enter and take possession of their patrimony, physically ejecting the offenders. 'Lat hym therfore that before hes stollin, steill na mare; but rather lat him wyrk with his handes, that he may be helpful to the pure'.[3]

Chapbooks also date from the sixteenth century. The word derives from Old English *céap*, meaning barter or dealing, an element found in 'chapman', hence a dealer or merchant. By the sixteenth century a chapman was understood to be an itinerant, a hawker or pedlar. A chapbook was thus any book purchased from a chapman, though in a more technical sense it was usually of eight pages made from a single sheet of paper printed on both sides and twicefolded. Some examples extend to twenty-four pages or even longer, but most were cheap, nasty and short. Like broadsides, they enjoyed a lifespan of almost half a millennium extending from the time of the medieval makars through to the eve of World War I. Constant favourites were Blind Harry's *Wallace*, which consistently far outsold John Barbour's *Brus*, and *The Whole Prophecies of Scotland*, first published in 1603, incorporating much earlier vaticination and which, though cast in the obscure language favoured by the genre, remained popular in the late nineteenth century. Chapbooks, designed for folk who were recently or just becoming literate, covered almost every imaginable subject. They were salacious and sanctimonious, adventurous and advisory, romantic and revolutionary, political and protesting, historical and histrionic, literary and licentious, religious and reactionary. They recycled medieval ballads and last year's news. They shamelessly stole from mainstream publications and from other chapbooks. Woodcuts were reused, irrespective of relevance.[4] But they were hugely popular and they inspired the whole 'cheap literature' movement which was masterminded to a pinnacle of unprecedented success by the Chambers brothers of Peebles and Edinburgh.

The chapmen who peddled their wares were deemed to represent an underclass of conmen as repugnant as they were irresistible. They operated in cities and towns but also in the countryside where they were often welcomed as a source of news and gossip as well as for their packs containing all sorts of items and knick-knacks designed to be as appealing to women as the chapmen themselves supposedly were, 'buskin braw the bonny sex', in their own minds and those of suspicious husbands.[5] Alexander Wilson, later to become famous as the pioneering ornithologist of America, became a chapman to support his poetry writing. He eloquently conveyed the wretchedness of the chapman's lot, saddled with a huge pack in often atrocious weather. He also wrote some wonderfully scatological pieces to advance the class war. It was his radicalism that forced him to America. One of the best known chaps is Dougal Graham's *John Cheap the Chapman* which, while providing a forum for jokes and insults at the expense of chapmen, probably gives a fairly accurate impression of how they were regarded. As well as womanising, they were prodigious drinkers and had vast appetites which were so seldom satisfied by niggardly farmers that they were often in competition with canines for the contents of the dog bowl. They were mischief-makers, playing tricks on the folk around the farms and widely suspected of thieving. They also did a bit of barbering, buying hair from countrywomen for wig-making. Graham was a chapman himself before he became the 'skellat bellman' of Glasgow and thus knew of what he wrote. William Cameron of Glasgow, known as 'Auld Hawkie', penned his own life story, in which he boasted of fights, cons, commissions and high jinks which included selling chapbooks containing only blank paper and punting the dying speech of a condemned criminal, who was in fact reprieved, to the crowds arriving for the execution.[6]

Graham's *John Cheap* and his *History of the Haverel Wives* are probably the best of his output for those in search of the manners of the eighteenth century's subordinate classes, but there are numerous other fields yielding rich harvests. Many broadsides and chapbooks celebrated the community camaraderie of the marketplace or the fair. Glasgow Fair was inaugurated in 1197. Each year, as documented in the city's earliest records from the sixteenth century, the 'Peace of Glasgow Fair' was reiterated, specifically banning any hurt, trouble, fighting or feuding, and almost every year the peace was infringed, even by merchants and crafts of whom more exemplary behaviour was expected. By the nineteenth century the fair was held on Glasgow Green. A broadside describes the booths, games, horse riding, theatre and acrobats on show. There is also mention of panoramas, magicians, freak shows, a camera obscura, talking pigs, wild animals and a zebra which turns out to be 'nought but a cuddy ass painted'. Also painted were the lassies in their finery with plenty of music and drink on hand. One interesting aside features undercover police – 'Policemen disguised through the mob; / To see if they need a correction'.[7] An accompanying piece presents the downer to a fair at Paisley. John and Meg having made merry for a week are 'skint'. Clothes and household items have been pawned to pay for drink. Meg has been unfaithful and arrested for fighting. The solution is to have another drink and wait until New Year for the next blowout.[8] According to a song about New Year 1854, the lads have been saving their wages to celebrate with good rum and whisky while the lassies have been starving themselves in order to afford new dresses for the event. 'Brochy' (filthy or ugly) Betty Wilson will be looking for a man. Nell M'Cairtney plans to take her boyfriend to the theatre. There will be dancing on the Green. But typically, the pleasure is short lived and the aftermath displays black eyes, broken noses, people with the shakes and grotesque hangovers freezing at street corners having pawned hats, coats and shoes.[9]

The cultural inversion present in festivals, when normal social constraints are abandoned in a world briefly turned upside down, is also to be observed in a minor way in *Doings on Sunday Night*, when droves of urban dwellers regularly promenade. The crowd includes old bachelors chatting up young girls, old maids with their pet dogs and 'servant lassies, fat and plump, / with great big bustles on their rump'. Courtship, canoodling couples and members of both sexes on the lookout for prey are rife; girls of seventeen are 'doing the thing that is not right'. The moral is that lassies who allow the boys 'to get their petticoats up' on the Sabbath will end up in the family way, not the kind of activity normally associated with a Scottish Sunday, while reflecting the absence of opportunities for privacy in towns and no doubt exaggerating the degree of indulgence.[10]

Consumerism is rife at the market where young women dressed in their finery meet their would-be suitors strutting around, penny cigars stuck in their mouths. There are tasty snacks, plenty of drink and games to play as well as endless opportunities for flirtation: 'Betty and Sam are playing deeds that you shan't'.[11] Feeing day in Falkirk is one to celebrate the indispensable work of the ploughmen who till the land to supply crops; they are also skilled in the non-violent training of the wildest horses for the plough. People come from all around for the day and most end up in the pub.

> May success the Ploughmen's labours crown;
> May Ploughmen's wages ne'er come down;
> May plenty in our land aboun'
> By the labours of the Ploughmen![12]

Less optimistic are the haymakers. Tanned dark, hot and sweating – 'poor is our daily reward' – they nonetheless feel more privileged than 'the pale faces over the loom', trapped in the gloom of the city. In the description of outdoor toil there is an echo of slavery and servitude in hot climes. In a tale of the Bethune brothers, 'the illegitimate' through constant exposure to 'an almost tropical summer', is sunburned or 'so completely tanned, that he might have been mistaken for a native of some more southern latitude'.[13] The haymakers invite urban ladies to visit the countryside:

Your garments will take no stain from the burs,
And a freckle won't tarnish your smile.

Rural landscapes provide the softest carpets and unrivalled healthy perfumes.[14]
A merry but ambitious ploughboy is sung as he becomes a footman, a butler,
and a tradesman who cheats his customers and diddles his employer on his way
to becoming a politician, eventually acquiring a seat in the Lords.[15] Novel agricultural practices are exhilaratingly lauded in *A New Song, Sung at the Meeting of
the Perthshire Florist and Vegetable Society*; unusually, it is actually dated to 1808.
In land once barren are now grown melons and pineapples, geraniums and
carnations, as orchards, hothouses and vegetable gardens flourish.[16] An ironic
song begins by celebrating an excellent harvest but quickly becomes a protest
about monopolies, greedy millers who contaminate the meal they grind by
mixing it with dust, bakers who collude in price fixing, hucksters and forestallers
of all kinds and farmers who allegedly throw grain into the sea rather than sell
it cheaply. Meat is hopelessly expensive. The price of liver, on which the poor
depend, is unprecedently high and even sheep's heid costs tenpence![17] Similar
in tone is a song to the tune of 'The Good Old Days of Adam and Eve':

> Our working men like slaves do toil, merchants like princes live,
> There [*sic*] motto is 'we will take all' they never think to give,
> When bread is dear and victualling high, and wages still the same,
> How can a man in decency his family maintain.[18]

Poverty is a depressingly recurrent theme of both broadsides and chapbooks.
Scotland's Stagnation attributes national poverty to the outbreak of the Crimean
War with a chorus of:

> Tens of thousands out of work, what will the country come to?
> I cannot think, says everyone, where all the trade is gone to.

Tradesmen cannot make sales. 12,000 snobs or snabs (cobblers) and 10,000 weavers
are unemployed. Doctors and lawyers are crying poverty. Not even thieves and
prostitutes can make a living.[19] A still familiar refrain concerns three Glasgow
bigwigs condemned for spending ratepayers' money, which should have gone
to the poor, on a junket to London.[20] Equally recognisable is a pauper who is
expected to live on half a sovereign a month, or half a crown a week. He asks a
minister what sort of a sermon he would preach for an equivalent sum:

> Now all you jolly gentle folks that's waxen rather fat,
> Apply unto the parish and you'll soon get rid o' that;
> Twa months will make you lank and lean, and supple as a leek,
> Pay washing, bed and board like me, on half a crown a week.[21]

An uplifting broadside, *Dialogue between Death and a Sinner Composed by a Sunday
School Teacher*, was designed to be sold by the unemployed.[22] It was believed that

much poverty was caused by alcohol during a century in which many of the well-intentioned were obsessed with temperance or abolition. The *Drunkard's Child*, reduced to beggary, 'Hungry, cold, distracted and wild', has lost a father to drink and mother to a broken heart.[23] A wife-beating drunk is reformed when he signs the pledge.[24] Another sheet deplores wastrels who drink, indulge in gaming and beat their wives:

> To the tap shop they go then without dread or fear,
> With a pipe or a pot of good ale or strong beer.
> Tho' the landlord will serve and come at your call,
> When your monies are gone he will laugh at your fall.
>
> With the money you take him he's filling his bags,
> While your family are clothed in tattars and rags,
> And the best roast and boil'd to his table is brought,
> While your own wife and children eat potatoes and salt.

The landlady has fine clothes while the drunkard's wife is in tatters. Yet the song advises moderation, not necessarily total abstinence:

> Strong ale at the first it was sent for our good,
> To strengthen our bodies and nurture our blood,
> But drink to excess why it must be confessed,
> That it oftentimes makes a man worse than a beast.
>
> That others shou'd drink and spend all they can,
> That's no reason you should act the same plan;
> Tho' they swear, lie and swager [*sic*] and drink till they burst,
> Be advised and think of your families first.[25]

The makers of broadsides and chapbooks seem to have early seized on the literary possibilities of the railway as metaphor, as in what must be the earliest commuter chap printed. A piece in a style which prefigures William Topaz McGonagall commemorates the opening of the Glasgow and Ayr Railway in 1840. The bard relates his impressions of the thunderous noise, the train flying like the wind, and a tunnel that reminded him of a coalpit. Dashing away from Paisley, 'My head it got dizzy, they ran so quick, / Some more on the train like me got sea sick'. Another marked the inauguration of the Greenock and Paisley Railway in 1841.[26]

One ingenious item is *Railroad to Hell: Or, If You Will, From Dissipation to Poverty, and from Poverty to Desperation, The Line begins in a Brewery and runs through all Public Houses, Dram Shops and Jerry Shops, in a zig-zag direction until it lands in the Kingdom of Hell*. Taverns are the railways to Hell, while their barrels are 'the engines that make men rebel', though far too many women also indulge.[27] The idea that pubs were for men only did not prevail in nineteenth-century Scotland, at least in the cities. A couple of broadsides by named authors are also concerned to communicate the temperance message. William Miller, who contributed to the *Whistle Binkie* series, depicts 'the drouthie, drouthie chiel, wi' the red plooky face, who' 'Daised and half doited stoytes fae place to place', while John Barr celebrates domestic bliss in the household of a reformed alcoholic.[28] Daniel Norris has a composition about Watty, a pillar of the community who runs teetotal meetings but who carries on imbibing and succeeds in having his illegitimate child fathered on a Glasgow lamplighter.[29]

Intoxication often led, of course, to crime. Dozens of cheap prints were concerned in one way or another with executions. Typically, the condemned person regrets that s/he did not heed parental advice while lamenting leaving aged parents to fend for themselves. Archibald Hare, 'inflamed by drink', murdered Ronald MacGregor in Blantyre for no apparent reason. James M'Donnell brutally beat his pregnant girlfriend with a loaded whip; she survived long enough to report him before she died: 'this girl was a servant maid and I a farmer's son'. He expressed sorrow from his heart, asking all Christians to pray for him when he came to stand on the trap-board below the gallows.[30] A story 'to make the blood run cold' was that of Betsy Smith, pleading for the life of her unborn child as her lover knifed her to death:

> Twice more then with the fatal knife he pierced her body through,
> Her throat was cut from ear to ear, most dreadful for to view;
> Her arms and hands and beauteous face he cut and mangled so.
> While down upon her lily white breast the crimson blood did flow.[31]

Margaret Bell murdered her child by throwing it into a pond at Crofton Bleachfield, Paisley. She slept at the site but when workers found the baby she fled only to be arrested and condemned. Remarkably, a public petition saved her from the gallows and she was transported, as another broadside recounts, warning other young maidens about 'false-hearted young men'.[32]

One of the most remarkable doomed prisoner episodes concerns twenty-year-old murderer, thief and conman David Haggart, about whom there survives a chapbook as well as his autobiography, the sales of which he intended would support his parents. In addition, in the condemned cell he was examined by the phrenologist George Combe, while his publications, his execution and the events leading to it were widely scrutinised in the press. Unlike most of the condemned, he attempted, in his autobiography, to justify his crime and to set the record straight on certain other matters. He was executed at Edinburgh on 18 July 1821 in scenes not entirely devoid of pathos.[33] Though they should not be mentioned on the same page as Haggart, the state murder of James Wilson, Andrew Hardie and John Baird showed so-called justice at its worst. All were caught up in the extravagantly named 'Radical War' of 1820. Wilson was with a group that processed from Strathaven to the outskirts of Paisley expecting to meet up with other protesters. Hardie and Baird joined a party of weavers advancing from Stirling with the idea of commandeering the iron-works at Falkirk, only to be stopped at Bonnymuir by troops. All three were arrested and barbarously executed.[34]

The Bonnymuir Rising is recounted by one of the transported, addressed to 'Ye True Sons of Freedom', as he returns after twelve years in Botany Bay. Wilson, Hardie and Baird he regards as martyrs, as might be expected. His own mother does not recognise him but she offers him lodging even if she has to 'lie on the ground'. At that point he reveals his identity to the joy of all.[35] Another transportee condemned to 'drag a wretched life, in chains, upon a distant shore' blames poverty and political apathy for his plight:

> Oh would our rulers make a law for man to earn his bread,
> And make sufficient wages to keep his wife and children fed.
> The children would have less to do, and half their pay might be
> Devoted to the public good, and bless society.
> The Prisons would be empty soon, and transport ships would then
> Bring o'er the seas a load of corn and not a load of men!
> Act after act our rulers make but one they will not do,
> To do to others as they would – themselves be done unto.[36]

Political ballads, broadsides and chapbooks are numerous. In *The White Cliffs of Albion*, Libertie's Queen appears to warn Britain's rulers that though they have forged chains she will not permit them to be used on British subjects, who will 'live to be free, or die to a man':

> Reform it, Reform it, they shouted aloud,
> And the breath from their voices soon formed a cloud
> In which she departed, and gave then a nod,
> Saying, the wish of the people's the will of a God.[37]

In the last line we have to wonder whether the people are the god, or if the indefinite article was introduced to avoid charges of blasphemy!

In one song a milkmaid's interest in a collier intensifies when she discovers he is a member of the trade union. It turns out that her father had been a pitman, reinforcing the popular adage that only miners' daughters married miners:

> Come all you noble gentlemen, wherever that you be,
> O, never pull their wages down to break their unity;
> You see they hold like brothers, like sailors on the sea,
> To do their best endeavours for their wives and family.
>
> We've steam upon the ocean, we've steam upon the land,
> And what can we do now at all without our colliermen?
> They send their coal above the ground the country all round,
> We know they work both night and day with danger under ground.[38]

And so the lass wins her collier, 'as black as any sloe'.

There is a great deal of information in both ballad and chapbook about the perennial *querelles des femmes*, more prosaically known in English as 'The Battle of the Sexes'. This tradition is manifested in some of our earliest ballads, many of which continued to appear in broadside form into the late nineteenth century.

Those same ballads relate many tales of sibling rivalry, of paternal disapproval of daughter's liaisons, of sons too strongly attached to their mothers, of *in extremis* infanticide and incest, but above all of gutsy women who defy the androcentric and authoritarian conventions of contemporary society. Janet, the heroine of *Tam Lin*, for example, defies her father's order to avoid Carterhaugh, the residence of the ballad's eponym who preys upon young women, by deliberately seeking out her seducer. Pregnant, she refuses her father's suggestion of marriage with a member of his household. She considers abortion but, on learning that Tam Lin is in fact a mortal, she follows his instructions to liberate him from Fairyland by means of an ordeal as she clings to him while he undergoes several shape-shiftings. The sixteenth and seventeenth centuries produced further examples of independent women who took charge of their own lives. One defiant beauty tells her lover that if he chases other women she will pursue other men. Another arranges the murder of her husband for wife beating and pays the supreme penalty.[39]

While there is no doubt that such ballads contained an apotropaic element, a warning of what could happen to foolish young maidens, songs of the later period were much more overtly didactic, often communicating a specific moral. *Woman the Joy and the Pride of the Land* is a paean to marriage. A virtuous woman is a jewel who will provide her husband with adoring children, tempting him out of the alehouse, tending him in sickness and looking after his every need. When he returns home, there is food on the table, everything is prepared for his comfort and whatever he desires his wife will fetch; 'His linen is clean and his bed is got ready'.[40] On the other hand, an amusing song has a woman boast that she is ninety-five, 'and to keep single I contrive'. Men are deceitful and fickle. She celebrates her childlessness: 'Matrimony with sorrow begins . . . There is naught but strife in a wedding ring'. She rejoices that she has avoided having 'to wash and brew, / And mend the holes in his stockings too'.[41] Another woman wishes her drunken husband dead but, having dreamed that he had expired, she is so full of remorse that she decides to stand by him in hope of reforming him.[42] One man laments that woman is the torment of man. He has to do the chores and make his own breakfast, has to tolerate her absences and her endless nagging, her physical assaults; however she turns out to be alcoholic.[43] A bachelor announces that he wants a wife with money to supply his considerable wants; another laments the bane of a gossiping wife. A recurring theme is that of the deceitful spouse. In many songs the girl or the boy fancies the other who says s/he is already spoken for. After very little persuasion, s/he succumbs to the entreaties of the other who then rejects her/him because, if they have proved unfaithful once, they will again in the future.[44]

An old maid of forty-five is desperate for a man, even one who would spend all his money in the tavern:

> Come landsmen come princes, brewers and bakers,
> Fiddlers, fifers, tailors, or weavers.

Ragmen, or madmen, foolish or witty,
Do not let me die a maid, marry me for pity.

She is rewarded with a chimney sweep.[45] Countless other chapbooks and broadsides deal with similar themes. Many are touching, some hilarious and others plain daft, such as the man who compares his girlfriend to a roasting duck.[46] Many chaps deal with courtship, irrespective of class or social position, of the joyous occasions that weddings were, and of the difficulties of married life, child rearing and economic pressures. A history of affective relationships could be traced through these ballads, songs and chapbooks. Houghmagandie (fornication) is also a popular subject in chapbook literature, possibly a direct reflection and a critical counterpoint to the Kirk's obsession with illicit sex as recorded in sessions and presbyteries.[47]

THE PERIODICAL PRESS

The periodical press is one other source of potential assistance to ethnologists. To date, newspapers have probably received more attention from researchers than the other periodicals. Comparatively ignored, however, are tale collections in which there was significant popular interest throughout the nineteenth century. Tales were often initially published in serial form or in periodicals and then collected in books. Some retold old and familiar stories but even tales of which the authors are known can be and were considered as traditional because of the style in which they were written, often containing much vernacular dialogue. Some tales drew upon traditional themes such as retelling of ballads but the effect was enhanced by the real or supposed circumstance that the authors were of the people. Several who were employed in quite lowly occupations wrote straight out of their own experiences, their stories sometimes close to autobiographical. In addition, some publications claimed to print material hitherto existing only in the oral medium.

One stunning survival, fragments of which have been traced to the thirteenth century, is the ballad of the murderous Lamkin, the stonemason who, unpaid for his work by Lord Wearie, murders his wife and child with the aid of a vicious wet nurse. In 1909 a contributor to *The Border Magazine* reported that he heard the story narrated by a nonagenarian with reference to Bonkyl Castle in Berwickshire. In this version, the psychopath is named Langkin and is eventually hanged on a tree 'which still stands to this day' while the nurse is condemned to 'a cauldron of lead'. The narrator confided that, when she was a girl, 'she knew a very old man named Gillies who declared that he had seen the cauldron'.[48] The tree and the cauldron may not be convincing but this was an attempt to locate a migratory ballad in a very specific location. Such traditional literature, so far rather ignored by scholarship, is one other possible vast source for ethnological enquiry.

The collectors and creators of such material were all, to some extent, influenced by three great inspirational figures beginning with the incomparable phenomenon of James Macpherson's translations (or imitations) of Ossianic poetry. The belief that Ossian was a Gaelic bard who flourished long ago in the distant past implied that he inhabited a world as old as, and possibly older than, that of Greece and Rome, and the possibility that the vernacular languages of Europe, those of the people at large, might preserve valuable information about the literature and history of ancient non-classical times.[49] Ossian was the spur to collectors of folk tales, poems and songs in their own backyards. A second influence was none other than Robert Burns who was viewed as the supreme poetic recorder of change, of a way of life on the verge of disappearing. The first collection of Burns' poetry, edited by James Currie, was notable not only for the voluminous personal correspondence which accompanied the texts but also for an essay on the life of the Scottish peasantry.[50] Other poets were revered for their creative output; Burns apparently could not be understood outside of his personal context. Was any other poet accorded similar treatment? Most editors allow the poetry to speak for the poet rather than providing pages of biographical information, let alone a dissertation on the nature of the wider society which sustained and supported the bard. Currie set the pattern for future editors, and for the Burns cult which became obsessed with recovering every single detail, however trivial, about the poet's existence, while stimulating widespread popular curiosity about, and interest in, agricultural Scotland on the part of those who had left the land as well as those who remained. The Burns phenomenon rendered study of the Scottish folk and their traditions respectable. The third influence was Walter Scott who combined tradition, history, personal genealogy and location to such telling effect, first in his *Minstrelsy of the Scottish Border* and later in his novels. Though he did not admit the collaboration until 1830, Scott was ably assisted in the production of *Minstrelsy* by John Leyden whose poems from the 1790s drew upon the traditions of his native Border country and who thus spearheaded a movement in which others apart from Scott participated.[51]

John Jamieson, for example, published his *Etymological Dictionary of the Scottish Language*, a veritable compendium of Scottish folklore, in 1808. That same year Henry Duncan, minister of Ruthwell in Dumfriesshire, later famous as the founder of savings banks, released the first issue of his *Scotch Cheap Repository*, which published couthy stories with a Christian moral, later gathered in book form as *Moral Tales*.[52] When R H Cromek produced his *Remains of Nithsdale and Galloway Song with Historical and Traditional Notices Relative to the Manners and Customs of the Peasantry* (1810), much of his unacknowledged material was supplied by Allan Cunningham. Most of the latter's folk and sociological information was sound but in a manner worthy of Macpherson he represented many of his own ballad and song compositions as traditional. James Hogg, the Ettrick Shepherd, also polished a number of traditional tales, while remaining much more deeply involved in, and sensitively respectful of, the folk tradition than Scott.[53]

Whatever our reservations about Scott's reputation, the immensity of his achievement cannot be denied. He, too, taught, like Burns, that humble humanity had its part to play in history and in so doing influenced generations of historians. A year after Scott's death, John Gordon Barbour produced *Unique Traditions Chiefly of the West and South of Scotland*, praising the late 'great traditionary novelist of Caledonia'.[54] The word 'traditionary' was to enjoy something of a vogue throughout the nineteenth century. The *Oxford English Dictionary* equates 'traditional' and 'traditionary' but neither Barbour nor anyone else could have described Scott as a 'traditional novelist'; rather, 'traditionary' implies the privileging of tradition, of that which is handed down, often orally, from generation to generation. Barbour claimed that he collected and recorded 'legends and traditions most meriting of being preserved' from Perthshire to Galloway. While some of his pieces are redolent of personal discussions and visits to sites of antiquarian interest, others, as in all such collections, suggest improved versions of tales acquired by the light of the lamp rather than the peat fire. Towns and cities were sources of oral material as much as country districts. John Francis Campbell of Islay, for example, collected Gaelic tales in Paisley later in the century.

A young man named John Mackay Wilson, born to Scottish parents in Tweedmouth, Northumberland, was responsible for a new departure in launching *Wilson's Tales of the Borders: Historical, Traditionary and Imaginative*, the first part of which was published in November 1834. When later published in book form, the title page added *And of Scotland: with an Illustrative Glossary of the Scottish Dialect*. Wilson exhausted himself producing the weekly series, which within six months was selling 30,000 copies each issue. Having taken to the bottle, he died aged thirty-one in 1835. The editorship was taken over by his brother and then by the pious Alexander Leighton.[55] Many well known writers contributed tales, such as Alexander and John Bethune, James Maidment, Hugh Miller and David Moir, though all appeared anonymously. The collection is now often plundered by growing numbers of modern storytellers who adapt and modify the tales so bringing them back into the oral tradition. In many there is a thin line between 'traditionary' and 'imaginative' but the point is that not a few, whether original or not, claimed to be traditional tales and thus to shed light on the manners and customs of former days. The series was collected in six volumes in 1840 (some 464 tales), in ten volumes from 1857–9 and in twenty-four in 1869. In signing off, when the series terminated, the editor modestly celebrated a work comprising 'the best collection of original tales extant'.

There was clearly a demand for such material, satisfied today by movies and television soaps. The final contribution to the series is entitled *The Last Tale: A Dream*, in which the contributing writers attend a wake-like gathering in the 'Border Tale Room' of the Hen and Chickens Tavern. 'The Border Tales are about to close. The writers of that inimitable work are holding their last meeting here tonight . . . The Border Tales are at an end and when shall we see such a work again?' By and by, individuals who had featured in earlier stories arrive to complain of authorial license but ultimately to commiserate and converse. Eventually they are joined by a procession of characters that had appeared in various tales, probably to make the point that there is no such thing as a truly original tale. Finally compositors and devils (printers' errand boys) march in, one carrying a black cushion with a sheet of paper on it. Edged in black it bears the title, 'The Last Tale', which it cannot be because we, the readers, are complicit in the telling of the tale about the last tale![56]

One entry which appears in *Wilson's Tales* is 'The Lykewake' by Hugh

Miller, the stonemason of Cromarty, who went on to become a great figure in the Free Church of Scotland and a deservedly popular writer on the subject of geology. Before achieving fame, he conscientiously collected folktales in his neighbourhood. 'The Lykewake' is so accurate an account as to almost pass for an ethnological case study. 'Lyke' is a corpse or body while the 'wake' (watch) is the vigil over the corpse before burial. Miller introduces his tale by reflecting that at a wake one ponders, in silence on death, the last great mystery, and yet gradually the folk present start to discuss what they know about the 'state and place' of death, recounting their experiences 'of the occasional visits of the dead, and all that in their less taciturn and more social moments they have communicated to the living'. Such at least is the case at country wakes for in the towns, 'a cold and barren scepticism has chilled the feelings and imaginations of the people'. The writer and an acquaintance attend the wake of an elderly woman. The storyteller describes lykewakes of the past at which music and dance, food, drink and games all featured. He is, of course, correct because Church and State both legislated against such frequently rowdy celebration in favour of respectful lamentation and contemplation.

In the room where the body was laid out in a white dress, elaborately stitched in a flower pattern, all the furniture had been hung in white; the floor had been swept and sanded. A small plate containing salt was placed on the corpse's chest. On arrival, both men were given a dram and a seat by the fire as they joined five other mourners. Each then tells a story relating to death, their way of coping with the situation and their grief. A woman told of the deceased's passing, a man had a tale of second sight, another spoke of a kelpie, a second woman had a ghost story. There was an account of the apparition of a vicious factor and another concerning a monopolistic meal-monger; in both tellings, the revenants suffered the replications for which they were hated in life. For example, the dead grain dealer, who had a reputation in life for depriving others by stealing or hoarding grain, wandered around begging a handful of meal because he was starving. Four of the stories were in Scots and all contain interesting social detail.[57]

The Bethune brothers contributed to *Tales of the Borders*. In 1838 Alexander published his *Tales and Sketches of the Scottish Peasantry*, one of the first books on the subject to be written, so to speak, from the inside. Alexander was born in 1804, John in 1811, both in Fife. Aged fourteen, Alexander began work as a labourer, mainly employed as a stone breaker and drainer; every morning for the first year his joints 'creaked like machinery wanting oil'. At times John joined him, but he became a gardener. Both were adversely affected, though John more so, by working in drains up to their knees in water. For twenty-two years they inhabited a house whose roof let in rain and whose floor was frequently flooded; they used stepping stones to reach their bed, the clothes of which were often soaking. Both considered the rich as ignorant as themselves, preferring poverty and obscurity, independence of thought and principle, to fawning patronage. Both brothers authored *Lectures on Practical Economy* aimed at the uneducated reader. Both published their first tales in *Chambers's Edinburgh Journal*. John died in 1839, aged just twenty-eight. In writing John's *Life* and editing his poems, Alexander noted that 'he lived poor, toiled hard and died early' but since the lives of both brothers were so close and intertwined he, in effect, produced an autobiography of two impoverished Scottish peasants, displaying a depth of experience that had characterised the earlier *Tales*.[58]

1843 saw the publication of *Historical and Traditional Tales in Prose and Verse Connected with the South of Scotland, Original and Select* by John Nicolson whose more famous brother was William Nicolson, the 'Bard of Galloway'. A former weaver and soldier, John worked as a chapman before becoming a printer and bookseller in Kirkcudbright. He acknowledged the source of most of his items, his aim being to illuminate,

> those particulars which are generally overlooked, or but slightly treated of in history – to exhibit our ancestors . . . in the privacy of their own homes and their various social relations. The peasant, the farmer, and the laird will be found, each breathing his characteristic notions and prejudices, and living amongst the quaint customs of a by-gone race.

He included his brother's much-loved poem, *The Brownie of Blednoch*, in the collection and he was the first to write about the 'Murder Hole' of which S R Crockett made such good use in *The Raiders*. The brownie was the cherished fantasy of the work-stretched and exhausted because he would labour for no more reward than a bowl of porridge. Indeed, if given greater payment, he would disappear along with his supranatural labouring capacities, never to be seen again.[59] He is known as the Glashan or the Gruagach of Gaeldom.[60] Nicolson produced an absorbing collection, recognising that the traditional material constituted 'the pendant of history'.

The late nineteenth century was described in *The Border Magazine*, launched in 1896, as 'the day of the magazines . . . multiplying around us in every department of Literature, Art and Science'. It aimed 'to illustrate what is passing in the present' rather than dwelling upon the region's rich and varied 'Literary, Historical and Romantic Associations of the past', while admitting that the last named aspects could not be ignored, 'for the past and the present are so inseparably united in the history of the Border Country, that one is simply the complement of the other'.[61] The magazine provided stories, poems, reminiscences, history, scenery and sites catering mostly but not exclusively to the nostalgia industry. There was actually an earlier magazine of the same title which launched in 1863 and survived for only six issues. Its aim was to treat of 'the past and present condition of our native country and its inhabitants, their language, works, social condition, and development'. The intention was to cover such subjects as archaeology, flora and fauna, 'the customs, proverbial sayings and traditions of Border-life', geology, agriculture, fine arts, manufacturing, landscape, literature, history, heritage and 'hundreds' of Border tales.[62] The first volume of the 1896 reincarnation featured 'Personal Recollections of the Border Country', battlefields, Tom Fox the collector of pontage for the Dryburgh Suspension Bridge, the 'Gonial Blast', Katie Dunn ferrywoman at Abbotsford, Border Societies (furth of the region), natural history, the story of 'Canonbie Dick and the Horses', the Wallace Statue and plenty of poetry. The magazine ran until 1931, too often reading like the cultic newsletter of worshippers at the shrine of Walter Scott. Rather similar in tone and content, though less Scott-fixated, was *The Gallovidian* which first appeared in 1899, struggling on until 1949. It undertook to

> sing the songs of the southern land, and bear tales told of her sons in bygone times with all the glamour the past can impart. The legend and the fireside are ever dear to patriotic hearts, and few there be who do not delight in the weal of the land that bore them.

Despite this rather inauspicious beginning, the first issue did carry some articles of contemporary interest such as 'Provincial Patriotism', 'The Student's Return to Galloway', 'What we want more of and what we want less of in Galloway by A Galloway Farmer' and 'Galloway Football'. Alongside articles on local history, there were traditional tales, too much verse and much material of ethnological interest.[63] One quaint innovation was the failed attempt to re-badge Dumfries and Galloway as 'Galfresia'! Despite some similar well-intentioned if misguided excursions, *The Border Magazine* and *The Gallovidian* between them have a great deal to offer ethnologists, covering as they do the major part of the Southern Uplands and often written by locals for locals.

William Donaldson has correctly pointed to the significance of such publications as the *People's Journal* and the *People's Friend* in the provision of popular tales written or recycled by amateur writers who wrote from the perspective of their own occupations and situations, often in the vernacular.[64] Such publications, however, had many precedents, though the publications he discusses were part of the flood following the repeal of the Stamp Act in 1855, making periodicals and newspapers very much cheaper. Newspapers are an obvious source for the study of ethnology. When the *Scotsman* launched on 25 January 1817 it spoke grandly of governments dedicated to the principles of freedom finding support among the people at large. Unfortunately the paper did not carry a great deal of information about Scottish folk since, in its earlier phases, it was largely devoted to national British and foreign news. Even local papers were often digests of national newspapers but matters rapidly improved during the first half of the nineteenth century offering almost limitless opportunities for ethnological studies. John Burnett has expertly demonstrated their potential in his study of Scottish sport, in which he makes excellent use of the medium, and he offers a case study in this chapter.[65] The present writer has found the local press invaluable in the study of such subjects as agricultural improvement and emigration, as well as late examples of witch accusations.[66]

Henry Duncan and other producers of moral tales knew very well that the best way to impact upon those they wished to reform was to speak to them in their own language, in terms they would understand. Newspapers soon learned the same trick. In the years just before the 'Radical War', there were profound fears on the part of some members of the Establishment that Britain was on the verge of a revolution and that the radicalism of industrial workers would spread to the countryside, which was experiencing a severe economic downturn due to the end of the Napoleonic wars. Some opinion detected a solution in emigration, hitherto regarded as a highly controversial topic but now seen as a possible mechanism for ridding Scotland of the disaffected. John McDiarmid, editor of the *Dumfries and Galloway Courier*, a paper founded by Henry Duncan, came up with an interesting and highly appropriate metaphor when he wrote that 'emigration operates as a drain and it is just as useful in thinning an extra population as extended rows of tiles are in carrying off surface water'. The practical farmers and all who worked on the land among his readership would have asked how well these tiles were operating. Were they performing a useful function? Where did the drains lead? Was the land better for being drained? Were the tiles taking off too much of the surplus? Did they represent a sensible solution to a perceived problem? In so doing, they would have been acting like conscientious students of ethnology.

CASE STUDY: NEWSPAPERS AND THE GLASGOW FAIR IN THE NINETEENTH CENTURY

John Burnett

From its inauguration in 1197 until about 1800, Glasgow Fair was like hundreds of others all over Europe; it was primarily for buying and selling animals and goods, and attracted the whole community.[67] It then changed rapidly: the commercial side of it became much less important, and the quantity and variety of entertainment increased.[68] Before 1800 there is little evidence for what happened at it, but after that it is covered in the newspapers, sometimes in considerable detail. Newspapers provide a way of investigating popular entertainment in the nineteenth century, and are particularly valuable because they record the changing character of the acts over the years as the showmen tried to increase their novelty value and therefore their profits. Newspapers have the advantage that most statements are precisely dated allowing comparative study of continuity and change. Until the 1840s the Fair was focused on Glasgow Green. Then leisure opportunities began to alter[69] and increasing numbers went 'doon the watter' by river steamer and railway to the Coast (Glaswegians did not call it the seaside) and in 1871, the shows were moved from the Green to the East End of the city and became relatively inconspicuous.

Newspapers have been published in Glasgow continuously since 1741.[70] The longest-running started as the *Glasgow Advertiser* in 1783 and became the *Glasgow Herald* in 1802.[71] Before 1859 it was produced two or three times a week, and since then it has been a daily paper. At various points it has been accompanied by five or more competitors but throughout the nineteenth century it was the largest and, to the historian, the most useful. Evening newspapers, starting with the *Evening Times* in 1876, were different, containing far more local news and being aimed at working people rather than the middle-class audience of the morning papers. There were weekly newspapers such as *Glasgow Citizen*, part of whose readership was the mass who could not afford the *Herald*. Glasgow had two weekly magazines of gossip and humour, *The Bailie* (1872–1926) and *Quiz* (1881–98), which say amusing things about the Fair. One trade paper is useful for the Fair, though it is not a trade paper in the normal sense. This is *The Era*, a Sunday paper published in London from 1838 which was read by show people and contains advertisements for performers for the Fair such as one for 'dramatic and gymnastic clog dancers and dog men'.[72]

Local newspapers existed on the Clyde Coast at Greenock (1802) and Ayr (1803) early in the century, but they were published in the more important destinations only after large numbers of Fair folk had started to go there, for example at Rothesay (1857), Dunoon (1871) and Largs (1877). They provide local stories and perspectives. Unlike the Glasgow papers, they sometimes carry significant material about the Fair at times other than in mid July, at the beginning and end of the summer season, for example.

Some idea of the place of the Fair in the world as reflected in a newspaper can be gained if we look at the *Herald* for Fair Monday, 1854. Its eight pages include three-and-a-half pages of advertisements, four pages of British and Scottish news and two columns – less than half a page – on Glasgow. The report of the Fair, covering both the Green and the Coast, is just over 500 words long. In other words, it takes up less than 1 per cent of that edition of the *Herald* or, since the paper appeared at that time twice a week, 0.008 per cent of its content over the whole year.

What kind of evidence is available for the Fair? When it was on the Green, newspapers tell us the names of the principal showmen and the character of the larger entertainments such as plays in temporary theatres, panoramas and menageries. Petty crime, particularly pickpocketing, is often mentioned. When the people go to the Coast, the numbers travelling are given, but rarely in a way which allows clear comparison between successive years. Novelties were attractive to journalists, and a number of them appeared at the end of the nineteenth century, including the helter-skelter, cinematograph, and motor car.

There are, however, limitations in the information available. What is on the page is often bland and repetitive from year to year: most of what the ethnologist would like to know was being spoken, not written down.

> The arm of labour was almost entirely suspended; the furnaces were blown out; the steam-looms stood still; the hammer was at rest; the shuttle ceased to ply, and thousands of our working population, who constitute the industrial power of Glasgow, had bedecked themselves in their Sunday's best.[73]

Thus the *Glasgow Herald* described the Fair in 1844 in picturesque words, but of how much value are they to the ethnologist?

Information can be uncomfortably vague. At the beginning of one July, the *Buteman* said that visitors to Rothesay were bathing, paddling, boating, fishing, cycling, promenading and playing tennis and bowls, though there was no evening entertainment.[74] This is good, solid information, but it leaves two large areas of doubt. First, who was doing these things and what do the words mean; for example, does fishing mean sea-fishing or angling, and if it is more probable that the fish were being sought in the sea, did the fishers have rods or were they using lines? What did they hope to catch? Second, the list sounds like the activities enjoyed by the better off: it may not have applied to the Fair folk.

Sometimes there is an enjoyable vividness in the descriptions; in 1854 it was said that the weather had been good, unlike the previous year when 'even habitually sober people flew to the bottle to drown their chagrin, and raise some heat in their half-starved bodies'.[75] The question of what people did on Sundays at the Coast is hardly ever mentioned. Traders must have taken on extra workers for the summer, and particularly for the Fair, but only one instance has emerged explicitly in the case of Catherine Macpherson, a Dunoon restaurateur, who engaged a Glasgow baker for the month of July 1898, and asked him to hire another man for Fair week, but had to dismiss them because they neglected their work.[76] Very occasionally, something poignant appears, as when a correspondent remembered that in Mumford's puppet theatre, the 'Portuguese hymn' was played while The Babes in the Wood were ascending to heaven. This music is today better known as 'Adeste Fideles' or 'O Come All Ye Faithful' – 'My attention was slightly distracted by an elder brother who accompanied me entering into a discussion with two washer-women sitting behind us, on the propriety of introducing church music in a show'.[77] Where else could one find this kind of evidence of the nature of the piety of working people?

One has to be aware of the personal bias of the observer. When the Fair on the Green started to go downhill, a journalist said that 'The jokes and wry-mouths of the Merry Andrews have at length become stale, flat and unprofitable, the tumblers and touters are getting shabby in appearance; and the brass instruments are affected by bronchitis, and are dying for want of wind'.[78] The author's aim is to impress the reader with the quality of his writing and of his cynicism. He certainly says that his enjoyment of the Fair has lessened, but the quotation is as much a series of judgments as a statement of facts, and many who were there may have disagreed with him. Otherwise, why did they keep going to the Fair?

It can be difficult to see what a writer is saying when disapproval is expressed through euphemisms. 'The Scottish nation . . . has still to learn the true philosophy of holidaying; for the common course of events proves that a pleasure trip as often as not belies its name'.[79] A second journalist was more explicit when he predicted that the Glasgow workman will show his faults from Saturday to Monday of Fair.[80] Both men were talking about excessive drinking of alcohol. It is easy to miss euphemism, as when in 1872 three riveters rowed a small boat upriver from Port Glasgow 'to take strawberries'. On the return journey the boat capsized and one man was drowned.[81] Strawberries, perhaps; whisky, certainly. There are few reports as blunt as this one, recording the evening arrivals at the Broomielaw: 'drunken men, drunken wives, sleeping or crying children, draggled petticoats, and scowling faces mingle together'.[82]

Local newspapers often go into more detail than the city ones. Marymass (originally the Feast of the Assumption) was celebrated in Irvine in the middle of August. In 1861, the *Ardrossan & Saltcoats Herald* complained of:

> Oaths vomited forth in fearful profusion, chiefly by colliers . . . Streets very throng till near midnight, when the curtain drops, and conceals much that it is desirable for the sake of our common humanity should be hid.[83]

Three decades later behaviour was better and attitudes to it more relaxed. In 1894 two navvies and their wives were fined for fighting: 'the women were taken in a machine to the Police Office, yelling all the way'.[84] In 1896 most of the convictions stemmed from alcohol: drunk in the High Street, drunk in Bank Street, drunk on a hot potato machine.[85] In some years, the Ayrshire papers provided more useful detail on Marymass than the Glasgow ones did on the Fair.

However, editors saw local news as being less important than national events. For example, King William IV died in the summer of 1837, and for three weeks the *Ayr Advertiser* carried no local news, though it did print a diagram of the king's funeral procession. Coverage of Glasgow Fair in 1895 was limited by accounts of the speeches given by candidates at a General Election.

As well as evidence, newspapers can help us to find a sense of contact with the past. The following dialogue was reported in 1891. It makes the objective point that the Fair was remembered throughout the year, but it says more.

Anticipating Vinegar Hill:
Bob (aged seven, to his sister Kate) – Come an' play at a show. You'll be the fat lady, an' I'll be the showman.
Kate (aged five) – No! that'll no dae. You'll be the learned pig. Come an' play.[86]

Across a century, we hear the reality of childhood and family life.

NOTES

1 'The Laird o' Loanhead's Description of the Farmers', Glasgow University Library (GUL), Mu23-y1:103. This chapter draws heavily upon the website *Glasgow Broadside Ballads. The Murray Collection* by David Hopkin and Valentina Bold which conveniently provides copies of the Glasgow University Library GUL Mu23 series. See: http://www.gla.ac.uk/t4/dumfries/files/layer2/glasgow_broadside_ballads/ [accessed May 2011].

2 This widening gulf is often noticed in the pages of *New (Second) Statistical Account of Scotland*.

3 Cowan, 2007, 14–16.

4 See Cowan and Paterson, 2007, 11–40. This study, *The Glasgow-Strathclyde Chapbooks Project*, supported by the British Academy, focused on The Murray Collection of Chapbooks in GUL. Since David Murray bought up the end-run stock of certain Glasgow chapbook printers the collection is centred overwhelmingly on chaps dating from the late eighteenth and the nineteenth centuries.

5 Fenton and Leitch, 2010.

6 Cowan and Paterson, 2007, 24–31.

7 'Glasgow Fair on the Banks o' the Clyde', GUL Mu23-y1:022.

8 'The Week After the Fair', GUL Mu23-y1:022.

9 'A Song on the New Year', GUL Mu23-y1:058.

10 'Doings on a Sunday Night', GUL Mu23-y1:066.

11 'Humours of this Town!', GUL Mu23-y1: 023.

12 'The Falkirk Ploughmen', GUL Mu23-y1: 023.

13   Bethune, A and J. *Tales of the Scottish Peasantry*, London and Glasgow, 1884, 254.

14   'Song of the Haymakers', GUL Mu23-y1: 043.

15   'The Plough Boy', GUL Bh13-c.2; Cowan and Paterson, 2007, 131–2.

16   'A New Song, Sung at the Meeting of the Perthshire Florist and Vegetable Society', GUL Bh13-d.3; Cowan and Paterson, 2007, 77–9.

17   'Fine Harvest Weather', GUL Bh13-c.11; Cowan and Paterson, 2007, 83–5.

18   'A New Song on the Times', GUL Mu23-y3:021.

19   'Scotland's Stagnation! Or, Where is all the Money gone?', GUL Mu23-y1:073.

20   'Who Diddled the Paupers?', GUL Mu23-y3:008.

21   'The Pauper and the Minister', GUL Mu23-y3:008.

22   'Dialogue between Death and a Sinner Composed by a Sunday School Teacher', GUL Mu23-y1:028.

23   'The Drunkard's Child', GUL Mu23-y1:012.

24   'The Drunkard Reclaimed', GUL Mu23-y1:024.

25   'A Word of Advice', GUL Mu23-y1:054.

26   'The Opening of the Glasgow and Ayr Railway', GUL Mu23-y3: 033; 'The Greenock Railway', GUL Bh13-c.3; Cowan and Paterson, 2007, 358–61.

27   'Railroad to Hell', GUL Mu23-y1:057.

28   'The Drouthie Chiel; The Unco Change', GUL Mu23-y3:034.

29   'Watty; or The Glasgow Teetotal Party', GUL Mu23-y2:010.

30   'Lament of Archibald Hare', GUL Mu23-y1:007; 'James M'Donnell', GUL Mu23-y1:079.

31   'Murder of Betsy Smith', GUL Mu23-y1:092. The fact that this murder took place near Manchester in no way diminished the horror of the crime.

32   'Lamentation of Margaret Bell at present under Sentence of Death in Paisley Jail', GUL Mu23-y1:092; 'Margaret Bell's Lament', GUL Mu23-y1:095.

33   'The Life and Adventures of David Haggart', GUL Bh13-c.38; Cowan and Paterson, 2007, 362–81.

34   Ellis and Mac a' Ghobhainn, 1970, *passim*. See also Cowan and Paterson, 2007, 136–8, on the suggestion that *agents provocateurs* played a role in this sad affair.

35   'The Convict's Return', GUL Mu23-y1:104.

36   'Farewell Address to their Countrymen and Friends, of all those unfortunate Men who received their Sentences of Transportation, at the present Circuit Court, by the Judges on the Western Circuit', GUL Mu23-y1:089.

37   'The White Cliffs of Albion', GUL Mu23-y1:050.

38   'The Pitman's Union', GUL Mu23-y1:015.

39   Cowan, E J. Sex and violence in the Scottish ballads. In Cowan, 2000, 99–110; Henderson and Cowan, 2001, 153–7.

40   'Woman the Joy and the Pride of the Land', GUL Mu23-y1:011.

41   'I'm Ninety-Five', GUL Mu23-y2:015.

42   'The Wife's Dream', GUL Mu23-y1:103.

43   'A Woman is the Torment of Man', GUL Mu3-y1:114.

44   There are dozens of songs on this theme. For example, 'The Blooming Rose of Banbridge Town', GUL Mu23-y1:015; 'The Braes of Strathblane', GUL Mu23-y1:044; 'The Glasgow Factory Lass', GUL Mu23-y1:010.

45   'The Chimney Sweeper's Wedding!', GUL Mu23-y1:047.

46   'A Choice Duck', GUL Bh 13-d.25; Cowan and Paterson, 2007, 226.

47   Cowan and Paterson, 2007, 159–240.

48   Border rhymes and folklore, *The Border Magazine*, 14 (1909), 179–80. On 'Lamkin' see Cowan, 'Sex and Violence', 110–12.

49 Stafford, 1988, *passim*.
50 [Currie], 1813, I, 2–31.
51 On Leyden see Henderson and Cowan, 2001, 195–7.
52 Duncan, 1848, 69–77.
53 Hogg, 1872.
54 Barbour, 1886, 11.
55 There is a helpful article online by Mike Yates, 'John Mackay Wilson and his tales of the Borders'. Available at: www.borderstraditions.org.uk/1033 [Accessed May 2011].
56 *Wilson's Tales*, 1840, VI, 312.
57 *Wilson's Tales*, 1840, IV, 41–8. On Hugh Miller as folklorist see also Henderson, 2003.
58 Bethune, 1884, 9–30.
59 Nicolson, 1843, 80–4; Henderson and Cowan, 2001, 49–50, 54–6.
60 Campbell, 1861, I, 33.
61 *The Border Magazine*, 1 (1896), 10.
62 *The Border Magazine*, 1:1–6 (1863).
63 *The Gallovidian: An Illustrated Southern Counties Quarterly Magazine*, 1 (Spring 1899).
64 Donaldson, 1986; Donaldson, 1988.
65 Burnett, 2000.
66 Cowan, 1977-87. But see now for a much fuller discussion, Beals, 2011, 159–96. On witches see Cowan and Henderson, 2002.
67 Fisher, 1994, 134–6.
68 King, 1987.
69 Maver, 2005.
70 Fisher, 1994, 242–50.
71 Its title was reduced to *The Herald* in 1992.
72 *The Era*, 25 June 1865, 16c.
73 *Glasgow Herald*, 15 July 1844.
74 *Buteman*, 1 July 1893, 2e.
75 *Glasgow Herald*, 17 July 1854, 5c.
76 *Dunoon Herald*, 12 August 1898, 2f.
77 *Glasgow Herald*, 13 May 1863, 6d.
78 *Glasgow Herald*, 16 July 1864, 4f–g.
79 *Glasgow Herald*, 13 July 1881, 6d.
80 *Buteman*, 21 July 1894, 2f.
81 *Greenock Times*, 20 July 1872, 1c.
82 *Buteman*, 26 July 1873, 3b.
83 *Ardrossan & Saltcoats Herald*, 31 August 1861.
84 *Ayr Advertiser*, 30 August 1894, 5g.
85 *Ayr Advertiser*, 27 August 1896, 5d.
86 *Bailie*, 3 June 1891, 10.

BIBLIOGRAPHY AND FURTHER READING

Barbour, J G. *Unique Traditions Chiefly of the West and South of Scotland* (1883), London and Glasgow, 1886.
Beals, M H. *Coin, Kirk, Class and Kin Emigration: Social Change and Identity in Southern Scotland*, Bern, 2011.
Burnett, J. *Riot, Revelry and Rout: Sport in Lowland Scotland Before 1860*, East Linton, 2000.
Campbell, J F. *Popular Tales of the West Highlands*, 4 vols, Edinburgh, 1861.

Cowan, E J. Agricultural improvement and the formation of early agricultural societies in Dumfries and Galloway, *The Transactions of the Dumfriesshire and Galloway Natural History and Antiquarian Society*, 3rd series, 53 (1977–8), 157–67.

Cowan, E J, ed. *The Ballad in Scottish History*, East Linton, 2000.

Cowan, E J. Scotching the beggars: John the Commonweal and Scottish history. In Murdoch, A, ed., *The Scottish Nation. Identity and History. Essays in Honour of William Ferguson*, Edinburgh, 2007.

Cowan, E J and Henderson, L. The last of the witches? The survival of Scottish witch belief. In Goodare, J, ed., *The Scottish Witch-hunt in Context*, Manchester, 2002, 198–217.

Cowan, E J and Paterson, M. *Folk in Print: Scotland's Chapbook Heritage 1750–1850*, Edinburgh, 2007.

[Currie, J, ed.] *The Works of Robert Burns with An Account of his Life and A Criticism on his Writings. To which are prefixed, some observations on the character and condition of the Scottish Peasantry* (1800), 4 vols, 7th edn, London and Edinburgh, 1813.

Donaldson, W. *Popular Literature in Victorian Scotland: Language, Fiction and the Press*, Aberdeen, 1986.

Donaldson, W. *The Language of the People: Scots Prose from the Victorian Revival*, Aberdeen, 1989.

Duncan, G J C. *Memoir of the Rev. Henry Duncan, D.D. Minister of Ruthwell*, Edinburgh, 1848.

Ellis, P B and Mac a' Ghobhainn, S. *The Scottish Insurrection of 1820*, Edinburgh, 1970.

Fenton, A. The people below: Dougal Graham's chapbooks as a mirror of the lower classes in eighteenth-century Scotland. In Gardner-Medwin, A and Hadley Williams, J, eds, *A Day Estival*, Abedeen, 1990, 69–80.

Fenton, A and Leitch, R. Itinerant traders in Scotland, *Review of Scottish Culture*, 22 (2010), 18–34.

Ferguson, J P S. *Directory of Scottish Newspapers*, Edinburgh, 1984.

Ferguson, R S. Chapbooks in the Library of the Society of Antiquaries, *PSAS*, 15 (1894), 338–45.

Fisher, J. *The Glasgow Encyclopedia*, Edinburgh, 1994.

Gifford, D, ed. *The History of Scottish Literature vol. 3: Nineteenth Century*, Aberdeen, 1988, 203–15.

Harvey, W. *Scottish Chapbook Literature*, Paisley, 1903.

Henderson, L and Cowan, E J. *Scottish Fairy Belief: A History*, Edinburgh, 2001.

Henderson, L. The natural and supernatural worlds of Hugh Miller. In Borley, L, ed., *Celebrating the Life and Times of Hugh Miller: Scotland in the Early 19th Century*, Cromarty Arts Trust, 2003, 89–98.

Hogg, J. *The Works of the Ettrick Shepherd Tales and Sketches*, 2 vols, London, Edinburgh and Glasgow, 1872.

King, E. Popular culture in Glasgow. In Cage, R A, ed., *Working Class Glasgow 1750–1914*, London, 1987, 142–87.

MacCulloch, J. *The Highlands and Western Islands of Scotland*, 4 vols, London, 1824.

Mackenzie, A. *Newsplan: report of the NEWSPLAN project in Scotland*, London, 1994.

McNaughtan, A. A century of Saltmarket literature, 1790–1890. In Isaac, P, ed., *Six Centuries of the Provincial Booktrade in Britain*, Winchester, 1990, 165–80.

Morris, J. Scottish ballads and chapbooks. In Isaac, P and McKay, B, eds, *Images and Texts: Their Production and Distribution in the 18th and 19th Centuries*, Winchester, 1997, 89–111.

Neuberg, V E. *Chapbooks: A Guide to Reference Material on English, Scottish and American Chapbook Literature of the Eighteenth and Nineteenth Centuries*, 2nd edn, London, 1972.

Maver, I. Leisure time in Scotland during the nineteenth and twentieth centuries. In Beech et al., eds, *Scottish Life and Society. A Compendium of Scottish Ethnology, Volume 9: The Individual and Community Life*, Edinburgh, 2005, 174–203.

Nicolson, J, ed. *Historical and Traditional Tales in Prose and Verse Connected with the South of Scotland, Original and Select*, Kirkcudbright, 1843.

Roscoe, S and Brimmell, R A. *James Lumsden & Son of Glasgow: Their Juvenile Books and Chapbooks*, Pinner, 1981.

Roy, G R. The Brash and Reid editions of 'Tam o' Shanter', *Burns Chronicle*, 98 (1989), 38–44.

Roy, G R. Robert Burns and the Brash and Reid chapbooks of Glasgow. In Schwend, J, Hagemann, S and Valkel, H, eds, *Literatur im Kontext*, Frankfurt, 1992, 53–67.

Roy, G R. Some notes on Scottish chapbooks, *Scottish Literary Journal*, 1 (1974), 50–60.

Smith, R. Poets and peddlars, *Aberdeen Leopard*, 150 (July 1990), 18–19.

Stafford, F F. *The Sublime Savage: A Study of James Macpherson and the Poems of Ossian*, Edinburgh, 1988.

Wilson's Tales of the Borders: Historical, Traditionary and Imaginative, 6 vols, London, Edinburgh and Glasgow, 1840.

22 Gaelic Language and Lexicography

CATRIONA MACKIE AND LORNA PIKE

LANGUAGE, LEXICOGRAPHY AND ETHNOLOGY

Ethnology covers all aspects of life, and these are expressed through language. Language is a fundamental part of how we communicate with one another, how we view reality and, ultimately, of who we are. In a complementary relationship with material evidence, linguistic evidence forms an essential part of ethnological enquiry into how individuals interact with one another and their environment.

Evidence of language can be found in a variety of sources, both documentary and oral, but it is in dictionaries that this language is explained, and it is in historical dictionaries that it is explained most fully. Unlike Scots and English, Gaelic does not yet have an historical dictionary, and must rely instead on those compiled by individual lexicographers over the last 250 years. These dictionaries are based largely on the limited language experience of the individuals who compiled them. In contrast, a historical dictionary is entirely evidence-based, with a selective corpus of material from the language providing its foundation. Definitions are supported by referenced quotations from throughout the history of the language, with senses presented in chronological order providing the dictionary user with a full understanding of how a word has developed through time and a direct route to the original sources. The historical dictionary illumines our understanding of every aspect of life, drawing its evidence from such areas as agriculture, building, manufacturing, burgh records, legal records, wills, personal diaries, private correspondence and literature. Where appropriate, and this is particularly apposite in Gaelic culture, it draws upon oral evidence. Thus, first-hand information from the users of the language underpins the definitions and the language is allowed to speak for itself.

Dictionaries, and most particularly historical dictionaries, are therefore of primary importance to the ethnologist since they can supply a great deal of valuable information beyond defining the words that we use. In the case of historical dictionaries, exemplified by quotations, this information is first-hand. A well-constructed historical dictionary can provide information that illustrates the culture of a particular society (both material and non-material) and the way in which that culture has changed over time, by documenting the history of the language, using referenced examples. Dictionaries come in many sizes and formats, and all of them, to a greater or lesser extent, express a view of reality. It is important that this view is from the perspective of the source language and not the target language in which it is defined.

The following overview of existing Gaelic dictionaries[1] attempts to provide an introduction to lexicographical resources with comment on their usefulness to ethnologists. They are viewed in terms of their compiler(s), the reason for compilation, and coverage.

Gaelic is served by a number of dictionaries, none of which has been compiled with the needs of the ethnologist uppermost in the compilers' minds. They have been produced with the aim of eliminating, preserving, describing, defining and explaining the Gaelic language, with cultural and ethnological requirements at best secondary and at worst incidental. For some time to come, these dictionaries will be all that will be available for interpretation of written evidence. It is important to consider first, on a more detailed level, those which will be of greater use to the ethnologist.

The First Gaelic Dictionary

The first dictionary of Gaelic was produced at the request of the Society in Scotland for Propagating Christian Knowledge (SSPCK), which aimed to eliminate the Gaelic language by making English the language of instruction in Highland and Island schools.[2] Gaelic was to be used as a learning aid to hasten its own demise. The method of teaching religious texts through the medium of English had resulted in learning by rote without comprehension. In order to enable children to improve their understanding of the Bible, Gaelic was introduced as a means of instruction after the scholars had learned to read the texts in English. The intention was that this method would accelerate understanding of English. Published in 1741, *Leabhar a Theagasc Ainminnin* was compiled by Alexander MacDonald (Alasdair Mac Mhaighstir Alasdair) from Ardnamurchan, a well-known poet highly skilled in the Gaelic language. The framework for the dictionary was *A New Vocabulary for the Use of Schools* printed by Mr James McEwing in 1720.[3] This was a Latin–English vocabulary and MacDonald substituted Gaelic for the Latin. The vocabulary of around 4,000 entries[4] is grouped under ninety-seven headings and consists chiefly of lists of nouns, although MacDonald added some common adjectives. Headings are varied, covering topics such as the Deity, heaven, fire, air, water, earth, man, victuals, drink, diseases, faculties of the soul, virtues, vices, crimes, magistrates of a burgh, servants, tradesmen, stones, metals, plants and herbs, fruit trees, barren trees, animals, insects, fishes, birds, beasts, whole-footed beasts, cloven-footed beasts, city, house, rooms, household furniture, kitchen furniture, brewing vessels, cloth-making, horse furniture, husbandry, milling, school, college, time, shipping, warfare, coins, weights, measures, numbers, and names of men and women. Coverage is wide and includes concepts unfamiliar in Gaelic culture. MacDonald gives many words for the first time in their Scottish as opposed to their Irish forms. He also added a thirty-two page appendix containing words and terms for divinity, facilitating the reading of published Gaelic sources such as Carswell's translation of the *Book of Common Order* (1567) and his translation of Calvin's *Catechism* (1631).

Robert Armstrong's *A Gaelic Dictionary*, published in 1825, heralded the start
of a period in which Gaelic lexicography flourished and peaked, reflecting
progress in the lexicography of the British Isles at the time. Armstrong was the
son of a schoolmaster in Dull and Kenmore and was educated at St Andrews
University. He trained for the ministry but chose instead to start a boarding
school in London for the sons of noblemen. Armstrong showed an acute
awareness of the challenges of lexicography. His aims were threefold: to give
information to those who did not know Gaelic; to add to the knowledge of
scholars who did; and to provide a basis to assist future lexicographers. The
role of lexicography as descriptive, not prescriptive, was now established. His
dictionary was structurally more advanced than its predecessors and was the
first to give referenced quotations. This followed the pattern of Johnson in
English and Jamieson[5] in Scots. The Gaelic–English section contains an estimated
34,000 headwords, many of which can be accounted for by Armstrong's aim to
improve accessibility for the learner by giving separate entries for features that
may prove problematic, such as plurals and declining prepositions. The English–
Gaelic section lists roughly 33,600 headwords. The coverage is generally good,
with a range of registers included. However, the dictionary is predominantly
aimed at readers of Ossian and the Bible, and is biased towards the use of
Ossianic texts for illustration.

The Highland Society's Dictionarium Scoto-Celticum, *1828*

Only three years later the Highland Society dictionary of 1828, *Dictionarium Scoto-
Celticum*, was produced for a European audience and contained a Latin–Gaelic
vocabulary in addition to Gaelic–English and English–Gaelic sections. The work
was overseen by a committee set up in 1806 and compiled by the Rev. Dr John
Macleod, minister of Dundonald; Mr Ewen MacLachlan, a native of Lochaber
and a schoolmaster in Aberdeen; Rev. Dr Alexander Irvine of Little Dunkeld;
and the Rev. Alexander Macdonald of Crieff. The *Dictionarium's* title page demonstrates just how ambitious this project was: 'A Dictionary of the Gaelic Language;
comprising an ample vocabulary of Gaelic words, as preserved in the vernacular
speech, manuscripts, or printed works, with their signification and various
meanings in English and Latin, illustrated by suitable examples and phrases,
and with etymological remarks, and vocabularies of Latin and English words,
with their translation into Gaelic. To which are prefixed, an introduction explaining
the nature, objects and sources of the work, and a compendium of Gaelic
grammar.'

The dictionary aimed to include on the whole those words that were
actually in use, making it a potentially useful tool in ethnological studies relating
to the nineteenth century. Meanings are listed in the order of most common to
least common, and referenced quotations are given from written sources and
'common speech'. In practice, manuscript material was rarely used, chiefly due
to the premature death of Ewen MacLachlan, who died leaving only a few

transcribed. Definitions are more explanatory than in previous dictionaries, suggesting thorough investigation of the evidence and a deeper understanding of the needs of the user. Obsolete words are marked by an asterisk and presented in a smaller typeface. Some of these are Irish items included for etymological reasons. Others that will be of interest to ethnologists are terms for objects that were no longer used at the time of publication or whose use in society had changed. These are included 'especially when they alluded to historical facts descriptive of Celtic languages and manners'.[6]

The Gaelic–English section lists an estimated 10,000 headwords and the English–Gaelic section, based on Todd's 1818 revision of Johnson's dictionary, around 37,000. The list of abbreviations used includes languages and dialect areas, names of authors and works cited, including dictionaries, and may itself yield information useful in ethnological study.

The compilers placed great importance on etymology, doubtless reflecting the contemporary views that led to the establishment of the Philological Society in 1842, the body that in 1857 called for a new English dictionary. This resulted in the eventual publication of the *Oxford English Dictionary* (*OED*, 1884–1928), a work whose methodology would change lexicography forever and greatly enrich the interpretation resources available to ethnologists. The impact of the Highland Society dictionary would have been much greater had it not been beset by problems, not least the untimely death of Ewen MacLachlan. Delays meant that O'Reilly's *Irish–English Dictionary* (1817) and Armstrong's dictionary (1825) both appeared first. However, the Highland Society dictionary was a great achievement in its own time and many subsequent dictionaries, including Dwelly's work,[7] owe it a great debt.

MacBain's Etymological Dictionary, *1896*

Another major milestone in Gaelic lexicography was Alexander MacBain's *Etymological Dictionary of the Gaelic Language* published in 1896 and listing almost 8,000 headwords. MacBain, born in Glen Feshie, Badenoch in 1855, was an excellent scholar, producing many key texts in mythology, philology, history and onomastics. The dictionary was undoubtedly his greatest work. It was pioneering in nature for the late nineteenth century and, although much of it has been superseded, it still earns respect from modern scholars. Gaelic dictionaries that had touched on etymology, namely Armstrong, the Highland Society and MacLeod and Dewar[8] had done so in a basic and not especially informative way. MacBain, in contrast, had done thorough and extensive research, as illustrated by his impressive list of works and authorities. Gaelic, and indeed Celtic, lexicography had reached a higher level. For the first time, the language had been placed in a wider Indo-European context. The final output is more comparative than etymological, since MacBain was comparing data across many linguistic boundaries rather than using detailed internal evidence. The typography in the dictionary makes it very user-friendly, especially the use of bold type for the main headword. This follows the pattern of the *OED*, the first fascicle of which had been published in 1884.

Edward Dwelly's Gaelic Dictionary *and Appendix*

In 1911, Edward Dwelly's dictionary, *A Gaelic Dictionary*, later *Faclair Gàidhlig gu Beurla le Dealbhan*, completed publication. In stark contrast to his predecessors, Dwelly was born into an English family with no Scottish connections. It may be partly this background that led him to produce the most ethnologically aware dictionary of Gaelic, which has not yet been superseded.

He began learning the language during his schooldays and, by the age of twenty-two, felt that his progress was impeded due to being based in London. In 1887, he joined the 5th Volunteer Battalion Argyll and Sutherland Highlanders as a piper and, in 1891, the 1st Volunteer Battalion Seaforth Highlanders (Gairloch). It was in this year that Dwelly moved to the Highlands and, according to report, achieved such a level of fluency that he was able to pass as a native speaker. He had been collecting Gaelic words ever since he could remember and now began to increase his collection of lexicographical material for his own use. In 1896 he married Mary MacDougall, a native Gaelic speaker from Ardchattan, and they lived in Perthshire and Inverness-shire before moving to Kent in 1900. It was at this time that he decided to publish as a dictionary the material he had collected.

The basis of the dictionary was MacLeod and Dewar's work supplemented by other dictionaries, specialist vocabularies and word lists. Many other words appear in print for the first time in this dictionary, which includes an estimated 82,000 headwords, considerably more than any Gaelic dictionary existing at that time. It was compiled with the beginner in mind, with some definitions accompanied by illustrations. Local terms are included, particularly for implements and their parts; many of these terms would have been lost but for Dwelly's meticulous fieldwork and methodology. Illustrated entries, in particular, provide great riches for the ethnologist, increasing understanding of topics such as parts of a horse's harness, boats, implements, cuts of meat, buildings, weaving, fishing and piping.[9]

Dwelly held the view that the difference between the Irish and the Scots was geographical and not racial, repudiating the accusations of those who said that Irishisms should not be included in dictionaries of Scottish Gaelic. He criticised those who took this view and yet did not object to the use of English and Scots words pronounced and spelled according to Gaelic rules. In his dictionary, all such words are defined as 'Gaelic spelling of . . .', in an attempt to expel anglicisms from the language.

In addition to his 'outsider's view', which undoubtedly enriched the ethnological aspect of his work, and his unquestionable lexicographical ability, Dwelly was supported by a very fine team: his wife, the best academics of his time including Dr W J Watson, later to become Professor of Celtic at the University of Edinburgh (1914–38), and a network of informants from throughout Scotland.

A list of proper names, including place-names, countries, surnames and languages listed under their English form, is given along with a list of people and places mentioned in old Gaelic folktales and poetry, and an essay on the commercial value of Gaelic which echoes many views held today. Dwelly's dictionary is a valuable repository for the language and culture, and an essential resource and first port of call for ethnologists. It is now available and searchable online, although the illustrations are not included in this format.

In 1991, the Appendix to Dwelly was published, edited by the late Douglas Clyne, a medical practitioner with a great interest in the Gaelic language. Following his death, the editing was completed by Professor Derick Thomson (1921–2012) a native speaker from Lewis and Professor of Celtic at the University of Glasgow between 1963 and 1991. This Appendix had been more or less compiled when Dwelly's work completed publication in 1911, but he lacked the funding to produce it. Users should note that it has not been updated in any way since Dwelly's time. Items important to Gaelic culture have been well researched. For example, there are three columns of information under *bàta* 'a boat', and also additional names for harness, parts of a byre, words for the parts of a mill, a still, and a peat spade, and detailed definitions of words to do with weaving. Dwelly also seems to have absorbed some Scots terms, possibly supplied by his informants, which he uses with or without comment.

As expected, most of the material in the Appendix relates to the early part of the alphabet. It contains additional words and additional meanings for some words already in the dictionary. The editors have dealt with Dwelly's notes, such as checking those items in the Highland Society dictionary that he thought were still in use. Only those that were obsolete in Dwelly's time are marked as obsolete in the Appendix.

Clyne has compiled an invaluable index of around 19,000 items, enabling the user to make full use of the Appendix. Regrettably, the symbols used to indicate several works as sources, namely MacBain's dictionary, Cameron's collection of plant names, Carmichael's collection of bird names, Gillies' names of diseases, MacEachen's dictionary and the Highland Society dictionary, have not been reproduced in print in the list of authorities or the text of the Appendix. Users who are particularly interested in the sources should be aware of this, especially since, in the original dictionary, most of the material with no identified source is from MacLeod and Dewar.

Gaelic Dictionary, 2004

In the twenty-first century, Boyd Robertson, a native speaker from North Uist and currently Principal of Sabhal Mòr Ostaig, and Ian MacDonald, also a native speaker from North Uist, now Director of the Gaelic Books Council, have produced a first-rate dictionary, aimed primarily at learners. Published in 2004, the *Gaelic Dictionary* was produced to accompany the *Teach Yourself Gaelic* course but stands, entirely on its own merits, as an excellent basic modern dictionary of the language. The Gaelic–English section includes some 6,500 headwords and the English–Gaelic around 10,500. The vocabulary range is wide and encompasses cultural topics such as crofting, weaving and shinty. The entry structure is simple and very user-friendly, giving a dictionary that provides a useful starting point for ethnologists with no knowledge of Gaelic. The compilers acknowledge their debt to existing dictionaries, particularly MacBain's *Etymological Gaelic Dictionary* and Dwelly's *A Gaelic Dictionary*.

Other works which were drawn upon are Thomson's *New English–Gaelic*

Dictionary and Cox's *Brìgh nam Facal*, Clò Ostaig's *An Stòr Dàta Briathrachais Gàidhlig, Faclair na Parliamaid* (2001), *Faclair Ùra Gàidhlig*, the Secondary Review Group's word list for schools, and two Irish dictionaries, Tomás de Bhaldraithe's *English-Irish Dictionary* and Séamus Mac Mathuna and Ailbhe Ó Corráin's *Pocket Irish Dictionary*.

ADDITIONAL WORKS OF USE TO THE ETHNOLOGIST

The above works might be regarded as the primary lexicographical resources in Gaelic available to ethnologists. Others, described below, may in their own way be useful and should not be dismissed out of turn.

William Shaw, a native of Clachaig in Arran, educated in Ayr and at the University of Glasgow, produced the first full-scale dictionary of the language, in alphabetical order. He was an acquaintance of Samuel Johnson, whose *A Dictionary of the English Language* had been published in 1755. Shaw published *A Galic and English Dictionary* in 1780, with the aim of preserving a language that he believed was dying. His work was basic, and his major focus seems to have been to record rather than to inform or analyse. The lack of editorial method is doubtless due to the stringent financial circumstances under which he was working. For the modern user, however, the dictionary is significant for the compiler's knowledge of Arran Gaelic.

Fifteen years later, Robert MacFarlan, the first and only 'Professor of Gaelic' elected by the Highland Society, published his *Nuadh Fhoclair Gaidhlig agus Beurla*. He also noted the decline of Gaelic in his dictionary, the main aim of which was to standardise Gaelic orthography. He set out to compile a dictionary for the antiquarian and those entering the service of the Church. The range of vocabulary is fairly wide, covering everyday items, geographical features, agricultural terms, military terms, personal names, place-names, and Biblical words and names. His work does not progress Gaelic lexicography much beyond that of Shaw and will be of limited use to ethnologists.

During the nineteenth century, the amount of printed material available in Gaelic increased as religious texts were complemented by secular texts and the first Gaelic journals. There was a growing demand for dictionaries and it is hardly surprising that there was a prolific lexicographical output at this time. In his dictionary of 1815, *Focalair Ùr Gaelig agus Beurla*, Peter MacFarlane, a schoolmaster in Appin and a translator of religious works into Gaelic, set out to explain the language. His work is the first indication of learners being considered in Gaelic dictionary-making and represented significant progress in Gaelic lexicography. It has a clear layout, and is far more structured than previous dictionaries. However, the dictionary merely translates, giving Gaelic equivalents for the English with no indication of which option to choose in a particular context where more than one option is given. Nevertheless, in the Gaelic–English section, the occasional use of examples of usage and also some indication of sources represent a major step forward. The coverage is good, with a well-chosen basic vocabulary of everyday Gaelic, enabling the user to read the religious and vernacular verse of the time. The dominant dialect is that of mainland Argyll.

The fundamental need for a concise, derivative moderately priced dictionary that would make the language accessible to a larger number of people was recognised by the Rev. Dr Norman MacLeod (Caraid nan Gaidheal), from Morvern, and the Rev. Dr Daniel Dewar from Glen Dochart. They had been asked to manage the production of two Gaelic periodicals begun by the Very Rev. Dr Baird, who was Principal of the University of Edinburgh from 1793 until his death in 1840. MacLeod was in charge of *An Teachdaire Gaelach* ('The Gaelic Messenger') and Dewar of *Ceithir Searmoinan* ('Four Sermons'). In the course of their work, they realised that the lack of a concise and moderately priced dictionary of Gaelic was an obstacle to the progress of education in the Highlands and undertook to supply such a dictionary. Published in 1831, *A Dictionary of the Gaelic Language* was founded on the authoritative lexicographical foundation provided by Armstrong's and the Highland Society's dictionaries. MacLeod and Dewar added further material and the work was seen through the press by MacFarlane, editor of *Focalair Ùr Gaelig agus Beurla*. While greatly improving accessibility to lexicographical resources for the general populace in the nineteenth century, this dictionary does not add much to previous resources for present-day ethnologists.

Neil MacAlpine, born in Islay in 1786 and a schoolmaster and student of divinity, was the first to attempt to provide pronunciation. His task was not simple, since Gaelic is a phonetically elaborate language. Published in 1832, his dictionary, *A Pronouncing Gaelic Dictionary* (first edition entitled *The Argyleshire Pronouncing Gaelic Dictionary*), was a remarkable achievement as it was produced before the establishment of the International Phonetic Alphabet (IPA) in 1888. MacAlpine devised his own system for representing the sounds of the language using examples from English, Gaelic, Scots and French. The entry structure is very simple. Definitions generally take the form of synonyms as opposed to explanations. It is interesting to note that Scots also finds its way into definitions, indicating a level of cultural interaction with Scots-speaking areas. In terms of lexicography, it does not match the quality of MacLeod and Dewar and it will be of limited use to ethnologists.

The next Gaelic dictionary, *Faclair Gailig us Beurla*, was published in 1842 and compiled by Ewen MacEachen, who was born in Arisaig in 1769. He trained for the priesthood at Valladolid in Spain, where he was an excellent scholar, particularly in Logic and Mathematics. While acknowledging the availability of useful lexicographical resources for the language, he felt strongly that a dictionary of 'pure Gaelic' was needed. He was particularly concerned about orthography and the fact that the inconsistent spelling in the Gaelic Bible was regarded as a standard. His work, which resumed a prescriptive role, was based on MacLeod and Dewar's dictionary. Definitions are very simple and consist of synonyms. Scots words are occasionally used in definitions and are labelled as such. This dictionary seems to have been compiled more for MacEachen's own satisfaction than the needs of the language.

Five years later, in 1847, the English–Gaelic section of MacAlpine's dictionary, *An English–Gaelic Dictionary; Being Part Second of the Pronouncing Gaelic Dictionary*, was published. Its compiler was John MacKenzie, born in Gairloch in 1806, a prolific publisher of Gaelic texts who had shown as a child that he had a good ear for language and music. The dictionary has simple definitions consisting of synonyms. This simplicity makes it less informative for ethnologists. Like MacEachen, MacKenzie's main aim seems to have been to present a fixed spelling system for the language.

Malcolm MacFarlane was a native Gaelic speaker from Dalavich, Lochaweside. His family moved to Paisley when he was a boy. He became a land surveyor by profession and also an active promoter of the Gaelic language. His *Am Briathrachan Beag / The School Gaelic Dictionary* was published in 1912. The quality of information and the level of coverage of standard Gaelic vocabulary are good, but definitions are simple. Probably because MacFarlane would also have felt at home in Scots, he occasionally gives the Scots equivalent. Sometimes the words are related, e.g. *bonnach/bannock* 'a cake'; other times MacFarlane apparently intends to show there is an equivalent, e.g. *fochann/braird* 'first shoots of corn'. This work was not highly successful and will be of limited use to ethnologists.

Malcolm MacLennan was born in 1862 in Cnip, Lewis and moved to Canada where he was educated at McGill University and became a minister. He returned to Scotland in 1897. MacLennan set out to produce a one volume Gaelic–English English–Gaelic pronouncing and etymological dictionary for students, since Gaelic was by now a subject qualifying for graduation in the arts in the Scottish universities. Published in 1925, *A Pronouncing and Etymological Dictionary of the Gaelic Language* was based on the dictionaries of MacBain, MacEachen and MacAlpine. It was very user-friendly in appearance, but MacLennan reproduced his sources somewhat slavishly. His work was somewhat inconsistent and lacked a sound methodology. In its favour, new material was added, giving a more northerly bias than previous works and it was, and still remains, the dictionary giving information on most aspects of the language.

Henry Cyril Dieckhoff, who was born in Russia and studied at Edinburgh University before becoming a priest at Fort Augustus Abbey, compiled *A Pronouncing Dictionary of Scottish Gaelic*. Published in 1932, it focused on the pronunciation of natives of Glengarry, Inverness-shire, born in the second half of the nineteenth century. Some comparisons are given with Moidart and, to a lesser extent, Lochaber. For dialectologists and phoneticians, this dictionary will always be a valuable resource.

At this time, Irish, Scots and English were making great progress in the field of lexicography with the compilation of multi-volume historical dictionaries that would provide excellent resources for ethnologists. Despite many positive developments for Gaelic in the twentieth century, Gaelic lexicographical resources remained unchanged until 1979 and the publication of *Abair Faclan!* This was a pocket dictionary aimed at learners, compiled by John (Jake) MacDonald and Ronald Renton, both teachers of Gaelic. With its very clear, simple format, the dictionary more than fulfilled its aims and is of immense value to learners. However, it is of limited use from an ethnological point of view.

In 1981, Professor Derick Thomson compiled the *New English–Gaelic Dictionary* in response to the needs of contemporary learners. Although basic in lexicographical terms, it provided the dictionary-using public with a modern vocabulary. It was revised in 1994 with the addition of terms for such items as 'computer', 'job description' and 'space-shuttle'. It will not be sufficiently informative for ethnologists and, indeed, Thomson recommends that Dwelly be consulted where more detail is required.

In 1991, Richard Cox's Gaelic–Gaelic dictionary, *Brìgh nam Facal*, was published. The first monolingual Gaelic dictionary, it was compiled for the younger student but is also a useful resource for learners. The vocabulary range is wide but it will only serve ethnological enquiry from within Gaelic. Regrettably, from this perspective, it is still the only monolingual Gaelic dictionary.

In 1993, Robert Owen's *Gaelic–English Dictionary* was published. Compiled in response to the twentieth century surge in interest in Gaelic and for use in conjunction with Thomson's *New English–Gaelic Dictionary*, it has a simple format and will be of limited use to ethnologists.

The twenty-first century has seen an increase in lexicographical activity in Gaelic. Angus Watson identified the need for a detailed but accessible dictionary of the language covering a wide range of registers and including formal, traditional and colloquial forms of speech. His *Essential Gaelic–English Dictionary* was published in 2001 and has good all-round up-to-date coverage. Watson also includes Scots equivalents, both to define more clearly and as a personal choice, to encourage users to think of the two languages as existing side by side. Examples are taken from modern poetry and modern and traditional song, implying that this dictionary may be useful for the ethnologist. The *Essential English–Gaelic Dictionary* followed in 2005, providing a complementary resource.

Colin Mark produced *The Gaelic–English Dictionary*, published in 2003, which has more to offer the more advanced student. It gives many examples of usage covering a wide range of vocabulary. These are drawn from the periodical *Gairm* but, unfortunately, they are unreferenced, although they may still be of some use in ethnological study. Like Watson, Mark also includes some Scots in his definitions.

In addition to dictionaries, there are other published sources available for the study of Scottish Gaelic terminology, many of which focus on a particular dialect area. These include Fr Allan McDonald's *Gaelic Words and Expressions from South Uist and Eriskay*, first published in 1958, and Roy Wentworth's *Gaelic Words and Expressions from Wester Ross*. Over the years, a number of articles have been published in the *Transactions of the Gaelic Society of Inverness* detailing words and phrases from different parts of the country, many of which are not found in existing Gaelic dictionaries.[10]

HISTORICAL DICTIONARIES AND ETHNOLOGY

Coming as it does so directly from the language itself, the historical dictionary constitutes the memory of a culture and its people as well as a description and explanation of their language and its structures from the earliest evidence to the present day. It has more to offer the ethnologist than any other type of dictionary. Because of the fundamental importance of language and culture, it is not merely a linguistic resource. It provides interpretation and clarity that is crucial to our understanding of ourselves and each other, in a way that no electronic corpora, however large, could ever achieve. The lexicographer, a 'linguistic ethnologist', has the privilege of entering the lives of our ancestors and accepting the challenge of providing a lucid output to aid our understanding of our past. The challenge is immense, but so are the rewards. The lexicographer must produce a finished entry that will accurately reflect the raw material on which it is based and present a true view of reality from the perspective of the source language. Senses must clearly show the semantic development of the word; syntax and morphology must be explained where necessary; orthography must be clearly displayed; and phonology, exemplified by rhyme, must be shown. All of this information is based on material in the quotations, and they make the historical dictionary stand apart from all others as a cultural and ethnological resource. They are selected extremely carefully as regards their foundational role in the entry and are fully referenced to allow the user to access the sources and additional information. For the dictionary user, the historical dictionary, through the quotations and the metalanguage, aims to answer six basic and essential questions: what?, how?, who?, where?, when? and why? Each must be considered on a diachronic and synchronic level.

What? This is the most fundamental question to which the dictionary user is seeking an answer. *What* is the object denoted by the word? *What* does the word mean? The quotations set out to exemplify the knowledge required in order to understand the answer to these questions. For example, it may be possible to include dimensions, colour or composition of the object being described.

How? The dictionary should explain *how* a word is used in the language, *how* an object is used in the culture, *how* an action is performed, *how* a thing is manufactured, etc.

Who? This question cannot always be answered, but wherever possible the identity, gender or position in society of the speaker/writer should be indicated. This type of information is also important in sociolinguistic study.

Where? It must be made clear *where* a word is used in terms of its register and geographical distribution. Selected quotations must clearly reflect both.

When? The dictionary must place all usages in their historical context. Explicit dating of every quotation tells the user *when* a word was used in a particular sense and whether it is still current.

Why? This is one of the most important questions asked by ethnologists. If the dictionary answers the five questions above, the user should be in possession of knowledge that goes some way to explaining *why* a particular context is the way it is, *why* particular people do things in particular ways, etc.

In short, the historical dictionary sets out to tell us why a culture is the way it is, what it is, how it got there, who is part of it, where they lived and when. Thus, historical dictionaries, through an in-depth description of language, are fundamentally about the human condition both at a personal and a societal level.

Since the early nineteenth century, Gaelic lexicography has fallen behind that of other European and Celtic languages. The inadequacy of Gaelic resources is particularly stark when viewed in the context of its nearest geographical neighbours, Scots and English, both of which are served by world-class, multi-volume historical dictionaries. The lack of a comparable historical resource for Gaelic has been keenly felt by Celtic scholars and Scots and English lexicographers.[11] There are over 1,500 references to Gaelic in the online *Dictionary of the Scots Language* (*DSL*)[12] and twelve Gaelic dictionaries[13] that use Scots terms in their definitions. Clearly, identification of the interfaces between these two languages will stimulate a great deal of research in the field of Scottish ethnology. The potential for such research is discussed below, and has been ably demonstrated by Fenton, in his study of the Scottish kiln.[14]

Gaelic is, in a sense, fortunate in that it can now draw upon the established expertise available in Scotland to create the historical dictionary for Gaelic. Historical lexicography in Scots is part of an unbroken tradition reaching back to Sir James A H Murray, first editor of the *OED*, and a native of Denholm near Hawick. His colleague, Sir William Craigie, from Dundee (who learned some Gaelic from his maternal grandfather), was the first editor of the *Dictionary of the Older Scottish Tongue* (*DOST*) which completed publication, under the editorial direction of Marace Dareau,[15] in 2002. On the completion of *DOST*, it was recognised that the opportunity should be grasped to maintain historical lexicographical skills in Scotland and to transfer them to Gaelic. This led to the formal establishment in 2003 of the Faclair na Gàidhlig project,[16] which will produce a historical dictionary of Scottish Gaelic compiled on principles developed from those applied in *OED* and *DOST*.

Faclair na Gàidhlig is currently in its foundational stages, with dictionary compilation scheduled to begin in 2015. Lexicographical structures designed specifically to meet the needs of Gaelic are being formulated and sample entries, accompanied by detailed instructions for compilation, will be used in staff training. The electronic corpus from which the dictionary will draw its evidence is being compiled at the University of Glasgow under the auspices of the Digital Archive of Scottish Gaelic.[17] Given sufficient funding and a dedicated staff of adequate size, it would be theoretically possible to have a full historical dictionary of Gaelic by 2035. For a project of such magnitude, this is a comparatively short duration. In terms of what it will achieve for the language and the culture, it is a resource well worth the wait.

USING DICTIONARY EVIDENCE

The study of language can illuminate all areas of ethnology, but perhaps most particularly material culture, where the study of terminology can focus on the names given to particular objects or implements.[18] Such terms are fully described and explained in a historical dictionary.

The existing complement of Scottish Gaelic dictionaries does not contain the detail or the breadth of information that can be found in a good historical dictionary, and can best aid the ethnologist when studied alongside other sources, such as first-hand documentary and oral sources, and existing historical dictionaries in other languages, such as *DSL* and *OED*. Unfortunately, most of the existing Gaelic dictionaries do not provide quotations that exemplify the meanings of words and provide links to source material. Those that do frequently do not provide references, or provide references that are so vague as to be almost untraceable. The Highland Society's dictionary of 1828, for example, uses references such as '*Oran.*, Gaelic Song' and '*MSS.*, Gaelic Manuscripts of Highland Society of Scotland', without providing further clarification.

A good example of the way in which the use of existing dictionaries can add to the study of material culture in Gaelic can be found in Quye and Cheape's article on the 'arisaid', a high-status article of woman's clothing that was already going out of fashion by the eighteenth century.[19] A thorough examination of the material held in Scottish museums, along with a review of documentary sources (both prose and verse), artwork and dictionary evidence enabled the authors to develop a clear picture of the changing use of this garment. Similarly, *DOST*'s compilers, whose starting point was the written evidence, had an excellent and profitable working relationship with staff in Scottish museums and with folklorists and ethnologists on the staff of the School of Scottish Studies. It is anticipated that Faclair na Gàidhlig will enjoy the same exchange of expertise.

Using dictionaries to aid in the study of ethnology has been made easier by the recent digitisation of many of the older Gaelic dictionaries, which are now out of copyright. Many of these dictionaries are now available online (from sites such as the Internet Archive and Google Books)[20] as PDF files, or in other fully searchable formats. This allows users to search the full text of a dictionary for a Gaelic or an English term, not just the headword. In some cases a Gaelic term is given as a definition in the English–Gaelic section of a dictionary, even though it does not appear as a headword in the Gaelic–English section. For example, in MacLeod and Dewar's dictionary, the Gaelic word *tallaid* does not appear as a headword in the Gaelic–English section of the dictionary but appears twice as a definition in the English–Gaelic section, under the headwords 'partition' and 'partywall'.

Linguistic Variation over Space and Time

Searching for English headwords can also throw up alternative Gaelic terms and variant spellings, which sometimes represent dialectal forms of words. The word *tallaid*, for example, is given by Dwelly as a Badenoch term for a partition. Other dictionary forms for the same feature include *talaint* (a term from Gairloch), *talainte, callaid, tallan,* and *talan*.[21] The word *talan* is defined by Dwelly as '[p]artition, division wall', and he further notes that in Lewis, the *talan* is the '[p]artition in blackhouses about 3ft high, for separating the portion occupied by the cattle'. In documentary sources, we also find the terms *fallan* (from St Kilda) and *hallan* (from Canna).[22]

Searching historical dictionaries in related languages can provide additional information about a particular term or concept. Following on from the above example, the word *hallan*, with its variant forms, including *halling, halland, hallant, halan, halend, hallen, hallon* and *hal(l)in* appears in Scots as:

> An inner wall, partition or screen erected in a cottage between the door
> and the fireplace to act as a shield from the draught of the door, gen.
> composed of mud or clay mixed with stones or moulded over a wood
> and straw framework . . .; also used to denote a similar partition of stone
> or clay in a byre or stable or between the living room and the byre;
> The inside porch, lobby or passage formed by such a partition;
> An outer wall before a door to stop wind;
> A cottage, house, dwelling;
> A buttress placed against a weak wall to prevent it from falling;
> A hen-roost (only evidenced in Orkney).[23]

Earlier uses of the word, from the sixteenth and seventeenth centuries, provide two further definitions:

> A partition or door-screen in a room; and
> A covering screen erected above a shop-door[24]

These terms do not seem to appear in Irish or in Manx, which perhaps suggests a borrowing into Scottish Gaelic from Scots. The Scots connection is further attested by the fact that in parts of Ulster, the jamb wall that is built between the hearth and the front entrance to the kitchen is known as the *hollan, hallun,* or *hallan wall*.[25]

In addition to variant spellings, the meaning of a particular term can also change between dialects. The wall construction common in the Scottish Hebrides during the nineteenth century was that of an inner and an outer wall of stone or turf, with the space between filled with earth and clay. This infill, or hearting, was called variously *uadabac, uatabac,* or *ùireabac*.[26] Dwelly's definition of a similar term *udabac*, however, reads:

> Porch, outhouse. 2 Buttress or support, usually of stone, built against a
> wall. 3 Wall about 6 ft high and 7 ft or 8 ft long, built in front of a main
> door at a distance of about 4 ft from it to break the force of the wind. They
> were common in the north of Skye till quite recently and may still be seen
> in some parts. 4 Backhouse.

He also notes that the Uist form of the word is *ùdabac*. The etymology of this word has yet to be determined, although MacBain suggests that it may come from the Norse *úti-bak*, meaning 'out-back'. Through a careful study of the written and oral evidence, Faclair na Gàidhlig will attempt to show the distribution, geographically and over time, of these various definitions, thus providing a valuable insight into the spread of language and culture throughout Gaelic-speaking Scotland.

Thomson's article on 'Words and expressions from Lewis' shows the range and breadth of terminology peculiar to a particular dialect (in this case, various townships in the Isle of Lewis), which is not, of course, restricted to material objects, but includes terms of endearment, physical and mental characteristics, and illnesses.[27]

Cross-Cultural Comparisons

The creation of Faclair na Gàidhlig will enable a fuller understanding not only of Scottish Gaelic language and culture but also of the linguistic and cultural relationship between Gaelic and Scots, and between Highland and Lowland Scotland. It will also enable a fuller comparison with the Irish material contained in the *Dictionary of the Irish Language*, and with *Foclóir na Nua-Ghaeilge* (Dictionary of Modern Irish) when that project is complete.

The value of examining Gaelic terminology alongside its Scots equivalent has been attested above, but the study of language can also contribute to the study of material culture across countries, as well as cultures. Current dictionaries in Scottish Gaelic, Irish and Manx allow for limited comparison of terminology in order to better understand the relationships between these cultures. Research recently undertaken by Mackie compared terminology relating to vernacular housing using dictionaries compiled by Dwelly (Scottish Gaelic), Dinneen (Irish), and Cregeen and Kelly (Manx), and a number of additional documentary sources.[28] In particular, the study focused on an examination of the bed alcove (also known as the bed-outshot), a common feature of vernacular housing in parts of northern and western Ireland.[29] This feature had its counterpart in the bed alcoves of Lewis and St Kilda, and in the *neuk-beds* of Orkney. Examining the related terminology between Gaelic Ireland and Scotland allows for an extra level of comparison of the material culture, and shows that much stands to be gained by studying these languages and cultures side by side.

In Ireland, the bed alcove was known by a variety of names, in Irish and in English. Examples include *cúilteach, cúiltheach, cúileach, cailleach, cúilleaba, póca, outshot, bed-pocket, pouch* and *cooltye. Cúilteach* (coming from *cúil*, meaning 'corner, nook' and *teach*, meaning 'house') and *cailleach* (the word for an old woman) were arguably the most commonly used terms in Irish. Interestingly, Dinneen notes that the term *cuileach* (which he states is properly *cúilteach*) was pronounced as *cailleach*. In an article published in 1938, Seán Mac Giolla Meidhre noted that the term *cailleach* actually came 'from the screen (*cailleóg*) which was hung in front of it'.[30] This seems to refer to the practice of screening the bed off from the rest of the room by the use of curtains or wooden doors. Interestingly, *culóg* (which is not given by Dinneen) was one of the terms listed for the bed-outshot in the Irish Folklore Commission's questionnaire on traditional housing.

The Hebridean beds seem to have been known by the terms *crùb* (possibly coming from the verb *crùb*, 'to crouch') and *leabaidh b(h)alla* ('wall bed'). Armstrong (1825), the Highland Society (1828), and MacLeod and Dewar (1831) all list the word *cùilteach*. The definitions 'bed' and 'bedroom' are given by both the Highland Society and MacLeod and Dewar. Armstrong defines it as a 'place full of corners' or, rarely, a 'bakehouse' – a definition which came from Shaw's dictionary of 1780.

The term *cailleach* is listed in all existing Gaelic dictionaries, but not in this context. However, three sources from Lewis do describe the use of the term *cailleach* in relation to beds, in this case in shieling huts. One reference comes from the *Celtic Review*, where a short article on the Lewis shieling huts, written by Lewis schoolchildren, mentions that the sleeping space in the hut was called the *cailleach* and that it was made up of grass and rushes spread on turves.[31] The other reference is from Donald MacDonald's book on *The Tolsta Townships*, where he notes that:

> The living space was utilised as in the small shielings, but the bed was much bigger. The stone platform might be 5 feet in width, and there was a stone-coping along its front to keep the bedding, and sometimes the inmates, from dropping on to the floor. This coping was always covered with dry turf and was called the cailleach, old woman.[32]

In this second example, it is interesting to note that the term *cailleach* referred not to the bed but to the turf-topped stone coping that bounded it, which was also used as a seat. This term is still known in Lewis today. Given Mac Giolla Meidhre's assertion that the *cailleach* was really the screen (*cailleóg*) that was hung in front of the bed, could it be that in the shieling huts of Lewis it came to be associated with the *edge* of the bed? Or did the terms develop separately in Ireland and in Lewis? Armstrong lists the term *caille*, meaning a veil or a hood: 'Hence cailleach, *an old woman.*'

The third reference from Lewis is from Thomson, who gives the term *a' chailleach* as being 'the line of turf bounding the bed in an *àirigh*' (shieling).[33] This definition is not given by Dwelly. However, as Thomson notes, a semantic connection can be made with the term *cailleach-baic*, given by Dwelly as: 'In cutting peats, the outside peat in a bank.' The Highland Society's dictionary lists the following definitions of the word *bac*: 'A bog, or marsh' and 'A pit, or ditch', both of which they state comes from the 'Northern Highlands'. *Bac-mòine* [sic] is given as meaning 'A turf-pit'. Interestingly, Dwelly's informant for the term *cailleach-baic* was A Henderson of Ardnamurchan. Perhaps this suggests a different etymology for the terms *uadabac*, *ùdabac*, *uatabac* and *ùireabac* than that suggested by MacBain, with *bac* perhaps representing the turf infill between the inner and outer stone wall. Thomson gives a similar definition for the term *ceap*, as 'the edge or boundary of the bed, in old shielings. Also used for sitting on.' He notes that Dwelly's definition differs slightly: 'Sort of sofa or couch formed of peats, placed between the fire and the bed in the *bothan-àiridh*, and used as a seat.' This perhaps suggests that the Scottish Gaelic term *cailleach*, meaning the row of turves at the edge of the bed in a shieling hut, derived from the peat that was used to construct it.

Bed outshots or alcoves were not known on the Isle of Man, although the terms *cuillee*, *cuillee-lhie*, and *thie-chooyl* are given for 'bedroom' and 'backroom'. The Manx word for old woman, *caillagh*, does not appear to have been used in this sense.

CONCLUSION

In summary, although Gaelic does not yet have its own historical dictionary, the dictionaries that do exist contain much of value to the ethnologist. Ethnologists are advised to consult Dwelly in the first instance, since this is the most informative dictionary on an ethnological level. Other more useful works are: Mac Mhaighstir Alasdair's dictionary, the earliest published dictionary; Armstrong's dictionary, the Highland Society's dictionary and MacBain's dictionary. The one-volume Robertson and MacDonald *Gaelic Dictionary* is a reliable starting point for those unfamiliar with Gaelic.

When complete, Faclair na Gàidhlig will provide an invaluable resource with which to study the history, culture, and languages of Scotland, and will allow more detailed comparisons with Irish and Manx Gaelic.

The debate about the relationship between language and culture is a familiar one in linguistics and its associated disciplines. However, it cannot be doubted that the study of a language can bring us closer to an understanding of that language's culture and its people. As Witold Rybczynski declares:

> Words are important. Language is not just a medium, like a water pipe, it is a reflection of how we think. We use words not only to describe objects but also to express ideas, and the introduction of words into the language marks the simultaneous introduction of ideas into the consciousness.[34]

NOTES

1 Another account justifying the need for a historical dictionary of Gaelic is published as Pike, 2008, 525–40.

2 'In June 1725 the Society proposed "to get a good English and Irish vocables composed, for a help to the more Speedy teaching the Schollars the most usual and familiar English words" (SRO GD 1/2/344).' Source: Withers, 1982, 40. See also Campbell, 1937, and MacDonald, 1741, Dedication.

3 It has not been possible to locate this edition. The eighth edition of *A New Vocabulary for the Use of Schools* (1749) contains the following statement reproduced from the first edition and which refers to the composers of the vocabulary: *'But because several English Words are not understood by Children, and the Generality of our People, it was judged necessary to join the Scottish Names to such of them as seemed to need Explanation.'* ('To the Reader', pp 1–2.) Printed in Edinburgh by T & W Ruddimans, but with no indication as to who the composers were. This indicates that a similar situation existed in Scots.

4 In each dictionary, the number of headwords has been estimated by selecting six pages at random and counting the headwords. The mean number of headwords for one page was calculated from the sample and multiplied by the total number of pages in the dictionary to give an estimated total number of headwords.

5 Jamieson, 1808. Jamieson was the first to include referenced quotations in historical order.

6 Highland Society, 1828, v.

7 Dwelly, 1902–11.

8 MacLeod and Dewar, 1831.

9 See, for example, entries for *acfhuinn* 'harness', *cairt* 'a cart', *crann-nan-gad* 'a plough used in the Western Isles', *bàta* 'a boat', *closach* 'a carcase', *taigh* 'a house', *beart-fhigh eadaireachd* 'a weaver's loom', *dorgh* 'a handline for fishing' and *pìob* 'a bagpipe'.

10 MacDonald, 1934–36; MacInnes, 1974–76; Thomson, 1976–78.

11 Ethnologists should note that the OED now employs a Celtic etymologist. Updates to the online dictionary, <www.oed.com> (subscription site) are added quarterly. In the absence of a historical dictionary of Gaelic, the OED etymology should be regarded as authoritative for those words in English that are derived from Gaelic.

12 URL, <www.dsl.ac.uk>, the electronic edition of the *Dictionary of the Older Scottish Tongue* and the *Scottish National Dictionary*.

13 See MacDonald, 1741; Highland Society, 1828; MacLeod and Dewar, 1831; MacAlpine 1832; MacEachen, 1842; MacBain, 1896; Dwelly, 1902–11; MacFarlane, 1912; Dwelly, 1991; Watson, 2001; Mark, 2003; and Robertson and MacDonald, 2004.

14 Fenton, 1974.

15 Marace Dareau was involved in editing *DOST* from 1968–2001 and was Editorial Director from 1997–2001. From 2002–05, she was Editorial Director of Scottish Language Dictionaries and is now Principal Editor. She is Editorial Consultant for Faclair na Gàidhlig.

16 Faclair na Gàidhlig is an inter-university initiative involving the universities of Aberdeen, Edinburgh, Glasgow, Strathclyde and Sabhal Mòr Ostaig UHI. Since its establishment in 2003, it has received funding from Bòrd na Gàidhlig, the Carnegie Trust for the Universities of Scotland, the Gaelic Language Promotion Trust, the Leverhulme Trust, the Scottish Funding Council and the Scottish Government.

17 Information on the Digital Archive of Scottish Gaelic (DASG) can be accessed at <www.gla.ac.uk/schools/humanities/research/celticgaelicresearch/ currentresearchprojects/digitalarchiveofscottishgaelicdasg/> [accessed November 2012].

18 See Kay, 1997, for a more general discussion on 'Historical semantics and material culture'.

19 Quye and Cheape, 2008.

20 Internet Archive, <www.archive.org>; Google Books, <http://books.google.co.uk/>

21 Dwelly, 1911; Armstrong, 1825; Highland Society, 1828; MacLeod and Dewar, 1831; McDonald, 1958.

22 MacKenzie, 1905, 401; Walker, 1989, 48. Other dictionary terms for a partition or party wall include *fraigh, fraidh, lantair, cailbhe, balladh dealachaidh, balla meadhonach,* and *balla tarsuing*.

23 *DSL*.

24 *DOST*.

25 Gailey, 1984, 165; Evans, 1942, 68.

26 Sinclair, 1953; Fenton, 1995, 11; Thompson, 1976–78, 176. Other terms include *glutaran, glutaranadh, glutarman,* and *talamh balla*, which literally translates as 'earth wall'.

27 Thomson, 1976–78, 173–200.

28 Dinneen, 1904; Cregeen, 1835; Kelly, 1866. This research was presented at the Edward Lhuyd International Conference in Aberystwyth in July 2009.

29 A more detailed examination of this feature is published in Mackie, 2013.

30 Mac Giolla Meidhre, 1938, 196–200.

31 Anon, 1909, 237.

32 MacDonald, 1984, 159.

33 Thomson, 1976–78, 175.

34 Rybczynski, 1987, 20–1.

A New Vocabulary in English & Latin for the Use of Schools, Edinburgh, 1749.

Airidh air Urram – An t-Athair Cyril Dieckhoff. Biographical information from BBC Radio nan Gaidheal, 18 December 2000.

Anon. Scenes in Lewis, *Celtic Review*, 5 (1909), 235–52.

Armstrong, A. *A Gaelic Dictionary*, London, 1825, available online at <http://www.archive.org details/gaelicdictionaryooarmsuoft> [accessed November 2012].

Black, R. The Gaelic Academy: The cultural commitment of The Highland Society of Scotland, *Scottish Gaelic Studies*, 14 (1986), 1–38.

Black, R. Unpublished biography of John MacKenzie. In the possession of the author, Ronald Black.

Campbell, J L. The first printed Gaelic vocabulary, *Scots Magazine*, 28 (December 1937), 51–7.

Carswell, J. *Foirm na n-urrnuidheadh*, Edinburgh, 1567.

Carswell, J. *Adtimchiol an Chreidimh*, Edinburgh, 1631.

Cox, R A V. *Brigh nam Facal*, Glasgow, 1991.

Cregeen, A. *A Dictionary of the Manks Language*, Douglas, 1835.

Dieckhoff, H C. *A Pronouncing Dictionary of Scottish Gaelic*, Edinburgh and London, 1932.

Dinneen, P S. *An Irish–English Dictionary*, Dublin, 1904.

Dwelly, E. *A Gaelic Dictionary*, Herne Bay, 1902–11, available online at <www.cairnwater. co.uk/gaelicdictionary/> [accessed November 2012].

Dwelly, E. *Appendix to Dwelly's Gaelic–English Dictionary*, edited from manuscript by Douglas Clyne, completed by D S Thomson, Glasgow, 1991.

Evans, E E. *Irish Heritage*, Dundalk, 1942.

Fenton, A. Lexicography and historical interpretation. In Barrow, G W S, ed., *The Scottish Tradition, Essays in Honour of Ronald Gordon Cant*, Edinburgh, 1974, 243–58.

Fenton, A. Words and things in Gaelic Scotland. In Bronner, S J, ed., *Creativity and Tradition in Folklore: New Directions*, Logan, UT, 1992, 223–36.

Fenton, A. *The Island Blackhouse*, Edinburgh, 1995.

Gailey, A. *Rural Houses of the North of Ireland*, Edinburgh, 1984.

Gillies, W and Pike, L. Gaelic lexography. In Macleod and McClure, 2012, 197–261.

Highland Society. *Dictionarium Scoto-Celticum: A Dictionary of the Gaelic Language*, Edinburgh and London, 1828, available online at <www.archive.org/details/dictionariumscoto1high> [accessed November 2012].

Jamieson, J. *An Etymological Dictionary of the Scottish Language*, Edinburgh, 1808.

Johnson, S. *A Dictionary of the English Language*, London, 1755.

Kay, C J. Historical semantics and material culture. In Pearce, S M, ed., *Experiencing Material Culture in the Western World*, Leicester, 1997, 49–64.

Kelly, J. *The Manx Dictionary in Two Parts*, Douglas, 1866.

McDonald, A. *Gaelic Words and Expressions from South Uist and Eriskay*, Dublin, 1958.

MacAlpine, N. *A Pronouncing Gaelic Dictionary*, Edinburgh, 1832, available online at <www.archive.org/details/argyleshirepronooomaca> [accessed November 2012].

MacBain, A. *Etymological Dictionary of the Gaelic Language*, Inverness, 1896. <www.smo. uhi.ac.uk/gaidhlig/faclair/macbain/> [accessed November 2012].

MacDonald, A. *Leabhar a Theagasc Ainminnin*, Edinburgh, 1741.

MacDonald, D. Some rare Gaelic words and phrases, *TGSI*, 37 (1934–36), 1–54.

MacDonald, D. *The Tolsta Townships*, Tolsta, 1984.

MacDonald, J A and Renton, R. *Abair Faclan!*, Glasgow, 1979.

MacEachen, E. *Faclair Gailig us Beurla*, Perth, 1842.

MacFarlan, R. *Nuadh Fhoclair Gaidhlig agus Beurla*, Edinburgh, 1795, available online at <archive.org/details/newalphabeticalvoomacf> [accessed November 2012].

MacFarlane, M. *The School Gaelic Dictionary*, Stirling, 1912.

MacFarlane, P. *Focalair Ùr Gaelig agus Beurla*, Edinburgh, 1815.

Mac Giolla Meidhre, S. Some notes on Irish farm-houses, *Béaloideas*, 8 (1938), 196–200.

MacInnes, J. Some Gaelic words and usages, *TGSI*, 49 (1974–76), 428–55.

MacKenzie, J. *An English–Gaelic Dictionary; Being Part Second of the Pronouncing Gaelic Dictionary*, Edinburgh, 1847.

MacKenzie, J B. Antiquities and old customs in St Kilda, Compiled from notes made by Rev. Neil MacKenzie, minister of St Kilda, 1829–43, *PSAS*, 39 (1905), 401.

Mackie, C. The bed-alcove tradition in Ireland and Scotland: reappraising the evidence, *Proceedings of the Royal Irish Academy*, 113c (2013), 309–40.

MacLennan, M. *A Pronouncing and Etymological Dictionary of the Gaelic Language*, Edinburgh, 1925.

Macleod, I and McClure, J D, eds. *Scotland in Definition: A History of Scottish Dictionaries*, Edinburgh, 2012.

MacLeod, N and Dewar, D. *A Dictionary of the Gaelic Language*, Glasgow, 1831, available online at <archive.org/details/dictionaryofgaeloomacl> [accessed November 2012].

Mark, C. *The Gaelic-English Dictionary*, London and New York, 2003.

Matheson, A. *Carmina Gadelica – Hymns and Incantations with Illustrative Notes on Words, Rites, and Customs, Dying and Obsolete, Orally Collected in the Highlands and Islands of Scotland by Alexander Carmichael*, 6 vols, Edinburgh, 1971.

Meek, D E, ed. *Caran an t-Saoghail*, Edinburgh, 2003.

Miracles of a word hunter, *Daily Express*, 25 August 1911.

Owen, R C. *The Modern Gaelic–English Dictionary*, Glasgow, 1993.

Pike, L. Supporting the language, defining the way: Gaelic dictionaries, past, present and future. In Ó Baoill, C and McGuire, N, eds, *Caindel Alban Fèill-Sgrìobhainn do Dhòmhnall E Meek*, Aberdeen, 2008, 525–40.

Quye, A and Cheape, H. Rediscovering the Arisaid, *Costume*, 42 (2008), 1–20.

Robertson, B and MacDonald, I. *Gaelic–English Dictionary*, London, 2004.

Rybczynski, W. *Home: A Short History of an Idea*, Harmondsworth, 1987.

Shaw, W. *A Galic and English Dictionary*, London, 1780.

Sinclair, C. *The Thatched Houses of the Old Highlands*, Edinburgh, 1953.

Some notes on a well-known work and its little-known author, *Celtic Review*, 15 (1909), 193–202.

Thomson, D S. Words and expressions from Lewis, *TGSI*, 50 (1976–78), 173–200.

Thomson, D S. *The New English–Gaelic Dictionary*, Glasgow, 1981.

Thomson, D S, ed. *The Companion to Gaelic Scotland*, Oxford, 1983.

Walker, B. Edited notes on Hebridean buildings from Åke Campbell's field notebooks of July 1948, *Vernacular Building*, 13 (1989), 48.

Watson, A. *The Essential Gaelic–English Dictionary*, Edinburgh, 2001.

Watson, A. *The Essential English–Gaelic Dictionary*, Edinburgh, 2005.

Wentworth, R. *Gaelic Words and Expressions from Wester Ross*, Inverness, 2003, available online at <www.smo.uhi.ac.uk/gaidhlig/wentworth/> [accessed November 2012].

Withers, C W J. Education and anglicisation: The policy of the SSPCK toward the education of the Highlander, *Scottish Studies*, 26 (1982), 37–56.

23 Ethnology and the Dictionaries of Scots

KEITH WILLIAMSON

INTRODUCTION

This chapter outlines how the *Dictionary of the Older Scottish Tongue* (*DOST*) and the *Scottish National Dictionary* (*SND*), and works related to them, can be used as tools for ethnological enquiry. The content and structure of these dictionaries are discussed below. First the inextricable relationship between ethnology and the study of languages will be examined.

WÖRTER UND SACHEN/WORDS AND THINGS

The great flourishing of enquiry into the history and development of languages during the ninteenth century was accompanied by an interest in the cultures of the speakers of these languages. There arose a view among a number of linguists that one could not understand the history of words without understanding the culture in which the words were used – essentially those 'things' within the cultural milieu to which the words referred. This knowledge was viewed as essential when working out the etymology of a word, particularly in the development of its senses through time.

Similarly, in linguistic geography the nature of the things to which different dialectal words referred became a concern. This was a prominent interest among investigators of the Romance languages. For example, Jules Gilliéron (1854–1926) wrote a series of studies on words collected for the Atlas Linguistique de la France (1902),[1] wherein he attempted to account for the words' histories through understanding the external world of the words and their users as well as of their forms. And Jacob Jud and Karl Jarberg's *Sprach- und Sachatlas Italiens und der Südschweiz* (1929–56)[2] tells us in its title that it is concerned with material culture as well as with language. The maps in this atlas not only show distributions of different words and different forms of words for 'the same thing', but they also contain line-drawings of the objects referred to by the words, showing characteristic differences in the shape or structure of the referents in different places. This kind of approach came to be known early on as '*Wörter und Sachen*' (Words and Things). Accessible accounts of the development of this work may be found in Iorgu Iordan's *Introduction to Romance Linguistics* (1937).

Words refer to or stand for or symbolise (in sound or in writing) things in the external world as perceived by human beings. Things include other people and our individual perceptions of and reactions to them. Things may be concrete entities: natural ones, such as trees and plants, rivers and seas, plains and mountains, animals; man-made ones such as houses, boats, ploughs, printing presses. Things may be abstract entities, intangible to the 'five senses' but perceivable emotionally, such as love, anger, fear, curiosity; and intellectually, such as words and morphemes themselves and their construction into utterances, logical lines of argument, numbers and the operations carried out with them. Of course, these things may come together in reality: for example, numbers and their operations may be conjoined with a weighing apparatus such as a set of scales and other measuring instruments which are part of the material culture.

Speakers (and writers) engage with each other and with the world through a common language, in informal interaction with co-speakers (or with readers) or in formal description, argument and analysis. It is through a common language – or common variety of a language – that speakers in a community share and exchange experiences of the world about them, and especially of their milieu and culture. A language encodes a culture, but also it is an integral part of the culture and is shaped by the culture. Knowledge of a language is part of our internalisation of the world about us. We process the world internally through the power of symbolic reference, which arguably is the key cognitive ability that human language is built on. That is, part of engaging with the world is not directly with 'real world' things, but with the interaction of word and referent (our mental representation of the thing – the 'meaning' of the word). Thus, the language we use is akin to another sense through which, individually and collectively, we both apprehend and engage with the community of which we are a part. The language of a community maintains words and uses them in ways that reflect this engagement with the world. The lexicon of the language has been shaped by its history – the activities, linguistic and non-linguistic of the preceding generations of speakers. A community lives on through time carrying its word-stock. It sheds words from it to leave a word-trail behind it in time; it replenishes it through internal processes of sense-extension and diminution, compounding of elements and through borrowing from other varieties or from the standard language as the milieu and culture change. These new elements are also subject to subsequent shedding, replacement or remoulding. By exploring the lexis within a community across space and through time, we can come to understand much about the manners of living and views of the world of its members, present and past.

DICTIONARIES

A dictionary is primarily a work of reference organised to give information about the lexis of a language or of some variety of a language. Depending on the scope of the dictionary, it may also provide information about grammatical categories of the words, and perhaps also about the historical, and geographical currency of the words. It may offer information about the relationship of the words to words in other related languages – earlier or contemporary – in an etymological note. The emphasis in all of this is clearly linguistic. Yet dictionaries have significance for ethnological study, for the words that they contain and define are a refraction of the culture of the speakers of the language recorded in the dictionary. In a synchronic sense, each word references a fragment of the culture or society. Each such fragment may be multi-faceted, each facet holding the part-image of some characteristic of the culture. Seen this way, a dictionary is a linguistically (more precisely, orthographically) arranged repository of such fragments. To see the fragments in an ethnological way, the problem is then how to retrieve them and rearrange them to reveal a mosaic picture of some thing or things that pertain to the culture.

DICTIONARIES OF SCOTS

The lexical history of Scots from its twelfth-century Anglic origins to the present day has been recorded in two major dictionaries: the *Dictionary of the Older Scottish Tongue* (*DOST*) and the *Scottish National Dictionary* (*SND*).

Structure, Scope and Character of the Dictionaries

DOST covers Scots from its origins in the twelfth century up to 1700; *SND* covers Scots from 1700 to the present day. These dictionaries were originally produced and continue to exist in printed form: twelve volumes of *DOST* (1931–2002) and ten volumes of *SND* (1931–76). However, there are also freely available online versions of the two dictionaries, brought together as the Dictionary of the Scots Language (DSL).[3] For *SND*, this also includes a second supplement (SNDS2, 2005) (volume 10 of *SND* contains the first supplement). Further, in 1985 the *Concise Scots Dictionary* (*CSD*) was published,[4] followed in 1981 by *The Scots Thesaurus* (*ST*). *CSD* is a digest of material in *DOST* and *SND* in a single volume. Since *DOST* was some way from completion in 1985, *CSD* lacks *DOST* material covering the letters R through Z. For this stretch of the alphabet, Scots material was abstracted from the Oxford English Dictionary (*OED*).[5] A revision of *CSD* is under way at the time of writing and it will incorporate new material from the since-completed *DOST*.

In the introduction to *DOST* in volume 12, it is stated that the dictionary:

> is intended to exhibit and illustrate the whole range of the Older Scottish vocabulary, as preserved in literary, documentary, and other records, down to the year 1600, and to continue the history of the language down to 1700, so far as it does not coincide with the ordinary English usage of that century. Words not found before 1600 are also included when they are not current, or are not used in the same sense, in English of the period, or when they have some special bearing on Scottish history or life. The closing of the record with 1700 rests on the practical ground that after that date few traces of the older literary language remain, and Scottish survives only as a dialect, differing so much both in form and vocabulary from the earlier standard that the two periods can be fully and consistently treated only in separate dictionaries.[6]

The *Scottish National Dictionary*

deals with (1) Scottish words in existence since c.1700 (a) in Scottish literature, (b) in public records, (c) in glossaries and in dictionaries, (d) in private collections, (e) in special dialect treatises, and (2) Scottish words gathered from the mouth of dialect speakers by competent observers. The general vocabulary will include (1) Scottish words that do not occur in St.Eng. except as acknowledged loan words; (2) Scottish words the cognates of which occur in St.Eng.; (3) words which have the same form in Sc. and St.Eng. but have a different meaning in Sc. – i.e. so-called Scotticisms; (4) legal, theological or ecclesiastical terms which, within our period, have been current in Scottish speech – e.g. *liege pousté, avizandum, action sermon*; (5) words borrowed since c.1700 (from other dialects or languages) which have become current in Gen.Sc., or in any of its dialects, especially Gaelic words in counties on or near the Sc.Western limit and Gipsy words in the Border counties.[7]

Accessing Information in the Dictionaries

Undoubtedly, finding information in the dictionaries and making connections between different pieces of information is easier in the online DSL. It is possible to search for words or parts of words in different parts of the dictionaries' entries: the full entry itself; headword forms; geographical labels; full citations; work titles; authors; quotation text; etymologies; senses; dates. DSL is under continuing refinement with the aim of providing improved search facilities and it offers considerable advantages over the printed volumes of *DOST* and *SND*. Of course, the printed volumes may be used also, albeit the results may be obtained more slowly and with less ease sometimes. Whether the online versions or the printed editions are to be used, the same general principles obtain and the objective remains the same, of gathering together linguistic fragments to construct from them a mosaic of some thing.

What Kinds of Information do the Dictionaries Provide?

DOST and *SND* do not have the same format and vary in the kinds of information they provide. Consider these entries, treating the equivalent of 'Standard English' *hood*.

DOST: Hude

Hude, Huid, n.[1] Also: hode, hud, hwd(e, hwid, howde. [North. ME. *hude* (c 1400), midl. and south. *hood, hode, hod*, OE. *hód*.]
    1. A hood, a covering for the head (and shoulders), worn by both men and women.
    In common use in the 15th and 16th cents. (a) [Michaele dicto Redhode; 1293 *Highland P*. II. 128.] His mekill hude [E. *hud*] helit haly The armyng that he on hym had; Barb. xviii. 308. Thai . . . send out archeris a thousand With hwdis of; *Ib*. xix. 332. He . . . kist his hud done oure his

face; *Leg. S.* xxiii. 269. Quhen he has endyt that werk he sal be payt of v marcis and a gown with a hude til his rauarde; 1394 *Liber Aberbr.* 43. That the commonis wifis . . . wer nouther lange tail na syde nekit hudis; 1429 Acts II. 18/2. A hud of Ynglys broun; 1456 *Misc. Bann. C.* III. 94. Thow put off syne . . . thi ald hud, becaus it is thred bar; *Wall.* vi. 449. Bocht . . . ij ellis of Inglis grene and tua ellis of reid to be to the King ane greit hude . . . . Item. j ell of tartor to lyne the hud; 1494 *Treas. Acc.* I. 224. For thre elne wellus to the Quene for hir hudis; 1507 *Ib.* IV. 29. v qhyt cat skyns with diuers furryngs of hwds; 1530 *Lindores Chart.* 33. Twa fransche hwdis of welwott and thair strippis; 1546 *Acta Conc. & Sess.* XXII. 126 b. Thair huddis, thair cheynes, thair garnysynges; *Maitl. F.* xxxiv. 43. That hude, sir, is gude, sir, To hap your brain-sick heid; *Montg. Ck. & Slae* 867. Ane veluot hude and ane paire of dressingis; 1628 *Edinb. Test.* LIV. 329. Nyn cramed littell hudis; 1643 *Ib.* LX. 234.

SND: Huid

HUID, n., v. Also *hud(e)*; *heud*, and in sense I. *heuld*, *huild* (Ork.); *heed*, *heid* (n.Sc.), in sense I. 4. (1); dims.

hu(i)die, hoodie, hødi; hødek, huddik, huddack in sense I. 4. (3) (Sh.); derivs. *huidan, heudin, huddin, hødin, hooden, -in; hiddin, hidden, hithin; heedin* (n.Sc.), esp. in sense I. 4. (1). Sc. forms and usages of Eng. *hood*. [I., m. and s.Sc. *hød, hyd*; Ork. + *høld*: n.Sc. *hid*] I. n. 1. As in Eng., a covering for the head; *specif.* in dim. a sunbonnet worn by field-workers (Rxb. 1923 Watson W.-B., *huidie*; Ork., Ags. 1957). Also fig. in phr. *to put the huidie on*, to cap, to top (Ib.).

*Ork. 1920 J. Firth *Reminisc.* 111:
The women attired in striped petticoats, white "hubbies" (shirt blouses) and "hoodies" (cotton sun-bonnets) and with bare feet, raked and gossiped.

Hence *hoodie*, (a) a hired mourner, a mute, "this designation seems to have originated from their wearing hoods" (Edb. 1825 Jam.), phs. also by association with HUIDIE, the hooded crow, q.v.; (b) by a sim. extension of meaning, a nun of a black-robed order (Ayr. 1929).

2. One of a pair of sheaves of corn placed on the top of a *stook* (Rxb. 1923 Watson W.-B., Rxb. 1957), or corn stack (Rxb. 1957), to shelter it from the weather; gen. used *attrib.* in comb. *hood-sheaf, -sheave*, id. (Sc. 1825 Jam.), also *fig.* = the final touch, the "lid," the last word or straw, a parting drink (see Ags. 1857 quot.) (Fif. 1957), and as a v. = to protect with a *hoodsheaf*. Cf. II. 2. and heid-sheaf s.v. HEID, n., 5. Combs.

*Kcb. 1789 D. Davidson *Seasons* 96:
One forms the stook wi' nice-directing eye, Another following after, crowns with hoods.

*Per. 1799 J. Robertson *Agric. Per.* 159:
The two hood sheaves are . . . laid on in opposite directions, as a covering.

*Ayr. 1830 *Brit. Husbandry* (Burke 1840) III. i. 43:
In this precarious climate, oats ought always to be hoodsheaved too.

*Dmf. 1830 W. Bennet *Traits Sc. Life* II. 211:
Its [a plaid's] skirts spreading over the shoulders, in the form of a hood sheaf upon a stook of corn . . .

SND contains information about pronunciation which *DOST* lacks (though *CSD* supplies some information about pronunciation for pre-1700 forms). *SND* also gives indications of provenance for the illustrative quotations. In this case, *SND* has a sense 2 that is not recorded in Older Scots: 'One of a pair of sheaves of corn placed on the top of a stook . . . or corn stack . . ., to shelter it from the weather.'

Investigation of the 'same word' in *DOST* may require looking up different headwords according to the spelling, cf. Gefe, Geve, Geif, Gif, etc, as separate headwords for GIVE. A grasp of the different kinds of information and their display in each of the dictionaries is essential for their use as investigative tools.

The Dictionaries as Resources for Scottish Ethnology: An Example

The use of the dictionaries of Scots as resources and tools for ethnological study will now be exemplified. An ethnological enquiry may range in scope enormously, from a study of a community – be it a country or some culturally defined region within it – to the manufacture of a tool and its use or the ingredients and preparation of a specific dish. An example will be to extract material from the dictionaries relating to HARVEST, denoting a thing to be studied. Of course, our thing can be divided into other things connecting to activities, methods, tools, customs and belief. One thing leads inevitably to another and that to others. Indeed, that is the very of essence of doing 'lexicographical ethnology', as we might term this exercise.

It might be useful to consider the thing rather as the theme of the study – the overarching idea. Encompassed by this is a set of topics, being more narrowly defining of certain aspects of the theme. But the aim should not be a rigid categorising. Rather, we have to think of the topics as fuzzy and overlapping at different points.

For the theme and its topics there is a set of questions which provide the general frame of the lexico-ethnological enquiry. These are summarised in Figure 23.1.

Some pre-knowledge of the principal thing, things relating to it or things which it subsumes, is to be supposed. One might therefore simply decide to look up words which refer to these things.

> WHO? The focus of the enquiry is the protagonists or other participators in an activity, e.g. the possessors of certain skills, the users of a tool, a storyteller and his or her audience.
> WHY? The motivation for carrying out an activity; the goal of an activity.

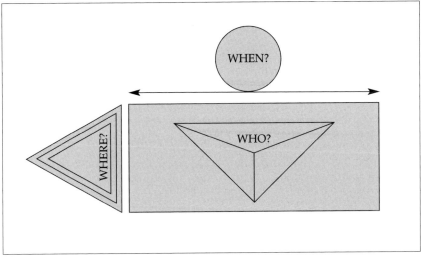

Figure 23.1 A frame for lexico-ethnological enquiry.

> HOW? The method and means of doing something. The behaviour of
> the protagonists.
> WHAT? The objects, artefacts involved in an activity, e.g. tool, musical
> instrument, ingredients of a dish.
> WHEN? and WHERE? define the spatio-temporal frame for the
> instances of a topic, e.g. 1850–1900, the south-west of Scotland.
> WHEN? can be considered to have two dimensions: (i) linear time and
> (ii) cyclical time. (i) corresponds to the conventional 'arrow of
> time', and instances of topics, as dated in the dictionary quota-
> tions, can be placed sequentially along it. (ii) correpsonds to activ-
> ities and events that recur, such as seasonal activities, like
> harvesting. Arguably, a cyclical pattern is abstracted from linear
> time – the instances that recur become types rather than tokens of
> the activity. The activity is assumed to recur following some
> general path, albeit there may be perceived changes in the
> specifics.
> WHERE? involves concentricity – the general area of investigation and
> specific areas of different extents within this, e.g. SCOTLAND –
> NORTH-EAST – INVERURIE PARISH – SUNNYSIDE FARM;
> WEST COAST – FISHING VILLAGE – BOAT.

Along the various dimensions of this frame can be assembled the senses and
the information to be found in the dictonaries' illustrative quotations. These are
the pieces which form the patterns of the mosaic we are reconstructing.

A useful starting-point is the *ST*. This organises material from the *CSD*
into semantic categories. There are fifteen main categories, each further subdivided.

Section 7 relates to FARMING. Under this are seventeen first-level subcategories and these in turn are further subdivided into second-level subcategories. Under FARMING is the subcategory 7.7 Crops, with six subcategories:

7.7   Crops
7.7.1 Crops: ploughing
7.7.2 Crops: manure
7.7.3 Crops: sowing
7.7.4 Crops: harvest work
7.7.5 Crops: harvest celebrations
7.7.6 Crops: processing

For this example, we want to focus on the subcategories 7.7.4–6. The information in the *ST* entries is quite basic: a headword, comprising a single lexical item or a phrase; a definition; and one or more labels indicating the geographical scope of the word.[8] A word or phrase may be precede by '†' to indicate that it is 'obsolete' in the sense that, for it, 'we have no evidence in the twentieth century'. There may also be a comment about what area of activity the word is used.[9] The format may be illustrated by two entries taken from 7.7.4 Crops: harvest work:

> **clype** *rick-building* the person who passes hay or sheaves from the forker to the builder *SW* [i.e. south-west]

> **†darg** the amount (meadow) which can be mowed in a day.

Having identified the thematic categories, the next stage is to select and organise into a finer categorisation words which refer to things which, judged from their definition, merit collection. The aim is to put together a corpus of words organised by their reference to things. It is akin to organising pieces that might make up different patterns within the mosaic of the overall theme – getting further information about the words from: (1) *CSD*, important for establishing variant spellings and useful for obtaining dates and etymological information; (2) *SND* and *DOST*.

More information about a word – its variant spellings, other senses, pronunciation(s), chronology, etymology – can be found in *CSD*. Working from the *ST*, it is probably best to approach *SND* and *DOST* through the *CSD* entry. This gives an overview of the word beyond the specific scope of its meaning in a *ST* entry. If we look up darg in the *CSD* we find

> **darg**[1] &c *16-*, **dairk** *la16–17*, **dark** &c *la16-* **dawerk** &c *15-16* [darg, derg, d r ; *dark &c; * dew rk, * d -] n **1** a day's work *15-*. **2** work, chf **the** *etc* **day's darg** *19-*. **3** the result or product of a day's work *la15-*, *now Edb.* **4** *chf* **darg** the amount (of meadow) which can be mowed in a day *la16-17*.
> *vi, only* **darg** 1 work, toil *la19*, *now Bnf Abd Fif.* 2 *chf agric* work by the day *la19-e20*.
> **darger, darker** a casual unskilled labourer *18-*, *now Bnf Abd Fif* [*cf* Eng *daywork*]

From this entry we can see a wider context of the word. The specific sense 4 of 'the amount (of meadow) which can be mowed in day' is seen to be restricted to the sixteenth and seventeenth centuries. The other senses refer to work in a more general way, but within the course of a single day. Sense 3, 'the result or product of a day's work', seems to have become restricted to Edinburgh, although the sense goes back to the fifteenth century.

If one is moving on to explore words in *SND* and *DOST*, especially important is identification of variant spellings. In *DOST* 'the same word' may occur under separate headwords according to the spelling, so that 'the same word' may have to be looked up in different places in the dictionary.

DOST:

Darg, *n*. Also: darge, darig(g.
[Variant of **Dark** *n*., with unusual change of *k* to *g*.] 1. A day's work, spec. of harvest-work.

Dark, *n*. Also: **darke**.
[Reduced from **Dawark** Cf. **Dairk**.] = **Darg** *n*.

Dawerk, Dawark, *n*. Also: **dawerke, dawwerk; dawork, dawirk**.
[Variants of **Daywerk**, with shortened first syllable. Cf. also **Dark** and **Darg** .] 1. A day's work, esp. in field labour. (a)

(Schere-dawark,) S(c)heir(e)-dawark, -dawirk, -darg, *n*. Also: **s(c)hear, sheere-**, and **-darrack, -durg; -day-wrok**. [**Scher(e** *v*. and **Dawerk** *n*. or **Darg** *n*.] A day's shearing, or reaping, at time of harvest, performed as a feudal service to a superior.

SND:

CLYPE, Clipe, n.5 and v.5 1. n. "In rick-building the one who passes on the hay or sheaves [from the forker] to the builder" (Dmf. 1925 W. A. Scott in *Trans. Dmf. and Gall. Antiq. Soc.* 21, *clipe*; Kcb.4 c.1900, *clype*).
 2. v. To pass sheaves from the forker to the builder of a stack.
 *Kcb.9 1936:
 Auld Edgar wis biggin' a soo stack. He had a boy clipin' an' he wis fairly tearin' on.
 [Same as **Clype**, v.1; a curious extension from a non-physical to a physical action – from the passing on of information to the passing on of sheaves.]

Methodology

The basic term that defines the investigation, I will call the *theme*, being HARVEST. This provides the starting-point. Within the theme a set of subsidiary *topics* is identified. In relation to the theme of HARVEST, the initial topics to explore would be those subsuming the different activities and processes – feeing of labour; reaping; gathering, binding and stacking; threshing. These provide key words through which to discover information in the DSL's illustrative quotations (IQs). Useful sources to identify topics are the *ST* and the *Historical Thesaurus of English*.[10] But topics and sub-topics will also arise in the course of investigating the information in DSL, particularly the IQs.

Once an initial list of topics has been established, the next stage is to search DSL. The words are entered in the search box. The section of the DSL to be searched is set to 'senses', and the sections of DSL are selected, e.g.

Here, 'cut' has '*' added to it, which is the wildcard character, i.e. it stands for a string of one or more characters following 'shear'. This allows discovery of senses containing forms such as 'shears', 'sheared', 'shearing'. In the example, the 'All DSL Texts' are specified for searching. However, one can select only one part of DSL or a combination of parts. The parts are:

(1) DOST itself and DOST Adds

The DOST Adds contains material drawn from the three supplements which were published in each of the first three printed volumes of *DOST* (A–C, D–G and H–L). 'It contains only additional senses and/or quotations, and editorial amendments. All complete new entries have been moved from their original place in these supplement sections and incorporated into the DOST main text file.'[11]

(2) SND, SND Suppl, SND New Suppl

The SND Suppl was added to the printed volume 10 in 1976. The New Suppl was added to DSL in 2005. It contains material published since 1976 from various written sources, including newspapers, and oral sources, 'acquired on the whole by casual means'. The contributors for oral sources included correspondents from various parts of Scotland and contributors to the Scottish Language Dictionaries website, which produces DSL.[12]

In response to the search specified for 'cut', a list of words is returned in the left-hand window, and the entry relating to the first of these is displayed in the main window.

Depending on the temporal scope of the investigation, one might want to omit either the *DOST* or the *SND* materials.

The next stage is to go through the list of entries, looking for the senses relevant to the topics of the theme. Many words returned will have senses that refer to quite other things. For example, 'LORNE SAUSAGE' can be disregarded in relation to the theme and topic, since we are interested in harvesting of crops. Other words, such as Kerve or STOO, although they denote actions of cutting, are not applied to crops and so can be disregarded.

With Scher(e and SHEAR, we find more material of relevance. *DOST* s.v. Scher(e, S(c)heir, *v.* gives Scher(e with specific senses.

> 10. To cut (corn , grass, etc.), ? chiefly or only with a reaping-hook or sickle, with a view to using it for a specific purpose.

and

> 10. d. *absol.* To cut standing crops.

SND, s.v. SHEAR, v., n., has

ADDS	1. (100)	Hill, *n*
DOST	2. (73)	Cut, *v*
DOST	3. (71)	Scher, *v.*
SNDS	4. (70)	CHACK, *n*
SNDS2	5. (70)	MALKIE, *n*
SNDS2	6. (70)	LORNE SAUSAGE, *n*
SND1	7. (60)	CUT, *v*
DOST	8. (50)	Kerve, *v*
DOST	9. (40)	Maw, *v*
SND1	10. (40)	CUT, *n*
SNDS	11. (35)	BUN, *ppladj*
SNDS	12. (35)	BREIST, *n*
SND1	13. (34)	PEAT, *n*
DOST	14. (31)	Cut, *n*
SND1	15. (26)	STOO, *v*
DOST	16. (26)	Hew, *v*
DOST	17. (26)	Cow, *v*
DOST	18. (26)	Strik, *v*
SND1	19. (23)	SHEAR, *v*
SND1	20. (21)	KIRN, *n*

Found 621 DSL Entries containing "cut" in the Field

Displaying 1 - 20 of 621 entries

> 1. As in Eng., to cut. Specif., *tr.* or *absol.*, to reap (corn), to cut crops with a sickle, to ac[t] as a harvester (Sc. 1799 W. Mitchell *Scotticisms* 76, 1808 Jam.; Uls. 1880 Patterson *Gl.*; Cai. 1904 E.D.D.; Per., Fif., Lth., Ayr. 1915–26 Wilson; I.Sc., Ags., Per. 1970). Now only dial. in Eng. Sim. used of peat-cutting (Ork. 1970). Phr. *to shear aff*, to finish the reaping of one's own rig. See **Affshearing**.

Within the entry *SND* also gives various derivatives and compounds:

> Hence ‡(1) *shearer*, one who reaps corn, a sickleman, harvester (Sc. 1782 J. Sinclair *Ob. Sc. Dial.* 179, 1808 Jam.; Per., Fif., Lth., Ayr. 1915–26 Wilson; Sh., ‡Cai. 1970). Combs. (i) *shearers' ale*, beer given to shearers at harvest; (ii) *shearer's bannock, -bap, -bun*, a large roll of bread or bun used in snacks on the harvest field (Lth. 1926 Wilson Cent. Scot. 205, Lth. 1970, bap); (iii) *shearers' bread*, id.; (iv) *shearers' market*, a hiring fair for harvest hands; (v) *shearer's rowe*, = (ii) above; (vi) *shearer('s) scone*, id. (Ags., Per., Fif., Bwk. 1970); (2) *shearin*, (i) reaping or cutting, hence, by metonymy, harvest (Sc. 1808 Jam., Add.; Per. 1915 Wilson L. *Strathearn* 270; Uls. 1953 Traynor). Also attrib., as in combs. *shearing claes, shearing heuk*, a sickle, *shearing silver*,

a payment made by a tenant to his landlord in lieu of service at harvest, *shearing time, south shearing,* harvest work in the south, in reference to the migration of workers from Bnff. to Ags. and Per. during this period of the year; . . .

Under sense 3., in 'comb[ination]s', is:

> (i) *shear-darg,* a day's work in harvest performed as a feudal service to a landlord;

Immediately one can see that these provide information for specific topics. And, indeed, perusal of these will suggest topics or subtopics. Thus, *shearer's ale, shearer's bannock, -bap, -bun,* bread, scone all give terms relating to FOOD AND DRINK in relation to the main theme.

But the main idea is to mine the IQs. We will want to keep in mind the frame of reference in Figure 23.1 above. The IQs will supply answers for all or some of the general questions posed in the frame of reference. In particular, *SND* gives information on WHERE?, usually at the level of (pre-1975) county, but sometimes a place more local is specified with the IQ itself. Both *DOST* and *SND* give dates to answer (linear) WHEN? Cyclic WHEN? may be inferrable from the text of the IQ. WHO? HOW? WHAT? WHY? are also to be sought within the text of the IQs.

The IQs may not be always very informative and may vary in length from a short phrase to an extensive paragraph or more. For example, *SND* s.v MAIDEN, *n., v.* has for sense 5:

> ‡5. The last bunch of corn to be cut on a particular farm at harvest time, frequently shaped and decorated in the image of a maiden and regarded as a symbol of the corn spirit (Rxb. 1923 Watson *W.-B.*; Fif. 1926 Wilson *Cent. Scot.* 254; ‡ne., em.Sc.(a) 1962). Hence, by extension: the harvest-home feast and celebrations, the Kirn. In mod. usage occas. applied to the last load of corn to be brought home at harvest time (Per. 1915 Wilson *L. Strathearn* 257; Fif.17 1951).

This is illustrated with the IQs:

> *Per. 1734 Atholl MSS.*:
>   3 Bottles of Whiskie to the shearers when they got his Graces Maiden
> . . . 0. 3s. 0.
>   *Sc. 1786 G. Robertson Har'st Rig (1801) 42*:
>   For now the Maiden has been won, And Winter is at last brought
> in.
>   *Per. 1795 Stat. Acc.*[1] XIX. 550*:
>   The fortunate lass who took the maiden was the Queen of the feast.
>   *Fif. 1806 A. Douglas Poems 144*:
>   The master has them bidden Come back again, be't foul or fair,

'Gainst gloamin', to the Maiden.

    *Gall. 1822 *Scots Mag.* (Oct.) 421:

This is the handful of oats which has been cut last the preceding harvest dressed up into the shape and designation of a maiden.

    *Ags. 1830 A. Balfour *Weeds* 166:

According to general custom, a handful of oats in the straw, fancifully plaited and decorated with ribbons, was fastened to the wall above the mantel-piece, as last year's maiden.

    *Fif. 1864 *St. Andrews Gaz.* (1 Oct.):

The "Loans' maiden" is not a mere sham, as too many of our "maidens" are now-a-days, but a thoroughly substantial affair, and partakes largely of the "patriarchal feasts" of the past.

    *Per. 1885 E. J. Guthrie *Old Sc. Customs* 130:

It was generally so contrived that this [maiden] fell into the hands of one of the prettiest girls in the field; it was then decked up with ribbons, and brought home in triumph to the sound of bagpipes and fiddles. A good dance was given to the reapers, and the evening was devoted to merriment. Afterwards the "Maiden" was dressed out, generally in the form of a cross, and hung up, with the date attached to it in some conspicuous part of the house.

    *Fif. 1962 *Scots Mag.* (June) 210:

The lucky one who brought the Maiden got a silver piece and a dram. The Maiden was plaited and hung on the kitchen ceiling till next harvest, for luck.

These provide information from a range of dates (1742–1962) and geographical areas, and provide different pieces of information. The most extensive observation is Per. 1885. Ags. 1830 and Fife 1864 give some detail about the dressing-up of the sheaf and its import. However, these pieces of information cannot be connected directly, as they have different provenances and dates. If one wishes to find more IQs from the same source, one can enter all or part of the text of the source for the IQ and search under 'full entry'. If 'Fif. 1962 Scots Mag. (June) 210' is input, another IQ is retrieved:

For dinner it was a shearer scone and a quart bottle of light beer. (2) (i)

This comes s.v. SHEAR n., v., where (2) (i) is a reference to a block of text relating to compounds, in this case *shearer scone*.

    The general questions can sometimes be used to specify the search for material. For example:

    WHAT? 'last sheaf'. Enter this for a search of full citations. Retrieved are

Found 9 ESND Entries containing "last sheaf" in the Field		
SND1	1. (100)	KIRN, *n*
SND1	2. (95)	MAIDEN, *n*
SNDS2	3. (82)	MAIDEN, *n*
SNDS2	4. (82)	CLYACK, *n*
SND1	5. (49)	HEID, *n*
SND1	6. (47)	MUCKLE, *adj*
SND1	7. (47)	WEIR, *v*
SND1	8. (24)	CLYACK, *n*
SND1	9. (24)	GRANNIE, *n*

Note that both MAIDEN and CLYACK have entries in SNDS2. In SNDS2, s.v. CLYACK is another IQ with a description of the tradition of the 'last sheaf':

> *ne.Sc. 1952 John R. Allan *North-East Lowlands of Scotland* (1974) 190:
> At the cutting of the corn, he said, the last sheaf was taken by the youngest person in the field; it was bound in the shape of a woman and called the clyack sheaf, or the maiden. That sheaf was carried home with honour and hung above the hearth.

The first sentence of this IQ is also found s.v. MAIDEN for SNDS2.

However, there are limitations to the way the search engine is set up at the time of writing. Consider WHEN? and WHERE? It is possible to search by 'date' and 'geographical label'. However, searching by 'date' can really only be done with any accuracy by specifying a full year, e.g. '1962', which for *SND* and Suppls retrieves 282 entries. A search for 'Fif.' by 'geographical label' produces 3,726 entries. In either case each entry would have to be consulted for relevance. Boolean searches are also possible, viz. 'Fif. AND 1962'. This produces 136 entries, but within the entry 'Fif.' and '1962' are more likely than not to be attached to different quotations, so that '1962' may be associated with an IQ relating to some other county than Fife. DSL lacks an advanced search engine that would allow searches for IQs which contain a date (or, better, a range of dates) AND/OR a geographical label. WHEN? and WHERE? have to be answered by organising appropriately the IQs retrieved by other search paths.

The processes of the chosen theme HARVEST can be considered in terms of:

> WHO? labour: feeing; roles of men, women, children in the tasks of harvesting, e.g.
>
> s.v. TASK, n., v. Sc. usages: I. *n.* 1. As in Eng., a fixed quantity of work, piece-work. Deriv. *tasker*, one paid by the specified task he accomplishes, a piece-worker, esp. a flail-man, a thresher of corn (Lth. 1808 Jam.), in Eng. dial. gen. applied to a reaper . . .
> *
> e.Lth. 1795 *Stat. Acc.*[1] II. 353:
> The taskers are those employed in threshing out the corn; and they receive one boll of every 25 for their labour.

WHAT? types of crop to be harvested; tools and machinery, such as scythes, sickles, threshing tools and machines; food and drink; celebrations at the end of harvest; e.g.

> s.v. HEUK, *n.*[1], *v.*[1] . . . I. n. 1. As in Eng., a reaping hook, a sickle. Hence by metonymy a reaper (Sc. 1825 Jam.).
>
> s.v. SCYTHE *n., v.* . . . .

(3) *Sc. 1844 H. Stephens *Bk. Farm* III. 1055:
The scythe-sickle is so called, because of its being provided with a cutting edge.

HOW? methods of working: in reaping, binding and stacking; e.g. s.v. PIRL v., n.

*Sc. 1890 H. Stephens *Bk. of Farm* V. 76:
A very common and effective plan of stooking pursued in certain exposed districts of the west and south-west, is to set up two pairs of sheaves, the one pair at right angles to the other instead of side by side, as in an ordinary stook ... This system is called "pirling", and, unless in particular districts, was probably more common half a century ago than now.

WHERE? geographical area specified in the sources of the IQs. WHEN? date specified in the sources of the IQs. WHY? motivation for the activities; e.g. s.v. HEUK,

(9) *Sh. 1937 J. Nicolson *Yarns* 85:
When the last "rig" was completed [at harvest time] it was customary to "cast da heuks." This was done by one individual taking hold of the various sickles by their points, and tossing these collectively backwards over the shoulder, at the same time repeating the following: – "Whaar 'ill I in winter dwell, Whaar 'ill I in voar dell, Whaar 'ill I in simmer fare, Whaar 'ill I in hairst shaer?" The direction in which each person's sickle pointed was supposed to answer those queries, but if one had stuck into the ground, that was taken as an indication that its owner was not destined to live very long.

and compare with

(11) *Lth., *Teviotd. 1825 Jam.:
Throwing the hooks. This is done immediately after *crying the kirn.* The *bandster* collects all the reaping-hooks; and, taking them by the points, throws them upwards: and whatever be the direction of the point of the hook, it is supposed to indicate the quarter in which the individual, to whom it belongs, is to be employed as a reaper in the following harvest. If any of them fall with their points sticking in the ground, the persons are to be married before next harvest; if any one of them break in falling, the owner is to die before another harvest.

Sources for the IQs such as records, histories, memoirs, diaries might seem to be most relevant for factual information. Many IQs in the DSL come from 'literary' texts, but these should not be dismissed as sources. They can as well record accurately the activities of everyday life. An observant writer of fiction – of poetry as well as prose – can describe the details of farming and community life. From

Scottish literature, one can cite the description of growing and harvesting flax from Robert Henryson's poem 'The Preiching of the Swallow' or the depiction of life in a north-east farming community in Lewis Grassic Gibbon's *Sunset Song*.

Organising the Data – Arranging the Pieces in the Frame

What is to be done with the material extracted from the dictionaries? Clearly, it needs to be organised in some way appropriate to the investigator's aims. The aims will vary according to interests and research questions. And the organisation will likely be a preliminary stage. That said, two possible approaches to organising the data may be considered: (1) a thesaurus-style classification; (2) a conceptual map.

The arrangements of material in *The Scots Thesaurus* have already been outlined. It offers one arrangement of some words. The ethnological investigator may well find it convenient to make a different – perhaps finer – thesaurus-type organisation of the data.

A conceptual map might be a more creative and heuristic way to look at the data. While there exist computer programs (some free) to make such maps (as, for example, 'mind maps'), one can just as easily draw them on a sheet of paper. Essentially, a conceptual map allows one to make connections between data and concepts, linking ideas with different colours and forms of line, for example. Connections can be hierarchical (as in the *ST* arrangement), but they can go anywhere one likes. One connection can lead to another and to another, so cross-linking information. A piece of information can have more than one significance. An IQ can illustrate more than one concept.

CONCLUSION

The above has been but a general and roughly sketched introduction to the use of *DOST* and *SND* for ethnological study. Without doubt, jointly and severally, they are a superb resource ready for exploitation by anyone studying the everyday life of Scotland's people from the medieval period to the present day. Material culture, customs and belief, literature, song, education, law, philosophy are all represented in rich detail.

NOTES

1 Gilliéron and Edmont, 1902–15.
2 Jaberg, Jud, Scheumeier, Rohlfs and Wagner, 1929–56.
3 <http://www.dsl.ac.uk/dsl/> [accessed February 2012].
4 Robinson, 1985.
5 Robinson, 1985; Dareau and MacLeod, 2009.
6 *DOST* vol. 12.
7 *SND*, Introduction, 36.
8 A list of geographical labels and their significations is given on pp. xv–xvi.
9 See *ST* Intro, xv.

10 The Historical Thesaurus of English was a project at Glasgow University running
    from 1965 to 2009, and on completion was published as *The Historical Thesaurus of
    the Oxford English Dictionary* (*THOED*). It was also published electronically
    in OEDOnline in 2010.
11 *DSL*, Introduction.
12 SNDS2, Introduction.

BIBLIOGRAPHY AND FURTHER READING

Dareau, M and MacLeod, I. Dictionaries of Scots. In Cowie, A P, ed., *The Oxford History of
    English Lexicography*, 2 vols, Oxford, 2009, 303–25.
Dareau, M G. Dictionary of the Older Scottish Tongue. In Macleod and McClure, 2012, 116–
    43.
Gilliéron, J. *Pathologie et thérapeutique verbales, résumé de conférences faites à l'Ecole Pratique des
    Hautes Etudes*, Neuveville, 1915.
Gilliéron, J. *Généalogie des mots qui désignent l'abeille: d'apres l'Atlas linguistique de la France*,
    Paris, 1918.
Gilliéron, J and Edmont, E. *Atlas linguistique de la France*, Paris, 1902–15.
Iordan, I. *An Introduction to Romance Linguistics: Its Schools and Scholars* / by I. Iordan; Transla-
    tion [from the Rumanian], in Parts Augmented and Revised by J. Orr, [with a Supplement
    'Thirty years on' by R. Posner], 2nd edn, Oxford, 1970.
Jaberg, K, Jud, J, Scheumeier, P, Rohlfs, G and Wagner, M L. *Sprach- und Sachatlas Italiens und
    der Südschweiz*, Zofingen, Ringier, 1929–56.
Kay, C and Mackay, M A, eds. *Perspectives on the Older Scottish Tongue*, Edinburgh, 2005.
Macleod, I. Scottish National Dictionary. In Macleod and McClure, 2012, 144–71.
Macleod, I and McClure, J D. *Scotland in Definition: A History of Scottish Dictionaries*,
    Edinburgh, 2012.
Rennie, S. Jamieson and the nineteenth century. In Macleod and McClure, 2012, 60–84.
Rennie, S. *Jamieson's Dictionary of Scots*, Oxford, 2012.

DICTIONARIES

The Concise Scots Dictionary, editor-in-chief Mairi Robinson, Edinburgh, 1985.
Craigie, W A, Aitken, A J, Stevenson, J A C et al., eds. *A Dictionary of the Older Scottish Tongue*,
    Chicago, Aberdeen, Oxford, 1931–2002.
Macleod, I with Macafee, C, Cairns, P and Martin, R. *The Scots Thesaurus*, Edinburgh, 1990.
Grant, W and Murison, D, eds. *The Scottish National Dictionary*, Edinburgh, [1931]–76.
The Dictionary of the Scots Language / Dictionar o the Scots Leid, online free-access versions
    of *SND* and *DOST*, Edinburgh, <www.dsl.ac.uk/dsl/>.

24 Creating a Digital Corpus of Ethnological Material

ANDREW WISEMAN

Those who make a study of the humanities now have available to them increasingly useful computer-based tools which can be used to produce digital collections. These digital collections or corpora are accessible either directly or over the internet. Such digital technology thereby has the potential to open up an archive or collection to a potential global audience. By being formed into a digital corpus, the data contained within these collections and archives can be easily sorted, searched and analysed. In a sense these developing tools lead to the creation of new material. Each digital corpus carries and presents the data at a remove from its creation but at the same time allows for ease of study. These digital corpora therefore have the potential to enable deeper analysis of a wider range of sources by general as well as academic users. In this brief discussion the use of such a digital corpus by ethnologists will be examined with reference to the Calum Maclean Collection.

Examples of online resources that contain relevant material for those studying Scottish ethnology include Tobar an Dualchais/Kist o Riches, which gives access to a wide variety of original fieldwork recordings drawn together from the archives of the School of Scottish Studies, BBC Scotland and the National Trust for Scotland's Canna Collection, and Pròiseact MhicGilleMhìcheil MhicBhatair/The Carmichael Watson Project, which makes available the collection of the pioneering folklorist Alexander Carmichael (1832–1912). The *Statistical Accounts of Scotland* website and various geo-referencing Digimap projects created and maintained by the University of Edinburgh's EDINA also contain evidence that is likely to be of interest to ethnologists. Similar projects furth of Scotland which are of an ethnological interest include Struth nan Gàidheal/Gael Stream, containing archival sound recordings, hosted by St Francis Xavier University at Antigonish, Nova Scotia; Cainnt mo Mhàthar/My Mother's Tongue; and, a remarkable initiative, An Drochaid Eadarainn/The Bridge Between Us, which provides an interactive online social space specifically, though not exclusively, aimed at the Gaelic community of Nova Scotia.[1] Such a service invites users to actively participate and share knowledge about ethnological materials, thereby embracing their social dimension.

Further linguistic and lexicographical projects that are of interest to those in the field of ethnological study are the inter-university initiative Faclair na Gàidhlig/Dictionary of the Scottish Gaelic Language[2] and the online DSL (Dictionar o the Scots Leid/ Dictionary of the Scots Language),[3] which contains two major historical dictionaries: *A Dictionary of the Older Scottish Tongue* (*DOST*) and *The Scottish National Dictionary* (*SND*).

Such resources complement and resonate with one another as they serve very similar purposes with regard to conservation and dissemination of hitherto difficult-to-access materials. They are therefore very much wedded to the concepts which underpin Pròiseact Chaluim MhicGilleathain/Calum Maclean Project, which is used in this discussion as an illustrative case study.

The AHRC-funded Calum Maclean Project offers, in digital format, an accessible and flexible research resource to a major collection of material which is central to Scottish ethnology. The collection consists of just over 13,000 manuscript pages of transcriptions of mainly Scottish Gaelic material from the fieldwork of Raasay-born Calum Iain Maclean (Calum Iain MacGilleathain, styled Calum Iain mac Chaluim 'ic Chaluim 'ic Iain 'ic Tharmaid 'ic Iain 'ic Tharmaid, or more simply Calum an Tàilleir) (1915–1960), folklorist and author of *The Highlands* (1959). The bulk of his collecting career was carried out in the Scottish Highlands and Islands first under the aegis of the Irish Folklore Commission (IFC), also known as Coimisiún Béaloideasa Éireann (founded in 1935), where he was trained. He commenced collecting in Ireland and then Scotland between 1946 and 1951, latterly at the University of Edinburgh's School of Scottish Studies between 1951 and 1960.

By way of encouragement, the founder and director of the IFC, James Hamilton Delargy (Séamus Ó Duilearga) (1899–1980), wrote this in a long letter of 17–19 October 1946 to Maclean:

> Always remember that . . . we are behind you. You are doing more important cultural work than anyone else in Scotland, for what you are doing is immortal; and when all the polemics of the day & all the headlines in the daily paper are forgotten, your work will remain.[4]

Delargy clearly understood the immense importance of the collecting which Maclean was then undertaking in the Southern Hebrides, mainly in Barra, Benbecula and South Uist. Maclean is arguably one of the greatest twentieth-century collectors of Scottish Gaelic oral traditions and his fieldwork legacy is rivalled only by those collections made during the nineteenth and early twentieth centuries by such assiduous collectors as John Francis Campbell of Islay, styled Iain Òg Ìle (1822–1885), Alexander Carmichael, as mentioned previously, John Dewar (1802–1872) and Fr Allan McDonald, styled Maighstir Ailein (1859–1905). Donald Archie MacDonald (1929–1999), Calum's successor in the School of Scottish Studies, later made almost 900 recordings of Gaelic lore, largely narratives.

CALUM MACLEAN'S FIELDWORK COLLECTION

During the fourteen years of his collecting career, Maclean recorded a remarkable amount of oral material, which he subsequently transcribed. In addition, he kept a daily record of and observations about his various work activities in his fieldwork diaries. An excerpt from an early diary entry from 1945 sets out the mission statement for the collecting that he carried out at the behest of the IFC:

Thòisich mise, Calum I. Mac Gille Eathain, a' cruinneachadh beul-aithris agas litreachas beóil ann an eilean Ratharsair am paraiste Phort-righeadh anns an Eilean Sgitheanach air an 19mh lá de 'n Dùdhlachd (Nodhlaig) 1945. Rugadh mi agas chaidh mo thogail anns an eilean seo. An uair a bha mise òg bha tòrr dhaoine anns an eilean seo aig a robh sgeulachdan agas seann-òrain nach deachaidh a sgrìobhadh sios riamh is nach téid a sgrìob-hadh sios gu bràth. Tha an t-seann-fheadhainn an nis marbh agas thug iad gach rud a bha aca leotha do'n uaigh. Có dhiubh tha cuid de dhaoine ann fhathast a chuimhneachas bloighean de na h-òrain a bhiodh aca agas bloighean de'n t-seanchas eile cuideachd. Shaoil mi gu robh barrachd òran air am fàgail anns an eilean seo na bha de aon rud eile. Uime sin chuir mi romham na h-òrain a sgrìobhadh sios uile mar a chuala mi aig na daoine iad. Ach sgrìobh mi sios cuideachd gach rud a thachair rium. Tha fhios agam gu bheil sinn tri fichead bliadhna ro anamoch gu tòiseachadh air an obair seo, ach dh'fhaoite gu sàbhail sinn rud air chor eigin fhathast, mun téid e uile a dhìth.[5]

I, Calum I. Maclean, began two days ago to collect the oral tradition of the island of Raasay. I was born and reared on this island. When I was young there were many people here who had tales and songs which had never been written down, and which never will be, since the old people are now dead, and all that they knew is with them in the grave. There are still some people alive who remember some of the songs and traditions of their forefathers, and as it seemed to me that there are more songs than anything else available, I decided to write down those which I could find. I realise that we are sixty years late in beginning this work of collection, but we may be able to save at least some of the traditional lore before it dies out.

This was written at the outset of Maclean's successful collecting sortie in his native Raasay. The IFC director decided in 1946, on the basis of that fieldwork trip, to send Maclean back to his homeland so that he could continue to collect, on a full-time basis, the fast-dying Gaelic traditions of the Hebrides and the mainland Highlands. By February 1946, Maclean had amassed a great deal of lore from his own relations, mainly from his maternal uncle, Angus Nicolson, styled Aonghas Shomhairle Iain 'ic Shomhairle (1890–1965), and his paternal aunt Peggie MacLean, styled Peigi Chaluim Iain Ghairbh (1869–1950). Maclean's Raasay collection was mainly songs along with associated stories about their provenance and background.[6] Reflecting on his experience of collecting in Raasay, Maclean wrote the following to his brother Sorley:

But I enjoy my work very much. The folklore business became more inter-esting according to how you master the proper system of approach. Raasay is a wonderful type of place to work. It is small and sea-contained. It has fishermen and crofters, land and sea, birds, fish and animals, old ruins, groves, buailes, ghosts, fairies, oral tradition, local history and everything that comes within our scope. It would take a good collector three years to cover it all.[7]

The bulk of Calum Maclean's fieldwork manuscripts are in the curatorial care of University College Dublin's National Folklore Collection, with the remainder housed in the School of Scottish Studies Archives at the University of Edinburgh. In Edinburgh there are twenty-eight notebooks (SSS MSS 1–28), containing around 440,000 words, and in Dublin there are twenty-four notebooks, of which nineteen contain transcriptions of oral traditions along with five fieldwork diaries[8] which, all together, contain upwards of 2.1 million words amounting to around twenty-five million characters. In addition to this, Maclean also collected a fair amount of Irish material in Connemara.[9]

The majority of his collection consists of Scottish Gaelic folklore, primarily tale texts along with more than 300 song texts together with two full-length autobiographies of two major Scottish Gaelic storytellers, Duncan MacDonald, styled Donnchadh mac Dhòmhnaill 'ic Dhonnchaidh (1882–1954) from Snishival, South Uist[10] and Angus MacMillan, styled Aonghas Barrach MacGilleMhaoil (1874–1954) from Griminish (see Fig. 24.1), Benbecula.[11]

Figure 24.1 Angus MacMillan, Griminish, Benbecula, recording on the Ediphone for Calum Maclean in 1947. National Folklore Collection, University College Dublin.

On an auspicious spring day in 1947, Maclean met two of the most remarkable storytellers he was ever to meet – Duncan MacDonald (Fig. 24.2) and Angus MacMillan. Both these men were to relate hundreds of stories for Maclean on an Ediphone recording device (see Fig. 24.1), which he would later transcribe word for word in order that a permanent written record of them could be created and preserved. Such oral narratives ranged from long romantic tales to shorter historical legends, from genealogy to place-name lore, from humorous anecdotes to supernatural tales about ghosts, second sight, and fairy lore. A story recited by Angus MacMillan has the distinction of being the longest ever to have been recorded in Western Europe. Called 'Alasdair mac a' Chèaird' ('Alasdair son of the Caird'), it took nine hours to tell and over a week to transcribe. MacMillan had over forty of these stories in his repertoire, each of which took around three hours to tell, whereas MacDonald's longest story, 'Sgeulachd Mhànuis' ('The History of Manus'), was short by comparison, taking only one and a half hours to tell.

Maclean was one of the first professionally trained fieldworkers to undertake the systematic collection of the old Gaelic songs, stories, customs and traditions in the Highlands and Islands with modern recording apparatus. Therein lies the importance of his work. It should also be borne in mind that Maclean was not alone in his endeavours, as others were also collecting oral traditions in the Southern Hebrides around this time. For example, Kirkland Cameron Craig (d. 1963) published some of Duncan MacDonald's stories.[12] John Lorne Campbell, styled Fear Chanaigh (1906–1996), also recorded a significant amount of material in South Uist from such tradition bearers as Angus MacLellan, styled

Figure 24.2 Duncan MacDonald, Snishival, South Uist. Photograph taken at Callanish while attending an International Conference on Folklore in 1953 at Stornoway. School of Scottish Studies Archives, University of Edinburgh.

Aonghas Beag mac Aonghais 'ic Eachainn 'ic Dhòmhnaill 'ic Chaluim 'ic Dhòmh-naill (1869–1966) from Locheynort[13] and, in Barra, from John MacPherson, styled The Coddy (1876–1955).[14] John Lorne Campbell also edited an earlier collection of half a dozen stories from Barra and Uist[15] recorded from two Barra tradition bearers, Murchadh an Eilein and James MacKinnon, styled Seumas Iain Ghunnairigh (1866–1957) from Northbay, and from the poet and South Uist tradition bearer Johnny Campbell, styled Seonaidh mac Dhòmhnaill 'ic Iain Bhàin (1859–1944) from Glendale. The important difference was that Maclean had institutional support, initially from the IFC and, afterwards, from the School of Scottish Studies, whereas Campbell was an independent scholar relying upon a private income.

A good deal had been done previously by way of collecting old stories in the Highlands by John Francis Campbell of Islay and his team of collectors but, lacking any means of making mechanical recordings, their task of writing down such tales from dictation was a highly laborious one. John Francis Campbell himself acknowledged that his collection in no way exhausted the stories then current in the Highlands by concluding his monumental four-volume *Popular Tales of the West Highlands* (1860–62) with the admission that 'whole districts are yet untried, and whole classes of stories, such as popular history and robber stories, have yet been untouched'.[16]

A very brief biographical account of Maclean's life puts his work as a collector, folklorist, author and ethnographer into the context of his career both in the employment of the IFC, and at the School of Scottish Studies. Through the far-sightedness of Delargy, Maclean was first offered a post as a part-time collector in 1946 at the IFC, which later became full-time. After collecting in Connemara on the west coast of Ireland, Maclean was transferred to the IFC's headquarters in Dublin where he undertook further training in cataloguing and archival techniques under the supervision of his colleague Sean O' Sullivan (Seán Ó Súilleabháin) (1903–1996).[17]

In January of 1951, Maclean was sent from the IFC for an initial period of three years, which subsequently became permanent, and was appointed the first collector at the newly founded School of Scottish Studies, where he continued his fieldwork throughout Scotland.[18] Soon after this, Maclean was enabled to spend a nine-month research sabbatical (from late summer 1951 to May 1952) at Uppsala University in Sweden, which was then at the forefront of folklore, dialectology, methodology, cataloguing and archival techniques. Having studied there under Professors Dag Strömbäck (1900–1978) and Åke Campbell (1891–1957), Maclean later set up an index system for Scottish folklore at the School of Scottish Studies based on that of Uppsala.

Some three years before he passed away, Maclean reflected upon the episte-mological motivation of collecting and was quite unambiguous when he made the point that to try and divorce the collection of oral tradition from the nation-alistic context of 'the folk' was ill conceived, for:

> Gaelic songs, stories and legends may be collected and recorded for one of two reasons: for the purposes of purely academic, scientific study on

the one hand or, on the other, as part of a definite policy to save a vital and integral part of the nation.

There were thus 'two approaches: the scientific and the aesthetic or nationalist, and of the two I think the latter more important.'[19]

OVERVIEW OF THE CALUM MACLEAN PROJECT

The Calum Maclean Collection Online Catalogue[20] is hosted by the University of Edinburgh in collaboration with University College Dublin (UCD). The project's primary aim was to publish Calum Maclean's fieldwork transcriptions as well as his diaries as an online digital archive so that his vast legacy would be available to a wider audience. A representative sample of Maclean's manuscript materials was selected along with a technological consultation for the most effective methodology for making them available online, which was conducted through a pilot project. This proof of concept established a firm foundation for the project itself with regard to methodology and technical aspects of creating a large linguistic corpus of Gaelic folklore texts using the Text Encoding Initiative (TEI) to store eXtensible Markup Language (XML) files in a database-driven searchable website. This overarching aim of the project may be subdivided as follows:

- Creation of searchable digitally based collection of Gaelic oral narratives;
- Provision of an online searchable catalogue to meet diverse research requirements;
- Provision of secure and managed access to a rich digital resource.

The texts from which XML files were created using the TEI format were then presented online through a searchable XML Relational Database (RDB). This digital collection provides a powerful and adaptable resource for folktale research, but also a major Scottish Gaelic language corpus. The digitisation process began with producing Tagged Image File Format (TIFF) images from either microfilm or from the original manuscript notebooks. The resulting TIFF images were used for the production of texts which were re-keyed (using a double-entry method to minimise errors) into an XML template. From these raw XML files the resulting texts were collated during the process of markup using TEI,[21] an internationally recognised standard for the production of electronic texts. The XML files were verified against a Document Type Definition (DTD) to ensure that they were well-formed and valid. As the process proceeded, the texts were added and stored in an XML RDB. Through a web interface specifically designed to query the texts stored in the database, the results of any given search were then rendered for display using a Cascading Stylesheet (CSS), which published the resultant files in a web browser. As stated, the process of digitisation began with the production of TIFF images and the resultant derived Joint Photographic Experts Group (JPEG) file format was used to make the images available alongside the edited texts.

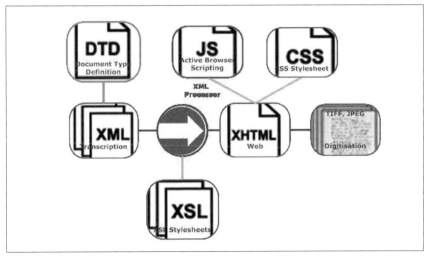

Figure 24.3 Data Flow Diagram, Andrew Wiseman, 2010.

A guiding principle of the markup procedure was to approximate as faithfully as possible the original documents in order that each notebook could be preserved along with its content. Fortunately, Maclean's hand is well-formed and can, for the most part, be read with relative ease, which made the re-keying process not only more accurate than it would have been otherwise but also meant that the process of textual editing was simpler (see Fig. 24.3).[22]

The features of XML are such that they provide flexibility in order to convey emendations such as deletions, supralinear additions, marginalia and so on which reflects, to some extent, the immediacy of the actual original transcriptions. Many would heartily agree with Maclean when he wrote:

> Fresh items were continually added, and it was almost impossible to keep the transcription of material apace with the accumulation of records. The transcription was, of course, nothing but the purest drudgery.[23]

The project could not have existed without the great amount of transcription work which Maclean undertook, sometimes in very trying circumstances and, it may be remembered, in relative isolation from either Dublin or Edinburgh, but which was ultimately very much worthwhile. If it were not for Maclean's selfless toil then a great deal of valuable oral material would have passed out of living memory.

A TRANSCRIPTION EXAMPLE FROM
THE CALUM MACLEAN COLLECTION

Out of more than around 4,000 items that are currently available, a short narrative concerning fairy belief will suffice in order to give a representative sample of

Figure 24.4 John MacDonald of Highbridge, Brae Lochaber. School of Scottish Studies Archives, University of Edinburgh.

the corpus. The following story was collected from John MacDonald of Highbridge (1876–1964), known locally as Iain am Bàrd or Iain Beag (see Fig. 24.4), from Brae Lochaber,[24] and was transcribed on 18 February 1951, shortly after being recorded. From his diary entry of that day, it may be assumed that after he had earlier met John MacDonald, Maclean probably went back to his lodgings and continued with transcribing until he travelled the short distance from Spean Bridge to Highbridge to fetch his informant:

> Chaidh mi dha'n Aifreann tràth anns a' mhaduinn an diugh. An déidh dhomh tighinn dachaidh thug mi greis a' sgrìobhadh gus an robh am dinnearach ann. An uair sin chaidh mi a mach agas thachair Iain Mac Dhomhnaill, am Bàrd, rium. Chan fhaca mi e an diugh idir agas bha mi air son gun tigeadh e a nall e dh' innseadh sgeulachdan domh. Thuirt e gun tigeadh e aig ceithir uairean feasgar. Chaidh mi a null g'a iarraidh agas thug mi liom a nall e a dh' ionnsaigh an taighe. Bha latha mór againn an diugh cuideachd le naidheachdan agas thug e grunn mór dhiubh dhomh. Bha e comhla rium gus an robh e mu naoi uairean a's t-oidhche.[25]

> I went to Mass early this morning. After I came home I spent a while writing until dinner time. I then went out and happened to meet John MacDonald, the Bard. I hadn't seen him at all today and I wanted him to come over to tell me stories. He said that he would come at four o'clock this afternoon. I went over to fetch him then and I took him over to the house. We had another great day today with regard to [recording] anecdotes

and he gave me a great many of them. He was in my company until around nine o'clock at night.

Indeed, the very first recordings that Maclean made in 1951 for the School of Scottish Studies included no less than 524 Gaelic tales (mainly short, pithy items that were part of the local *seanchas* or historical lore) from this roadman, encountered, as Maclean wrote, 'in the dead of winter, and Lochaber lay white and deep in snow'.[26] The title of this particular narrative item is 'Fear a chunntais na sìdhchean' – 'The man who counted the fairies':[27]

Bha an sluagh anns an dùthaich seo air an cuideachadh gu math tri(ch)c leis na sìdhchean (F346). Tha àite anns an dùthaich seo ris an abair iad an Ràth, thall am Bracleitir. Agas bha duine a' fuireach ann ris an abradh iad Ailean Mór an Ràth agas iomadh duine air thoiseach air an àm aig Ailean Mór an Ràth. Agas bha fear a' dol seachad aig Geàrrlochaidh, dìreach mu choinneamh an Ràth: tha iad glé theann air a chéile, ach gu bheil an abhainn a' ruith sìos eatorra, Abhainn Spèan. Bha oidhche bhriagha ghealach ann. Agas gu dé b' iongnadh leis ach an t-àite làn sìdhchean a' ruith air ais 's air adharst ag obair air an ar[a](bh)ar (F455.6.8.1). Agas 's ann dar a rachadh càch mu thàmh air an oidhche, 's ann a bha à-san a' tighinn a mach a dh' obair (F348.8). Agas thuirst e ris fhéi':
    'Chuala mi iom[a]radh riamh air nan cunntadh tu na sìdhchean nach fhai(ch)ceadh tu tuillidh iad (F381). Nach fhiach mi sin a dhèanadh,' thuirst ris fhéi'.
    Shuidh e agas bha e 'gan cunntas. Agas b'e sin an obair. Bha iad cho colta' ri chéile a chuile h-aon dhiubh a' ruith air ais 's air adharst. Is thuirst e:
    'Is iomadh cunntas a rinn mi riamh air meanbh-chruidh 's air crodh, air spréidh agas an iomadh àite, ach bheat seo na thachair riamh or[a]m.'
    Chum e air cunntas gus an dàinig e a dh' ionnsaigh ciad gu leith.
    'Ma ta, chan 'eil mi ro-chinnteach a bheil iad agam uile. Ach 's e an t-aon rud a chuala mi: nam bitheadh iad air an cunntas cearst, nach bitheadh iad ri fhai(ch)cinn tuillidh.'
    Agas chum e air a thuras. Dar a thàinig a' sluagh a mach 's a' mhaduinn, b' iongnadh leotha a chuile sguab de'n ar[a](bh)ar cho seasgair, tioram air a chur air dòigh agas air a thughadh. Agas thug iad taing seachad: na bu có a rinn e, gur h-iad an sgioba a bha tapaidh. Agas cha deach na sìdhchean fhai(ch)cinn tuillidh. Agas feumaidh a' fear a chunnt iad, gun robh iad air an cunntas cearst. Mar a tha a' fa(ch)cal ag ràdha: 'Ma chunntas e a dh' ionnsaigh a h-aon iad, chan fhai(ch)c thu a h-aon dhiubh tuillidh.'[28]

Maclean also rendered a close translation of the above tale:

The folk in this country were often helped by the fairies (F346). There is a place in this district which they call the Ràth, over in Brackletter. And there was a man living there whom they called Big Allan of the Ràth, and many other people lived there before the time of Big Allan of the Ràth. And a certain man was passing by Gearrlochy, over opposite the Ràth; the two places are very close to one another except that the river runs down between them, the Spean river. It was a fine, moonlit night, and to his amazement the place was full of fairies who ran hither and thither as they harvested the corn (F455.6.8.1). And it was when other people went to rest at night that they came out to work (F348.8). And he said to himself:

'I have always heard it said that, if you counted the fairies (F381), you would not see them again. Should I not try to do that,' said he to himself.

He sat down and counted them. And that was some job. They were all so alike running to and fro. And he said:

'I have made many reckonings of sheep and of cattle, of herds, and I did so in many places but this has surpassed anything that I have ever come across.'

He continued counting until he came to a hundred and fifty.

'Indeed, I am not sure that I have them all, but the one thing I did hear is that, if they are counted properly, they would not be seen again.'

And he continued on his journey. When the folk came out in the morning, they were amazed to find every sheaf safe and dry, stacked and thatched. And they expressed their thanks: whoever did it, it was done by an agile team. And the fairies were not seen again. And it must have been the person who counted them did count them properly. As the saying has it, 'If he counts them to the exact figure, you will not see one of them again.'

A summary of the above tale, taking in all the salient aspects of the narrative, may be given as follows:

Local people were greatly helped by the fairies (F346). There was a man who stayed at Ràth, in Brackletter, Lochaber, called Ailean Mór an Ràth. A man was going past Gairlochy just opposite Ràth separated by the River Spean. It was a beautiful moonlit night and what he saw was amazing: the fairies were running up and down working on the corn (F455.6.8.1). After the people had gone to bed, the fairies were coming out to work (F348.8). He said to himself that he always heard that if you count the fairies then you'd never see them again (F381). He sat down and started counting – it was hard work as they all looked similar. Many a time he had counted cattle, sheep and herds but this surpassed him. He got to one-hundred and fifty but he wasn't quite sure that he had them all. But one thing he was sure of is that if he counted them all they'd never be seen again. The man continued on his journey. Next day, the people were amazed to see all the corn harvested and all in sheaves. They gave thanks to whoever had done the work. The fairies were never seen again. The man who counted them must have done it correctly. As the saying has it: 'If he counts them to the exact figure, you will not see one of them again (F381).'

Bu tu an cuireach nèo-sgàthach
'S an toir't sàthailte a mach.

(XVI)

Ceist nam Ban th'n tìr Abrach
Bho Dhochann-fhasaidh an fheòir:
Leitir Fhionnlaigh nam Badan,
Far an stadadh a' slògh.
Bho thaobh Lòchaidh nam Bradan,
Is bho thaobh Loch Airceig nam bò—
Slàn-ghuisgeach Chloinn Chamarain,
Laoch g'am ainim Domhnall òg.

Iain mac Dhomhnaill a dh'innis:

18 : 2 : '51

Fear a chunntais na sìdhchean

Bha an sluagh anns an dùthaich seo air
an cuideachadh gu math tric (h) leis na sìdhchean.
Tha àite anns an dùthaich seo ris an abair
iad an Ràth thall am Bracleitir. Agus tha
duine a' fuireach ann ris an abradh iad
Ailean mòr an Ràth, agus ismath duine air
thoiseach air an àm aig Ailean mòr an Ràth.
Agus bha fear a' dol seachad aig Beàrrlochaidh
dìreach mu choinneamh an Ràth. Tha iad glé
theann air a chéile, ach gu bheil an abhainn

As can be seen from the above example the story is replicated from the transcription made by Maclean, to which a summary has been appended. Motifs, where appropriate, were then identified and added to the transcribed narrative where they occurred as well as to the summary, allowing any researcher, even without any prior reading knowledge of Scottish or Irish Gaelic, access to the resource. During this process appropriate keywords were also added for the sake of making searching and retrieval more accessible. The most suitable genre classification for each item, generated from an in-house created list of hierarchical descriptions, moving gradually from the general to the particular, was identified for this tale, which turned out to be Tale/Legend/Supernatural/Fairy; and, in this instance, a 'local' taxonomy was also identified and appended which was F115 – Fairies Help at Harvest. So far this example has only dealt with the body of the text, but all the metadata – such as the information concerning the informant's details, date, place, provenance (of the material if available) and so on – were then added to the header. A proforma used by the IFC was the source for metadata creation which, in most cases, had been appended to each section of the manuscripts for each of the individual informants. The accuracy of this information, reflected in the resultant metadata creation, depended not only upon the reliability of the information itself but also upon Maclean, who was assigned responsibility for noting down such details. Such metadata are vital for information retrieval and thus searches may be based on title, name of reciter, location, recording date, classification or keywords. After each item was proofread it was ready to be uploaded into the RDB and so published electronically. It was deemed necessary to compare the re-keyed texts from the supplied XML files with the manuscripts in order to maintain accuracy, including paragraphing, spelling, punctuation and so on. The markup of the texts involved the following steps:

- Insertion of tags for names, places, titles, contractions, foreign words, emendations, notes and so on;
- Replacing entities such as accents, contractions, and special symbols to accord with their ISO equivalents;
- Assigning motifs where they occur in the main text and to the summary;
- Assigning a genre to a given text;
- Assigning keywords to the text;
- Assigning a taxonomic classification to a text if it had been identified either as an International Tale (AT/ATU),[29] a Migratory Legend (ML),[30] a Witch-type (Wi)[31] or Fairy-type (Fa)[32] legend;
- Checking the validity of the marked-up XML text against the DTD (Document Type Definition).

One clear editorial advantage of electronic publication is that content can be either updated or, indeed, expanded. Through the use of keyword and free-word text searching, the user has the ability to find materials of interest. The benefits of such online resources may be summed up as preservation as well as access, as the material was preserved through digital conservation and therefore is more readily accessible. The resultant resource, through the use of modern technology, can be disseminated to anyone with an interest in ethnological studies, especially of a Scottish provenance.

Commenting upon the legacy left by Maclean, Basil Megaw (1913–2002), the first director of the School of Scottish Studies from 1957 to 1969, wrote:

> The full significance and range of the oral material preserved as a result of Calum Maclean's work in Scotland will only become apparent after years of study, but already Scandinavian and other scholars who have had access to it have expressed their admiration for the skill and care displayed in the recording, no less than the intrinsic value of the material. The unique combination of his inherited gifts, training and experience, lend particular weight to his own final conclusion that, for richness in oral tradition, no area in these islands – not excepting even the west of Ireland – can compare with South Uist.[33]

The resultant digital corpus of ethnological data will make the material more widely available than it has ever been previously and therefore attractive to researchers from various field and disciplines as well as to a wider public audience. The primary audience for such a research resource includes those with an interest in the following subject-related areas: ethnology (especially from a Scottish and Irish perspective), narrative studies, Celtic studies, linguistics, anthropology and oral history. It is envisaged that the corpus will be used in a variety of ways, providing up-to-date tools for interdisciplinary research, which may include at least some of the following: analysis of stylistics and folklore language register; oral formulae; word frequency; dialectology; discourse analysis; geographic distribution of folktales and motifs; comparative studies; and lexicography. The addition of English summaries has the effect of widening access to the contents of the corpus to users with no previous knowledge of either Scottish or Irish Gaelic.

    Additional benefits of this corpus may include, but are not limited to, aspects such as providing an up-to-date tool for interdisciplinary research by allowing access to an electronic catalogue, where researchers can compare materials through an easy-to-use web interface, together with a flexible tool for searching. Every effort has been made to ensure electronic publication is of a high standard, which it is hoped will encourage further research in folktales and song – whether in an academic context or by a more general audience, particularly those with an interest in Gaelic oral traditions. Classifying the tale texts into different genres, such as international and migratory folktales as well as identifying motifs, allows for comparison with similar linguistic and folkloristic corpora and will hopefully attract a more academic audience, whether on a national or international scale.

    An electronic resource such as the Calum Maclean Project could be easily replicated for any other folklore collections. When major Scottish folklore collections such as those of Dr Robert Craig Maclagan,[34] Campbell of Islay,[35] John Dewar,[36] Fr Allan McDonald,[37] Francis Diack,[38] Cyril Dieckhoff,[39] Rev. Charles Robertson Montcrieff,[40] Donald John MacDonald[41] and others are made available in a similar format (or with formats complying with emerging technologies) as that used for the production of the Calum Maclean Project's electronic catalogue, then a truly significant series of ethnological resources will result that rivals, or even surpasses, those currently accessible. Such collections, when made available, would, of course, not only complement one another but would also be first-class, stand-alone resources that will not be limited to ethnological research.

Despite the use of current technology with regard to ethnological material, this area remains underdeveloped. There is great potential for far more information to be made available. Given that information technology is being harnessed, and together with established and emerging international standards and formats for electronic publication, there is far greater scope to open up archival materials for research purposes to a wide range of the humanities and social sciences. For example, there is enormous potential in archives in Scandinavia or those in the National Folklore Collection at UCD.[42] Of course, raw materials – such as transcriptions, sound recordings, films, videos, questionnaires and such like – have to exist in the first instance, but if they are made available, and if the appropriate resources can be put in place, then any given country or ethnic identity can potentially create an ethnological resource of not only national but also international importance. Scotland is well served with regard to the availability of such rich raw sources and taking into consideration the projects for online dissemination listed at the start of this chapter, may rightly be described as being at the forefront of creating ethnological digital resources.

Transcriptions and recordings of materials, made at the behest of either the IFC or the School of Scottish Studies, are remarkable for a variety of reasons. For example, Calum Maclean preserved precious cultural artefacts that were in danger of disappearing. He left a treasure-trove for future generations and made an outstanding contribution to the preservation of Scotland's intangible cultural heritage. Elsewhere, Maclean wrote that:

> Although the academic folklorist may be concerned only with the collection and study of material before it becomes too late, he may, unconsciously, participate in the efforts towards the preservation and rehabilitation of the language.[43]

Calum Maclean may not have foreseen the manner and form that his fieldwork legacy was going to take, but doubtless he would have been satisfied that this store of knowledge, the product of his commitment to working in the field, is being not only preserved but made readily available to anyone who has an interest in Gaelic cultural history and oral tradition.

1 Sruth nan Gàidheal/Gael Stream, <http://gaelstream.stfx.ca/>; Cainnt mo
  Mhàthar/My Mother's Tongue, <www.cainntmomhathar.com/>; An Drochaid
  Eadarainn/The Bridge Between Us, available as a prototype at
  <http://demo.headspacedesign.ca/androchaid/> [all accessed November 2012].

2 Faclair na Gàidhlig/Dictionary of the Scottish Gaelic Language,
  [accessed November 2012].

3 DSL, [accessed November 2012].

4 For a full edition of this letter, see Wiseman (forthcoming).

5 IFC MS 1026, fo. 1a.

6 IFC MS 1026–1027; Maclean 1942–50, 176–92.

7 NLS MS.29536, fo. 26.

8 IFC MSS 1026–1031, 1053–1054, 1111, 1129, 1153–1156, 1171, 1179–1183, 1300–1302.

9 IFC MSS 840, 851, 868, 926, 969, 1025 and 1142.

10 MacGilleEathain, 1954, 170–4; MacMhathain, 1949, 59; Maclean, 1956, 31–2; Maclean,
   1975, xiv. Maclean recorded Duncan MacDonald's biography, see IFC MS 1180,
   111–256. See also Draak, 1957, 47–58; Campbell, 1952, 1–5; Campbell, 1954, 473–4.

11 Maclean, 1952, 126–9; Maclean, 1956, 29–31; MacGilleEathain, 1954, 170–4; Maclean,
   1975, xiii–xiv; Maclean, 1979, 64. Maclean also recorded Angus MacMillan's
   biography, for which see IFC MS 1180, 301–548.

12 MacDhomhnaill, 1950.

13 MacLellan, 1997.

14 MacPherson, 1992.

15 Campbell, 1939.

16 Campbell, 1890, iv, 428.

17 Maclean, 1975, ix.

18 A few years later, the School received the generous gift from the IFC of microfilm
   copy of all the Scottish material collected for them by Maclean.

19 Maclean, 1957, 27.

20 Pròiseact Chaluim MhicGilleathian/Calum Maclean Project,
   <www.celtscot.ed.ac.uk/calum-maclean/> [accessed March 2012].

21 For more imformation about the TEI, see <www.tei-c.org/index.xml> [accessed
   November 2012], where detailed guidelines are available as well as listings of many
   scholary projects using this standard for the production of electronic texts.

22 In 1956 Maclean was struck down by cancer, necessitating the amputation of his left
   arm the following year. Despite this setback Maclean continued fieldwork and was
   assisted with transcription work by Liza Sinclair, who was employed by the School of
   Scottish Studies for this purpose.

23 Maclean, 1956, 30.

24 Maclean, 1956, 33; Maclean, 1975, xiv; 20.

25 NLS, MS. 29795, fo. 29r.

26 Maclean, 1956, 33.

27 This and other oral narratives about fairies from Lochaber clearly made an impression
   on Maclean, for he produced an article about them, complete with translations and
   notes, Maclean, 1960.

28 CIM I.I.3, TSB 3, 279–81. It is likely that Maclean's transcription method was guided
   by Angus McIntosh in rendering pre-aspiration and the development in many Gaelic
   dialects of *rt* to *rst*. Jackson rightly points out that 'Maclean spells always *c(hc)*, but
   this is phonetically a serious misrepresentation, and I have substituted *(ch)c*

throughout; and instead of *rst* he writes the *s* suprascript, which is unnecessary and might cause typographical difficulties.' Following Jackson's recommendations I have adopted the same method. Jackson, 1971–73, 161, n. 3.

29 See Aarne, 1964; Uther, 2004.

30 See Christiansen, 1958.

31 See Bruford, 1967.

32 See MacDonald, 1994–95.

33 Megaw, 1960, 122–3.

34 The Maclagan Manuscripts (1893–1902), the fruits of a decade's collecting by Dr Robert Craig Maclagan (1839–1919), are now held in the School of Scottish Studies Archives at the University of Edinburgh.

35 John Francis Campbell of Islay's Papers (MSS.50.1.1–51.2.7; MSS.2993–2994) are in the National Library of Scotland, Edinburgh. Five additional volumes of travel correspondence to his family, 1859, 1877, 1879–81 are part of the Bromley Davenport Muniments in the Department of Manuscripts, John Rylands Univerity Library at the University of Manchester.

36 The Dewar Manuscripts (seven volumes), along with translations (nineteen volumes) made by Hector MacLean, are housed in the archives of Inveraray Castle, Argyllshire. Microfilm copies of the manuscripts are available for consultation at the School of Scottish Studies Archives, University of Edinburgh.

37 Fr Allan McDonald's folklore collection is now scattered throughout three archives: Glasgow University Library (GUL MS Gen 1090(28) [Folklore MS V]; Gen 1090(29) [Folklore MS VI]; Edinburgh University Library (CW 58A [Folklore MS 1]; CW 58B [Folklore MS II]; and Canna House Archive (CH2/1/1/13/128/1).

38 Aberdeen University Library (MSS 2276, 2636, 2771).

39 Scottish Catholic Archives (FA200).

40 Many of his manuscripts are housed in the National Library of Scoltand, as well as a few in the Centre for Research Collections at Edinburgh University Library.

41 Donald John MacDonald, styled Dòmhnall Iain mac Dhonnchaidh (1919–1989), was a son of Duncan MacDonald and an able tradition bearer as well as a bard in his own right. His manuscript collection of South Uist oral traditions of around 6,000 pages in length was bequeathed to the School of Scottish Studies, University of Edinburgh.

42 One of the projects undertaken by the National Folklore Collection UCD is the digitisation of John McKeagney's collection of folklife and archaeological artifacts. In addition, the mission statement of the Irish Virtual Research Library & Archive (IVRLA) states that the project was conceived as a means to preserve elements of UCD's main repositories and to increase and facilitate access to this material through the adoption of digitisation technologies. Greater amounts of material, particularly that of an ethnological provenance, will be available in the near future, such as the Schools' Folklore Scheme (1937–38), an initiative for children from all around Ireland who collected more than half a million manuscript pages of folklore material and local history.

43 Maclean, 1957, 27.

Aarne, A. *The Types of Folk-tale: A Classification and Bibliography*, Folklore Fellows Communications no. 184, Helsinki, 1964.

Almqvist, B. Irish Folklore Commission: Achievement and legacy, *Béaloideas*, 45–7 (1977–79), 6–26.

Briody, M. The collectors' diaries of the Irish Folklore Commission: A complex genesis, *Sinsear*, 9 (2005), 27–45.

Briody, M. *The Irish Folklore Commission 1935–1970: History, Ideology, Methodology*, Studia Fennica Folkloristica 17, Helsinki, 2007.

Bruford, A. Scottish Gaelic witch stories: A provisional type-list, *Scottish Studies (SS)*, 11 (1967), 13–47.

Buzzetti, D. Digital representation and the text model, *New Literary History*, 33 (2002), 61–88.

Campbell, J F. *Popular Tales of the West Highlands* [1860–62], 4 vols, rev. edn, Paisley, 1890.

Campbell, J L. *Sia Sgialachdan a Chruinnich 's a Dheasaich Iain Latharna Caimbeul ann am Barraidh 's an Uidhist a Deas / Six Gaelic Stories from Barra and South Uist*, Edinburgh, 1939.

Campbell, J L. Portrait of a bard, *Scots Magazine*, 58:1 (1952), 1–5.

Campbell, J L. Duncan of the Stories, *Scots Magazine*, 61:6 (1954), 473–4.

Christiansen, R T. *The Migratory Legends: A Proposed List of Types with a Systematic Catalogue of the Norwegian Variants*, Folklore Fellows Communications no. 175, Helsinki, 1958.

Cumming, J. The Text Encoding Initiative and the study of literature. In Schreibman, S and Siemens, R, eds, *A Companion to the Digital Literary Studies*, Oxford, 2008, 451–76.

Douglas, F M. The Scottish Corpus of Texts and Speech: Problems of corpus design, *Literary and Linguistic Computing*, 18:1 (2003), 23–37.

Draak, M. Duncan MacDonald of South Uist, *Fabula: Journal of Folklore Studies*, 1 (1957), 47–58.

Jackson, K. The baby without a mouth, *Béaloideas*, 39–41 (1971–73), 157–64.

Henderson, H. Calum Maclean 1915–1960, *Tocher*, 39 (1985), 81–8.

Hockey, S. *Electronic Texts in the Humanities*, Oxford, 2000.

Ide, N. Encoding standards for large text resources: The Text Encoding Initiative, *International Conference On Computational Linguistics: Proceedings of the 15th Conference on Computational Linguistics*, 1 (1994), 574–8.

Ide, N and Sperberg-McQueen, C M. The TEI: History, goals, and future, *Computers and the Humanities*, 29:1 (1995), 5–15.

Kirschenbaum, M. Editing the interface: Textual studies and first generation electronic objects, *TEXT*, 14 (2002), 15–51.

Lysaght, P. Swedish ethnological surveys in the Western Isles of Scotland, 1939, 1948: Some data from Ireland, *ROSC*, 6 (1990), 27–51.

McCarty, W. *Humanities Computing*, Basingstoke and New York, 2005.

MacDonald, D A. Migratory legends of the supernatural in Scotland: A general survey, *Béaloideas*, 62–3 (1994–95), 29–78.

MacDhomhnaill, D. *Sgialachdan Dhunnchaidh: Seann Sgialachdan air an gabhail le Dunnchaidh MacDhomhnaill ac Dhunnchaidh, Uibhist a Deas, mar a chual e aig athair fhein iad 1944*, ed. K C Craig, Glasgow, 1950.

Maclean, C I. Traditional songs from Raasay and their value as folk-literature, *TGSI*, 39–40 (1942–50), 176–92.

Maclean, C I. Hebridean storytellers, *ARV: Journal of Scandinavian Folklore*, 8 (1952), 120–9.

Maclean, C I. Hebridean traditions, *Gwerin*, 1:1 (1956), 21–33.

Maclean, C I. Folklore and Gaelic, *Ossian*, (1957), 27–9.

Maclean, C I. International folk-tales in the archives, *SS*, 2 (1958), 113–17.

Maclean, C I. Fairy stories from Lochaber, *SS*, 4 (1960), 84–95.

Maclean, C I. *The Highlands* [1959], rev. edn, Inverness, 1975.

MacLellan, A. *Stories from South Uist* [1961], ed. John L Campbell, Edinburgh, 1997.

MacGilleathain, C I. Aonghus agus Donnchadh, *Gairm*, 10 (1954), 170–4.

MacPherson, J. *Tales from Barra Told by the Coddy* [1960], ed. John L Campbell, Edinburgh, 1992.

Megaw, B R S. The late Calum I. Maclean, *SS*, 4 (1960), 121–3.

Morrison, A, Popham, M and Wikander, K. *Creating and Documenting Electronic Texts: A Guide to Good Practice*, Oxford, 2002. (Online version, <http://ota.ox.ac.uk/documents/creating/cdet/> [accessed March 2012].)

Nellhaus, T. XML, TEI, and digital libraries in the humanities, *Libraries and the Academy*, 3:1 (2001), 257–77.

Newall, V. Séamus Ó Duilearga, *Folklore*, 92:1 (1980), 113.

Nicolaisen, W F H. Calum I. Maclean (1915–1960), *Fabula: Journal of Folklore Studies*, 5 (1962), 162–4.

Schreibman, S, Siemens, R and Unsworth, J. *A Companion to Digital Humanities*, Oxford, 2004.

Uther, H. *The Types International Folktales: A Classification and Bibliography: Based on the System of Antti Aarne and Stith Thompson*, Helsinki, 2004.

Wiseman, A E M. 'Your work will remain': A letter from James Hamilton Delargy to Calum Iain Maclean, dated 17–19 October 1946, *SS*, 36 (forthcoming).

Wynne, M, ed. *Developing Linguistic Corpora: A Guide to Good Practice*, Oxford, 2005. (Online version, <http://www.ahds.ac.uk/creating/guides/linguistic-corpora/index.htm> [accessed March 2012].)

ONLINE RESOURCES

All websites last accessed March 2012.

An Drochaid Eadarainn / The Bridge Between Us, <demo.headspacedesign.ca/androchaid/>

Cainnt mo Mhàthar / My Mother's Tongue,

Dictionar o the Scots Leid / Dictionary of the Scots Language,

Digimap Collections [subscription site] , <edina.ac.uk/digimap/>

Faclair na Gàidhlig / Dictionary of the Scottish Gaelic Language,

Pròiseact Chaluim MhicGilleathian / Calum Maclean Project, <www.celtscot.ed.ac.uk/calum-maclean/>

Pròiseact MacGilleMhìcheil MhicBhatair / The Carmichael Watson Project,

Scottish Corpus of Texts and Speech,

Sruth nan Gàidheal / Gael Stream, <http://gaelstream.stfx.ca/>

Sounds, <http://sounds.bl.uk/>

Statistical Accounts of Scotland [subscription site with some free access], <http://edina.ac.uk/stat-acc-scot/>

Text Encoding Initiative, <www.tei-c.org/index.xml>

Tobar an Dualchais / Kist o Riches,

25 Photography

ANDREW BLAIKIE

INTRODUCTION

Given the ubiquity of the photographic image, the range of sources available for contemporary research is vast. However, historical materials are limited by several factors, the first of which is chronological. Compared with storytelling and the written tradition, or with visual forms such as art and engraving, photography is a relatively new practice. No photographs exist anywhere before the mid nineteenth century, although photography was at that time being pioneered by Scots, so there is some excellent early material on Scotland. A second, related, problem is technological. Victorian cameras were fragile yet cumbersome; the difficulties of transporting and setting up heavy equipment severely restricted dexterity, and long exposure times and single-shot sessions precluded spontaneity or capturing subjects on the move. While these problems present more of an obstacle regarding images of people than those of objects or landscapes, the need for light, before innovations such as the camera flash (1930), also means that environments in which much time was spent – domestic interiors and dimly lit workplaces – were infrequently recorded. The advent of cheap, portable and easy-to-use cameras led to photography becoming a popular medium in the twentieth century, this democratisation occasioning a considerable expansion in the distribution of potential source material. Third, despite the burgeoning range of material, archived and otherwise, the pattern of sources displays a number of biases amongst photographers, curators, scholars and in the popular imagination. Motives, perceptions, fashions and changing interests dictate that some types of people, places, objects, buildings, pastimes and occasions have been selected rather more frequently than others. These three concerns frame the central challenges for historical picture research, and it is with them in mind that the characteristics of photographic practice, archival and popular coverage should be considered.

RANGE OF SOURCES

Sources may be conveniently divided into those deliberately amassed as ethnological evidence and those that are useful though created for other reasons. The former include the collections of those with avowedly antiquarian and folkloric interests such as Erskine Beveridge (1851–1920), Margaret Fay Shaw (1903–2004), Werner Kissling (1895–1988), and Alasdair Alpin MacGregor (1899–1970), each of whom aimed to document 'traditional' island cultures during the early to mid twentieth century. Alongside the Royal Commission on the Ancient and Historical Monuments of Scotland (RCAHMS), which has focused upon archaeological and topographical site information (and which houses the Beveridge collection), these photographers highlighted relationships between human cultures and their settings while, since 1959, the Scottish Life Archive at National Museums Scotland (NMS) has gathered an immense number of photographs from private individuals, together with several collections (including those of Shaw and MacGregor), as a documentary resource for both material culture and social history in urban, rural, industrial and maritime communities. Most of this illustrative material dates from after 1880. Besides these national archives, country life museums and heritage centres and independent museums hold significant collections, some of which concentrate on specific trades or industries – for example the Scottish Fisheries Museum in Anstruther or the Scottish Mining Museum at Newtongrange. At its establishment in 1951, the School of Scottish Studies at the University of Edinburgh considered photography 'a primary means of documenting houses, structures, agricultural and domestic equipment and craftwork'.[1] In the years following, fieldwork in urban and rural contexts has extended the range of topics represented in its photographic and film archive to include working practices, customs, rites of passage, community activities, singing, storytelling and portraits of tradition bearers.

The second category of archive incorporates collections of the work of photographers which often includes images of ethnological value but whose output was driven by other motives, the first of which is commercial. The firm of George Washington Wilson and Co., which produced postcards and lantern slides for the mass market during the second half of the nineteenth century, is particularly prominent, as is their great competitor James Valentine and Co. Their extensive collections are held at the universities of Aberdeen and St Andrews respectively. The latter also houses the archive of Robert Moyes Adam, whose material was used extensively by the *Scots Magazine* and in mid twentieth-century travel guides, while several collections of material by local photographers, professional and amateur, exist in regional centres. For example, the Shetland Museum's Photographic Archive holds 80,000 photographs dating from the early 1870s onwards.[2] Complementing these are the collections developed from what might be termed 'indigenous photography', including the various *comuinn eachdraidh*, the local history societies established in the Western Isles during the 1970s. Stemming from the widespread revival of interest in local histories and cultures and from the boom in genealogical research, these collections incorporate material from local photographers, the local press and family albums. Most of these sources have been digitised, allowing internet access to a sizeable proportion of material. Such collections are by no means confined to islands or rural areas, and several towns and urban districts have online collections (see, for instance, Springburn Virtual Museum). Pilot research may be conducted into many of the above collections via SCRAN, an online educational resource and effectively a meta-archival sample containing around 340,000 photographic images and multimedia files. Including the NMS and RCAHMS among its principal founders and working in partnership with over 300 cultural institutions, SCRAN also gathers material from independent sources such as regional and national newspaper collections. Photojournalism represents a largely untouched genre in ethnological research. However, press photographers, as well as contributing to substantial archives among some local newspapers,[3] conducted revealing assignments on aspects of Scottish life and culture for magazines such as *Picture Post* (1938–57), and extensive examples of the published and unpublished work of Bert Hardy, Malcolm Dunbar, Haywood Magee, Raymond Kleboe, Thurston Hopkins and others may be accessed from the Getty Images online archive.

Although the above sources incorporate material from many individual photographers, others (or their estates) have maintained independent collections. Some, such as Oscar Marzaroli, whose images document so much of the changing social and physical landscape of Glasgow between the 1950s and 1980s, also published compilations of material that represent valuable sources in their own right. The same applies to Gus Wylie (the Hebrides), Tom Kidd (Shetland) and, *par excellence*, Paul Strand (the Uists). Others, such as Chick Chalmers in the mid 1970s, who 'created a catalogue of Orkney pictures that rivalled Tom Kent's of half a century before', did not publish their projects, although many individual images may be consulted.[4] Glyn Satterley's photographs of life on Highland sporting estates in Caithness and Sutherland present a rare visualisation of hunting, shooting and fishing within the rural economy.[5]

THE THEMATIC LEGACY

Embracing genres as diverse as portraiture, landscape, documentary, tourism, wildlife, family snaps and even fine art, photographers display a range of predispositions. Nevertheless, some generic perceptions affected their selection of subjects and how they chose to picture them. Photographs imitate the artistic conventions of the period. Thus the photographic pioneers Hill and Adamson acknowledged the influence of Vermeer in their depiction of multi-generational family groups in Newhaven, while the late nineteenth-century tradition of social realism is reflected in portrayals of elderly sailors as the maritime counterparts of the salt of the earth. In many ways an attempt to illustrate a distinction between civilised metropolitan society and its 'backward' rural periphery, such a vision finds a counterpart in the portrayal of character 'types', designed to reflect a symbiotic relationship between particular kinds of peoples and places. Although most evident in the Victorian imperialist imagery to which visual anthropologists have become critically sensitive, this ecology of the image bears heavily across the photographic spectrum.

The Royal Anthropological Institute Photographic Collection contains photographs of native 'types', including: '"Murdoch McRae, a pure highlander living at Fort Augustus; native of Kintail . . . never had trousers on but once" – Carte-de-visite, photographed by MacFarlane, *c*.1878. Type "B", vol. 2, no. 24. Selected by Dr Beddoe, BAAS "Racial Committee" Albums (RAI, 2987).'[6] Such a depiction of 'a pure Highlander' found popular resonance in, for example, the *Illustrated London News* (1930), which referred to a tableau of St Kilda portraits as 'island types',[7] and continued into mid twentieth-century social stereotyping. Finlay, for instance, portrays 'Scottish types', including the 'Highland crofter', 'Lowland miner', 'Hebridean woman' and 'East Coast fisherman'.[8] While the distinctiveness of each signals sociological distance from the mainstream of 'modern' everyday life, an implied eugenicism was also applied by philanthropic organisations concerned with 'saving' children – morally and physically – from the evils of poverty in the urban slums. The NSPCC and Dr Barnardo's Homes photographed ragged children ('street arabs') before and after 'rescue' and relocation to children's homes, starkly contrasting clothing, posture and facial expressions to suggest the transformation from 'savage' to 'civilised'.[9] Equally, the relationship between people and their environment has frequently been contrived to suggest harmony. Strand's 1950s portraits of Uist folk standing against stone croft walls or juxtaposed with images of wave-sculpted rock were intended to show that 'nature and architecture had come to reflect the personality of the people'.[10] What each has in common is the application of a convention where distinctive physiognomic and bodily features and clothing are set within a specific environmental frame as though it were somehow natural. That it may not have been so raises questions about how, ironically, in the very quest for authenticity – or, rather, what they ideally regarded as such – some photographers in fact fabricated their images. While evidence sometimes exists to indicate this, assessment frequently depends upon the interpretative skills of the researcher. Images of peasant couples standing by their homes might suggest respectability (upright, sprucely dressed families in well-tended gardens) or poverty (arthritic elders beside crumbling walls). Such associations could imply social comment (documentary), or testimony to a once proud but rapidly disappearing way of life (romanticism), or simply be seen as realist depiction. One needs to question whether these individuals were representative of their wider community or whether they were posed so as to make a point.

Certainly, in the early twentieth century there existed a strong preservationist impulse to record the 'ways of life' of 'traditional' communities seen to be threatened by the advances of modernity. M E M Donaldson (1876–1958) thus explained her criterion for what to picture: 'Considerations of fast disappearing aspects of life and of interesting subjects not usually photographed . . . have dictated my choice.'[11] Reinforced by the curatorial desire to capture traces of vanishing customs, artefacts, people and practices, such thinking led to a selective national inventory that paradoxically made central geographically and economically peripheral locations and activities. Thus the six main photographic collections in the Scottish Life Archive indicate distinct bias towards fishing and crofting, focusing respectively on Fife fishing villages, Foula (Shetland), the Uists, Coll, Ardnamurchan, Morar and Arisaig, St Kilda and Lewis.[12] Meanwhile, very few images of heavy industry exist. Fisherfolk, crofting and island life have not been regarded as pivotal to mainstream economic history, but they have been culturally important as emblems of difference, hence their appeal to ethnologists, albeit that the photographers, far from being driven by an impulse for social realism, were romantically motivated. 'One must deplore the passing of the picturesque primitive cottages of the natives, notably of the thatch, in favour of corrugated or tarpaulin roofs, and other equally hideous features,' continued Donaldson.[13] The demon here is modernity and all its emblems. Yet rather than capture scenes of social conflict, as might say photojournalists or sociologists conducting visual ethnographies, these photographers highlighted the battle between man and the land or people and the elements. Where cultural disharmony is accentuated, as it has been more recently, the emphasis is on distinctive alternatives rather than on people compromising with change. James Nicolson says of Tom Kidd's Shetland portfolio: 'Inevitably the photographs highlight the difference between the old and the new, contrasting the ugly steel structure of the oilmen with the simple basic tools of the crofter as he wields his scythe or tar brush'.[14]

SELECTIVITY

Within this overarching if sometimes implicit critique of modernity, some subjects have gained fuller coverage than others. As already mentioned, peripheral rural locations and their attendant occupations predominate in the record.[15] Equally, but this time because they signify the failings of modernisation, slums – particularly in Glasgow and Dundee – command rather more attention than other living spaces. The trope of 'endurance in the face of adversity' found in rural and Highland and Island documentary has a vivid counterpart in images of the urban poor.[16] And in both these types of setting children and older people are over-represented at the expense of other age groups. While there was 'a long-standing concern amongst photographers of the Western Isles to portray children in both sentimental and naturalistic ways',[17] in Glasgow the ongoing association between children, slums and street photography is reflected in a documentary lineage begun by Thomas Annan in the 1860s, continued in the photojournalism of Bert Hardy in the 1940s and further advanced by Oscar Marzaroli and Joseph McKenzie in the 1960s. Yet motives vary: whereas Annan, commissioned by the City of Glasgow Improvements Trust, was illustrating the state of the housing stock and children occupied the foreground inadvertently, both Hardy's and Marzaroli's images are used deliberately to underline tenement experience as the essence of community. The relationship between welfare and environment, read from clothing, facial and bodily features, informed diagnoses of vulnerable types found in the photographic records of Glasgow City Archives, which also show images of interventions such as sun-lamp treatment for rickets. Meanwhile, the dialectic between urban deprivation and the putative benefits of the countryside is evident from pictures of boarded-out children in, for example, the Comunn Eachdraich Bharraidh collection.[18]

Scenes and subjects are frequently chosen by photographers because it is assumed that these will soon no longer be there to picture. Older people were so frequently selected because they stood as the final bearers of vanishing skills and ways of life: the last of the handloom weavers, last shoemaker in Selkirk, the bellman of Newburgh or, in the case of one decrepit elderly couple beside a dilapidated blackhouse, 'The Last of the Cottars'.[19] Here photographs became a means of archiving for posterity; they are the visual equivalent of sound recordings of folk speaking a disappearing language. As with the interviewer in search of the nonagenarian, an important aim was to capture images of traditional but declining crafts, dress styles and lifestyles before they disappeared forever. Thus, while older relatives appear in many family portraits, they are frequently cast in generationally specific occupational roles – baiting fishing lines, as wise elders, or as local characters, such as Westray's 'Willie o' the blacksmith's'.[20] Another reason elders predominate amongst the images of rural and island people is that they are in fact representative of the ageing demography of communities whose youth has emigrated or left the land for the cities. Again, modernity looms large.

The sociability of work is evident throughout the record. Because fishing involved a range of tasks – cleaning, baiting and preparation of the lines – performed by family members, photographs of fisherfolk are often portraits of whole families. However, the very ordinariness and privacy (and low light quality) meant that household interiors often went unrecorded. For example, among the 64,483 online images in the Shetland Museum's Photographic Library, just 122 are catalogued under 'domestic interiors', as against 1,843 for 'croft buildings' in general.[21] Similarly, Kidd has commented:

> Of the dozens of photographs held by the [Scottish Life] Archive, only one shows the interior of a bothy, so the habit of displaying some of their contents provides us with visual evidence of the living conditions and pastimes of the bothy men to back up written and oral sources.[22]

Women have been significantly under-represented because many private, domestic roles do not figure, and because they were often passive onlookers on more public occasions.[23] The late-Victorian 'New Woman' and society belle were photographed because of their professional rank or fashionable attire, while the fishergirl carried an element of the fading picturesque. However, although domestic servants formed the largest female occupational group, their mundanity and low social status kept them largely out of the frame. Moreover, although there were 400 times as many female clerks in 1911 as there had been in 1868, the camera did not penetrate into offices to record the phenomenon. Not only was the great exodus of young women from the land and into the towns and cities never effectively captured, there is no visual archive of the two massive occupational groups at either end of the process.[24] By contrast, the iconic popularity of older women at spinning wheels or carrying creels has resulted in their over-representation, while some figures – like some activities – have gained a prominence disproportionate to their social significance. This is particularly so in the case of multiple portraits of legendary 'local characters', eccentrics who were remarkable precisely because of their atypicality.[25]

COMMUNITY ARCHIVES

Traditionally, researchers making cultural comparisons used a vocabulary based on a vision of difference or 'otherness', whereas the indigenous cultural account emphasises the continuity of community – its memory, genealogy and self-definition. While those with directly ethnological concerns photographed places where customs, working practices, objects and patterns of culture persisted, having been superseded elsewhere, their perspectives were very much those of the interested outsider. By contrast, since the 1970s the development of community archives garnered from the pictures taken by local people, as well as the more recent posting of collections (or 'galleries') of local and family history societies and heritage centres online, has fostered an insider approach. For some, this initiative has seen the growth of an 'empowering narrative of community endurance and progressive change',[26] photographic collections comprising not just folk histories of 'personalities', events, streets, landmarks, customs, skills and local stories, but also the construction of virtual communities, a 'reckoning of kin' which, like the naming of family boats, or cataloguing of place names or archaeological sites, establishes which families once lived and worked in which places.[27] To this extent, photographs act as a form of collective remembrance, constituting 'the storage system for the social order'.[28]

As well as consulting public evidence, such as postcard scenes, and particularly the work of local photographers, both amateur and professional, whose work constitutes the mass of material already held in many local and regional archives, indigenous archives are inevitably genealogical. They draw upon private material, such as snapshots, yet extend their reach diasporically to connect with those family and community members who have long since migrated from an area. Importantly, in areas with a long tradition of outmigration and depopulation, such as the Highlands and Islands or the rural Lowlands, they provide means of documenting the past that account for dispersion.[29] Indeed, these archives provide a focal point and clearing house connecting locals with kin scattered around the globe. A major source is family albums which are, of course, highly selective in their coverage, creating a myth of continuity through images of happy occasions while omitting significant but unpleasant aspects of family life such as illness, death, divorce or estrangement of relatives – and often, in their record of occasional formality rather than everyday processes, disguising normal attire, poverty or domestic disorder. Like diaries and memoirs, family photographs reflect not what the historian would necessarily wish to document but what the sitters considered it worthwhile to preserve. There is a sense in which family pictures are public statements about private lives. Poses are carefully choreographed for the benefit of others, often, by implication, future generations. The family snapshot thus complements pictures of school groups or work teams in its explicit appeal to posterity.

Because different types of archive co-exist, for most communities there is no single definitive inventory or visual record. While the researcher can compare images from various collections, photographs have their own biographies, migrating between contexts as they pass from photographers to families and communities and then to curators. The pattern of appropriation this reflects can have important consequences for interpretation, since an image can mean different things to each of these constituencies. In general, photographers take the pictures and the archivists subsequently classify them. However, sometimes families and communities intervene in the process. There is a photograph in the Shetland

Museum taken around 1910 by local photographer Peter Halcrow. It was captioned by the curator as 'Robert and Laurina Smith, Aith'. The text was subsequently crossed through and the scribbled lines 'Peter says no!! Possibly one of his brothers' added below. Nevertheless, the evidence of such active renegotiation remains hidden from the online image which, having been lifted from the card mount on which the captioning occurs, is simply labelled 'Unknown elderly couple'.[30] This example demonstrates how interpretation can be steered by the combination of image and text. It also counsels doing research, wherever possible, with the original photographs physically to hand. Years later, several pictures from Halcrow's family collection formed part of a local community exhibition in Cunningsburgh, his birthplace. Locals who viewed these images did two significant things: first, they helped to name the places where the pictures had been taken and the individuals and their family relationships; second, where captions already existed, they queried the details, frequently amending or supplementing them. In terms of how the labelling process operates, if not in its ethnographic significance, this negotiation of tensions between photography, identity and (re)-appropriation compares with, say, investigations of 'Indianness' by Native American artists and writers.[31] In their detail, accompanying captions serve to contextualise and explain images which may otherwise be highly ambiguous and capable of endless interpretation. In the case of the photo-essay, and especially with photojournalism, providing such a steer is quite deliberate, as it is with the descriptions that accompany many catalogued images. Nevertheless, as the above example illustrates, in foreclosing alternative readings it needs to be borne in mind that labelling an image powerfully influences what the viewer sees.

SITUATED CHRONOLOGIES: ST KILDA

Since ethnology is concerned with relationships between peoples, places and times, visual images are only valuable when they can be set in context. This may seem self-evident, yet it must be a prime consideration in assessing the uses of photographic material. What we might call situated chronologies may be constructed through careful triangulation between sources. Some continuity can be glimpsed when comparing early photographs with previous engravings. The first photographs of the Western Isles – for example those of St Kilda by F W L Thomas in 1860 – can be situated by considering the engravings made from Moses Griffith's drawings to illustrate Thomas Pennant's *A Tour in Scotland, and Voyage to the Hebrides* (1772). As Pennant's personal draughtsman, Griffith sketched on location. Like the travelling artists of the earlier nineteenth century, his material provides an important comparative backdrop, although it needs to be borne in mind that painters were at least as prone to invention and embellishment as photographers. In turn, photographs from a century later, such as those by George Washington Wilson and Co., may be compared with Thomas' collection. In this way, 'an eighteenth-century travel book, the personal album of a mid-nineteenth century antiquarian and a commercially produced sequence of lantern slides . . . each play[ed] a vital role in generating knowledge about the isles', albeit their different intentions and aesthetics must be evaluated.[32] Indeed, what might look like similarities may be the result of deliberate attempts to pose individuals or capture settings so as to conform anachronistically to their earlier likenesses. Because of such considerations, it is important to assess all possible sources for a particular place. For instance, images of cragsmen fowling on the St Kilda cliffs – a practice vital to the islanders, who depended on seabirds for their survival – may be found in the watercolours of Sir Thomas Acland (1812), Washington Wilson's 1886 lantern slide sequence, the pictures taken by the naturalist Kearton brothers during 1896, and the photographs of Robert Atkinson, who visited the islands along with some natives returning for the summer in 1938, some eight years after Hirta was evacuated. Their veracity or otherwise may be deduced by reference to the written accounts dating back to Martin Martin's 1698 sojourn and Macaulay's 1758 description, and much more broadly to the voluminous bibliography of several hundred articles pertaining to these islands as well as to the many photographs taken by tourists to St Kilda on the thrice-yearly steamship visits between 1877 and the 1930s. The film *St Kilda: Britain's Loneliest Isle* (1923), also features cragsmen abseiling down cliffs.[33] Such repeated images contribute to the familiar iconography of St Kilda – an island whose traditions are represented as at once primitive, exotic and democratic. Spring comments that:

> of the various photographs that constitute an ethnographic reading of the St Kildan way of life, several characteristics . . . stand out – notably a concentration on the 'otherness' of their way of life with its emphasis on work rather than leisure activities . . . the self-conscious employment of direct address, and the clear association of the inhabitants of the island with the landscape they inhabit or the natural things they harvest.[34]

Knitting was St Kilda's staple, and its knitters provide an enduring motif. Yet, in themselves, the photographs of these women tell us nothing of the socially conflicted experiences through which they lived. Let us consider the visual biography of Ann Ferguson/Gillies. Washington Wilson's lantern slide sequence *The Outer Hebrides* (1886) ends with a picture entitled 'Group with Queen' (Fig. 25.1). Although the attached commentary simply refers to St Kilda having a queen 'who is said to be the best looking woman on the Island', we know from other sources that the person in question was Ann Ferguson, aged 20, who sat second from right amongst a group of seven women and young girls. Martin Padget notes that: 'While the exposure was made the five women took leave of their knitting; in all likelihood they were making socks, scarves or gloves for sale to visiting tourists.'[35] Two large tweed plaids hang from the wall behind the group. This is the first of several images of Ann Ferguson/Gillies taken between 1886 and 1938 that provide clues to the relationship between knitting, tourism and representation on St Kilda. Far from being a long-held 'primitive' tradition, the title of Queen of St Kilda had originally been bestowed by the Duke of Atholl on Betty Scott during his visit in 1858. Padget informs us further that:

> when it became known beyond St Kilda that Ann was to marry John Gillies in 1890, the Sutherland resident James Gall Campbell, in a gesture both

philanthropic and exploitative, collected funds with which to create a library for the community and to purchase various gifts for the new couple.

He then arranged for a steamer to convey 'myriad wedding presents of dubious worth' to St Kilda to coincide with the wedding and, crucially, fifty visitors, including 'several professional and amateur photographers, an artist, and several newspaper reporters'. Clearly designed as a crude publicity stunt, it is perhaps unsurprising that the wedding did not take place when planned, since Campbell's intervention 'was looked upon dimly by the islanders and their resident minister'.[36] In regard to what is nowadays known as 'ethnic tourism', many anthropologists and sociologists point to 'staged authenticity', the performance of 'pseudo events' or practices as though these were real, for the benefit of those seeking novel experiences.[37] While this episode illustrates the extent to which some parties went to arrange performances for the benefit of a gullible public hungry for exotic images, there is also considerable evidence suggesting that the St Kildans themselves exploited photographers, including tourists with cameras, by producing the required poses in return for payment. Some photographers wishing to retain integrity disputed this, at least when it came to their own endeavours.[38]

Revealing the layers of invention and interpretation demands careful inves-

Figure 25.1 Group with Queen, St Kilda, 1886. Photograph by George Washington Wilson. © National Trust for Scotland. Licensor <www.scran.ac.uk>

tigation. Here comparison between photographs and moving film is illuminating. The 1923 documentary *St Kilda – Britain's Loneliest Isle* shows women and children running away and hiding their faces, preceded by the caption 'Timid – they never saw a movie cameraman before'. Nevertheless, a number are shown spinning for the benefit of onlooking tourists, while Ann Gillies appears posting mail for a visitor at the islands' post office. A later photograph of Ann Gillies by Alasdair Alpin MacGregor (Fig. 25.2) shows her sitting alone, needle in hand, with a fleece and various knitted garments including socks, gloves and a blanket. Using the image to illustrate a book on Scottish women in pictures, a historian captioned the photograph as follows: 'Mrs Gillies, one of the last St Kildans, seated in front of her house. This photograph was taken the day before St Kilda was evacuated, in August 1930. She calmly continued to knit, using wool plucked from the local Soay sheep and spun at home. Most of her own clothes would have been dyed and woven or knitted on the island.'[39] At face value the image is a classic example of the fusion of old age and a fading local craft, given added poignancy by its timing – a dignified memento of the end of a marginal way of life. MacGregor's image was one of several close-ups of islanders taken on the day prior to evacuation before he, along with all members of the press, photographers and cameramen, was required to depart the island by the Scottish Office, which wished to avoid publicity. But while Mrs Gillies may appear to have been comfortable enough, the photograph sits uneasily within a disturbing context. John Ritchie's clandestine film *Evacuation of St Kilda*, made on the day of the evacuation and suppressed until 1979, reveals a picture somewhat at odds with the pre-existing visual record. An extract from the shot list reads:

> Old woman knitting socks outside her cottage. Photographer paid her £2.00 for the privilege of taking this shot . . . Another woman knitting outside her house takes fright at the camera and three times runs away to escape into the house . . . One woman hides her face. Woman's back to camera . . . Old man smoking pipe outside his house. Younger man picks up stone to throw at the camera . . . Group of people outside house. Woman sitting disconsolate.[40]

Several women, including Ann Gillies, are shown sitting at their spinning wheels. At one point Ann is also depicted knitting, but this time standing with her back to the camera and clearly trying to avoid being filmed. Thus, MacGregor's photograph of a seemingly composed Mrs Gillies, in lending itself to a romanticised view of placid acceptance, disguises some rather ugly social tensions.

Compiling footage for his own film about the islands in 1967, Christopher Mylne remarked:

> there is a world of difference between the people of 1908 going about their daily business [in *St Kilda – Its People and Birds*] and the camera-shy 'natives' of 1923 onwards hiding their faces from the inquisitive gaze of the tourists and their cameras.

Figure 25.2 Ann Gillies, St Kilda, 28 August 1930. Photograph by Alasdair Alpin MacGregor. © National Museums Scotland. Licensor <www.scran.ac.uk>

Mylne attributes this shift to the islanders' growing aversion of a community in decline to the ghoulish 'unfeeling curiosity' of outsiders.[41] Yet, as Spring points out, some press photographs were also taken of the evacuation: 'A full page spread appeared in the *Illustrated London News*. These pictures, with the islanders seemingly proudly displaying their possessions, seem to tell a very different tale from the jumbled images collected by Ritchie.'[42] The ambiguity of possible narratives indicates the value of multiple-source – and in this case dual-media – research in teasing out complexities hidden behind isolated single images.

When, in 1938, photographer Robert Atkinson visited St Kilda, he found that Ann Gillies, her son and Finlay MacQueen had returned to spend the summer there. His subsequent publication *Island Going* (1949) included groups of images of MacQueen snaring puffins and Ann at her spinning wheel (Fig. 25.3). Padget comments:

> Mrs Gillies resumed her former life on the island with enthusiasm and vigour. Atkinson describes her as 'always busy, carding and spinning, knitting socks and gloves, baking oatcakes and scones, scrubbing the floor.' She also scraped crotal off rocks with an old hoe so as to dye wool. She was kept busy by her domestic routine and creating knitwear that was sold to visiting tourists.[43]

Figure 25.3 Mrs John Gillies Snr spinning, St Kilda, 3 August 1938 (outside No. 11). Photograph by Robert Atkinson. Reproduced by permission of the School of Scottish Studies Archives, University of Edinburgh.

Likewise, the sequences of photographs demonstrating Finlay MacQueen's fowling exploits 'echo[ed] the photographs created by the Kearton brothers forty years before'.[44] Together, these two elderly protagonists – Ann Gillies was now 73 and Finlay MacQueen 79 – outlived their community in their representation of its staple activities. In this sense they had become living museum exhibits.

CONCLUSION

The St Kildan case study serves to remind us of some key characteristics, possibilities and limitations of photographs as an ethnological source. Since the photographic medium began less than two centuries ago, we are restricted to the evidence of modern times. Nevertheless, the earliest photographs may be set alongside visual sources such as sketches and engravings and pre-existing written accounts. Since the Victorian era, the emergence of other media such as postcards and moving film allows for direct visual comparisons. The changing technology of the camera, particularly its portability and ease of use allied with reduced cost, have facilitated such things as indoor photography and the family snapshot, latter-day advantages not evident from the pre-1930 record for St Kilda but important in other settings, rural as well as urban–industrial.[45] The textual surround of many photographs, including captioning, is important, ostensibly in placing images within their factual context, but equally, and sometimes misleadingly, as evidence of the biases of photographers, scholars and curators. The photographs of Ann Ferguson/Gillies taken at various points between 1886 and 1938 provide a personal biography while denoting the ongoing and iconic significance of knitting and spinning wool as activities among women of all ages. But they also act as reference points for a study of different motives, fabrications and interpretations that together invent and deconstruct the collective understanding and mythology of these islands. Taken as seen, the images look remarkably similar, appearing to reflect an enduring tradition exemplified by one of its hardy practitioners. However, while most pictures of Mrs Gillies were taken for ethnological reasons and show her posed to demonstrate her craft, some images from the filmed record suggest she was less comfortable in a public role at the time of St Kilda's evacuation. This said, the last pictures of her, which capture a seasonal return to the island from which she had migrated eight years previously, do indicate a rare tenacity.

Each picture of Mrs Gillies tells a different story, but these stories can only be unearthed by interrogating the context: who took the picture and why? What was the relationship between photographer and subject? This means asking questions of the authenticity of the image: to what extent might the portrait or scene have been deliberately staged, and by whom – photographer, sitter, or both acting in concert? And how was the picture subsequently used? How, in turn, have all these factors influenced interpretation? The ideological force of a vision that saw the Highlands and Islands and rural Scotland in general as places of antique and backward ways of life to be contrasted with modern civilisation has been pervasive, reaching its apogee in the most physically remote of the Western Isles. St Kildans were in part the atypical limit case, but they have also come to exemplify stereotypical, above all selective, ethnological traits. Among these, older people, and particularly local 'characters' such as Mrs Gillies, feature as final exemplars of vanishing skills; fowling, knitting and spinning are constant visual themes. The very fact that St Kilda was chosen as a location by so many photographers and tourists reflects the bias toward particular types of places as suitable for observation and record. Against the highlights, there were the omissions: images do exist, but how many now recall photographs of the minister and the manse on Hirta? Were any snapshots taken by St Kilda folk themselves? And, if so, do they collectively amount to an alternative account or social history? The researcher's priorities in addressing these questions will depend in part upon disciplinary approach: ethnologists may be more interested in material culture, anthropologists in customs and kin structures, sociologists in differing perceptions of social conflict and cohesion. This said, there is a high degree of overlap in the conceptual and methodological rigour required to interpret photographs in the historical record. Reading from the perspective of the digital twenty-first century, much of the equipment and techniques used by photographers in the period between 1840 and 2000 may seem quaint and limited. Nevertheless, in the visual material they generated there remains a rich and continually debated legacy of ethnological data.

BIBLIOGRAPHICAL ESSAY

A number of secondary sources provide useful guidance, beginning with overviews. Tom Normand's *Scottish Photography: A History* ranges widely though genres, amongst which the discussions of landscape, portraiture and rural and Highland documentary are most relevant, while John Hannavy's *A Moment in Time: Scottish Contributions to Photography, 1840–1920* gives potted biographies of around thirty photographers, illustrated with samples of their work. See also Sara Stevenson and A D Morrison-Low, *Scottish Photography: A Bibliography, 1839–1989*. Two volumes based on material available in the Scottish Ethnological Archive (now Scottish Life Archive) – Dorothy Kidd, *To See Oursels: Rural Scotland in Old Photographs* and Leah Leneman, *Into the Foreground: Scottish Women in Photographs* – reflect widely on the coverage of rural life and women respectively, while Alexander Fenton's magisterial *The Northern Isles* makes extensive use of photographs, many again from the Scottish Life Archive, in detailing the material culture of Orkney and Shetland. His book *Scottish Country Life* has a 22-page introduction illustrated mainly by photographs from the Scottish Life Archive followed by seventy pages of colour pictures of rural scenes and activities from all over Scotland, taken by himself over a thirty-year period, from 1959 to 1989.

A hitherto unknown source is the material in the Gothenburg Museum in Sweden, which includes photographs of a number of house interiors in Lewis with central hearths, and neat sketches showing the position of the furniture. These flow from the first known field research trip to Scotland, in 1934, made by the ethnologists Sven T Kjellberg and Olof Hasslöf, to study the material culture of the Outer Isles. This source has been published in Alexander Fenton's *A Swedish Field Trip to the Outer Hebrides, 1934* (2012). Another regional overview, although this time focused specifically upon the image-makers, is Martin Padget's *Photographers of the Western Isles*. Beyond providing close biographical detail on those who pictured the Hebrides and their output between 1843 and the present day, the author gives space to themes such as folklore, community and contemporary photography. The journal *Studies in Photography* (previously *Scottish Photography Bulletin*) is a helpful source for Scottish material. Anne MacLeod, *From an Antique Land: Visual Representations of the Highlands and Islands 1700–1880* explores ethnological motives behind paintings and drawings.

Biographies and research into the work of individual photographers frequently address matters of ethnological interest. This is obviously so in Michael Russell's *A Different Country: The Photographs of Werner Kissling*, which includes over 100 of Kissling's images of the Hebrides (especially South Uist and Eriskay), Dumfries and Galloway, and the Borders, and Lesley Ferguson's compilation *Wanderings with a Camera in Scotland: The Photography of Erskine Beveridge*, which covers particularly Fife, Argyll and the Highlands and Islands. Shorter, location-specific studies include Sara Stevenson's *Hill and Adamson's Fishermen and Women of the Firth of Forth* (on the maritime community of Newhaven) and A L Fisher's paper 'Thomas Annan's *Old Streets and Closes of Glasgow*' (on urban slums) while, somewhat broader in scope, Roger Taylor's *George Washington Wilson: Artist and Photographer, 1823–93* ranges across many areas of Scotland. Though diverse in its topic choice, Washington Wilson and Co. was a commercial enterprise; Robert Morris' *Scotland 1907: The Many Scotlands of Valentine and Sons, Photographers* reflects the range of material covered by another commercial concern, whose tourist-minded marketing similarly captured many places and social activities. Donald MacLeod's *Nis Aosmhor: The Photographs of Dan Morrison* contributes a scarce example of selected work by an amateur Lewis photographer working in one community from 1936 to 1990.

Post-1945 visual accounts published by photographers themselves include, most famously, Paul Strand and Basil Davidson's *Tir a' Mhurain / Outer Hebrides* and, more recently for the same region, Gus Wylie's *The Hebrides, Patterns of the Hebrides* and *The Hebrideans*.[46] In their depiction of communities at the crossroads of change, these examples are complemented by Tom Kidd's *Life in Shetland* and, for Glasgow, Oscar Marzaroli's *Shades of Grey: Glasgow, 1956–87* and *Glasgow's People, 1956–68*; Joseph McKenzie's *Pages of Experience: Photography, 1947–87* (pp. 24–35) and *Gorbals Children: A Study in Photographs*; and David Peat's *An Eye on the Street: Glasgow 1968*. Iconic images of Glasgow by Bert Hardy and Humphrey Spender and, importantly, many photographs of other Scottish towns and cities, are the subject of photo-essays in the popular magazine *Picture Post*, which flourished briefly between 1938 and 1957. These can now be consulted online at www.gale.cengage.co.uk/picturepost (a subscription site), while the photographs (including many that did not appear in final published articles) are accessible via the Getty Images website. Andrew Blaikie's paper 'Photography, childhood and urban poverty: Remembering "The Forgotten Gorbals"' discusses Glasgow's photographic imagery in these and other sources. It is nevertheless noticeable that while island and rural areas, especially remote ones – and, contrastingly, urban settings, notably impoverished ones – have caught the eye of many photographers, great swathes of seemingly unremarkable suburban Scotland remain either unpictured or unanalysed.

Despite what I have characterised above as the pervasiveness of the critique of modernity, much social science research in photography concerns contemporary ethnography rather than historical ethnology.[47] However, for cultural studies, geography and sociology respectively, see Ian Spring's 'Lost land of dreams: Representing St Kilda'; Fraser MacDonald's 'Geographies of vision and modernity: Things seen in the Scottish Highlands'; and Andrew Blaikie's 'Photographs in the cultural account: Contested narratives and collective memory in the Scottish Islands'. For social history, although English rather than Scots, Raphael Samuel's *Theatres of Memory* (pp. 315–77) provides four fascinating essays, while Elizabeth Edwards' 'Photographic "types": The pursuit of method' is particularly insightful about the imperialist racial classifications of early anthropologists.[48]

Several potentially valuable areas remain largely unresearched. Despite the significance of migration, no single photographic study of Scotland's diasporic communities exists, although scattered images do appear in histories of New World communities.[49] Immigrant groups are not yet well served, although Owen Logan's projects problematise the role of documentary in exploring difference, photographing minority groups including the Sikh community and Scots-Italians.[50] Meanwhile, his 'Oil Lives' work – a series of ten commissioned digital composite images, based on several participants in an oral history project, 'Lives in the Oil Industry (Oral History of the UK North Sea Oil and Gas Industry)' – captures images of a surprisingly little examined contemporary industry.[51] Photographs by Hermann Rodrigues and poems by Bashabi Fraser are combined in *Ragas and Reels* (2012) to illustrate contemporary links between Scotland and South Asia. An emerging field of visual analysis is rephotography. This involves observing historic images then taking contemporary images of exactly the same site. Although this very rarely involves human subjects, the practice facilitates detailed comparisons of buildings, streets, crofts, farms and factories.[52] Similarly, the uploading of then-and-now images on the internet by individuals and local history societies has blossomed.[53]

Finally, and most informatively, Ian MacKenzie's 'Festivals, faces and fire: A survey of fieldwork photography' is an autobiographical conference paper delivered by the late photographer at the School of Scottish Studies in Edinburgh, which provides illuminating advice and reflection on the process of ethnological photography as well as details of archival sources.

1 Padget, 2010, 139.
2 Online availability varies. For example, only 348 images are accessible out of over 50,000 in the Orkney Library archive. Glasgow Digital Library provides access to several collections, including Virtual Mitchell (indexed by area, street and subject), in which a sample of 9,000 images may be browsed.
3 Sam Maynard's many thousands of photographs for the *Stornoway Gazette* and *West Highland Free Press* between 1980 and 2000 are one exceptional instance.
4 Normand, 2007, 120. Some 279 photographs taken by Chalmers in the mid 1970s may be viewed via SCRAN.
5 Normand, 2007, 119–21.
6 Poignant, 1992, 59.
7 Spring, 1990, 166.
8 Finlay, 1945, 9.
9 Abrams, 1998, reproduces good examples.
10 Shaw, 1978, n.p.
11 Padget, 2010, 160–1.
12 William Easton, H B Curwen, Cathcart, Robert Sturgeon, M E M Donaldson and Alasdair Alpin MacGregor Collections.
13 Quoted in Padget, 2010, 161. Donaldson attributed some crofters's reticence about being photographed to superstition, although they may simply have been reacting to her inquisitive gaze. The Lewis Association published a critique of MacGregor's overly sentimental visions of Gaeldom.
14 Nicolson, 1980, n.p.
15 So do the figures of peasant and seaman, exemplars in the art of storytelling. Samuel, 1994, 323, notes how in this 'iconography of the national past . . . lifestyle rather than politics or economics became the subject of history's grand narratives'.
16 Normand, 2007, 102–3.
17 Padget, 2010, 133.
18 Abrams, 1998, 43, 50.
19 Kidd, 1992, 75, 112; Charnley and Miket, 1992.
20 Photographed by R H Robertson. Other Orkney 'characters' include Willie Laughton, alias 'Skatehorn', and Annie Harper, the bearded fortune teller, both pictured repeatedly by Tom Kent.
21 The same technical difficulty partly explains the absence of photographs of dark places such as mines and industrial workshops.
22 Kidd, 1992, 142. Farm servant crews, pictured by itinerant photographers, used everyday objects humorously to symbolise their tough domestic arrangements. The loaf of bread being attacked by a saw is a common motif.
23 Kidd, 1992, 131.
24 Leneman, 1993, 33, 65, 52.
25 See note 21. Blaikie, 2001, 354–5, found the sub-categories 'Kay [photographer] personalities', 'personalities – Rattar', 'Stout personalities', 'personalities – Peterson', 'Manson – personalities' and 'personalities – smaller collections' in the Shetland Museum catalogue.
26 Padget, 2010, xxv.
27 Cohen, 1987, 58–60.
28 Douglas, 1987, 70.

29 For migrants of the second generation and after, photographs may act as agents of transmission for postmemories, 'experiences that preceded their births but that were nevertheless transmitted to them so deeply as to seem to constitute memories in their own right' (Hirsch, 2008, 103).

30 Blaikie, 2010, 186.

31 Lippard, 1993.

32 Padget, 2010, 9–10, 114.

33 Fenton, 1997, 510–23, provides comparative visual detail for Orkney and Shetland.

34 Spring, 1990, 161.

35 Padget, 2010, 93.

36 Padget, 2010, 93–4.

37 MacCannell, 1973.

38 Padget, 2010, 94–5.

39 Leneman, 1993, 72.

40 Spring, 1990, 164.

41 Quoted in Spring, 1990, 164. These films may be accessed via the Scottish Screen Archive.

42 Spring, 1990, 165. This photo-essay, subtitled 'Island types; and scenes of departure', included an image of a woman 'selling homespun tweed', but none of spinning or knitting.

43 Padget, 2010, 107.

44 Padget, 2010, 107.

45 While Kissling photographed the interior of a Uist blackhouse in 1934, the photographs of hearths in Fenton, 1997, 195–204, demonstrate the value of earlier indoor photography. See Lloyd, 1948, for examples of Bert Hardy's tenement interiors.

46 Padget, 2010, 218–24, discusses these.

47 Cf. Pink, 2001.

48 See also Edwards, 1992.

49 Basu, 2007, discusses the photographs taken by 'homecoming' tourists.

50 Logan, 1994.

51 See also Kidd and Morton, 2004. The oral history project was carried out by the British Library National Life Story Collection and the University of Aberdeen.

52 Rohde, 2010.

53 See the BBC's Scotland's Landscape web pages, <www.bbc.co.uk/scotland/landscapes>.

BIBLIOGRAPHY AND FURTHER READING

Abrams, L. *The Orphan Country: Children of Scotland's Broken Homes from 1845 to the Present Day*, Edinburgh, 1998.

Basu, P. *Highland Homecomings: Genealogy and Heritage Tourism in the Scottish Highland Diaspora*, London, 2007.

Blaikie, A. Photographs in the cultural account: Contested narratives and collective memory in the Scottish islands, *Sociological Review*, 49:3 (2001), 345–67.

Blaikie, A. Photography, childhood and urban poverty: Remembering 'The forgotten Gorbals', *Visual Culture in Britain*, 7:2 (2006), 47–68.

Blaikie, A. *The Scots Imagination and Modern Memory*, Edinburgh, 2010.

Charnley, B and Miket, R. *Skye: A Postcard Tour*, Waternish, 1992.

Cohen, A. *Whalsay: Symbol, Segment and Boundary in a Shetland Island Community*, Manchester, 1987.

Douglas, M. *How Institutions Think*, London, 1987.

Edwards, E. Photographic 'types': The pursuit of method, *Visual Anthropology*, 3 (1990), 35–58.

Edwards, E, ed. *Anthropology and Photography, 1860–1920*, London, 1992.

Fenton, A. *Scottish Country Life*, Edinburgh, 1989.

Fenton, A. *The Northern Isles: Orkney and Shetland* (1978), East Linton, 1997.

Fenton, A, compiler and editor, with Mark A Mulhern. *A Swedish Field Trip to the Outer Hebrides, 1934*, Edinburgh, 2012.

Ferguson, L. *Wanderings with a Camera in Scotland: The Photography of Erskine Beveridge*, Edinburgh, 2009.

Finlay, W I R. *Scotland*, Oxford, 1945.

Fisher, A L. Thomas Annan's *Old Streets and Closes of Glasgow, Scottish Photography Bulletin*, Spring 1987.

Fraser, B and Rodrigues, H. *Ragas and Reels: Visual and Poetic Stories of Migration and Diaspora*, Edinburgh, 2012.

Hannavy, J. *A Moment in Time: Scottish Contributions to Photography, 1840–1920*, Glasgow, 1983.

Hirsch, M. The generation of postmemory, *Poetics Today*, 29:1 (2008), 103–28.

Kidd, D I. *To See Oursels: Rural Scotland in Old Photographs*, Glasgow, 1992.

Kidd, T and Morton, T. *Black Gold Tide: 25 years of Oil in Shetland*, Lerwick, 2004.

Leneman, L. *Into the Foreground: A Century of Scottish Women in Photographs*, Stroud, 1993.

Lippard, L R, ed. *Partial Recall: Photographs of Native North Americans*, New York, 1993.

Lloyd, A L. The forgotten Gorbals, *Picture Post*, 31 January 1948, 11–16.

Logan, O. *Bloodlines*, Manchester, 1994.

McKenzie, J. *Pages of Experience: Photography, 1947–87*, Edinburgh, 1987.

McKenzie, J. *Gorbals Children: A Study in Photographs*, Glasgow, 1990.

MacCannell, D. Staged authenticity: Arrangements of social space in tourist settings, *American Journal of Sociology*, 79:3 (1973), 589–603.

MacDonald, F. 'Geographies of vision and modernity: Things seen in the Scottish Highlands', DPhil thesis, University of Oxford, 2003.

MacKenzie, I. Festivals, faces and fire: A survey of fieldwork photography by Ian MacKenzie for the School of Scottish Studies, 1985–2005. Paper delivered at the conference Dialect and Folk Life Studies in Britain: The Leeds Archive of Vernacular Culture in Context, University of Leeds, 19 March 2005. Available online at, <www.ed.ac.uk/schools-departments/literatures-languages-cultures/celtic-scottish-studies/archives>.

MacLeod, A. *From an Antique Land: Visual Representations of the Highlands and Islands 1700–1880*, Edinburgh, 2012.

MacLeod, D. *Nis Aosmhor: The Photographs of Dan Morrison*, Stornoway, 1997.

Marzaroli, O. *Shades of Grey: Glasgow, 1956–87*, Edinburgh, 1987.

Marzaroli, O. *Glasgow's People, 1956–68*, Edinburgh, 1993.

Morris, R. *Scotland 1907: The Many Scotlands of Valentine and Sons, Photographers*, Edinburgh, 2006.

Nicolson, J R. Introduction. In Kidd, T, *Life in Shetland*, Edinburgh, 1980, n.p.

Normand, T. *Scottish Photography: A History*, Edinburgh, 2007.

Padget, M. *Photographers of the Western Isles*, Edinburgh, 2010.

Peat, D. *An Eye on the Street: Glasgow 1968*, Edinburgh, 2012.

Pink, S. *Doing Visual Ethnography*, London, 2001.

Poignant, R. Surveying the field: The making of the RAI photographic collection. In Edwards, 1992, 42–73.

Rohde, R F. Written on the surface of the soil: Northwest Highland crofting landscapes of

Scotland during the twentieth century. In Webb, R H, Boyer, D E and Turner, R M, eds, *Repeat Photography*, Washington, DC, 2010, 247–61.

Russell, M W. *A Poem of Remote Lives. Images of Eriskay 1934: The Enigma of Werner Kissling 1895–1988*, Glasgow, 1997.

Russell, M. *A Different Country: The Photographs of Werner Kissling*, Edinburgh, 2003.

Samuel, R. *Theatres of Memory*, London, 1994.

Shaw, M F. *Paul Strand: The Hebridean Photographs*, Edinburgh, 1978.

Spring, I. Lost land of dreams: Representing St Kilda, *Cultural Studies*, 4:2 (1990), 156–75.

Stevenson, S and Morrison-Low, A D. *Scottish Photography: A Bibliography, 1839–1989*, Edinburgh, 1990.

Stevenson, S. *Hill and Adamson's Fishermen and Women of the Firth of Forth*, Edinburgh, 1991.

Strand, P and Davidson, B. *Tir a' Mhurain / Outer Hebrides*, London, 1962.

Taylor, R. *George Washington Wilson: Artist and Photographer, 1823–93*, Aberdeen, 1981.

Wylie, G. *The Hebrides*, Glasgow, 1978.

Wylie, G. *Patterns of the Hebrides*, London, 1981.

Wylie, G. *The Hebrideans*, Edinburgh, 2004.

ONLINE RESOURCES

All websites last accessed March 2011.

BBC Scotland's Landscape, <www.bbc.co.uk/scotland/landscapes/what_are_rephotographs. shtml>

Getty Images, <http://gettyimages.com>

Glasgow Digital Library, <http://gdl.cdlr.strath.ac.uk>

Orkney Library Photographic Archive, <www.orkneylibrary.org.uk/html/photoarchive.htm>

Scottish Screen Archive, <http://ssa.nls.uk>

SCRAN, <www.scran.ac.uk>

Springburn Virtual Museum, <http://gdl.cdlr.strath.ac.uk/springburn/springindexcomm unity.html>

Index

'Flashbacks' series, 387
Haggart's, 468
in Maclean's collection, 525
musicians', 220
in periodicals, 471
Scottish History Society publications, 388
social organisation, 318, 321
working-class people, 378, 396
Ayrshire Archives, 428

Bacchilega, C, 447
Bacon, Sir Francis, 104
Badenach, J, 372
Badenach, Dr James, 373
Badenoch District Council, 130
Baillie, Lady Griselle, 388
Baird, Very Rev. Dr, 492
Baird, John, 468, 469
Bakhtin, M, 286, 303
ball games, 298–303, 304–5
ballad metre, 272, 273
ballads, 236–7, 250, 449
    Aberdeen University archives, 390
    broadsides and chapbooks, 463, 464,
        469–70
    collection/publication, 17, 27, 117, 237,
        238, 242, 245, 246, 247–8
    Crawford Ballads Collection, 393
    English influence, 239, 242
    Gaelic, 259–60, 264, 272
    Hogg's poetry, 451
    Lamkin, 471
    'popular song', 244
    regional, 242
    Scott and, 117, 237, 246, 247, 448
    Soutar's poetry, 452
    Spark's *The Ballad of Peckham Rye*, 456
    see also Macpherson, James
Ballantyne Commission, 431
Ballantyne, R M, 457–8
Banff and Buchan District Council, 134
bank archives, 153, 382, 391
Bank of Scotland, 153
Bannatyne, George, 449
Baptie, D, 228
Baptist church, 153, 273
Barbour, John, 448, 463
Barbour, John G, 472–3
Barke, James, 456
baron courts, 112, 426
Barr, John, 468
Barrie, J M, 455

Barrow, Prof. G W S, 332
Barry, Tom, 373–4
Basile, Giambattista, 196
Bateman, Meg, 378
Bauman, R, 288
bawdy songs, 247, 250, 270
BBC, 61, 156–7, 243, 258, 275, 351, 522
Beamish open-air museum, 129
Beaton, Alex, 239
Beckett, J V, 372, 383
Beddoe, Dr, 543
Beethoven, Ludwig van, 247
Belgium, 123, 127
Bell, Eric, 134
Bell, Margaret, 468
Bell, Patrick, 52, 111
Ben Lawers Historic Landscape Project,
    181–2
Ben-Amos, Dan, 195
Benfey, Theodor, 197
Bennett, Alan, 124
Bennett, Margaret, 59, 296
Berger Gluck, S and Patai, D, 84
Bertaux, Daniel, 74
Bertaux-Wiame, Isabelle, 74, 77
Bethune, Alexander and John, 465, 473,
    474–5
Bettelheim, B, 447
Beveridge, C and Turnbull, R, 179
Beveridge, Erskine, 541, 542, 556
Beveridge, J, 334
bibliographies, 393, 394, 425, 429, 430
Biggar fire-building contest, 303–4, 305
Biggar Gas Works, 150
Birmingham University, 361
Bishops' (Gresham) Committee, 431, 432
Black, G F, 329
Black, Ronald, 290, 295
Blackhall, Sheena, 453
Blacking, John, 218
Blaeu, Willem, 394
Blaikie, Andrew, 556, 557
Blair Castle archive, 389
Blair, Hugh, 349
Blair-Imrie, Hugh, 434
Blind Harry, 449, 463
BLITON (Brittonic Language in the Old
    North) database, 333
Bloch, Marc, 109
Board of Agriculture, 156, 383, 411–13, 434
Board of Ordnance, 427
Boas, Franz, 200

Boccaccio, Giovanni, 195
Boece, Hector, 448–9
Bogle, Eric, 240
Bohlman, Philip, 218
BOPCRIS (British Official Publications
    Collaborative Reader Information
    Service), 430
Borland, K, 84
Boswell, James, 290
Boud, R C, 384
Boulton, Sir Harold, 222
Bourne, Henry, 25
Braco, Lord, 376
Brand, John, 25, 26, 27, 53, 283
Breadalbane, earls of, 145
Bremond, Claude, 201
brewing industry, 153, 382, 390, 391, 392
The Bridge Between Us (online social space),
    522
Bringéus, Prof. Nils-Arvid, 60, 126–7
British Association for Local History, 169
British Ethnography Committee, 19
British Library, 148, 149, 155–6, 393, 427
British Linen Company, 388
British Museum, 104
British Newspaper Archive, 427
British Sign Language (BSL), 5, 8
British Steel records, 154
Brittany, 318
broadsides, 241, 244, 245, 458, 462–84
Broadwood, Lucy, 53
Brody, Alan, 281
Brooke-Freeman, Eileen, 330
Brooksbank, Mary, 237
Broom A M, 382
Broughton House, 250
Brown, Mrs, of Falkland, 242
Brown, Callum G, 420
Brown, George Douglas, 455
Brown, George Mackay, 453, 455
Brown, Thomas, 424
Bruce, George, 453
Brueghel, Pieter, the Elder, 305
Bruford, Alan, 58, 59, 207
Buccleuch, dukes of, 145, 389
Buchan, David, 242, 451
Buchan, John, 455
Buchan, Norman and Janey, 249
Buchan, Peter, 196, 206, 247, 397
Buchan-Hepburn, Sir George, 170
Buildings at Risk register, 149
Bulloch, James, 420

Bunessan Mill, 169
Bureau for Lesser Spoken Languages, 97
Burger, Gottfried, 246
burgh courts, 422, 427
burgh records, 150, 151, 152, 219, 331, 428
Burke, Peter, 39–40, 41, 117
Burma, 32
Burne, Charlotte, 29
Burnett, John, 377, 378, 476
Burns, Robert
    collector, 50–1, 185, 228, 246, 350
    influence, 472
    letters, 219, 376
    'Merry Masons' tune, 226
    oral sources, 448, 450
    Scots Musical Museum, 228, 246
    Scots songs, 237, 244, 246, 247
        broadcasts, 243
        broadsides, 463
        Centre for Robert Burns Studies, 249
        'Katherine Ogie', 241
        Eddi Reader and, 250
        recordings, 239, 248
Burnside, John, 453
Burrell Collection, 99
Burrell, Sir William, 387
Burt, Edward, 374
Burton, J H, Masson, D and Hume Brown, P,
    334
Business Archives Council, 382
Business Archives Council for Scotland
    (BACS), 153
business records, 153–4, 380–2, 391
    Dundee University archives, 152
    Glasgow University archives, 151, 153,
        390
    maps and plans, 386
    National Library of Scotland (NLS), 148,
        390
    National Records of Scotland (NRS), 145,
        153, 154, 380, 382, 392, 397
    National Register of Archives for
        Scotland (NRAS), 144, 153, 382, 397
    RCAHMS, 149
    Scottish Business Archive, 390
    Scottish History Society publications, 388
    surveys of, 392
    use, 381–2, 395, 397
Busk, Rachel Harriette, 32
Butcher, David, 415, 419
Bute, Marquesses of, 144
Butt, John, 382

Byron, Reginald, 318

Cregeen, A, 499
Cregeen, Eric, 58, 59, 65, 132, 318, 350–1, 358, 365
Cregneash, 129
Cripps, Judith, 426
Crockett, S R, 455, 475
Croker, Thomas C, 27
Cromartie, earls of, 389
Cromek, R H, 472
Cromek, Robert, 247
Crook, Alice, 337
Cruickshank, Graeme, 165
Cunningham, Allan, 28, 240, 247, 451, 472
Currie, James, 472
Cushnie Estate papers, 379
custom and belief, 29, 278–315
    antiquarianism and, 25–6
    comparative ethnology, 21, 282, 283–4, 301, 302
    Grimm's and Wright's work, 27
    Regional Ethnology of Scotland Project, 8
    School of Scottish Studies' work, 57, 59, 60, 61

Daiches, David, 321
Dale, David, 138, 177
d'Alembert, Jean le Rond, 120
Dalhousie, earls of, 145
Dalyell, John G, 218
Dàn (Gaelic verse form), 259–61
dance, 27, 249
    see also sword dances
dance music see puirt à beul
Danish Folk Museum, 35
Dareau, Marace, 496
Darwin, Charles, 197
Dasent, George W, 32, 53
databases see electronic resources
Dauney, W, 228
David I, king of Scots, 106
Davidson, Basil, 556
Davidson, George, 130
Davidson, H R Ellis, 447
de Bhaldraithe, Tomás, 491
De Luca, Christine, 453
Dean Orphanage and Cauvin Trust, 389
Defoe, Daniel, 374
Dégh, Linda, 60, 194, 203, 204
Delargy, Prof. James H, 55, 56, 57, 62, 523, 527
Den Gamle By, 35
Denmark, 19, 20, 35, 41, 239, 318, 373
Denton, Howard, 321

Department of Agriculture and Fisheries, 146
descriptive transcription, 220, 229
Deutsches Hirtenmuseum, 118
Devine, T M, 380
DeWalt, K M, and DeWalt, B R, 73, 80
Dewar, Rev. Dr Daniel, 488, 489, 490, 492, 497, 499
Dewar, John, 33, 523, 536
Dewar, John, and Sons, 153
Diack, Francis, 536
Diageo archives, 153
Dialect Society, 28
    see also English Dialect Society
dialects see language
Diamond, Hanna, 86
diaries, 154, 291, 372–4, 381, 387, 388, 395, 396, 398
diaspora communities see emigrants
Dick Bequest, 385
Dickson, Joshua, 228
Dickson, W K, 334
dictionaries, 5, 34, 506–7
    Brand's work, 26
    Gaelic, 54, 485–501, 522
    Halliwell-Phillipps' work, 27
    historical dictionaries, 485, 493, 494–8
    School of Scottish Studies and, 57, 63, 497
    Scots, 50, 53, 54, 319, 472, 507–21, 522–3
        see also Dictionary of the Older Scottish Tongue (DOST); Scottish National Dictionary (SND)
Dictionary of the Older Scottish Tongue (DOST), 54, 507, 522
    compilation, 54, 57, 496
    use, 49, 319, 508–9, 510, 512, 513, 514, 515
Dictionary of the Scots Language (DSL), 54, 496, 497, 507, 508–10, 512–19, 522
Dictionary of the Scottish Gaelic Language, 496, 497, 498, 499, 501, 522
Diderot, Denis, 120
Dieckhoff, Henry C, 493, 536
diffusionists see evolutionists/diffusionists
Digital Archive of Scottish Gaelic, 496
digitised texts, 219, 296, 392, 393–4, 429–30, 436, 522
    see also electronic resources
Dilworth, W H, 375
Dineen, P S, 499
directories, 424–5, 430
Dixon, Norman, 331
Donaldson, G, 334
Donaldson, Prof. Gordon, 144

music, 227
The National Archives in London (TNA), 155, 156
National Library of Scotland, 148, 156, 392–3, 394, 427, 429, 430
National Records of Scotland (NRS), 388, 392, 397, 423, 429, 436
National Trust for Scotland, 392
newspapers, 427, 429
onomastic research, 331, 333, 337
oral history, 348
parish registers, 222, 430
photographs, 150, 542–3, 548, 556
private accounts, 391–4, 397–8
public accounts, 428–30, 436
School of Scottish Studies' archives, 9, 60–1, 185, 249, 275, 351–2, 522
Scots songs, 242, 244, 248, 249
Statistical Accounts, 219, 296, 429, 436, 522
sword dances, 280
wills and testaments, 147, 429, 430
witchcraft, 423
see also Alexander Carmichael Project; Calum Maclean Project; *Dictionary of the Scots Language (DSL)*; PEARL Project; Scottish Archive Network; Tobar an Dualchais/Kist o Riches
Elias, Norbert, 39
Elinor, Gillian, 363
Ellis, Sir Henry, 26, 27, 283
Elphinstone Institute, 61, 249
Elphinstone, Margaret, 456
emigrants
  fiction by, 457
  folk narrative, 205, 208
  Gaelic songs, 238, 240, 267
  letters, 376, 394, 396
  National Records of Scotland (NRS) material on, 389, 425
  photographs and, 547, 557
  Scots songs, 238–9, 240, 241
  Tiree, 318
Emmerson, G S, 227
Empire Exhibition (Scotland), 127
Enerstvedt, Åse, 60
English Dialect Society, 29
  see also Dialect Society
English Place-Name Society, 329, 331, 333
English Short Title Catalogue (ESTC), 393, 429
Erdélyi, Zsuzsanna, 33
Erixon, Prof. Sigurd, 14, 19, 38, 42, 55, 56, 105, 108, 316

Erskine, John, of Carnock, 388
Erskine, John F, 411
estate papers, 378–80, 389, 392, 395
  archives, 152, 379–80, 391
  maps and plans, 386, 389, 394
  National Library of Scotland (NLS), 148, 390
  National Records of Scotland, 145
  Scots outwith Scotland, 156
ethics, 81–6, 87, 220, 225–6, 363
'Ethnographical Investigations in the British Isles' committee, 28–9
Ethnographical Survey of Ireland, 29
ethnography, 16, 19, 20, 37, 72–3, 164
Ethnological Society of London, 16
Ethnological Society of New York, 16
'ethnology'
  defining, 20–3, 42, 181
  'folklife' and, 15, 19–20
  term origin, 16
  see also applied ethnology
ethnomusicology, 218
European Ethnological Research Centre (EERC), 8, 61, 66, 386–8
European ethnology, 15, 19, 20, 23, 42, 108
Evans, E Estyn, 36–7, 39, 109, 130
evolutionists/diffusionists, 30–1, 34, 197–8
exhibitions, 64–5, 99–100, 101, 126, 127, 178–9
  see also Great Exhibition, London (1851); Highland Exhibition; Royal Highland and Agricultural Show

Faclair na Gàidhlig, 496, 497, 498, 499, 501, 522
Faculty of Physicians and Surgeons in Glasgow, 152
  see also Royal College of Physicians and Surgeons of Glasgow
Fahrenheit, Daniel, 118, 119
fairytales (*märchen*), 17–18, 27, 193–4, 195, 196
  Gaster's view of, 31
  Holbek's work, 202
  McRitchie's view of, 32
  Müller's view of, 197
  'The man who counted the fairies', 531–2, 534
  see also folktales
faiths *see* churches/religions
Fallersleben, A H Hoffmann von, 37
family history, 106, 107, 144, 148, 425, 426
family records, 376, 378, 389, 390, 391, 395, 547

museums, 19, 117
   see also folk museums
pure and applied studies, 24
Volkskunde, 15, 17–18, 20, 21, 22, 23
see also material culture; social
   organisation
folklore, 18–19, 27–33, 53, 197
   antiquarianism, 24–7
   folklife and, 14, 19
   Gaelic, 31, 33, 53, 525
   Haddon's work, 21
   Ireland, 27, 32, 33, 108–9, 204, 287, 288, 435
      see also Irish Folklore Commission
   personal narratives as, 195
   Smout on, 164
   term origin, 18, 53, 197, 282
   see also oral tradition
Folklore Association, 198
Folklore Institute of Scotland (FIOS), 56, 257,
   258
Folklore Society, *see* Folk-lore Society
folksongs *see* songs
folktale indexes/classifications, 27, 193–5,
   198–9, 207, 534, 535
folktales
   comparative ethnology, 27, 32, 198–9,
      200, 203, 207–8
   Evans' work, 36
   fairytales contrasted with, 194
   Grimm brothers, 17–18, 32, 53, 195,
      196–7, 202, 206, 282, 283
   Lang's view, 197–8
   paradigmatic model, 201
   in periodicals, 471–4
   psychoanalytic approach, 202–3
   Regional Ethnology of Scotland Project, 8
   School of Scottish Studies' archives, 58,
      207, 208
   structural analysis, 201–2
   see also fairytales (*märchen*); Gaelic
      folktales; literary sources; narratives
Forbes of Callendar papers, 150
Forbes, Prof. Eric, 165
Ford, Grace, 415
Ford, Percy, 415
Forde, C Daryll, 37, 38
Fortier, A M, 81, 83
Fourth Statistical Account, 170, 408, 410
Fox, Tom, 475
Fox, Wilson, 431
France, 20, 40, 74
   ball games, 301

linguistic atlas, 34, 505
melodies from, 263
museums, 118, 122
oral tradition collecting, 350
Perrault's tale collection, 196
surnames, 334
van Gennep's work, 286
see also Société d'Ethnologie de Paris;
   Société ethnologique de Paris
franchise courts, 422
Franz, Marie-Louise von, 202
Fraser, Bashabi, 457, 557
Fraser, George Macdonald, 457
Fraser, Hamish, 146
Fraser, Ian, 58, 329–30
Fraser papers, 378
Frazer, Sir James G, 281, 283–4
Free Church, 147, 153
Freeman, Fred, 248
Freemasons' Walk, Rosehearty, 220–7
Freud, Sigmund, 202
Friel, George, 456
Frimannslund (Holmsen), Rigmor, 317,
   318–19
Frisch, Michael, 348
Fyfe, J G, 373
Fyffe, James, 388
Fyffe, Will, 243

Gael Stream, 522
Gaelic ballads, 259–60, 264, 272
Gaelic betrothal ritual, 280
Gaelic bibliography, 393
Gaelic dictionaries, 54, 485–501, 522
Gaelic folklore, 31, 33, 53, 525
Gaelic folktales, 207, 208, 260, 489, 525, 526,
   528, 529–34
Gaelic funeral invitations, 320–1
Gaelic language, 5, 97, 229, 243, 258,
   485–504
   see also Gaelic dictionaries; Irish Gaelic
Gaelic place-names, 328, 332, 333, 489
Gaelic poetry, 33, 219, 258–65, 272, 449, 489
Gaelic Society of Inverness, 170, 494
Gaelic songs, 55, 238, 240, 257–77
   bagpipe music and, 217
   Maclean's collection, 525, 526
   School of Scottish Studies' work, 57, 58,
      61, 63, 258, 264
   Scots songs and, 238, 247, 251
   Tiree, 318
Galileo, 117

folktale collection, 207
Gaelic songs, 57, 58, 63, 258, 264
local history societies, 165
material culture, 56, 57, 60, 61, 62
music, 56, 57, 58, 61, 62
onomastics, 56, 57, 58, 60
oral history, 59
oral tradition, 56, 350–2
place-names, 56, 58
Scots songs, 58, 60, 61, 248, 250
social organisation, 58, 59, 317–23
travelling people, 57, 207, 250
Schrager, Samuel, 74, 75
'Scope and Methods of Folk Life Research'
   symposium, 19, 24
Scotch songs, 241
   see also Scots songs
'Scotland's People', 430
Scots dictionaries, 50, 53, 54, 319, 472, 507–21,
   522–3
   see also *Dictionary of the Older Scottish*
      Tongue (DOST); Scottish National
      Dictionary (SND)
Scots language, 5, 97, 229, 243, 449
Scots songs, 236–56
   archives, 390
   broadsides and chapbooks, 469–71
   lyric songs, 237, 241, 247, 451
   political songs, 237, 247, 249, 469
   School of Scottish Studies' work, 58, 60,
      61, 248, 250
   see also ballads; Burns, Robert; children's
      songs; Scotch songs; Ulster Scots
      songs
Scots Thesaurus (ST), 320, 507, 511–12, 514,
   520
Scott, Betty, 549
Scott, Cathie, 57
Scott, David, of Dunninald, 156
Scott, Dufton, 225
Scott, Gavin, 376
Scott, James, 294
Scott, Sir Walter
   ballads, 117, 237, 246, 247, 448
   collection work, 51, 185, 245, 350, 451, 473
   Croker's work and, 27
   folklore-based literature, 28, 219, 291–2,
      453–4, 472–3
   on guisers, 279
   The Minstrelsy of the Scottish Border, 52,
      61, 237, 241–2, 247, 451, 472
   poetry by, 450–1

sword dances, 279–80, 291–2, 294
Scottish Agricultural Industries Work Study
   in Agriculture, 64
Scottish Agricultural Museum *see* Royal
   Highland and Agricultural Show; West
   Kittochside
Scottish Anthropological and Folklore
   Society, 55, 56, 62
Scottish Archive Network (SCAN), 143, 151,
   152, 392, 397, 426, 428, 429
Scottish Bibliographies Online, 393, 429
Scottish Book Trust, 249
Scottish Brewing Archive, 153, 390, 391, 392
Scottish Burgh Records Society, 150
Scottish Burgh Survey, 149
Scottish Business Archive, 390
Scottish Catholic Archives, 152, 428
Scottish Catholic Historical Association, 420
Scottish Church History Society, 420
Scottish Civic Trust, 167
Scottish Cooperative Wholesale Society, 384
Scottish Council on Archives (SCA), 143
Scottish Country Life Museums Trust, 65,
   130, 133, 135, 136
Scottish Cultural Resources Access Network
   (SCRAN), 66, 298, 542–3
Scottish Culture & Traditions (SC&T), 249
Scottish Department of Agriculture and
   Fisheries, 146, 414, 431
Scottish Development Department, 146, 431
Scottish Dialects Committee, 54
'Scottish Documents', 430
Scottish Episcopal Church, 153
Scottish Ethnological Archive *see* Scottish Life
   Archive
Scottish Exhibition of National History, Art
   and Industry, 127
Scottish Fisheries Museum, 542
Scottish Genealogy Society, 167
Scottish Government, 418, 430, 436
   see also Lord Advocate's department;
      Scottish Office
Scottish History Society, 165, 373, 382, 388,
   420, 422, 426
Scottish Home and Health Department, 146,
   414, 431, 432
Scottish Industrial Archaeological Survey,
   149
Scottish Jewish Archives Centre, 153, 428
Scottish Labour History project, 351
Scottish Labour History Society, 164, 167
Scottish Language Dictionaries Limited, 54

Smout, T C, 109–10, 163–4, 166, 170, 171, 351,
352, 375
Social History Curators' Group, 64
Social History and Industrial Classification
(SHIC), 64
social organisation, 14, 17, 19, 58, 59, 316–23,
354–8
see also anthropology; community studies
Social Science Research Council (SSRC), 59,
318
Societá italiana di antropologia e di
etnologia, 16
Société d'Ethnologie de Paris, 16
Société ethnologique de Paris, 16
Société internationale d'Ethnologie et de
Folklore *see* International Society for
Ethnology and Folklore (SIEF)
societies' records, 223, 331, 383–5, 390, 391, 392
Society of Antiquaries of London, 28, 104
Society of Antiquaries of Scotland, 51, 110
John Jamieson and, 52
local history, 165, 167
Mitchell and, 6, 107
museum, 51, 104, 120
Royal Anthropological Institute and, 55
Society of Archivists, 388, 425–6
Society for Folk Life Studies, 20, 36, 65
Society Instituted in Scotland for the Benefit
of the Sons and Daughters of the Clergy,
410
Society for Name Studies in Britain and
Ireland, 329
Society in Scotland for Propagating Christian
Knowledge (SSPCK), 486
sociology, 21, 34–7, 39–40, 316
songs, 227, 236–77
Aberdeen University archives, 390
collection work, 17, 32, 42, 50
Greig–Duncan collection, 60, 222, 248, 326
instrumental music and, 217
onomastics and, 326
Regional Ethnology of Scotland Project, 8
Sweden, 42, 239
see also ballads; bawdy songs; children's
songs; Gaelic songs; political songs;
religious songs; Scots songs; work-
related songs
Sorenson, Janet, 246
sound recordings
archives, 9, 157
School of Scottish Studies' archives,
8–9, 57, 63, 157, 229, 250, 274, 351

Scottish Jewish Archives Centre, 153
Scottish Life Archive, 154
see also International Society of
Sound Archives (IASA)
custom and belief and drama, 296–7
Gael Stream, 522
Gaelic song, 262, 271, 274
music, 218, 220, 228
research method, 72, 345, 346–7, 348
School of Scottish Studies' archives, 8–9,
57, 63, 157, 229, 250, 274, 351
see also *Scottish Tradition* LP/CD series
Scots songs, 239, 248
Scottish Jewish Archives Centre, 153
Scottish Life Archive, 154
Scottish Sound Archive, 9
SCRAN (Scottish Cultural Resources
Access Network), 298
see also Scottish Tradition LP/CD series
'Sources in Local History' series, 66, 386–7
Soutar, William, 452
South East of Scotland Working People's
History recordings, 59
South Kensington Museum (later Victoria
and Albert Museum), 100
South Ronaldsay and Burray Agricultural
Society, 384
Spark, Muriel, 454, 456
Spence, Charlie and Moira, 135
Spender, Humphrey, 556
Spiers of Glasgow, 131
sport-related songs, 237, 251
Spottiswoode, John, 374
Spring, Ian, 549, 553, 557
Springburn Virtual Museum, 542
Spufford, M, 40
Stafford Record Office, 156
Stahl, Sandra, 195
Stair Society, 422
Stationery Office publications, 415–16
Statistical Accounts, 3, 51, 408–11, 434
digitised texts, 219, 296, 429, 436, 522
local history, 164, 166, 167, 168–9, 170,
171
music, 219
Sinclair's *Analysis*, 414, 434
see also *Fourth Statistical Account; New
Statistical Account; Old Statistical
Account; Third Statistical Account*
Stekert, Ellen J, 246
Stell, E, 227
Stephenson, John, 318